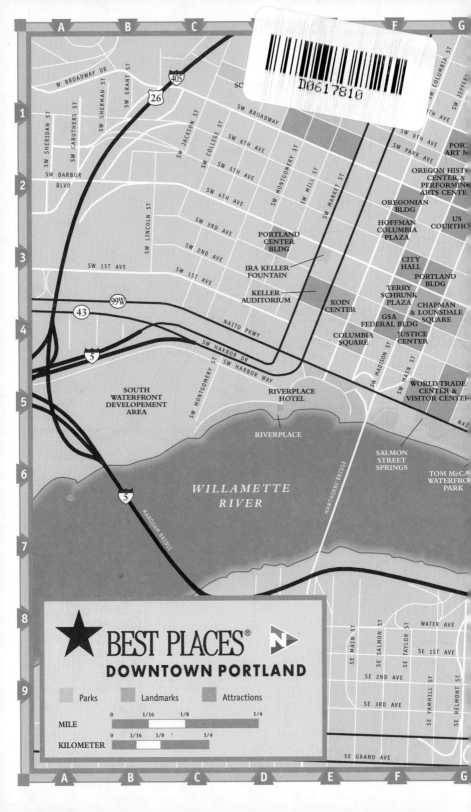

| A | B | C | D | E | F | G |

1
W BROADWAY DR
SW SHERIDAN ST
SW CARUTHERS ST
SW SHERMAN ST
SW GRANT ST
405
26
SC
SW BROADWAY
SW JACKSON ST
SW COLLEGE ST
SW 6TH AVE
SW MONTGOMERY ST
SW MILL ST
SW MARKET ST
SW COLUMBIA ST
SW JEFFERS
SW 9TH AVE
SW PARK AVE
PORT
ART M

2
SW BARBUR
BLVD
SW 5TH AVE
SW 4TH AVE
OREGON HIST
CENTER &
PERFORMIN
ARTS CENTE
OREGONIAN
BLDG
HOFFMAN
COLUMBIA
PLAZA
US
COURTHO

3
SW LINCOLN ST
SW 3RD AVE
SW 2ND AVE
SW 1ST AVE
SW 1ST AVE
PORTLAND
CENTER
BLDG
IRA KELLER
FOUNTAIN
KELLER
AUDITORIUM
KOIN
CENTER
CITY
HALL
PORTLAND
BLDG
TERRY
SCHRUNK
PLAZA
CHAPMAN
& LOUNSDALE
SQUARE

4
99W
43
5
NAITO PKWY
SW HARBOR DR
SW HARBOR WAY
GSA
FEDERAL BLDG
COLUMBIA
SQUARE
JUSTICE
CENTER
SW MADISON ST
SW MAIN ST

5
SOUTH
WATERFRONT
DEVELOPEMENT
AREA
SW MONTGOMERY ST
RIVERPLACE
HOTEL
WORLD TRADE
CENTER &
VISITOR CENTER
NA

6
5
RIVERPLACE
SALMON
STREET
SPRINGS
TOM McCA
WATERFRO
PARK
WILLAMETTE
RIVER
MARQUAM BRIDGE
HAWTHORNE BRIDGE

7

8
SE MAIN ST
SE SALMON ST
SE TAYLOR ST
WATER AVE
SE 1ST AVE
SE 2ND AVE

★ **BEST PLACES**® **N**

DOWNTOWN PORTLAND

9
Parks   Landmarks   Attractions
SE 3RD AVE
SE YAMHILL ST
SE BELMONT ST

MILE
0   1/16   1/8   1/4

KILOMETER
0   1/16   1/8   1/4

SE GRAND AVE

| A | B | C | D | E | F | G |

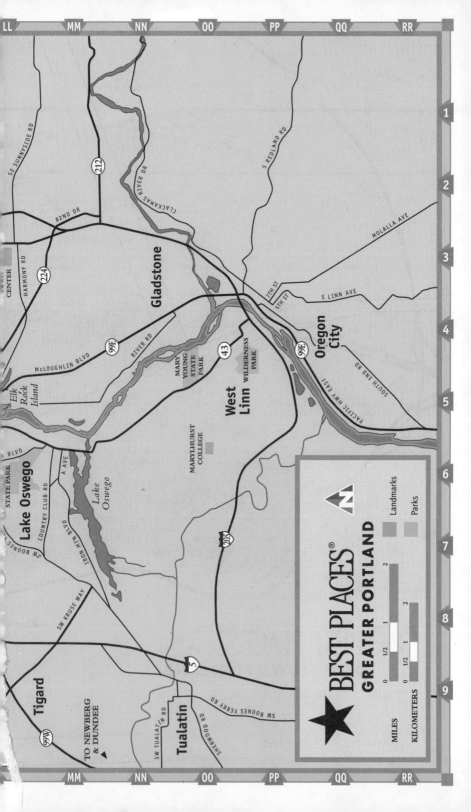

Praise for Best Places® Guidebooks

"Best Places *covers must-see portions of the West Coast . . . with style and authority. In-the-know locals offer thorough info on restaurants, lodgings, and the sights.*"
—NATIONAL GEOGRAPHIC TRAVELER

"Best Places *are the best regional restaurant and guide books in America.*"
—THE SEATTLE TIMES

". . . *travelers swear by the recommendations in the* Best Places *guidebooks...*"
—SUNSET MAGAZINE

"Known for their frank yet chatty tone . . . "
—PUBLISHERS WEEKLY

"Best Places Portland *is the guide that makes all the others roll over and play dead.*"
—THE OREGONIAN

"*For travel collections covering the Northwest, the* Best Places *series takes precedence over all similar guides.*"
—BOOKLIST

"Best Places Northwest *is the bible of discriminating travellers to B.C., Washington and Oregon. It promises, and delivers, the best of everything in the region.*"
—THE VANCOUVER SUN

"*The best guide to Seattle is the locally published* Best Places Seattle . . . "
—JONATHAN RABAN, MONEY MAGAZINE

"*Funny, conversational writing and clever sidebars make* Best Places Vancouver *an enjoyable read.*"
—VANCOUVER MAGAZINE

"Best Places San Francisco *has frank assessments of restaurants and accommodations* . . . "
—THE SEATTLE TIMES

TRUST THE LOCALS

The original insider's guides, written by local experts

COMPLETELY INDEPENDENT
- No advertisers
- No sponsors
- No favors

EVERY PLACE STAR-RATED & RECOMMENDED

★★★★   The very best in the region

★★★   Distinguished; many outstanding features

★★   Excellent; some wonderful qualities

★   A good place

NO STARS   Worth knowing about, if nearby

MONEY-BACK GUARANTEE
We're so sure you'll be satisfied, we guarantee it!

HELPFUL ICONS
Watch for these quick-reference symbols throughout the book:

 FAMILY FUN

 GOOD VALUE

 ROMANTIC

 UNIQUELY PORTLAND

BEST PLACES®

PORTLAND

Edited by
KIM CARLSON
CARRIE FLOYD

EDITION 5

SASQUATCH BOOKS
SEATTLE

Printed in the United States of America
Distributed in Canada by Raincoast Books, Ltd.

Fifth edition
07 06 05 04 03 02 01   5 4 3 2 1

ISBN: 1-57061-267-6
ISSN: 1095-9742

Series editor: Kate Rogers
Cover and interior design: Nancy Gellos
Cover photograph: Rick Dahms
Maps: GreenEye Design
Composition: Patrick David Barber and Holly McGuire

SPECIAL SALES

BEST PLACES® guidebooks are available at special discounts on bulk purchases for corporate, club, or organization sales promotions, premiums, and gifts. Special editions, including personalized covers, excerpts of existing guides, and corporate imprints, can be created in large quantities for specific needs. For more information, contact your local bookseller or Special Sales, Best Places Guidebooks, 615 Second Avenue, Seattle, Washington 98104, 800/775-0817.

SASQUATCH BOOKS
615 Second Avenue
Seattle, Washington 98104
206/467-4300
books@SasquatchBooks.com
www.SasquatchBooks.com

CONTENTS

Acknowledgments and Contributors

In 2000, *Money* magazine bestowed Portland with its most livable big city award, the latest feather in what has become a very decorated urban cap. By most measures—strong employment, options for leisure time, gorgeous setting, livable neighborhoods—this is one gem of a city. *Best Places Portland* is an easy book to fill: at the turn of the millennium the City of Roses is defined by its stunning parks, enticing restaurants, a multitude of transportation options, and what we hope is an increasingly bolstered arts scene.

But subject matter alone doesn't make a book, and we couldn't have put this one together without the stellar contributions of the following people: Michaela Lowthian Bancud, *Portland Tribune* feature writer; Byron Beck, special sections editor for *Willamette Week;* Liz Brown, a regular contributor to health-related publications and the *Portland Tribune;* Gail Dana, writer for *Our Town* and the *Business Journal;* Troy DuFrene, freelance writer and former fishmonger now living in the Bay Area; Karen Foley, *Fresh Cup* editor and *Willamette Week* contributor; Jen Lane, publisher of *BarFly* (a free monthly guide to Portland's bars and clubs); Ethan Machado, freelance writer and former Portlander now residing in Evanston, Illinois; Maureen Mackey, writer of all trades; James McQuillen, classical music critic for the *Oregonian* and freelance food writer; Terry Richard, outdoor and travel writer for the *Oregonian* and the editor of *Inside Out Oregon* (Sasquatch Books); Jennifer Sargent, traveler and writer; David Sarasohn, associate editor and restaurant reviewer for the *Oregonian;* Elizabeth Steiner, family practice physician with a weakness for books; Sarah Thomas, Portland-based travel writer; William Tripp, architect and writer; and Erika Troseth, *Business Journal* copy editor and writer.

At Sasquatch Books, we'd like to thank Kate Rogers, Laura Gronewold, and Justine Matthies for their cheerful guidance along the way. Essential to the project were copy editor Rebecca Pepper, proofreader Kris Fulsaas, word processor Sarah Campbell, and indexer Miriam Bulmer. As always, you the reader are the ultimate reviewer. Let us know of places we've misjudged or missed altogether. We love to hear from you.

—*Kim Carlson and Carrie Floyd*

About Best Places® Guidebooks

People trust us. Best Places® guidebooks, which have been published continuously since 1975, represent one of the most respected regional travel series in the country. Each guide is written completely independently: no advertisers, no sponsors, no favors. Our reviewers know their territory, work incognito, and seek out the very best a city or region has to offer. Because we accept no free meals, accommodations, or other complimentary services, we are able to provide tough, candid reports about places that have rested too long on their laurels, and to delight in new places that deserve recognition. We describe the true strengths, foibles, and unique characteristics of each establishment listed.

Best Places Portland is written by and for locals, and is therefore coveted by travelers. It's written for people who live here and who enjoy exploring the city's bounty and its out-of-the-way places of high character and individualism. It is these very characteristics that make *Best Places Portland* ideal for tourists, too. The best places in and around the city are the ones that denizens favor: independently owned establishments of good value, touched with local history, run by lively individuals, and graced with natural beauty. With this fifth edition of *Best Places Portland*, travelers will find the information they need: where to go and when, what to order, which rooms to request (and which to avoid), where the best music, art, nightlife, shopping, and other attractions are, and how to find the city's hidden secrets.

We're so sure you'll be satisfied with our guide, we guarantee it.

NOTE: *The reviews in this edition are based on information available at press time and are subject to change. Readers are advised that places listed in previous editions may have closed or changed management, or may no longer be recommended by this series. The editors welcome information conveyed by users of this book. A report form is provided at the end of the book, and feedback is also welcome via email: books@SasquatchBooks.com.*

How to Use This Book

This book is divided into eleven chapters covering a wide range of establishments, destinations, and activities in and around Portland. All evaluations are based on numerous reports from local and traveling inspectors. Best Places® reporters do not identify themselves when they review an establishment, and they accept no free meals, accommodations, or any other services. Final judgments are made by the editors. **EVERY PLACE FEATURED IN THIS BOOK IS RECOMMENDED.**

STAR RATINGS (FOR TOP 200 RESTAURANTS AND LODGINGS ONLY) Restaurants and lodgings are rated on a scale of one to four stars (with half stars in between), based on uniqueness, loyalty of local clientele, performance measured against the establishment's goals, excellence of cooking, cleanliness, value, and professionalism of service. Reviews are listed alphabetically, and every place is recommended.

★★★★ The very best in the region

★★★ Distinguished; many outstanding features

★★ Excellent; some wonderful qualities

★ A good place

NO STARS New or undergoing major changes

(For more on how we rate places, see the Best Places Star Ratings, below.)

PRICE RANGE (FOR TOP 200 RESTAURANTS AND LODGINGS ONLY) Prices for restaurants are based primarily on dinner for two, including dessert, tax, and tip (no alcohol). Prices for lodgings are based on peak season rates for one night's lodging for two people (i.e., double occupancy). Peak season is typically Memorial Day to Labor Day; off-season rates vary but can sometimes be significantly less. Call ahead to verify, as all prices are subject to change.

$$$$ Very expensive (more than $100 for dinner for two; more than $200 for one night's lodging for two)

$$$ Expensive (between $65 and $100 for dinner for two; between $120 and $200 for one night's lodging for two)

$$ Moderate (between $35 and $65 for dinner for two; between $75 and $120 for one night's lodging for two)

$ Inexpensive (less than $35 for dinner for two; less than $75 for one night's lodging for two)

RESERVATIONS (FOR TOP 200 RESTAURANTS ONLY) We used one of the following terms for our reservations policy: reservations required, reservations recommended, no reservations. "No reservations" means either reservations are not necessary or are not accepted.

ADDRESSES AND PHONE NUMBERS Every attempt has been made to provide accurate information on an establishment's location and phone number, but it's always a good idea to call ahead and confirm. All listings here are in Portland unless otherwise specified. If an establishment has two Portland-area addresses, we list both at the top of the review. If there are three or more locations, we list only the main address and indicate "other branches."

CHECKS AND CREDIT CARDS Many establishments that accept checks also require a major credit card for identification. Note that some places accept only local checks. Credit cards are abbreviated in this book as follows: American Express (AE); Carte Blanche (CB); Diners Club (DC); Discover (DIS); Japanese credit card (JCB); MasterCard (MC); Visa (V).

EMAIL AND WEB SITE ADDRESSES Email and web site addresses for establishments have been included where available. Please note that the web is a fluid and evolving medium, and that web pages are often "under construction" or, as with all time-sensitive information, may no longer be valid.

MAP INDICATORS The letter-and-number codes appearing at the end of most listings refer to coordinates on the fold-out map included in the front of the book. Single letters (for example, F7) refer to the downtown Portland map; double letters (FF7) refer to the Greater Portland map on the flip side. If an establishment does not have a map code listed, its location falls beyond the boundaries of these maps (for example, Vancouver, Washington, locations).

HELPFUL ICONS Watch for these quick-reference symbols throughout the book:

 FAMILY FUN Family-oriented places that are great for kids—fun, easy, not too expensive, and accustomed to dealing with young ones.

 GOOD VALUE While not necessarily cheap, these places offer you the best value for your dollars—a good deal within the context of the city.

 ROMANTIC These spots offer candlelight, atmosphere, intimacy, or other romantic qualities—kisses and proposals are encouraged!

 UNIQUELY PORTLAND These are places that are unique and special to the City of Roses, such as a restaurant owned by a beloved local chef or a tourist attraction recognized around the globe. (Hint: If you want to hit several of these special spots at once, turn to the Top 20 Attractions in the Exploring chapter. They're all uniquely Portland!)

 Appears after listings for establishments that have wheelchair-accessible facilities.

INDEXES In addition to a general index at the back of the book, there are five specialized indexes: restaurants are indexed by star-rating, features, and location at the beginning of the Restaurants chapter, and nightspots are indexed by features and location at the beginning of the Nightlife chapter.

MONEY-BACK GUARANTEE Please see "We Stand by Our Reviews" at the end of the book.

READER REPORTS At the end of the book is a report form. We receive hundreds of reports from readers suggesting new places or agreeing or disagreeing with our assessments. They greatly help in our evaluations, and we encourage you to respond.

BEST PLACES® STAR RATINGS

Any travel guide that rates establishments is inherently subjective—and Best Places is no exception. We rely on our professional experience, yes, but also on a gut feeling. And, occasionally, we even give in to a soft spot for a favorite neighborhood hangout. Our star-rating system is not simply a checklist; it's judgmental, critical, sometimes fickle, and highly personal. And unlike most other travel guides, we pay our own way and accept no freebies: no free meals or accommodations, no advertisers, no sponsors, no favors.

For each new edition, we send local food and travel experts out to review restaurants and lodgings anonymously, and then to rate them on a scale of one to four, based on uniqueness, loyalty of local clientele, performance measured against the establishment's goals, excellence of cooking, cleanliness, value, and professionalism of service. That doesn't mean a one-star establishment isn't worth dining or sleeping at—far from it. When we say that all the places listed in our books are recommended, we mean it. That one-star pizza joint may be just the ticket for the end of a whirlwind day of shopping with the kids. But if you're planning something more special, the star ratings can help you choose an eatery or hotel that will wow your new clients or be a stunning, romantic place to celebrate an anniversary or impress a first date.

We award four-star ratings sparingly, reserving them for what we consider truly the best. And once an establishment has earned our highest rating, everyone's expectations seem to rise. Readers often write us letters specifically to point out the faults in four-star establishments. With changes in chefs, management, styles, and trends, it's always easier to get knocked off the pedestal than to ascend it. Three-star establishments, on the other hand, seem to generate healthy praise. They exhibit outstanding qualities, and we get lots of love letters about them. The difference between two and three stars can sometimes be a very fine line. Two-star establishments are doing a good, solid job and gaining attention, while one-star places are often dependable spots that have been around forever.

The restaurants and lodgings described in *Best Places Portland* have earned their stars from hard work and good service (and good food). They're proud to be included in this book—look for our Best Places sticker in their windows. And we're proud to honor them in this, the fifth edition of *Best Places Portland*.

PLANNING A TRIP

PLANNING A TRIP

How to Get Here

BY PLANE

The good news is that **PORTLAND INTERNATIONAL AIRPORT**, or **PDX** (503/460-4234; www.pdxairport.com), is served by most major airlines, with excellent connections from points around the Pacific Northwest and beyond. The bad news is that the airport is forever in a state of expansion, which can mean difficult parking, unexpected gate changes, and long walks from the terminal to baggage claim. Allow plenty of time— 30 minutes at least, especially during rush hours—to get from the airport into town, and the same to get back to the airport. Portlanders and visitors alike look forward to **SEPTEMBER 2001**, which is the scheduled completion date of the extension of eastside light rail—aka **AIRPORT MAX**—a 37-minute trip from Pioneer Courthouse Square to the station near baggage claim at PDX. Cost will be $1.50.

All major **CAR RENTAL** companies operate from the airport. **TAXIS** and **SHUTTLES** are readily available on the lower deck; after picking up your baggage, cross the first roadway, which is reserved for passenger pickup, and proceed to the commercial roadway. Expect to pay about $25 for the trip downtown. Another way to get from the airport to downtown (and back) is on the **GRAY LINE OF PORTLAND AIRPORT EXPRESS** (503/285-9845); cost is $15 one-way or $30 round trip, and buses leave every 45 minutes from the second roadway as you exit baggage claim. The route covers most major downtown hotels; let the driver know where you're headed when you board the bus. The most economical trip ($1.15) into the city is via **TRI-MET** (503/238-7433). Catch bus number 12 outside the baggage claim area; the ride downtown takes about 45 minutes, along Sandy Boulevard. Before the no. 12 hits downtown, it makes a stop at the Hollywood MAX station. Travelers heading toward Gresham or Hillsboro can use their transfers to board light rail here.

PARKING (503/288-PARK; 800/PDX-INFO) at PDX comes in three flavors, and where you park probably depends on how long you'll be there. The **ECONOMY LOT**, at $48 per week, is a good bet for extended parking; the **LONG-TERM LOT**, at $12 per day, is designed for parking over a one- or two-day period; and the **PARKING GARAGE**, or short-term parking ($1.50 per half hour), is best for quick trips. Call ahead for space availability.

BY BUS

Near Union Station, just north of Old Town, is the **GREYHOUND** station (550 NW 6th Ave; 800/231-2222, or locally, 503/243-2357), with a complete schedule of buses each day. Both the train station and the bus station are within walking distance of the downtown core known as "Fareless Square," where you can ride MAX or Tri-Met buses for free, and where Tri-Met buses and MAX trains pick up passengers for trips into downtown and beyond, to most suburbs in the metropolitan area.

BY TRAIN

AMTRAK (800/872-7245 for reservations or 503/273-4866 for a recording of updated arrival and departure times) operates out of the lovely Union Station (800 NW 6th Ave) just north of downtown Portland (look for "Go By Train" written in neon on the tower). With its prominent clock tower, great curving entrance, and muscular features, this romantic structure memorializes the bygone era of the great railways. Trains come from and head for points north, east, and south daily.

BY CAR

Most drivers come into Portland via either **INTERSTATE 5**, which runs north-south, or **INTERSTATE 84**, which runs into town west from the Columbia Gorge. **HIGHWAY 26** goes east to Beaverton and then on to the Oregon Coast; south of Portland, **INTERSTATE 205** loops off I-5 to the east and passes near Lake Oswego, West Linn, Oregon City, and Milwaukie, among other towns, before connecting back to I-5 north of Vancouver, Washington. **INTERSTATE 405** loops off I-5, skirting the western edge of downtown. Rush hours in Portland can mean stand-still traffic, but if you arrive midday (after 9am but before 3pm) or after 7pm, you should have clear sailing into town.

When to Visit

Portland is in bloom—culturally speaking—year-round. When to visit is strictly a matter of preference, but there are a few constants that can make planning a trip a little bit easier.

WEATHER

Unless you plain don't mind getting soaked—and many natives own neither slicker nor umbrella—bring something water-resistant no matter what the season. Portland skies are ever-changing, but the common denominator is precipitation. All this rain does pay off, though: Portland boasts close proximity to fabulous skiing on Mount Hood, lush year-round parks, and a temperate clime that makes it OK to have hot chocolate or ice cream pretty much any time of year.

Outside of the snow on the nearby mountains, frozen, fluffy white flakes are generally feared. Childrens' peals of "No school!" may seem premature when only a trace of snow is visible, but they know that the City of Roses is the city that closes when snow falls. Still, snow rarely lasts long on city streets (not because plows remove it, but because it simply melts), so enjoy the dusted evergreens while you can. If you visit in winter, be prepared for bus delays and traffic snarls on those rare occasions when snow falls.

Portland's true summer runs from July to early October, so sun worshippers should time their trips accordingly. Bring the shades and—gasp!—sunscreen. Allergy sufferers will find May and June the toughest going for sensitive eyes and noses, but they can still enjoy the fulsome beauty of Bridgetown's gardens. Early spring is redolent with its magnolia, cherry, and plum blossoms; June's end sees the full explosion of Portland's famous International Rose Test Garden.

Average temperature and precipitation by month

Month	Daily Max. (degrees F)	Daily Min. (degrees F)	Monthly Precipitation (inches)
JANUARY	45.4	33.7	5.35
FEBRUARY	51	36.1	3.85
MARCH	56	38.6	3.56
APRIL	60.6	41.3	2.39
MAY	67.1	47	2.06
JUNE	74	52.9	1.48
JULY	79.9	56.5	0.63
AUGUST	80.3	56.9	1.09
SEPTEMBER	74.6	52	1.75
OCTOBER	64	44.9	2.67
NOVEMBER	52.6	39.5	5.34
DECEMBER	45.6	34.8	6.13

Source: U.S. National Oceanic and Atmospheric Administration

TIME

Portland is on Pacific Standard Time (PST), which is three hours behind New York City, two hours behind Chicago, one hour behind Denver, one hour ahead of Anchorage, and two hours ahead of Honolulu. Portland is 17 hours behind Tokyo and 8 hours behind London. Daylight savings time begins in early April and ends in late October.

WHAT TO BRING

The Portland fashion aesthetic is ever evolving, but most locals aren't too picky (much to the dismay of some bigger-city transplants). Rule of thumb for tourists: dress for comfort, with good walking shoes a must. Men may want to pack a jacket for dinner, but it won't be required anywhere; women, as usual, have more choices: dresses, skirts, or pants are all fine, and you should know that many people—though not everyone—will be wearing jeans, T-shirts, and Nikes (or the equivalent) no matter what day of the week it is. If you want to draw attention, dress Miami Beach; to blend, think fleece and cotton.

PORTLAND ON THE PAGE

The best way to experience Portland, like any other city, is to get out, get wet (if necessary), and see it for yourself. You can read about the city's bridges, its roses, its parks and shops and restaurants, but until you actually *do* Portland, your impressions will be borrowed ones.

Still, we can't help but think that our first trip to Paris was enhanced by reading *A Movable Feast*, and we loved visiting New York after spending an entire childhood reading about it—in *Stuart Little, Harriet the Spy*, and *Cricket in Times Square*, to name a few beloved, dog-eared titles.

Below is a short Portland reading list. For more ideas, visit any of the bookstores listed in the Shopping chapter; many have sections that feature the works of local authors.

Ramona the Pest lives in Northeast Portland, as her author, Beverly Cleary, once did. Any of the Ramona books are almost sure hits with children (and their grown-ups); *Ramona Quimby, Age 8* is an all-time favorite. To see a tribute to Beverly Cleary, check out the Ramona, Henry Huggins, and Ribsy statues in Grant Park (between the tennis courts and NE 33rd Ave).

Local publisher Timber Press recently published William J. Hawkins III and William F. Winnigham's *Classic Houses of Portland, Oregon: 1850–1950*. Complete with black-and-white photos, this book tells stories of many local residences. *One City's Wilderness: Portland's Forest Park*, by Marcy Cottrell Houle, includes an excellent map of the 5,000-acre park, plus trail descriptions. Hot off the press is *Wild in the City: A Guide to Portland's Natural Areas*, edited by Mike Houck and M. J. Cody, a must-have blueprint for the urban naturalist.

Author and cooking teacher extraordinaire James Beard grew up in Portland during the early part of the 20th century. His book *Delights and Prejudices* contains lavish passages about Portland markets, the city's social life, the summer trip to the Oregon Coast on the train, and other aspects of life in Portland 100 years ago. *The Solace of Food: A Life of James Beard*, by Robert Clark, affords a broader view of Beard's world than Beard himself could offer.

A hard-to-find book that's worth seeking out is *The Portland Bridge Book*, by Sharon Wood. With complete descriptions of Portland's many bridges, this book is a treasure for visitors and residents alike.

Oregon's beloved poet William Stafford taught for years at Portland's Lewis and Clark College and contributed much to the literary life of his adopted city until his death in 1993. *The Way It Is: New and Selected Poems* is an invaluable collection of Stafford's work.

Finally, Sasquatch Books's own *Portland Cheap Eats* gives you 200 ideas about where to eat—on the cheap.   —*Kim Carlson*

Essentials for all seasons include a water-resistant shell; comfortable, water-resistant shoes; sunglasses (rain or shine); lip balm; and a mind toward layering: summer days are often cool in the mornings and evenings, so pack a jacket—even in August.

General Costs

Visitors are often surprised to find that Oregon has no sales tax (hence higher income and property taxes than many states), making it a shoppers' paradise—and ensuring that there's always a tax revolt in the works. All in all, the Portland area has a robust economy, driven by a broad base of services and industry. Manufacturing industries here include machinery, electronics, metals, transportation equipment, and lumber and wood products. High technology plays a huge role in the economy as well, with some 1,000 high tech companies in the metro area, the largest of which is Intel. Among the other large companies in the Portland area, a few internationally well-known names stand out, including Nike, Columbia Sportswear, and Adidas.

The residential real estate market in Portland has been stratospheric for years, but if you're planning only a visit to the City of Roses, you might find some good deals on bedrooms. It's a buyer's market in the luxury hotel trade in downtown Portland—at least until the demand catches up to the supply. In the last few years a number of new downtown hotels, large and small, have opened for business—with more scheduled to open in the near future—and now there are too many to fill on a regular basis. Inquire about special rates and packages; you might find a bargain, or at least a set of amenities (maybe a shopper's package or a romance package) that will make your hotel stay memorable.

Prices at Portland restaurants may be above the national average, but for visitors who are used to eating out in San Francisco or Seattle (Portland's closest big-city neighbors), dinner in the City of Roses may seem like a bargain.

Average costs for lodging and food

Double room
INEXPENSIVE	**$50–$75**
MODERATE	**$75–$135**
EXPENSIVE	**$135 AND UP**

Lunch for one (including beverage and tip)
INEXPENSIVE	**$6–$10**
MODERATE	**$11–$18**
EXPENSIVE	**$19 AND UP**

Beverages
PINT OF MICROBREW	**$3.50**
12-OUNCE HOUSE COFFEE	**$1.15**
GLASS OF WINE	**$5–$7**

Other common items
MOVIE TICKET	**$6.75**
ROLL OF FILM	**$4**
TAXI	**$2.50 PICKUP; $1.50 PER MILE**
LOCAL ROCK SHOW	**$5–$20 PER TICKET**
ADMISSION TO OREGON ZOO	**$4–$6**

Tips for Special Travelers

FAMILIES WITH CHILDREN

If you think your child has ingested something toxic, call the Poison Control Center (800/452-7165). To report child abuse, call the Child Abuse Hotline (503/731-3100). For other emergencies, dial 911. Legacy Emanuel Hospital and Health Center (2801 N Gantenbein Ave; 503/413-2200; map:FF6) has an excellent children's facility; Legacy Good Samaritan Hospital and Medical Center is close to the downtown center (1015 NW 22nd Ave; 503/413-7711; map:GG7) in Northwest Portland. Another close-in hospital is the Providence St. Vincent Medical Center (9205 SW Barnes Rd; 503/216-1234; map:HH9).

Most major hotels can arrange for baby-sitters if notified in advance. The Northwest Nannies Institute (503/245-5288) places course graduates for live-in or daily care throughout the metro area. Care Givers Placement Agency (503/244-6370) also matches families with daily or overnight nannies. Metro Child Care Resource and Referral (503/253-5000) offers free information on day care services in the tri-county area.

Many young families move to Portland with the idea that it is a great place to raise children—and they're right. Not surprisingly, there is plenty to do here for children of all ages. The new Children's Museum (across from the zoo in Washington Park; 503/823-2227; map:HH7), slated to open in spring 2001, is a local philanthropic success story. Check out the climbing structure and the waterworks. Both the Oregon Zoo (4001 SW Canyon Rd; 503/226-1561; map:HH7) and OMSI, the Oregon Museum of Science and Industry (1945 SE Water Ave; 503/797-4000; map:HH6), are top-notch family standbys.

For an up-to-date overview of possibilities, pick up a copy of *Portland Parent* (503/638-1049; www.parenthoodweb.com) or *Portland Family Magazine* (503/255-3286; www.portlandfamily.com). These free publications have activity calendars and can be found at coffee shops and newsstands. When copies are scarce, try Finnegan's Toys and Gifts (922

7

SW Yamhill St; 503/221-0306; map:H2) or Rich's Cigar Store (820 SW Alder St; 503/228-1700; map:I3{RP3}).

For a copy of the Official Oregon Kids Travel Guide and Explorer Passport, call the state tourism commission (800/547-7842) or visit the web site, www.traveloregon.com. The guide features youngsters sharing their favorite activities, and the passport lets young travelers collect stickers from designated Oregon attractions.

Watch for this icon throughout the book; it indicates places and activities that are great for families.

SENIORS

In Multnomah County, the Aging Services Department operates a Senior Helpline (503/248-3646), which assists seniors with information about health services, low-income housing, recreation, transportation, legal services, volunteer programs, and other matters. In Clackamas County, call the Area Agency on Aging (503/655-8640); it has a counterpart in Washington County (503/640-3489). Seniors Ala Cart Transportation Services (503/591-9161) operates what is essentially a senior-citizen taxi. The pickup charge is higher than a standard taxi, but the cost per mile is lower, making it an economical option for longer excursions. Senior citizens and people with disabilities receive free transportation when participating in activities sponsored by the Portland City Parks Program for Disabled Citizens and Senior Leisure (503/823-4328).

PEOPLE WITH DISABILITIES

Public transportation in Portland, on Tri-Met buses and MAX trains, is wheelchair accessible. Press the blue button outside the MAX doors for ramp access. The doors will remain shut longer than the doors for foot traffic, but don't panic—the beeping sound means that the ramp is being lowered. The Arc of Multnomah County (503/223-7279) offers services for people with disabilities, including in-home and center-based respite care. Call well in advance to take advantage of this service.

Trips Inc. Special Adventures (800/686-1013) has provided chaperoned excursions for people with developmental disabilities since 1991. Many Trips Inc. adventures are out-of-state, but check with the office for in-state camping and rodeo offerings. To contact people who are deaf or hearing- or speech-impaired, call the Oregon Telecommunications Relay Service (800/735-1232 or TTY 800/735-2900).

WOMEN

Portland is a relatively safe place, but as in most cities, women travelers should take extra precautions at night. The Women's Crisis Line number is 503/235-5333. For health and reproductive services, call Planned Parenthood (503/775-0851).

PET OWNERS

Many hotels allow pets, including 5th Avenue Suites (506 SW Washington St; 503/222-0001; map:H4) and the Hotel Vintage Plaza (422 SW Broadway; 503/228-1212; map:I4). Only two city parks allow dogs to run off the leash: Gabriel Park (the off-leash area is at SW 45th Ave, near SW Vermont St; map:JJ8) and Chimney Park (9360 N Columbia Blvd; map:DD7).

GAYS AND LESBIANS

Portland is in all things low-key, but its gay scene—particularly in the area of downtown nightclubs—is growing. Pick up a copy of *Just Out* (503/236-1252; www.justout.com), a free weekly source for gay news, arts, and community events. For a complete rundown of gay-friendly businesses, pick up a copy of *Portland's Gay & Lesbian Community Yellow Pages*. The free directory is published annually and can be found at most coffee shops and the like. To scope out the city before arriving, visit the directory's web site (www.pdxgayyellowpages.com). Another web site to check out is www.pdxpride.com. The Gay Resource Connection operates a hotline (800/777-2437) and will provide referrals for both services and activities.

FOREIGN VISITORS

Oregon has long had a relationship with its neighbor across the Pacific—Japan—and Portland continues to fuse its down-to-earth sensibilities with a cosmopolitan flavor. Some tour companies will track down a translator if they know in advance which language is needed, or inquire through the Portland Oregon Visitors Association (503/222-2223). Visitors from around the globe can contact their local consulates.

Exchange currency at any main bank branch, at the American Express Travel Agency (1100 SW 6th Ave; 503/226-2961; map:H4), or at Travelex America (503/281-3045), located at Portland International Airport across from the United Airlines ticket counter. Money can also be swapped at the Thomas Cook counter inside Powell's Travel Store in Pioneer Courthouse Square. Ask about commission charges, or call 800/CURRENCY.

For general visa information, contact the U.S. Immigration and Naturalization Service (511 NW Broadway; 503/326-3006; map:L4). Portland is home to a number of foreign consulates, some large, some small.

CZECH REPUBLIC, 10260 SW Greenburg Rd, Ste 560, Tigard, 503/293-9545

CYPRUS, 1235 SW Myrtle Ct, Portland, 503/293-9545

DENMARK, 888 SW 5th Ave, Portland, 503/802-2131

DOMINICAN REPUBLIC, 921 SW 6th Ave, Portland, 503/499-4200

FIJI, PO Box 2, Portland, 503/231-4649

FINLAND, 2730 SW Cedar Hills Blvd, Beaverton, 503/526-0391

FRANCE, PO Box 751, Portland, 503/725-5298

GERMANY, 200 SW Market St, Ste 1695, Portland, 503/222-0490

GREAT BRITAIN, 1300 SW 5th Ave, Ste 2300, Portland, 503/227-5669

GUATEMALA, 921 SW 6th Ave, Portland, 503/499-4200

ITALY, PO Box 82303, Portland, 503/234-1437

IVORY COAST, 6316 SW Peyton Rd, Portland, 503/244-2293

JAPAN, 1300 SW 5th Ave, Ste 2700, Portland, 503/221-1811

KOREA, 707 SW Washington St, 503/224-5560

MALAYSIA, 18697 SE Semple Rd, Clackamas, 503/658-3633

MEXICO, 1234 SW Morrison St, Portland, 503/274-1442

NETHERLANDS, 1001 SW 5th Ave, Ste 1800, Portland, 503/222-7957

NORWAY, 5441 SW Macadam Ave, Ste 300, Portland, 503/221-0870

SWEDEN, 15537 Village Park Ct, Lake Oswego, 503/697-3200

THAILAND, 121 SW Salmon St, Ste 1430, 503/221-0440

WEB INFORMATION

Portland is a surfer's dream—web surfers, that is. Among the best general interest sites include those for the Portland Oregon Visitors Association (www.pova.com) and the Portland Chamber of Commerce (www.pdxchamber.com). For information on local microbreweries, see www.oregonbeer.com; for local wineries, head to www.oregonwine.com; and for a local foodies' calendar, go to the web site for *Northwest Palate Magazine* (www.nwpalate.com). For the *Oregonian*'s calendar of events, go to www.oregonlive.com; and for *Willamette Week*'s calendar of events, see www.willametteweek.com. Finally, to check current weather conditions, visit www.channel6000.com/weather.

LAY OF THE CITY

LAY OF THE CITY

Orientation

The mighty **COLUMBIA RIVER** and the oft-bridged **WILLAMETTE RIVER** set the blueprint for Portland. In fact, natural landmarks eliminate the need for a compass, at least when skies are clear. Mount Hood marks the east like a glistening guardian, Washington's Mount St. Helens, known for its flat top, marks the north, and the verdant green West Hills mark, appropriately, the west.

The Willamette enters town from the south, dividing Portland's east from its west, and Burnside Street separates north from south. The light rail, known as MAX, runs basically east-west. Each quarter of town has its own flavor, and new cultural ecosystems are always emerging. **PIONEER COURTHOUSE SQUARE**, Portland's public red-bricked plaza, marks central downtown. A preponderance of the bricks are engraved with names of donors to what some call Portland's living room. Portlanders gather here for lunch, people-watching, and many events; the visitors center relocated here in the summer of 2001.

PGE PARK (known until recently as Civic Stadium—home to minor league baseball) is approximately 12 blocks to the west (a five-minute MAX ride), and the **ROSE GARDEN** (aka the Rose Quarter—home of the Trail Blazers and the site for big-name touring concerts) is about a 15-minute MAX ride to the east.

Heading slightly downhill from Pioneer Courthouse Square, visitors on the weekend will find lots to look at and smell at Portland's **SATURDAY MARKET**. Here, under the Burnside Bridge, artisans hawk their wares and steamy fried food makes mouths water. Just across the street is **TOM MCCALL WATERFRONT PARK**, a riverside stretch of grass (for picnickers and Frisbee throwers) and paths (for runners and cyclists). This park, once a strip of highway, is the spot for summertime festivals.

Northwest of Pioneer Courthouse Square, across Burnside from PGE Park, is Portland's trendy **NORTHWEST NEIGHBORHOOD**. Shoppers along NW 23rd Avenue and gallerygoers in lower Northwest's Pearl District will find getting around as easy as A-B-C, 1-2-3. The north-south avenues march westward in numerical order, and the east-west streets (Burnside through Wilson) are helpfully named in alphabetical order. The top of the neighborhood, at the end of NW Thurman Street, marks the beginning of 5,000-acre **FOREST PARK** with its 23-plus-mile Wildwood Trail.

On the east side of the river, car travelers will find Grand Avenue and Martin Luther King Jr. Boulevard speedy north-south through streets. **NORTHEAST PORTLAND** has been home to a recent economic upswing, coming both from external gentrification and community-based business development. Broadway is the most developed in this regard, and it is

THE SCALE OF ONE CITY: PORTLAND ARCHITECTURE

In great cities the urban fabric and the buildings are woven together to form one rich, continuous tapestry. As each new building finds its place in the city, it also shapes and defines the city to come. Portland is such a place. The city's small size, gentle terrain, abundant street trees, and temperate climate make it a pedestrian's paradise.

It is not surprising then, that one of the defining characteristics of Portland architecture lies in how buildings meet the street. As you walk around Old Town or along First and Second Avenues, take notice of the mostly two- to three-story buildings with brick bearing walls, heavy timber framing and cast iron facades. These early commercial buildings of the Cast Iron era (erected in the mid 1800s) exemplify the intimate scale of the street space. With several buildings per block, each with its own style of doors and windows, there's a pleasing and friendly rhythm along the sidewalk.

In the mid-town area near Pioneer Courthouse Square you'll find buildings of the Terra Cotta era, from the early twentieth century. Typically these buildings cover a half or full block and are about ten stories tall, the height made possible by steel structures and elevators. The **Meier & Frank Building** and the **Pacific Building** (both designed by A. E. Doyle), to the north and south of Pioneer Courthouse respectively, exemplify this style. With these taller buildings and their continuous pattern of windows the character of the street space changes: as proportions grow taller, the scale becomes grander and the sidewalk cadence more regular.

During the early modern period—beginning just after the Second World War—buildings continued to adhere to the existing patterns while experimenting with new materials and structural systems. The **Equitable Building** by Pietro Belluschi (now called the Commonwealth Building; 421 SW 6th Ave) is an outstanding example of these combined principles. Its elegantly proportioned and carefully detailed aluminum and glass curtain wall—the first of its kind in the U.S.—still meets the street in a respectful and thoughtful manner.

The streetscape of Portland changed dramatically in the 1960s when large skyscrapers began to appear. For the first time buildings were set back from the street, erected on plazas or plinths. The imposing scale of these structures and their lack of street level commercial space made them inhospitable, especially on sloping sites. Unfortunate examples include **Standard Plaza** (by Skidmore, Owings & Merrill; 1100 SW 6th Ave) and the **First National Center** (by Charles Luckman & Assoc., now the Wells Fargo tower; 1300 SW 5th Ave). This era also brought us places like the **South Auditorium** urban renewal area (south of Market St, originally laid out by S.O.M.), where streets disappear altogether to be replaced with office and condominium towers surrounded by green space.

Portland's infamous flirtation with Postmodernism, best represented by Michael Grave's **Portland Building** (completed in 1982), returns to the Terra Cotta era principle of filling out the block—at least at the lower levels—and it deserves credit for attempting a new pattern at street level: an arcade. Unfortunately the arcade is dark and difficult to access on the sloped streets, and lacks the retail density Graves envisioned. Perhaps the most important legacy of this building is *Portlandia*, the famous statue above the entrance that has become one of Portland's icons.

For a good look at Portland's contemporary scene, take a walk through the **Portland Center** project (designed by Thomas Hacker & Associates) at Portland State University (SW 6th Ave and Mill St), which has creatively opened up the interior of the block to form a south-facing public courtyard. Also, the recent redevelopment of old industrial buildings in the Pearl District such as the **Wieden & Kennedy Building** (NW 13th Ave and NW Everett St; Allied Works Architecture) and new loft buildings such as the **McKenzie Lofts** (NW 11th Ave and NW Glisan St; Ankrom Moison) marry innovation with a respect for original patterns, continuing the tradition of architecture that has given Portland its unique character.

To learn more about Portland architecture visit the American Institute of Architects/Portland (315 SW 4th Ave; 503/223-8757; www.aiaportland.com) and the Oregon History Center (1200 SW Park Ave; 503/222-1741; www.ohs.org).   —*William Tripp*

near to downtown and the Lloyd Center neighborhood—home to the eastside business community, the Rose Quarter, and the city's convention center. In the residential Northeast neighborhoods, pedestrians will have the best luck exploring NE Alberta, Killingsworth, and Fremont Streets, east to the Alameda neighborhood.

SOUTHEAST PORTLAND is to downtown what Berkeley is to San Francisco. Home to Portland's hippified element, Southeast is the place to relax. SE Hawthorne, Belmont, and Clinton Streets are good bets for bargain-hunting moviegoers, thrift-store devotees, and shoppers of all persuasions. **MOUNT TABOR PARK** marks the eastern edge of this neighborhood. A view of downtown from the top and the endless staircases that mark the back entrance make this a popular spot for runners and relaxers alike.

Visitor Information

People have been moving to Portland at such a clip that sometimes it seems as if there's been another homesteading act. A good place to start for both visitors and new Oregonians is the **PORTLAND OREGON VISITORS ASSOCIATION** (POVA), located on the ground floor of the World

Trade Center building (corner of SW Salmon St and Naito Pkwy; 503/222-2223; www.pova.com; map:F3). Here shelves are well stocked with brochures in English—ask about foreign-language guides to the area. Inside the center, visitors can surf the POVA web site and purchase discounted tickets to events happening that day. If you're planning a convention, you might want to look into the **OREGON CONVENTION CENTER** (literally—take their virtual tour at www.oregoncc.org). The CitySearch web site (www.portland.citysearch.com) offers food and music reviews, and www.oregonlive.com, maintained in cooperation with the *Oregonian,* lets surfers stay up-to-date with local news stories and arts coverage. Find out more about the **CITY OF PORTLAND**—everything from which parks have dog runs to how city government is run—at www.ci.portland.or.us. Finally, the **PORTLAND CHAMBER OF COMMERCE** (221 NW 2nd Ave; 503/228-9411; www.pdxchamber.org) can answer questions about doing business in Portland.

Getting Around

BY BUS OR MAX

TRI-MET (503/238-7433, www.trimet.org) operates both the city bus system and the sleek Metropolitan Area Express—**MAX**—trains; tickets for the two systems are interchangeable. Almost all the bus lines run through the Portland Transit Mall (SW 5th and 6th Aves, downtown); MAX lines also pass through downtown and currently extend east to Gresham and west to Hillsboro.

Buses run north across Burnside all the way to the Tri-Met North Terminal, just past the Greyhound station and just across the street from Union Station. The terminal is now the first stop on the transit mall and serves as a pit stop for bus drivers, providing a place to park their buses while they take a break and wait to complete their schedule.

Travelers in the downtown area can ride buses or MAX for free anywhere in the 300-block **FARELESS SQUARE**. The square extends from I-405 on the south and west, to NW Hoyt Street on the north and the Willamette River on the east.

Fares outside the square are $1.20 for travel in two zones (from downtown to residential areas within the metropolitan area) and $1.50 for three zones (necessary for travel from downtown to most parts of Tigard, Beaverton, Gresham, Milwaukie, Lake Oswego, and the airport). Youth tickets are 90 cents per ride, and as many as three children age 6 and younger can ride free with a fare-paying customer. All-day tickets are $4; a special three-day visitors pass is $10. Honored citizens—those 65 and older or disabled—can catch a bus for 60 cents per ride or pay $14 for a monthly pass. Tickets can be purchased on the bus (exact change only) or at MAX stops. **TRI-MET'S CUSTOMER ASSISTANCE OFFICE** is in the middle of Pioneer Courthouse Square, in the center of downtown. Open weekdays from 9am to 5pm, this is the place for face-to-face route information or ticket purchases. MAX trains run on the honor system; that is, MAX drivers never check fares. However, Tri-Met inspectors do randomly request proof of fare payment on buses and MAX, and passengers who haven't paid are fined or cited in district court.

Starting from Hillsboro in the west, MAX winds through Beaverton, making its first Portland stop at the Oregon Zoo. From there it stops in the Goose Hollow neighborhood at SW Salmon Street and 18th Avenue, passes through downtown and Old Town, crosses the Steel Bridge, and continues on the east side, swinging by the Oregon Convention Center and the Lloyd Center before making its way to Gresham. Glass-covered stations along the way maintain schedule information and ticket machines. The comfortable trains run every 15 minutes most hours of the day—more frequently during rush hour—every day of the week. Trains are generally spacious during non-rush-hour times, but they get packed (although not quite Tokyo-style) during the morning and evening commute.

Of the 20 stops between downtown and Hillsboro, 9 accommodate a total of 3,700 parked vehicles. Hang on to your transfer and check out the public art at these stations. Architects, artists, and engineers collaborated to create individual identities for each station. Art brochures are available on MAX trains and buses.

You can take your bike on the bus (or on the train). All Tri-Met buses are outfitted with bike racks, as is MAX; purchase a good-for-life bike pass for $5.

BY STREETCAR AND TROLLEY

The **PORTLAND STREETCAR** (www.portlandstreetcar.org) opens in summer 2001, whisking travelers from Portland State University, through the downtown core, into the Pearl District, and up to NW 23rd Avenue. Book lovers will appreciate the stop smack in front of Powell's Books, but there are plenty of other intriguing stops along the way. Streetcars will run from 6am to midnight, seven days a week, with cars arriving every 10 minutes during the day and less frequently at night .

Another option is the oak-paneled and brass-belled **VINTAGE TROLLEY** (503/323-7363), which follows the MAX route from the Lloyd Center in Northeast Portland to the downtown turnaround at SW 11th Avenue and back. Top speed is 35 miles an hour, and rides are free. The round-trip ride takes about 40 minutes, and trolleys run about a half hour apart, Sunday afternoons only.

BY CAR

Although Portland is relatively easy to navigate using mass transit, you may want a car for driving to wineries or to the Columbia River Gorge or Oregon City. Most major **RENTAL CAR** companies have offices at the airport; some have locations throughout the metro area. Here are local numbers for some of the larger ones: Enterprise, 800/736-8222 (multiple locations throughout the city); Thrifty, 503/254-2277; Hertz, 503/249-8216; Avis, 503/249-4950; Dollar, 503/249-4792; and Budget, 503/249-6500. If you're a member, you can pick up free maps and route advice at the **AUTOMOBILE ASSOCIATION OF OREGON** (600 SW Market Ave; 503/222-6734; map:E2); if not, try the **PORTLAND OREGON VISITORS ASSOCIATION,** at the corner of SW Salmon Street and Naito Parkway (503/222-2223; map:F5).

The best bet for **PARKING** downtown is in one of the six **SMART PARK** garages; many merchants will validate your parking ticket for one or two hours of free parking with a minimum purchase of $25. You can find these garages at SW First Avenue and Jefferson Street; SW Fourth Avenue and Yamhill Street; SW Third Avenue and Alder Street; SW 10th Avenue and Yamhill Street; SW Naito Parkway and Davis Street; and under O'Bryant Square, at SW Park Avenue and Stark Street. Of course, many other parking garages exist downtown, but their rates are usually higher for short-term usage.

Driving in Portland is generally not hard, once you figure out the woven pattern of one-way streets downtown (although beware of the tangle beneath the Morrison Bridge's west entrance). A warning about crossing town: the bridges of downtown Portland open regularly for Willamette River traffic; always expect a delay—so you won't be surprised when there is one.

BY TAXI

Portland is not New York City, and cabbies are not used to being flagged down on the street. You'll have better luck finding a phone and calling for one. Your options? Portland Taxi (503/256-5400), Broadway Cab, Inc. (503/227-1234), Radio Cab (503/227-1212), and Green Cab (503/252-4422). At press time, all four companies charged identical pickup and per-mile rates, so let cabbie availability be your guide. If you're headed to the airport, expect to pay about $25.

BY BICYCLE

In 1999, *Bicycling* magazine ranked Portland the number-one city in the United States for cyclists. New bike lanes are still being added to the city streets, and even the police operate a cadre of bike patrollers. Portland is flat enough that it can be enjoyed by bike, so go for it even if you aren't an ironman or ironwoman.

The **YELLOW BIKES** are Portland's famous on-again off-again experiment with bike sharing. The solid yellow cycles can (sometimes) be found unlocked against buildings or trees. Take one for a spin around town, then leave it in a moderately visible spot. The bikes last as long as the honor system prevails.

For bicycle-centric maps of the city, visit the **BICYCLE TRANS-PORTATION ALLIANCE** (1117 SW Washington St; 503/226-0676; map:I2). The BTA is a great source for bike advocacy and up-to-date cycling information.

Finally, if the idea of cycling yourself is too taxing, call the **PORT-LAND RICKSHAW COMPANY** (503/704-4797; open May–Oct). Owner Jean Poulot will send a new-fashioned rickshaw your way.

Essentials

PUBLIC REST ROOMS

The most centrally located public rest rooms downtown are those in Pioneer Courthouse Square (701 SW 6th Ave; map:H3), near the Tri-Met office. The lobby opens at 8:30am and closes at 5pm weekdays and is open during the afternoon on weekends (hours vary). Farther south, there are public rest rooms in the Clay Street parking garage (map:E3) between SW Third and Fourth Avenues. Restrooms are also available at Pioneer Place, Meier and Frank, and Nordstrom.

MAJOR BANKS

The usual West Coast suspects can be found downtown. Most offer money exchange services but will cash personal checks only for account holders. Call for branch locations and hours: Bank of America (503/279-3445), Bank of the West (503/225-1776), Key Bank (503/323-6767), US Bank (503/872-2657), Washington Mutual (503/238-3100), and Wells Fargo (503/886-3330).

POLICE AND SAFETY

In serious, life-threatening emergencies, dial 911. In nonemergency situations, dial 503/823-4636 for Portland Police information, or 503/823-3333 to make a report. Unlike the downtowns of many American cities, Portland's hops into the night, making it safe for walking, but if you're out after dark, let common sense be your guide: know your destination. Another commonsense tip: Don't leave your valuables in the car, anytime.

HOSPITAL AND MEDICAL/DENTAL SERVICES

Several hospitals provide physician referrals, including Adventist Medical Center (10123 SE Market St; 503/256-4000; map:GG2) and Eastmoreland Hospital (2900 SE Steele St; 503/234-0411; map:HH4). Providence Portland Medical Center (4805 NE Glisan St; 503/215-1111; map:GG4) and Providence St. Vincent Hospital (9205 SW Barnes Rd;

503/216-1234; map:HH9) share a referral line, 503/215-6595. Legacy Health System, which locally comprises both Emanuel Hospital and Health Center (2801 N Gantenbein Ave; 503/413-2200; map:FF5) and Good Samaritan Hospital and Medical Center (1015 NW 22nd Ave; 503/413-7047; map:FF6), also have one physician referral line, 503/335-3500. The Multnomah Dental Society (503/223-4731) provides emergency and routine referral service at no charge.

POST OFFICE

Three full-service post offices are located in the downtown core. Across the street from Pioneer Courthouse Square, Pioneer Station (520 SW Morrison St; map:H3) is open Monday through Friday from 8am to 5pm; University Station (1505 SW 6th Ave; map:E2) is just blocks from Portland State University and is open Monday through Friday from 7am to 6pm and Saturdays from 10am to 3pm. For the best choice of stamps, visit the main office at 715 NW Hoyt Street (map:M4). It is open Monday through Friday from 7am to 6:30pm and on Saturdays from 8:30am to 5pm. Call 800/275-8777 to locate additional branches.

GROCERY STORES

Grocery shoppers in Portland have many choices: Fred Meyer (aka "Freddy's"), the most central of which is just off W Burnside Street near PGE Park (100 NW 20th Ave; 503/273-2004; map:GG7), has for many years been the local favorite. Others prefer the upscale feel of Zupan's (3301 SE Belmont St; 503/239-3720; map:HH5), the quasi–health food offerings at Nature's (3535 NE 15th Ave; 503/288-3414; map:FF5), or the variety of QFC (7525 SW Barnes Rd; 503/203-0027; map:HH9).

PHARMACIES

National giant Rite Aid has several locations in Portland; call 800/748-3243 to find the one nearest you. Ditto Walgreens (800/925-4733). Several grocery stores (Fred Meyer, Safeway) contain pharmacies also. For downtown-area delivery, go to Central Drug Co. (538 SW 4th Ave; 503/226-2222; map:H5); for deliveries in Northwest Portland, go to Nob Hill Pharmacy (2100 NW Glisan St; 503/227-1489; map:GG7).

DRY CLEANERS, TAILORS, AND LAUNDROMATS

Many hotels offer room-service dry cleaning and laundry services, or they can direct you to the closest place that does. One of the most convenient dry cleaners in the downtown area is Bee Tailors and Cleaners (939 SW 10th Ave; 503/227-1144; map:G2), open weekdays and Saturday mornings. Bee offers curbside service; just honk. Or try Levine's, with several branches downtown and the main location at 2086 W Burnside Street (503/223-7221; map:GG6). Near the Oregon Convention Center, New China Laundry and Dry Cleaners (105 NE 8th Ave;

PLACES OF WORSHIP

Portland has an abundance of places to pay reverence, many downtown. Here is a short list for visitors to the city—the devout and curious alike—to consider.

The **First Christian Church** (1315 SW Broadway; 503/228-9211) is a modern place downtown on the South Park Blocks, where anyone is invited to attend either a tradional or more informal Sunday Christian service.

A long-beloved church, also on the South Park Blocks, is the **First Congregational Church** (1126 SW Park Ave; 503/228-7219), built in 1895. The impressive Venetian Gothic building provides seating for some 900 worshippers; the church is also often used for lectures sponsored by Literary Arts (see the Performing Arts chapter).

Covering a full city block, **All Saints Episcopal Church** (4033 SE Woodstock Blvd; 503/777-3829) has long been a Southeast Portland landmark, a multi-use facility for the Westmoreland and Eastmoreland neighborhoods.

Synagogues in Portland accommodate reform, conservative, and orthodox communities. The reform congregation of **Temple Beth Israel** (1972 NW Flanders; 503/222-1069) was the first to be founded in Oregon, in 1858.

On the edge of the Laurelhurst neighborhood sits the immense **Greek Orthodox Church** (3131 NE Glisan St; 503/234-0468), which hosts a lavish Greek festival each fall.

A centrally located Roman Catholic church, where classical concerts are sometimes performed, is the **St Philip Neri Catholic Church** (SE 18th Ave and SE Division St; 503/231-4955).

The **West Hills Friends Church** (7425 SW 52nd Ave; 503/246-7654) holds Quaker services every Sunday in the Maplewood neighborhood of Southwest Portland.

The **Dharma Rain Zen Center** (2539 SE Madison St; 503/239-4846) is a Zen Buddhist Temple, where members and nonmembers alike can meditate and learn about Buddist teachings.

Finally, downtown once again is the location of the city's largest Unitarian Universalist congregation (indeed one of the largest such congregations in the country). **First Unitarian Church** (1011 SW 12th Ave; 503/228-6389) hosts several Sunday morning services. —*Kim Carlson*

503/239-4100; map:GG6) offers delivery service. Many do-it-yourself laundries are tucked into neighborhood commercial centers or located in strip malls, so you can do your errands while your clothes wash.

LEGAL SERVICES

The Oregon State Bar Lawyer Referral Service (5200 SW Meadows Rd, Lake Oswego; 503/684-3763; map:LL8) has offered referrals since 1971.

Expect to pay $35 for an initial office consultation, after which you'll be charged the firm's normal hourly rates. A reduced-fee program is available.

BUSINESS, COPY, AND MESSENGER SERVICES

For high-quality business copy services, Clean Copy (1704 SW 6th Ave; 503/221-1876; map:D1) features offset printing, color laser copies, and photocopying, and has desktop publishing services, plus free parking and delivery to the PSU campus. Kinko's (many locations throughout the metro area; downtown at 1503 SW Park Ave; 503/223-2056; map:E1) is usually helpful and friendly—even at 3am—although these shops do high-volume business, and small jobs sometimes don't get the attention they deserve. You can rent Macintosh computers or PCs by the hour here, and color laser copiers and fax service are also available. Lazerquick Copies (1134 SW 5th Ave; 503/228-6306; map:F3) offers more than 30 locations throughout the Portland metro area. This is a homegrown company that began its modest operations in a small Tigard house. Today, in addition to its offset printing and high-speed copying services— and a savings of 3 cents per copy over Kinko's in the do-it-yourself department—Lazerquick provides a host of computer and digital imaging solutions. All branches have scanners and rent Macs and PC-platform workstations.

At the Ladd Carriage House (1331 SW Broadway; 503/222-1313; map:F3), personalized secretarial services are the specialty. Word processing, tape transcription, and mailing services are available at an hourly rate. A pleasant conference room can be rented by the hour in this house that was once a livery stable. Sixteen offices are rented privately here; an answering service and mailbox can be rented for most any length of time.

It seems that whenever someone wants to send something by messenger in this city, they invoke the verb "Pronto," as in "I'll Pronto it over to you." Pronto Messenger Service (503/239-7666) is a Portland favorite, especially for crosstown deliveries. For deliveries farther afield, try TranServ Systems (503/241-0484).

PHOTOGRAPHY EQUIPMENT AND SERVICES

Film can be dropped off for developing at most major grocery stores, but for special treatment, helpful staff, and custom orders, head for the downtown Shutterbug (540 SW Broadway; 503/227-3456; map:I3), where all color film development is done on-site. For a full selection of the most newfangled photography equipment, Camera World (400 SW 6th Ave; 503/205-5900; map:I4) is the spot.

COMPUTER RENTALS AND REPAIRS

Bit-by-Bit (9203 SW Nimbus Ave, Beaverton; 520-0218; map:JJ9) is a well-established, nationwide rental service that will rent you an IBM-compatible PC and even deliver and set it up for you anywhere in the

Portland metro area. They also lease notebooks, laptops, and Macintoshes, as well as peripheral equipment. Twenty-four-hour service is available. For repairs, the Computer Store (700 NE Multnomah St; 503/238-1200; map:GG6) is the place to take an ailing Macintosh.

PETS AND STRAY ANIMALS

If you see a stray or any animal in need of help, or if you've lost your furry travel companion, call the Multnomah County Animal Control (503/248-3066) or the nonprofit Oregon Humane Society (503/285-0641). For emergency medical care for your pet, call the highly respected Dove Lewis Emergency Animal Hospital (1984 NW Pettygrove St and branches; 503/228-7281).

SPAS AND SALONS

In Portland, hair is big—big business, that is. There are many reputable hair salons in the city, and sometimes the best stylists are hiding out in small neighborhood salons; ask a local who's got a great cut for a suggestion. Or check out one of these larger salons, listed for each quadrant of the city: in Northeast, Gary Luckey Hair Design (4016 NE Fremont St; 503/281-7831; map:FF5); in Southwest, Robert's of Portland (5131 SW Macadam Ave; 503/222-4301; map:JJ6); in Southeast, La Belle Vie (Clackamas Town Center; 503/652-1618; map:KK3); and in Northwest, Aphrodite (1100 NW Glisan St; 503/223-7331; map:GG6). For spa suggestions, see "City Spas" in the Lodgings chapter.

Local Resources

NEWSPAPERS AND PERIODICALS

The lone daily in Portland, the OREGONIAN (503/221-8327), has been published since 1850 and reigns as the king of print journalism in the city. A telephone information service, Inside Line, is available from the newspaper. Call 503/225-5555 to hear everything from lottery results to movie schedules. The newspaper doesn't maintain its own web site, but you can find much of what's in the *Oregonian* on www.oregonlive.com.

The *Oregonian* is joined on Wednesdays by WILLAMETTE WEEK (503/243-2122; www.willametteweek.com), a free, thought-provoking, irreverent, sometimes controversial newsweekly covering politics, the arts, and civic matters. Both papers contain substantial and useful entertainment calendars. (The *Oregonian*'s "A&E" is published on Fridays.) Newcomer the MERCURY (503/294-0840; www.portlandmercury.com) is a weekly aimed at a more decidedly 20s crowd; it also offers alternative news and arts coverage. OUR TOWN (503/224-1774; www.ourtown mag.com) covers the downtown core, with features on fashion, residential interiors, travel, and entertainment. The BUSINESS JOURNAL

(503/274-8733; www.bizjournals.com/portland) and the **DAILY JOURNAL OF COMMERCE** (503/226-1311; www.orenews.com/directory/portcomm. html) cover the city's business beat. **THE COLUMBIAN** (503/224-0654) is the daily paper in Vancouver, Washington. The **ROCKET** (503/242-9896; www.musicuniverse.com), published every other Wednesday, is a joint Seattle–Portland source for local music and semi-punk news. **JUST OUT** (503/236-1252; www.justout.com) is Portland's free gay and lesbian newsletter, available, like the other free papers, at various locations about town. Finally, parents appreciate the free **PORTLAND PARENT NEWS-MAGAZINE** (503/638-1049; www.portlandparent.com) for its calendar and tot-related news.

PUBLIC LIBRARIES

The **MULTNOMAH COUNTY LIBRARY** has 15 branches throughout the city, with film, tape, and book borrowing plus other services. The library sponsors a variety of films, lectures, and programs for children. Portlanders are exceedingly proud of their **CENTRAL LIBRARY** (801 SW 10th Ave; 503/248-5123; map:H1), which was completely remodeled in the mid-1990s; in 1998 voters also approved funds for upgrading many branch libraries. Cardholders are entitled to one hour of Internet access per day; visitors can obtain a 24-hour card for Internet use. Clackamas County has 10 city libraries and 3 county libraries. Call individual branches for hours and events. The **BEAVERTON CITY LIBRARY** (12500 SW Allen Blvd, Beaverton; 503/644-2197; map:II9), Washington County's biggest, is available for use by citizens in Washington, Multnomah, or Clackamas Counties and is open seven days. Although Washington County's 11 libraries are individual, nonbranch entities, they all share databases.

MAJOR BOOKSTORES

Powell's City of Books (NW 10th Ave and W Burnside St; 503/228-4651; map:J2) is the nation's largest independent bookseller, and despite a recent labor-union controversy, the store remains a Portland favorite. Occupying an entire block, Powell's has color-coded rooms and free maps to the store to help bookworms find their way around. Specialty satellite stores buttress the million-plus volumes. The major chains have made their way into Portland in recent years—most with an in-house coffee shop. Borders (503/220-5911; map:G5) is conveniently located on the light rail line at SW Third Ave and Morrison St; Barnes & Noble is on the east side at 1231 NE Broadway (503/335-0201; map:GG6).

RADIO AND TV

KBOO radio is a true labor of love for each of its hundreds of volunteers. The station has been on the air since 1975, and visitors will find it a great way to tap into Portland's vibrant eclectic communities. Tune into Iranian music, local newshounds, ditties from Holland, or local hip-hop megastars. Pick up a schedule at the station (20 SE 8th Ave; 503/231-8032; map:GG5) and listen your way to Portland's epicenter. The city does, of course, offer standard radio and TV fare. Headbangers and honky-tonks will soon find their homes on the dial; cable-access scholars and soap-opera junkies can get comfy on the couch. Here's the basic rundown:

Radio Stations

NEWS	750 AM	KXL
COUNTRY	970 AM	KUPL
TALK, NEWS, SPORTS	1190 AM	KEX
JAZZ	89.1 FM	KMHD
ECLECTIC	90.7 FM	KBOO
NATIONAL PUBLIC RADIO	91.5 FM	KOPB
CLASSIC ROCK	92.3 FM	KGON
NEW/ALTERNATIVE ROCK	94.7 FM	KNRK
DANCE/ROCK	95.5 FM	KXJM
OLDIES	97.1 FM	KKSN
COUNTRY	99.5 FM	KWJJ
TOP 40	100.3 FM	KKRZ
ADULT CONTEMPORARY	103.3 FM	KKCW
ADULT CONTEMPORARY	105.1 FM	KRSK

TV Stations

ABC	2	KATU
CBS	6	KOIN
NBC	8	KGW
PBS	10	KOPB
UPN	12	KPTV
FOX	49	KPDX

INTERNET ACCESS

The branches of the Multnomah County Library all have Internet access; see Public Libraries, in this chapter, for further information. Another place to get on-line is at the visitors center (corner of SW Salmon St and Naito Pkwy; 503/222-2223; map:E5; after summer 2001, in Pioneer Courthouse Square; map:H3), run by the Portland Oregon Visitors Association.

UNIVERSITIES AND COLLEGES

For a city its size, Portland has many institutions of higher learning. Portland State University, the state's urban university, is located at the south end of the South Park Blocks (724 SW Harrison St; 503/725-3000; www.pdx.edu; map:E1). The Oregon Health Sciences University, in Southwest Portland (3181 SW Sam Jackson Park Rd; 503/494-8311; www.ohsu.edu; map:HH6), is the only academic institution in the state devoted exclusively to the study of health. The Oregon Graduate Institute of Science and Technology (20000 NW Walker Rd, Beaverton; 503/748-1121) is the only private graduate school of science and engineering in the Pacific Northwest. In North Portland, the University of Portland (5000 N Willamette Blvd; 503/943-7911; www.up.edu; map:EE8) was founded early in the 20th century by the Catholic archbishop of Oregon. Another private institution, Pacific University, was founded in 1842 in nearby Forest Grove (2043 College Wy; 503/357-6151; www.pacificu.edu). Nationally renowned for its academic rigor and free-thinking student body, Reed College is located in Southeast Portland off Bybee Boulevard (3203 SE Woodstock Blvd; 503/771-1112; www.reed.edu; map:II5). Founded in 1867, Lewis and Clark College, a liberal arts school known for its international programs, is located off SW Terwilliger Boulevard in Southwest Portland (0615 SW Palatine Hill Rd; 503/768-7000; www.lclark.edu; map:JJ6). Lewis and Clark is also home to the acclaimed Northwestern School of Law. Marylhurst University, once a women's college, became coeducational in 1976 (just more than a mile south of Lake Oswego at 17600 SW Pacific Hwy; 503/636-8141; www.marylhurst.edu; map:MM6). Warner Pacific College (2219 SE 68th Ave; 503/517-1000; www.warnerpacific.edu; map:HH4) is a liberal arts school affiliated with the Church of God. On the opposite side of town is another Christian school, Concordia University (2811 NE Holman St; www.cu-portland.edu; 503/288-9371).

Community colleges also abound. Portland Community College (503/244-6111; www.pcc.edu) has three campuses in the metropolitan area: Cascade Campus (705 N Killingsworth St; map:EE5), Rock Creek Campus (17705 NW Springville Rd; map:EE9), and Sylvania Campus (12000 SW 49th Ave; map:JJ7); Mount Hood Community College is located in Gresham (26000 SE Stark St; 503/491-6422; www.mhcc.cc.or.us/); and Clackamas Community College is in Oregon City (19600 S Molalla; 503/657-6958; www.clackamas.cc.or.us/). The Pacific Northwest College of Art (1241 NW Johnson St; 503/226-4391; www.pnca.edu) and the Oregon College of Art and Craft (8245 SW Barnes Rd; 503/297-5544; www.ocac.edu) both grant bachelor of fine arts degrees.

Important Telephone Numbers

EMERGENCY: POLICE, FIRE, AMBULANCE	**911**
DIRECTORY ASSISTANCE	**411**
AAA (Automobile Association of America), Portland office	**503/222-6734**
AIDS HOTLINE	**503/223-AIDS**
ALCOHOLICS ANONYMOUS	**503/223-8569**
AMTRAK	**800/872-7245**

ANIMAL CONTROL — 503/248-3066

AUTO IMPOUND — 503/823-0044

BETTER BUSINESS BUREAU — 503/226-3981

BIRTH AND DEATH RECORDS (Oregon Vital Records) — 503/731-4095

BLOOD DONATION — 503/284-4040

CHAMBER OF COMMERCE — 503/228-9411

CHILD ABUSE HOTLINE (Multnomah County) — 503/731-3100

CITY OF PORTLAND (general information) — 503/823-4000

COAST GUARD — 503/240-9310

emergencies: 503/240-9300

CONSUMER HOTLINE — 503/229-5576

DRUNK DRIVERS HOTLINE — 800/24-DRUNK

ENVIRONMENTAL PROTECTION AGENCY — 503/326-3250

FBI — 503/224-4181

HEALTH INFORMATION AND REFERRAL — 503/248-3816

HUMANE SOCIETY (lost pets) — 503/285-0641

IMMIGRATION AND NATURALIZATION SERVICE

(information hotline) 800/375-5283

INTERNAL REVENUE SERVICE — 800/829-1040

MARRIAGE LICENSES AND PASSPORTS — 503/248-3027

PARKS AND RECREATION INFORMATION — 503/823-2223

PERMIT CENTER INFORMATION — 503/823-7310

PLANNED PARENTHOOD — 503/775-0861

POISON CONTROL CENTER — 503/494-8968

POST OFFICE INFORMATION — 800/ASK-USPS

POWER OUTAGES (24 hours) — 503/464-7777

RECYCLING INFORMATION — 503/234-3000

RED CROSS — 503/284-1234

ROAD CONDITIONS — 800/977-6368 or 503/588-2941

STATE PATROL (Monday–Friday) — 503/731-3020

SUICIDE PREVENTION, MENTAL HEALTH CRISIS, AND CHEMICAL DEPENDENCY — 503/215-7082

TICKETMASTER — 503/224-4400

TIME, TEMPERATURE, AND WEATHER (KXL) — 503/243-7575

TRI-MET — 503/238-RIDE

VISITOR INFORMATION — 503/222-2223

VOTER INFORMATION — 503/248-3720

WOMEN'S CRISIS LINE (sexual assault, domestic violence) — 503/235-5333

TOP 200 RESTAURANTS

Restaurants by Star Rating

★★★★

Genoa
The Heathman Restaurant
  and Bar
Paley's Place

★★★★☆

Cafe Azul
Castagna
Joel Palmer House
Wildwood

★★★

Briggs and Crampton's
  Table for Two
Bugatti's Ristorante
  Italiano
Cafe des Amis
Caprial's Bistro
Couvron
El Gaucho
Ezparza's Tex-Mex Cafe
Fishtales
Higgins
Jake's Famous Crawfish
Lemongrass Thai
  Restaurant
Lucy's Table
McCormick & Schmick's
  Seafood Restaurant
Morton's of Chicago—
  The Steakhouse
Red Hills Provincial Dining
Restaurant Murata
Tapeo
3 Doors Down
Tina's
Winterborne

★★★☆

Assaggio
Bread and Ink Cafe
Caffe Mingo
Compass World Bistro
Gino's Restaurant
Horn of Africa
Hudson's Bar & Grill
Il Piatto
Khun Pic's Bahn Thai
Laslow's Northwest
L'Auberge
Mother's Bistro & Bar

¡Oba!
Papa Haydn
Pazzo Ristorante
Pho Van
Red Star Tavern & Roast
  House
Ruth's Chris Steak House
Saucebox
Serratto
Southpark
Sungari Restaurant
Syun
Typhoon!
Veritable Quandary

★★

Al-Amir
Alexis
Basta's
Beaches Restaurant & Bar
Berbati
Bernie's Southern Bistro
Besaw's
Bijou Cafe
Black Rabbit Restaurant
  and Bar
Bombay Cricket Club
  Restaurant
Brasserie Montmartre
BridgePort Ale House
Byways Cafe
Campbell's Bar-B-Q
Chez Grill
Clarke's
Colosso
Counter Culture
Daily Cafe
DaVinci's Italiano
  Ristorante
Delta Cafe
Dundee Bistro
Fa Fa Gourmet
Fernando's Hideaway
Fratelli
Gourmet Productions
  Market
Grand Central Bakery and
  Cafe
Hall Street Bar & Grill
Hands On Cafe
Harborside
Henry Ford's

Henry's Cafe
Hiro
Ikenohana
Il Fornaio
Jarra's Ethiopian
  Restaurant
Jo Bar and Rotisserie
John Street Cafe
Ken's Home Plate
La Catalana
Le Bouchon
Legin
London Grill
Marco's Cafe and
  Espresso Bar
McCormick's Fish House
  and Bar
Montage
New Seoul Garden
Nicholas' Restaurant
Opus Too
The Original Pancake
  House
Oritalia
Pambiche
Paparrazzi Pastaficio
Paragon
Pavilion Trattoria
Plainfield's Mayur
Portland Steak and
  Chophouse
Riccardo's Restaurant &
  Espresso Bar
The Ringside
Roland's
Saburo's
Saigon Kitchen
Salvador Molly's
Sammy's Restaurant and
  Bar
Swagat
Sweetwater's Jam House
Thai Orchid
Thanh Thao
Three Square Grill
Todai
Umenoki
Wild Abandon
William's on 12th
Zell's: An American Cafe

★★
Alameda Brewhouse
Bush Garden
Chez Jose
Doris' Cafe
Esplanade
Fong Chong
Good Dog/Bad Dog
Holden's
India House
Ivy House
Jake's Grill
Koji Osakaya
La Calaca Comelona
Marrakesh
Metronome
Milo's City Cafe
Noho's Hawaiian Cafe
Obi
Pasta Veloce
Pho Hung
Pizzicato
Red Electric Cafe
Ringside East
Rustica
Sayler's
Stickers Asian Cafe
Tennessee Red's Country
    Cooking

★
Abou Karim
Albertina's
Anne Hughes Kitchen
    Table Cafe
Aztec Willie & Joey Rose
    Taqueria
Bai Tong
Bangkok Kitchen
Billy Reed's
Brasilia
Cafe du Berry
Casablanca
Caswell
Clay's Smokehouse Grill
Czaba's Barbecue and
    Catering, Inc.
Dan and Louis' Oyster
    Bar
El Burrito Loco
Escape From New York
    Pizza
Fat City Cafe
Foothill Broiler
Fusion
Giant Drive-In
Good Day
Hoda's Middle Eastern
    Cuisine

House of Asia
Hunan
J&M Cafe
Kornblatt's
La Buca
La Prima Trattoria
Little Italy's Trattoria
Little Wing Cafe
Lorn and Dottie's
    Luncheonette
Misohapi
Morning Star Espresso
Nancy Lee's Pharmacy
    Fountain
Old Wives' Tales
Raccoon Lodge
Taqueria Chavez
Tara Thai Northwest
Thai Little Home
Vista Spring Cafe
Wild Heron Cafe
Wu's Open Kitchen
Yen Ha

UNRATED
Bluehour

Restaurants by Neighborhood

ALAMEDA/BEAUMONT
Alameda Brewhouse
Pizzicato
Winterborne

NE ALBERTA ST
Bernie's Southern Bistro

BEAVERTON
Beaches Restaurant & Bar
Bush Garden
Hall Street Bar & Grill
Ikenohana
McCormick's Fish House
    and Bar
New Seoul Garden
Pavilion Trattoria
Pho Hung
Sayler's
Swagat

BELMONT
Bangkok Kitchen

Genoa
Hoda's Middle Eastern
    Cuisine
Khun Pic's Bahn Thai
Sweetwater's Jam House
Wild Abandon

**BURLINGAME/
CAPITOL HILL**
Chez Jose
Henry Ford's
The Original Pancake
    House
Thai Orchid

CHINATOWN
Fong Chong
Good Day

DAYTON
Joel Palmer House

DOWNTOWN
Al-Amir

Brasserie Montmarte
Bush Garden
El Gaucho
Fernando's Hideaway
Good Dog/Bad Dog
The Heathman Restaurant
    and Bar
Higgins
Hunan
India House
Jake's Famous Crawfish
Jake's Grill
Koji Osakaya
London Grill
Lorn and Dottie's
    Luncheonette
McCormick & Schmick's
    Seafood Restaurant
Morning Star Espresso
Morton's of Chicago—
    The Steakhouse
Mother's Bistro & Bar

Oritalia
Pasta Veloce
Pazzo Ristorante
Pizzicato
Portland Steak and
   Chophouse
Red Star Tavern & Roast
   House
Restaurant Murata
Ruth's Chris Steak House
Saucebox
Southpark
Todai
Sungari Restaurant
Typhoon! on Broadway
Veritable Quandary

DUNDEE
Dundee Bistro
Red Hills Provincial Dining
Tina's

EAST SIDE, CLOSE IN
Albertina's
Anne Hughes Kitchen
   Table
Caswell
Daily Cafe
Il Piatto
J&M Cafe
La Calaca Comelona
La Catalana
Lemongrass Thai
   Restaurant
Montage
Nicholas' Restaurant
Old Wives' Tales
William's on 12th
Zell's: An American Cafe

GOOSE HOLLOW
Couvron

GRESHAM
El Burrito Loco
Pasta Veloce
Pizzicato
Roland's
Thai Orchid

HAWTHORNE
Bombay Cricket Club
   Restaurant
Bread and Ink Cafe
BridgePort Ale House
Casablanca
Castagna
Chez Grill

Compass World Bistro
Grand Central Bakery and
   Cafe
Jarra's Ethiopian
   Restaurant
Ken's Home Plate
Thanh Thao
3 Doors Down

HILLSBORO
Syun

HILLSDALE
Pizzicato
Red Electric Cafe
Salvador Molly's
Three Square Grill

IRVINGTON
Marco's Cafe and
   Espresso Bar

LAKE OSWEGO
Clarke's
Giant Drive-In
Gourmet Productions
   Market
Hiro
Riccardo's Restaurant &
   Espresso Bar
Wild Heron Cafe
Wu's Open Kitchen

LAURELHURST
Esparza's Tex-Mex Cafe
La Buca East
Pambiche
Pizzicato

**LLOYD CENTER/
NE BROADWAY**
Aztec Willie & Joey Rose
   Taqueria
Chez Jose
Colosso
Grand Central Bakery and
   Cafe
Koji Osakaya
Metronome
Milo's City Cafe
Paparrazzi Pastaficio
Rustica
Saigon Kitchen

MILWAUKIE
DaVinci's Italiano
   Ristorante

MULTNOMAH
Fat City Cafe
Grand Central Bakery and
   Cafe
Marco's Cafe and
   Espresso Bar

NORTHEAST
Albertina's
Billy Reed's
Counter Culture
Doris' Cafe
Grand Central Bakery and
   Cafe
Horn of Africa
Lemongrass Thai
   Restaurant
Pho Hung
Ringside East

**NORTH PORTLAND/
ST. JOHNS**
Czaba's Barbecue and
   Catering, Inc.
El Burrito Loco
John Street Cafe
Taqueria Chavez

NORTHWEST
Basta's
Besaw's
Briggs and Crampton's
   Table for Two
Cafe des Amis
Caffe Mingo
Escape From New York
   Pizza
Foothill Broiler
Il Fornaio
Jo Bar and Rotisserie
Kornblatt's
La Buca West
Laslow's Northwest
L'Auberge
Lucy's Table
Marrakesh
Misohapi
Nancy Lee's Pharmacy
   Fountain
Paley's Place
Papa Haydn
Pizzicato
The Ringside
Sammy's Restaurant and
   Bar
Serratto
Swagat

Tapeo
Tara Thai Northwest
Thai Orchid
Typhoon!
Umenoki
Wildwood

OLD TOWN
Abou Karim
Alexis
Berbati
Bijou Cafe
Dan and Louis' Oyster Bar
Lorn and Dottie's
   Luncheonette
Obi
Opus Too

PEARL DISTRICT
Bluehour
Byways Cafe
Cafe Azul
Fratelli
Holden's
Ken's Home Plate
Le Bouchon
Little Wing Cafe
¡Oba!
Paragon

PORTLAND HEIGHTS
Nancy Lee's Pharmacy
   Fountain
Plainfield's Mayur
Vista Spring Cafe

RALEIGH HILLS
La Prima Trattoria
Raccoon Lodge

RIVERPLACE
Esplanade
Harborside

ROSE CITY
Yen Ha

SELLWOOD
Assaggio
Gino's Restaurant

SOUTHEAST, BEYOND 39TH
Campbell's Bar-B-Q
El Burrito Loco
Fusion
Legin
Pho Hung
Sayler's
Tennessee Red's Country
   Cooking

SE CLINTON & DIVISION
Clay's Smokehouse Grill
Henry's Cafe
Little Italy's Cucina
Noho's Hawaiian Cafe
Saigon Kitchen

SW MACADAM/ JOHNS LANDING
Bai Tong
Brasilia
Cafe du Berry
House of Asia
Koji Osakaya
Noho's Hawaiian Cafe

TIGARD
Pasta Veloce
Wu's Open Kitchen

TROUTDALE
Black Rabbit Restaurant
   and Bar

TUALATIN
Bush Garden

WEST LINN
Bugatti's Ristorante
   Italiano
Thai Orchid

WEST SLOPE
Hands On Cafe
Pizzicato

WESTMORELAND
Caprial's Bistro
Fishtales
Ivy House
Papa Haydn
Pizzicato
Saburo's
Stickers Asian Cafe

WOODSTOCK
Delta Cafe

VANCOUVER, WA
Beaches Restaurant & Bar
Hudson's Bar & Grill
Fa Fa Gourmet
Little Italy's Trattoria
Noho's Hawaiian Cafe
Pizzicato
Thai Little Home
Thai Orchid

Restaurants by Food and Other Features

AMERICAN
Albertina's
Beaches Restaurant and Bar
Besaw's
Black Rabbit Restaurant and Bar
Bread and Ink Cafe
Byways Cafe
Fat City Cafe
Hall Street Bar & Grill
Harborside
Henry Ford's
Jake's Grill
London Grill (The Benson Hotel)
Montage
Mother's Bistro & Bar
Nancy Lee's Pharmacy Fountain
Red Star Tavern & Roast House
Sammy's Restaurant and Bar
Three Square Grill
Zells: An American Cafe

BAKERIES
Grand Central Bakery and Cafe
Il Fornaio

BARBECUE
Campbell's Bar-B-Q
Clay's Smokehouse Grill
Czaba's Barbecue
Doris'cafe
Tennessee Red's Country Cooking

BENTO
Misohapi

BRAZILIAN
Brasilia

BREAKFAST
Besaw's
Bijou Cafe
Bread and Ink Cafe
Byways Cafe
Cafe du Berry
Fat City Cafe
Foothill Broiler

The Heathman Restaurant and Bar
J & M Cafe
John Street Cafe
Lorn and Dottie's
Kornblatt's
Marco's Cafe and Espresso Bar
Milo's City Cafe
The Original Pancake House
Red Electric Cafe
Wild Heron Cafe
Zells: An American Cafe

BREWPUBS
(See also Nightlife chapter)
Alameda Brewhouse
BridgePort Ale House
Raccoon Lodge

BRUNCH
Bread and Ink Cafe
Compass World Bistro
Dundee Bistro
Esplanade at RiverPlace
Hands on Cafe
Il Fornaio
Jo Bar and Rotisserie
London Grill
Papa Haydn
Red Star Tavern and Roast House
Sammy's Restaurant and Bar
Three Square Grill
Veritable Quandary
Wild Abandon
Wildwood

BURGERS
Beaches Restaurant and Bar
Besaw's
Bijou Cafe
Billie Reed's
Bread and Ink Cafe
Byways Cafe
El Gaucho
Fat City Cafe
Foothill Broiler
Giant Drive-In
Jamie's

Jo Bar and Rotisserie
John Street Cafe
L'Auberge
Marco's Cafe
Mother's
Paragon
The Ringside
Zell's: An American Cafe

CAJUN/CREOLE
Montage
Sweetwater's Jamhouse

CAMBODIAN
House of Asia

CARIBBEAN
¡Oba!
Salvador Molly's
Sweetwater's Jam House

CHINESE
Fa Fa Gourmet
Fong Chong
Good Day
Hunan
Legin
Sungari
Wu's Open Kitchen

COFFEEHOUSES
(See also Nightlife chapter)
Anne Hughes Kitchen Table
Daily Cafe
Il Fornaio
Marco's Cafe and Espresso Bar
Morning Star Espresso

CONTINENTAL
Clarke's
London Grill (The Benson Hotel)
Roland's

CUBAN
Pambiche

DESSERTS, EXCEPTIONAL
Bluehour
Bread and Ink Cafe
Cafe Azul
Castagna

The Heathman Restaurant
and Bar
Higgins
L'Auberge
Papa Haydn
Paley's Place
Pambiche
Wildwood

DIM SUM
Fong Chong
Legin

EAST AFRICAN/
ETHIOPIAN
Horn of Africa
Jarra's Ethiopian
Restaurant

ECLECTIC
Caswell
Compass World Bistro
Counter Culture
FusionGourmet
Productions
Hands on Cafe
Henry's Cafe
Metronome
Old Wives' Tales
Paragon
Wild Abandon
William's on 12th

FAMILY
Alexis
Aztec Willie & Joey Rose
Taqueria
Bai Tong
Byways Cafe
Dan & Louis' Oyster Bar
Doris' Cafe
Fat City Cafe
Fong Chong
Foothill Broiler
Giant Drive-In
Gino's Restaurant
Good Dog/Bad Dog
Il Fornaio
Ivy House
Jamie's
Legin
Marco's Cafe and
Espresso Bar
New Seoul Garden
Old Wives' Tales
The Original Pancake
House
Pho Van

Pizzicato
Salvador Molly's
Thanh Thao
Todai
Vista Spring Cafe
Wu's Open Kitchen

FIREPLACE
Esplanade
The Heathman Restaurant
and Bar
Hudson's
Il Fornaio
Jake's Famous Crawfish
Joel Palmer House
L'Auberge
¡Oba!
Paragon
Plainfield's Mayur
Red Hills Provincial Dining
The Ringside
Sayler's
Tina's

FRENCH
Brasserie Montmartre
Cafe des Amis
Castagna
Couvron
The Heathman Restaurant
and Bar
L'Auberge
Le Bouchon

FUSION
Oritialia

GOOD VALUE
Albertina's
Anne Hughes Kitchen
Table
Bai Tong
Delta Cafe
Doris' Cafe
Good Day
Gourmet Productions
Henry's Cafe
Holden's
Horn of Africa
Legin
Metronome
Pasta Veloce
Pho Hung
Pho Van
Taqueria Chavez
Thanh Thao

GOURMET TAKE OUT
Gourmet Productions
Ken's Home Plate

GREEK
Alexis
Berbati
Nicholas' Restaurant

HAWAIIAN
Noho's Hawaiian Cafe

INDIAN
Bombay Cricket Club
India House
Plainfield's Mayur
Swagat

ITALIAN
(See also Pizza)
Assaggio
Basta's
Bugatti's Ristorante
Italiano
Caffe Mingo
Castagna
DaVinci's Italiano
Ristorante
Fratelli
Genoa
Gino's Restaurant
Il Fornaio
Il Piatto
La Buca
La Prima Trattoria
Little Italy's Trattoria
Paparrazzi Pastaficio
Pasta Veloce
Pavilion Trattoria
Pazzzo Ristorante
Riccardo's Restaurant
Rustica
Serratto
3 Doors Down
Veritable Quandary

JAPANESE
Bush Garden
Hiro
Ikenohana
Koji Osakaya
Misohapi
Murata
Obi
Saburo's
Syun
Todai
Umenoki

JEWISH
Bread and Ink Cafe
Kornblatt's
Mother's Bistro & Bar

KOREAN
New Seoul Garden

LATE NIGHT
Brasserie Montmartre
Caswell
Montage

LATIN AMERICAN
¡Oba!
Salvador Molly's

LUNCH ONLY
Albertina's
Brigg's and Crampton's
    Table for Two

MEDITERRANEAN
Bluehour
Fishtales
Lucy's Table
Southpark

MEXICAN
Aztec Willie & Joey Rose
    Taqueria
Cafe Azul
El Burrito Loco
La Calaca Comelona
¡Oba!
Taqueria Chavez

MIDDLE EASTERN
Abou Karim
Al-Amir
Hoda's Middle Eastern
    Cuisine
Nicholas' Restaurant

MILK SHAKES
Bijou Cafe
Byways Cafe
Fat City Cafe
Foothill Broiler
Giant Drive-In
Jamie's
Mother's Bistro & Bar
Nancy Lee's Pharmacy
    Fountain
Vista Spring Cafe

MOROCCAN
Casablanca
Marrakesh

NORTHWEST
Atwaters
Bluehour
Caprial's Bistro and Wine
Compass Cafe
Dundee Bistro
Esplanade
Hands on Cafe
The Heathman Restaurant
    and Bar
Higgins
Hudson's Bar & Grill
Joel Palmer House
Laslow's Northwest
Paley's Place
Pavilion Trattoria
Red Hill's

PROVINCIAL DINING
Tina's
Wild Abandon
Wildwood

ONION RINGS
Alameda Brewhouse
Portland Steak and
    Chophouse
The Ringside
Ruth's Chris Steak House
Salvador Molly's
Wildwood

OUTDOOR DINING
Basta's
Beaches Restaurant & Bar
Black Rabbit Restauant
    and Bar
Bugatti's Ristorante
Castagna
Chez Jose East
Compass World Bistro
Hall Street Grill
Hands on Cafe
Harborside
Henry's Cafe
Ivy House
Joel Palmer House
Laslow's Northwest
L'Auberge
Paley's Place
Riccardo's Restaurant
Salvador Molly's
Sammy's Restaurant and Bar
Tapeo
Typhoon!
Veritable Quandary
Wildwood

OYSTERS
Bluehour
Dan & Louis' Oyster Bar
Jake's Famous Crawfish
Montage
Wildwood

PAN-ASIAN
Misohapi
Saucebox
Stickers Asian Cafe

PIZZA
Beaches Restaurant & Bar
BridgePort Ale House
DaVinci's Italian
    Ristorante
Escape from New York
    Pizza
La Prima Trattoria
Pizzicato
Vista Spring Cafe

PRIVATE ROOMS
Atwaters
Black Rabbit
Caprial's Bistro
Serratto

ROMANTIC
Assaggio
Bluehour
Cafe des Amis
Caffe Mingo
Couvron
Fernando's Hideaway
Genoa
Gino's
The Heathman Restaurant
    and Bar
Henry's Cafe
Il Piatto
Joel Palmer House
Lucy's Table
Marrakesh
Paley's Place
Sungari Restaurant
Veritable Quandary
Wild Abandon

SEAFOOD
Dan & Louis' Oyster Bar
Fishtales
Hall Street Grill
Harborside
Jake's Famous Crawfish
Lemongrss
Legin

McCormick & Schmick's
Opus Too
Southpark
Typhoon!
Winterborne

SOUP/SALAD/ SANDWICH

Anne Hughes Kitchen
   Table
Bijou Cafe
Daily Cafe
Grand Central Bakery and
   Cafe
Hands on Cafe
Holden's
J & M Cafe
John Street Cafe
Little Wing Cafe
Marco's Cafe & Espresso
   Bar
Morning Star Espresso
Nancy Lee's Pharmacy
   Fountain
Red Electric Cafe
Wild Heron Cafe

SOUTHEAST ASIAN

Bai Tong
Bangkok Kitchen
House of Asia
Khun Pic's Bahn Thai
Lemongrass Thai
Pho Hung
Pho Van
Saigon Kitchen
Tara Thai Northwest
Thai Little Home
Thai Orchid
Thanh Thao
Typhoon!
Yen Ha

SOUTHWESTERN

Chez Grill
Chez Jose/Chez Jose East
Esparza's Tex Mex

SOUTHERN

Bernie's Southern Bistro
Delta Cafe
Doris' Cafe
Montage
Sweetwater's Jam House
Tennessee Red's Country
   Cooking

SPANISH

Colosso
Fernando's Hideaway
Fishtales
La Catalana
Tapeo

STEAK HOUSES

El Gaucho
Henry Ford's
Jake's Grill
Morton's of Chicago
Opus Too
Portland Steak and
   Chophouse
The Ringside
Ruth's Chris Steak House
Sayler's

SUSHI

Bush Garden
Hiro
Ikenohana
Koji Osakaya
Misohapi
Murata
Obi
Saburo's
Syun
Todai
Umenoki

THAI

Bai Tong
Bangkok Kitchen
House of Asia
Khun Pic's Bahn Thai
Lemongrass Thai
Saigon Kitchen
Tara Thai Northwest

Thai Little Home
Thai Orchid
Thanh Thao
Typhoon!

UNIQUELY PORTLAND

Anne Hughes Kitchen
   Table
Bijou Cafe
Caprial's Bistro
Hands on Cafe
The Heathman Restaurant
   and Bar
Henry Ford's
McCormick & Schmick's
Paley's Place
Papa Haydn
The Ringside
Southpark
Wildwood

VEGETARIAN/VEGAN

(See also ethnic
   restaurants)
Counter Culture
Old Wives' Tales
Vita Cafe

VIETNAMESE

House of Asia
Pho Hung
Pho Van
Saigon Kitchen
Thanh Thao
Yen Ha

VIEW

Atwaters
Beaches Restaurant and
   Bar
Esplanade at RiverPlace
Harborside

WINE BAR

(See also Nightlife chapter)
Assaggio
Dundee Bistro
Southpark

RESTAURANTS

Abou Karim / ★

221 SW PINE ST, OLD TOWN; 503/223-5058

The best way to dine here is to gather at least three friends for a Mezza: a quartet of kebabs supported by baba ghanouj, hummus, tabbouleh, falafel, dolmas, and a range of other Middle Eastern soul food. Relaxed, moderately priced, and roomy, Portland's long-established downtown Middle Eastern restaurant has a broad, loyal following—despite some stiff competition around town. Abou Karim is an inviting place to put away some pita—and it offers a wide range of kebabs, grilled chicken, and lamb dishes, and a particularly addictive, smoky baba ghanouj. Finish up with Lebanese coffee, and set out for a riverside stroll. *$$; AE, MC, V; checks OK; lunch Mon–Fri, dinner every day; full bar; reservations recommended; map:I5*

Alameda Brewhouse / ★★☆

4765 NE FREMONT ST, BEAUMONT; 503/460-9025

Located in the heart of the Beaumont neighborhood, this family-friendly brewpub draws out the locals like ants to a picnic with its handcrafted ales made distinct with ingredients like sage, juniper, and Willamette Valley fruit. Inside this lofty warehouse, folks perch on stools along the sinuous bar or crowd into one of the honey-colored slat-backed booths (which in the right light look like harvest wheat sheaves) to nibble on above-average pub fare: superb smoked chicken quesadillas with chipotle accents, salmon gyros with a dilly tzatziki, Cajun calamari, and lemon-pepper chicken strips with pesto-cilantro ranch dressing. Larger plates include thick fish-and-chips, huge slabs of baby back ribs, a generous burger with traditional garnishes, whiskey-chipotle barbecue chicken, a noteworthy Reuben, and other classic sandwiches. If you're still hungry, try the home-baked pies or exquisite cheesecakes. If you're still thirsty, you can take home a 32-ounce carryout of beer. *$$; AE, MC, V; checks OK; lunch, dinner every day; full bar; reservations required; map:FF4 &*

Al-Amir / ★★

223 SW STARK ST, DOWNTOWN; 503/274-0010

There may be some clash between the exterior decorations on the old Bishop's House and this restaurant's interior, which exudes Middle Eastern warmth, but the menu resolves everything. In Portland's most elaborate and satisfying Lebanese restaurant, the smoky, intense baba ghanouj and the creamy hummus are outstanding, but the kitchen's reach is extensive. It does a particularly savory job on meats: the shish kebab, lamb vibrant with spices and juices, highlights a menu that stretches to *kharouf muammar,* a huge pile of moist, faintly sweet lamb chunks; and *dujaj musahab,* a charcoal-grilled chicken breast in lemon and olive oil.

Don't depart without trying the dolmas. A little Lebanese beer makes the light through the bishop's stained-glass windows shine even more brightly. *$$; AE, MC, V; no checks; lunch Mon–Fri, dinner every day; full bar; reservations recommended; map:I5* &

Albertina's / ★

424 NE 22ND AVE, NORTHEAST; 503/231-0216

This place should be honored for good karma alone. Except for the head chef and kitchen manager, all help in the former orphanage is volunteer, and revenues are used to support the Albertina Kerr Center for the Treatment of Physically and Emotionally Disturbed Children. The inexpensive three-course lunch also happens to be quite good: the menu, which changes weekly and is surprisingly inventive, starts with an appetizer, soup, or salad; is followed by an entree such as quiche lorraine, orzo shrimp salad, or chicken pot pie; and then finishes with dessert, maybe raspberry ginger cream or lemon ice cream. There are two seatings daily, at 11:30am and 1pm, and reservations are recommended. Next door in the Economy Jar you'll find heirloom jewelry and china sets to pass down through your own family. *$; MC, V; checks OK; lunch Mon–Fri; beer and wine; reservations recommended; map:FF5* &

Alexis / ★★

215 W BURNSIDE ST, OLD TOWN; 503/224-8577

This boisterous institution of a Greek restaurant is a family operation that makes every diner feel like a cousin: the welcome here is warmer than the flaming *saganaki* (Greek cheese ignited with ouzo). On their journey toward substantial, fork-tender lamb dishes and other entrees, diners are slowed by plump grape-leaf packets, terrific calamari, and the little pillows of filo and feta known as *tiropitas*. While being entertained by the appetizers, try not to be filled up by them; moussaka and lamb souvlaki await, and you wouldn't want to miss them. Baskets of addictive warm house bread come with the meal—and if you like what you taste, take heart: Alexis sells it retail, along with various other specialties. The food could even distract you from the belly dancers. *$$; AE, DC, MC, V; no checks; lunch Mon–Fri, dinner Mon–Sat (belly dancers Fri–Sat); full bar; no reservations necessary; map:J5* &

Anne Hughes Kitchen Table Cafe / ★

400 SE 12TH AVE, SOUTHEAST; 503/230-6977

Some know Anne Hughes from her coffee room at Powell's Books; others might remember her from the poster she posed for sans clothes a few years back (for art's sake, OK?). And then there are those who've made her acquaintance at this cozy soup kitchen in Southeast Portland. Lunch here means three soups a day—maybe carrot with ginger cream, chicken Thai coconut, or butternut squash chili—served with French bread, focaccia, or corn bread. Also offered at lunch are a couple of different sandwich choices (along the lines of turkey, ham, or cheese) and salads. The cafe doubles as a neighborhood coffeehouse, making it a good place to stop in the morning for pastry and coffee, or to read the paper in the afternoon with a cappuccino and a slice of homemade marionberry pie. *$; no credit cards; checks OK; lunch Mon–Fri; beer and wine; no reservations; map:GG5* ॐ

Assaggio / ★★☆

7742 SE 13TH AVE, SELLWOOD; 503/232-6151

Assaggio takes pasta very seriously—and it's taught Portlanders to take it seriously enough to wait in line for it. This booming neighborhood trattoria, which draws steadily from other neighborhoods, offers more than a dozen different pastas each night, and people who have trouble choosing only one can order a trio. It could be penne with pepperoni, a carbonara, or a pungent puttanesca, or some toothsome Neapolitan noodle you've never encountered. In any case, it's likely to be lively and highly substantial. You might want to start with the nifty bruschetta, the crimini mushrooms, or the smoked-trout mousse, but be careful—the real theme here is carbo loading, and you don't want to fill up too early. The rooms where this all happens are as colorful and satisfying as the pasta. In the adjoining wine bar, Enoteca, you can order from the same menu while imbibing one of the 12 Italian wines offered by the glass. *$$; AE, MC, V; local checks only; dinner Tues–Sat; beer and wine; reservations recommended; assaggio@aol.com; www.assaggiorestaurant.com; map: JJ5* ॐ

Aztec Willie & Joey Rose Taqueria / ★

1501 NE BROADWAY, NE BROADWAY (AND BRANCHES); 503/280-8900

In one corner of this cavernous room, with its flying-saucer tables and high turquoise ceiling, is an attractive bar that serves up myriad kinds of frosty margaritas in enormous glasses large enough to bathe in. But while Aztec Willie is a distinctive bar, it's much more besides. Like its sister taquerias Santa Fe (831 NW 23rd Ave; 503/220-0406; map:GG7) and Mayas (1000 SW Morrison St; 503/226-1946; map:H2), the restaurant's strength lies in the variety of items available on the cafeteria-style menu. Diners move down a line, choosing between burritos, tacos, and enchiladas, a half-dozen kinds of each, including such stars as the vividly flavored chile verde taco, the chicken mole enchilada, and the chiles rellenos. If you're not up for a margarita, you can cool the heat of your meal with *horchata* or fresh lemonade. Especially in the summer, when diners can avail themselves of the outdoor seating, Aztec Willie is a good late-night spot—it's open until 2am—and dinner is available until midnight. It's also a good spot for people out with kids earlier in the day: in the opposite corner from the bar is an inviting glass-walled playroom. *$–$$; AE, DIS, MC, V; no checks; lunch, dinner every day; full bar; no reservations; map:FF5* ॐ

Bai Tong / ★

6141 SW MACADAM AVE, JOHNS LANDING; 503/452-4396

You have become an official Portlander when you can order in a Vietnamese restaurant without a menu. What the city lacks in inspired Chinese dining it more than makes up for with scores of simple and tasty Southeast Asian places that can turn out a good curry—yellow, green, or red. Inconspicuously set off Macadam Avenue, Bai Tong offers an extensive menu of Vietnamese standards in a comfortably modern setting. (It may lack the funky character of the eastside Thai and Vietnamese places, but you will always find parking, and no one nearby will try to sell you a beaded bracelet.) Keeping with the time-honored custom of Asian restaurants, lunch at Bai Tong starts with complimentary soup: a clean and light hot-and-sour that makes a good starter before you dig into one of the richer dishes on the menu. Begin your meal with *miang kum*— spinach leaves stuffed with dried shrimp, peanuts, and coconut—or incredibly fresh salad rolls with tofu. Noodle dishes are worthy, led by a pad thai—neither too sticky nor too sweet. Curries are rich and redolent of kaffir lime leaf and ginger. The whole fried fish is an experience in itself: crispy golden and just hard enough to eat to stimulate conversation between precious bites. *$; MC, V; no checks; lunch Mon–Fri, dinner every day; beer and wine; no reservations; map:JJ6* &

Bangkok Kitchen / ★

2534 SE BELMONT ST, BELMONT; 503/236-7349

Despite the fact that new owners have taken over what was known as an institution under the tutelage of Srichan Miller and her family (see reviews in this chapter of Lemongrass Thai Restaurant and Khun Pic's Bahn Thai), locals still frequent this no-frills Thai restaurant for the unadorned basics of Southeast Asian cooking: hot-and-sour soups, pungent curries, tangy seafood salads, and lively noodles. On a good day, the flavors dance on the palate, reminding diners that a dousing of spices can do the spirit good. Favorites include the whole crisp sea bass in a concentrated chile sauce; the marinated prawns with baby corn, mushrooms, and bamboo shoots; and the basic tofu with fried rice. Soup orders are very large, so prepare to split it with friends. Also, check the daily special board for more inventive and daring dishes. Whatever you order, the laid-back staff will make you feel at home. *$; MC, V; no checks; lunch Mon–Sat, dinner every day; beer and wine; no reservations; map:GG5* &

Basta's / ★★

410 NW 21ST AVE, NORTHWEST; 503/274-1572

Basta's continues doing what it has done well since it opened: serving well-priced and mostly reliable Italian fare in a Tuscan-fun atmosphere (a former fast-food hangout nicely modified into an art-filled trattoria). Although the diners on the patio might be casually attired, there's a well-dressed Caesar salad on the menu, and deftly pan-fried oysters. The emphasis is on pasta, with about a dozen shrewd entrees offering flavors ranging from wild mushrooms to duck. But there are some choices for carnivores, and the kitchen has a way with lamb—especially the slow-cooked lamb shank in an herby tomato-pancetta sauce. Breads are irresistible. *$$; AE, MC, V; checks OK; lunch Mon–Fri, dinner every day; full bar; reservations recommended; map:GG7*

Beaches Restaurant & Bar / ★★

1919 SE COLUMBIA RIVER DR, VANCOUVER, WA; 360/699-1592
Perched above the Columbia River, with an open view and a contemporary interior, Beaches has become a favorite of Vancouver residents and their guests. Its easygoing casualness pleases suits, shorts, and kids alike, who all come for the simple menu of pizzas and other specialties baked in their wood-burning oven, meal-size salads, pastas, steamed mussels, and half-pound burgers. It offers a few comfort-food signatures such as the popular Jack Daniels flamin' wings, seafood cioppino, and hot berry cobbler. The swinging bar fills up seven nights a week, and there's a growing, reasonably priced wine list. A slightly different menu can be found at the new Beaches in Beaverton (14450 SW Murray Scholls; 503/579-3737)—and a completely different view. *$$; AE, DC, MC, V; checks OK; lunch, dinner every day; full bar; reservations recommended; www.yagottahavefun.com; map:BB5* ৬

Berbati / ★★

19 SW 2ND AVE, OLD TOWN; 503/226-2122
Skip the noisy atmospherics—inside and outside—and concentrate on the consistently good Greek food. Order a tableful of appetizers—the creamy tzatziki, delicious dolmas, and the refreshingly unadulterated Greek salad—and expect to be perfectly satisfied, and possibly full before you get any further. Sautéed prawns are a signature dish, but the menu runs wide. The chicken souvlaki is served alongside a lemon-spiked potato wedge. The *tiropita*—a hot, cheese-filled pastry—is so smooth it cries out for an accompanying glass of pine-scented retsina. And the calamari is simply the best fried squid in town. Berbati's Pan occupies the other side of the building, with live music and a bustling scene. If anything, Berbati has just become more of a hangout—but we've been hanging out here all along. *$$; AE, DIS, MC, V; no checks; dinner Tues–Sun; full bar; no reservations; map:J6* ৬

Bernie's Southern Bistro / ★★

2904 NE ALBERTA ST, ALBERTA ST; 503/282-9864
The restaurant is a long way from the South, but the menu gets pretty close. The cornmeal-fried oysters are crunchy and fresh, the fried chicken hot and tangy, and the desserts—especially the ones involving pecans—

endearing. (Watch closely for pumpkin-praline cheesecake.) You can even get grits, although it's unclear why you'd want to. Bernie's covers a fair amount of southern territory, from Cajun to Carolina, but manages it gracefully and skillfully, especially when it involves fins or tails—notably blackened catfish, aggressive barbecued shrimp, and various dishes starring crayfish. Inside the cool, darkened space—and we mean dark—this place can feel like midnight on the bayou. (Outside in summer the patio is splendid.) The service is warm and gentle (they're always truly glad to see y'all) and so are the prices. *$$; AE, MC, V; no checks; dinner Tues–Sat; full bar; reservations recommended; map:FF5* &

Besaw's / ★★

2301 NW SAVIER ST, NORTHWEST; 503/228-2619
Besaw's has seen changes in chef and menu, but nothing seems to shake the powerful loyalty and affection of its customers. It's currently operating on a high level of imagination. The core menu may run to Mother's meat loaf and roast chicken, but its nightly specials expand to include dishes like habanero-glazed pork chop and bronzed scallops. At weekend breakfast, when enthusiasm may burn hottest, hearty servings of farmer's hash or French toast might be bolstered by hand-lettered specials such as poached eggs on crab cakes over yakisoba noodles with Thai curry hollandaise, or grilled salmon Benedict. In the best tradition of the neighborhood cafe, Besaw's serves three squares a day in a bright, high-ceilinged dining room that beckons the neighbors—as well as others from well beyond the reaches of Nob Hill—to come back for repeat performances. The place has been here since the turn of the century, and it has aged beautifully; everything seems polished, from the mirror above the bar to the gracious service. *$–$$; MC, V; checks OK; breakfast, lunch, dinner every day, Sun brunch; full bar; reservations recommended; map:GG7* &

Bijou Cafe / ★★

132 SW 3RD AVE, OLD TOWN; 503/222-3187
The constantly changing lunch menu may produce items such as a summer fruit and nut salad, an avocado-grapefruit salad, or steamed fish with red curry sauce and basmati rice. Specials mingle with the standards, including red snapper hash and Japanese noodle salad, and lunches are popular enough that you can get crowded out of the tables and up to one of the counters. But the real crush still happens mornings, especially weekend mornings, when the lines stretch out the door for grilled cinnamon bread, terrific scrambled eggs, and sometimes three kinds of pancakes. The Bijou, with its gleaming mirrors and almost-as-gleaming hardwood floors, long ago attained breakfast-landmark status in Portland, and the remodeling of neither the restaurant nor the entire surrounding neighborhood has changed its position. Tofu and granola still pop up in various places on the menu, but they're now joined by micro-

brews and local wines. And since the breakfast menu is served all day, you can pick just the right vintage to go with a blueberry pancake. *$$; MC, V; local checks only; breakfast, lunch every day; beer and wine; no reservations; map:J5* &

Billy Reed's / ★

2808 NE MARTIN LUTHER KING JR BLVD, NORTHEAST; 503/493-8127
Billy Reed's is the restaurant equivalent of Dorothy's house—one afternoon it fell from the sky, landing in the Standard Dairy Building on NE Martin Luther King Jr. Boulevard. The vast space—with a polished, if sterile and commercial-looking, ambience—has a bizarre Disney quality to it. Not every night, but most, you can catch rousing tunes from a live squeeze-box-and-fiddle combo, trawl for love without fear of cold elbows at the heated (for some unimaginable reason) granite bar, check your e-mail at the lounge's free Internet connection, or board a bull-painted mini-bus with a dozen other revelers to be shuttled to a Blazer game. Chef Pascal Chureau's large menu is full of fun caricatures of southern American regional favorites: fried chicken, chicken-fried steak, a "Kentucky" chicken dish that marries mushrooms and bacon with the ubiquitous bourbon sauce that must run in rivers through the streets of Louisville. Bar food is solid here, including an excellent made-from-scratch burger and unique appetizers, like a cheese and potato pancake with enough gooey richness to comfort the colicky child in any of us. Choices are, for the most part, well prepared and satisfying. Extreme hunger is a requisite for dinner at Billy Reed's: the portions are monstrous, with dinners dragged to the table groaning on thick oval platters that would do justice to any Thanksgiving turkey. *$$; AE, MC, V; checks OK; lunch, dinner every day; full bar; reservations recommended; wwwstandarddairy.com; map:FF5*

Black Rabbit Restaurant and Bar / ★★

2126 SW HALSEY ST, TROUTDALE; 503/492-3086
One thing that strikes a guest immediately at Edgefield, the estate home of Black Rabbit Restaurant and a smattering of smaller, less formal eateries and watering holes, is that everyone seems to be having a good time. Even the people who work here are smiling. One reason may be that there's something for everyone to like on these 25 acres. That's true of Black Rabbit Restaurant, too: not only is there the large, pleasant dining room, with its white-clothed tables and booths along the perimeter, but there's also a bar serving light meals and, outside, a New Orleans–style courtyard that is Edgefield's most elegant and romantic spot for supping on a summer evening. What the menu lacks in surprises it makes up for in successes. Variations on the meat-and-potato theme result in dishes like beef tenderloin with garlic mashed potatoes and roasted game hen with stuffing. The grilled pork chops encrusted with

herbs and served with roasted potatoes in a garlicky butter and the sautéed prawns spiked with poblano chiles and lime juice rarely disappoint. When the food matches the Columbia Gorge-ous setting, when the wind carries to your nose the scent of herbs from the nearby estate gardens or the smell of hops from the on-site brewery, and when there's a bed-and-breakfast room right upstairs reserved in your name, Edgefield's Black Rabbit is a great place to spend a Saturday evening. *$$–$$$; AE, DIS, MC, V; local checks only; breakfast, lunch, dinner every day; full bar; reservations recommended; www.mcmenamins.com* &

Bluehour / [unrated]
250 NW 13TH AVE, PEARL DISTRICT; 503/226-3394

Bruce Carey (of Zefiro and Saucebox fame) has undoubtedly raised the bar in Portland for dining in style. Every detail of Bluehour's urban-chic dining room, set within the prestigious Wieden & Kennedy building in the heart of the Pearl District, begs to be noticed: panels of shimmering kelp-colored fabric draped to the floor, beveled screens that reflect light from the upper walls, black walnut floors, and a fleet of designer leather chairs. No less deserving of attention is Kenny Giambalvo's menu, an intriguing swath of Mediterranean classics with unusual and lavish flourishes. Giambalvo's take on *insalata caprese* pairs heirloom tomatoes with *burrata*—a fresh mozzarella with a creamy center. A plate of humble potato gnocchi goes uptown when bathed in a fragrant black truffle and fontina sauce. Fresh lemon taglioni practically steal the show when served alongside seared yellowfin tuna. In its infancy there is already a lot to like—from the handsome room to the thoughtful wine list and Mandy Groom's splendid desserts—but it remains to be seen whether the sum of its parts will live up to its captivating appearance. *$$$; AE, DC, MC, V; checks OK; lunch Mon–Fri, dinner Mon–Sat; full bar; reservations recommended; www.bluehourestaurant.com; map:K1* &

Bombay Cricket Club Restaurant / ★★
1925 SE HAWTHORNE BLVD, HAWTHORNE; 503/231-0740

This lively little restaurant on Hawthorne serves familiar Indian food—curries, vindaloo, tandoori, biryani—and a small selection of Middle Eastern dishes, while the TV on the bar broadcasts recorded cricket matches. If cricket is not your thing, never mind; once you've tasted your first mango margarita and dipped a samosa into the tangy tamarind chutney, you'll find yourself distracted by the potential of such intriguing flavors. Focus in on chewy naan stuffed with onions and spices, succulent tandoori chicken, and garlicky-hot fish vindaloo. The only disappointment is that the condiments that usually accompany an Indian meal—mango chutney, yogurt raita, and dal—have to be ordered separately here. *$$; AE, DIS, MC, V; no checks; dinner every day; full bar; reservations recommended; map:GG5* &

Brasilia / ★

6401 SW MACADAM AVE, JOHNS LANDING; 503/293-2219

Roberto Silva and Caio Oliveira, the same folks who used to run B.J.'s Brazilian Restaurant in Westmoreland, have moved across the river to this more spacious location, with a substantial and sometimes lively bar scene. The menu remains pretty similar: a reasonably sized, reasonably priced, reasonably good evocation of Brazilian cuisine. Soups and stews remain the strong point—although some of the spicier chicken dishes might deserve some attention—and the headliner is still the *feijoada,* a crowded Brazilian stew of black beans, pork bits and sausages, and some spices that never made it into a cassoulet. After some exposure to Brazilian sugarcane liquor, it all seems even more intriguing. Live music Thursday through Saturday. *$$; MC, V; local checks only; lunch Mon–Fri, dinner Mon–Sat; full bar; reservations recommended; brasilia2k@aol.com; map:JJ6* &

Brasserie Montmartre / ★★

626 SW PARK AVE; DOWNTOWN; 503/224-5552

Over the past few years, Brasserie Montmartre's kitchen has gone through more fast shuffles than its strolling magician—but in both cases, things have ended up working out. There are several places to eat in Portland after midnight, but there's only one real restaurant at that hour. Until 1am weekdays, and 3am on weekends, Brasserie offers everything from veal with mushrooms to eggs Benedict to Beluga caviar. It also offers a burst of glass and wood enclosing the flashy black-and-white checked floor, and framed crayon drawings on the walls. The major ingredient may be the scene—Doc Martens and suits, nightly local jazz with no cover, and dancing—but the food deserves notice. The cuisine may not be subtle and exquisite, but dishes like red snapper sautéed with crabmeat and tea-smoked duck are solid and reliable. Whatever the hour, it's surprising how consistent it is—and it's always a good time for the sweetly succulent crab cakes or the roast lamb sandwich on focaccia. *$$; AE, DC, DIS, MC, V; no checks; lunch, dinner every day, brunch Sat–Sun; full bar; reservations recommended; map:H2* &

Bread and Ink Cafe / ★★★

3610 SE HAWTHORNE BLVD, HAWTHORNE; 503/239-4756

If a restaurant could ever manage to survive just on the strength of its blintzes, the beloved Bread and Ink might succeed. Sure, there are lots of other striking dishes in this homey, light-filled bistro in the heart of the funky Hawthorne District—sizable sandwiches, impressive baked desserts including a legendary cassata, and a serious hamburger, with homemade condiments that do it justice. There are reasons the place— with intriguing framed line drawings on the walls, crayons on the table, and huge windows onto Hawthorne—has become a neighborhood landmark. But the blintzes, delicately crisped squares of dough enfolding cheese, are hallowed—especially with Bread and Ink's raspberry jam. Dinner, with serious efforts such as poached salmon in ginger fumet and pork loin served with herbed polenta, also has its fans. *$$; AE, DIS, MC, V; checks OK; breakfast, lunch, dinner Mon–Sat, brunch Sun; beer and wine; reservations accepted; map:JJ5* &

BridgePort Ale House / ★★

3632 SE HAWTHORNE BLVD, HAWTHORNE; 503/233-6540
Given the upscale—especially for Hawthorne—menu and tony interior, it's easy to forget that this enterprise was spawned by a brewpub: Bridge-Port Brewing Company. Taupe green walls and cherry booths surround the cask-mounted open bar, the biggest draw for the twentysomething crowd. Everyone else grabs a table and dives into the menu: terrific pizzas (Italian sausage with roasted red peppers; grilled zucchini, mushroom, olive, tomato, and pesto) baked in the wood-fired oven in back; knife-and-fork sandwiches with exotic fillings of wood-roasted oysters or grilled chicken and caramelized onions; and tasty salads. A grilled egg-plant sandwich and veggie pot pie ensure that vegetarians needn't feel slighted. House specialties like penne with sun-dried tomato pesto, and even the New York strip steak, pair well with the BridgePort beer on tap. To top it all off, try the marbled fudge brownie served warm with vanilla ice cream, or an old-fashioned root beer float. *$$; MC, V; checks OK; lunch, dinner every day; beer and wine; no reservations; www.firkin. com; map:HH5* &

Briggs and Crampton's Table for Two / ★★★

1902 NW 24TH AVE, NORTHWEST; 503/223-8690
Though the Portland culinary scene has changed considerably since Table for Two burst onto the pages of the *Wall Street Journal* and *People* magazine, there's still nothing like it. One table, one lunch, two people. Still at 8:30am sharp on the first business day of the quarter, people leap for their phones to snag a reservation in the following three months. For $75, not counting wine or tip, a couple gets a four-course lunch worth lingering over. It might be halibut steaks with a red pepper salsa or roasted rack of lamb in a saffron-tomato demi-glace, ending with an orange-mascarpone tart. Though there is no set menu, don't worry about being served something you fear (the week before your reservation, one of the cooks calls to find out what you do or don't like and then takes it from there). It's like dining at the house of friend who happens to be a very good cook, but you get to bring the friend. Within such an intimate setting (with no one waiting for your table) people have been known to make lunch last until dinner. Last minute reservations can be made in the event of a cancellation; don't be afraid to call. *$$$; MC, V; checks OK; lunch Tues–Fri; beer and wine; reservations required; map:FF6*

Bugatti's Ristorante Italiano / ★★★

18740 WILLAMETTE DR, WEST LINN; 503/636-9555

Lydia Bugatti and John Cress's endearing Italian restaurant in West Linn features fine Italian wines, seasonal foods, and a menu that changes every few weeks. Anytime, keep watch for rigatoni carbonara and spaghetti frutti di mare. Recently highlights on the menu included a grilled chicken risotto and veal with shallots and grilled asparagus. There's a nice olive oil spiked with garlic for bread-dipping, but save room for dazzling desserts such as the cloudlike tiramisu. The well-dressed yet simple dining room is quite large, but reservations are a good idea; it's a popular place. Those who can't get in can now console themselves with a spot at Bugatti's Caffe and Pizzeria in downtown West Linn (1885 Blankenship Rd; 503/557-8686) open every day for lunch and dinner. *$$; V; local checks only; dinner every day; beer and wine; reservations recommended; map:NN5* &

Bush Garden / ★☆

900 SW MORRISON ST, DOWNTOWN (AND BRANCHES); 503/226-7181

There's an extensive Japanese menu here, with table-produced *shabu shabu* and sukiyaki and several unexpected offerings such as scallop *batayaki* and different views of tofu, along with the widest choice of tatami rooms in Portland. But the most interesting options come through the sushi bar, where you can expertly rattle off words like *uni, ama ebi,* and *toro;* point and look hopeful; or just ask the chef to surprise you. Chefs here turn out versions of sushi and sashimi not found elsewhere— Alaskan roll with surimi and smoked salmon, fiery spicy tuna maki, pungent pickled plums. They also like to show off; ask for a translation of the day's specials. Or just leave it to the chef's inspiration, and end up with something like a deliciously crunchy, sweet soft-shell spider crab roll. Bush Garden has now burst out to the suburbs in Tualatin (8290 SW Nyberg; 503/691-9777) and Beaverton, adding a noodle house to Beaverton's Uwajimaya Asian supermarket. *$$; AE, DC, DIS, MC, V; no checks; lunch Mon–Fri, dinner every day; full bar (downtown), beer and wine (Tualatin); reservations recommended; map:H3* &

Byways Cafe / ★★

1212 NW GLISAN ST, PEARL DISTRICT; 503/221-0011

The American Roadtrip sets the theme of what was formerly known as Shakers, where hundreds of salt and pepper shakers lined the walls and those waiting for a table on the weekend waited outside, rain or shine. Now instead of condiment novelties, state plates and pendants fill the room, and a Viewfinder graces every table. Although the nineties saw a number of owners come and go, each with his or her own moniker, this place has stayed true to form. Longtime employee Collin McFadyen moved from the back seat (she was one of the original Shakers cooks) to the front when she took ownership, and she continues to drive home a menu not unlike that of the original: simple, wholesome, no-frills diner food in lumberjack-sized portions. Breakfast customers load up on griddlecakes, omelets, Scottish oatmeal, bangers, corned beef hash, or Meg's Vegetarian Hash. The lunch menu includes burgers (with a very popular ground turkey version), grilled sandwiches, soups, onion rings, and fries. The corned beef, cooked on the premises and used in the best-selling morning hash, towers between two slices of rye bread slathered with homemade horseradish sauce, and is just one example of the generous serving sizes (keep this in mind when you order the fries; a half-order easily feeds two). Of course there are milkshakes, served the old-fashioned way in a tall glass with extra in a tin cup on the side. *$; no credit cards; checks OK; breakfast every day, lunch Mon–Sat; beer and wine; no reservations; map:L2*

Cafe Azul / ★★★⯪

112 NW 9TH AVE, PEARL DISTRICT; 503/525-4422
Ever since Claire Archibald brought—with her sister Shawna—her skillful, strikingly authentic Mexican cuisine from McMinnville to the Pearl District, this restaurant has been rising in local estimation. Now the warm, high-ceilinged room draws a steady stream of diners eager for thick, rich moles, prawns rubbed with achiote and garlic paste, and cornhusk-wrapped tamales filled with wild mushrooms or chicken and plantain. Make a choice from a range of different, carefully described tequilas, and accompany it with a handmade corn tortilla taco filled with Yucatan-style pork. Flavors here are vivid and unexpected, with punchy chiles and unusual salsas. The creativity spreads buoyantly into dessert, with incredible house-made ice creams, either scooped into a trio or fashioned into a red banana ice cream sundae with chocolate, caramel, and candied peanuts. This is more than you've been accustomed to spending for Mexican food, but you've probably never had Mexican food anything like this. If getting a reservation poses a problem, consider eating at the diminutive bar, where the company is usually good and the margaritas better. *$$$; DIS, MC, V; checks OK; dinner Tues–Sat; full bar; reservations recommended; map:K3* &

Cafe des Amis / ★★★

1987 NW KEARNEY ST, NORTHWEST; 503/295-6487
People often come to Dennis Baker's polished little restaurant knowing what they'll order before they ever sit down. The specialties are legendary—Dungeness crab cakes, fillet of beef in port garlic sauce, salmon in a sorrel sauce, duck in blackberry sauce—and diners are more likely to have a hunger for one of them than to wonder what's new on the menu. They're also drawn by cobblers and fruit tarts that look like they've just been glazed in a Boulevard St. Germain pâtisserie, and the crème brûlée to die for. Specials, such as a melting lamb shank, are not to be played down or overlooked. Sidewalk tables and a bistro menu of

lighter dishes (chicken au poivre, steamed mussels, salmon salad) are the latest changes to this Northwest favorite, bringing it up to near-perfect status in our estimation. *$$–$$$; AE, MC, V; checks OK; dinner Mon–Sat; full bar; reservations recommended; map:GG7*

Cafe du Berry / ★

6439 SW MACADAM AVE, CORBETT; 503/244-5551

Good news: breakfasts at Cafe du Berry are sublime, especially the house specialty, French toast served with a sprinkling of berries. The toast arrives like an edible cloud on a plate—light, sweet, and delicious—and is served alongside a heap of well-cooked hash browns. Order a side of the country sausage (even our friend who usually eats vegetarian does), a glass of fresh-squeezed orange juice (you take oranges and you juice them, right? So why does this juice taste better than others we've had?), and a steaming cup of coffee, and you've got a dream breakfast that may just take you right through the lunch hour. Which is good news, indeed, especially when you get to the bad news: lunches and dinners here tend to be priced a bit steeply, and although the quality of the food stays high throughout the day, there may be too many other good dinner places in Portland—that are perhaps a little less rough around the edges—to eat here during the latter part of the day. Our advice: stick to Cafe du Berry in the morning, when the cheerful yellow light in the upstairs dining room almost makes us forget we're on busy Macadam Avenue and not on a hidden alley in Paris. *$$–$$$; AE, DIS, MC, V; no checks; breakfast, lunch every day, dinner Wed–Sat; beer and wine; reservations recommended; map:JJ6*

Caffe Mingo / ★★⯪

807 NW 21ST AVE, NORTHWEST; 503/226-4646

The dishes that made this tiny, exquisite trattoria an immediate smash when it opened a few years ago are still drawing crowds that spill out the door while waiting for a table. Diners eagerly wait in line for the spiedini with prawns and croutons, the gorgonzola and walnut raviolini, and the grilled portobello mushrooms. But Caffe Mingo has also gotten a bit more ambitious, with such items as grilled rare tuna with tapenade and spaghetti with hot pepper flakes and shrimp. (You can also now spend $100 on the reserve wine list.) Still, it remains a solid, inviting version of Italian cafe cuisine, and the somewhat expanded menu—and prices—won't put a deep dent in your wallet. A seat in back gets you a close-up view of the kitchen preparing your dinner; a seat in front just lets you watch people waiting for your table. *$$; AE, DC, DIS, MC, V; local checks only; dinner every day; beer and wine; reservations recommended; map:GG7* &

Campbell's Bar-B-Q / ★★

8701 SE POWELL BLVD, SOUTHEAST; 503/777-9795

People who come into this little house along Powell Boulevard and inhale deeply get more of a barbecue hit in one breath than some places provide in a rack of ribs. The dining area is quaint, the servers are cheerful and efficient, and side dishes, especially the potato salad and the corn bread, are inviting. But what packs the place is an exuberant vision of barbecue. Pork ribs, slathered with smoky brown-sugar sauce, are messy and satisfying. There are plenty of other options too, including smoked turkey, chicken, beef, and sausages. Campbell's sauce has more zip to it than you generally find up here in the Northwest; as they might say in the heart of barbecue country, this is right good Q. A space is available for parties, though some people claim any meal here is a party, and the party's never over until they've run out of peach cobbler. *$–$$; AE, DIS, MC, V; no checks; lunch, dinner Tues–Sun; no alcohol; no reservations; map:HH3*

Caprial's Bistro / ★★★

7015 SE MILWAUKIE AVE, WESTMORELAND; 503/236-6457

In recent years Caprial Pence has expanded her reach in lots of different directions, from broadcast of her national public television cooking show to the publication of ever more cookbooks—to enlarging the size of her restaurant. The original storefront is now a larger, warmer, more colorful space, with big soft chairs and walls as flashy as the cuisine: a night's offerings might include wok-steamed fish with persimmon compound butter or panseared duck breast with pomegranate glaze. There's still the Hot as Hell Chicken at lunch (grilled chicken with chile sauce over pungent peanutsauced pasta), along with creative sandwiches and salads. Mark Dowers has brought additional skills to the kitchen, and Melissa Carey is an impressive dessert chef; raspberry/blackberry linzertorte with caramel sauce can affect both your eating and your TV viewing habits. The menus shift around but never stray too far from the Northwest; dishes just get here in a different way. Paying homage to the original bistro, pre-Caprial, one of the walls is lined with wine bottles; sadly, the wines are no longer priced at retail with a minimal corkage fee, but it's still a fun way to peruse the list. *$$–$$$; MC, V; checks OK; lunch, dinner Tues–Sat; full bar; reservations recommended; caprial@caprial.com; www.caprial.com; map:JJ5* &

Casablanca / ★

2221 SE HAWTHORNE BLVD, HAWTHORNE; 503/233-4400

This Moroccan hot spot spellbinds diners with elaborate atmosphere and decoration—a swirl of billowing fabric and exotic music, and even an occasional outburst of belly dancing—and food that provides its own richness. Dinner begins with enticing appetizers, and flaky filo pastries enfold seafood or chicken. Entrees run to couscous, kebabs, and tagines, intense Moroccan stews. Baklava is rich, sweet, and flaky as you'd expect from a place that specializes in filo. And if, in this crazy world, the problems of two little people don't amount to a hill of beans, at least it's worth finding out what Casablanca does with beans, notably lentils and garbanzos. *$$; MC, V; local checks only; lunch Mon–Fri, dinner every day; beer and wine; reservations recommended; map:HH5* &

Castagna / ★★★½

1752 SE HAWTHORNE BLVD, HAWTHORNE; 503/231-7373

Bucking the trend of high-profile, dramatic dining, Castagna has slowly and steadily won over Portland diners. Understated elegance sets the tone, from the sparsely decorated dining room to the straight-forward, deftly executed menu. Together Monique Siu, one of the founding troika of the late Zefiro, and her husband Kevin Gibson (formerly of Genoa, La Catalana, and Zefiro) have created a very comfortable restaurant, softly lit and as easy on the ears as it is the eyes. Subtle, clean flavors distinguish the kitchen, drawing inspiration from classic French and Italian dishes, and highlighting what the current season and local purveyors have to offer. Though the menu changes frequently, standbys include oysters on the half shell, butter lettuce salad with vinaigrette Royale, and grilled Prime Angus N.Y. steak with a heap of shoestring potatoes. With dishes like a mixed grill of quail, lamb chop, and fennel sausage with flageolet beans or a Breton fish stew, some recall the early days of Zefiro, though the finesse is pure Castagna. Zefiro was a key player in the formation of NW 21st Avenue's restaurant row; likewise Castagna may help elevate the heat along Hawthorne Boulevard. At press time, Cafe Castagna, an adjoining bistro, just opened. The menu here is more casual and less pricey—Caesar salad, country pâté, plate-size pizzas, roast chicken—but the setting is no less refined than its parent restaurant. only louder. *$$$; AE, MC, V; checks OK; dinner Tues–Sat; full bar; reservations recommended; map:HH5* &

Caswell / ★

533 SE GRAND AVE, SOUTHEAST; 503/232-6512

A change in ownership has done little to change the feel of this place, which is an edgy bar backed up by an adventurous kitchen. The best things on the menu are the smaller plates (such as bruschetta with goat cheese and sweet red peppers) and the distinctive signature dishes, like *vatapa*, a Brazilian dish combining prawns and salmon in coconut milk, lime, and ginger, and Island Witch, a hefty calzone stuffed generously with potatoes, peppers, and garlic. Other than the *vatapa* (which will set you back $14.95), the average plate—including a variety of pizzas and pasta—rings in under $10. What was once a cherished secret among Southeast Portlanders is now a popular hangout replete with regulars from near and far. And when it comes to cocktails, when was the last time someone squeezed the orange juice to order for your drink? *$; AE, MC, V; no checks; dinner Mon–Sat; full bar; no reservations; map:H9* &

Chez Grill / ★★

2229 SE HAWTHORNE BLVD, HAWTHORNE; 503/239-4002

As you might be able to tell from the dramatic decor and the fondness for wordplay evident in the name of its bar (Chez's Lounge), Chez Grill is the upscale cousin of Chez Jose (see review in this chapter). Innovative Mexican-inspired cuisine is also the rule here, though the approach is more refined and generally takes its cues more from Sante Fe and California than from south of the border: chipotle aioli graces fried calamari; the baked avocado comes laden with polenta and toasted hazelnuts; and the pan-roasted chicken breast is stuffed with goat cheese and cilantro pesto and accompanied by a coulis of tomato, mango, and chile. Entrees include a New Mexican–style paella, with achiote-infused rice and chorizo; lamb shank braised in tomato-chipotle broth and served with nopalito-potato salad; and a grilled pork loin adobado that comes with grilled corn and tomatillo salsa. There's light fare late into the night, including fish tacos and a Caesar salad with a Southwestern twist, and plenty of people come just for the house margarita and stacks of warm, fresh tortillas. *$$–$$$; MC, V; no checks; lunch, dinner every day; full bar; reservations recommended; map:HH5* &

Chez Jose / ★★☆

8502 SW TERWILLIGER BLVD, BURLINGAME; 503/244-0007
2220 BROADWAY, NE BROADWAY; 503/280-9888

The larger, flashier Northeast outpost of this local Southwestern favorite has a bar and a slightly bigger menu, but most dishes appear in both places, to general satisfaction. Chicken breast with spicy peanut sauce, grilled shrimp with chipotle honey dip, and the weird but truly addictive squash enchiladas span both sides of the Willamette, as do the specials on each blackboard. Sometimes a bowl of the rich black bean soup with a dollop of sour cream is all you need. The original Chez Jose recently underwent a modest remodel and still attracts Lewis and Clark College hangers-on. Chez Jose East, on trendy NE Broadway, has a lot more seating, a booming bar, and garden tables outside when it's not raining. There's a kids menu, too, and at the eastside location kids eat for free every day from 5pm to 7pm with the purchase of an adult entree. *$–$$; MC, V; no checks; lunch Mon–Sat, dinner every day; full bar; reservations recommended; map:FF5, map:JJ6* &

Clarke's / ★★

455 2ND ST, LAKE OSWEGO; 503/636-2667

Transplanting himself from downtown Portland, where he produced an alluring menu before Toulouse decided it really wanted to be a bar, British-born Jonathan Clarke has scored a solid hit in a place where upscale dining has been a sometime thing. Even allowing for its location, tucked into a strip mall, Clarke's is a serious, skillful restaurant, and its proprietor has a sure sense of what to do with dishes such as Muscovy duck, goat cheese soufflé, and fresh fish. Notably, he has shrewd ideas about gravlax and roast Cornish game hen. Presentations are particularly interesting, fitting into the attractiveness of the restaurant (especially if you don't look out the window). OK, it's a storefront (actually, a couple of storefronts), but inside, it's all grace and soft lights. At lunchtime the place is more casual—expect interesting twists on sandwiches and pasta, as well as soup and salad—but no less popular. *$$; AE, DIS, MC, V; checks OK; lunch Tues–Fri, dinner Tues–Sat; full bar; reservations recommended; map:LL6* ⅋

Clay's Smokehouse Grill / ★

2932 SE DIVISION ST, SOUTHEAST; 503/235-4755

There are two schools of barbecue: if it has sauce it's not real barbecue and if it doesn't have sauce it's not real barbecue. Clay's Smokehouse falls into the category of "more sauce is better," especially when it comes to the brisket sandwich—a delicious heap of hickory-smoked beef, onions, melted cheddar cheese, and the sweet and tangy Smokehouse barbecue sauce. All sandwiches and barbecue come with home fries drizzled with garlicky sour cream and an unusual and tasty coleslaw enlivened with ginger and chile. The smoker on the premises comes into contact with almost everything on the menu—the vegetables in the red bean and smoked vegetable chili, the salmon gracing the spinach salad, and the barbecued quarter-chicken served with hot links. Smoky and casual, this is the kind of place that is comfortable for both kids and bikers. *$; AE, DIS, MC, V; no checks; lunch, dinner Tues–Sun; beer and wine; reservations recommended; map:HH5* ⅋

Colosso / ★★

1932 NE BROADWAY, NE BROADWAY; 503/288-3333

Patrons at Colosso know that sharing an assortment of tapas, a bottle of sherry, and a stirring conversation with a table full of friends is a rich way to spend the evening, without becoming poor in the process. In two low-lit, bronze-painted dining rooms, owner Julie Colosso and her staff cook up a dozen tapas and nearly half that many full dinners. Look for garlicky, piquant prawns in olive oil and sautéed mushrooms with sherry and lemon thyme mounded on a thick slice of grilled bread. The menu changes twice yearly (with the two seasons in Portland, Colosso jokes), and there's always a long list of creative cocktails and nonalcoholic drinks made with such tantalizing ingredients as fresh grapefruit juice, coconut milk, or random pickled vegetables. By the looks of things, diners enjoy the drinks almost as much as the food, and at night the place turns into a hipster hangout. *$$; MC, V; no checks; dinner every day; full bar; no reservations; map:FF5* ⅋

Compass World Bistro / ★★☆

4741 SE HAWTHORNE BLVD, HAWTHORNE; 503/231-4840
Though the Compass hops at night with a dressy, global menu that highlights a new cuisine every quarter (French, Italian, Mediterranean, and American Bistro, respectively), it's the brunch that fans come back for again and again. Everything is thoughtfully prepared here, from the old favorites—plump spinach-mozzarella omelets, feather-light pancakes—to the extraordinary, such as French toast stuffed with a delicate apricot-currant cream cheese and sprinkled with strawberries and sliced almonds, a combination so flavorful you might forgo syrup. The breakfast burrito is a black bean and vegetable omelet folded into a flour tortilla, served alongside a beautiful oven-roasted potato-and-caramelized-yam combination and melt-in-your-mouth sweet corn pudding. The garden area out back, complete with fountain, attractive plantings, and a sizable number of tables, is another reason to head in this direction. But that doesn't mean this is a fair-weather cafe only; dressed up with upholstered banquettes and warm colors with gold accents, the dining room is a lovely place to dine on both standard and extraordinary fare. *$$; AE, DIS, MC, V; checks OK; dinner Tues–Sat, brunch Sat–Sun; beer and wine; reservations recommended; www.compassworldbistro.com; map:HH4*

Counter Culture / ★★

3000 NE KILLINGSWORTH ST, NORTHEAST; 503/249-3799
"Cuisine Nurturing Community" is the motto of this understated, light-filled bistro, which has recently gone over to a 100 percent vegan menu, with no animal products whatsoever. In a working-class neighborhood where some businesses sport iron bars across their windows, Counter Culture has made a strong commitment to creating a community center for the people who live and work here. Prices have edged up recently, but they're still reasonable, and there's no scrimping on either the decor or the flavor-packed menu. Breakfast and lunch went out with the meat, but there's still weekend brunch with organic coffee, French toast, biscuits and gravy, and a variety of scrambles. The dinner menu changes frequently; past entrees have featured sweet potato–ginger cakes topped with scallions, salad rolls, and Counter Culture's own twist on pad thai. Save room for dessert—spice and carrot cake or pôts de crème (bearing in mind that even the desserts here are vegan; the faux cream cheese and crème brûlée represent an impressive culinary sleight of hand). Everything can be ordered to take home, too. With such good vibes and great food, it's a shame that this bistro can't be located within walking distance of everyone's home. *$–$$; AE, MC, V; checks OK; dinner Tues–Sat, brunch Sat–Sun; beer and wine; reservations recommended; www. foodline.com; www.counterculture.com; map:EE5* ♿

A TIME FOR TEA

With beer and coffee already fully injected into the consciousness of Portlanders, many locals are looking for the next best libation. Thank goodness for tea. Portland has become somewhat of a pilot city for the American premium tea revolution, with a slew of tea companies, teahouses, and tea schools offering people the best Camellia sinensis has to offer. And while visiting one of the city's teahouses or shops is a worthwhile endeavor, you may want to experience tea where it's the brew of choice, not an after-thought to coffee. Fortunately, Portland has some offbeat tea venues that offer a unique perspective on the leaf while taking in some of the city's most fascinating landmarks, from afternoon tea at a historic downtown hotel to a traditional Japanese tea ceremony illustrating the complexity and history of this beguiling brew.

The **Heathman Hotel** (101 SW Broadway; 503/241-4100) is, in the opinion of many, Portland's most distinguished hotel. Teeming with impressive art, elegant furnishings, and a sophisticated history, it houses one of Portland's finest restaurants and remains one of the favorite places to sit back with a glass of Scotch or, in the case of some, a cup of tea. On weekends guests gather in the hotel's luxurious lounge for tea and finger foods. True to the English tradition, the tea of choice is black, and the selection of food includes scones, cookies, and turkey salad croissants. Tea at the Heathman is especially popular around Christmas (between Thanksgiving and New Year's, tea is served every day), but space is often limited, so reserve a table to avoid disappointment. The price for adults is $14.95, less for children.

Among Portland's well-respected tea schools is **Wakai Dokokai** (503/236-4948), where students learn about Japanese tea culture and the "way of tea." Classes are ongoing, but on the last Tuesday of every month instructors invite visitors to take part

Couvron / ★★★

1126 SW 18TH AVE, GOOSE HOLLOW; 503/225-1844

This 32-seat, award-winning jewelbox of an upper, upper-scale restaurant gets more and more elaborate, but Tony Demes' skills can keep up with it. Couvron now offers three seasonally changing prix fixe menus: vegetarian at $65, seven-course at $75, and nine-course Chef's Grand Menu at $95. The presentation is as elaborate as the menu—each dish is highly architectural, stacked into hillocks or condominiums—and the descriptions are equally so. Diners might choose between pan-roasted Maine diver scallops served with crème fraîche, melted leeks, hand-pressed herb pasta, and lobster glaze or cherry-wood smoked Oregon quail served with a salad of assorted autumn garden vegetables with summer truffles, Italian white truffle oil, and port sauce. Demes is equally

in an elaborate Japanese tea ceremony. Join 10 other guests in finding respect, purity, harmony, and tranquillity in a bowl of green tea, and get a glimpse into the history of this intriguing ritual. The ceremony usually lasts about two hours, and reservations are required. The cost is $10.

If you're fascinated by the idea of the Japanese tea ceremony but you're not inclined to participate, **Portland's Japanese Garden** (611 Kingston Ave; 503/223-1321), demonstrates the ritual to the public during the summer months. Here in Portland's own garden of Eden a trained tea master explains the technique involved in the ceremony and offers visitors a bit of Japanese history. Demonstrations are held from May through September on the third Saturday of each month at 1 and 2pm. Price of admission to the garden is $6 for adults, $4 for senior citizens, and $3.50 for students and children; there is no additional charge to observe the ceremony.

Portland's newest—and perhaps most picturesque—teahouse resides in the new **Classical Chinese Garden** (NW 3rd and Everett; 503/228-8131). The two-story Tower of Cosmic Reflections looks out over the bridged lake and surrounding garden, with glimpses of the city beyond its walls. Looking inward there are beautifully-carved wood tables and benches, potted orchids, and attractively displayed teapots and cups. Visitors to the teahouse take in the tranquility while sipping from a pot of Chinese tea (White, Oolong, Green, Pu-er, or Red) and sampling tea snacks: spicy peanuts, pressed plums, almond cookies, and coconut tarts. The teahouse, run by The Toa of Tea (see Coffee and Tea in the Shopping chapter), maintains the same hours as the garden and requires admission to the garden ($6 for adults; $5 for seniors, students, and children 6-18; children 5 and under free). —*Karen Foley and Carrie Floyd*

particular about all of his ingredients, flying in his seafood from Maine and selecting local organic vegetables. He makes it all work; a several-hour meal here is lovely and inviting, right down to the closing chocolate afterthoughts. It's also heartening to see a place with a cheese course. The dining rooms may feel a bit small and crowded, but the location is striking—Couvron is directly on the new westside light rail line, and really deserves its own station. *$$$; AE, MC, V; local checks only; dinner Tues–Sat; beer and wine; reservations required; map:GG6*

Czaba's Barbecue and Catering, Inc. / ★

5907 N LOMBARD ST, ST. JOHNS; 503/240-0615
When you see the giant black oil drums smoking out front, it's not too hard to guess what the menu is likely to be. It may not be classic barbecue—classic barbecue sauce doesn't have apricot and citrus elements—but it works, and people pile in here for pork and beef ribs, hot links, chicken, and catfish in adjustable degrees of heat. Michael "Czaba"

Brown, who somehow found barbecue inspiration while growing up in Portland, also puts effort and imagination into side dishes, such as Southern succotash, cabbage salad, and vivid garlic toast. Come Thanksgiving you can bring in your own turkey to be smoked—but do call ahead. *$; DIS, MC, V; no checks; lunch Tues–Fri, dinner Tues–Sat; beer and wine; reservations recommended; map:EE7*

Daily Cafe / ★★

1100 SE GRAND AVE (REJUVENATION HOUSE PARTS), SOUTHEAST; 503/234-8189

Food and Bloom, one of Portland's bigger and better-known catering companies, oversees this sweet little cafe tucked into the southwest corner of Rejuvenation House Parts. Those weary of the remodel can break for fortification, refueling over one of the many delicious sandwiches, a bowl of heart-warming soup with grilled bread, a latte, or a cup of coffee. Others, addicted to the currant-orange scones and black truffle chocolate cookies or curious to sample one of the delicious daily specials, stop into the cafe with no intention of going anywhere but here. Enormous double-hung windows and just the right fixtures (suspended from the incredibly high ceilings) bring plenty of light to the room, while marble-topped tables and the painted mosaic cement floor lend a certain charm. *$; MC, V; no checks; breakfast, lunch every day; no alcohol; no reservations; map:EE5* &

Dan and Louis' Oyster Bar / ★

208 SW ANKENY ST, OLD TOWN; 503/227-5906

Tourists who visited Portland before the advent of the automobile came to this Old Town establishment for seafood. Now diners come for an alternative to the preciousness of the year 2000 restaurant cuisine. Just about everything here is deep-fried or stewed, although a few grilled items peep through. Among the place's charms are its value ($9.95 for the classic oyster fry, served alongside a hunk of sourdough and a haystack of iceberg lettuce sprinkled with tiny pink shrimp) and its coffee and pie (the marionberry is wonderful). Among its problems are efficient but unexciting preparations and friendly but not especially swift service. The decor is family-friendly, with a lot to look at, from plates on the walls to maritime bric-a-brac everywhere, and you get the feeling that the Wachsmuth family has held their restaurant together through thick and thin for almost a century, serving up oyster stew every single day. *$; AE, DC, DIS, JCB, MC, V; local checks only; lunch, dinner every day; beer and wine; reservations recommended; map:J6*

DaVinci's Italiano Ristorante / ★★

12615 SE MCLOUGHLIN BLVD, MILWAUKIE; 503/659-3547

This place is a major secret that the residents of Milwaukie obviously want to keep to themselves. Patrick Conner brings his San Francisco cooking experience to bear on a substantial Italian menu with multiple veal dishes, cioppino, specialties from the various regions of Italy, and pizza to go—and he manages it all with prices that don't shock the suburban market. Elegance and suave service are not the hallmark here, but solid, skillful Italian cuisine (check out the scaloppine with mushrooms or artichoke hearts) brings in local crowds and some well-informed westsiders. Admittedly, the outside doesn't look like a place that orders its own abalone flown up from San Francisco, but don't be dissuaded; Conner can connect Milan and Milwaukie. *$$; AE, MC, V; no checks; dinner Tues–Sun; full bar; reservations recommended; www.davincis italiano.com; map:LL5* &

Delta Cafe / ★★

4607 SE WOODSTOCK BLVD, WOODSTOCK; 503/771-3101

Just up the boulevard from Reed College is this hip hangout, decorated with ropes of Mardi Gras beads in the windows and Klimt reproductions on the walls, and serving steaming plates of Southern cooking on Formica-topped tables. The menu is pure Elvis, with some Cajun/Creole influence as well: fried chicken, blackened catfish, jambalaya, pork ribs, collard greens, mashed potatoes, corn bread, succotash, and apple-cheddar pie for dessert. No grits, but if it's comfort food you're after, you can get a substantial portion of mac-n-cheese for $3.50, with a hot biscuit alongside. If your thirst matches your appetite, wash it all down with a fresh-squeezed lemonade spiked with Jack Daniels, or order the 40-ounce Pabst Blue Ribbon that comes in a champagne bucket. No matter what you get, you'll still find it difficult to spend $15 for dinner. The Delta's major drawback has been a long, long wait for a table, but a just-completed expansion should help. *$; no credit cards; checks OK; lunch Sat–Sun, dinner every day; full bar; no reservations; map:II4* &

Doris' Cafe / ★★☆

325 NE RUSSELL ST, NORTHEAST; 503/287-9249

Here's the first thing to ask yourself about a visit to Doris' Cafe: how many days of salad will it take to balance an order of fried chicken wings? What's not a question is whether it's worth it; it's all tang and crunch. The rest of the chicken doesn't do badly here either, either fried or barbecued, in a smoky sauce more sweet than angry. Then there's everything else on the extensive soul food menu, from smothered roast beef to the legendary rib tip sandwiches, and sides that may make it hard for you to pick just two. (Fortunately, the corn bread doesn't count as a choice.) The bar has expanded the options, and the cool, attractive space with wood floors and high ceilings is also one of the few places around where Portlanders of all races regularly mingle. Just by themselves, the buttery pound cake and the mousse-like sweet potato pie could draw a crowd, and the barbecue smoker out in the driveway is a powerful advertisement. *$; AE, DIS, MC, V; local checks only; breakfast Sat–Sun, lunch, dinner every day; full bar; no reservations; map:EE5* &

Dundee Bistro / ★★

100-A SW 7TH ST (RTE 99W), DUNDEE; 503/554-1650

This new casual wine-country restaurant offers a sweeping view of the surrounding hills and vineyards, and a kitchen that can make you pause and take in the view. It may not be quite comparable with Tina's or Red Hills, its near neighbors, but its Painted Hills beef tenderloin or free-form ravioli are more than enough to justify a ride. As the name suggests, this place offers more options than elegant full dinners—making it a great place to stop on the way through—and the vanilla crème brûlée can follow any kind of meal you design. Dundee Bistro may be especially inviting on a summer Sunday, for a brunch of smoked-salmon eggs Benedict with a glass of local (as in up the hill) sparkling wine. Time things just right and you can precede your dinner or follow your brunch with a stop at the inviting Ponzi wine bar just across the hall. *$$; AE, MC, V; local checks only; lunch, dinner Tues–Sat, brunch Sun; full bar; reservations recommended* &

El Burrito Loco / ★

1942 N PORTLAND BLVD, NORTH PORTLAND (AND BRANCHES); 503/735-9505

The namesake creation is a fresh, floury tortilla wrapped—like a pair of pants that you can't quite button—around a chile relleno, strips of tender beef, and refried beans. It's the kind of thing that you occasionally have to have right this moment. And so are the tacos: a choice of meat folded into soft corn tortillas with cilantro, onions, and lime. Other standards on the menu range from predictably plump burritos to the sopping chile

rellenos. The *horchata*, a Mexican rice drink, outdoes an American soda any day. Service is prompt, as the young Mexican male staff takes special pride in making this restaurant run on a dime—which is a little less than what you'll pay for your meal. Takeout is big business here—could it be the dive decor?—although there are a few tables and some spare copies of Latino newspapers to peruse. *Hasta luego;* we know you'll be back for more. Two other locations worth noting: in Southeast (3162 NE 82nd Ave; 503/252-1343; map:GG3) and Gresham (18238 SE Division St; 503/669-1253). *$; MC, V; no checks; lunch, dinner every day; no alcohol; no reservations; map:EE5*

El Gaucho / ★★★

319 SW BROADWAY (BENSON HOTEL), DOWNTOWN; 503/227-8794

This new branch of the serious Seattle steak house, ensconced in Portland's classic Benson Hotel, is all dark shadows and leaping flames, from the open kitchen grills at the back to the flaming shish kebabs served tableside. There's nothing subtle about the strengths here; the beef is stunning, and nothing else quite lives up to the same high standard. If your company has just gone public, the chateaubriand for two at $82 offers a dazzling display of tenderness and flavor, and the tableside carving—completed by whisking together a sauce of beef juices, Worcestershire, and Dijon—will entertain you. (Anything tableside is performance art; El Gaucho may hold the record for most ingredients in a Caesar salad, and for readiness to cut loose with the anchovies.) A Frenched rib steak rounds up the beef flavor of an entire cow. Waiters presenting shish kebab torches spread light into the dark booths and across the center tables, adding an element of performance to what would otherwise be a private, clubby dining room. The restaurant is becoming the Portland HQ of visiting NBA teams, providing a whole other kind of beef. *$$$; AE, DC, MC, V; checks OK; lunch Mon–Fri, dinner every day; full bar; reservations recommended; www.elgaucho.com; map:I3* &

Escape From New York Pizza / ★

622 NW 23RD AVE, NORTHWEST; 503/227-5423

On NW 23rd Avenue, amid many espresso cafes and hopelessly haute houseware shops, sits a dependable slice of pizza. As the name suggests, the pizza here is classic Gotham pie—thin almost waiflike crust, spicy aromatic tomato sauce, and a goopy layer of cheese. It's the closest thing Portland has to New York ferry pizza—just as greasy and floppy. Sadly, there are but a few choices of toppings available: your basic cheese, pepperoni, or a two-topping special will have to do. Then again, it's not for ingenuity or gourmet pretensions that EFNYP succeeds. Rather, it's the muscle memory your stomach experiences after downing a soda and gorging yourself on one of these slices. *$; no credit cards; local checks only; lunch, dinner every day; beer and wine; no reservations; map:GG7*

Esparza's Tex-Mex Cafe / ★★★

2725 SE ANKENY ST, LAURELHURST; 503/234-7909

People may wonder how a Tex-Mex restaurant has become a landmark in Portland—but the surprise doesn't survive the first visit, or certainly not the first smoked beef brisket taco. By then, new visitors have already been educated by a restaurant resembling a San Antonio garage sale, a stunning jukebox, and a sweeping array of tequila bottles. That lets them decide just which tequila goes with the Cowboy Tacos, filled with thick slabs of smoked sirloin, barbecue sauce, guacamole, and pico de gallo; or the Uvalde, a smoked lamb enchilada; or some nopalitos—the best cactus appetizer around (if you like cactus). The menu and specials have the reach of Texas—from red snapper to smoked pork loin stuffed with spiced buffalo, and from ostrich enchiladas to calves'-brain tacos. Watch the blackboard—and the satisfied faces of other diners—to catch the latest inspiration of Joe Esparza. Esparza's is so much fun you might not appreciate how good it is—and it's so good you might not realize how much fun you're having. *$$; AE, DC, DIS, MC, V; no checks; lunch, dinner Tues–Sat; full bar; reservations recommended; map:GG5* &

Esplanade / ★★

1510 SW HARBOR WY (RIVERPLACE HOTEL), RIVERPLACE; 503/295-6166
In a restaurant with a splendid river view but a kitchen that's struggled to stay afloat, French chef Pascal Sauton is making some progress. The theme is Northwestern with a French accent, which in summer might produce braised halibut cheeks with a roasted pepper oil, or in winter perhaps pork loin with a Normanesque apple cider cream or roasted Oregon venison in a chestnut sauce. A survivor from the succession of chefs is a thick, deeply rich lobster bisque, crowded with lobster chunks. As always, the room is stunning, with the river rolling past, the marina in the foreground, and, if you're lucky, a mountain in the background. Some think the view is even better in the morning, as the sun casts a glow on your eggs Benedict. *$$$; AE, DC, MC, V; checks OK; breakfast, dinner every day, lunch Mon–Fri, full bar; reservations recommended; www.riverplacehotel.com; map:D5* &

Fa Fa Gourmet / ★★

11712 NE FOURTH PLAIN BLVD, VANCOUVER, WA; 360/260-1378
As culinary trends have shifted in the Portland area over the years, Chinese food has taken it on the chin—no pun intended—and good Chinese restaurants have become scarce. To those who have bemoaned the loss, it will come as a pleasant surprise that there's great Hunan and Sichuan cuisine to be had across the river in Vancouver. From a semi-open kitchen looking out onto a bright dining room come the myriad items that make up Fa Fa's voluminous menu, which features both unusual dishes and familiar favorites such as kung pao chicken, Sichuan beef, and lo mein. Whether you try something new or stick to the tried and true, you can't go wrong. Crispy prawns with walnuts unite savory and sweet by combining breaded fried shrimp with honey-roasted walnuts; orange beef does something similar with its combination of fried flank steak and orange sauce. Fa Fa is strong on seafood, from crispy shrimp served with chili sauce to whole fish in bean sauce to five different preparations of lobster (call ahead), and it also offers plenty of vegetable concoctions and steamed dishes for dieters. Everything is prepared to order from fresh ingredients, so even if you order an old standby, it is likely to taste better than you remember it from elsewhere. Prices are reasonable, especially at lunch, and the beverage list includes several Northwest wines and beers. *$–$$; MC, V; no checks; lunch Mon–Sat, dinner every day; full bar; reservations recommended; wwwfafagourmet.com; map:AA3* &

Fat City Cafe / ★

7820 SW CAPITOL HWY, MULTNOMAH VILLAGE; 503/245-5457
Diners in general are fading bits of American culinary history, and this particular one has its own place in Portland's past: it's where Mayor Bud Clark (a regular even now, many years after he left office) fired his police chief back in 1987. History is also all around—this part of Portland, Multnomah Village, used to be a separate town, and now it's well known as one of the top antique shopping districts in the region. Inside is the classic narrow layout of booths and a counter, with walls covered in traffic signs and old Monopoly boards for menus. The menu is exactly what you'd expect. For breakfast, there are monster stacks of pancakes, eggs every which way, and legendary hash browns; for lunch, substantial burgers, great sandwiches, and legendary milkshakes. The name has less to do with any geographic location than with how you're going to feel after you've eaten here. There's no such thing as a small meal at the Fat City Cafe, so you might want to opt for a spot at the counter and have the benefit of gravity to help you get out your seat. *$; MC, V; no checks; breakfast, lunch every day; no alcohol; no reservations; map:JJ7*

Fernando's Hideaway / ★★

824 SW 1ST AVE, DOWNTOWN; 503/248-4709
Light an impossibly heavy cigarette, drink a lot of wine, and watch two or three of Pedro Almodovar's films before going to Fernando's Hideaway. The restaurant drips with a seedy, lived-in sensuality that confirms it as the most romantic and seductive of Portland's Spanish eateries. It's roaring bar is a first-rate singles scene, and the downstairs area hosts salsa dancing and flamenco exhibitions. Come to have fun, and don't be surprised if you do something that would shock your mother. But the food, on the whole, is hit or miss. The tapas menu is full of what you would expect: shrimp sautéed in spicy oil, marinated octopus, thick slices of potato omelet. Any of them can be good snacks while drinking, but not enough to carry an evening. Dinners can be more ambitious, with safe bets on the three house specialties: paella (on Sunday only if you call 24 hours in advance), *arroz negro* (risotto cooked with squid ink), and *fideua* (a dish like a pasta-paella). Desserts are impressive— a Catalan crème brûlée flavored with cinnamon and lemon, and a tangy lemon ice—and the extensive wine list offers a range of good value. *$$; AE, MC, V; checks OK; dinner Tues–Sun; full bar; reservations recommended; marcha2000@aol.com; www.opentables.com; map:F6* &

Fishtales / ★★★

1621 SE MILWAUKIE AVE, WESTMORELAND; 503/239-5796
When Fishtales describes its identity as Mediterranean seafood, it isn't kidding; several times a week, it flies in seafood from Spain. That means a range of shellfish, such as unexpectedly shaped clams—notably Spanish

razor clams that actually resemble razors—and multiple kinds of shrimp: brilliant red caballeros and huge, clawed langostinos, which Americans rarely encounter. It must also be a striking experience for the seafood, plucked from the Mediterranean, flown to Portland (by way of Miami), and then delivered into the hands of Serge Selbe, the Laotian-born chef/owner. It all ends in a splendidly happy outcome (OK, maybe not for the fish), with Fishtales' dazzling dishes such as the pan-seared Mediterranean seafood platter, whole sea bass baked in salt, and paella for two or more. (The Laotian themes surface occasionally, too, in whispers of lemongrass in otherwise Mediterranean marine life.) Look for the intoxicating lobster bisque with truffle ravioli. The vividness of the food rivals the brilliance of the colorful dining room; hands down, fins up, this is the most orange restaurant in Portland. Fishtales is a dramatic addition to the Portland restaurant world, even allowing for commuting. *$$$; AE, MC, V; no checks; lunch Tues–Sat, dinner Mon–Sat; beer and wine; reservations recommended; map:JJ5* &

Fong Chong / ★★

301 NW 4TH AVE, CHINATOWN; 503/220-0235

In a three-block stretch of Portland's Chinatown, there are now enough dim sum places to cause serving-cart gridlock, but it's not just Fong Chong's historical reputation as the local shining dim sum star that should make you maneuver to this one. Along with vibrant humbao buns and addictive sticky rice in a lotus leaf, you might find something surprising, such as shallot dumplings—and implausible but heartwarming pork cookies. The much larger House of Louie, under the same ownership, is across the street. But whether it's the Chinese grocery next door or because the place is crowded and loud or because watching the carts maneuver through the tables is like watching the Super Mario Brothers, we like Fong Chong better. It's fun, inexpensive, and tasty. At night, Fong Chong is transformed into a quiet Cantonese eatery, with average preparations and a few surprises. *$; MC, V; no checks; lunch, dinner every day; full bar; no reservations; map:K5* &

Foothill Broiler / ★

33 NW 23RD PL, NORTHWEST; 503/223-0287

Come in at noon and you'll find yourself waiting in line—possibly longer than you might have expected—with socialites, construction workers, and realtors talking deals. Burger patties come in three sizes—none will put you out more than $4.50—with good French fries or baked beans alongside. And if the burgers may be less expensive than at some other places in Portland, they're no less serious. Foothill Broiler may be a step-up-from-a-cafeteria kind of place, where you can have a cupcake or a bowl of spaghetti and a malted milkshake, but people line up for the meaty hamburgers and the fine layer cakes, cheesecakes, and pies. Tilework, framed prints, and unexpected skylights in the back raise the interior from merely cafeterian to almost stylish. *$; MC, V; checks OK; breakfast, lunch, dinner Mon–Sat; no alcohol; no reservations; map:FF6* &

Fratelli / ★★

1230 NW HOYT ST, PEARL DISTRICT; 503/241-8800

After a bumpy start in the restaurant-saturated Pearl District, Fratelli has leveled itself to become one of the better dinner options in the neighborhood. The narrow entry hallway parallels the long dining room, with its two-story ceilings and its spare wooden tables and chairs, illuminated if not by late afternoon sun, then by candlelight. The kitchen fills the back of the room. The Italian menu is as minimalist as the dining room, with a couple of antipasti, about a half-dozen starters, and the same number of entrees—rounded out with one or two daily specials. The menu changes to reflect the season, but if spring beans with arugula and octopus are available, order them: it's a textured and satisfying dish, with hints of lemon providing a welcome freshness. The ravioli stuffed with goat cheese and graced with grilled onion shoots and marjoram is also memorable, and the house lasagne, with its layers of beef, pork, and béchamel, is a menu regular and a rich favorite. Service here is smart, the mostly Italian wine list impressive (there's also a limited bar), and the location unbeatable for its proximity to the district's galleries and nightspots. *$$; AE, DC, MC, V; no checks; dinner Tues–Sun; beer and wine; reservations recommended; map:L2* &

Fusion / ★

4100 SE DIVISION ST, SOUTHEAST; 503/233-6950

This combination neighborhood cafe/retro house-furnishings shop draws its ideas from a wide variety of sources, but usually manages to keep them straight on the plate. You can skip from Thai Spinach Fusion—spinach leaves to be filled with ginger, lime, dried shrimp, peanuts, coconut, and chutney—to a mouth-filling salmon fillet marinated in soy, ginger and wasabi, or cut sideways to a sizable Fusion burger before ending up with a rich chocolate pôt de crème. Prices are reasonable, servers are friendly—even if wearing black—and there's always something to look at, either the Division Street scene out the window or a sofa in the back that looks as though it belonged to your grandmother. This is the kind of neighborhood place that can create neighbors. *$; MC, V; checks OK; , breakfast Sun, lunch, dinner Tues–Sat; beer and wine; no reservations; map:HH4* &

Genoa / ★★★★

2832 SE BELMONT ST, BELMONT; 503/238-1464

Dinner here always begins with a reverent recitation, and just hearing the dishes feels good in the mouth: maybe Sardinian-style swordfish cooked in a sauce of tomatoes, saffron, mint, and chiles, or roasted poussin stuffed with homemade ricotta, marjoram, and pancetta. And at Genoa, that would be the fifth course, a.k.a. the entree. At this point the diner would already have enjoyed antipasto—perhaps rabbit preserved in oil like tuna and then served with a pickled Black Mission fig over wild greens—followed by a bowl of Sicilian-inspired gazpacho, surpassed only by fresh egg pasta tossed with chanterelles and black olives, then a fish course of Puget Sound mussels fried in a light batter and served with lemon. The elaborate, minuetlike seven-course menu (with a four-course option on weekdays) changes every two weeks, and for almost 30 years Portlanders have been returning to see what's up next. Co-owners Kerry DeBuse and Cathy Whims (also the executive chef) have been leading Genoa to ever new triumphs, sweeping the local *Zagat* and *Gourmet* magazine polls and cooking a Columbus Day dinner at James Beard House in New York. It's a very special-occasion restaurant; diners may have to spend some time training for the three-hour meal (with no choices except entree and dessert), and some time recovering from it. But at least once or twice in the meal, Genoa will leave you stunned—often at the pasta course, especially if it is *ravioli di zucca,* thin sheets enfolding squash, sweet potato, and biscotti crumbs. Looking for highlights, it doesn't seem fair even to count the powerhouse dessert tray, with a double-digit range of choices from homemade fig ice cream to a creation that mixes fruit and chocolate into a result as intricate as a palazzo. The famously dark dining room has lightened a bit—although it's still Portland's immediate image of an intimate dinner. *$$$; AE, DC, MC, V; checks OK; dinner Mon–Sat; full bar; reservations required; www.genoarestaurant.com; map:GG5*

Giant Drive-In / ★

15840 SW BOONES FERRY RD, LAKE OSWEGO; 503/636-0255

The Giant Filler Burger at this 900-square-foot burger joint resembles a natural wonder, Devil's Tower with cheese. There are some 30 specialty burgers topped with the likes of soy sauce and pineapple, but the Filler is the one diagrammed on the company T-shirt: two burgers, ham, bacon, egg, cheese, and the kitchen sink. In case that's not enough for you, have an order of fat fries—make it the Cajun ones, so you can have some spice with your cholesterol. Less ambitious appetite? Order the Skinny, with a real ice cream milkshake. You'll swear you've died and woken up in 1955. And if the thick, addictive shake isn't enough of a dessert, try the homemade pecan pie. There is no real drive-in, but takeout is an option.

$; no credit cards; local checks only; lunch, dinner every day; no alcohol; no reservations; map:LL7

Gino's Restaurant / ★★☆

8057 SE 13TH AVE, SELLWOOD; 503/233-4613

What was formerly the Leipzig Tavern, a smoky, dark watering hole frequented by those more interested in drinking than eating, has transformed into the delightful Gino's. This is not trendy Italian dining, with every shape of pasta under the sun and dish names that run on for two lines; it's just great, honest Italian food. The main dining room sports red-and-white checked tablecloths and is best for gathering a larger group to feast on steamed clams, stellar Caesar salad, wonderful garlic bread, and pasta. For the latter, expect generous portions along the traditional meat-and-tomato theme; there's also *vongole* (clam) pasta, a mussel and puttanesca pasta to die for, and a ravioli daily special. (The adjoining bar is better for couples, with its cozy booths and quieter acoustics.) The wine list is one of the best in the city. Owner Marc Accuardi is no slouch when it comes to wine: he knows what the good bottles are, he knows you shouldn't drink it too young, and he knows that it's a crime to make people pay too much for it. He features notable producers and remarkable prices, and his list is worth the trip across town many times over. The place can get crowded, but you can eat at the bar—hey, with food and wine like this, you'd eat on the floor. *$$; MC, V; checks OK; lunch Sat, dinner every day; full bar; reservations recommended; accuardi@earthlink.com; map:JJ5*

Good Day / ★

312 NW COUCH ST, CHINATOWN; 503/223-1393

This large-sized Chinatown eatery is seriously informal but also seriously good. It has a wide range of dishes not common in the American Chinese restaurant world—you don't have to order any dish on the menu that features the word "blood"—but it's also solid on standards: pot stickers, egg rolls, a vast serving of wonderfully sweet barbecued pork. This, however, is the place to be experimental. Just a little bit of boldness will get you to impossibly aromatic clay-pot dishes and Winter Garlic Fragrant Chow Mein, every word of which is true. Set out for fried fresh milk with spare ribs—the ribs are fine, and the milk has a seductive coconut ambience— or duck with ginger sauce. Before long, you'll understand why those tables occupied by large Chinese-American families keep the lazy Susan in constant motion. Dining here is dramatic, and at utterly minimal cost. The whole experience may lead you to conclude that ambience is highly overrated. *$; AE, DIS, MC, V; no checks; lunch, dinner Wed–Mon; beer and wine; no reservations; map:J5* ♿

Good Dog/Bad Dog / ★★

708 SW ALDER ST, DOWNTOWN; 503/222-3410

A downtown hot dog stand with pedigree, Good Dog/Bad Dog offers a dozen different sausages laden with fried onions in crusty baked rolls. It may be a challenge to your digestive system, but your tongue won't be complaining as you work your way through Oregon smokies, British bangers, garlic sausages, and specials like Louisiana tasso. They're all made in-house and are undeniably flavorful—if not always fiery. Potato salad, chili, and baked beans can be ordered alongside, as can soda pop or microbrews. Wacky owners and a setting more uptown than ballpark add to this charming mix, a whole new take on man's best friend. *$; MC, V; no checks; lunch, dinner every day; beer only ; no reservations; map:H3* &

Gourmet Productions Market / ★★

39 B AVE, LAKE OSWEGO; 503/697-7355

Blessed are those who live or work close enough to take advantage of this catering company turned small cafe/market. It really doesn't get much better than this: high-quality, reasonably priced food packed to go in the same amount of time it takes to drive through a fast-food window. Many people fax in their orders (503/697-5040) during the afternoon, swing by after work to pick up their bounty, and head home with such eclectic entrees as grilled pork loin with a Chinese plum sauce, jerk chicken, or homemade ravioli. There's always a half-dozen or more salads and side dishes (from roasted beets to quinoa salad, dressed up with yellow bell peppers, pine nuts, garlic, apricots, and fresh herbs), and about a dozen entrees. And for lunch, a number of sandwiches are worth considering: perhaps the luscious rendition of chicken salad—chunks of chicken breast, dried apricot, and toasted almonds—on focaccia, or the turkey Cobb. Items change with the season's bounty; every week brings something new, and there's always something yummy for dessert. Lots of gourmet products surround the four gingham vinyl–covered tables: sea salt, brown cane-sugar cubes, crackers, and many reasonably priced, individually recommended bottles of wine takeout only. *$; AE, MC, V; checks OK; lunch, dinner Mon–Fri; wine only; no reservations; map:LL5* &

Grand Central Bakery and Cafe / ★★

1444 NE WEIDLER ST, NORTHEAST (AND BRANCHES); 503/288-1614

Everyone knows that the secret to making a good sandwich is good bread. Operating on that premise, Grand Central makes some of the best sandwiches in town: Black Forest ham and Swiss on sour rye, roasted chicken and cranberry chutney on como, hummus and tomato on yeasted corn. The sack lunch, which includes one of these sandwiches plus a bag of chips, pickle wedge, and cookie, makes for a tasty and reasonably priced meal (it's only a buck over the price of the sandwich). Tables, countertop seating, wine by the glass, and an expanded menu have successfully changed this spot's image from bakery to cafe. In addition to all the yummy breads and pastries, Grand Central sells marvelous cakes—chocolate, lemon, and carrot—by the slice or to take home whole. Other branches sell the same delicious breads, pastries, and sandwiches, with limited seating (2230 SE Hawthorne Blvd; 503/232-0575; map:HH5 and 3425 SW Multnomah Blvd; 503/977-2024; map:JJ7). *$; MC, V; local checks only; breakfast, lunch, dinner every day; beer and wine; no reservations; map:FF5* &

Hall Street Bar & Grill / ★★

3775 SW HALL BLVD, BEAVERTON; 503/641-6161
Summer evenings, a huge tent out back fills up with seekers after coconut shrimp, bouillabaisse, and prime rib; winters, people sit around the huge bar and fill up the dining room. The owners' smashing success with ¡Oba! (see review in this chapter) in the Pearl District hasn't taken away from the most popular restaurant in Washington County, with its plump crab cakes that satisfy equally well as a starter or as dinner; and steak-cut salmon served with roasted vegetables that just might make anyone forget that such a thing as beef exists. (Burning under the grill are local vineyard cuttings, giving salmon and seafood specials an inviting, tangy undertone.) The rock salt–roasted prime rib is a permanent menu fixture—a favorite that has been known to sell out quickly—and the grilled steaks are terrific. A superb burnt cream with a hard sugar crust is a signature favorite, but you might be lured away by the chocolate banana pudding. *$$; AE, DC, MC, V; checks OK; lunch Mon–Fri, dinner every day; full bar; reservations recommended; map:HH9* &

Hands On Cafe / ★★

8245 NW BARNES RD, WEST SLOPE; 503/297-1480
If only every institute of higher learning had a cafeteria like this one. The campus of the Oregon College of Art and Craft may seem an unlikely place to sit down to dazzling baked goods—from scones to solid breads to stunning, ever-changing desserts—but the ovens here are as artful as the kilns next door. Low-key lunch and early dinner (5:30–7:30) menus stress salads, soups, and stews, but this is not standard salad-bar fare: fresh tuna and pasta salad with capers, a cabbage roll stuffed with ground veal, white bean pâté on focaccia. At the popular Sunday brunch, the inspiration ranges from the Pacific Northwest to New Orleans to Peru. Pumpkin bread and bowls of strawberries sprinkled with candied ginger will keep you busy while you wait (and you might have to wait a bit longer than you'd like) for the main course to arrive. *$; no credit cards; checks OK; lunch Mon–Fri, dinner Mon–Thurs, brunch Sun; no alcohol; reservations recommended; map:HH9* &

Harborside / ★★

0309 SW MONTGOMERY ST, RIVERPLACE; 503/220-1865
On a warm Portland afternoon—and there really are such things—Harborside may have the best location in the city, with a sweeping view of the Willamette, terraced seating, and ranks of tables out on the promenade. What's been a more casual branch of the McCormick & Schmick empire now has a fairly elaborate menu, more like Jake's, with Northwest wild salmon specials, macadamia-crusted halibut, and wild Columbia sturgeon with a medley of Oregon mushrooms. On any Portland evening, the Pilsner Room brewpub next door—run by Hood River's Full Sail Ale folks—gets almost as full. Those looking for something more casual with their beer, or some Oregon white wine, can relax into Apple Whisky Salmon Salad or scallop and halibut ceviche. People who get enough maritime impact from the view might try a steak or porterhouse pork chop with caramelized peaches—and there are lots of designer pizzas. *$$; AE, DC, DIS, JCB, MC, V; no checks; lunch, dinner every day, brunch Sun; full bar; reservations recommended; www.mccormickandschmicks.com; map:C5* &

The Heathman Restaurant and Bar / ★★★★

1001 SW BROADWAY, DOWNTOWN; 503/241-4100
Philippe Boulot, who came to Portland by way of Paris and New York, has produced a consistently impressive kitchen, to go with a dining room that continues to be the center of Portland power breakfasts and lunches. And after making his own strong statements about Northwest cuisine, such as a stirring salmon in a pesto crust with a shard of crisp salmon skin planted on top, Boulot has returned to his Gallic roots. That means leg of lamb cooked for seven hours and Alsatian stuffed veal breast. Of course, there are still heartening Northwestern dishes, such as roast venison wrapped in smoked bacon or the appealing crab cakes in a red curry butter sauce. The king salmon hash prevails at breakfast, and lunch produces its own creations, including rich soups, pungent salads, and heartening stews. Evenings bring jazz, and brandy from upstairs and downstairs bars. All possible excuses should be sought for the dessert creations, such as a recent chocolate pear tart with pear brandy sauce and dulce de leche ice cream. Boulot regularly brings in guest chefs, visiting friends from France and New York; the chocolate pear tart suggests but one reason why they come. Though the hotel has recently been sold, there are no anticipated changes for the restaurant. *$$$; AE, DC, DIS, MC, V; checks OK; breakfast, lunch, dinner every day; full bar; reservations recommended; www.heathmanhotel.com; map:G2* &

Henry Ford's / ★★

9589 SW BARBUR BLVD, CAPITOL HILL; 503/245-2434
Back before people went around dusting alligator tails with cumin, there was another American cuisine, and Henry Ford's is what it was all about: huge slabs of red meat, simply prepared but of high quality, preceded by a shrimp cocktail or stuffed mushrooms, and followed by damn-your-arteries cheesecake. Before such a meal, people didn't sip white wine, they belted down serious cocktails. Henry Ford's vividly evokes that cuisine, partly because much of the staff—and the customers—date from it. (The average server seems to have been here since the Nixon administration, and then there's Lyle at the piano bar.) Lately at Henry Ford's, a whole new generation—possibly fleeing one too many medallions of Chilean sea bass—has discovered the appeal of such unpretentious cuisine, and of a real whiskey sour. If you like porterhouse, this restaurant captures it brilliantly. And the carrots in brown sugar glaze alone could have you voting for Eisenhower. The restaurant is not visible from Barbur Boulevard; look carefully as you approach the intersection with Capitol Highway. *$$$; AE, DC, MC, V; checks OK; dinner every day; full bar; reservations recommended; www.henryfords.com; map:JJ7* &

Henry's Cafe / ★★

2508 SE CLINTON ST, CLINTON ST; 503/236-8707
Restaurants are like love affairs: when you least expect it, one comes along and steals your heart. Henry's, a lovely cafe painted in various coffee shades, with lots of dark wood, fir floors, soapstone tables, and a long bar that runs the length of this narrow storefront, is serious crush material. And it's not just another pretty face, either. The breakfast menu satisfies a variety of appetites, from simple pastries to the upgraded continental, called "Parisian Brunch" here (French press coffee, a bowl of seasonal fruit, a croissant, and jam), and heartier plates like three-egg omelets and potato-vegetable hash. There are only a few choices for lunch—spinach salad, soup du jour, and a handful of sandwiches—but lots of coffeehouse specialties. Whether it's for breakfast or between meals, you'll find plenty to choose from within the glass case: pastries, zucchini bread, cookies, tortes, and cakes. Dinner, a relatively new thing at Henry's, is unbelievably reasonable; for less than $12 you can sup on a pork chop with mashed potatoes, sautéed prawns, or pan-seared salmon. *$–$$; MC, V; no checks; breakfast, lunch every day, dinner Wed–Sun; beer and wine; no reservations; map:II5* &

Higgins / ★★★

1239 SW BROADWAY, DOWNTOWN; 503/222-9070
Greg Higgins cooks with skill and principle, distilling dazzling dishes from the Northwest soil and seas. Dedicated to local producers and the idea of sustainability, Higgins sets out deft, creative cuisine such as medallions of

pork loin and foie gras, or crab and shrimp cakes with chipotle crème fraîche, or perhaps a saffron bourride of regional shellfish. Part of Higgins' policy is to maintain a vegetarian component of the menu, which can mean a forest mushroom tamale with hazelnut mole and tangerine salsa, or a black- and white-truffle risotto. Spectacular presentation endures, especially in desserts, which might be a roasted pear in filo or a chocolate-almond-apricot tart. An inviting bistro menu—with offerings ranging from smoked goose to Higgins' signature sandwich, house-cured pastrami with white cheddar—beckons those seeking less formality to the bar. Every day at lunch, the question arises: how does a place dedicated to sustainability and authenticity produce such a good burger? *$$–$$$; AE, DC, MC, V; checks OK; lunch Mon–Fri, dinner every day; full bar; reservations recommended; higgins@europa.com; map:F2*

Hiro / ★★

6334 SW MEADOWS RD, LAKE OSWEGO; 503/684-7521

People elsewhere in Portland may sulk over the Lakers, but this unexpected little sushi bar in a Lake Oswego shopping center is always a home for Trail Blazer memorabilia and Trail Blazers—it's a hangout for team members, many of whom live in the suburb. It also features exquisite, impressive sushi. Behind the bar, Hiro himself assembles elaborate rolls and sushi pieces using ingredients of remarkable freshness and sometimes unusual identity: monkfish liver? The nightly specials board contains marine offerings uncommon in the region, such as a particularly rich variety of yellowtail, and there's usually toro, the fatter slices of tuna belly. When he's not sculpting small gems for the bar, Hiro is often assembling vast arrays of sushi to go. Everyone seems to know everybody here—even if no Blazers show up. *$$; AE, MC, V; no checks; lunch Mon–Fri, dinner Mon–Sat; beer and wine; reservations recommended; map:MM8* &

Hoda's Middle Eastern Cuisine / ★

3401 SE BELMONT ST, BELMONT; 503/236-8325

Husband and wife Hani and Hoda Khouri have quickly established a hotbed for vibrant Middle Eastern food. (Hoda is the daughter of Nicholas, founder of Nicholas' Restaurant; see review in this chapter.) From the wonderful pita bread—which arrives puffed up like a Chinese lantern, then slowly deflates—to the smoky baba ghanouj, one gets the sense that the food here is well tended. So is the restaurant's ambience; fir floors, white walls, various tea sets, and hanging plants make for a pleasing place to share a mezze plate. Other things worth trying include a tangy, parsley-friendly tabbouleh and a tasty kofta kebab (skewers of spiced ground beef). The lunchtime sandwiches are packed with flavor as well and make for a great lunch on the go. *$; no credit cards; checks OK; lunch, dinner Mon–Sat; beer and wine; reservations recommended; map:GG5* &

Holden's / ★★

524 NW 14TH AVE, PEARL DISTRICT; 503/916-0099

With the relocation of ad mavens Wieden and Kennedy to their new post-modern digs in the Pearl District, the value of a table at lunchtime went way—way!—up. Creative types need their down time, too, and a swarm of restaurateurs have opened in the Pearl to make it happen. When Margot Leonard sold Bima, she opted to pour her energy into Holden's around the corner. Since then she has transformed the former after-thought of Bima into a bustling lunch counter that fills up the locals' needs for both good food and high visibility. Everything at Holden's starts from scratch. Fish tacos are made with freshly grilled tuna, chicken salad arrives with tender chunks of white meat tossed in a not-too-heavy mayonnaise, and all of the sandwiches are delicious, with vegetarian options abounding. Drinks are self-serve, and the big cookies are a point of great weakness. *$; MC; local checks only; breakfast, lunch every day; beer and wine; no reservations; map:L1* &

Horn of Africa / ★★★

3939 NE MARTIN LUTHER KING JR BLVD, NORTHEAST; 503/331-9844

As the name implies, the cuisine featured behind this simple purple store-front in Northeast Portland comes from the area stretching from Ethiopia to Somalia. That doesn't stop most people from referring to it as an Ethiopian restaurant—and indeed, there are obvious similarities, such as the meats braised in spicy, flavorful sauces and the spongy bread used to scoop and sop it up. But here the bread is called *biddeena* rather than *injera,* the palette of spices is different, and the food is less likely to make you feel like you've been sucking on a flamethrower. A favorite is *lukkuu akhaawi,* spiced and grilled chicken in a sauce that's rich but not oily, spicy but not too hot. Like similar preparations of lamb and beef, it comes with red lentils, onions, and saffron rice (the *biddeena* can be had as a side). Vegetables get like treatment in other dishes: carrots, potatoes, and onions become infused with the flavors of garlic, cumin, coriander, and other spices as they slowly cook to softness. *Missira,* a savory com-bination of stewed green lentils, onions, garlic, olive oil, and a medley of African spices, shows off the intriguing range of East African flavors. The atmosphere is decidedly spare and casual, but it's a comfortable place thanks to Mohammed and Khadija Yusuf, the gracious owners, who will treat you like family. *$; MC, V; checks OK; lunch Tues–Fri, dinner Tues–Sat; no alcohol; no reservations; map:FF6* &

House of Asia / ★

7113 SW MACADAM AVE, MACADAM VILLAGE; 503/452-5002

This pleasant little shopping mall storefront run by the Chhim family has become so popular so quickly that already it's considerably expanded its menu. It still includes graceful bows to many parts of East Asia, from satay to pad thai to teriyaki and California roll, but there's Cambodian cuisine at the core here definitely worth dipping into. For a taste of Cambodia, order the nifty sour chicken soup with shrimp and the capacious rice flour crêpe folded around shrimp, chicken, onions, and bean sprouts. The key here is to order the things you've never heard of before, confident that very modest prices and very gracious service will keep you from getting into too much trouble. And not only is *kroeung samott cha khney* lots of fun to say and order, but the gingered seafood is tasty and substantial—with three different colors of onions. And you can't go wrong washing down your entree with a young coconut milk drink or Thai iced tea. *$; AE, MC, V; no checks; lunch Mon–Sat, dinner every day; beer and wine; reservations recommended; houseofasia@yahoo.com; www.house ofasiapdx.com; map:JJ6* &

Hudson's Bar & Grill / ★★☆

7801 NE GREENWOOD DR (HEATHMAN LODGE), VANCOUVER, WA; 360/816-6100

Perhaps by design, the name of this place is less imposing than the setting. Hudson's is the restaurant of the Heathman Lodge, an enormous log edifice that would look perfect for its setting—a wooded area several miles up the Columbia Gorge from downtown Vancouver—if it weren't on the fringes of a sprawling commercial development. Like its Portland cousin, the Heathman Restaurant and Bar, Hudson's aims high, and if the execution is not on a par with that justly famed establishment, the place is still worth a visit. Chef Mark Hosack balances routine fare—steak and onion rings, Reubens—with innovative Northwest preparations, which dominate the dinner menu. Items like venison with apple bacon and sweet potato hash stand out, along with the Northwest seafood stew; pan-roasted halibut with manila clams, chorizo, roasted tomatoes, and harissa mayonnaise; and salmon cakes. Hosack doesn't restrict himself to seasonal and local ingredients, but he certainly makes better use of them than the chefs in most hotel restaurants. Big flavors are the rule, as are big portions. The excess carries over to the wine list: while it features an abundance of interesting Northwest wines, it also includes many mediocre ones at unreasonable prices. *$$$; AE, DC, DIS, MC, JCB, V; local checks only; breakfast, lunch, dinner every day; full bar; reservations recommended; info@heathmangroup.com; www.heathmangroup.com/hotels andrestaurants* &

Hunan / ★

515 SW BROADWAY, DOWNTOWN; 503/224-8063

Although the cuisine here is not exactly cleaver-cutting-edge, it's consistent and popular, especially come lunchtime. The specialties here have been on the menu for more than two decades, and diners—especially lunchers—are still streaming in for them. Lake T'ung T'ing Shrimp, dumplings in hot oil, and beef with orange flavor grace the menu. The restaurant's versions of the spicy standards—General Tso's chicken, twice-cooked pork, dry-sautéed string beans—are pungent and swift to appear. Then there's the tropical fish, swimming around with the help of hoisin sauce. *$$; MC, V; no checks; lunch, dinner every day; full bar; no reservations; map:I3*

Ikenohana / ★★

14308 SW ALLEN BLVD, BEAVERTON; 503/646-1267

The suburban strip-mall storefront opens into a modest space (with a tiny sushi bar in one corner) where Japanese paper screens and lanterns give a private and charming feel, and even when things are busy, it's not noisy. The menu allows a wide range of options, from sushi and sashimi to tempura, katsu dishes, teriyaki, and noodles. You can't go wrong here: the sashimi is elegantly presented and very fresh and firm. A plentiful plate of sushi includes wonderful mackerel and eel. Even the simple yakisoba noodles are spicy and cooked just right. If you look like you don't know how to mix the wasabi and soy sauce for the sushi, the friendly waitstaff will show you. *$; MC, V; no checks; lunch Mon–Fri, dinner every day; beer and wine; reservations recommended; map:II9*

Il Fornaio / ★★

115 NW 22ND AVE, NORTHWEST; 503/248-9400

Good Italian family dining isn't exactly commonplace in Oregon. With a limited ethnic population, Portland's premier pasta places tend to require lots of lire. This California chain eases the situation, and its wide range of choices—from multiple pastas to crisp pizzas to chicken grilled under a brick and mesquite-grilled lamb chops—are generally reliable and consistently inviting. The room is huge and at dinnertime is often filled with both diners and aromas, and one of the attractions here is that while the aromas are rich, the diners don't have to be. A mellower time is in the mornings, when smaller groups toy with cappuccino and whatever the bakers have just brought from the ovens (there are fresh pastries every morning). The menu goes on an annual tour of Italy; any particular month will find full offerings—from the breads to the wines—of any place from Sicily to the Veneto. *$$; AE, DC, MC, V; local checks only; lunch, dinner every day, brunch Sun; full bar; reservations recommended; www.ilfornaio.com; map:GG6* &

Il Piatto / ★★★

2348 SE ANKENY ST, BUCKMAN; 503/236-4997

Portland thrives on restaurants like this: a cozy, ever-inviting nook tucked quietly into a residential neighborhood, almost qualifying as a secret. Chef Eugene Bingham has created a restaurant that draws fans from across the city, with nearly 20 pastas—notably a punchy puttanesca—

deft risottos, and signature dishes such as pork saltimbocca and wild mushroom crêpes with smoked pear crème fraîche. It's a particularly good place for midweek lunches, discreet and otherwise. The attraction is heightened by decor resembling an overstuffed Venetian apartment, complete with a comfy sofa on which to wait for your table, and personable service. *$$; AE, MC, V; checks OK; lunch Tues–Fri, dinner every day; beer and wine; reservations recommended; map:GG5* &

India House / ★★☆

1038 SW MORRISON ST, DOWNTOWN; 503/274-1017

The tandoori chicken here could draw people right off the light rail trains that run by the door, and the crispy pakoras can cause them to miss the next train. Some Portland Indian restaurants may be more elaborate and formal, but this storefront has consistently and skillfully maintained its place near the top of the list of local Indian eateries. This pleasant restaurant serves the full range of Indian food with a consistency that has attracted a solid, happy constituency of downtown diners. Dishes from north and south India, including tandoori-roasted specials, make weekend dinner a crowded, festive affair, and the daily lunch buffet has caught on, too. Bring a group to adequately sample the generous menu. *$$; AE, DC, DIS, MC, V; no checks; lunch Mon–Sat, dinner every day; beer and wine; reservations recommended; map:H2* &

Ivy House / ★★☆

1605 SE BYBEE BLVD, WESTMORELAND; 503/231-9528

It's a toss-up who likes this place more—kids or their parents. While the wee ones divide their time between the playroom and the table, Mom and Dad sip killer wine from lovely crystal goblets and sup on grilled hanger steak served with onion confit and mashed potatoes. The enthusiastic owner, Brian Quinn, met his wife, Lisa, while they were both in cooking school; their combined interest in fine food and wine is made evident in both the entirely grown-up menu—chinook salmon baked with a hazelnut crust and served with a cider-Riesling reduction—and the uncanny wine list—which ranges from easy-drinking Northwest and California wines to triple-digit, vintage Bordeaux. The Quinns' attention to detail (sip cups, $1 kid meals, and a Brio train track) reflects their parenting experience and sensitivity to dining with children. For some it might seem all too familiar—a little sticky and tattered, with toys scattered on the floor—for dinner out. A look around the room, however, reveals many without kids seated near the front of the house or on the outside patio. *$$; MC, V; checks OK; lunch Mon–Fri, dinner every day, brunch Sat–Sun; beer and wine; reservations recommended; map:JJ5*

J&M Cafe / ★

537 SE ASH ST, SOUTHEAST; 503/230-0463

A comfortable spot in the soon-to-be-hip eastside industrial area, the J&M Cafe is a morning person's dream come true. High ceilings and light, bright windows fill the spacious dining room with sun (or a gray local version thereof). An old-fashioned lunch counter, warm furniture, and colorful diptych furnish the dining room, set off by a self-service coffee station. One of the few kitchens around that will still baste an egg, J&M builds its eponymous breakfast plate with two of the buttery eggs atop English muffins with cheese and bacon. The egg scrambles are all good choices, made that much better by the splendid breakfast potatoes that accompany them. French toast is thin and crisp and magnificent with fresh strawberries. Consider the pasta specials at lunch, which, when not loaded with too much cheese, can be very satisfying. The afternoon menu is rounded out with a selection of interesting sandwiches, in particular the J&M grilled cheese—a layering of grilled onions, tomatoes, and fontina with red pepper pesto on a sturdy como bread—and salads. *$; no credit cards; local checks only; breakfast every day, lunch Mon–Fri; no alcohol; no reservations; map:I9* &

Jake's Famous Crawfish / ★★★

401 SW 12TH AVE, DOWNTOWN; 503/226-1419

This is the place that spawned an empire; any day now, owners Bill McCormick and Doug Schmick will announce that they have restaurants in as many places as they get their fish from. The core of it all is the fresh list at the top of the menu, with seafood from Fiji to Maine to Arkansas to New Zealand. The fish might appear in a shiitake-soy-ginger glaze, or blackened with corn-pepper relish, or in a bouillabaisse. Jake's is strong on tradition, from the polished wooden fixtures to the waiters' white jackets, but on the menu there's constant experimentation; read carefully. The combination of old tradition and new ideas applied to very fresh seafood could keep Jake's going for another 100 years. And there are lots of folks in the bar who are in no hurry at all. Jake's was an early fan of Oregon wines, and it has also assembled a powerful dessert tray, where tradition and innovation also combine; the three-berry cobbler endures, but the equally legendary chocolate truffle cake has been revised, and actually intensified. *$$; AE, DC, MC, V; no checks; lunch Mon–Fri, dinner every day; full bar; reservations recommended; www.mccormickandschmicks.com; map:I2* &

Jake's Grill / ★★⯪

611 SW 10TH AVE (GOVERNOR HOTEL), DOWNTOWN; 503/241-2100

Sure, this is McCormick & Schmick, so there is some fresh seafood. But it's also a three-meal-a-day Governor Hotel dining room, and a steak house feels right in this grandly restored building. Choose from eight kinds of juicy steak and fist-thick double lamb chops. The range is wide, with a comfort-food section of meat loaf and macaroni (almost too pedestrian) and more interesting sandwiches and salads, such as blackened rockfish and spinach, Dungeness crab roll, and smoked salmon club. Appetizers and desserts are familiar from the other M&S outposts, along with the high-ceilinged, turn-of-the-century saloon decor. The styles shift during the day: lunch is casual, while the dinner mood gets more flashy. You really should dress for that huge wood-and-glass bar and the lamb chops, though happy hour draws in a more dress-downed crowd. *$$–$$$; AE, DC, MC, V; no checks; breakfast, lunch, dinner every day; full bar; reservations recommended; www.mccormickand schmicks.com; map:I2* &

Jarra's Ethiopian Restaurant / ★★

1435 SE HAWTHORNE BLVD, HAWTHORNE; 503/230-8990
Jarra's, after years still Portland's prime place to go for an explosive, sweat-inducing Abyssinian stew, has had different incarnations, and this may be the most formal. Rising from the basement of an old Portland home up to the main floor, this is the neighborhood's unequaled heat champ. Jarra's is the restaurant to teach you what's wat: made with chicken, lamb, or beef, the *wat* (stews) are deep red, oily, and packed with peppery after-kicks. Full dinners come with assorted stewed meats and vegetables, all permeated with vibrant spices and mounded on *injera*—the spongy Ethiopian bread that doubles as plate and fork. *$; MC, V; no checks; dinner Tues–Sat; full bar; reservations recommended; map:HH5* &

Jo Bar and Rotisserie / ★★

715 NW 23RD AVE, NORTHWEST; 503/222-0048
Papa Haydn's younger sibling has emerged as a big player in the NW 23rd Avenue restaurant stakes, with loyal customers returning to feast on succulent chicken, duck, pork loin, and leg of lamb roasted in one of the two huge wood-burning ovens that blaze along the back wall. Burgers and breads also go through the fire. Salads, such as smoked salmon and caviar on wild greens, are inventive and inviting. Service and desserts can be uneven, but the restaurant bloodlines here are terrific. Weekend brunch breaks away from standard fare, serving up chilaquiles, frittatas, and brioche French toast. *$$; AE, MC, V; checks OK; lunch Mon–Sat, dinner every day, brunch Sun; full bar; reservations recommended; map:GG7* &

Joel Palmer House / ★★★½

600 FERRY ST, DAYTON; 503/864-2995
 Jack and Heidi Czarnecki came to Oregon to find the perfect marriage of wild mushrooms and civilized pinot noir, and they've created a restaurant that no gastronome will want to miss. Jack is the author of authoritative, prize-winning books on mushroom cookery, and mushrooms are

the earthy foundation of a menu that freely reaches into myriad cuisines—Mexican, Chinese, and Polish, to name just three—to create food that says "this is the place." Seasonal ingredients make for an ever-changing menu, but depending on what's popping up in the woods, you might find suillis soup, sautéed chanterelles on a bed of shredded filo, portobello stuffed with blue cheese and hoisin sauce, morel enchiladas, porcinis in puff pastry, and various other mycological marvels. You haven't lived until you've had Heidi's three-mushroom tart, which, as the menu says, is "what wild mushrooms are all about." The Joel Palmer House is not just for mushroom enthusiasts—Jack's deft touch extends to everything from a fiddlehead salad with beet sauce to intriguing preparations of lamb, salmon, pork, and the occasional exotic meat such as ostrich. A well-chosen selection of wines, especially local pinot noirs, will complement your meal perfectly, and Heidi's exquisite desserts will cap it off. Yes, Dayton is a 45-minute drive from Portland, but a meal at the Joel Palmer House is worth every minute, and then some. *$$$; AE, DIS, MC, V; checks OK; lunch Tues–Fri, dinner Tues–Sat; full bar* &

John Street Cafe / ★★

8338 N LOMBARD ST, ST. JOHNS; 503/247-1066

The John Street Cafe is a beacon of hospitality in the St. Johns neighborhood. Jamie and Marie Noehren's second incarnation of the much missed Tabor Hill Cafe in the Hawthorne District, the John Street Cafe manages to make guests feel as though they are dropping in on good friends for a meal—albeit friends who are handy in the kitchen. Children are liable to be whisked away by the grandfatherly owner for a tour of the kitchen, appearing later with silly grins and massive homemade cookies. Coffee cups rarely go unfilled. Breakfast can be had light—with fresh fruit, granola, or yogurt—or more substantial with any of several exotic omelets (roasted peppers, goat cheese, chicken sausage, etc.) or a variety of pancakes. Generous sandwiches, burgers, and salads round out the lunch menu. The Reuben is among the best in town: toasted sour rye, heaps of corned beef, Gruyère, Russian dressing, and a very tangy sauerkraut. A delicious combination of roasted vegetables, Jack cheese, and black beans makes for a vegetarian sandwich that tastes better than it eats—don't be surprised when black beans shoot out onto your plate. *$; MC, V; local checks only; breakfast, lunch Wed–Sun; no alcohol; no reservations; jmarine@spiritone.com; map:DD8* &

Ken's Home Plate / ★★

1852 SE HAWTHORNE BLVD, HAWTHORNE; 503/236-9520
1208 NW GLISAN ST, PEARL DISTRICT; 503/517-8935

After just about a year, Ken Gordon's snappy takeout place has expanded its success to a second outlet in the trendy Pearl District across the river. The offerings are identical in the two locations—in fact, everything's cooked in Southeast—but the new Pearl premises open at 7am for breakfast pastry. So now there are two places to get Gordon's dozen or so outstanding daily entrees—interesting, well-executed, and authentic dishes from around the globe, prepared on the premises and ready to heat and serve in the privacy of your own home. Gordon's skill and use of high-quality ingredients are evident in the *bastilla* (Moroccan chicken pie), highly seasoned Tuscan meat loaf, salmon fillet en croûte, and chicken pot pie, to name but a few of the dozens of dishes in his repertoire. The many excellent entrees can be ordered by the pound, à la carte, or, for $6.75 to $8.50, with your choice of an accompanying side dish or salad. For dessert, the bittersweet chocolate pudding grows addictive. Ken's takeout menu changes daily, with a few standards (stuffed chicken breasts) usually available. In both storefronts, there are a few tables for sit-down diners. Ken's also caters a wide range of events, small or large, and with advance notice can prepare a special takeout meal for a crowd. *$–$$; MC, V; checks OK; lunch, dinner Tues–Sat (Hawthorne), breakfast, lunch dinner Tues–Sat (Pearl District); beer and wine; no reservations; map:HH5, map:L2*

Khun Pic's Bahn Thai / ★★☆

3429 SE BELMONT ST, BELMONT; 503/235-1610
It may have been destiny that led Mary Ogard to open Khun Pic's Bahn Thai, or maybe just family ties: her mother, Srichan Miller, started a local revolution in Thai cooking when she opened Bangkok Kitchen, and sister Shelley Siripatrapa continued the tradition at her renowned restaurant, Lemongrass. Ogard's place, like her sister's, is an old house, though gold-painted woodwork and other touches of opulent exotica give it a style of its own. The menu is spare to the point of austerity, with just over a half-dozen offerings augmented by a special or two. Thai papaya salad is delicious and refreshing, and the hot-and-sour soup with prawns is spicy and flavorful but not too rich; there's also a terrific vegetarian pad thai chock-full of vegetables and various excellent curries with chicken, prawns, vegetables, and occasionally something unusual like catfish. Give yourself time if you're planning on eating at Khun Pic's Bahn Thai, because Mary is doing everything in the kitchen while her sometimes harried but gracious and affable husband, Jon, tends tables—but don't let the wait deter you from experiencing one of Portland's most distinctive Thai restaurants. *$$; no credit cards, checks OK; dinner Mon–Sat; beer and wine; reservations recommended; map:HH5*

Koji Osakaya / ★★☆

7007 SW MACADAM AVE, SOUTHWEST (AND BRANCHES); 503/293-1066
Sushi bars are everywhere, but this operation is clearly one of the better full-service Japanese restaurants around—especially since it's multiplied by three. From the original place in Southwest Portland—with sumo

wrestling broadcasts—to the tiny, always jammed place downtown (606 SW Broadway; 503/294-1169; map:H3) to the newest outpost in the trendy NE Broadway neighborhood (1500 NE Weidler St; 503/280-0992; map:FF5), Koji's offers a wide Japanese menu. Besides the basic teriyakis, there are a bunch of slurpy Japanese noodle soups (hold to the pork-bone broth), multiple donburis in elaborate arrangements atop oversized rice bowls, and pungent appetizers of vividly flavored bits of meat or tofu. The sushi bar is wide-ranging—try the salmon box sushi—and check out the day's specials; the chef may be doing something inspiring with ramen. If there have to be chain restaurants, Koji may have the strongest links. *$$; AE, MC, V; no checks; lunch, dinner every day; beer and wine; no reservations; map:JJ6* &

Kornblatt's / ★

628 NW 23RD AVE, NORTHWEST; 503/242-0055

Given the dearth of good New York Jewish delis in Portland, we're hoping that Kornblatt's new owners, Joe and Christine Rosenkrantz, will follow through on their pledge of improvements and more New York. Kornblatt's is still the best place for chewy home-baked bagels (in a wide range of flavors) to meet tangy flown-in smoked fish. And considering the mileage from Brooklyn, the corned beef and pastrami is fairly plausible; the custom of unexpected hot toppings atop bagels may take some more getting used to. Breakfast is our favorite meal of the day here, a variety of savory and sweet in large portions: corned beef hash, blintzes, matzo brei, French toast, and eggs scrambled with lox and onions. As more changes come, hopefully nothing will disturb the bowl of pickles on the table, or some legitimately NY by NW service. *$; MC, V; checks OK; breakfast, lunch, dinner every day; beer and wine; no reservations; map:GG7* &

La Buca West / ★
La Buca East / ★

2309 NW KEARNEY ST, NORTHWEST; 503/279-8040
40 NE 28TH AVE, LAURELHURST; 503/238-1058

La Buca stands apart as a place to sup on uncomplicated pasta dishes, panini sandwiches, and salads, all at friendly prices. After developing a strong following at his beachhead location just off NW 23rd Avenue, owner Scott Mapes opened an equally successful eastside spot. Although La Buca East lacks the charm of the original (and loses points for awful overhead lighting), it offers more elbow room for slurping noodles. Both eateries utilize a no-frills, order-at-the-counter approach to keep customers and orders moving along. You can guide yourself through a dignified Italian meal if you order correctly. The filling "bread spreads"—sun-dried tomato, basil, and the salty, savory olive—taste great generously slathered atop slices of Grand Central bread. House salads are hearty and big enough to split, and the pesto mashed potatoes worthy of repeat orders. But wait—save room for the pasta! Dishes such as the penne puttanesca and the basic spaghetti with garlic and red pepper work their minimalist charm. For lunch try one of the sandwiches, such as the grilled chicken with pesto, fontina, and tomato. *$; MC, V; checks OK; lunch Mon–Sat, dinner every day; beer and wine; no reservations; map:GG7, map:GG5* &

La Calaca Comelona / ★★☆

1408 SE 12TH AVE, SOUTHEAST; 503/239-9675

As owner Patricia Cabrera proudly declares, they don't make burritos at "The Hungry Skeleton," a brightly painted cantina crammed with rustic wooden furniture, suspended skeletons, and Frida Kahlo and Diego Rivera reproductions. The menu features more authentic fare than what normally passes as Mexican cooking: behind the scenes at this colorful establishment, the kitchen turns out its own tortillas, chorizo sausage, and daily salsas. What this means for those who sup here: knock-your-socks-off tacos (try the oven-roasted marinated pork and pineapple). Your choice of grilled steak, chorizo, or chicken can also be wrapped into a taco, featured on a combination plate, or worked into a quesadilla. Vegetarians can feast on the sopa: a pillow of masa topped with queso fresco, lettuce, tomatoes, onion, guacamole, and sour cream. There are also fresh (as in made-to-order) juices, including the "Oasis," a tantalizing concoction made with oranges and cactus juice. Also on the beverage list are cinnamon-laced hot chocolate and—it was only a matter of time—margaritas. *$; DC, DIS, MC, V; checks OK; lunch Tues–Sat, dinner Mon–Sat; beer and wine; no reservations; map:HH5* &

La Catalana / ★★

2821 SE STARK ST, SOUTHEAST; 503/232-0948

This was one of the first Spanish restaurants to blaze trails to Portland a few years ago; now there are several more. La Catalana has held its own, though, mainly because the food in this sweet, relaxed place bursts with flavor, color, and intrigue. A half-dozen entrees share the menu with a strong list of tapas; paella is a specialty, but you might also try the grilled salmon fillet served with a minty salsa. Among the tapas are beautifully roasted padron peppers that are just spicy enough to heighten the flavors in a mild salad of tomato and *mahon* (Spanish goat cheese). Razor clams are lightly floured and fried in butter and olive oil with a burst of lemon—and a little magic. Servers here seem to know when you want to be left alone, or when they might ply you with samples from the kitchen. Lemon ice cream is luscious served in a hollowed-out lemon. La Catalana expanded a while back (adding a limited bar), making reservations less crucial; but if you prefer an intimate setting, call ahead and ask to be seated in the original dining room. *$$; no credit cards; local checks only; dinner Wed–Sun; beer and wine; reservations recommended; map:GG5* &

La Prima Trattoria / ★

4775 SW 77TH AVE, RALEIGH HILLS; 503/297-0360

Hidden in the shadow of Fred Meyer and a suburban strip mall, La Prima Trattoria lacks what you might call "street appeal." But never mind; the food is good, if not memorable, and the interior far more attractive than what you might expect—especially if you sit with your back to the parking lot. For lunch there are "wood-fired" pizzas with enough diverse ingredients perched atop the "fresh-made peasant crust" to spell out good value. Dinner consists of basic red-sauce standards with elaborations, like a linguine bolognese—a traditional rib-sticking meat sauce gussied up with sage. For dessert, try the Venetian classic, tiramisù; the La Prima Trattoria version forgoes the traditional coffee for the south-of-the-border sizzle of a Kahlua-espresso sauce pooled beneath sodden ladyfingers and mounds of cream. *$$; AE, MC, V; checks OK; lunch Mon–Fri, dinner every day; beer and wine; reservations recommended; map:II8*

Laslow's Northwest / ★★☆

2327 NW KEARNEY ST, NORTHWEST; 503/241-8092

The year 2000 brought a shift in location to Laslow's without missing a beat either on the floor or in the kitchen. After making a strong showing in what other restaurateurs found a challenging location on NE Broadway, Connie and Eric Laslow opened a second location in the more restaurant trendy Northwest. For a short while they ran both places, then closed the original one to focus on the Northwest location. Though eastsiders miss the proximity, the experience of dining with the Laslows hasn't really changed. Within a similar setting (a tastefully appointed refurbished house) guests savor dishes that have become menu mainstays since the early days of Laslows: grilled Bosc pear salad, hibiscus-rubbed duck breast, cherrywood-smoked Argentine beef fillet, and the now-legendary pumpkin-custard crab cakes. *$$$; AE, MC, V; local checks only; dinner every day; full bar; reservations recommended; www.laslows.com; map: GG7*

L'Auberge / ★★☆

601 NW VAUGHN ST, NORTHWEST; 503/223-3302

This longtime establishment may no longer be among the hottest of the city's upscale restaurants, but it remains a solid, comfortable, deeply pleasant place to spend an evening. The casual bistro menu, served near the warm fireplace up in the bar area—a softly lit den of respite in the winter months—and on the outside deck in summer, is a powerful draw. Specialties include L'Auberge's classic pâté, steamed mussels and clams, and each evening's pasta. Downstairs, in the dining room, dishes such as a richly moist and flavorful apple cider chicken breast can be warming; one attractive option of the new style is smaller bistro servings of some of the restaurant entrees, such as salmon pavé in a bacon cream or filet mignon. In either place, just remember to end with L'Auberge's dessert menu, including the hallowed poached lemon cheesecake—still dazzling—or the intense chocolate mousse. *$$–$$$; AE, DC, MC, V; local checks only; dinner every day; full bar; reservations recommended; map:FF7*

Le Bouchon / ★★

517 NW 14TH AVE, PEARL DISTRICT; 503/248-2193

The word "bistro" is tossed around loosely in the present restaurant world, but this tiny, loud storefront in the Pearl District reminds you that it sounds best in a French accent. The menu is studded with French standards—onion soup, escargots, and pâté. The authenticity continues

through entrees and desserts, from entrecôte in red wine sauce through—*naturellement*—a potent chocolate mousse. There may be questions here about decibel level and the acrobatics needed to get around the closely packed tables, but that's part of the atmosphere. These folks know what they're doing—and it's worth it to listen to them discuss it. *$$; AE, DIS, MC, V; no checks; lunch Fri, dinner Tues–Sat; beer and wine; reservations recommended; map:L1*

Legin / ★★

8001 SE DIVISION ST, SOUTHEAST; 503/777-2828

At first glance, this huge, garish building among the fast-food architecture of SE 82nd Avenue looks like the chop suey palace of all time. It's only when you get inside and see the huge Chinese menu and the multiple tanks of live seafood that you discover one of the best Chinese restaurants in town. There are items here you just won't find elsewhere

in Portland—bamboo marrow, two kinds of shark fin soup—and you can accompany them with live geoduck or a whole tilapia. Try anything that's alive when you order it, try to find a place for the pepper and salt lobster, and take a shot at something you don't recognize—Cantonese ham, maybe. Although dim sum lunch is served every day, the dim sum on Sunday is not to be missed, if only to watch the dispensing of all the chicken feet and siu mai in the world. *$$; MC, V; no checks; lunch, dinner every day; full bar; no reservations; map:HH3* &

Lemongrass Thai Restaurant / ★★★

1705 NE COUCH ST, NORTHEAST; 503/231-5780

The big news at this exquisite Thai restaurant in an elegant old Portland Victorian house is that there's now red curry. To understand why this is so exciting, you need to have tasted Shelley Siripatrapa's green curry and yellow curry. Tastes here are bright and sharp, sweet and hot and tangy, from emerald pools of green curry to snap-your-eyes-open shrimp with garlic and basil. Siripatrapa has a magical touch with seafood; her shrimp is a good example, snuggled into pad thai noodles or just floating in a clear-your-sinuses broth of lemongrass, kaffir lime, and chile. She also produces a stunning peanut sauce, and in her new inspiration of prawn satay the two specialties come together dramatically. There's a choice of heat intensity, but getting much past mild takes you into a place of pain (you have to wonder about the scale of 1 to 10 when your eyes smart at 2). There are no reservations, and nothing is cooked ahead of time; you'll wait for a table, and then wait again at your table. But after you do, you'll come back and wait again. *$$; no credit cards; checks OK; lunch Tues–Fri, dinner Tues–Sat; beer and wine; no reservations; map:GG6*

Little Italy's Trattoria / ★

901 WASHINGTON ST, DOWNTOWN VANCOUVER, WA; 360/737-2363
316 SE 123RD AVE, CASCADE PARK (VANCOUVER, WA); 360/883-1325
Although Italian cuisine has come a long way in the last two decades, it's still nice to find a place that embodies the Italian restaurant of our youth: red checked tablecloths, a satisfying plate of noodles and sauce, buttery garlic bread, and a bowl of spumoni ice cream to top it all off. This pleasing trattoria offers something for everyone in the family: baked rigatoni with Italian sausage for your meat-loving brother, pizza margherita for your sister with Portland airs, Caesar salad for Mom, veal parmigiana for Grandpa, and spaghetti with butter and cheese for Junior. To wash it all down there's a small selection of mostly Italian wines (with the requisite bottle of chianti), Peroni beer, Italian sodas, and espresso drinks. Most recently, the noodle has stretched to the other side of the Columbia, with a new branch in Southeast, Little Italy's Cucina (2601 SE Clinton St; 503/239-4306; map:II5). *$; MC, V; no checks; lunch Mon–Sat, dinner every day; beer and wine; reservations recommended; map:BB6* &

Little Wing Cafe / ★

529 NW 13TH AVE, PEARL DISTRICT; 503/228-3101
Barbara and Bob Weisman run a brisk countertop lunch business and a limited yet inviting dinner hour. Lunch is all about sourdough bread sandwiches, highlighted by the chicken sandwich with avocado, bacon, and blue cheese. It's possible to eat on the cheap by ordering a classic peanut butter and jelly, leaving an extra buck for one of those loved chocolate chip cookies. The evening menu offers sandwiches as well, augmented by more serious entrees such as mustard-crusted salmon served atop herb pancakes and broccolini. Specials change often, with a seasonal emphasis. The restaurant opened seven years ago as the Little Wing Cookie Company and has grown up along with the area, even if its humble Formica tables might suggest that it hasn't exactly kept up with the times. *$; AE, MC, V; checks OK; lunch Mon–Sat, dinner Tues–Sat; beer and wine; no reservations; map:L2* &

London Grill / ★★

309 SW BROADWAY (BENSON HOTEL), DOWNTOWN; 503/295-4110

At the core of the Benson Hotel, this place has been a Portland institution since before software, or jogging, or even Mark Hatfield—definitely a 20th-century classic. The overstuffed seats and rococo chandeliers speak to a traditional idea of what a power restaurant should be, and much of the menu harkens back to that ideal: chicken Oscar, veal medallions, chateaubriand for two. On the other hand, there are signs of today: bronzed ahi fillet in a Sichuan glaze, and medallions of Northwest ostrich—although presented in the crabmeat-and-béarnaise Oscar manner. London Grill has deeply loyal fans, high-quality ingredients—its seafood treatments may be traditional, but it's treating fine seafood—and a harpist. The service is highly professional, although it seems fewer dishes now involve tableside preparation. The longest wine list in town is especially strong on French bottlings; settle into your cushy chair as you consider your decision. *$$$; AE, DC, MC, V; checks OK; breakfast, lunch, dinner every day, brunch Sun; full bar; reservations recommended; www.bensonhotel.com; map:I3* &

Lorn and Dottie's Luncheonette / ★

322 SW 2ND AVE, OLD TOWN; 503/221-2473

This clean, well-lighted space might surprise you on your first visit—especially if you're expecting a casual luncheonette. At Lorn and Dottie's, situated on the edge of Old Town, brass nameplates mark the booths of regulars, the waiter wears a bow tie, and hot coffee is poured with frequency. A basic eggs, ham, and toast breakfast is actually eggs, several slices of Canadian ham, savory potato pancakes served alongside a dish of applesauce, and a thick slice of cinnamon bread (or jalapeño corn bread or banana nut bread—or, of course, basic toast). Regulars also like the Italian eggs, with sausage and Parmesan, or the decadent apple pancake. Lorn and Dottie's is open until 2pm daily, serving classic lunchtime fare (hamburgers, sandwiches, chef's salad) at midday, but on the weekends breakfast is the only meal available. *$; MC, V; no checks; breakfast every day, lunch Mon–Fri; no alcohol; no reservations; map:I6* &

Lucy's Table / ★★★

704 NW 21ST AVE, NORTHWEST; 503/226-6126

When you walk through the door of Lucy's Table, you enter one of the city's most inviting spaces: a sumptuous dining room appointed in rich jewel tones with funky lighting and provocative art on the walls. The knowledgeable (and, incidentally, jaw-droppingly gorgeous) waitstaff will pamper you and guide you through the exotic fusion swirl of rising-star chef Alex Pitts' menu. You may need to loosen your cuffs and tie to properly enjoy the pomegranate-basted ribs, but this is a small sacrifice to make for these sweet and smoky morsels. The charred squid is tender and surprisingly balanced against a deep-dish olive bread, and an unusual second course of cold almond and garlic soup provokes both contemplation and discussion. When it comes to the beautifully presented entrees, Pitts turns a deft hand with seafood and prime cuts of beef, also making allowances for vegetarian diners with grace and style. Fetching, toothsome desserts—flourless chocolate cake, crème brûlée, homemade ice creams—warrant sacrifice. Owner Peter Kost stocks an impressive and reasonably priced cellar of local and imported wines. *$$$; AE, DIS, MC, V; checks OK; dinner Mon–Sat; full bar; reservations recommended; map:GG7* &

Marco's Cafe and Espresso Bar / ★★

7910 SW 35TH AVE, MULTNOMAH VILLAGE; 503/245-0199
3449 NE 24TH AVE, IRVINGTON; 503/287-8011
In the stroller's paradise of antique-rich Multnomah, Marco's has near-landmark status. The sunny dining rooms have high ceilings and intriguing prints on the walls, and there's a rack of reading material by the front door. Breakfast, served until late afternoon, includes French toast stuffed with apples and cinnamon, homemade pastries, and savory dishes such as huevos rancheros, all in nap-inducing portions. For lunch there's a variety of organic burgers, delicious main-course salads large enough to share, and an ever-changing lineup of soups. In the evening,  Marco's turns into an imaginative dinner operation, with a different menu every night featuring entrees such as spanakopita, chicken Roma, and sweet corn and smoked tomato quesadillas, as well as pastas and a good variety of vegetarian dishes. Marco's mulligatawny, served on Thursday, has attracted something of a following of its own, and the desserts, also Marco's own, never fail to satisfy a sweet tooth. With the new location in Irvington, a trip to Marco's no longer involves a daunting trek for eastsiders, and at both locations, children fit right in. *$$; AE, DC, DIS, MC, V; local checks only; breakfast, lunch every day, dinner Mon–Sat; beer and wine; no reservations; map:JJ7, map:FF5* &

Marrakesh / ★☆

1201 NW 21ST AVE, NORTHWEST; 503/248-9442
Step into Marrakesh and take a magic carpet ride to a place where low lights reveal tapestried walls, and yards of fabric are draped tentlike from the ceiling. The appeal at this exotic restaurant is in the atmosphere and drama of the evening; unfortunately, the food falls short of fabulous, but you'll probably be so occupied with the scene that you won't notice. At one of the knee-high dining tables, get comfortable on a cushion: you're here for five courses. The meal begins with the customary finger-washing ceremony and ends with the sprinkling of orange water over your hands. In between, you eat without the benefit of utensils (unless you order something like couscous, in which case you might wangle a fork). The first

course is a cumin-and-coriander lentil soup, and next comes an eggplant salad. The sweetened *bastela royale* (chicken pie) paves the way for your entree—maybe lamb with eggplant or braised hare in a rich cumin and paprika sauce. The easiest way to sample the fare is to go with three friends and order the Royale Feast. *$$; AE, DC, DIS, MC, V; no checks; dinner every day; beer and wine; reservations recommended; map:FF7* ᪴

McCormick & Schmick's Seafood Restaurant / ★★★
McCormick's Fish House and Bar / ★★

235 SW 1ST AVE, DOWNTOWN; 503/224-7522
9945 SW BEAVERTON-HILLSDALE HWY, BEAVERTON; 503/643-1322

True, this place is the template of the chain of M&S Seafood Restaurants dotting the country. But you have to admire a restaurant where the fresh fish offerings include blue nose grouper from Gisborne, New Zealand, cashew-crusted and served with hot Jamaican vanilla-rum butter sauce—especially when the kitchen can carry it off, which is usually the case. McCormick & Schmick's has a vast range of both seafood and imagina-

tion, from blackened Fijian escolar to pecan catfish with fried green tomatoes. The menu changes daily, but the place has its specialties, notably grilled alder-smoked salmon—with a smoke aroma that announces the restaurant a block away—and crab cakes and bouilla-baisse. M&S is frequently jammed, offering a lively bar scene, complete with a pianist and an extraordinary selection of single-malt Scotches. Expect a more casual mood and feel at the Beaverton outpost. *$$; AE, DC, MC, V; no checks; lunch Mon–Fri, dinner every day (downtown), lunch Mon–Sat, dinner every day (Beaverton); full bar; reservations recommended; www.mccormickandschmicks.com; map:H5* ᪴

Metronome / ★⯪

1426 NE BROADWAY, NE BROADWAY; 503/288-4300

The name of this bustling bistro is apt, not just because it reflects the owners' musical interests, but also because it suggests the rhythm of the place—which moves along steadily at a good clip. The colors of this bright and airy space are bold, as are the flavors of the dishes that make up an eclectic Italian-meets-Asian-in-the-Northwest menu. Asian touches predominate in the appetizers, such as curry soups, sliced ahi with lemon-wasabi vinaigrette, and spring rolls with spinach and shi-itake, while pastas, sandwiches, burgers, and bistro variations on the meat-and-potato theme—like grilled salmon with sorrel-caper butter and Yukon Gold potatoes—make up most of the entrees. Chef Mark Potovsky's presentation has flair, and his kitchen is generally up to satis-fying speedily all but the busiest weekend-night crowds. The wine list always has a few gems by the glass, and prices for both food and wine are very reasonable. Metronome is a good place to visit in the summer, when outdoor tables bring diners closer to the beat of this burgeoning neighborhood. *$$; AE, MC, V; no checks; lunch Tues–Fri, dinner Tues–Sun; full bar; reservations recommended; map:FF5* &

Milo's City Cafe / ★★

1325 NE BROADWAY, NE BROADWAY; (503)288-6456

This breakfast and lunch place has become so hot so quickly that on weekend mornings the only plausible approach is to drop off your name and then trot the block to Barnes & Noble to feed your soul. After you've thoroughly examined the Spiritual Growth section, Milo's might be ready to offer some French toast stuffed with Italian sausage or peanut butter and jelly, or a wide range of Benedicts and hashes that only start with terrific smoked salmon. Inside is a spacious, casual, new-looking storefront, but if you're lucky—and you've reached the right spiritual level—you might even get a table outside, where your crab cakes and eggs will be seasoned by strollers' envious glances. And although breakfast all day may be tempting, for those inclined to order more standard lunch fare come noon, there's lot to choose from: sandwiches, pasta, and entrees like chicken piccata or pan-fried oysters. *$; AE, MC, V; local checks only; breakfast, lunch every day; beer and wine; no reservations; skogland@msn.com; map:FF5* &

Misohapi / ★

1123 NW 23RD AVE, NORTHWEST; 503/796-2012

Once you get past the unforgivable pun, Misohapi is exactly the sort of place that you want to have right down the street: fast, fresh, and filling. The noodle dishes are all strong, anchored by a fine pad thai and accessorized by a loaded yakisoba and a lighter shrimp noodle bowl with fresh mint. For entrees, consider the ginger beef, the black bean garlic pork, or the interesting Southeast Asian spin on General Tso's chicken. If you're in a hurry, Misohapi promises real food, real fast. Choose the to-go bento (grilled skewers of beef or chicken with rice and cabbage salad) or the lunch special: soup or salad and one of the stir-fried entrees. When the weather allows, take your chopsticks to the street and draw envious stares from the motorists caught in interminable "Trendy-Third" traffic. A recent expansion has more than doubled the dining area, easing the lunch pileup. *$; MC, V; no checks; lunch Mon–Fri, dinner every day; beer and wine; reservations recommended; map:GG7* &

Montage / ★★

301 SE MORRISON ST, SOUTHEAST; 503/234-1324

It may come as a surprise that Portland's definitively hip late-night hangout is open for lunch. You won't get the 2am energy, but you'll get the same unexpectedly good, cheap Southern/Cajun cuisine. (When Montage says spicy, it's not kidding.) If you join the later, more alternative crowd, you may have to wait for a spot at one of the long tables for such Cajun specialties as Spicy Mac (glorified macaroni with Cajun gravy, jalapeños, tomatoes, and Parmesan), blackened snapper, or jambalaya topped with crab, rabbit sausage, or alligator meat. Dinners are both ambitious and unique—from spicy frogs' legs to alligator pâté to green eggs and Spam—and make up in visceral satisfaction what they lack in finesse. Round out your meal with a slice of pecan pie. The loud hum of conversation and music is punctuated with waiters' shouts to the open kitchen announcing shooters—oysters or mussels served in shot glasses. Lots of wines are offered by the glass and are promptly refilled in jelly jar–like vessels with a nod in the right direction. The snarky and sometimes indifferent waiters manage to look as if they're having as good a time as most of the guests. *$–$$; no credit cards; checks OK; lunch Mon–Fri, dinner every day; full bar; no reservations; map:HH6*

Morning Star Espresso / ★
510 SW 3RD AVE, DOWNTOWN; 503/241-2401
If everyone has, like a belly button, an attitude, then everyone should feel at home in this offbeat (OK, downright bizarre) java joint and sandwich shop in the heart of downtown. Note the sign on the counter that reads, "Please, if you're a junkie, don't ask for the bathroom key unless you purchase a sandwich. Thank you." The blaring eclectic music makes the espresso seem even stronger in the mornings as a steady stream of students, professionals, and shiftless types with time to kill parade to the counter to load up on typical coffee bar fare: bagels, pastries, and lattes. At lunch, however, Morning Star rises above the run-of-the-mill mud shack with an impressive menu of hearty sandwiches—all with cheeky names like "The Sandwich Formerly Known as Roast Beef" and "Bob." All are constructed on sturdy Grand Central bread and sent out with a few Tim's Cascade potato chips and a token fruit garnish. Recent speculation has wondered if the clientele at Morning Star would change much with the departure of the advertising hipsters at Wieden & Kennedy. The staff of Morning Star does not seem to think so; quoting one barista, "Good riddance." *$; no credit cards; local checks only; breakfast, lunch Mon–Sat; no alcohol; no reservations; map:H5* &

Morton's of Chicago—The Steakhouse / ★★★
213 SW CLAY ST, DOWNTOWN; 503/248-2100
Morton's is Vince Lombardi's idea of a steak house—bigger isn't just a better thing, it's the only thing. This is brought home to you early, in a live presentation of the menu that includes the brandishing of a potato the size of Idaho. In this new outpost of a national chain, the bill will be of similar size—and many of the steaks similarly impressive. The New York steak and the prime rib are particularly outstanding, rich and tender and aggressively flavorful. There are a few non-beef specialties, notably a lobster that figures live and squirming in the opening display, which

may be more up close and personal than you want to get with your entree. The menu also shines at the opening and closing, from smoked salmon and crab cocktails to cheesecake and soufflés. The service is uniformly dazzling—and it's not easy to be charming while hefting a potato that could be used in a shot put. *$$$; AE, DC, MC, V; checks OK; dinner every day; full bar; reservations recommended; www.mortons. com; map:D4* &

Mother's Bistro & Bar / ★★☆

409 SW 2ND AVE, DOWNTOWN; 503/464-1122

This is the way your mother should have cooked but almost certainly didn't, unless you're closely related to proprietor Lisa Schroeder. After cooking in Paris and New York, Schroeder opened the most comfortable of comfort-food restaurants in Portland, with offerings such as matzo ball soup, pot roast and chicken with dumplings. The place flies in H&H bagels from New York but cures its own smoked salmon. The substantial, three-meals-a-day menu is not only reassuring but impressively skilled, and every month Schroeder focuses on a mother of a different ethnic group, providing maternal specials ranging from Italian to Moroccan Jewish. The space is endearingly decorated in maternal memorabilia, from old advertisements to particularly heart-tugging prints. Inviting overstuffed furniture and a warm wooden bar outfit the bar, which serves mostly as a waiting area; it's hard to drink seriously in a place with a name like this. Unsurprisingly, Mother's turns out a mean cookie and wicked devil's food cake. *$$; AE, MC, V; no checks; breakfast, lunch Tues–Sun, dinner Tues–Sat; full bar; reservations recommended; map:I5*

Nancy Lee's Pharmacy Fountain / ★

2334 W BURNSIDE ST, PORTLAND HEIGHTS; 503/241-1137

This old, classic-looking soda fountain throwback inside the Town Pharmacy is the quintessential nostalgic "walk down memory lane." Before the Internet—or even before the VCR and DVD were invented—this was the kind of down-home, friendly place where regulars stopped in for seltzer water or an afternoon ice cream soda. Breakfast and lunch eventually became ritual, and as sure as the clock ticked, the omelets fluffed and the waitresses smiled. You could have walked in here 20 years ago and seen a similar scene: the long, angular counter set close to the kitchen, the waitresses dressed in aprons and skirts making small talk about the weather and refilling coffee cups. At lunchtime, sally up to the counter in a swivel chair and order a burger and an old-fashioned, real ice cream milkshake or a meat loaf sandwich with a cup of tomato soup. And while you're at it, bring along a copy of *American Heritage* to add to the nostalgia. *$; no credit cards; local checks only; breakfast, lunch Mon–Sat; no alcohol; no reservations; map:GG7* &

New Seoul Garden / ★★

10860 SW BEAVERTON-HILLSDALE HWY, BEAVERTON; 503/643-8818

The Korean population of Beaverton has been burgeoning, and this sweeping dining area is where they go for *bul kal bi* (*bul* meaning "fire," *kal bi* a kind of short rib) and celebration. In the center of the tables are gas grills, to be set afire for diners to cook raw beef, seasoned chicken, and marinated pork. It may take a little while to get the hang of it, but it's worth the effort—and it fascinates kids, once they figure out how to cook the meat and not themselves. Gracefully gowned waitresses will show you the process, but basically you're on your own, alone with the beef and the fire. Less pyromaniac diners may try soups or seafood, but be warned—they can be fiery in their own way. Soothe yourself by working through the *namul*, small salads that cover the table. There is bento to go at lunchtime and a lively nightclub late at night, where the emphasis is on Seoul music/karaoke. *$$; AE, MC, V; no checks; lunch, dinner every day; full bar; reservations recommended; map:II9* &

Nicholas' Restaurant / ★★

318 SE GRAND AVE, SOUTHEAST; 503/235-5123

A terrific dive with character, Nicholas' is almost always packed with enthusiastic fans of hearty, honest Lebanese fare at great prices. The basics—such as rich baba ghanouj, light and creamy hummus, crisp and flavorful falafel—are reliably excellent, and you can get them in a mountain of a mezze plate for a mere $7. There are substantial kebabs of vegetables, chicken, lamb, or beef, delicious lamb kofta, savory lentil soup, and an intriguing pizzalike *manakish,* which unites the flavors of thyme, sesame, and sumac. Everything at Nicholas' tastes fresh and healthy; that and the low prices help to explain the crowds. Be forewarned that Nicholas' serves no alcohol and takes no credit cards: bring cash or a check, have a glass of wine elsewhere, and revel in the food and atmosphere of one of Portland's most inviting hole-in-the-wall eateries. *$; no credit cards; checks OK; lunch, dinner every day; no alcohol; no reservations; map:I9* &

Noho's Hawaiian Cafe / ★★☆

2525 SE CLINTON ST, CLINTON ST (AND BRANCHES); 503/233-5301

This is a place to put away some serious food. Korean-cut short ribs, marinated in honey, garlic, and sesame seed sauce, are sublime; Phil's Ono Chicken is infused in a ginger sauce and cooked until the bird is as tender as tuna. As a matter of fact, ahi is available too, as is pork—sometimes as a special. Dinners are available in three sizes that translate—in our minds, at least—to medium, large, and mega-portions, and they come with rice and a macaroni or green salad. There's also a yakisoba noodle plate with four choices of sauce. Noho's is usually packed; if you can't get a table to put that food away on the premises, you might consider taking it home. Check out one of the other locations if you're in the area—or in the mood for the same food with a little more atmosphere—near Johns Landing (0515 SW Carolina St; 503/977-2771; map:II6) or the new Noho's in Vancouver (11820-G NE Fourth Plain Blvd; 360/883-3137). *$–$$; AE, MC, V; checks OK; lunch, dinner every day; no alcohol (Clinton St and Vancouver), beer and wine (Johns Landing); no reservations; www.nohos.com; map:HH5* &

¡Oba! / ★★☆

555 NW 12TH AVE, PEARL DISTRICT; 503/228-6161

Even for the ultrahip Pearl District, this place has created the buzz of all buzzes. With its flashy red walls and star-hung ceiling, and its sizzling bar scene, it's won awards for design. Diners have also given thumping approval to its cuisine, but nothing could be as hot as the ambience here. Chef Scott Newman's style is called Nuevo Latino, and the menu extends across everything Latin, from Brazilian *feijoada* to Cuban flank steak to fish Veracruz-style, from sangria to Brazilian sugarcane liquor. Some are big fans of the ribs with guava-habanero barbecue sauce, and others prefer putting together arrays of openers such as crispy shrimp tostadas and shiitake mushroom rellenos. Try to be beautiful, or at least very cool. *$$; AE, DC, MC, V; checks OK; dinner every day; full bar; reservations recommended; www.obarestaurant.com; map:L2* &

Obi / ★★☆

101 NW 2ND AVE, OLD TOWN; 503/226-3826

There is a standard Japanese menu here, but to order from it would be to miss the point. Obi is about sushi, a point clearly made by its signature T-shirt, showing owner Masahide Arima holding a large fish and a knife. At Obi, he combines these two elements strikingly, slicing and sculpting Tiger Eyes (salmon in a circle of squid), Crazy Rolls, and Rock 'n' Rolls. Each is creative and vividly fresh, and the menu goes on, regularly thickened with his new inspirations, as Arima spins tuna, salmon, flying fish eggs, avocado, and seaweed into unexpected new arrangements. Obi is a comfortable oasis in the midst of Old Town, but sushi like this—and even the T-shirts—would be welcome anywhere. *$$; AE, DC, DIS, MC, V; no checks; lunch Mon–Fri, dinner Mon–Sat; full bar; reservations recommended; map:J6*

Old Wives' Tales / ★

1300 E BURNSIDE ST, SOUTHEAST; 503/238-0470

When Holly Hart opened this restaurant in the early '80s, it doubled as a feminist gathering place, with a back room where men and women met for heated discussions and an indestructible playroom for the younger set. Now, although the playroom is still an important part of the ambience, the back room has long since become the "quiet room." The food and mood are the same as they were in the early days, and although intriguingly adult things are done to seafood, the motif continues to be whole-wheat correctness. On the menu you'll find Hungarian mushroom soup (something like a meatless stroganoff), vegetarian enchiladas, and carrot-cashew burgers, plus hot pastrami sandwiches or a chicken-topped Caesar for the unconverted. The children's menu meets parental approval—pancakes, grilled cheese, burritos—but kids will like it too. Even without a shorty in tow, it's a good place to meet for lunch—just ask for a table far away from the one in which half of the eight seats are high chairs. *$; AE, DIS, MC, V; checks OK; breakfast, lunch, dinner every day; beer and wine; reservations recommended; map:GG1* &

Opus Too / ★★

33 NW 2ND AVE, OLD TOWN; 503/222-6077

Whatever happens in food fashion—and this place isn't totally immune—the dominant theme here is always the searing mesquite grill and the fresh fish and great hunks of red meat that decorate it. Sure, there are a few other dishes, such as crab cakes and jambalaya, but basically you're looking at the grill, which stretches from gulf shrimp wrapped in pancetta to New Zealand rack of lamb. It's an excellent place to look, and the splendid protein is helped by béarnaise and beurre rouge sauces. There's a range of lunchtime sandwiches, and the atmosphere runs heavy at both meals. The decor is urban cool—tile floor, dark-wood booths, and a long swivel-chair bar overlooking the open kitchen and grills. A terrific sourdough bread is part of the deal, as is the live jazz that floats in from Jazz de Opus next door. A respectable wine list, fine desserts, and piles of fettuccine. *$$; AE, DC, MC, V; no checks; lunch Mon–Fri, dinner every day; full bar; reservations recommended; map:J6* &

The Original Pancake House / ★★

8600 SW BARBUR BLVD, BURLINGAME; 503/246-9007

Show some respect the next time you come here for Swedish or banana or simply perfect pancakes. In 1999, the Original Pancake House was designated by the James Beard Foundation as a regional landmark restaurant, a thick-battered legend. The question is whether, when the New York foundation folks came to present the award, they had to wait in line—the way people have been waiting patiently here since it opened in 1955. This place hums from the time it opens at 7am practically until it closes in midafternoon. The sourdough flapjacks—from wine-spiked cherry to wheat germ to a behemoth apple pancake with a sticky cinnamon glaze—are made from scratch. A good bet is the egg-rich Dutch baby, which arrives looking like a huge, sunken birthday cake, dusted with powdered sugar and served with fresh lemon. Omelets big enough for two (made from a half-dozen eggs) arrive with a short stack. The billing may mention just the pancakes, but this is a place that knows how to handle eggs. The service is cheerful and efficient; after all, there are people waiting for your table. *$; no credit cards; checks OK; breakfast, lunch Wed–Sun; no alcohol; no reservations; map:HH6*

Oritalia / ★★

750 SW ALDER ST (WESTIN HOTEL), DOWNTOWN; 503/295-0680
Portland's version of the restaurant that succeeded in San Francisco is heavy on the ambience—curtains, elaborate light fixtures, a dramatic stairway down from the street entrance—and its almost baroque presentations declare that this time, function may be chasing after form. Its sweeping fusion concept—Japanese/Italian specifically, East/West more broadly—can seem overdone, but it can also work, with admirable Dungeness spring rolls, tagliatelle with scallops and shiitake mushrooms, and tuna tartare on rice cakes turning out both satisfying and entertaining. And only here would cheesecake be served as a napoleon, obliging you to eat it as canapés. The restaurant's multicultural menu could be summed up—or stuck together—in a dish such as this: sea bass steamed in sake, accompanied by a Chinese black bean sauce, arugula, green bean tempura, and portobello mushroom. Though it covers a lot of ground, somehow it works. Oritalia, the restaurant of Portland's spanking new downtown Westin Hotel, certainly provides enough flash in the atmosphere to back up the surprises in the food. The key is to enter in the right spirit—and be surprised by nothing. *$$–$$$; AE, DC, DIS, MC, V; no checks; breakfast, lunch, dinner every day; full bar; reservations recommended; www.oritalia.net; map:I3*

Paley's Place / ★★★★

1204 NW 21ST AVE, NORTHWEST; 503/243-2403
What was a love affair has turned into a blissful marriage. Though it's been a few years since Vitaly and Kimberly Paley waltzed into Portland from New York and swept diners off their feet, Paley's continues to dazzle, warm, and thrill Portlanders. In a constant culinary orbit, Kimberly Paley circles the intimate, thoughtfully designed dining room, closely watching everything that her husband sends out from the kitchen, maintaining an atmosphere as artful as the food. In winter, their seasonal menu might offer crispy veal sweetbreads with a pomegranate demi-glace and a potato-bacon galette, or roasted rabbit with mustard cream and gruyère mashed potatoes. You might get started with warmed Pacific oysters served with leeks and a curry cream sauce over a cheddar biscuit or the mussels with aioli that have become a local addiction. Other seasons might bring a bisque of spring asparagus, broccoli, or steelhead set off by smoked seafood sausage. Menus change with the harvests, but the dessert tray is consistently impressive. From one of the city's best creme brûlées to the warm chocolate soufflé cake to homemade sorbets and ice creams, there's something to satisfy every sweet tooth. *$$$; AE, MC, V; no*

checks; dinner every day; full bar; reservations recommended; www. paleysplace.com; map:GG7

Pambiche / ★★

2811 NE GLISAN ST, LAURELHURST; 503/233-0511

To have experienced Pambiche without a crowd is to have dined here shortly after it first opened. With only 10 tables and limited counter seating, it's entirely common to wait for a table, growing ravenous and envious amid such good smells and vibes. Perhaps it's the otherworld feel of this tiny storefront, tucked behind a huge colonnade and painted—inside and out—in bold colors, that makes it so popular. Or the friendly staff, who slip in and out of English and Spanish. Maybe it's the lip-smacking yucca fritters, grilled Cuban sandwiches, or the *pollo criollo—* chicken stewed in a Creole sauce with fresh herbs and orange. Or possibly the large, full glasses of South American wines? And though it is most definitely the café con leche that draws in the neighbors between mealtimes, it's the dessert case that makes the largest impression anytime, day or night: classic tortes, cheesecakes, and tarts made exotic with tropical fruits, liqueurs, chocolate, and nuts. All in all, there are lots of things to like about this sweet little cafe, Portland's first exclusively Cuban restaurant. *$; MC, V; no checks; lunch, dinner Tues–Sat; beer and wine; no reservations; pambiche@bizland.com; www.apambichau.com; map:GG5*

Papa Haydn / ★★★☆

701 NW 23RD AVE, NORTHWEST; 503/228-7317
5829 SE MILWAUKIE AVE, WESTMORELAND; 503/232-9440

Portland's dessert headquarters—liable to appear at any point as dessert.com—trails waiting diners out of its doors the way it trails chocolate sauce across its cakes. The Northwest Portland outpost now extends across most of a block, incorporating Jo's Bar, a grill with different entrees from the restaurant but, of course, the same desserts. The desserts include dozens of choices, from huge architectural cakes such as Autumn Meringue (layers of chocolate mousse and meringue, festooned with chocolate slabs) and *boccone dolce* (a mountain of whipped cream, chocolate, meringue, and fresh berries) to cookies to house-made sorbets and ice creams. Before the last course, Papa Haydn offers salads and sandwiches (try the chicken club with avocado and sun-dried tomato mayonnaise) at lunch and daily dinner choices, such as pasta with scallops and Gorgonzola cream and filet mignon bresaolo. The Westmoreland location is more low-key with a few menu variances, but don't think that's a way to avoid the lines—it has most of the same desserts, and the many regulars know it. *$$; AE, MC, V; local checks only; lunch, dinner Tues–Sat, brunch Sun (Northwest), lunch Mon–Sat, dinner every day, brunch Sun (Westmoreland); full bar (Northwest), beer and wine (Westmoreland); no reservations; map:GG7, map:II5*

Paparrazzi Pastaficio / ★★

2015 NE BROADWAY, NE BROADWAY; 503/281-7701
Pasta places are as common these days as Spaghetti-os were in the '60s, but Paparrazzi's sweet potato–Parmesan ravioli with caramelized onion sauce is like nothing Chef Boyardee could ever have dreamed up. In all, there are some 20 pasta dishes to eat in or take out (a popular choice for nearby Irvington families), such as gnocchi topped with marinara or wide noodles flecked with radicchio and pancetta. There are a few thin-crust pizzas to choose from as starters, but if you're deciding between those and dessert, hold out for the divine, silky tiramisù (dessert offerings also include the locally rare cannoli). Besides the food itself, value is one of this restaurant's strengths: you can order the pasta dishes as a full dinner—which includes soup or salad, bread, entree, and ice cream—for about $15. (We usually spend $2.50 more and substitute the tiramisù for our dessert.) The bi-level interior is decorated with the work of the namesake photographers, but it has grown increasingly warm over time. *$$; MC, V; local checks only; dinner Tues–Sun; beer and wine; no reservations; map:FF5*

Paragon / ★★

1309 NW HOYT ST, PEARL DISTRICT; 503/833-5060
In this Pearl District hot spot, the buzz has been so loud that the neighbors complained. Since then the noise has been tuned down a bit—although it's still one of the livelier bar scenes around—and the kitchen has been tuned up. Chef Peter Dougherty turns out steady, sometimes dazzling dishes, such as smoked oyster chowder and a pork chop with Bing cherry–onion marmalade, along with more casual efforts like the two-hands Paragon burger. The kitchen also does interesting things with fresh fish, such as lavender-scented, rare-grilled tuna or pan-roasted halibut with a zinfandel reduction. And for dessert there are such striking numbers as a wild ginger crème brûlée and a deeply dense, deeply dark chocolate cake. Dougherty is skilled and creative, although you might enjoy his work more if you can get a table a little ways from the bar. Then again, why not try out a whole new pickup line: "Could I buy you a smoked oyster chowder?" *$$; AE, DC, MC, V; checks OK; lunch, dinner every day; full bar; reservations recommended; map:L1* &

Pasta Veloce / ★★½

1022 SW MORRISON ST, DOWNTOWN (AND BRANCHES); 503/916-4388
In its short life, Pasta Veloce has rocketed to the top of many a downtowner's list of favorite places to grab lunch, and now it's shot out to the burbs. When the owners of NE Broadway's neighborhood Italian restaurant Rustica decided to go after the noon crowd, they opened the airy two-tiered Pasta Veloce on the MAX line at SW Morrison Street, between 10th and 11th Avenues. Since 1997, Pasta Veloce has been feeding hungry clerks and businesspeople a steady diet of interesting pastas—such as

FISHING IN PORTLAND

Ask a Portlander to recommend a seafood restaurant and you will most often get steered to Jake's Famous Crawfish or McCormick & Schmick's (see reviews in this chapter). Although both offer fine preparations of fish, Portland also offers a whole world of exotic seafood just waiting to transport you—one bite at a time—without ever leaving the confines of the city.

It's raining. You sit at your desk and look longingly at your vacation photos, pining wistfully for the smells of the seaside grill in Cozumel, the fish taco stand in San Felipe. Fortunately for you, Claire and Shawna Archibald have made virtual vacations available at their thrilling and vibrant Cafe Azul (112 NW 9th Ave; 503/525-4422). With no more exertion than making a reservation, you travel to distant shores—or, at least, your palate does. On any given night, expect to find such exotica as a salad of smoked Hawaiian threadfish with fresh cactus paddles in a citrus dressing with tomatoes and onions; seviche of marinated scallops, rock shrimp, rockfish, and halibut on a crisp tortilla with savory black beans; and electric blue parrot fish wrapped in banana leaves with spices and chiles and roasted to a turn.

It's summertime. You're in Southeast—the Hawthorne District, and the heat is stifling on the street. You will wait for a long time to get a table at 3 Doors Down (1429 SE 37th Ave; 503/236-6886). The people-watching is good. Be patient. When you do get your table, pay close attention to the scallop dishes—the house specialties that have gathered a cultish following among lovers of fine seafood. Enormous rounds of diver-

penne with spinach, butternut squash, cream, and Parmesan. You order at the counter, then find a seat at one of the simple blonde tables downstairs or up—or take your boxed meal back to the lunchroom. It's satisfying fare that's not bad for you (unlike much fast food), and you can count on the wait being short. But a cheap eat? You'll see: a plate of pasta with a slice of hearty grilled bread alongside will cost around $5; add a green salad for another $1.95. And the red wine, itself a bargain at $3 a glass, is generously poured. The suburban outlets don't have quite everything the downtown cores do, but the pasta principles hold. Panini, too. Other locations are downtown (933 SW 3rd Ave; 503/223-8200; map:G4), Tigard (12700 SW North Dakota St; 503/521-1099; map:LL9), and Gresham (246 N Main Ave; 503/492-9534). *$; AE, MC, V; checks OK; lunch, dinner Mon–Sat; beer and wine; no reservations; map:I2*

Pavilion Trattoria / ★★

10700 SW ALLEN BLVD (GREENWOOD INN), BEAVERTON; 503/626-4550
It might seem that this restaurant, the most prominent hotel dining room in Washington County, changes its menu as often as the hotel rooms

caught sea scallops from the icy waters off Maine arrive at the table, seared on the outside and still quivering within, anointed with the most original sauces and garnishes around. Fresh, sweet peaches with basil-tinted cream one night and a confetti of roasted peppers and white corn with salty chunks of pancetta the next. Don't miss the seafood entrees either. The sautéed halibut in a porcini mushroom crust will haunt your dreams.

A little past midnight, Saturday. You're doing a passable job of holding down your chair in the prison-yard bright dining room of Golden Horse (238 NW 4th Ave; 503/228-1688). On the way to the dining room, you passed a churning saltwater tank; you peered inside at its doomed occupants. A half dozen resigned Dungeness crabs defy you to order them dismembered in black bean sauce, sluglike sea cucumbers await steaming with bok choy, and one or two geoducks gape lewdly, not seeming to care what happens to them (if you looked like a geoduck, would you?). But tonight a solitary eel nods its head above the surface of the water and mouths to you—"Eat me for God's sake, eat me!" And after 10 minutes of convincing the waitress that you wouldn't rather have the sweet and sour pork, a stout man in (you imagine) a bloody apron appears from the kitchen and seizes your eel by the neck. In less time than it takes for you to order another drink, your eel reappears, transformed by ancient Chinese secrets into clouds of ginger-scented steam and nuggets of glistening meat. Prices are ludicrously low here, and portions are ample. All seafood choices are respectable, consistent, and about as far removed from the ordinary as is possible. —*Troy DuFrene*

above change their sheets. Blasted out of its somnolent roots by the Heathman management group, it went to upscale Northwest, and then to Southwest-inflected, and now—as its name suggests—it's become Italian. Chef Benjamin Gonzalez has added a half-dozen reasonably priced pastas, a seafood risotto, and chicken saltimbocca to the menu, but he's kept some of the old favorites—Painted Hills rib-eye steak, oven-roasted rack of lamb, and pork tenderloin stuffed with candied fruit. On Sundays, the noontime sun shines through the skylight, beaming onto endless brunch tables laden with fresh seafood, waffles made to order, and enough desserts to get you through to Monday—if not Thursday. *$$; AE, DIS, MC, V; local checks only; breakfast, lunch, dinner every day, brunch Sun; full bar; reservations recommended; map:JJ9* &

Pazzo Ristorante / ★★☆

627 SW WASHINGTON ST (VINTAGE PLAZA HOTEL), DOWNTOWN; 503/228-1515

In the two years that he spent here, Kenny Giambalvo turned Pazzo into an exciting place to eat once again. With his departure to open Bluehour (Bruce Carey's new restaurant in the Pearl District; see review in this chapter), hopefully things will stay on track—and they should, given his replacement: Nathan Logan from LA's Drago Restaurant. This flashy hotel restaurant—in the posh Vintage Plaza Hotel—with a dining room perfumed by the wood grill, a lively bar, and wine cellar seating, has built its reputation on producing Northern Italian cuisine that's steadily interesting and not steadily predictable. Spaghetti wild with mushrooms, chunks of pancetta bacon, and garlic cloves is wonderful, and slices of rare Muscovy duck breast find a homey nest atop unexpected bitter greens. Warm up for it with an expensive antipasto and crisp grilled calamari. For breakfast and lunch, Pazzoria (621 SW Washington St; 503/228-1695) next door sets out pastries, panini, and pasta, and you can sometimes get a whiff of what's cooking on the grill. *$$; AE, DC, MC, V; no checks; breakfast, dinner every day, lunch Mon–Sat; full bar; reservations recommended; www.pazzo.com; map:I3*

Pho Hung / ★★☆

4717 SE POWELL BLVD, SOUTHEAST (AND BRANCHES); 503/775-3170
This is one of Portland's busiest beef noodle houses, its dining room a swirl of hungry families, rushing waiters, and steamy aromas of Vietnam's national dish—pho. For less than $5 you can immerse yourself in a curative bowl—"tureen" might be more accurate—of Vietnamese beef soup thick with rice noodles, thin slices of beef, fresh herbs, and sublime beef broth. Soups are served with a garnish plate of bean sprouts, basil, jalapeño, and lime wedges to sweeten or sour an already sinus-clearing experience; an assortment of Asian hot sauces and nuoc mam (fermented fish sauce) boost the megatonnage. Order with your brain and not your stomach; many people never even finish the small portion at $3.75. Though Portland foodies praise Pho Hung's beef broth, the chicken noodle soup is even better: a sweet and antibiotic broth with tangles of slippery noodles, scallions, and tender slices of chicken that actually taste like chicken. Finish your meal with Vietnamese hot or iced coffee (brewed to order and served with sweetened condensed milk), gratifyingly strong and tasty. In Vietnam they eat pho for breakfast, but here you can eat it morning, noon, and night at numerous branches throughout the city. *$; MC, V; no checks; breakfast, lunch, dinner every day; no alcohol; no reservations; map:HH4* ♿

Pho Van / ★★★

1919 SE 82ND AVE, SOUTHEAST; 503/788-5244

What was once a dive with great pho is now a lovely restaurant with great pho. Amid such stylish decor as slate floors, high ceilings, wood booths, and windows, it's hard to believe that the most expensive thing on the menu rings in at $7.95. Let the feast begin with fresh salad rolls and crispy rice-flour crêpes. Follow it with a bowl of pho, the heart-warming Vietnamese noodle soup that combines a wonderfully flavored meat broth with rice noodles, your choice of meat (round steak, shredded tripe, meatballs, lean brisket), and a heap of fresh flavors and textures to add to your liking—basil or mint leaves, chiles, lime, bean sprouts. Though it's easy to always order pho (even the small bowls are large here), the grilled entrees, like the lemongrass-marinated chicken on rice with a side of delicious pickled cabbage with carrots and daikon radish, are also very good. To wash it all down there's a bevy of exotic beverages—sour sop and jackfruit smoothies, fresh lime juice, coffee with condensed milk—as well as local and Asian beers. *$; DIS, MC, V; no checks; lunch, dinner every day; beer only; no reservations; map:GG3* &

Pizzicato / ★☆

705 SW ALDER ST, SOUTHWEST (AND BRANCHES); 503/226-1007

These yupscale pizzerias have cornered the market on quality gourmet pizza in a casual environment. While the service varies from location to location—and when it's busy it can get snarly—the most important aspect of eating here is decoding the various, often wild pizza combinations. The selection of gourmet sauces and toppings goes from the exotic (peanut sauce, chipotle, Thai chicken) to what you might call the Northwest sublime. For example, a wild-mushroom pizza is loaded with meaty chanterelles, roasted peppers, roasted garlic, onions, and chèvre—seemingly inspired from the culinary gods above. Even the plain cheese slices are usually spruced up with roasted herbs, garlic, and feta cheese. Better still, the slices are just plain big. Quick expansion has put a Pizzicato into most of Portland's prominent neighborhoods and bigger suburbs, as well as crossing the river into Vancouver. *$; AE, DC, DIS, MC, V; no checks; lunch, dinner every day; beer and wine; no reservations; map:H3* &

Plainfield's Mayur / ★★

852 SW 21ST AVE, PORTLAND HEIGHTS; 503/223-2995

In a city of extensive Indian menus, Plainfield's doesn't go that way; its menu is small, expensive, and skilled. This is a place for breast of duck in silken almond sauce with cheese-stuffed apricots, and tandoori rack of lamb. Plainfield's has been in business for more than two decades—much longer than any other Portland Indian restaurant—but its longevity doesn't distinguish it as much as do two other factors: its formality (china, crystal, and the absence of a messy lunch buffet) and its wine list (with Madeiras dating back to the 18th century). The tandoori dishes, roasted in authentic style in a huge oven, are highlights, but don't miss the biryanis, fragrant rice concoctions served with intriguingly edible silver foil—much as the maharaja might have had centuries ago. *$$; AE, DC, DIS, MC, V; checks OK; dinner every day; full bar; rich@plainfields.com; www.plainfields.com; map:GG7* &

Portland Steak and Chophouse / ★★

121 SW 3RD AVE (EMBASSY SUITES HOTEL), DOWNTOWN; 503/223-6200
Portland's wave of downtown steak houses—one in the '80s, six today—
was bolstered by this sizable entry in the downtown Embassy Suites, the
lovingly restored old Multnomah Hotel. Understandably, the restaurant
has a fair amount of polished wood and restoration itself, but also a very
snappy new martini list. If there's not much on the menu that you haven't
seen in other places, it still sends out solid, tasty hunks of beef in a comfortable atmosphere. There is much to be said for the prime rib, and the
place can surprise you in some ways, with a carved sirloin and spinach
salad, grilled portobello mushrooms, and Thai chicken and shiitake
mushrooms on angel hair pasta. The Colossal Onion Rings are, well,
colossal. The Portland Steak and Chophouse upholds its identity as a
Portland restaurant with a cedar-planked salmon fillet, and entree salads
and cafe meals appear for those watching their weight—or their wallet.
*$$$; AE, DC, MC, V; no checks; lunch, dinner every day, breakfast
Sat–Sun; full bar; reservations recommended; www.portlandchop
house.com; map:J5* &

Raccoon Lodge / ★

7424 SW BEAVERTON-HILLSDALE HWY, RALEIGH HILLS; 503/296-0110
If you are one of those people who dine by cravings, the Raccoon Lodge
(one of the most recent additions to the Portland brewpub scene) offers
one-stop shopping. For salty there's fries: shoestring, sweet potato, ale-
battered, Yukon Gold, and tater tots, all served by the half or full bucket,
with your choice of eight dipping sauces: Creole tomato, raspberry
habanero, and buttermilk ranch, to name only a few. If it's a hamburger
you're hankering after, you won't be disappointed, but you will be taxed
when it comes to the choices: one-third, two-thirds, or one pound?
Cheddar, Swiss, or jack? Caramelized onions, sautéed peppers, bacon, or
"smokin' red eye chili"? Other fixes worth indulging include the micro-
brews, a quaffable Bandit Amber and tasty Black Snout Stout, brewed on
the premises, and comfort food such as meat loaf with buttermilk mashed
potatoes or chocolate brownie pie. All of this upscale pub grub is served
in a "lodge" surrounded by strip malls; although the warmth of wood and
Pendleton blanket–upholstered booths—not to mention the mounted elk
head—lend a certain mountain charm, you'll never forget you're in the
middle of the burbs. *$–$$; AE, MC, V; checks OK; lunch, dinner every
day; full bar; no reservations; www.raclodge.com; map:I17* &

Red Electric Cafe / ★½

6440 SW CAPITOL HWY, HILLSDALE; 503/293-1266

This soup-and-sandwich roadside cafe redefines the genre: order a cup of
creamy tomato soup and you'll find it comes with pesto-graced crostini.
Put that cup of soup next to a grilled mozzarella and tomato sandwich

on Grand Central's toasted como bread, and you have an exciting, satisfying twist on classic lunch fare. And classics just get better with each Red Electric reworking: the BLT comes with pesto mayo, while lingonberries sweeten the smoked turkey sandwich. The special of the day might be a sloppy joe or a meat loaf sandwich, and there's always a choice of cold beer or fresh lemonade to go along with the half-dozen varieties of burgers. Breakfasts—the standards—are delicious and hearty, with a long list of ingredients to choose from for the omelets. And for dinner this little roadside cafe almost gets dressed up, with entrees like tiger prawn pasta, butternut squash ravioli, and salmon served with a tomato, caper, and kalamata olive relish and couscous. *$–$$; DIS, MC, V; no checks; breakfast, dinner Mon–Sat, lunch Mon–Fri, brunch Sun; full bar; no reservations; map:II7*

Red Hills Provincial Dining / ★★★
276 HWY 99W, DUNDEE; 503/538-8224
Red Hills Provincial Dining is a monument in Oregon wine country, and it shows up on the red-wine radar screens of many Portland fans as well. This country-house-turned-restaurant features a vineyard view from some tables and a simple dinner menu of a half-dozen items that changes weekly. The choices might run to venison medallions in marionberry demi-glace or pinot noir–braised lamb shanks on white beans. Watch for the crab cakes, with thick, sweet chunks of crab, served with tomato aioli. All the details are just right, whether it's bread dusted with fresh rosemary or a crisp salad of greens or lightly cooked vegetables. Desserts are interesting, too, like a rich, chewy fennel cake or raspberry-filled chocolate cake. Add to this an outstanding wine list, with a huge selection from all over the world, and you have a meal you'll want to linger over. *$$; MC, V; checks OK; lunch Tues–Fri, dinner Tues–Sun; full bar; reservations recommended*

Red Star Tavern & Roast House / ★★½
503 SW ALDER ST (5TH AVENUE SUITES), DOWNTOWN; 503/222-0005
In this lofty restaurant of the 5th Avenue Suites hotel, Rob Pando describes his cooking as regional American cuisine, from seared Nantucket scallops to Kansas City baby back ribs. He covers the continent impressively, using the huge wood-burning grill and rotisserie at the center of the restaurant, as well as exercising the kind of culinary skill that produces splendid crab-and-smoked-salmon cakes, or ravioli of winter squash and goat cheese. Also on the menu are some longtime favorites, including a skillet of moist corn bread and tangy barbecued pork. The range is considerable, portions are sizable, the atmosphere is entertaining—the tone reflects giant workingman murals of the restaurant's bounty—and you couldn't be closer to the middle of downtown. A great place for breakfasts, too. *$$; AE, DC, MC, V; no checks; break-*

fast, lunch, dinner every day; full bar; reservations recommended; www.kimpton.com; map:H4 &

Restaurant Murata / ★★★

200 SW MARKET ST, DOWNTOWN; 503/227-0080

There has been a small but significant breakthrough at Murata: Portland's best Japanese restaurant is now actually open on Saturday nights. For years, it was closed then, on the assumption that its core clientele was on the Delta nonstop back to Tokyo—a calculation that told you everything you needed to know about Murata. At the tiny sushi bar, the specials are listed in Japanese, with a "translation" underneath: Japanese names spelled out in English. But once someone has translated the specials, they're often worth the culinary gamble—crisp grilled sardines, mackerel necks, layers of deep purple tuna. Murata has a particular affinity for fish, displayed in terrific sushi, great grilled fish, and the *nabe*—huge bowls of stewlike soups, thick with seafood. The elaborate, prearranged Japanese multicourse banquet, *kaiseki,* runs as high as your wallet allows; it's the ideal way to celebrate your software company going public. *$$–$$$; AE, DC, JCB, MC, V; no checks; lunch Mon–Fri, dinner Mon–Sat; beer and wine; reservations recommended; murata@teleport.com; map:D3*

Riccardo's Restaurant & Espresso Bar / ★★

16035 SW BOONES FERRY RD, LAKE OSWEGO; 503/636-4104

Come summer, the backyard here blossoms, with a welcoming courtyard featuring flowers and fountain. The challenge is to get the diners to leave after dinner—especially considering the place's intriguing selection of grappas. Owner Richard Spaccarelli is a serious oenophile, as his more than 300 bottles of Italian-only wine (and Riccardo's own wine shop across the way) attest. The rising kitchen is strong on veal dishes, from an impressively meaty veal chop (with a lively brandy demi-glace) to a pungent, tender saltimbocca. The menu also includes juicy lamb chops and a half-dozen mostly meatless pastas, and it can surprise you with something such as a slow-roasted pork shank with garlic, sage, and rosemary. *$$; AE, DC, MC, V; checks OK; lunch Mon–Fri, dinner Mon–Sat; full bar; reservations recommended; map:MM8* &

The Ringside / ★★
Ringside East / ★★☆

2165 W BURNSIDE ST, NORTHWEST; 503/223-1513
14021 NE GLISAN ST, GLENDOVEER; 503/255-0750

Some national organization calls the Ringside one of the top 10 independent steak houses in the country, but nobody needed to tell Portlanders that. For 55 years, the restaurant has staked out the territory here, and the only real question for most fans of the Ringside is which cut—the New York, the filet mignon, or the prime rib? People come here for beef, and that's what they get—in large, juicy slabs. The steaks appear at the table in black cast-iron platters, preceded by the sound of sizzling. Against the designer starches of the newer steak houses, the Ringside holds to the standards—and doesn't charge extra for them. Starring on the side are the plump, light, slightly salty onion rings, made with Walla Walla Sweets, that single-handedly made the Ringside famous. For those with an aversion to beef, there is well-reputed fried chicken, and there's also something to be said for the seafood Caesar. The dignified black-jacketed and bow-tied waiters are eminently professional, and the wine list is substantial—especially if you're looking for something to go with beef. Lunch is served at the eastside location only. *$$; AE, DC, MC, V; checks OK; dinner every day (Northwest), lunch Mon–Fri, dinner every day (Glendoveer); full bar; reservations recommended; www.ringsidesteakhouse.com; map:GG7* &

Roland's / ★★

155 SE VISTA, GRESHAM; 503/665-7215

Roland's is the best reason to go to Gresham since MAX. Roland Blasi's traditional continental cuisine—sizable portions and strong flavors, gathered from his cooking odyssey through four continents—has taken root in Gresham. This is a very personal restaurant in feel and menu; Blasi draws ideas from the full range of European cooking, and comes up with some of his own. So you're offered not only a pungent gypsy chicken, but also a heartwarming pasta Angelo made with Italian sausage, and a deep, fragrant onion soup. *$$; MC, V; local checks only; dinner Tues–Sat; beer and wine; reservations recommended* &

Rustica / ★★

1700 NE BROADWAY, NE BROADWAY; 503/288-0990

The calamari, scampi, and gnocchi with grilled chicken are enough by themselves to draw a crowd to this cheerful, roomy trattoria, with its open kitchen and Italian street scene fresco covering the back wall. Prices are reasonable, with most pastas around $10, and some dishes—notably the carbonara and the seafood lasagne—are vivid and impressive. Lunchtime adds pungent panini: crusty sandwiches such as grilled eggplant with smoked mozzarella or nifty grilled sausages with caramelized onions and aioli. Either time offers one of the great desserts of the Pacific Slope: an ice cream sandwich of creamy gelato between two crisp Florentine cookies with a chocolate sauce drizzle. With its big, sweeping picture windows on bustling NE Broadway, this restaurant may be rustic in name, but its appeal is decidedly urban. For an inexpensive and quick meal, duck into the adjoining Pizza Luna (1708 NE Broadway; 503/335-3059), where the pizza by the slice is as large as it is tasty. *$$; AE, DIS, MC, V; local checks only; lunch Mon–Fri, dinner every day; full bar; reservations recommended; www.citysearch.com/pdx/rustica; map:GG5* &

Ruth's Chris Steak House / ★★☆

309 SW 3RD AVE, DOWNTOWN; 503/221-4518
When Portland became the 57th city gifted with a branch of this upscale New Orleans steak chain, it seemed another vindication of the city's rising status. And it turns out that Portlanders, those acolytes of salmon, couldn't pile in fast enough to pay $30 for a steak, presented on bone-white china in an atmosphere of high-cholesterol reverence. It also turned out that several of the steaks, notably the steer-sized porterhouse for two, were inspiring—rich and beefy, with an alluring tenderness. For diners who just had a porterhouse for two for lunch, there are sizable (and sizably priced) lobsters, and there's the chance to pick one that's alive—which is more than you can do with the steak. You'll be paying extra for everything else, but it's still worth exploring the various potatoes and the creamed spinach. The space is massive, and so are the portions; you'll still be eating your dinner for tomorrow's lunch. *$$$; AE, DC, MC, V; no checks; dinner every day; full bar; reservations recommended; www.ruthschris.com; map:I5* &

Saburo's / ★★

1667 SE BYBEE BLVD, WESTMORELAND; 503/236-4237
What draws diners from all over the city to Saburo's is neither the vintage Naugahyde banquettes nor the shoebox feel to the place. And, Buddha knows, it's not the wait, which has become as integral to the experience as a wasabi rush. No, what makes Saburo's a destination for sushi lovers is this simple formula: consistently fresh fish, generous portions, and fair prices. There's nothing slick or stuffy about Saburo's: no other sushi place in Portland captures the laid-back, funky feeling of an authentic Japanese neighborhood restaurant. Combination dinners feature teriyaki, tempura, or gyoza and come with salad, soup, rice, and ice cream. Bear in mind that the waiting list is consistently long because Saburo's is one of the best places in Portland to splurge on the raw stuff. *$–$$; AE, MC, V; no checks; dinner every day; beer and wine; no reservations; map:JJ5*

Saigon Kitchen / ★★

835 NE BROADWAY, NE BROADWAY; 503/281-3669
3829 SE DIVISION ST, SOUTHEAST; 503/236-2312
Still the spring roll for all seasons, the two branches of this restaurant are among the best of Portland's seemingly endless supply of Vietnamese eateries. The menu—more than 120 items long—features Thai dishes as well as the predominantly southern Vietnamese offerings. Standouts are the spicy soups—try the sour catfish concoction with pineapple—and the stews and ragouts, which go well with white or fried rice. Service is brisk and efficient at both busy locations. If the cheerful, enthusiastic waiters bring you a dish you didn't order, consider this: their unintentional error might be the perfect subliminal suggestion, because when it comes to

expanding your food horizons, you can't go wrong here. Enjoy patio dining at the branch on SE Division (which is closed on Sunday). *$; AE, DIS, MC, V; no checks; lunch Mon–Fri, dinner every day; beer and wine; reservations recommended for large parties; map:FF5, map:HH4 &* *(Broadway only)*

Salvador Molly's / ★★

1523 SW SUNSET BLVD, HILLSDALE; 503/293-1790

A recent expansion into the space next door has relieved some of the crush, but not necessarily any of the wait, at this bright and funky Caribbean/Latin American hot spot. From its humble beginnings in a tired little strip mall off the Beaverton-Hillsdale Highway, Salvador Molly's has grown in popularity, as fans have passed the word along that this place is outrageously fun. They come for the new Latin cuisine: Willapa Bay corn-crusted oyster tacos, mouth-sizzling jerk grilled chicken, jambalayas studded with shrimp and sausage, and the never-disappointing tamale of the day. They also come for the mood, which is just plain good. (Even if they can't stay, sometimes they come in for the hot sauces, which are available for purchase.) Nobody's in a hurry—and if you're in a hurry, you're sure to be disappointed—but that's part of what makes this place happen. What's the rush? Sip a margarita, crack a few peanuts, enjoy yourself. *$$; AE, MC, V; checks OK; lunch, dinner Mon–Sat; full bar; no reservations; map:JJ7 &*

Sammy's Restaurant and Bar / ★★

333 NW 23RD AVE, NORTHWEST; 503/222-3123

A list of the day's fresh fish—maybe six or eight choices—hangs proudly at either end of the dining room, noting one of the themes that's made this restaurant last in what had been a turnover spot. When Sam Pishue, founder and longtime successful proprietor of Opus Too (see review in this chapter), decided to open another restaurant, he stayed with what he knew. As a result, the best things here are hot off the grill—steaks, chops, and seafood—although the menu is flecked with pastas and Greek specialties. Subtlety may not be a strong point, but the meats are good, the room is comfortable, and the artfully assembled bar is popular and crowded. Sunday brunch is a particular success, especially on warm weekends, when brunchers spread out on the tables that stretch along NW 23rd, and the atmosphere of urban sophistication makes the just-baked cinnamon twists taste even better. *$$; AE, DC, DIS, MC, V; no checks; lunch, dinner every day, brunch Sat–Sun; full bar; reservations recommended; map:GG7 &*

Saucebox / ★★☆

214 SW BROADWAY, DOWNTOWN; 503/241-3393

This ultrahip, Pan-Asian shoebox of a restaurant has kept to the same basic, lively food presentations since opening in the mid-1990s, frequently inventing stylish new cocktails and overhauling entire displays of art to keep things lively. The menu here may be limited, but it's remarkably creative and satisfying—especially the Javanese salmon fillet crisped in soy, garlic, and ginger and then topped with frizzled leeks. Dumplings, curries, and noodles, and some stirring (and changing) entrees round out the menu. At lunchtime people come by for the inspiring Chinese roast pork sandwich or a plate of pad thai. The bar scene is hot, crowded, and forever young—especially after 10pm, when a disc jockey gets rolling. But the food has already been jumping all day. *$$; AE, MC, V; local checks only; lunch Tues–Fri, dinner Tues–Sat; full bar; reservations recommended; map:J4* &

Sayler's / ★★☆

10519 SE STARK ST, RUSSELLVILLE; 503/252-4171
4655 SW GRIFFITH DR, BEAVERTON; 503/644-1492

This place—or, rather, these places—could be called Portland's low-profile steak houses. They don't have all the high-protein hoopla of the downtown beef palaces, but for decades now, Sayler's has been setting out solid, reasonably priced steaks, and the crowds continue to come. The kitchen serves the basics here—steak and baked potato on a sizzling black iron platter—but the basics are done admirably, especially the filets. Fish and fried chicken are also available, but steaks are really the point, especially when they're served in an environment that's this relaxed. And the good value extends to Sayler's best and best-known deal: a 72-ounce sirloin absolutely free—if you eat it all in an hour. *$$; AE, DIS, MC, V; checks OK; dinner every day (SE Stark St), lunch Mon–Fri, dinner every day (Beaverton); full bar; reservations recommended; map:H9, map:II9* &

Serratto / ★★☆

2112 NW KEARNEY ST, NORTHWEST; 503/221-1195

For many years, loyalists came to Delfina's, a cornerstone on NW 21st Avenue's Restaurant Row, and when it closed in 1998, they squirmed, wondering what was next. "Slow food"—in contrast to the fast food that feeds so many of us—was next, and now lovely Serratto, with its tall windows open to the sidewalk, its golden light, and its exposed-beam ceilings, is building a reputation on fresh, flavorful food that is carefully prepared and skillfully presented. The slow food movement heralds from Italy, where the idea of wolfing down a Big Mac is about as appealing as eating a shoe. Slow food refers to the unfolding of the meal, not the service. So you can expect servers to be attentive and informative and the food to be first-rate Italian fare—but not the heavy marinara of your father's Italian restaurant. This menu emphasizes fresh ingredients: start with the supremely simple and delicious plate of mozzarella, bread, basil, and tomato; follow it with one of the half-dozen entrees—we've had good luck with fish and stuffed pastas like ravioli and agnolotti here—and finish with a dessert, maybe the suave panna cotta studded with blueberries. The restaurant is divided into sections: the main room, the vineira (wine bar), and well-designed private dining rooms that can seat as few as 15 or as many as 40. Here, slow is a state of mind, and who couldn't use a little change of pace now and then? *$$–$$$; AE, DIS, MC, V; no checks; lunch Mon–Fri, dinner every day; full bar; reservations recommended; map:GG7* &

Southpark / ★★☆

901 SW SALMON ST, DOWNTOWN; 503/326-1300

This Heathman Hotel offshoot, just behind the hotel and across the Park Blocks, has not only been reformatted under chef Paul Ornstein, it's been totally remodeled from its days as B. Moloch's. What had been a brewpub now opens into a sophisticated wine bar, and what was a deli-counter atmosphere is now all about polished wood and earth-toned columns. Overall, the general level of elegance has been raised considerably. Ornstein's bias lies in Mediterranean seafood, resulting in a menu that ranges from a rich paella to a powerful southern French fish soup. The day's catch drives innovation, and the wine treatment is equally creative, with wines grouped according to style rather than geography and a wine bar that offers flights of several treatments of one kind of varietal. And you have to like any place that offers a fresh-baked chocolate crostada. *$$; AE, DC, MC, V; lunch Mon–Sat, dinner every day, brunch Sun; full bar; reservations recommended; map:H2* &

Stickers Asian Cafe / ★☆

6808 SE MILWAUKIE AVE, WESTMORELAND; 503/239-8739

John Sinclair and Joan Frances spent several years in China eating different regional variations of pot stickers, the quintessential Sino street food. At their restaurant, Stickers, they cook and serve this and other snack foods of Asia on what has become the hot yuppie food corner of Westmoreland. Here the beautiful, artful surroundings belie the remarkably affordable prices for food that is grandly conceived and near-perfectly executed. The menu does not confine itself to China, but roams down to India and over to Thailand—curries, satays, and pad thai all have their place—yet never feels like contrived "Pan-Asian." The hot-and-sour soup with pot stickers is much thinner than what you might be used to from your corner Chinese place and more delicately flavored—and it's all for the better. The cold sesame noodle salad is refreshing and snappy, not heavily saturated with sesame oil. Double Happiness, the (4pm to 7pm) happy hour special for $5, consists of a plate of six pot stickers with the traditional dipping sauce and a well drink. Double indeed; it's worth doubling the order. The recent addition of weekday lunch offers the same menu at the same prices. *$–$$; AE, MC, V; checks OK; lunch Mon–Sat, dinner every day; full bar; no reservations; map:JJ5*

Sungari Restaurant / ★★★

735 SW 1ST AVE, DOWNTOWN; 503/224-0800

For many locals Portland hasn't been the same since Chen's Dynasty closed. However, with the opening of Sungari, the days of dining on intriguing Sichuan fare in hushed elegance have once again returned to downtown Portland. Owners Sunny Chen and Francis Koo, together with chef Zhi Wei He (all former employees of Chen's), have combined their talented resources into a lovely dining room and appealing menu. One of the best ways to get a taste of what the kitchen has to offer is to start with a sampler for two: barbecue ribs, spring rolls, fried prawns, and foil wrapped chicken. Follow this with something familiar—maybe Kung Pao Chicken—or one of the house specialties, like Crispy Scallops in Spicy Mandarin Sauce. Vegetables are treated with reverence here, lightly cooked and nicely spiced, like the Broccoli in Tangy Sauce (or asparagus when in season). The slightly off-center location has kept this newcomer rather sleepy, but it has too many good qualities—from the high ceilings and gracious service to the thoughtful wine list and fresh flavors—to remain a secret for long. *$$–$$$; AE, MC, V; no checks; lunch Mon–Fri, dinner Mon–Sat; full bar; reservations recommended; www.SungariRestaurant.com; map:G5* &

Swagat / ★★

2074 NW LOVEJOY ST, NORTHWEST; 503/227-4300
4325 SW 109TH AVE, BEAVERTON; 503/626-3000

Neither of the two locations of this fragrant, accomplished Indian restaurant—the suburban house-and-garage in Beaverton or the expansive restaurant-bar space in Northwest—are big on atmosphere. But if you close your eyes and breathe deeply, you can get closer to the spicy tandoori dishes and vindaloo stews that make Swagat so inviting. The range of choice here is substantial, from curries and samosas to South Indian specialties such as the oversized rice pancake dosas. Nothing will cost too much, especially the mandatory Indian restaurant lunchtime buffet. Swagat is also a fine place for vegetarians—unless atmosphere is a requirement. *$; AE, DIS, MC, V; no checks; lunch, dinner every day; full bar (Northwest), beer and wine (Beaverton); no reservations; map:GG7;* & *(Northwest only)*

Sweetwater's Jam House / ★★

3350 SE MORRISON ST, BELMONT; 503/233-0333

Out back of the renovated Belmont Dairy, Sweetwater's is sending up some serious heat in a damp climate. In a flashy version of Caribbean cuisine (and mood), the restaurant puts out peppered shrimp and goat curry that could cauterize your taste buds—better grab quickly for your bottle of Red Stripe beer or your lethal Rum Runner. Sweetwater's has an extensive list of Caribbean rums and does wicked things with them; it's a thumping bar scene. Barbecued ribs, jerk chicken, and stunning dark, molasses-infused corn bread are also highlights, along with spicy Caribbean vegetable options such as not-for-Thanksgiving curried pumpkin. And on those occasional days of Portland warmth, outside tables bring you slightly closer to Jamaica. The most recent addition—the adjoining, sultry Voudou Cafe—brings lunch to the table and overflow seating on busy weekends; expect a menu laden with Sweetwater favorites as well as new Creole dishes such as turtle soup, catfish, and po'boy sandwiches. *$–$$; AE, MC, V; no checks; lunch, dinner every day; full bar; no reservations; www.jamhouse.citysearch.com; map:GG5* &

Syun / ★★★½

209 NE LINCOLN ST, HILLSBORO; 503/640-3131

Among Portland-area Japanese restaurants, this one is close to Japan not only geographically but spiritually. Sake bottles line the walls, and impressive and unusual sushi moves the menu, along with a wide variety of Japanese small plates. Try the dumplings, at least while you're waiting for your sushi. Most places may not stack monkfish liver on their sushi—although it's Japan's version of foie gras—but it's a pretty good idea. Watch for the specialties, and move quickly when the list includes fresh clam. But dip into the hot dishes, too, in particular the tempura and seared beef slices. How deeply you want to dip into the long sake list—the restaurant is decorated in sake bottles—is up to you. A considerable part of the market here comes from the Hillsboro-area high-tech world, whose understanding of Japanese food is close-up and whose programming is probably helped by the sake. *$$; AE, DC, DIS, M, V; local checks OK; lunch Mon–Fri, dinner every day; full bar; reservations recommended*

Tapeo / ★★★

2764 NW THURMAN ST, NORTHWEST; 503/226-0409

To a deceptively modest storefront on a quiet Northwest Portland street, Ricardo Segura has brought the flavors of his native Spain—notably the flavors of serrano ham, salmon cured with manzanilla sherry, and boneless quail with bittersweet chocolate sauce. Thirty different tapas—small plates designed for casual munching—and a list of 20 sherries have captivated Portlanders accustomed to big entrees and pinot noir. In a place of powerful relaxation and an almost Iberian lack of hurry, diners might start by combining a few cold tapas—some marinated trout, or ham and cheese on thick toasted bread—with some hot items, such as a white bean stew or a *zarzuelita*, seafood in brandy, almonds, and cinnamon. Then, after some sipping and conversation, and some wiping of the empty plates with crusty bread, retrieve the menu and explore a bit further. As in a sushi bar, the bill can mount up, but it will record some striking flavors. Come summer, tables outside make NW Thurman Street seem even more southwest European. *$$; DIS, MC, V; no checks; dinner Tues–Sat; beer and wine; no reservations; map:GG7* ⅙

Taqueria Chavez / ★

2727 N LOMBARD ST, NORTH PORTLAND; 503/283-4655

Gone from Portland, forever if we're lucky, are the days of gringo-Mexican food dished up in glorified Denny's by aging waitresses from Des Moines. Any seasoned eater could order blind at Taqueria Chavez and be perfectly happy. Burritos are put together with creamy frijoles de olla, rice, and your choice of meat: the carne asada is tender and smoky from the grill, and the *lengua* (beef tongue) is simmered to tender perfection. Tacos come open-faced on double tortillas with the same choice of meats. Tamales here are less usual taqueria fare: pillows of masa with savory pork or chicken fillings are snugly wrapped in a cornhusk. Fiery, delicious salsas can be added with your own light or heavy hand—the green is citrusy with tomatillo, the red ablaze with chiles de arbol, and the salsa fresca all about jalapeño. In the finest taqueria tradition, the prices reflect the fact that food is for the hungry and not the bored. Keep this one on your list, and enjoy often. *$; no credit cards; checks OK; lunch, dinner every day; no alcohol; no reservations; map:DD5*

Tara Thai Northwest / ★

1310 NW 23RD AVE, NORTHWEST; 503/222-7840

There used to be three branches of this family-run Thai restaurant, but now there is only one; in 1998 owner Lavanny Phommaneth sold the Beaverton and Tigard restaurants in order to channel her time and energy into the Northwest location. Oh, the lucky residents of this neighborhood! Everything about this converted former home is pleasant: the modest but comfortable dining room, the understated but knowledgeable servers, the wonderfully fresh and flavorful food. The menu concentrates on the foods of northern Thailand and Laos, which translates into such recognizable dishes as fresh salad rolls, *tom kai kai* (ginger–coconut milk soup with chicken), green curry, and pad thai, as well as less familiar Lao specialties: *khao poon nam kai* (a delicious chicken–rice noodle soup flavored with fresh banana leaves, basil, and galangal) and *soop pak* (steamed vegetables in a roasted ginger paste). For dessert there's a murky gray—but nonetheless tasty—rice pudding with bananas and, in season, mangoes over sweet sticky rice in coconut milk. *$; AE, DIS, MC, V; no checks; lunch, dinner every day; beer and wine; reservations recommended; map:GG7* ᕼ

Tennessee Red's Country Cooking / ★☆

3330 SE 82ND AVE, SOUTHEAST; 503/775-9564
With its powerful smoke pits, Tennessee Red's can gild chicken, beef, and pork ribs; pork loin; and brisket with Texas, Carolina, Memphis, and Arkansas sauces—or an Oregon version with hazelnuts. The meat is juicy and deeply smoky, and the possible sides extend from corn bread to beans and rice to intense mashed potatoes. There are also a number of ambitious barbecue sandwiches, which require a hearty appetite and large hands—and a certain indifference to the cleanliness of your shirt. Most of the barbecue heads out the door, but if basic tables and chairs and lots of aroma fit your idea of ambience, you can consume your barbecue before it even thinks about cooling down. Breakfast here means chicken-fried steak, Denver omelets, and biscuits and gravy. *$; MC, V; no checks; breakfast, lunch, dinner every day; full bar; no reservations; map:HH3* ᕼ

Thai Little Home / ★

3214 E FOURTH PLAIN BLVD, VANCOUVER, WA; 360/693-4061
For many Vancouverites, this little Thai is home. Although it's not as fancy as similar joints across the river in Portland, Serm Pong and his family prepare fresh, home-cooked Thai food that locals like just fine. *Yum nuer* (sliced beef salad with cucumber, seasoned with chile and lime juice) rivals the popular *pra koong* (shrimp with chile paste, lemongrass, and lime juice); and we've enjoyed both *mee krob* (crisp Thai noodles) and chicken satay at the beginning of meals. Service is friendly, informed, and fast. *$; AE, DIS, MC, V; local checks only; lunch Mon–Fri, dinner Mon–Sat; beer and wine; no reservations; map:BB5*

Thai Orchid / ★★

2231 W BURNSIDE ST, NORTHWEST (AND BRANCHES); 503/226-4542
It's a weekday evening, but a stream of glossy, youthful Portlanders flow into this low-profile Burnside storefront. They're here for the Evil Jungle Noodles, or maybe the honey duck, or perhaps the catfish in chile sauce. Owners Na and Penny Saenguraiporn consistently produce reasonably priced—and more than reasonably spiced—Thai food. The place looks so mild, you may be surprised by both the size of the menu and the heat of the food, a fact not lost on faithful takeout customers. Entrees, especially seafood in chile sauce and a deep-fried whole fish, tend to be more interesting than appetizers. The beef salad is pungent and mouth-clearing—and now it's clearing mouths throughout the metropolitan area with outposts on SW Barbur Boulevard and in West Linn, Beaverton, Gresham, and Vancouver, Washington. *$$; AE, DIS, MC, V; no checks; lunch, dinner every day; beer and wine; reservations recommended; map:GG7*

Thanh Thao / ★★

4005 SE HAWTHORNE BLVD, HAWTHORNE; 503/238-6232

Unswervingly consistent and always busy, Thanh Thao may be the most competent Vietnamese kitchen in the city. Throngs of fiercely loyal patrons ensure long waits at peak hours; come early or late to avoid crowds, or battle your way into the nonexistent lobby to find a cramped space next to a dusty faux ficus. With few soft spots on the extensive menu, this is a safe place to be adventurous: tofu with basil groans with purple basil and mushrooms; salted squid, perfectly fried, arrives studded with bits of onion and green chile; shrimp and barbecued pork noodles marry warm bits of crispy pork to cold rice noodles dressed carefully with vinegar and fish sauce. Soups shine in general, but the hot-and-sour (served with the lunch special and disguised on the dinner menu as "soup of the day"), a mélange of tofu, exotic mushrooms, and Asian vegetables in an unctuous broth, can revive the dead. The menu is very vegetarian-friendly, but carnivore do-it-yourselfers should try the charbroiled beef. Thin slices of raw beef are brought to the table with a small propane grill and a vast array of raw vegetables, fruits, and rice pancakes. Not for the overly private, this dish will draw confused stares and jealous scowls from fellow diners as it hisses and pops on the table. *$; MC, V; local checks only; lunch, dinner Wed–Mon; beer and wine; reservations recommended; map:HH4*

3 Doors Down / ★★★

1429 SE 37TH AVE, HAWTHORNE; 503/236-6886

The people out on the street in front of this modest storefront aren't grabbing a smoke. They're waiting patiently—well, maybe not always patiently—for a table at this unpretentious, no-reservations Italian/seafood restaurant. The menu changes, but there's always the bountiful seafood fra diavolo, penne with vodka sauce, and Italian sausage and clams baked with a hint of Parmesan. The kitchen will also be doing skillful things with salmon—maybe roasting it with pancetta in a red-wine port sauce—and other fish, and will provide some heartening pastas—all in substantial portions. Desserts are splendid—perhaps banana cream pie or double chocolate mousse cake—and the service particularly warm. If the wait is long, you can head up to Hawthorne and window-shop the boulevard until your table is ready. *$$; AE, MC, V; checks OK; dinner Tues–Sat; beer and wine; no reservations; map:GG5* &

Three Square Grill / ★★

6320 SW CAPITOL HWY, HILLSDALE; 503/244-4467

A dash of French bistro, and a heaping plate of American comfort food with a bias for southern cooking, defines this determinedly down-home neighborhood cafe in the Hillsdale Shopping Center. Over the years Barbara and David Barber have culled a strong local following for brunch and lunch: deft omelets and French toast in the morning, and unusual sandwiches—pulled pork barbecue, for instance—and intricate hash dishes at noon. Three Square has also gotten attention for its particularly nifty mashed potatoes and its other interesting sides (like spicy garlic fries and collard greens in pot likker), but the news here now is an ambitious drive at dinner. Prices remain neighborhood-reasonable, but in addition to the popular lunch standbys there's a long list of specials every night, like steak frites, catfish étouffée, shrimp and grits, and herb-roasted chicken. More options, happy customers. *$$; MC, V; checks OK; lunch Tues–Fri, dinner Tues–Sat, brunch Sat–Sun; beer and wine; reservations recommended; www.threesquare.com; map:JJ7* &

Tina's / ★★★

760 SW HWY 99W, DUNDEE; 503/538-8880

This place has always had a great kitchen, and now it's got a comfortable dining room and an elegant bar. Owners Tina Landfried and husband David Bergen have now matched their vest-pocket herb-and-salad garden with a gleaming glass entryway, inviting you to stop and start working through the wine list. The half-dozen entree choices are on the chalkboard: if you're lucky, you might find the roasted duck breast with a ginger-fig sauce, marinated salmon atop udon noodles, or maybe braised rabbit with fresh morels. Stop on the way for the salmon spring rolls, clams steamed in Pernod, or a goat cheese soufflé fines herbes. For dessert watch for a potent chocolate hazelnut torte, or a creamy and deeply gingery custard. Tina's offers a good selection of local wines by the glass, all reasonably priced. It's a terrific place to relax and unwind after a wine-country day, but be careful what you say about the wine; its maker may be at the next table. *$$–$$$; AE, MC, V; checks OK; dinner every day; full bar; reservations recommended* &

Todai / ★★

340 SW MORRISON ST, DOWNTOWN; 503/294-0007

You have never seen so much sushi, and you have never seen so many people in quest of it. This new Portland branch of a California chain of Japanese seafood buffets draws crowds—especially on weekend evenings—of people in search of unlimited salmon-skin hand rolls for $22.95, the fixed buffet dinner price. (On Thursdays the price per person is $21.95; children 11 and under 5 feet, 4 feet, and 3 feet get respective price breaks.) The sushi is not at all bad, and if it's not comparable to some of the most exquisite sushi bars in town, the range of choice—and did we mention the unlimited quantity?—helps compensate. The hot side of the buffet is a more mixed catch; although it features multiple varieties of shrimp and regular appearances by fresh scallops and lobster, they tend to end up somewhat overcooked, and the teriyaki doesn't have quite the necessary gingery bite. Still, you can always head back for some more spicy tuna seaweed rolls—or off to the dessert buffet that extends about

15 feet, from East to West. *$$; AE, MC, V; no checks; lunch, dinner every day; beer and wine; no reservations; www.todai.com; map:H4* ⅃

Typhoon! / ★★⯪
Typhoon! on Broadway / ★★⯪

2310 NW EVERETT ST, NORTHWEST; 503/243-7557
400 SW BROADWAY (IMPERIAL HOTEL), DOWNTOWN; 503/224-8385

Typhoon! is blowing into a small empire. The original Northwest Portland space—where the atmosphere is a bit more upscale than much of the Thai competition in town—has been joined by a larger downtown location in the Imperial Hotel (called Typhoon! on Broadway), and the most recent expansions extend across the border to Kent and Seattle, Washington. Notice in the national food magazines can do that, and besides, Bo Kline is a deeply gifted chef. From openers of *miang kam* (spinach leaves to be filled with a half-dozen ingredients) and mouth-filling soups, the menu moves into a kaleidoscope of curries, inspired seafood dishes, and multiple pungent Thai noodle dishes. Try the King's Noodles, to know why it's good to be king. Scored into a checkerboard grid, a fried fish blossoms into a pinecone, and dishes with names such as Fish on Fire and Superwild Shrimp turn out to be named exactly right. Typhoon! also offers 150 different teas—including one that goes for $65 a pot. *$–$$; AE, DC, MC, V; no checks; lunch Mon–Sat, dinner every day; beer and wine; reservations recommended; map:GG7, map:I3* ⅃

Umenoki / ★★

2330 NW THURMAN ST, NORTHWEST; 503/242-6404

When a Japanese restaurant hangs a samurai sword over the sushi bar, it's serious. When it hangs out big signs about the fish available that day, take notice. A quick, skillful sushi chef does remarkable things with yellowtail and mackerel, especially when he combines them in a trademark roll called Saba Street. There's a mountainous roll of tuna and smoked salmon called—appropriately—Red Mountain, and California rolls and Umenoki's own San Francisco roll benefit from fresh real crabmeat instead of surimi. Hot dishes include crisp, greaseless tempura and specials such as New York steak teriyaki. Umenoki is a very comfortable, traditionally decorated Japanese restaurant—all blond wood and paper screens—but the sushi can have the impact of the samurai sword. *$$; MC, V; no checks; lunch Mon–Fri, dinner Mon–Sat ; beer and wine; reservations recommended; map:FF7*

Veritable Quandary / ★★⯪

1220 SW 1ST AVE, DOWNTOWN; 503/227-7342

A recent fire nearly wiped out this landmark restaurant on the fringes of downtown's financial district, and that would have been a tragedy—but the continuing tragedy is that there are so many otherwise food-savvy Portlanders who think that the VQ is more about scene than cuisine.

True, there was once a time when it was a bastion of burger-and-martini power lunches and after-work ogling and schmoozing at the bar, but under chef Anne Barnette the offerings have become much more refined, to the extent that it's worth making several trips to explore the menu. The predominant influence is northern Italian, even though you'll find a random smattering of elsewhere-oriented dishes that crop up here and there, especially among the appetizers. Winning starters include *bresaola* (a prosciuttolike cured beef), gnocchi with Gorgonzola, and a spinach salad with pancetta, blue cheese, and roasted wild mushrooms. Osso buco—braised veal shank with a smooth, rich wine and tomato sauce—is the star among the entrees; it comes with a creamy Parmesan risotto on a plate the size of a hubcap. Simpler dishes such as rosemary roasted chicken, braised rabbit, and grilled fish are also carefully prepared and reliably satisfying. Desserts range from good to stellar; don't miss the chocolate soufflé. Pastas and focaccia sandwiches dominate the lunch menu, which is ideally sampled on the VQ's patio on a warm day. The place tends to fill up before opera performances and other events at the nearby Keller Auditorium, so you might want to check the arts calendar before heading over on a weekend night. *$$–$$$; AE, DC, DIS, MC, V; no checks; lunch Mon–Fri, dinner every day, brunch Sat–Sun; full bar; reservations recommended; map:E4* &

Vista Spring Cafe / ★

2440 SW VISTA AVE, PORTLAND HEIGHTS; 503/222-2811
Portland Heights residents pack this place for gourmet pizzas, micro-brews, lusciously thick milkshakes, sandwiches, and pasta. Even if the pies lack some of the spark that pizza fiends have learned to expect in recent years, the crust is tasty and they're loaded with all the right toppings: olives, prosciutto, Thai chicken, sun-dried tomatoes, feta cheese. There's also chicken pot pie, sandwiches, and now (comfort food is comfort food, even in Portland Heights) macaroni and cheese. The red-ceilinged, low-lit room has a velvety feeling—with booths along the walls and strings of twinkling lights hung about. A welcoming spot with nice folks, too, it's the quintessential neighborhood cafe. *$; DIS, MC, V; checks OK; lunch, dinner every day; beer and wine; no reservations; map:HH7* &

Wild Abandon / ★★

2411 SE BELMONT ST, BELMONT; 503/232-4458

Wild Abandon is Portland's very own Madonna Inn or Hearst Castle of flamboyant gustatorial excess. The pocket-sized dining room more than makes up in sheer visual overload what it lacks in size. Golden fists emerging from the walls, sweeping romantic murals, and formal table services will transport even the weariest minds away from the rigors of daily life, making Wild Abandon one of the best dating destinations around. The menu carries on the rococo theme set by the interior. Start with an order of the lavish mussels tropicale—mussels steamed in coconut milk, lemongrass, and green curry—then proceed to the entrees, a range of innovative and carefully prepared dishes. Desserts—the rightful place for exotic opulence—are splendid. The tiramisù is lush with a bittersweet coffee-chocolate sauce, and the habanero-spiced rum and mango bread pudding is, amazingly, delicious. Wild Abandon has served a fine Sunday brunch for some time and, for now, also serves breakfast and lunch every day but Sunday. *$$; AE, DIS, MC, V; local checks only; breakfast Mon–Sat, lunch, dinner every day, brunch Sun; full bar; reservations recommended; map:HH5*

Wild Heron Cafe / ★

333 S STATE ST, LAKE OSWEGO; 503/635-3374
One of the region's nicer juice bars is in Lake Oswego, left over from the days when this place was run by the crew at Nature's. The restaurant changed hands a few years ago, but you can still get a fruity and/or veggie drink concoction with a name like Ruby Tuesday blended while you wait. The juice is orchard fresh, and the food is fine too: three meals a day with highlights such as French toast made with braided cardamom bread, a chicken burger with Wild Heron's own basil-garlic chicken sausage, and polenta lasagne. Desserts from Joseph's, a wholesale bakery that supplies coffeehouses, cafes, and dessert places around town, are encased in glass at the entry, lovely to look at, and almost as good to eat (try the double lemon cheesecake). The expansive dining room, though located in a bland Lake Oswego shopping mall, has a casual, eco-hip feel about it, with plenty of space for families, power lunchers, and even romance-seekers. *$$; MC, V; checks OK; breakfast, lunch, dinner every day; beer and wine; no reservations; map:MM5* &

Wildwood / ★★★½

1221 NW 21ST AVE, NORTHWEST; 503/248-9663
With a deft remodel of the main dining room, a gorgeous new cookbook, and a sustained buzz among diners, Cory Schreiber's Wildwood, long a fixture on NW 21st Avenue's restaurant row, has acheived the success that every restaurant hopes for. In 1998, Schreiber was named the James Beard top chef in the Northwest, but Portlanders had already grown to appreciate his dazzling touch, especially with local seafood. Among the standards on a changing menu are skillet-roasted mussels in tomato, garlic, and saffron, and crispy pizzas that might include bacon, Bosc pear, and sweet onion. He does steadily interesting things with salmon, such as giving it a mushroom and thyme crust, and with Muscovy duck breast. You also might see a mesquite-roasted pork loin chop with corn bread and bacon stuffing. The bar is rousing—the noise level hums all around the restaurant—and offers some more casual menu choices. Try the highly hospitable Sunday brunch, and don't miss the basket of breads. In

its open, boisterous style, Wildwood feels a bit like San Francisco, but it tastes like the best of Oregon. *$$$; AE, MC, V; no checks; lunch, dinner every day, brunch Sun; full bar; reservations recommended; cory@wildwoodpdx.com; www.wildwoodpdx.com; map:GG7* &

William's on 12th / ★★

207 SE 12TH AVE, SOUTHEAST; 503/963-9226

At 25—OK, by now he may be 26—Bill Henry has created an inviting, deft, and consistently interesting new restaurant. He shifts his menu continuously but has a close and enduring relationship with seared sea scallops, lamb with rosemary, and grilled quail—if you're lucky, nestled into a pile of pasta. Henry also has a fondness for squash, which pops up in soups, sides, and lasagne. What he lacks in age he makes up for in style and cheerful excess, sometimes going over the top—an attitude best reflected in the appetizer of baked Brie with brown sugar, pears, and hazelnuts. Though purists wince, it could be one of Portland's real guilty pleasures. Servers here are cheerful and visibly enthusiastic, as is the proprietor, who may bubble out of the kitchen to make sure you're enjoying everything. More than likely, you will be—and the lady sprawled across a divan in a painting taking up most of one wall looks pretty pleased herself. *$$$; DIS, MC, V; local checks only; dinner every day; beer and wine; reservations recommended; williamson12th@hotmail.com; map:HH6*

Winterborne / ★★★

3520 NE 42ND AVE, BEAUMONT; 503/249-8486

This tiny, almost ritualistic seafood restaurant steadily scores high in the Portland *Zagat* listings, suggesting that people know what they want. Since taking over, Alsatian chef Gilbert Henry has kept to the original style and much of the menu, including sautéed oysters, crab juniper with pears, and the potent Death by Chocolate. He does have his own style; there can't be many local restaurants that offer choucroute aux poissons. But aside from the sauerkraut, Gilbert has both upheld Winterborne's high reputation and brought his own ideas. The menu also includes another Henry specialty, Basil Thai Prawn—substantial shellfish laced with garlic, ginger, and coconut milk. Bringing new continental inspirations to Northwest seafood, this chef can stretch a halibut from Astoria to Alsace. Winterborne is a tiny place of perhaps 10 tables, and guests feel the warmth and care that such a size allows. *$$; AE, DIS, MC, V; local checks only; dinner Wed–Sat; beer and wine; reservations recommended; map:FF4* &

Wu's Open Kitchen / ★

17773 SW BOONE FERRY RD, LAKE OSWEGO; 503/636-8899
12180 SW SCHOLLS FERRY RD, TIGARD; 503/579-8899 &

 The flames leaping high behind the windows in the back of the restaurant are firing the large woks in the kitchen, and you can watch the cooks deftly preparing dishes while you wait for dinner. Chef Jimmy Wu's extended family helps run this place, serving a variety of spicy and not-so-spicy dishes from all over China (but the cooks reckon on the American palate—the hot dishes won't wilt too many taste buds). Seafood is fresh, vegetables are crisp, sauces are light, and service is speedy and attentive. Kids will feel right at home, and parents will appreciate the modest prices. Prepare for a wait on weekends—it has been discovered by locals. A second restaurant resides in Tigard. *$; MC, V; no checks; lunch, dinner every day; full bar; reservations recommended; map:MM8, map:KK9* &

Yen Ha / ★

6820 NE SANDY BLVD, ROSE CITY; 503/287-3698

In Portland, Vietnamese restaurants turn over faster than a good spring roll, but Yen Ha has endured. With 160 items, Portland's most extensive Vietnamese menu (and one of its oldest) offers a range of possibilities that invite intricate exploration. One short cut—which isn't that short—is Yen Ha's signature specialty, seven courses of beef, which sends bovine protein through soup, meatballs, skewers, and a delicate wrapping (with vegetables and spices) in rice paper. You might also try a messy, tangy whole Dungeness crab, game hen with coconut rice, or some remarkable things done with frogs' legs. Some local Vietnamese have been heard to mutter that the menu (and the spicing) has become a bit Americanized, but the crowd is consistently multicultural. The ambience is Formica and Budweiser; concentrate on all your beef. *$; AE, MC, V; no checks; lunch, dinner every day; full bar; no reservations; map:FF4* &

Zell's: An American Cafe / ★★

1300 SE MORRISON ST, BUCKMAN; 503/239-0196

Sure, lots of places pride themselves on their seasonally changing menu, but how many of them offer seasonally changing breakfast? At Zell's that can mean pumpkin pancakes or a fresh nectarine waffle—all skillfully produced. This is a place that will dare a German pancake with rhubarb. Zell's serves one of the best breakfasts in this time zone: a range of waffles and pancakes (try the ginger if they're available) and inspired eggs. To the trademark chorizo-and-peppers omelet has now been added a Brie-and-tomato effort and, if you're lucky, scrambled eggs with smoked salmon, Gruyère, and green onions. Lunchtime means a whole other set of specialties, from meat loaf and vegetarian sandwiches to clam cakes, but it's hard not to be overshadowed by the breakfasts. The catch, especially on weekend mornings, will be the wait for your table, but it probably won't be long enough for the nectarines to go out of season. Limited bar. *$; AE, DIS, MC, V; checks OK; breakfast, lunch every day; beer and wine; no reservations; map:GG5* &

LODGINGS

LODGINGS
Downtown/Southwest Portland

The Benson Hotel / ★★★

309 SW BROADWAY; 503/228-2000 OR 800/426-0670

Although the arrival of the 21st century has coincided with the arrival of a host of new luxury hotels in downtown Portland, the Benson, open since 1912, remains the grand dame of them all. Many locals who want to spend a night downtown opt for the Benson (rates start at $220 per night, but packages and special rates are often available), and it is still the first choice for politicos and film stars; with 287 rooms, there's space for everyone. The palatial lobby—a fine place to linger over a drink—features a stamped-tin ceiling, mammoth chandeliers, stately columns, and a generous fireplace, surrounded by panels of carved Circassian walnut imported from Russia. The guest rooms, though comfortable, lack the grandeur of the public areas, with modern furnishings in shades of black and beige. Characterized by service that's completely competent, though sometimes impersonal, the Benson is, literally and figuratively, quite corporate (it's run by WestCoast Hotels), but the place is well loved nonetheless. The London Grill (see review in the Restaurants chapter), with its white linens, upholstered chairs, tableside steak Diane, and formal service, caters to an old-fashioned dining crowd; the newer El Gaucho (also reviewed in the Restaurants chapter) features fresh seafood and steak and is also quite formal. *$$$$; AE, DC, DIS, JCB, MC, V; checks OK; www.bensonhotel.com; map:J3&*

Doubletree Red Lion Hotel / ★

310 SW LINCOLN ST; 503/221-0450 OR 800/222-TREE

This standard hotel in south downtown Portland sits close to a 1970s urban renewal project: handsome apartment towers by Skidmore Owings & Merrill are set amid sensitive landscaping and fountains by Lawrence Halprin. You can stroll from the hotel through the towers and greenspace to the Keller Auditorium, or west to Portland State University. The 235 rooms are unexciting, but some do look out onto a landscaped central courtyard with an outdoor pool. Business travelers appreciate the coffeemaker and ironing board in each room and the weight room, which is open around the clock; and everyone appreciates the rates, which, at $129/double (or less), are lower than those of many downtown hotels. *$$$; AE, DC, MC, V; checks OK; www.hilton.com/doubletree; map:B2&*

Embassy Suites Downtown Portland / ★★

319 SW PINE ST; 503/279-9000

The most interesting thing about this newish hotel on the edge of the downtown center is its pedigree: it's in the former Multnomah Hotel building, a lavish hostelry that hosted U.S. presidents and royalty, plus practically any Hollywood star who passed through town, until its closure in 1965. For the next 30 years the place led a sort of Orwellian existence as home to a large number of boxy federal offices until the Embassy Suites chain bought and remodeled it in 1997 in an effort to restore it to its original grandeur. The spacious lobby is probably the finest room, with its gilt-touched columns and player grand piano, but the Arcadian Gardens, where both a complimentary happy hour and a complimentary full breakfast are served, has a hollow, unfinished feeling. The Portland Steak and Chop House is a better dining option (see review in the Restaurants chapter). Guest rooms are relatively large with average furnishings but lots of nice touches—ample glassware, basic kitchen facilities, his and her television sets, and a coffee-table book describing the building's history. The hourglass-shaped pool, sunk beneath the ground in what was for years a parking lot, is great for the Pokemon set; there's also an exercise room and sauna, as well as a pair of spa pools. *$$$; AE, DC, DIS, MC, V; no checks; www.embassy-suites.com; map:I5* ♿

5th Avenue Suites / ★★★

506 SW WASHINGTON ST; 503/222-0001 OR 800/711-2971

Well-run, well-furnished, well-conceived: that sums up the 5th Avenue Suites. It's a delightful stay in the city center—for business travelers, yes, but excellent for families too. Most of the 221 rooms are spacious suites, but even those that are not have a sense of grandeur. Two sets of French doors usher guests in; yellow-and-white striped wallpaper makes the rooms look like well-wrapped presents. Each suite has three phones (with personalized voice mail and data ports), a couple of televisions, personal fax machines, plus such traveler-choice details as pull-down ironing boards and irons, plush cotton robes, and hair dryers. The workout room is open 24 hours. The staff is gracious and the bellhops are extremely attentive—and like its sister inn, the Hotel Vintage Plaza, 5th Avenue Suites welcomes the occasional dog or lizard. The Kimpton Group has covered its bases: everything from indoor parking with an unloading area to protect you from the (high) chance of rain to the stunning but welcoming lobby with its large corner fireplace, where you'll find complimentary coffee and newspapers in the morning, and wine tastings come evening. The Red Star Tavern & Roast House is a very good open-spaced bistro (see review in the Restaurants chapter), and there's an Aveda spa on the ground floor. *$$$–$$$$; AE, DC, DIS, JCB, MC, V; checks OK; www.5thavenuesuites.com; map:H4* ♿

CITY SPAS

Judging from the number of day spas in Portland, you'd think the locals were as stressed out as bustling New Yorkers. On the contrary, the proliferation of pampering oases is more likely a cosmopolitan outgrowth of the city's strong alternative—and preventive—medicine roots. Everything from the basic (a good manicure) to the exotic (an Ayurvedic facial) can be found among the diverse day spas in Portland. A sprawling Aveda Concept Salon and day spa called **Dosha** (2281 NW Glisan St; 503/228-8280) is the newest addition to the spa scene; it offers Ayurvedic pancha karma treatments found nowhere else in town. And you won't have to book an appointment with the best esthetician months in advance, as those big-city spa converts do. Most services at most spas are under a hundred dollars, but there are exceptions, of course. (Don't forget to tip.)

The chic salon at **Urbaca** (120 NW 9th Ave, Ste 101; 503/241-5030) is large and active, but the spa area is perfectly intimate. The soundproofed spa houses a few treatment rooms for massages and facials, and there's a serene lobby area for down time between treatments. Showers, a steam room, private changing rooms, and highly personal service top off a stellar setup. Try the Ultimate Urbaca: massage, facial, steam, manicure, pedicure, lunch, shampoo, cut and style, makeup—and even car detailing. **Salon in Vogue** (1721 SE Hawthorne Blvd; 503/228-8280; 2340 NW Westover Rd; 503/239-5395) looks like another salon from the outside, but this Aveda Concept Salon offers some excellent spa services in back: facials, aromatherapy massage, and hydrotherm massage (this is the only place it's available on the West Coast) are among them. For the chi-chi version of Aveda services, visit the **Aveda Lifestyle Store and Spa** (5th Avenue Suites, 500 SW Washington St; 503/248-0615). Facials are outstanding at both. **Pleiades** (1122 SE Ankeny St; 503/238-8089) is a cooperative spa run by six skilled women in a renovated Victorian house in Southeast. The spa offers discounts to Industrial Workers of the World members and those who use alterative transportation to get there (it's easy to get there by bus, too). Haircuts, vigorous Russian massage (highly recommended), Ayurvedic facials based on your constitution, or dosha, and other services are available at reasonable prices. Service is professional yet friendly. Finally, check out **Nature's Northwest** (3535 NE 15th Ave; 503/288-3414). The concept may sound unorthodox—a spa upstairs in a grocery store—but it works here. Services range from seaweed wraps with Vichy showers to Dr. Hauschka holistic skin care treatments with biodynamic farming-derived ingredients. The treatment rooms and equipment are top-notch. —*Liz Brown*

General Hooker's / ★

125 SW HOOKER ST; 503/222-4435

Many Portland bed-and-breakfast inns have a Rose Room (or some variation thereof), but at this conveniently located Victorian B&B, the Rose is *the* room. It has a private bath, a king-size bed, and a private entrance to the sun deck. Like the other rooms, the Rose has its own VCR (there's a collection of 4,000 films here), but the best show is of the city lights twinkling outside the window. The General itself is a tad cluttered—it's not a huge house—but still clean and well kept. A night in one of the two rooms separated by a shared bath can be a bit awkward, and the refrigerator in the upstairs hall feels a bit out of place. Kids (over 10 only) might appreciate the bunk room downstairs. There is half-price use of the nearby Metro YMCA; also within walking distance are the Duniway Park track, Terwilliger Boulevard bike path, and Lair Hill Market (for casual lunch or dinner) and public tennis courts. Downtown is five minutes by car or an easy bus ride away. *$$; AE, MC, V; checks OK; www.generalhookers.com; map:HH6* &

The Governor Hotel / ★★★

611 SW 10TH AVE; 503/224-3400 OR 800/554-3456

On the northwestern edge of the downtown core—and an easy walk from Powell's Books and the art galleries and shops of the Pearl District—sits the handsome Governor. The hotel's lobby is the first thing that impresses you: a dramatic mural depicting scenes from the Lewis and Clark expedition spans one wall, and Arts and Crafts–style furnishings, yards of mahogany, and a true wood-burning fireplace give the place a clubby feel. Alas, the 100 guest rooms are less dramatic: done in Northwest earth-tone pastels with a faint oak-leaf pattern wallpaper, they feature standard hotel furnishings. Some have whirlpool tubs, and suites feature gas-burning fireplaces, wet bars, and balconies. Almost all the rooms have big windows, but the upper-floor rooms on the northeast corner of the adjacent Princeton Building sport the best city views (you might ask for guest rooms 5013 and 6013, the only standard rooms with private balconies). The list of amenities is long; among them are 24-hour maid service and access to the business center, as well as use of the adults-only Princeton Athletic Club ($8 fee)—or you can call Studio Adrienne for an invigorating Pilates workout (it's under the same roof; best to call ahead at 503/227-1470 to book a session). The restaurant downstairs, Jake's Grill (a younger cousin of Jake's Famous Crawfish; see review in the Restaurants chapter), also provides better-than-average room service fare. *$$$–$$$$; AE, DC, DIS, JCB, MC, V; checks OK; www.gov hotel.com; map:I2* &

123

The Heathman Hotel / ★★★★

1001 SW BROADWAY; 503/241-4100 OR 800/551-0011

A refurbishment of all the guest rooms in 1998 has helped the intimate, elegant Heathman to keep pace with the competition—of which there is plenty these days. While its appeal is broad—excellent business services, a central downtown location, and fine artistic details—guests especially appreciate the meticulously courteous staff, who provide exceptional but low-key service from check-in to check-out. (Those not accustomed to the rain will appreciate the umbrella service, for instance.) The common rooms are handsomely appointed with Burmese teak paneling, and the elegant lobby lounge is a great place to enjoy afternoon tea or evening jazz performances. Among the 150 guest rooms, the Symphony Suites, with a sofa and king bed, and the Andy Warhol Suite, featuring original paintings, are our favorites. Depending on your interests, you might be impressed by the video collection, the library (with author-signed volumes), or the fitness suite (personal trainer available). The hotel itself features an impressive display of original artwork, from the Warhol prints to the fanciful Henk Pander mural on the east wall of the Arlene Schnitzer Concert Hall. And finally, you're just steps (or room service) away from one of the city's finest restaurants, where chef Philippe Boulot designs culinary masterpieces (see review of the Heathman Restaurant and Bar in the Restaurants chapter). Late in 2000, we held our breath as the Heathman was sold to the Rim Corporation of California; however, we've been assured that no changes to the hotel are expected. *$$$–$$$$; AE, DC, DIS, JCB, MC, V; checks OK; www.heathmanhotel.com; map:G2* &

Hotel Vintage Plaza / ★★★

422 SW BROADWAY; 503/228-1212 OR 800/243-0555

In a city that's becoming crowded with luxury hotels, the Vintage still shines, mostly because of what it offers for what you pay. Weekend rates are very competitive, making this an ideal destination for out-of-town shoppers who want to be in the center of the city—and feel like they're staying somewhere special. Located just blocks from Nordstrom and Pioneer Square, Vintage Plaza is run by the Kimpton Group, and like many other Kimpton hotels, its decor is elegant but not opulent. We appreciate the intimate scale of the place (107 rooms), the inviting lobby, and the gracious staff—including perfectly attentive bellhops. In the early evening, there are complimentary Northwest wines in the lobby; in fact, the wine theme extends to the guest rooms, some of which are newly decorated on a Tuscan theme. Even pets get royal treatment here (they're served treats at the front desk); just inquire well in advance. The best rooms are the top-floor starlight rooms with greenhouse-style windows (ask for one of the larger corner rooms) or one of the spacious bi-level suites. All rooms come with duo phone lines, complimentary shoe shine, nightly turndown service, morning coffee served in the lobby, and the newspaper delivered to your door. Pazzo Ristorante on the main floor serves excellent Northern Italian cuisine in a variety of settings (see review in the Restaurants chapter). Pazzoria Cafe, next door to the restaurant, sells pastries, crusty Italian breads, and panini sandwiches to take out or eat in. *$$–$$$; AE, DC, DIS, JCB, MC, V; checks OK; www.vintageplaza.com; map:I4* &

Imperial Hotel / ★

400 SW BROADWAY; 503/228-7221 OR 800/452-2323

You won't feel like royalty if you stay here, but if you don't have a king's booty at your disposal, the Imperial may fit the bill: central location, clean, fairly quiet, friendly—and room rates that are about half those of the more luxurious hotels on SW Broadway. You can request one of the newer rooms, which tend to be larger and sport new linens and furniture, or one of the older rooms, which are usually smaller, less expensive, and less appealing. Each room's bathroom, though recently remodeled, has retained its original charm, with tile floor and big porcelain tub. The folks here make you feel good: they'll park your car for you at all hours, and they'll even let you leave your baggage (locked) in the lobby for the afternoon after you've checked out. If you don't smoke, be sure to ask for a nonsmoking room (floors 2–6). An added draw: the better-than-average Thai restaurant Typhoon! (see review in the Restaurants chapter) has its downtown outpost in the hotel. *$$; AE, DC, DIS, MC, V; checks OK; www.hotel-imperial.com; map:I3* &

MacMaster House / ★★

1041 SW VISTA AVE; 503/223-7362 OR 800/774-9523

Everything here—from the florid furnishings and eclectic art to the mismatched, albeit lovely, china—reflects the dramatic personality of the host, Cecilia Murphy. It's a mix that is made more interesting by the contrasts—extravagant decor but quiet rooms, a country-paced breakfast in the heart of the city, a gracious and fiery innkeeper who is happy to give you the insider's view of Portland, if you seek it. This is the kind of place where you set the tone of your stay. The breakfast table is a great place to socialize, if you are so inclined, or, if you'd rather keep to yourself and have breakfast in your room, so be it. Although the massive portico flanked by Doric columns makes for an imposing exterior, the interior of this mansion feels more like Dr. Doolittle's library. Six rooms range from small and bookish to large and fanciful; all of them house antiques, four boast fireplaces, and two have private baths. Our favorite, the Artist's Studio on the third floor, has the feel of a Parisian garret apartment, complete with a claw-footed tub in the bath. Breakfast is a lavish affair fresh from the oven. Although this B&B is officially in Southwest Portland, it has the feeling of being in inner Northwest: you're two blocks from the entrance to Washington Park (which incorporates the Rose Garden, the

Japanese Garden, and Hoyt Arboretum) and a straight shot down to NW 23rd Avenue, with its multitude of shops and restaurants. *$$; AE, DIS, MC, V; checks OK; www.macmaster.com; map:GG7* ♿

Mallory Motor Hotel / ★

729 SW 15TH AVE; 503/223-6311 OR 800/228-8657

Some things never change; look no farther than the Mallory for evidence. Located just west of the downtown core, a 15-minute stroll to Pioneer Courthouse Square, the beloved Mallory remains the favorite lodging of many regular visitors to the City of Roses—and has been since they were kids. It's an older establishment in every sense, from the massive hunks of ornate wooden lobby furniture to the senior staff. It's also one of the best bargains in town, starting at $85 for a spotless double and topping out at $150 for a suite—so it's a good idea to reserve a room far in advance. The Mallory sits in a quiet area of town where its four-story garage makes parking a breeze. Have breakfast in the restaurant—simple, charming touches and almost motherly service—and dinner downtown. The quirky cocktail lounge draws in denizens from both the older and retro crowds. *$$; AE, DC, DIS, JCB, MC, V; checks OK; map:I1* ♿

Marriott Hotel / ★★

1401 SW NAITO PKWY; 503/226-7600

There's lots of glitter, bustle, and convention hustle at this behemoth hotel that would be a standard business lodging except for one important, redeeming quality: a terrific location, overlooking the Willamette River, that is convenient to downtown shopping and cultural centers. There are 503 rooms in the 14-story structure, and facilities include a 24-hour health club, an indoor pool, two restaurants, and two bars. A full remodel in 1999 replaced op art shock rugs with calmer carpets, dated gym equipment with cutting edge goodies, and standard coffee service with a Starbucks espresso stop in the lobby. Don't settle for the first price quoted—if you probe, you just might find that you qualify for more moderate prices (ask about weekend, seasonal, senior citizen, AAA, and other special rates). For a smaller Marriott option, check out the Portland Marriott City Center, a newer "boutique" hotel close to Pioneer Courthouse Square (520 SW Broadway; 503/226-6300; map:I4), or, for more space, reserve at the soon-to-be-completed Marriott Residence Inn in the RiverPlace district (2115 SW River Pkwy; 503/552-9500). *$$$; AE, DC, MC, V; checks OK; www.marriott.com; map:D4* ♿

The Paramount Hotel / ★★

808 SW TAYLOR ST; 503/223-9900 OR 800/426-0670

"Location, location, location" might be what sells a house, and in this case, it might also sell a room in a luxury hotel. Just down the street from the green South Park Blocks, the new Paramount is close to the Portland Art Museum, Nordstrom, the Portland Center for the Performing Arts, Pioneer Courthouse Square, and many other downtown attractions. So while the Paramount may not be perfect, it is convenient—or will be, eventually. At press time, the hotel, which has been open since early 2000, still doesn't have a restaurant or bar, although room service is being handled by the competent Southpark up the street (see review in the Restaurants chapter). Rooms are comfortable, although not extravagant, with black and tan interiors. All the amenities one would expect are here, including dual phone lines and in-room movie and game systems. Of the 154 guest rooms, we suggest you spring for the roomy executive room with Jacuzzi bath, although to celebrate your lottery win you might reserve one of the two grand suites with their fireplaces, terraces, and great views northward over the city. *$$$; AE, DC, MC, V; checks OK; www.westcoasthotels.com; map:G2* ♿

Portland Hilton / ★★

921 SW 6TH AVE; 503/226-1611

Set squarely in central downtown, this 24-story, 465-room lodging is already big, and it's going to get bigger—sort of. The new 20-story Portland Hilton Executive Tower will open in 2002, kitty-corner from the existing hotel, so there will be 327 more rooms. The guest rooms are compact, adequately furnished, and plainly decorated, but they are—technologically speaking—ahead of the pack, with high-speed Internet access, Web TV, and other features that techies and other business people especially savor (the work stations in the new rooms are exceptionally well thought out, complete with ergonomic chairs). Guests at both hotels have easy access to Portland's cultural attractions, downtown department stores and businesses, and PSU. The public areas of the existing hotel are impressive: there's a collection of artwork from prominent Oregon artists, a full-service athletic club, a covered swimming pool, the 6,800-square-foot Pavilion Ballroom (popular for weddings), and the street-side Bistro 921 with an open kitchen. Alexander's on the 23rd floor offers a view of the city over gourmet fare. A west-facing room on any of the floors above the 16th affords a lovely view of the city that stretches from the West Hills to St. Johns Bridge; an upper-floor room on the east side promises, in fair weather, a view of Mount Hood. *$$$; AE, DC, MC, V; checks OK; www.hilton.com; map:G2* ♿

RiverPlace / ★★★

1510 SW HARBOR WY; 503/228-3233 OR 800/227-1333

If you're looking for a room with a view, look no further than RiverPlace. The only downtown luxury hotel that fronts the busy Willamette River—and the boat show that comes with it—the European style RiverPlace (managed by the same hoteliers who run the grand Benson) is lovely to look at and glorious to look out from. The better rooms among the 84—doubles, suites, and condominiums—face the water or look north across park lawns to the downtown cityscape. Inside are plush furnishings, TVs concealed in armoires, and generously sized bathrooms. Complimentary continental breakfast can be brought to your room, along with your requested newspaper; massage and spa treatments are available by appointment. Use of the adjacent RiverPlace Athletic Club is complimentary, but on nice days there's plenty of opportunity for exercise right outside: wide, paved paths lead from the hotel through the fountains and monuments of Tom McCall Waterfront Park. Or you can sit outside and watch the stream of skaters whizzing by. Downstairs, the Esplanade restaurant makes a stunning location for a meal (see review in the Restaurants chapter). *$$$; AE, DC, MC, V; checks OK; www.riverplace hotel.com; map:D5* &

The Westin Portland / ★★★

750 SW ALDER ST; 503/294-9000 OR 800/937-8461

Downtown Portland is blessed with a healthy selection of distinctive upscale hotels. So the challenge for the new Westin was to create a big (205 rooms), new (opened in 1999) hotel that didn't feel like yet another cookie-cutter chain offering that left guests wondering whether this was Atlanta or Cincinnati or Portland. By almost every measure, they got it right. The ground floor lobby and desk have an intimate feel; a sitting room with a fireplace is comfortably separate from the bustle of guests checking in and out, and fine artwork adorns the walls. The knowledgeable and professional staff is pleasant and helpful. And finally, it's a handsome place; the architectural style suggests both modern and traditional (with lots of tile, even on the elevator floors). The rooms house tasteful modern furniture, a big television, fax machines (in some rooms), phones with data ports and voice mail, clock/radio/CD player, and uncommonly luxurious beds with down comforters and tons of pillows. But the bathroom is definitely worth the price of admission: a separate, spacious glass shower stall, nice deep tub, tile floor, and a big slab of marble for the counter. No pool, but there's a workout room with an array of weight and aerobic machines. Diners have many restaurants to choose from in the neighborhood, including pretty Oritalia downstairs (see review in the Restaurants chapter). *$$$; AE, CB, DC, DIS, JCB, MC, V; checks OK; www.westinportland.com; map:I3* &

North Portland/Jantzen Beach

Doubletree Hotel Columbia River / ★

1401 N HAYDEN ISLAND DR; 503/281-1500 OR 800/325-3535
This rambling 351-room motel is poised right on the Columbia River, a mere 7 miles north of downtown. For the sports minded it offers a small basketball court and a pool (seasonally) with a sun deck that virtually overhangs the river, and complimentary airport pickup. Nearby, there's the 27-hole Heron Lakes Golf Course (via a two-minute free shuttle), a jogging path, and a health club. Honeymooners and business people are everywhere (the riverfront executive suites—650 square feet, private deck, garden bathtub, and king-size bed—are in high demand). The dance floor at the informal Brickstones restaurant hops on Fridays and Saturdays. Next door is the Doubletree Hotel Jantzen Beach (909 N Hayden Island Dr; 503/283-4466); expect much the same. *$$; AE, DC, MC, V; checks OK; www.hilton.com/doubletree; map:CC6* &

Northeast Portland

The Clinkerbrick House Bed and Breakfast / ★★

2311 NE SCHUYLER ST; 503/281-2533
While Bob and Peggie Irvine's clinkerbrick house in the Irvington neighborhood is open to guests, it's really the top floor that's yours, and privacy (for all parties involved) is encouraged with a separate entrance and key. Upstairs there's a small kitchen and dining area where you can procure a snack, make a cup of tea, or even cook if you so choose. Of the three rooms, the largest is the only one with a private bath; it also has a canopy bed and a private balcony. Our favorite room, oddly enough, is the smallest one, where the sun (when out) seems to shine brightest. Peggie prepares a full breakfast: perhaps a gingerbread waffle served out on the brick courtyard when the weather allows. Two-night minimum, all weekends, summer months. *$; MC, V; checks OK; map:FF4* &

Doubletree Portland Lloyd Center / ★

1000 NE MULTNOMAH ST; 503/281-6111 OR 800/222-TREE

With 476 guest rooms, the Doubletree Lloyd Center is Oregon's second-largest hotel (the Portland Marriott is slightly bigger), making it a good choice for eastside conventions or seminars. The hotel itself features a number of well-organized meeting rooms, an exhibit hall, an outdoor pool, a workout room, and a courtesy airport van; a recent renovation spit-polished the lobby decor. A map in the lobby directs you to the hotel's three restaurants. Reserve an east-facing room above the fifth floor for a view of Mount Hood. The proximity to the Lloyd Center, the

ROOMS WITHOUT HONOR BARS

If you're familiar with Portland, you've probably seen or heard of Brian and Mike McMenamin's brewpubs and movie theaters. But have you heard of their hotels? Where you're actually welcome to take pitchers of Hammerhead to your room? Like all the McMenamins' establishments, the hostelries are tied together by a comfortable, quirky, slightly mystic decorating scheme—including paintings created by artists who are members of the staff. And by a chain of good karma.

One of the admirable things these guys do, besides provide appealing, mostly non-smoking spots to get out of the rain, is refurbish old, dilapidated buildings. Several sites are on the National Register of Historic Places and have interesting histories. **Edgefield**, a "destination resort" (20 minutes from downtown; see review in this chapter), was a former poor farm; the **Kennedy School** (see review in this chapter) in Northeast Portland was a grade school; and the **Grand Lodge** in Forest Grove (3505 Pacific Ave; 503/992-9533) was the former Masonic and Eastern Star Home.

These lodgings are not for everyone—true luxury seekers, those who avoid beer, or businesspeople in town for work may not want to stay here—but everyone agrees they are unique. Check out www.mcmenamins.com for descriptions of each establishment, menus, current movie offerings, and room rates. Next up: virtual beer?

—Kim Carlson

Rose Quarter, and the Convention Center makes this a sensible and adequate choice if you've planned activities nearby. *$$$; AE, DC, MC, V; checks OK; www. doubletreehotels.com; map:FF5* &

The Georgian House Bed and Breakfast / ★
1828 NE SISKIYOU ST; 503/281-2250
On a summer day most of the guests can be found outside in the garden amid the fragrant lavender and roses, perhaps helping themselves to the berries that grow along the back fence. Given the lovely grounds and quiet neighborhood, this Irvington B&B combines the respite of a country getaway with a convenient location (downtown is about five minutes away by car). Antique furniture and collectibles blend with a contemporary country motif for a style that, depending on your tastes, is either charming or cluttered. Upstairs rooms are all air-conditioned. Of the three upstairs rooms, we like the East Lake for its private veranda and the Lovejoy Suite for its claw-footed bathtub. Willie Ackley, the likable host, has guests sign up for breakfast. One caveat: for anyone who likes to sleep in, the sign-up times are shamefully early. *$–$$; MC, V; checks OK; map:FF5* &

The Kennedy School / ★★

5736 NE 33RD AVE; 503/249-3983

If you're not familiar with the McMenamin brothers' brewpub/movie theater/B&B enterprises, you may find this place perplexing, but if you're on the bus, so to speak, you're bound to like the Kennedy School. Located in a former Italian Renaissance–style public school building in the Concordia neighborhood of Northeast Portland, this enterprise is part community center, part meeting facility, part fun house. The Kennedy School features 35 bed-and-breakfast guest rooms--two to a classroom!--each featuring a private bath, the McMenamins' signature commissioned artwork (think Grateful Dead posters), Indonesian antiques, and, in some, chalkboards still in place. There are the requisite bars (Detention and Honors), a brewery, and a restaurant, with some not-so-common public areas as well: an excellent movie theater, a gymnasium, a wine bar/dessert room, a hot-water soaking pool for guests and community members, and a charming courtyard with a fireplace to warm you. *$$; AE, DIS, MC, V; checks OK; www.mcmenamins.com; map:EE5* ♿

The Lion and the Rose / ★★★

1810 NE 15TH AVE; 503/287-9245 OR 800/955-1647

Housed in a 1906 Queen Anne mansion in the Irvington district (not far from Lloyd Center), the Lion and the Rose maintains its status as one of Portland's more elegant B&Bs. The two hosts let few details go unchecked—from the candles in the baths to beverages in the refrigerator to the extra blankets upon request. The best rooms are the Joseph's (rich colors contrast with ample natural light) and the Lavonna (done in lavender and white, it boasts a spacious bay window reading nook); the place is indisputably decorated, with rich drapery, fine rugs, and antiques. Breakfast is lavish (available in the formal dining room), and tea is offered to guests from 4pm until 6pm. Those set on relaxing will appreciate the porch swing—roofed to guard against rain—but business travelers will also find plenty of phone lines and other amenities. *$$$; AE, MC, V; checks OK; www.lionrose.com; map:EE5*

Marriott Residence Inn/Lloyd Center / ★

1710 NE MULTNOMAH ST; 503/288-1400 OR 800/331-3131

This hotel near the Lloyd Center has 168 rooms that you might mistake, from the outside at least, for apartments. It's geared toward longer stays (four to seven days), and the longer you stay the lower your per-night charge. Each suite has a full kitchen, as well as a sitting area with a couch and a desk. Dual phone lines and data ports are provided in each room. Most rooms have wood-burning fireplaces. Extra conveniences include weekday dry cleaning and complimentary grocery-shopping services. There isn't much of a view and there's no restaurant, but a full breakfast buffet (daily) and afternoon hors d'oeuvres (Monday through Thursday) are served in the lobby. Three Jacuzzis and a heated outdoor pool are on the premises for guest use; an extra $5 a day gains you access to the Lloyd Center Athletic Club seven blocks away. *$$; AE, DC, DIS, JCB, MC, V; no checks; www.marriott.com; map:GG5* &

Portland Guest House / ★★

1720 NE 15TH AVE; 503/282-1402

Owner Susan Gisvold has created an urban retreat just off busy NE Broadway in the historic Irvington neighborhood. White carpets and antique linens lend the classy air of an intimate hotel, and comfortable mattresses ease the separation from home. Gisvold doesn't live here, but she's usually around long enough to advise you on Portland doings and make sure the flowers in the window boxes are watered. In the morning, she'll drop in to serve a home-cooked breakfast of lowfat cottage cheese pancakes, scones, fresh strawberries, and coffee or tea. Each of the seven rooms—five have private baths—has its own phone and clock (items not standard in many B&Bs), making this a good place for business travelers, too. Three of the rooms have multiple beds for travelers rooming together but sleeping separately. When the weather's warm, the garden brick patio is the spot to be; when it's not, relax in the simple parlor or set out to explore the many shops along NE Broadway. *$–$$; MC, V; checks preferred; www.teleport.com/~pgh/; map:GG7*

Portland's White House / ★★

1914 NE 22ND AVE; 503/287-7131

Owners Lanning Blanks and Steve Holden hired a historian to help with the restoration of this stately old home, built in 1911 of solid Honduran mahogany and oak by local timber baron Robert F. Lytle. Now the exquisite interior replicates the original Lytle home. On the outside, Portland's White House looks a bit like its Washington, D.C., namesake, complete with fountains, a circular driveway, and a carriage house that contains three newly converted guest rooms with baths. Inside are more guest rooms, all with private baths. The Canopy Room is especially inviting, with its large canopied bed and bright bath. The Garden Room's private terrace is nice in summertime. A full gourmet breakfast is served in the main dining room every morning. Evenings, wander down to the formal parlor for a glass of sherry or a game of chess. *$$; DIS, MC, V; checks OK; www.portlandswhitehouse.com; map:GG7*

Northwest Portland

Heron Haus Bed and Breakfast / ★★

2545 NW WESTOVER RD; 503/274-1846

Although Heron Haus is just blocks away from NW 23rd Avenue, its location, at the base of the West Hills, has a residential feel. The common areas in this 10,000-square-foot English Tudor home include a bright living room with a cushy sectional sofa, a mahogany-paneled library punctuated by an inviting window seat, and a brilliant sun room. Six guest rooms, each with a fireplace and private bath (one bathroom has a seven-nozzle shower), are comfortably furnished in pastels, with large brass beds, sitting areas, telephones, and TVs. The extraordinary bath in the Kulia Room features an elevated spa tub with a city view and all the deluxe bathing accoutrements one could want—from his-and-her robes to a rubber ducky. Guests can communicate between rooms via intercom or pick up their phone for service from the omnipresent innkeepers. Julie Keppeler caters to the business crowd (hence the reduced corporate rate and phone hookups). Breakfast, served in the dining room, is an elaborate cut fruit dish with pastries from Delphina's Bakery, three varieties of cereal, and designer coffees. *$$$; MC, V; checks OK; www.innbook. com/heron.html; map:GG7*

Portland City Center Hostel / ★

1818 NW GLISAN ST; 503/241-2783

Portland City Center Hostel is located in the Nob Hill neighborhood, where theaters, cafes, restaurants, shops, and brewpubs keep early-morning to late-night hours. Forest Park—the country's largest natural city park—is a healthy walk or bike ride away. Rooms here are strictly for travelers, unavailable to anyone residing within 30 miles of the hostel. The hostel features a coin-op laundry, a clean kitchen with room to store guests' food, and a clean, if simple, dining area. Separate men's and women's dorms have shared bathrooms, and a coed dorm serves couples traveling together or booked hostel overflow. Rules are standard. Call ahead for reservations. Forty-eight-hour cancellation call requested. A credit card is required for reservation, although traveler's checks or cash are fine for room payment. Children OK. No pets. Rooms are $15 a night for Hostelling International members, $18 for nonmembers. *$; MC, V; no checks; www.iyhf.org; map:GG7*

Silver Cloud Inn / ★

2425 NW VAUGHN ST; 503/242-2400

Location alone would recommend this motor hotel on NW Vaughn Street; the Silver Cloud sits just a block off NW 23rd Avenue, a nice walk from some of the city's more intriguing boutiques and coffee stops. Plus, there are three or four highly recommended restaurants within a few blocks, and Forest Park is just up the hill. But this place has more than its address going for it: it's clean and well priced, and has easy freeway access and plenty of parking. A continental breakfast featuring pastries from local bakeries is served with designer coffee, plus one night each week the Silver Cloud hosts a reception for guests—a nice touch for longer-stay visitors. *$$; AE, DC, DIS, MC, V; checks OK; map:GG7*

Southeast Portland

Century Garden / ★★

1960 SE LARCH AVE; 503/235-6846

The diminutive Century Garden offers two upstairs suites in a turn-of-the century house in Ladd's Addition, not far from SE Hawthorne Boulevard. In the Garden Room, lace curtains hang from birch-branch rods, framing windows that overlook narrow streets and leafy trees. The queen-size bed here looks feather soft beneath a cream-colored down comforter and blue-and-white sheets. Vintage and antique furniture tastefully decorates walls and fills corners. The Century Room has a queen bed, too, covered in quilts and pillows and located beneath windows that spill light everywhere. Guests share a bath with antique white porcelain fittings; everything is immaculately clean. Beyond the suites, the common guest room features a television, phone, microwave, refrigerator, and a collection of coffees and teas. Innkeeper Carol Olpin will prepare breakfast whenever you'd like it; gingerbread muffins are a constant, but you can choose the rest of your breakfast from a menu of standard items. In nice weather, meals are served on the back balcony overlooking a manicured garden. Take note: If your party wants both rooms, the price is excellent. *$$; MC, V; checks OK; www.centurygarden.com; map:HH6*

Portland International Hostel / ★

3031 SE HAWTHORNE BLVD; 503/236-3380

The Hawthorne district location for one of Portland's two official hostels couldn't be better for budget travelers; within blocks are great used bookstores, good eats, and plentiful coffee and microbrew hangouts. This place will seem familiar to those who know hostels: clean linens are available; check in by 10pm and enjoy 24-hour access with a security access code. Shared showers, bunk beds, blankets, a kitchen, and two small living areas are the amenities—plus all-you-can-eat pancakes come morning. The hostel encourages groups and has one private room, good for families. Hostelling International membership is not required but lessens the price; you can buy an HI membership ($25 for the year) when you arrive. Rooms are $15/night with membership, $18 without. *$; MC, V; no checks; www.iyhf.org; map:GG4*

Airport

Sheraton Portland Airport Hotel / ★★

8235 NE AIRPORT WY; 503/281-2500 OR 800/325-3535

Some Portlanders opt to spend the night here before an early flight: it's conveniently close to the terminal (FedEx planes load up next door, and Delta and United arrival and departure times are broadcast via video screen at the hotel's main entrance), and guests can park a car for up to 14 days with no charge. For the traveling businessperson as well, the airport's Sheraton tops the list. Inside, amenities abound: everything from meeting rooms and a small but complete complimentary business center (with a computer, a printer, a fax machine, and secretarial service) to an indoor swimming pool, sauna, and workout room. The mini-suites consider the personal needs of the businessperson, providing two phones, sitting areas, and jacks for computer hookup. Mount Hood stands tall to the east, but you'd never know it from the airport-facing rooms. *$$; AE, DC, JCB, MC, V; corporate checks OK; www.sheraton.com; map:EE3*

Beaverton

Greenwood Inn / ★

10700 SW ALLEN BLVD, BEAVERTON; 503/643-7444

Billed as a city hotel with resort-style comfort, this 251-room complex delivers, for the most part, on its promises. Located just off Highway 217 in Beaverton, and convenient to Tigard, the Greenwood Inn is well situated for those doing business in the Silicon Forest. A few of the suites have Jacuzzis, others have kitchens, and some rooms are set aside for guests with pets. The courtyard and trapezoidal pool are quite pretty. Inside the Pavillion Trattoria, the menu features Italian cuisine, the lights are soft, and the service treads the delicate line between chummy and concerned (see review in the Restaurants chapter). *$$; AE, DC, DIS, MC, V; checks OK; www.greenwoodinn.com; map:II9* &

Lake Oswego

Holiday Inn Crowne Plaza / ★

14811 KRUSE OAKS BLVD, LAKE OSWEGO; 503/624-8400

A business hotel without a doubt, the Crowne Plaza sits right off I-5 near Highway 217, one of the busiest intersections in Southwest Portland. The rooms are fairly standard, unless you request one of the posh rooms on the sixth floor—the concierge floor. All guests receive a free pass to a nearby athletic club, complimentary van service within 5 miles, and plenty of business services. There are a lounge and restaurant, an indoor/outdoor pool, a workout room, bicycles (there are trails behind the hotel), a sauna, and a whirlpool. Room rates plummet on the weekends. *$$; AE, DC, DIS, MC, V; checks OK; www.crowneplaza.com; map:KK8* &

Lakeshore Motor Hotel / ★

210 N STATE ST, LAKE OSWEGO; 503-636-9679 OR 800/215-6431
From the street or parking lot, Lake Oswego's Lakeshore Motor Hotel might look like any another motel located on a main thoroughfare through town, but this one happens to be near the new and impressive city park on the lake. And from inside one of the lake-facing rooms, the view out the window is uncannily rural and picturesque. All 33 guest rooms have a kitchenette and TV and are clean and plainly decorated. Although the one- and two-bedroom suites offer more room, the studios allow you a view of the water without getting out of bed. Guests have year-round use of the pool (heated only in summer), which is perched over the lake, and the lakeside rooms have private sun decks. An added bonus: Millennium Plaza Park, a sensational new city park on the lake, is right next door. *$$; AE, DC, DIS, MC, V; checks OK; map:LL6* &

Sauvie Island

Sauvie Island Bed and Breakfast / ★★

26504 NW REEDER RD; 503/621-3216
The best amenity at the Sauvie Island Bed and Breakfast is the front window in the dining room, which on a clear day affords views of Mount Rainier, Mount St. Helens, Mount Adams, and Mount Hood. It's a short walk from this cozy lodging to the beachfront, where swimming is easy in the summer and strolling, bird-watching, fishing, boating, and ship-viewing are year-round pleasures. This contemporary B&B is reached by a drive up a gravel path surrounded by berry vines and manicured greenery with a pretty inset walkway. Owner Marie Colasurdo, a white-haired wunderelder, greets you at the front door in a flowered apron and directs you to one of two sparkly clean guest rooms set off from the rest of the house by French doors. The Sunset Room, shaded by lace curtains that let the sun filter in over polished wood floors, has a queen-size bed, bookshelves, armoire, chest, clock, and phone. The River Room has a view of the Columbia and the mountains, a double bed, clock, phone, and more closet and move-around space. On a back deck, a Jacuzzi spa and outdoor picnic table are for the exclusive use of guests. Marie serves guests a full breakfast featuring possibly a soufflé one morning and a Belgian waffle the next. *$$; no credit cards; checks OK; www.moriah.com/sauvie; map:AA9*

Tigard

Embassy Suites Hotel / ★

9000 SW WASHINGTON SQUARE RD, TIGARD; 503/644-4000
While you might choose the Embassy Suites in downtown Portland for its history and character, *this* Embassy Suites is far less of a destination—unless you're here to shop or do business in Silicon Forest. An immense, suburban hotel adjacent to the sprawling Washington Square shopping complex in Tigard, Embassy Suites is about a 15-minute drive from downtown Portland. Hundreds of rooms (all with separate living room), an elaborate ballroom, and a swank conference center make it the neighborhood's biggest hotel. A business center kiosk in the lobby offers Internet access. Complimentary services for guests include full breakfast, transportation to a nearby athletic club or the mall, and the evening manager's reception—free drinks from 5:30pm to 7:30pm in the atrium. Restaurant and lounge are the usual Denny's-gone-velvet found in all hotels of this genre. Double occupancy begins at approximately $139, but ask about special rates. *$$$; AE, DC, MC, V; checks OK; www.embassysuites.com; map:JJ9* &

Troutdale

Edgefield / ★

2126 SW HALSEY ST, TROUTDALE; 503/669-8610 OR 800/669-8610
The McMenamin brothers of Portland microbrew fame did a terrific job of turning the former Multnomah County Poor Farm into a quirky but winning place to visit. There's the brewpub, of course, but there's also the movie theater, the winery, the distillery, the respectable Black Rabbit Restaurant and Bar (see review in the Restaurants chapter), the Power Station pub, the amphitheater (which draws some big-name bands in the summer), the 18-hole par 3 golf course, the meeting and party sites, and 114 guest rooms spread throughout three buildings. All are furnished with antiques and cozy linens and are embellished with custom artistry; most share a bath, although the 13 suites have private baths. Because Edgefield is billed as a European-style bed-and-breakfast, the first meal of the day is included in the room rate ($50 – $130), and glasses and pitchers are readily available for fetching beer. There is also a men's and women's hostel, a great alternative for the budget traveler, as well as family rooms that sleep up to six. The proximity to (and location away from) airport property makes Edgefield less conventional than the usual airport-area lodging alternatives. *$$; AE, DIS, MC, V; checks OK; www.mcmenamins.com* &

Vancouver, Washington

Heathman Lodge / ★★

7801 NE GREENWOOD DR, VANCOUVER, WA; 360/254-3100 OR 888/475-3100

Vancouver's first luxury hotel—run by the pros who until recently owned Portland's venerable Heathman—gives a distinct first impression: it is simply stunning but somewhat out of place. The hotel looms like a National Park lodge as you approach it from busy SR500, but it's set squarely in a Clark County suburb, near a mini-mall and high tech office space. Huge timbers support the porte cochere, and nearby a carved cedar totem pole and a bronze sculpture of a Chinook chief enrich your first impressions, which only grow more positive as you step inside. There's a striking lobby with a basalt fireplace, bright pool and exercise rooms, the top-drawer Hudson's Bar & Grill (see review in the Restaurants chapter), a range of suites and guest rooms attractively furnished in Northwest style (complete with bedspreads created by Pendleton), and plenty of amenities for the business traveler. Perhaps best of all is that promise of excellent, understated service for which the Heathman Lodge's parent company has made itself known. The lodge is unlikely to become a destination in itself because of the surrounding neighborhood, but for those travelers making Vancouver their destination, the Heathman Lodge should be at the top of their accommodations list. *$$$; AE, DC, DIS, MC, V; checks OK; www.heathmanlodge.com* &

EXPLORING

EXPLORING

Top 20 Attractions

1) WASHINGTON PARK

SW Park Pl, a block west (uphill) of Vista Ave; 503/823-2223 Portland is a city of parks: there are some 280 greenspaces in the city. At 4,683 acres, **FOREST PARK** (see separate listing in this section) is the most sprawling and primitive, while the 24-square-inch **MILL ENDS PARK** (SW Naito Pkwy and Taylor St) is decidedly the city's smallest. And lovely Washington Park may well be the most civilized.

The 546-acre plot, originally purchased by Portland's founders in 1871, is the home of several different gardens, including the well-kept trails of the **HOYT ARBORETUM** (see separate listing in this section) and the inspiring **VIETNAM VETERANS' LIVING MEMORIAL** (4000 SW Fairview Blvd, next to the World Forestry Center; 503/823-3654).

Whether to obtain a blossom-framed snapshot of Mount Hood or to scrutinize a new hybrid, the **INTERNATIONAL ROSE TEST GARDEN** (400 SW Kingston Ave; 503/823-3636) is an obligatory stop for any visitor to the Rose City. The garden (established in 1917) is the oldest continually operating testing program in the country. Thanks to its more than 8,000 plants—over 500 varieties—and a knockout setting overlooking downtown Portland, it's an unmatched display of the genus *Rosa*. The garden's 4½ acres are a riot of blooms from June through October, from dainty half-inch-wide miniatures to great, blowsy 8-inch beauties. Fragrant old-garden varieties fill the gap between the parking lot and the Washington Park tennis courts. While you're here, check out the new **ROSE GARDEN STORE** (850 SW Rose Garden Wy; 503/227-7033), which sells rose-themed merchandise, including rose-patterned tea sets and floral wreaths; proceeds from the store benefit the rose gardens and Portland parks youth programs.

The park also is home to the elegant **JAPANESE GARDEN** (see separate listing in this section), and in the northern end of the park, hiking trails meander through the woods. Also in the park is the **OREGON ZOO** (see separate listing in this section), famed for its successful breeding of Asian elephants. The westside light rail line, MAX (503/238-RIDE), stops at the zoo; take time to notice the geological time line exhibit that lines the walls of this 260-foot-deep train stop—the **DEEPEST UNDERGROUND TRANSIT STATION** in North America (elevators take you up and down in 20 seconds). At the entrance to the plaza aboveground sits a sculpture made from columnar basalt and etched granite, which tells the story of creating the light rail tunnel. Those who arrive at the zoo by car take a chance with overflow parking, especially on the weekend.

TOP 20 ATTRACTIONS FOR PORTLAND

1) Washington Park
2) Central Downtown, Pioneer Courthouse Square, South Park Blocks
3) Tom McCall Waterfront Park/ RiverPlace
4) Portland Art Museum
5) Oregon Museum of Science and Industry (OMSI)
6) Japanese Garden
7) Oregon Zoo
8) Pearl District
9) Northwest Portland

10) Hoyt Arboretum
11) Oregon History Center
12) River Cruises on the Columbia and Willamette Rivers
13) End of the Oregon Trail Interpretive Center/ Oregon City Historic Sites
14) Powell's Books
15) Breweries and Brewpubs
16) Hawthorne District
17) Pittock Mansion
18) Fort Vancouver National Historic Site
19) Saturday Market
20) Antiquing in Sellwood

In the vicinity of the zoo is the educational **WORLD FORESTRY CENTER** (see Museums in this chapter). One-way roads wind through Washington Park, and in warm-weather months a narrow-gauge train runs through the zoo to the Rose Garden (see Train and Trolley Tours in this chapter). Other facilities include four lit tennis courts, covered picnic areas, an archery range, a playground, public rest rooms, and an outdoor amphitheater that features free musical and stage performances in summer (call 503/823-2223 for schedule). In 2001, the **CHILDREN'S MUSEUM** will move into the old OMSI building, across the parking lot from the zoo (see Museums in this chapter). *www.parks.ci.portland. or.us/parks/washington.htm; map:GG7*

2) CENTRAL DOWNTOWN, PIONEER COURTHOUSE SQUARE, SOUTH PARK BLOCKS

The area bordered by I-405 on the west and south, W Burnside on the north, and the Willamette River on the east Portland has good reason to be proud of its downtown. While most cities in America have allowed the malling of suburbia to drain the life from the downtown core, the City of Roses has not. Whatever the season, you will see people taking to the streets downtown: during the day it's a thriving business and retail center; at night, restaurants, hotels, and festivals of one sort or another attract tourists and residents alike. Thanks to the city's half-size city blocks and pedestrian-friendly planning, a good way to see the downtown is to walk, and a good place to start your tour is the visitors information center at the **PORTLAND OREGON VISITORS ASSOCIATION** (POVA), in the World

Trade Center (corner of SW Salmon St and Naito Pkwy; 503/222-2223; map:F5; open Mon–Sat; moving to Pioneer Courthouse Square in summer 2001). Get yourself free copies of "Powell's Walking Map of Downtown Portland" and the "Portland Visitor's Map"; kids have their own guide, the colorful "Portland City Kids Fun Book." POVA has information on just about anything you might want to do in the Rose City. While you're exploring downtown, keep an eye out for the green-jacketed **PORTLAND GUIDES**, employees of the Association for Portland Progress, who roam the downtown core in pairs just to answer questions about the city.

The Association for Portland Progress also sponsors the **SMART PARK** garages. A minimum $25 purchase at major downtown retailers buys one or two hours of **FREE PARKING** at these lots. For more information, see the Lay of the City chapter. You should also know that public transportation is free in the downtown core, in the area called "Fareless Square" bounded by the Willamette River on the east, Interstate 405 on the south and west, and NW Irving Street on the north.

Portland's downtown owes its lived-in feel in part to its "living room": the Will Martin–designed **PIONEER COURTHOUSE SQUARE** (map:H3). The city's first public school occupied this site, as did its most magnificent hotel—look for the hotel's wrought iron gate on the east side of the square. An eyesore of a parking garage stood here after the hotel was demolished, until the city resolved to turn it into public space, with the help of a clever funding campaign: most of the square's 45,000 bricks bear the names of individual contributors who chipped in to pay for the project. It now hosts political rallies, concerts (many at no charge), flower shows, and people-watching daily.

On the lower level of the bi-level square, by the fountain, is the **TRI-MET CUSTOMER SERVICE OFFICE** (and, in summer 2001, the visitors center). **PUBLIC REST ROOMS** are found in the Tri-Met offices; **POWELL'S TRAVEL STORE** is also located in the square's southeast corner. Next to the **STARBUCKS** at its northwest corner is the 25-foot-tall **WEATHER MACHINE,** which at noon spews mist and predicts rain, sun, or storms with a fanfare of trumpets. Adjacent to the square are two big department stores and a bank (**MEIER & FRANK** at SW Sixth Avenue and Morrison Street, **NORDSTROM** on SW Broadway between Morrison and Yamhill Streets, and **WELLS FARGO** in the American Bank Building on SW Morrison Street between Sixth Avenue and Broadway) and of course the stout **PIONEER COURTHOUSE**, with a gracefully refurbished post office on the main floor. From the cupola of this historic building you get great views of the city—next to the eight windows are historic photos of the area you're looking at so you can see how the city has changed. (To get to the cupola, take the elevator to the third floor, turn left, go through the door, and walk two flights up.)

Two blocks east of the square is downtown's principal shopping complex, **PIONEER PLACE** (503/228-5800), between SW Third and Fifth Avenues and SW Yamhill and Morrison Streets. This cheerful shopping mall recently doubled its size with a second block-sized mall, which connects with the original via a sky bridge over SW Fourth Avenue. **SAKS FIFTH AVENUE** (850 SW 5th Ave) anchors both; its main store is on SW Yamhill between Fourth and Fifth Avenues. Among the highly touted retail shops in the original airy four-level pavilion are those familiar to other Rouse development projects, such as Seattle's Westlake Center and New York's South Street Seaport: the San Francisco–based cookware store **WILLIAMS-SONOMA**; established clothing shops such as **EDDIE BAUER, TALBOT'S**, and **J. CREW**; and the eclectic **SHARPER IMAGE** and **MUSEUM COMPANY**. Surrounding the lovely three-story rose fountain in the center of the new addition are several stores new to Portland: **BARCELINO** sells upscale international clothing for men and women, **JOHNSTON & MURPHY** retails classic shoes and belts, and **APRIL CORNELL** offers French country clothes and home furnishings. You can buy sport shoes at the **NEW BALANCE** store, French soaps and lotions at **L'OCCITANE EN PROVENCE**, and completely natural lotions and oils at **ORIGINS**. Then you can eat your fill at **TODAI'S** Japanese seafood buffet (see review in the Restaurants chapter).

To the west and south of Pioneer Courthouse Square, on SW 10th Avenue between Yamhill and Taylor Streets, is the **MULTNOMAH COUNTY CENTRAL LIBRARY**. Beautifully restored in the mid-1990s at a cost of $24 million, it is an architectural gem worth a visit even if you're not feeling bookish. The **FRIENDS LIBRARY STORE** (503/988-5911), a gift shop for bibliophiles, is just off the lobby, and there's even a Starbucks cafe on the main floor.

Portland's has many other signature buildings. On SW Fifth Avenue between W Burnside and SW Oak Streets is the tallest, the **US BANCORP TOWER**, known to locals as "Big Pink" and offering a terrific view from **ATWATER'S** restaurant on the 30th floor. South on Broadway between SW Salmon and Main Streets is another pink-tinted and affectionately nicknamed structure, **1000 BROADWAY**—the "Ban Roll-On Building"—which houses a deli, a retail space, and a set of cinemas, the **BROADWAY METROPLEX**.

The most controversial of downtown's architectural landmarks is Michael Graves's love-it-or-hate-it postmodern **PORTLAND BUILDING** (1120 SW 5th Ave), on which crouches **PORTLANDIA**, an enormous hammered-copper statue. City offices are located here and next door at the lovely **CITY HALL**, which recently underwent a total renovation to take it into the next century.

Closer to the river, the bold brick **KOIN CENTER** (SW Clay St and 3rd Ave), like a blue-tipped pen, has left its indelible mark on Portland's skyline; inside are six cinemas and offices for its namesake, KOIN-TV. Kitty corner to KOIN, across SW Third Avenue and Clay Street, are the 18-foot cascades of the **IRA KELLER FOUNTAIN**, designed specifically with summer kid-fun in mind. Across from that is the **KELLER AUDITORIUM** (formerly the Civic Auditorium), where many local and traveling performers take the stage. **PUBLIC REST ROOMS** are located on the main floor of the Clay Street parking garage, between SW Third and Fourth Avenues.

Farther west, a peaceful component of Portland's downtown is the elm-lined oasis known as the **SOUTH PARK BLOCKS**. If Pioneer Courthouse Square is the heart of the city, the Park Blocks are its green backbone; sandwiched between SW Park and Ninth Avenues, the blocks are reserved almost entirely for public use. In 1852 a 25-block stretch running parallel to Broadway was set aside for a park. However, in 1871 eight blocks ended up in private hands, and they continue to be developed.

The South Park Blocks (demarcated on street signs as the Cultural District) begin in a pedestrians-only zone on the **PORTLAND STATE UNIVERSITY** campus and continue north for 12 blocks, hedged neatly along the way with student apartments, upscale condominiums, and public institutions such as the **PORTLAND ART MUSEUM** (between SW Jefferson and Main Sts; see separate listing in this section), the **OREGON HISTORY CENTER** (between SW Jefferson and Madison Sts; see separate listing in this section), and the **PORTLAND CENTER FOR THE PERFORMING ARTS** and **ARLENE SCHNITZER CONCERT HALL** (between SW Madison and Salmon Sts). The park continues to the doorstep of the private Arlington Club on SW Salmon Street, where nearby you'll find **SOUTHPARK**, a Mediterranean seafood restaurant (look up on the corner of the building for an eyeful of salmon) and a bustling **DIEDRICH COFFEE PEOPLE**. In summer months the **PORTLAND FARMERS MARKET** sells fresh produce in the South Park Blocks near Salmon Street on Wednesdays from 10am to 2pm and on Saturdays farther south near Portland State from 8am to 1pm.

Sculpture abounds in the South Park Blocks. Tipped-over granite monoliths adorn the three-church block between SW Columbia and Jefferson Streets, Theodore Roosevelt and his horse guard the next block north, and a somber statue of Abe Lincoln stands outside the art museum's North Wing. At the **PORTLAND CENTER FOR THE PERFORMING ARTS** (1111 SW Park Ave; 503/796-9293) be sure to view the Henk Pander mural *Portland Town* through the glass on the west side of the building. Just across SW Main Street (this block is closed during concerts) is the larger **ARLENE SCHNITZER CONCERT HALL**, aka "The Schnitz," a plush and ornate theater that's home to the Oregon Symphony and the Portland

Arts and Lectures Series. Purchase tickets for events at either location through the Portland Center for the Performing Arts.

The Park Blocks seem to end on SW Salmon Street, but they pick up again at SW Washington Street and **O'BRYANT SQUARE** (named for Portland's first mayor, Hugh Donaldson O'Bryant), with a jet engine–like fountain encircled by brick steps, a good spot to catch noontime rays in summer. (See Skidmore/Old Town/Chinatown in the Neighborhoods section of this chapter for a description of the North Park Blocks.) *Map:A1–J6*

3) TOM MCCALL WATERFRONT PARK/RIVERPLACE

On the west side of the Willamette River from the Marquam Bridge north to the Steel Bridge; 503/823-2223 It is a rare city that has both the planning sense and the political will to reclaim territory taken over by the automobile, but that is precisely what Portland did at the eastern edge of its downtown. In the early 1970s, Portlanders decided they didn't like the way the city had grown—an expressway called Harbor Drive impeded access to the otherwise scenic Willamette River. So the Portland Development Commission did what the locals asked: it took the road away and replaced it with a showcase riverfront park.

TOM MCCALL WATERFRONT PARK (named for the governor credited with giving Oregon its reputation as a "green" state) has become indispensable. Its showplace sweeping lawns are the hardest-working turf in the city; from Cinco de Mayo through Labor Day, it's rare to find a weekend when something (the Rose Festival, park concerts, the Bite) isn't going on here. The riverside promenade is shared by anglers, walkers, runners, Rollerbladers, and cyclists, and in the summer, many cool off with a dash through the **SALMON STREET SPRINGS** fountain at the foot of SW Salmon.

Toward the southern end of the park sits **RIVERPLACE**, a complex that includes the elegant **RIVERPLACE HOTEL**, a health club, condominiums, and a short promenade lined with specialty shops. Farther to the south, there's covered parking, more shops, apartments, and the efficient **STANFORD'S RESTAURANT AND BAR** (1831 SW River Dr; 503/241-5051), which provides a business atmosphere for riverfront power lunches. South of RiverPlace stands a recently completed development that brings together apartment buildings with the new world headquarters for PG & E Gas Transmission Northwest—thus establishing an attractive "mixed-use" neighborhood.

In the middle of the park sits **MCCALL'S WATERFRONT CAFE** (1020 SW Naito Pkwy; 503/248-9710), a fine place to congregate on a sunny day. The promenade stretches north under the Burnside Bridge, passing on its way the mast of the USS *Oregon* at the **BATTLESHIP OREGON MARINE MEMORIAL**. Beyond it lies the **WATERFRONT STORY GARDEN**— a whimsical tribute by artist Larry Kirkland to storytellers of all ages, complete with etchings in granite and cobblestone of animals, queries ("What do you remember?"), and "safe havens." Next, the walkway passes 100 Japanese cherry trees in the **JAPANESE-AMERICAN HISTORICAL PLAZA**, which honors the Japanese-Americans interned during the Second World War. Memorable quotes by Oregonians who were interned are set in boulders along the pathway. To the north, at the foot of the Steel Bridge, sits the **FRIENDSHIP CIRCLE**, a sculpture that emits the sounds of a Japanese flute and drum and honors the strong sister-city relationship between Portland and Sapporo, Japan. The park ends just beyond, but the walkway continues north another quarter mile or so.

If you can't take in the entire 2-mile stretch of Waterfront Park all at once, at least check out **MILL ENDS PARK**, located in the SW Naito Parkway median at Taylor Street. A plaque at the site tells how a hole for a lamppost became the smallest park in the nation; despite its size, weddings are occasionally held at the spot. *Map:A5–M5* &

4) PORTLAND ART MUSEUM

1219 SW Park Ave; 503/226-2811 The Portland Art Museum—or PAM—is the oldest art museum in the Pacific Northwest; its southernmost building, designed by Portland's venerable architect, the late Pietro Belluschi, is a landmark structure on the South Park Blocks. The museum's permanent holdings span 35 centuries and include Native American art, tribal art of Cameroon, prehistoric Chinese artifacts, and modern European and American sculpture and painting. Thanks to an ambitious capital campaign, the museum has recently added new galleries for permanent exhibits, including Centers for Native American Art and Northwest Art, two new galleries for special exhibitions, a new community education center, and a new museum shop and cafe. Furthermore, its courtyard has been transformed into an inviting sculpture garden featuring historic and contemporary work from the museum's collection.

PAM attracts some of the world's top touring exhibitions: the Imperial Tombs of China, Splendors of Ancient Egypt, and Stroganoff: The Palace and Collections of a Russian Noble Family. Every Wednesday from October through April, PAM lets down its hair after work and warms up with two hours of live music in the North Wing, at 5:30pm. Tickets for Museum After Hours are $6, $3 for museum members. Admission to the museum is $7.50 for adults, $6 for seniors and students 16 and over, and $4 for children 2–15. *Tues–Sat 10am–5pm; www.port landartmuseum.org; map:F1* &

5) OREGON MUSEUM OF SCIENCE AND INDUSTRY (OMSI)

1945 SE Water Ave; 503/797-4000 The 219,000-square-foot Oregon Museum of Science and Industry (OMSI), with its spectacular view of downtown from the east bank of the Willamette, is a delightful diversion no matter the weather—and it's not just for kids.

The facility features six immense exhibit halls, a planetarium that doubles as a theater in the round, an IMAX theater, a riverfront cafe, and a naval submarine, the USS *Blueback*, which is permanently docked for tours for those 4 years and older (admission is $3 extra).

You can't miss this angular brick showpiece, domed with a copper cap topped by a Ferrari-red smokestack and a glass pyramid atrium. The 18½-acre industrial location (formerly owned by Portland General Electric Company, which donated the land) is appropriate for a museum where science and industry are the emphasis: the Marquam Bridge soars just above, and a PGE substation still operates at one corner of the property.

Inside, you can poke around an old turbine, stand on a platform and feel an earthquake, touch a tornado in the Natural Science Hall, observe nutrient cycling in the Greenway, or cruise the Internet in the High Tech Hall. The numerous hands-on exhibits are popular with people of all ages, but for the very young—and their grateful parents—there's Discovery Space, a children's room with tennis balls to feed into a pneumatic tube, a Lego table, and live reptiles. The Murdock Planetarium features a new state-of-the-art Digistar projection system, which displays 10 times as many stars as the former system and can simulate three-dimensional space travel (admission is $3 extra).

Traveling exhibits—robotics, for example, or early humans—prove educational as well as entertaining. Museum admission is $6.50 for adults, $4.50 for seniors and children 4 to 13; Omnimax (the IMAX theater) admission is an additional $6.50 for adults, $4.50 for seniors and children (ask about the $15 package admission if you'd like to see everything). After Labor Day until mid-June every Thursday after 2pm, OMSI offers two for the price of one admission to all attractions. Evening laser-light extravaganzas in the planetarium cost $6.50. Memberships are available. *Every day 9:30am–7pm (mid-June–Labor Day); Tues–Sun 9:30am–5:30pm (after Labor Day–mid-June); www.omsi.edu; map:A9* &

6) JAPANESE GARDEN

611 SW Kingston Ave; 503/223-1321 In 1988, the Japanese ambassador to the United States pronounced this the most beautiful and authentic Japanese garden outside of Japan, and it continues to enthrall visitors. An extraordinarily peaceful spot, it actually comprises five gardens: the traditional Flat Garden, the secluded and flowing Strolling Pond Garden, the Tea Garden with a *chashitsu* (ceremonial teahouse), the stark Dry Landscape Garden, and a miniature Natural Garden. In contrast with the exuberant rose blossoms down the hill, this is an oasis of lush greenery, winding paths, and tranquil ponds. Flowering cherries and azaleas accent the grounds come spring; in summer, the Japanese irises bloom, and in autumn, the laceleaf maples glow orange and red. Eaves and posts of the Japanese pavilion frame the Flat Garden to the west and Mount Hood to the east. A shop in the garden stocks books on such topics as the art of Japanese flower arranging and traditional tea ceremonies, and one on Portland's garden itself. Admission is $6 for adults, $4 for seniors, and $3.50 for students and children over 5. Guided public tours are offered daily at 10:45am and 2:30pm, April through September. *Every day 10am–7pm (Apr–Sept), 10am–4pm (Oct–Mar); map:HH7*

7) OREGON ZOO

4001 SW Canyon Rd; 503/226-1561 What began over a century ago as a seaman-turned-veterinarian's menagerie on SW Third Avenue and Morrison Street has since grown into an outstanding 64-acre zoo in Washington Park, winning awards for exhibits showcasing the lush flora and fauna of the Cascades as well as the colony of endangered Peruvian Humboldt penguins, well protected (and thriving) here.

Born in 1962, Packy—the first Asian elephant born in the Western Hemisphere—blazed the trail for the pachyderm breeding program. Now, some two dozen newborns later, the elephant program continues apace, with excellent viewing opportunities no matter the weather. The zoo has a complex chimpanzee exhibit, featuring an arena architecturally designed with the natural behavior of the chimps in mind. The African savanna exhibit features black rhinoceros, giraffes, impalas, zebras, and birds; the African rain forest exhibit features hourly rainstorms and more than two dozen animal species, including the naked mole-rat.

The newest exhibit is Great Northwest: A Crest to Coast Adventure, where visitors can journey through lush mountain forests and wild coast-lines. It's being completed in phases, the first of which was Cascade Crest, where mountain goats roam a simulated rocky cliff face, and the second was Steller Cove—home to Steller's sea lions. Eventually, the completed exhibit will include black bears, wolverines, bald eagles, and other Northwest animals in a 90-year-old forest on the north end of the zoo. The Cascade Grill restaurant, which looks out over an alpine setting, serves better-than-average zoo food; its carpet and metalwork chande-liers are commissioned art pieces that reflect the Pacific Northwest.

During warm-weather months you can catch the small steam train that chugs through the zoo and down to the Rose Garden ($2.75 for adults; $2 for seniors and children 3–11); in spring and for special events the train makes a shorter run around the zoo's perimeter. On the second Tuesday of each month, zoo admission is free after 1pm; regular admis-sion is $6.50 for adults, $5 for seniors, and $4 for kids 3–11. On summer evenings crowds throng to the grassy outdoor amphitheater for live music concerts. In fall, the zoo hosts a World Animal Festival, and on the weekend before Halloween, kids trick-or-treat and go on a scavenger hunt at the zoo's Howloween celebration. In December, the Zoo Lights Festival is an incandescent holiday tradition. *Every day except Christmas; gate hours are 9am–6pm (Apr 1–Sept 30), 9am–4pm (Oct 1–Mar 31); visitors can stay in the zoo for 1 hour after the gate closes; www.oregonzoo.com; map:HH7* &

8) PEARL DISTRICT

North of Burnside to NW Marshall St between NW 8th and 15th Aves
In the last 15 years, warehouses and wholesalers' storefronts in the aged industrial Northwest Triangle district have taken on new lives. Empty spaces have been turned into clean-lined art galleries, antique show-rooms, furniture stores, bookstores, and lofts for upscale urban dwellers. Construction and renovation continue along the cobblestone streets (built at the turn of the century from stones used as ballast by sailing vessels); the current multiblock redevelopment of the former Henry Weinhard's brewery on W Burnside Street is the latest, but certainly not the last, office/retail/housing metamorphosis to take place. When the dust finally clears, the area will be substantially transformed—and considerably more populated.

The Pearl is *the* place to gallery-browse, especially on the FIRST THURSDAY of each month, when galleries throw open their doors to show off their collections (see Galleries in this chapter) and beautiful people stroll the sidewalks. If you're lucky enough to catch First Thursday on a warm evening, the show on the sidewalk may be the best: artists of all stripes come to hawk their wares, creating a vibrant street scene.

Besides the fine art galleries, the Pearl District is saturated with "functional art" galleries and hot furniture stores. Among them: P. H. REED (1100 NW Glisan St; 503/274-7080), for a variety of stylish, con-temporary furniture and lighting designs; LUX LIGHTING (1109 NW Glisan St; 503/299-6754), for lamps that have life even when they're turned off; and FULL UPRIGHT POSITION (1200 NW Everett St; 503/228-6190), for modern home furnishings. PACIFIC ORIENT TRADERS (221 NW 11th Ave; 503/241-9914) and GALLERY ZEN (525 NW 10th Ave; 503/221-3184) specialize in antiques and furniture from Asia, while DOMA (205 NW 10th Ave; 503/222-7366) features contem-porary home furnishings from China, Indonesia, and Japan; CIRCA (1204 NW Glisan St; 503/221-1269) is filled with fine antiques and home accessories from Europe, and A PLACE IN TIME (526 NW 13th Ave; 503/227-5223) sells hand-painted plates and other tabletop accessories.

Nearby are a few of the district's interesting retail outlets: check out the WHOLE NINE YARDS (1033 NW Glisan St; 503/223-2880) for gorgeous fabric; **HANNA ANDERSSON** (327 NW 10th Ave; 503/321-5275), for colorful cotton kids' clothing; **AUBERGINE** (1100 NW Glisan St; 503/228-7313), for fine women's clothing; **DIECI SOLI** (304 NW 11th Ave; 503/222-4221), for April Cornell linens and Italian pottery; and **DEHEN KNITTING COMPANY'S FACTORY OUTLET STORE** (924 NW Flanders St; 503/222-3871)—the place to buy that letter jacket you could only earn in high school. **DESPERADO** (1321 NW Hoyt St; 503/294-2952) sells everything western, from apparel to accessories; the **FRENCH QUARTER** (536 NW 14th Ave; 503/223-3879) retails fine European linens; **CAPTAIN'S NAUTICAL SUPPLIES** (138 NW 10th Ave; 503/227-1648) sells everything you need to navigate—charts, maps, navigation and weather instruments, and binoculars; and **VISAGE EYEWEAR** (810 NW 12th Ave; 503/944-5475) is the place to find perfect, artful frames.

A couple of notable bookstores are here: **MORRISON BOOKS** (530 NW 12th Ave; 503/295-6882) specializes in books on photography, art, and architecture in fine and rare editions; **POWELL'S CITY OF BOOKS** (1005 W Burnside St; 503/228-4651) features a city block's worth (68,000 square feet!) of new and used books (see separate listing in this section). A visit to this literary institution is a tour in itself, especially with its new four-story addition and art gallery, so finish by resting your feet in the **ANNE HUGHES COFFEE ROOM**, in the southwest corner of the store. You can also get your coffee fix at **TORREFAZIONE ITALIA** (1140 NW Everett St; 503/224-9896) or the **PEARL BAKERY** (102 NW 9th Ave; 503/827-0910), where you can also get uncommonly good pastries and sandwiches. If tea's what you want a cuppa, the **TEA ZONE** (510 NW 11th Ave; 503/221-2130) sells teas from around the world by the cup and by the tin in its elegant and cozy tea room, as well as miniature teapots from China and Japan. At **750 ML.** (232 NW 12th Ave; 503/224-1432), a small corkage fee allows you to choose a bottle of wine from the racks and enjoy it in the comfy shop along with breads and cheeses. For more substantial fare, stop in for lunch at **IN GOOD TASTE** (231 NW 11th Ave; 503/241-7960), a cooking school and gourmet shop that serves a bistro lunch; **LITTLE WING CAFE** (529 NW 13th Ave; 503/228-3101), for homemade soups and a huge array of cookies; or **HOLDEN'S** (524 NW 14th Ave; 503/916-0099), a deli serving soups and sandwiches. More food, too: **KEN'S HOME PLATE** (1208 NW Glisan St; 503/517-8935) offers such tempting goodies as Tuscan meatloaf and tomato feta tart and has a few tables for diners to eat there, too.

One of Portland's oldest microbreweries, **BRIDGEPORT BREWERY & PUB** (1313 NW Marshall St; 503/241-3612) serves exceptional pizza along with its tasty beer (see the separate Breweries and Brewpubs listing in this section); or select beer from over 30 different microbrews at **MICKEY FINN'S** (1339 NW Flanders St; 503/222-5910) to eat with your salad, fish and chips, or burger. Lively **PARAGON RESTAURANT AND BAR** (1309 NW Hoyt St; 503/833-5060) serves Northwest cuisine for lunch and dinner; **¡OBA!** (555 NW 12th Ave; 503/228-6161) offers a festive array of Latin American–influenced cuisine; and **CAFE AZUL** (112 NW 9th Ave; 503/525-4422) specializes in authentic regional dishes from Oaxaca and southern Mexico. One of the Pearl's newest restaurants is **BLUEHOUR** (in the Wieden & Kennedy building at the corner of NW 12th Ave and Everett St; 503/226-3394), created by the founder of long-time Portland favorite Zefiro (R.I.P.). (See the Restaurants chapter for reviews of all four.)

On the eastern edge of the Pearl, the **NORTH PARK BLOCKS** stretch from W Burnside Street to NW Glisan Street. Find walking paths, basketball courts, and playground equipment in this five-block stretch; watch for Art in the Pearl, which takes place over the Labor Day weekend. Bordering the park are retail shops, lofts, and the granite colonnade and courtyard of the majestic Italian Renaissance U.S. Customs House. *Map:K2–3 and N2–3*

9) NORTHWEST PORTLAND

North of W Burnside St, centered on NW 21st and 23rd Aves For thousands of Portlanders, "Northwest" means home, but for nonresidents it mostly means shopping and dining along two of the most bustling avenues in the city. Lively, urbane NW 23rd Avenue purposefully combines elements of funk with high fashion, making for a smart street scene, while two blocks away, NW 21st Avenue continues to be home to a variety of excellent restaurants despite the loss of a few longtime favorites.

In block after block along NW 23rd Avenue—from W Burnside Street to NW Thurman Street—there's a wealth of cosmopolitan attractions. (It helps in orienting yourself to know that the streets in this part of town are named in alphabetical order from south to north: Burnside, Couch, Davis, and so on.) Down the avenue, many Victorian homes have been remodeled into small retail enclaves, and attractive new developments have also been built, nosing out less sightly structures. "Trendy-Third," as it's affectionately known, draws an eclectic crowd: neighborhood first-graders on scooters weave among open-mouthed tourists, determined shoppers busily compare goods in the many housewares and clothing stores, and the cafe crowd lingers at tables along the sidewalk (and this crowd may surprise you: look for the lineup of Harleys parked every evening outside the local Starbucks). It's easy to pass a day here. Parking can be tough; your best bet for spaces is on the east-west cross streets. Or take Tri-Met (503/238-7433). After July 2001, you'll have yet another transportation option: the Portland Streetcar will run from Portland State University through downtown and the Pearl District to NW 23rd Avenue (www.portlandstreetcar.org).

A good way to see NW 23rd Avenue is to walk up one side and down the other. In the **UPTOWN SHOPPING CENTER** (W Burnside St and NW 24th Ave), check out the fabulous takeout at **ELEPHANT'S DELICATESSEN** (13 NW 23rd Pl; 503/224-3955); **PHIL'S UPTOWN MEAT MARKET** (17 NW 23rd Pl; 503/224-9541), where special orders are no problem; the district's utterly dependable **UPTOWN HARDWARE** (27 NW 23rd Pl; 503/227-5375); and **FOOTHILL BROILER** (33 NW 23rd Pl; 503/223-0287), a top-drawer cafeteria.

Nearby is the playful **TWIST** (30 NW 23rd Pl; 503/224-0334), offering colorful earthenware, glassware, and furniture, and **SMITH & HAWKEN** (26 NW 23rd Pl; 503/274-9561), which elevates gardening to an art form—and a consumerist enterprise. A bit to the north is the big clapboard **WESTOVER PLACE**, where you'll find acre-sized pancakes at the **CAMEO CAFE** (2340 NW Westover Rd; 503/221-6542) and the city's original—and many say best—bento spot, **BIG DAN'S WEST COAST BENTO** (2346 NW Westover Rd; 503/227-1779).

Speaking of food, this part of town has some of the best around. Pizza lovers can choose between classic East Coast style (**ESCAPE FROM NEW YORK PIZZA**, 622 NW 23rd Ave; 503/227-5423) or a little more tarted-up (**PIZZICATO**, 530 NW 23rd Ave; 503/242-0023). Get a thick corned beef sandwich and all the pickles you can eat at **KORNBLATT'S DELICATESSEN** (628 NW 23rd Ave; 503/242-0055); a towering, intense Autumn Meringue at **PAPA HAYDN** (701 NW 23rd Ave; 503/228-7317); a tasty salad or burger at **JO BAR ROTISSERIE** (715 NW 23rd Ave; 503/222-0048); or a scoop of Black Tiger (espresso ice cream) at the mod **COFFEE PEOPLE** (533 NW 23rd Ave; 503/221-0235). On hot days, you can sip cold drinks alfresco at **SAMMY'S RESTAURANT AND BAR** (333 NW 23rd Ave; 503/222-3123). Coffee flows freely here, but the best places to linger over an Americano and a few biscotti are **TORREFAZIONE ITALIA** (838 NW 23rd Ave; 503/228-2528) or the funkier **COFFEE TIME** over on NW 21st Avenue (712 NW 21st Ave; 503/497-1090), open 24 hours.

The area's bustling restaurant scene shows no sign of fading, thanks to newcomers that have replaced longtime favorites. These include **LASLOW'S** (2327 NW Kearney St; 503/241-8092) for Northwest cuisine with a French accent; **SERRATTO** (2112 NW Kearney St; 503/221-1195) for Italian food in a classy setting; and **LUCY'S TABLE** (706 NW 21st Ave; 503/226-6126) for Mediterranean-inspired food.

Old standbys include two Italian stars: **BASTAS** (410 NW 21st Ave; 503/274-1572), which serves outstanding pasta, and **CAFFE MINGO** (807 NW 21st Ave; 503/226-4646), which regulars frequent for its tradition of well-prepared food in a setting at once romantic and convivial. Two of the hottest restaurants in town, cutting-edge **WILDWOOD** (1221 NW

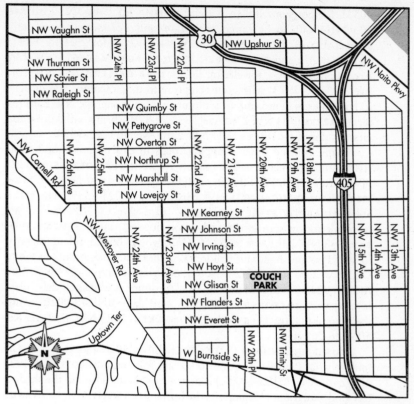

NORTHWEST PORTLAND

21st Ave; 503/248-9663) and diminutive **PALEY'S PLACE** (1204 NW 21st Ave; 503/243-2403) sit across from one another on NW 21st Avenue.

If you're dining in, stock up at **CITY MARKET NW** (735 NW 21st Ave; 503/221-3007), where the finest pasta, seafood, fruits, vegetables, and meats are gathered under one roof, and stop at **LINER & ELSEN LTD.** (202 NW 21st Ave; 503/241-9463) for the perfect bottle of wine.

On NW 23rd Avenue at Pettygrove Street is the home of **CLEAR CREEK DISTILLERY** (1430 NW 23rd Ave; 503/248-9470), which rivals European brandy makers with its pear and apple eaux-de-vie and its grappa.

Even Martha Stewart would have a ball shopping NW 23rd Avenue, where shops offer every "necessity" for the home. Standouts among these are **RESTORATION HARDWARE** (315 NW 23rd Ave; 503/228-6226), for upscale fixtures and accessories; the recently expanded **KITCHEN KABOODLE** (404 NW 23rd Ave; 503/241-4040), for everything from lawn furniture to egg timers; **URBINO** (521 NW 23rd Ave; 503/220-

0053), for gorgeous Italian pottery; **MAMMA RO** (940 NW 23rd Ave; 503/241-4960) for ceramic tableware and accessories from Italy; **SOULEIADO** (529 NW 23rd Ave; 503/464-9211) for cheerful French country decor; and **THE COMPLEAT BED & BREAKFAST** (615 NW 23rd Ave; 503/221-0193), for elegant linens. **IMBA GALLERY** (818 NW 23rd Ave; 503/295-2973) sells stone sculpture from Zimbabwe and displays its larger pieces in its outdoor sculpture garden. Longtime NW 23rd resident **DAZZLE** (704 NW 23rd Ave; 503/224-1294) brims with kooky artifacts, as does **3 MONKEYS** (803 NW 23rd Ave; 503/222-9894).

Fashion is the other shopping focus in this neighborhood, from stylish undergarments meant for few to see (**JANE'S OBSESSION**, 728 NW 23rd Ave; 503/221-1490) to stylish spectacles that help you to see (**REYNOLD'S OPTICAL**, 625 NW 23rd Ave; 503/221-6539). The venerable **ELIZABETH STREET** (635 NW 23rd Ave; 503/243-2456) has women's cotton sportswear and rayon dresses, and at **ZELDA'S SHOE BAR** (633 NW 23rd Ave; 503/226-0363), you're bound to find footwear to suit. Hip and handknit children's clothes hang downstairs at **MAKO** (732 NW 23rd Ave; 503/274-9081); **BEDTIME STORIES** (524 NW 23rd Ave; 503/223-7492) sells upscale kids' furniture as well as clothes. Teens love **URBAN OUTFITTERS** (201 NW 23rd Ave; 503/248-0020), while their moms find traveling clothes at **TIMBUKTU** (2323 NW Westover Rd; 503/226-2694).

MUSIC MILLENNIUM (801 NW 23rd Ave; 503/248-0163) is to CD junkies what Powell's Books is to literary folk, and **CHILD'S PLAY** (907 NW 23rd Ave; 503/224-5586) is a wall-to-wall toy store. In the shadow of Good Samaritan Hospital sits the hospitable **TWENTY-THIRD AVENUE BOOKS** (1015 NW 23rd Ave; 503/224-5097).

After dark, cinema lovers ease into the rocking chairs that serve as seats at one of Portland's favorite movie houses, **CINEMA 21** (616 NW 21st Ave; 503/223-4515), for art-house and foreign flicks.

For additional information on establishments listed here, see the Restaurants and Shopping chapters. *Map:FF7*

10) HOYT ARBORETUM

4000 SW Fairview Blvd; 503/228-8733 Sweeping views, 10 miles of trails, and more than 850 species of trees and shrubs—all neatly labeled—make up Washington Park's 175-acre tree garden. It's an international collection of woody plants, including the nation's largest assortment of conifer species. Blossoms dust the Magnolia Trail in spring; a three-quarter-mile section of the Bristlecone Pine Trail is paved for wheelchair access. In the arboretum's southwest corner is the Vietnam Veterans' Living Memorial, an inspiring outdoor cathedral commemorating Oregonians who died in that war. Maps are available at the arboretum's visitor center (9am–4pm), and weekend guided walks (April through

October, 2pm) begin there. A few of the trails are wheelchair accessible. *Grounds open every day 6am–10pm; visitor center open 9am–4pm every day except Thanksgiving, Christmas, and New Year's Day; www.parks.ci.portland.or.us/parks/hoytarboretum.htm; map:HH7*

11) OREGON HISTORY CENTER

1200 SW Park Ave; 503/222-1741 An eight-story-high trompe l'oeil mural welcomes you to enter the brick courtyard of the Oregon History Center, one of the landmark buildings in the South Park Blocks. The center, which is the headquarters of the Oregon Historical Society, houses a museum, archives, a research library, and a store, all open to the public.

The museum's exhibits range from Native American artifacts to the actual penny used in the coin toss that decided Portland's name to a multimedia exhibit that explores Portland's light rail system. The archives consist of manuscripts, oral histories, and more than 2 million photographs, prints of which are available for purchase. The museum store, at SW Broadway and Madison, sells gifts, jewelry, and books. Admission is $6 for adults, $3 for students, and $1.50 for children 6–12. Seniors get in free on Thursdays. *Tues–Sat 10am–5pm; Sun noon–5pm; Thurs until 8pm; www.ohs.org; map:F2* &

12) RIVER CRUISES ON THE COLUMBIA AND WILLAMETTE RIVERS

Before the arrival of railroads and paved roads, people could hail a steamboat just about anywhere between Portland and Eugene, Astoria and The Dalles. Stern-wheelers still navigate the waters of the Columbia and Willamette Rivers and offer some relief from today's crowded highways—but also, more importantly, give patrons an opportunity to see the region from a riverine viewpoint.

From its summer base about 45 minutes east of Portland, the sternwheeler *Columbia Gorge* (a triple-deck paddle wheeler) voyages through the dramatic Columbia River Gorge. Sound a bit touristy? There are plenty of Portlanders who've taken the scenic trip several times and still love it. In early October, the 147-foot vessel returns to Waterfront Park in Portland, where it takes guests up and down the Willamette River on dinner-dance, lunch, and brunch cruises, special holiday cruises, and cruises for chartered wedding receptions and company outings. Fares range from $12.95 to $37.95. Call ahead for the exact schedule; 503/223-3928. *www.sternwheeler.com;* &

The *Rose*, a 92-foot stern-wheeler replica, sails from the OMSI dock on the east side of the Willamette. The downriver trip gets quite industrial, passing shipyards, grain terminals, 7 of Portland's 12 bridges, and perhaps the world's largest dry dock. The more scenic direction is upriver toward Milwaukie, passing Sellwood, Oaks Park, Johns Landing, and gracious old homes on the bluffs overlooking the Willamette. The 130-

passenger, double-deck stern-wheeler is often privately chartered, but public cruises are available; prices are $25 for brunch, $35 for dinner. Call for the schedule; 503/286-7673. *www.sternwheelrose.com*

The *Portland Spirit* and its sister crafts, the *Willamette Star* and *Crystal Dolphin*, offer fine dining, dancing, and sightseeing cruises up and down the Willamette River. The *Portland Spirit* leaves from its berth near the Salmon Street Springs in Tom McCall Waterfront Park; catch the *Willamette Star* and *Crystal Dolphin* at the RiverPlace Marina. You may want to reserve this activity for special occasions: Dinner cruises have climbed over the $50 mark, a midday lunch tour costs around $30, and the Sunday champagne brunch cruise is around $35 (all prices are lower for seniors and children). Two less expensive options are available without dining: evening dance cruises are available Saturday night for $10, and sightseeing tours costs $15. Charters are available; call 503/224-3900. *www.portlandspirit.com;* &

WILLAMETTE JETBOAT EXCURSIONS offers perhaps the most exciting way to experience the Willamette River on a public boat—if you don't mind the possibility of getting splashed. Their open-air jetboats ride close to the water and take sightseers upriver, past riverfront homes—the spectacular and the modest—all the way to Willamette Falls in Oregon City and downriver to Portland's cargo docks and shipyards. The two-hour, 37-mile boat tours depart from OMSI every day from the end of April to the middle of October. Adults are $25, children (4–11) are $15, and kids 3 and under are free. You can also plan a trip for 20 or more people that includes lunch or dinner at a riverside park. Call for the schedule and reservations; 503/231-1532. *www.jetboatpdx.com*

13) END OF THE OREGON TRAIL INTERPRETIVE CENTER/ OREGON CITY HISTORIC SITES

1726 Washington St, and other locations in Oregon City; 503/657-9336 Under the Paul Bunyan–sized covered wagons in Oregon City, the **END OF THE OREGON TRAIL INTERPRETIVE CENTER** houses a mixed-media dramatization about life 150 years ago—"The Spirit Lives On"— as well as costumed history interpreters who teach Oregon Trail 101 (do you know how eggs were transported before egg cartons?). There are exhibits of artifacts and heirlooms from the trail as well. Admission is $5.50, $4.50 for seniors, $3 for children 5 to 12, and children under 5 are free. You'll want to call ahead to check show times; you won't be allowed in unless you're in the tour, except to see a few exhibits and the well-stocked museum store. *Mon–Sat 9am–5pm, Sun 10am–5pm; www.endoftheoregontrail.org; map:OO3* &

In addition to being the official end of the Oregon Trail, Oregon City lays claim to many firsts—among them the first public library west of the Rockies (1842), the first incorporated city west of the Rockies (1844), and the first navigation locks in the Northwest (1873). Much of the city's history is portrayed in murals on its downtown buildings. **THE OREGON CITY MUNICIPAL ELEVATOR** (at the foot of the bluff on 7th St), one of only four municipal elevators in the world, takes you from the town's river level up to the top of the bluff, where, a few blocks away, you'll find the **MCLOUGHLIN HOUSE NATIONAL HISTORIC SITE** (713 Center St; 503/656-5146). Dr. John McLoughlin, the "Father of Oregon," built this house when he was forced to retire as chief factor of the British Hudson's Bay Company at **FORT VANCOUVER** (see separate listing in this section). Here you can learn how McLoughlin helped claim the Oregon Territory for the United States and see some of the home's original furnishings, including the dining room table and chairs, the Staffordshire china, and the hand-carved bed from Scotland. Admission is $4 for adults, $3 for seniors, $2 for children 6–17. *Tues–Sat 10am–4pm, Sun 1pm–4pm (Feb–Dec), closed holidays; www.mcloughlinhouse.org; map:OO7*

About 10 blocks south, along the **MCLOUGHLIN PROMENADE**, the **CLACKAMAS COUNTY HISTORICAL MUSEUM** (211 Tumwater Dr; 503/655-5574) has ancient petroglyphs, a 12-foot-high statue of Lady Justice, and the original plat map of San Francisco, which was filed in 1850 in Oregon City, site of the only federal courthouse in the Oregon Territory. From the museum's third floor you get a panoramic view of Willamette Falls, where Native Americans gathered for centuries to catch and trade salmon, and where, later, settlers used the river's power for saw, grain, and paper mills. Adult admission is $4; less for seniors and children. *Map:OO7*

14) POWELL'S CITY OF BOOKS

1005 W Burnside St; 503/228-4651 National bookseller chains can open as many superstores in town as they please, but Powell's will always be top dog in Portland. Even those who prefer smaller, more intimate bookstores find themselves lured to Powell's out of sheer gluttony. With more than a million volumes filling a city block at the main Burnside store, it is most definitely the largest bookstore in the country—and tourists should plan at least an afternoon here, if just to say they've seen it.

The store provides maps to guide buyers through its dozens of sections, from Automotive to Zen. Tucked into the maze are a rare-book room, the Anne Hughes Coffee Room, and a children's book area. Several times each week, touring authors of national repute read from their work in the Pearl Room, part of the store's latest expansion. The Pearl Room also houses the Basil Hallward Gallery, which displays art and photography from local—and international—artists. The new northwest entrance to the store is anchored by the Pillar of Books—a nine-foot column of Tenino sandstone in which eight of the world's great books have been carved. Powell's even has a **PARKING GARAGE** (enter on NW 11th Ave).

Powell's also has spawned offspring, each with its own specialty. **POWELL'S TRAVEL STORE** (SW 6th Ave and Yamhill St; 503/228-1108), in the southeast corner of Pioneer Courthouse Square, carries guidebooks to everywhere. On your way out of town at the airport, check out **POWELL'S BOOKS AT PDX** (503/249-1950), which stocks mostly new volumes. A few blocks from the main store, **POWELL'S TECHNICAL BOOKSTORE** (33 NW Park Ave; 503/228-3906) has the city's best selection of computer, electronics, and engineering books. **POWELL'S BOOKS IN BEAVERTON** (8725 SW Cascade Ave, Beaverton; 503/643-3131) has an excellent children's selection, but much more. Finally, **POWELL'S ON HAWTHORNE** (3723 SE Hawthorne Blvd; 503/238-1668) carries a healthy selection of new and used general titles, while two stores down, **POWELL'S BOOKS FOR COOKS AND GARDENERS** (3747 SE Hawthorne Blvd; 503/235-3802) specializes in—what else?—cookbooks and gardening guides. *Powell's main store is open every day 9am–11pm; www.powells.com; map:J2* &

15) BREWERIES AND BREWPUBS

Since Henry Weinhard proposed pumping beer through the Skidmore Fountain more than 100 years ago, Portlanders have loved beer. Today, although Weinhard's beer is brewed elsewhere (and the former brewery is being developed into housing and retail space), the city has almost as many places to drink beer as there are to drink coffee. More than 40 craft breweries and brewpubs call Portland home—more per capita than any other American city (check out www.oregonbeer.com for a listing). The Northwest in general—and Portland in particular—is the national center for craft breweries: small, independent companies that turn out specialty beers, generally in small batches and according to traditional methods. Aficionados argue that Northwest brews are distinctly different from even the best imports. They claim that the western barley, hops from the Willamette and Yakima Valleys, and Cascade water give local concoctions their particular character.

Although the location in Northwest Portland's industrial zone isn't simple to find, you'll know you've arrived at the **PORTLAND BREWING COMPANY'S BREWHOUSE TAPROOM AND GRILL** (2730 NW 31st Ave; 503/228-5269; www.portlandbrew.com; map:FF7) when you see the giant gleaming copper kettles at the entrance. Some of the best brew in the city is made here. Sample the ever-popular MacTarnahan's Ale, Zig Zag River Lager, Haystack Black Porter, or Original Honey Beer with grilled Copper River salmon in season, halibut fish and chips, or steamed clams cooked in beer. Through picture windows behind the bar, you can watch the brewers at **BRIDGEPORT BREWERY & PUB** (1313 NW Marshall

St; 503/241-3612; www.bridgeportbrew.com; map:N1) at work. The comfortable pub, with its library of periodicals and exceptionally good pizza, encourages lingering over award-winning Bridgeport IPA, Blue Heron Ale, Bridgeport Amber, and seasonal brews. In the summer the best tables are out on the loading dock under ropes of leafy green hops.

Head to the waterfront along the RiverPlace esplanade for **FULL SAIL BREWING COMPANY'S** Portland brewery. Tours are by appointment only (0307 SW Montgomery St; 503/222-5343; www.fullsailbrewing.com; map:C5), but you can see the works from the adjoining pub (**HARBORSIDE PILSNER ROOM**; 503/220-1865) and sample 12 beers, including their best-selling Amber Ale, Golden Ale, and Nut-Brown Ale.

WIDMER BREWING COMPANY is one of the finer Portland breweries, which may be why Anheuser-Busch recently purchased distribution rights for their beer. Widmer brews the city's favorite hefeweizen in its facility on an industrial byway in North Portland. Free tours (with beer sampling) are available Fridays at 3pm and Saturdays at 1pm and 2pm—to go on a tour simply show up at the attached beer hall, the attractive **WIDMER GASTHAUS** (955 N Russell St; 503/281-3333; www.widmer.com; map:FF6), which also is a fine place to sample Widmer suds with a plate of sausage and kraut or a pretzel.

One brewery that's garnered attention on the international level is **HAIR OF THE DOG** (4509 SE 23rd Ave; 503/232-6585; www.teleport.com/~beer/hairofthedog.html; map:HH5), which produces sublime "bottle-conditioned" (it improves with age) strong beer. British beer writer Michael Jackson has picked them as one of the best breweries in the country, and their Adam beer is one of his personal favorites. It's a small operation, but the beer makers at Hair of the Dog are happy to give tours (call ahead).

Technically, the McMenamins joints all over town are not breweries, they're brewpubs. The difference? A brewery is exactly what it claims to be—sometimes with a pub or tasting room attached. A brewpub is more of a novelty—a brewery that makes its beer only for a particular bar or, in the case of McMenamins, a group of bars. Most will give tours by prior arrangement only, though there's always a place to get a peek at the process. Of the dozens of McMenamins pubs in Portland and other Oregon cities, only a handful have in-house breweries. In Portland, try the **FULTON PUB AND BREWERY** (0618 SW Nebraska St; 503/246-9530; map:HH6), the original **HILLSDALE BREWERY AND PUBLIC HOUSE** (1505 SW Sunset Blvd; 503/246-3938; map:II7), **KENNEDY SCHOOL** (5736 NE 33rd Ave; 503/249-3983; map:EE5), or **RINGLER'S** (1332 W Burnside St; 503/225-0543; map:J1). **CORNELIUS PASS ROADHOUSE AND BREWERY** (4045 NW Cornelius Pass Rd, Hillsboro; 503/640-

6174), in a huge, inviting farmhouse, is favored by the techies who work in the neighborhood (www.mcmenamins.com).

There are also a number of popular brewpubs in town that aren't owned by the McMenamin brothers, including the **ALAMEDA BREW-HOUSE** (4765 NE Fremont St; 503/460-9025; map:FF4), the **LUCKY LABRADOR BREWPUB** (915 SE Hawthorne Blvd; 503/236-3555; www.luckylab.com; map:D8), and **PHILADELPHIA'S STEAKS & HOAGIES** (6410 SE Milwaukie Ave; 503/239-8544; www.teleport.com/~beer/philadelphias.html; map:JJ5), where you can get Philadelphia cheese steaks along with a variety of handcrafted ales.

One way to sample brews from several different places is to head down to Tom McCall Waterfront Park the last full weekend in July for the **OREGON BREWERS FESTIVAL** (503/778-5917; www.oregonbrewfest.com) to sample beers from about 70 different craft breweries.

16) HAWTHORNE DISTRICT

Along SE Hawthorne Blvd from SE 17th Ave to 43rd Ave The lengthy strip that is Hawthorne Boulevard might well be considered Portland's own little Haight-Ashbury. And while those who dream about the Summer of Love feel right at home here among the purveyors of tie-dye and incense, an increasing number of upscale retail shops and eateries are locating here as well. As commercial activity creeps east and west along the boulevard, this district—just southeast of downtown—may come to resemble a funkadelic, four-lane version of NW 23rd Avenue.

On Hawthorne, espresso can be quaffed at such corporate coffeehouses as **STARBUCKS** (3639 SE Hawthorne Blvd; 503/234-1757) and **DIEDRICH COFFEE PEOPLE** (3500 SE Hawthorne Blvd; 503/235-1383) or in the cozier confines of the très comfy **COMMON GROUNDS COFFEEHOUSE** (4321 SE Hawthorne Blvd; 503/236-4835) or the popular **CUP AND SAUCER** (3566 SE Hawthorne Blvd; 503/236-6001). For an ice creamy pickup, try the Coffee Olé at **BEN & JERRY'S** (1428 SE 36th Ave; 503/234-2223). The **HAWTHORNE COFFEE MERCHANT** (3562 SE Hawthorne Blvd; 503/230-1222) sells gourmet coffee beans, tea, and candies.

The bustling boulevard also offers a good representation of international cuisines. The wonderfully idiosyncratic **BREAD AND INK CAFE** (3610 SE Hawthorne Blvd; 503/239-4756) serves up one of the city's finer hamburgers as well as pastas, fish, luscious desserts, and a Yiddish brunch with blintzes that keep you full all day. Just down the street is **NICK'S FAMOUS CONEY ISLAND RESTAURANT** (3746 SE Hawthorne Blvd; 503/235-4024), otherwise known as Yankee Stadium West, where the chili dogs draw 'em in. **3 DOORS DOWN CAFE** (1429 SE 37th Ave; 503/236-6886) offers Mediterranean-inspired dinners in a warm, bistro-style setting. The **HAWTHORNE STREET CAFE** (3354 SE Hawthorne Blvd;

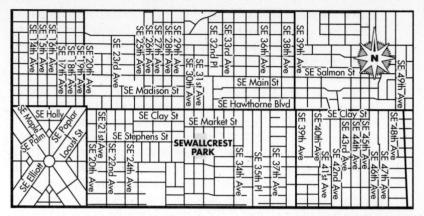

HAWTHORNE DISTRICT

503/232-4982) is a bright lunch spot serving a variety of sandwiches and salads; **GARBONZOS** (3433 SE Hawthorne Blvd; 503/239-6087) specializes in falafel, shawarma, baba ghanouj, and other Middle Eastern favorites; **THANH THAO** (4005 SE Hawthorne Blvd; 503/238-6232) is known for its Thai and Vietnamese dishes; and the garden behind the **COMPASS WORLD BISTRO** (4741 SE Hawthorne Blvd; 503/231-4840) may be the prettiest alfresco eating option in town (see review in the Restaurants chapter).

If pizza and a brewski with a movie is your thing, try the McMenamins' brightly colored **BAGDAD THEATER AND PUB** (3710 SE Hawthorne Blvd; 503/230-0895). Around the corner is **GREATER TRUMPS** (1520 SE 37th Ave; 503/235-4530), where you can sit back in luxury with port and a cigar, and down the boulevard is the classy **BRIDGEPORT ALE HOUSE** (3632 SE Hawthorne Blvd; 503/233-6540).

Book and music shoppers won't be disappointed by this neighborhood. **CROSSROADS** (3130-B SE Hawthorne Blvd; 503/232-1767) buys, sells, and trades LPs, tapes, and CDs, specializing in collectibles and hard-to-find records, while next door a fine collection of guitars, violins, flutes, and drums make a musical display at **ARTICHOKE MUSIC** (3130-A SE Hawthorne Blvd; 503/232-8845). Down the street, **MURDER BY THE BOOK** (3210 SE Hawthorne Blvd; 503/232-9995) buys, sells, and trades new and used thriller, spy, and mystery novels. **POWELL'S ON HAWTHORNE** (3723 SE Hawthorne Blvd; 503/238-1668) and **POWELL'S BOOKS FOR COOKS AND GARDENERS** (3747 SE Hawthorne Blvd; 503/235-3802) (see separate listing in this section) are outposts of the venerable downtown bookstore; the latter stocks a variety of cooking- and gardening-related accessories and gifts in addition to new and used books. With the recipe for culinary inspiration in hand, step next door to **PASTAWORKS** (3735 SE Hawthorne Blvd; 503/232-1010) to choose from a gala assortment of fresh pastas, cheeses, prepared antipasti, and imported foodstuffs. Find just the right bottle of wine at **PORTLAND WINE MERCHANTS** (1430 SE 35th Ave; 503/234-4399) or **MT. TABOR FINE WINES** (4316 SE Hawthorne Blvd; 503/235-4444).

Birds of many feathers will flock for a bath and a nibble at your house if you stock up at the **BACKYARD BIRD SHOP** (3572 SE Hawthorne Blvd; 503/230-9557), but beware—nearby the **CAT'S MEOW** (3538 SE Hawthorne Blvd; 503/231-1341) appeals to cat lovers and their felines. Outdoor adventurers can find all they need at **CLIMB MAX** (3341 SE Hawthorne Blvd; 503/797-1991); **PRESENTS OF MIND** (3633 SE Hawthorne Blvd; 503/230-7740) is crowded with cards, gifts, and pretty wrapping paper. Handcrafted pottery and the works of local artists fill the **GRAYSTONE GALLERY** (3279 SE Hawthorne Blvd; 503/238-0651), **ESCENTIAL LOTIONS & OILS** (3638 SE Hawthorne Blvd; 503/236-7976) specializes in custom-scented skin and bath products, and **THE THIRD EYE** (3950 SE Hawthorne Blvd; 503/232-3EYE) is known in the neighborhood as the "hippie department store," with its cornucopia of candles, tie-dye, black lights, posters, and smoke shop.

An eclectic array of vintage furnishings, antiques, and reproductions are bought and sold at **SOREL VINTAGES LIMITED** (3713 SE Hawthorne Blvd; 503/232-8482); **THE UPPER EAST: ANTIQUES** (4258 SE Hawthorne Blvd; 503/239-1900) repairs and sells antique clocks and other antiques; in the back of the store, **SOUTHWEST CONNECTION** (4258 SE Hawthorne Blvd; 503/235-0211) specializes in Southwest Indian art and jewelry. Colorful cotton and rayon clothes can be found at **M. SELLIN** (3556 SE Hawthorne Blvd; 503/239-4605), while **FYBERWORKS** (4300 SE Hawthorne Blvd; 503/232-7659) features unique, handmade clothing. Designer shoes from dressy to casual make their imprint at **IMELDA'S** (1431 SE 37th Ave; 503/233-7476), and moms-to-be and their offspring can dress stylishly with clothes from **GENERATIONS** (4029 SE Hawthorne Blvd; 503/233-8130), while every fashionable traveler knows about the **PERFUME HOUSE** (3328 SE Hawthorne Blvd; 503/234-5375), where you have a choice of 1,500 fragrances from around the globe. *Map:GG4–GG5*

17) PITTOCK MANSION

3229 NW Pittock Dr; 503/823-3624 Henry Pittock had the advantage of watching over Portland from two perspectives: from behind the founder's desk at the *Daily Oregonian* and, in his later years, from his home 1,000 feet above the city. The stately, 16,000-square-foot Pittock Mansion, built in 1914, stands on 46 acres that look across Northeast Portland to Mount Hood. The house stayed in the family until 1964, when the entire property was sold to the City of Portland for $225,000. Inside, a graceful staircase sweeps from the basement to the second story; another, less conspicuous stairway leads to the servants' quarters on the top floor. The 22 rooms, furnished with antiques, include an oval parlor and a Turkish smoking room. Regular tours are conducted in the afternoon, and the manicured grounds around the mansion and Pittock Acres (with numerous hiking trails) are open to the public until dark. Admission to the mansion is $5 for adults, $4.50 for seniors, $2.50 for kids 6–18, and free for children 5 and younger. *Every day noon–4pm except major holidays (Feb–Dec); www.mediaforte.com/pittock; map:FF7*

18) FORT VANCOUVER NATIONAL HISTORIC SITE

612 E Reserve St, Vancouver, WA; 360/696-7655 Anyone with even a mild curiosity about what life was like here in the last century should head to **FORT VANCOUVER**. First the headquarters of the Hudson's Bay Company (1825–49) and then a U.S. military post until 1860, it has been reconstructed as the **FORT VANCOUVER NATIONAL HISTORIC SITE.** Before you try to find your way to the fort, stop at the **FORT VANCOUVER VISITORS CENTER** (1501 E Evergreen Blvd; take I-5 north to Vancouver, then take the Mill Plain Blvd exit and follow the signs; 360/696-7655) to gather maps and visit the museum, which presents a 12-minute video of the fort's history. The old fort and officers' quarters are in different areas—a map will help.

The historic **1840S GARDENS OF FORT VANCOUVER** are flourishing. Some consider these early gardens the seedbeds of Northwest horticulture and agriculture; this is the first known organized local planting of vegetables, herbs, and flowers in a formal plot (reflecting the garden's English origins as well as some exotic additions such as purple Peruvian potatoes and West Indian gherkins). The original master gardener was Scotsman Billy Bruce, who learned his craft from the Royal Horticultural Society on the Duke of Devonshire's estates.

The grand officers' quarters along **OFFICERS' ROW** have all been restored. The **MARSHALL HOUSE**, named for commanding officer George C. Marshall, is the fort's showpiece and is furnished in antiques. The rest are townhouses and offices. The quarters of the Hudson's Bay Company's chief agent, Dr. John McLoughlin, who later founded Oregon City, are also impressive. Admission to the fort is $2 per person, $4 per family; children under 17 free. Tours are offered regularly. *Every day 9am–5pm (Mar 1–Oct 31), 9am–4pm (Nov 1–Feb 28), closed Thanksgiving Day and Dec 24th and 25th; www.nps.gov/fova;* &

19) SATURDAY MARKET

Under the Burnside Bridge at SW 1st Ave; 503/222-6072 In 1974 a group of Portland artists assembled the beginnings of what has become possibly the largest continuously operating outdoor craft market in the country. From March through December 24, every Saturday and Sunday and for the week before Christmas (called the Festival of the Last Minute), nearly 300 craft and food booths cluster under the Burnside Bridge and beyond to peddle handmade items ranging from stained glass to huckleberry jam, sweaters to silver earrings.

The food booths are often a few bites beyond what you'd expect from a cart. On any given weekend (and especially around holidays or during the summer), musicians, jugglers, magicians, face painters, and clowns please the crowd.

You can reach the Saturday Market via bus, rail, or car. Tri-Met (503/238-7433) is free in the heart of downtown, known as Fareless Square. MAX light rail—also free within Fareless Square—runs to the market every 15 minutes or so. Get off at Skidmore Fountain, right in the thick of things under the Burnside Bridge. Street parking is free on Sundays, but with a $25 purchase at the Market you can also get two hours of free parking at the **SMART PARK** garage on NW Davis Street and Naito Parkway.

While in the area, wander through the year-round stalls in the nearby **NEW MARKET VILLAGE** and the **SKIDMORE FOUNTAIN BUILDINGS** (see Skidmore/Old Town/Chinatown in the Neighborhoods section of this chapter). *Sat 10am–5pm; Sun 11am–4:30pm (Mar–Dec 24); every day the week before Christmas; www.portlandsaturdaymarket.com; map:J6 &*

20) ANTIQUING IN SELLWOOD

SE 13th Ave from Malden to Clatsop Sts   At the east end of the Sellwood Bridge is one of Portland's best areas to go antique shopping—13 blocks of antique and collectible stores. Sellwood, once a separate town on the east bank of the Willamette, was annexed to Portland in the 1890s, and it is proud of its past: shop owners have placed signs on their buildings identifying their original uses and construction dates. The better part of a day can be spent browsing in this old neighborhood, now a repository of American country furniture (both antique and new), lace, quilts, toys, hardware, china, jewelery, and trinkets.

Particularly noteworthy are **1874 HOUSE** (8070 SE 13th Ave; 503/233-1874), crammed with brass and copper hardware, light fixtures, and architectural fragments; and **R. SPENCER ANTIQUES** (8130 SE 13th Ave; 503/238-1737), with furniture and collectibles. **THE RAVEN** (7927 SE 13th Ave; 503/233-8075) features all things military. The rambling **GENERAL STORE** (7987 SE 13th Ave; 503/233-1321) is well stocked with antique furniture and glass and is housed in the 1905 Caldwell Grocery, whose back wall is the exterior of an old caboose from the Spokane, Portland, and Seattle Railway. The **SELLWOOD ANTIQUE MALL** (7875 SE 13th Ave; 503/232-3755) sells antique and nostalgic toys and household furnishings. For Asian antiques, try **KHAN'S ORIENTAL FURNITURE AND DECOR** (8085 SE 13th Ave; 503/230-8088). At the **HANDWERK SHOP**

SE Sellwood St   SE Rex St
SE Malden St
SE Lambert St
SE Bidwell St
SE Lexington St
SE Miller St
SE Nehalem St
SE Spokane St
SE Tacoma St
SE Tenino St
SE Umatilla St
SE Harney St

SE 13th Ave
SE 15th Ave
SE Milwaukie St
SE 18th Ave
SE 20th Ave
SE 22nd Ave
SE 23rd Ave
SE 16th Ave
SE 17th Ave
SE 6th Ave
SE 7th Ave
SE 8th Ave
SE 9th Ave
SE 11th Ave
SE 19th Ave
SE 21st Ave
SE 23rd Ave

99E

N

SELLWOOD

(8317 SE 13th Ave; 503/236-7870), you can buy high-quality new and old Mission-style furniture.

The **WEBFOOT BOOKMAN** (8235 SE 13th Ave; 503/239-5233) retails old books on Oregon and the West; further south, **FOLK ART FRIENDS** (8624 SE 13th Ave; 503/236-3255) offers interesting hand-crafted primitive home decor pieces. Garden gift shops have sprung up throughout the area; the best is **THE JEALOUS GARDENER** (8301 SE 13th Ave; 503/231-4500).

To restore your energy, try a breakfast specialty (served until 2pm) or sandwich at **MICHAEL'S SELLWOOD CAFE** (7937 SE 13th Ave; 503/231-6544). There are also several Italian eateries in the neighborhood: **PORTOFINO CAFFE ITALIANO** (8075 SE 13th Ave; 503/234-8259), **GINO'S RESTAURANT AND BAR** (8051 SE 13th Ave; 503/233-4613), and **ASSAGGIO** (7742 SE 13th Ave; 503/232-6151) are also good bets for dinner. (See also Westmoreland in the Neighborhoods section of this chapter.)

Neighborhoods

ALAMEDA/BEAUMONT

NE Fremont St between 41st and 51st Aves In the heart of the Alameda neighborhood, the portion of NE Fremont Street known as Beaumont has become a place where Portlanders like to shop, eat, and browse. At the area's west end is **THE ARRANGEMENT** (4210 NE Fremont St; 503/287-4440), a longtime neighborhood favorite, which sells a wide variety of gifts, flowers, jewelry, and clothing. Nearby, **GAZELLE** (4100 NE Fremont St; 503/288-3422) features natural fiber clothing, and further up, **STYLINIQUE** (4623 NE Fremont St; 503/284-9368) offers tops and pants for the teenage set. If you're in a creative mood, **FIRST IMPRESSION** (4803 NE Fremont St; 503/288-2338) has more ideas for rubber stamp art than you can imagine, and at **CHRISTMAS IN THE CITY** (4714 NE Fremont St; 503/281-2974) you can get Christmas decorations any time you want. This street is a good place for kids, too. Little ones can get books, games, music, and art supplies at **A CHILDREN'S PLACE** (4807 NE Fremont St; 503/284-8294); **CABBAGES AND KINGS** (4419 NE Fremont St; 503/284-5113) sells stuffed animals, fanciful statuettes, and kid-oriented knickknacks; and at **ANGEL FACE** (4225 NE Fremont St; 503/281-9890) Erin Sorenson makes personalized baby gifts and Snuggle Kits. For more-adult shopping, **BEAUMONT WINES** (5015 NE Fremont St; 503/331-3991) advises local hosts and hostesses what wines to serve at their dinner parties and offers drop-in tastings on Friday evenings from 5pm until 8pm.

When you get hungry, there's enough variety to satisfy just about any craving you might have. For light fare, get fresh bagels at **BAGEL LAND** (4118 NE Fremont St; 503/249-2848) or coffee and pastry from **JAVA MAN COFFEE** (4727 NE Fremont St; 503/287-5456) and **FAVORITES** bakery (503/282-2253), which share the same space. **PIZZICATO** (4217 NE Fremont St; 503/493-2808) sells gourmet pizza; **BRAVO!** (4110 NE Fremont St; 503/282-2118) specializes in large breakfasts and panini—Italian-style grilled sandwiches—as well as ice cream; **KIM HONG** (4239 NE Fremont St; 503/282-0456) serves Vietnamese food for lunch and dinner; **LEAF AND BEAN CAFE** (4936 NE Fremont St; 503/281-1090) makes a variety of vegetarian ethnic foods for breakfast, lunch, and dinner—think African peanut stew. The **ALAMEDA CAFE** (4641 NE Fremont St; 503/284-5314) serves fresh Northwest food; and at **SUZANNE'S** (3517 NE Fremont St; 503/282-4233) you can get homemade biscuits and breads with your meal. Longtime Portland favorite **STANICH'S** (4915 NE Fremont St; 503/281-2322) warns diners they have to relax and enjoy themselves because here burgers are not fast food. For a little more upscale pub atmosphere, try the **ALAMEDA BREWHOUSE** (4765 NE Fremont St; 503/460-9025). And in **WINTERBORNE'S** intimate dining room (3520 NE 42nd Ave; 503/249-8486) you can get some of the best seafood in town.

ALBERTA STREET

From NE 13th St to 30th St The best time to visit multi-cultural and arty NE Alberta Street is on the last Thursday evening of the month, when galleries and shops in a 20-block stretch come alive in a happy bustle of art, food, and bodies known as Art on Alberta (www.artonalberta.com) or Last Thursday (not to be confused with First Thursday downtown and in the Pearl District). The scene is quieter the rest of the time but is no less intriguing. NE Alberta is rapidly becoming not only a commercial success story but an ever-strengthening ribbon of community that ties together several residential neighborhoods (King, Vernon, Concordia, and Sabin). Yes, such restaurants as **BERNIE'S SOUTHERN BISTRO** (2904 NE Alberta St; 503/282-9864), **CHEZ WHAT?** (2203 NE Alberta St; 5023/281-1717), and the **VITA CAFE** (3024 NE Alberta St; 503/335-8233) fill the bellies of the locals; but those establishments' art-hung walls also fill more aesthetic cravings as well. A number of studios and art galleries line the street, including **GUARDINO GALLERY** (2939 NE Alberta St; 503/281-9048), **ONDA STUDIO AND GALLERY** (2215 NE Alberta St; 503/493-1909), and **GLASS ROOTS** (2921 NE Alberta St; 503/460-3137). You will see a Malcom X mural on one corner, a Mexican grocer on another, and an art exhibit of Central Asian textiles on a third. It all adds up to a lively, groovy, youthful scene—a diamond in the rough that is being polished all the time.

DOWNTOWN
See Top 20 Attractions in this chapter.

HAWTHORNE
See Top 20 Attractions in this chapter.

IRVINGTON
NE Broadway and NE Weidler Sts from NE 7th Ave to NE 24th Ave
One of Portland's oldest eastside neighborhoods, Irvington was developed as an exclusive residential area in the late 1880s and is filled with large homes, attractive gardens, and wide sidewalks. A stroll here is a pleasant outing.

On the neighborhood's south end, small stores, boutiques, restaurants, and coffee shops line NE Broadway and NE Weidler Street. **TRADE ROOTS** (1831 NE Broadway; 503/281-5335) is one of the best bets in the city for finding interesting folk art, clothing, jewelry, and gifts from developing countries around the world; if you're looking to make your own candles, cross Broadway to **RADIANCE** (1902 NE Broadway; 503/281-2438). Cooks (and brides) can find just what they need at **KITCHEN KABOODLE** (NE 16th Ave and Broadway; 503/288-1500). **GOODNIGHT ROOM** (1517 NE Broadway; 503/281-5516) carries everything for a small child's bedroom—toys, stuffed animals, cribs, mobiles, and more. **WORDS INK** (1139 NE Broadway; 503/284-4212) offers cards, posters, journals, and glassware that features the words and artwork of Mary Anne Radmacher; and **RENAISSANCE TILE** (1127 NE Broadway;

503/335-8575) is a fun place to browse even if you're not in the market for hand-made ceramic tile. **BROADWAY COFFEE TRADERS** (2130 NE Broadway; 503/281-3882) sells fine teas and teapots, coffee beans, and chocolate; **GREAT WINE BUYS** (1515 NE Broadway; 503/287-2897) has a great selection of Northwest wines; and the **MOUNTAIN SHOP** (628 NE Broadway; 503/288-6768) has everything you'll need for your outdoor adventure. One of Portland's best independent bookstores, **BROADWAY BOOKS** (1714 NE Broadway; 503/284-1726), often hosts readings by local artists.

You can find unique women's clothing at a variety of shops here: **BYRKIT** (2129 NE Broadway; 503/282-3773) sells casual clothes designed by Jan Byrkit; **VERGOTIS** (1713 NE 15th Ave; 503/284-4065) features dramatic slim styles, many by Kelli Vergotis; and at **MATISSE** (1411 NE Broadway; 503/287-5414) women can play dress-up like they did as children in Aunt Tess's attic—only this time the clothes are new, in sumptuous fabrics and colors.

Jewelers appreciate **DAVA BEAD** (1512 NE Broadway; 503/288-3991) for its beads of bone, glass, or semiprecious stones (if you need instruction in beading, take one of their classes); or paint your own pottery at **CERAMICA** (1428 NE Broadway; 503/460-9669).

Coffee here, as it is everywhere else, is serious business. **TORREFAZIONE ITALIA** (1403 NE Weidler St; 503/288-1608) and **PEET'S COFFEE & TEA** (1441 NE Broadway; 503/493-0192) are favorite neighborhood hangouts. Or you can make a meal out of fruit and yogurt smoothies at **BIBO JUICE** (1445 NE Weidler St; 503/288-5932). **MILO'S CITY CAFE** (1325 NE Broadway; 503/288-MILO) and **CADILLAC CAFE** (914 NE Broadway; 503/287-4750) have long lines for breakfast on weekend mornings. If pizza's what you're after, try **PIZZA LUNA** (1708 NE Broadway; 503/335-3059) or **PIZZA SCHMIZZA** (1422 NE Broadway; 503/517-9981). Fresh Northwest fare can be had at **METRONOME** (1426 NE Broadway; 503/288-4300); **DRAGONFLY** (1411 NE Broadway; 503/288-3960) serves food with an Asian flair; **RUSTICA** (1700 NE Broadway; 503/288-0990) features Italian food in its cheerful, mural-covered trattoria; and **SAIGON KITCHEN** (835 NE Broadway; 503/281-3669) is one of Portland's best Vietnamese restaurants. You can get Japanese food at **KOJI OSAKAYA** (1502 NE Weidler St; 503/280-0992); **AZTEC WILLIE AND JOEY ROSE** (1501 NE Broadway; 503/280-8900) offers a wide selection of Tex-Mex favorites from its cafeteria-style counter; wash them down with a frosty margarita from the bar. Hip **COLOSSO** (1932 NE Broadway; 503/288-3333) attracts locals with its delicious tapas and martinis; while the **ROSE AND THISTLE** (2314 NE Broadway; 503/287-8582) claims to be Oregon's only Scottish restaurant and pub and proves it by serving such goodies as Scotch egg and haggis.

IRVINGTON

If you're eating in, pick up everything you need at **IRVINGTON MARKET** (1409 NE Weidler St), which is home to **NEWMAN'S FISH COMPANY** (503/284-4537), **KRUGER'S PRODUCE** (503/288-4236), and the **CHESHIRE CAT** deli (503/284-5226).

LAKE OSWEGO

10-minute drive south of Portland on SW Macadam Ave; from E Ave south to Ridgeway and from 6th St east to the Willamette River Before the arrival of white settlers, Native Americans fished for abundant salmon in Lake Oswego, which they called Waluga for the wild swans that gathered here. White settlers first came in 1846; the town thrived with the Oregon Iron Company and later the Oswego Iron Company. As the iron industry declined, the 405-acre lake became a popular recreation area and the city grew around the lake, becoming an upscale community that now has a variety of interesting shops and restaurants.

To find Lake Oswego from downtown Portland, take SW Macadam Avenue 8 miles south; the road becomes State Street when you get into Lake Oswego. Or take the **WILLAMETTE SHORE TROLLEY** (503/222-2226) from RiverPlace along the Willamette River into Lake Oswego (see Train and Trolley Tours in this chapter). In downtown Lake Oswego, letter avenues (A, B, C, D) run perpendicular to State Street, numbered streets run parallel.

On Fifth Street between A and B Avenues, the **ELEGANT BASKET** (450 5th St; 503/636-4041) sells gifts, wines, and gourmet foods, and chocolate lovers can stock up at **BERNARD C. CHOCOLATES** (440 5th St; 503/675-7500). Everything you need for your feathered friends can be had at the **BACKYARD BIRD SHOP** (352 B Ave; 503/635-2044), where birdbaths and houses overflow into the front yard; just down the street, **ISABELLA'S** (519 3rd St; 503/699-1171) sells upscale elegant and casual women's clothing; and **LORD & NELSON** (269 A Ave; 503/697-9330) entices shoppers with beautiful Mariposa dinnerware, embroidered linen coasters, and olive oil–based Marseilles soaps. For Christmas ornaments—even in July—try **R. BLOOM'S** (449 3rd St; 503/636-5876), which also sells a wide variety of home accessories, flowers, and "Little Souls" dolls. If your child needs a bed for her teddy bear, stop by **RED COTTAGE DOOR** (425 2nd St; 503/635-3520), where you'll find a huge variety of handmade doll furniture and clothes. Toys, books, and baby clothes can be found at **BRIDGES** (402 N State St; 503/699-1322). Or get creative at **KILNMANJARO** (41 B Ave; 503/636-9940), where you can paint pottery in their colorful workshop.

For antiques, **SIXPENCE ANTIQUES** (148 B Ave; 503/699-6923) sells accessories, lamps, and small furniture, and **SQUIRE'S ANTIQUES** (340 1st St; 503/675-9002) buys, sells, and consigns high-quality antique furniture of all kinds.

When you get hungry, the thoroughly British **LADY DI COUNTRY STORE** (420 2nd Ave; 503/635-7298) serves tea with finger sandwiches and crumpets, or a heartier hot beef pasty—they also have British and South African food to take home. **DESANTO'S CAFE** (464 1st St; 503/699-1662) offers more conventional lunches; **PIKE'S DELI AND RESTAURANT** (467 3rd St; 503/636-7355) serves breakfast as well as lunch. For something a little more formal, try **CLARKE'S RESTAURANT** (in Country Square, 455 2nd Ave; 503/636-2667). Or pick up a bottle of wine and a tasty lunch at **GOURMET PRODUCTIONS** (39 B Ave; 503/697-7355) and eat it in **MILLENNIUM PLAZA PARK** (at the south end of 2nd Ave), an inviting public square that overlooks the lake and has a lovely fountain, benches, and tables for picnics and gatherings. The plaza also has public rest rooms. In summer, at lunchtime and in the evenings, concerts are held here (visit the Lake Oswego web site, www.ci.oswego.or.us, for more information). **WIZER'S** (330 1st St; 503/636-1414) is right next to the plaza and has a deli and wine store as well as a grocery. For dinner, good food, and outdoor tables on their dock on the lake, try **BLINN'S BOATHOUSE** (40 N State St; 503/636-4561), a favorite of locals, who often arrive by boat.

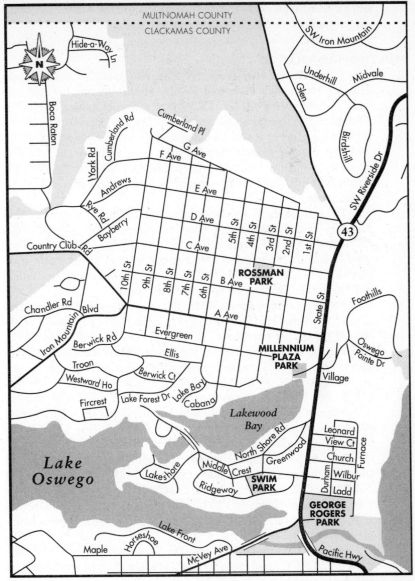

LAKE OSWEGO

If you prefer to eat looking out over the Willamette River, take State Street south from downtown and turn left on Foothills Road (follow signs to public parking), then follow Oswego Pointe Road to where it ends at **RAM BIG HORN BREWING CO.** (320 Oswego Pointe Dr; 503/697-

8818). You can eat here on an outside deck above the Willamette or take the footpath around back with its benches as well as high platforms for river viewing.

MULTNOMAH VILLAGE

Along SW Capitol Hwy from SW 28th Ave south to the overpass crossing Multnomah Blvd, and vicinity Hidden among the hills and vales of Southwest Portland is a jewel of a district known to most as Multnomah Village (although some long-time residents insist on calling it by its name when it was an independent town: simply Multnomah). Although antique shopping is a big draw here, there are enough other shops and hangouts—including the friendly **VILLAGE COFFEE** (7781 SW Capitol Hwy; 503/244-3954)—to give the area destination status for just about anyone.

The antique shops are sufficiently close together along SW Capitol Highway that browsing and window shopping are easy. **JK HILLS ANTIQUES** (7807 SW Capitol Hwy; 503/244-2708) specializes in china, crystal, and silverware, and **KEN SHORES ETC.** in **LE MEITOUR GALLERIES** (7814 SW Capitol Hwy; 503/293-0946) sells antiques and ethnic and fine arts and furniture from around the world.

For more contemporary finds, slip into **ANNIE BLOOM'S BOOKS** (7834 SW Capitol Hwy; 503/246-0053), arguably the finest small bookstore in the city. At **TOPANIEN** (7832 SW Capitol Hwy; 503/244-9683), soapstone sculpture from Kenya, handmade baskets from Ghana, Chulucana pottery from Peru, and other unusual imports entice gift buyers. **THINKER TOYS** (7784 SW Capitol Hwy; 503/245-3936) sells toys that delight and challenge the kids in your life—in a dazzlingly spacious 3,000-square-foot store. Up SW 36th Avenue, in the old neighborhood post office, **F. PALUMBO IMPORTS, LTD.** (3612 SW Troy St; 503/768-9168) sells ceramics and furniture, much of it Italian.

East on SW Capitol Highway is a multipurpose neighborhood treasure, the **MULTNOMAH ART CENTER** (7688 SW Capitol Hwy; 503/823-ARTS). Beyond the MAC, **EAST WEST TRIBAL RUGS AND ART** (7642 SW Capitol Hwy; 503/293-4330) sells reasonably priced Oriental rugs, and **ZINGO!** (7650 SW Capitol Hwy; 503/244-7381) features handmade jewelry and objets d'art.

Good eats are found here, too. One longtime favorite is **FAT CITY CAFE** (7820 SW Capitol Hwy; 503/245-5457), with its square breakfasts and fresh cinnamon rolls (get 'em early or they're gone). **THE GRAND CENTRAL BAKING COMPANY** (3425 SW Multnomah Blvd; 503/977-2024) serves tasty sandwiches made from its homemade breads—buy a loaf or three to take home. Two happy, all-day neighborhood restaurants are **MARCO'S CAFE AND ESPRESSO BAR** (7910 SW 35th Ave; 503/245-

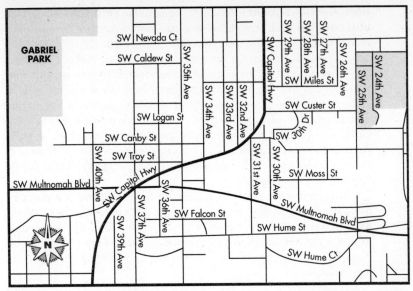

MULTNOMAH VILLAGE

0199) and **O'CONNOR'S** (7850 SW Capitol Hwy; 503/244-1690), the latter a late-night spot as well.

NORTHWEST PORTLAND

See Top 20 Attractions in this chapter.

PEARL DISTRICT

See Top 20 Attractions in this chapter.

SELLWOOD

See Top 20 Attractions in this chapter.

SKIDMORE/OLD TOWN/CHINATOWN

Between Naito Pkwy and 4th Ave from SW Oak St to NW Glisan St
Once the heart of the city's commercial core, the Skidmore and Old Town districts (Skidmore to the south of W Burnside, Old Town to the north), east and north of the present downtown, abound with art galleries, good restaurants, and nightclubs; Chinatown, with its magnificent gate on Fourth Avenue at W Burnside, is a relatively small area highlighted by the new classical Chinese garden. This area contains one of the largest collections of restored brick and cast-iron buildings in the country, making it popular with film producers for period movie sets.

At the center of the **SKIDMORE DISTRICT** is the city's oldest and most gracious fountain, **SKIDMORE FOUNTAIN** (where two women dispense the gift of water in drinking troughs for both man and beast), in cobblestone **ANKENY SQUARE**. Across the square, the **SKIDMORE FOUNTAIN BUILDING** has been remodeled as a mall with a number of tourist-oriented shops, including **AUSTRALIAN ORIGINALS** (28 SW 1st Ave; 503/228-4484), where you can get real didgeridoos, outback rain gear, and Uggs slippers. At the east end of the square, the **JEFF MORRIS FIRE MUSEUM** (55 SW Ash St) provides what is basically a window view of vintage fire engines; take a peek. West of Ankeny Square is a courtyard with an overflow of tables from the eateries inside the **NEW MARKET VILLAGE**, a magnificent brick and terra-cotta building dating back to 1872. Across the street, on weekends, a craft market bustles 10 months out of the year underneath the Burnside Bridge (see Saturday Market in Top 20 Attractions in this chapter).

Driving around Portland, it's easy to forget that this is a port city. You can regain a watery perspective at the **OREGON MARITIME CENTER AND MUSEUM** (113 SW Naito Pkwy; 503/224-7724), where the main exhibit is the steam-powered stern-wheeler *Portland* moored just across Tom McCall Waterfront Park from the museum building (see Museums in this chapter).

Hungry yet? You might down a few mollusks at the 93-year-old **DAN AND LOUIS OYSTER BAR** (208 SW Ankeny St; 503/227-5906). Or, at the foot of SW Ankeny Street on SW Second Avenue, there's **BERBATI RESTAURANT** (19 SW 2nd Ave; 503/226-2122), an excellent, casual Greek restaurant, and **BERBATI'S PAN** (231 SW Ankeny St; 503/248-4579), its connected nightclub.

Just south, along SW Second and SW First Avenues, are a handful of galleries. In the historic Hazeltine Building, the **ELIZABETH LEACH GALLERY** (207 SW Pine St; 503/224-0521) is a large, airy space representing many of Portland's well-known painters and photographers. **FIRST AVENUE GALLERY** (205 SW 1st Ave; 503/222-3850) exhibits fresh and technically accomplished Northwest contemporary artists; across the street, **ATTIC GALLERY** (206 SW 1st Ave; 503/228-7830) shows a variety of painters and sculptors. **PHOTOGRAPHIC IMAGE GALLERY** (240 SW 1st Ave; 503/224-3543) exhibits excellent prints from master photographers.

After a day's gallery-hopping, stop in at **MCCORMICK & SCHMICK'S SEAFOOD RESTAURANT** (235 SW 1st Ave; 503/224-7522) for some of the best happy-hour eats in town, **KELLS IRISH RESTAURANT & PUB** (112 SW 2nd Ave; 503/227-4057) for Celtic music and a creamy pint of stout, **ALEXIS** (215 W Burnside St; 503/224-8577) for Greek food in a relaxed atmosphere, or the more formal **PORTLAND STEAK AND CHOP HOUSE** (121 SW 3rd Ave; 503/223-6200) in the magnificently restored **EMBASSY SUITES HOTEL** (319 SW Pine St; 503/279-9000).

Down the middle of SW First Avenue runs the MAX light rail. Follow it north under the Burnside Bridge to the carefully restored historic district of **OLD TOWN**. At the corner of NW First Avenue and W Burnside Street is a store where everything is **MADE IN OREGON** (10 NW 1st Ave; 503/273-8354); in the same block, the **OLD TOWN ANTIQUE MARKET** (32 NW 1st Ave; 503/228-3386) provides space for 23 vendors. The popular **OREGON MOUNTAIN COMMUNITY** (60 NW Davis St; 503/227-1038) stocks a good variety of outdoor sports clothing and equipment—for sale and for rent; **COUNTRYSPORT** (126 SW 1st Ave; 503/221-4545) stocks everything a fly fisherman could possibly want. If leather's your thing, **OREGON LEATHER COMPANY** (110 NW 2nd Ave; 503/228-4105) sells all things leather: clothing, bags, saddles, sole and upper leathers, upholstery leather, and scrap leather.

Old Town has many great places to eat. From the upstairs windows of **LA PATISSERIE** (208 NW Couch St; 503/248-9898), watch the activity down in the streets while you eat a sandwich and a piece of cake. A block away, the neighborhood pizza shop is **OLD TOWN PIZZA COMPANY** (226 NW Davis St; 503/222-9999). If the weather's nice, you can pick up a box lunch at **FREDDIE BROWN'S DELI** (220 NW 2nd Ave; 503/222-4034) in the octagonal One Pacific Square building, where a plaque on side of the building notes the **HIGH-WATER MARK** of the flood on June 7, 1894 (about 3 feet above the present sidewalk level). **OPUS TOO** (33 NW 2nd Ave; 503/222-6077) is known for its excellent grilled fish. Next door, lights are low in **JAZZ DE OPUS** (33 NW 2nd Ave; 503/222-6077), a good choice for late-night drinks. **OBI** (101 NW 2nd Ave; 503/226-3826) creates innovative renditions of sushi, and **UOGASHI** (107 NW Couch St; 503/242-1848) is one of the most strikingly designed Japanese restaurants in Portland.

In the 1930s, the area between SW Ankeny and NW Glisan Streets and First and Sixth Avenues was known as Japantown, a bustling community with more than 100 businesses. To learn about the history of the Japanese in Oregon and for a walking map of Japantown, visit the **OREGON NIKKEI LEGACY CENTER** (117 NW 2nd Ave; 503/224-1458) (see Museums in this chapter).

Portland's diminutive **CHINATOWN** blends into Old Town at about NW Third Avenue; the **SERPENT-ADORNED ENTRANCE GATE** to Chinatown is on NW Fourth Avenue and W Burnside Street. In 1989, the area north of Burnside between NW Third and Sixth Avenues was designated a National Historic District, now the oldest and, technically, the largest in Oregon. It's still small enough that fiery red-and-yellow lampposts are needed to remind you of your whereabouts, though.

The highlight of Chinatown is the newly opened **CLASSICAL CHINESE GARDEN** (between NW 2nd and 3rd Aves and NW Everett and

Flanders Sts), a beautiful, serene oasis in the heart of Old Town (see "Garden of the Awakening Orchid" in this chapter).

While several restaurants here will fill a craving for good Chinese food, the oldest, **FONG CHONG** (301 NW 4th Ave; 503/220-0235), has been serving Portlanders since the 1930s and is half Oriental grocery, half restaurant—and Portland's finest dim sum parlor, a Sunday morning favorite.

One caveat: Although lawyers, architects, and artists dominate the work force in and around Old Town, the perpetually unemployed consider the area prime turf, too. Officially designated a "drug-free zone," Old Town has yet to be free of drug dealers, and while visitors should definitely visit this area, they may not want to linger long here after dark.

WESTMORELAND

Several blocks north and east of the antique lovers' mecca, Sellwood, Westmoreland has become a destination in itself. While there aren't as many antique stores here as in its sister neighborhood, Westmoreland has three large antique malls: **STARS** (7027 SE Milwaukie Ave; 503/239-0346), **STARS AND SPLENDID** (7030 SE Milwaukie Ave; 503/235-5990), and **MORE STARS** (6717 SE Milwaukie Ave; 503/235-9142). For a clothing bargain, try **SILVER LINING** (7044 SE Milwaukie Ave; 503/238-5578), an upscale women's consignment boutique; attractive wrapping paper, cards, and gifts can be had at **BRANCHES** (6656 SE Milwaukie Ave; 503/235-7124), and at **ON THE AVENUE** (7007 SE Milwaukie Ave; 503/236-7388), which shares its space and phone number with **FIREWORKS**, where you can paint pottery and then get it glazed and fired. Independent bookstore **WALLACE BOOKS** (7241 SE Milwaukie Ave; 503/235-7350) offers a houseful of new and used books and will help you track down that out-of-print volume. **THINKER TOYS** (1626 SE Bybee Blvd; 503/235-2970) sells toys to stimulate kids' minds, and at **HAGGIS MCBAGGIS** (6802 SE Milwaukie Ave; 503/234-0849) kids can buy funky shoes while their moms try on hats and slippers. Satisfy your sweet tooth at **SIMPLY IRRESISTIBLE** (1620 SE Bybee Blvd; 503/231-2960), fill up on gourmet pizza at **PIZZICATO** (1630 SE Bybee Blvd; 503/736-0174), indulge in the flavors of New Mexico at the **ADOBE ROSE CAFE** (1634 SE Bybee Blvd; 503/235-9114), or try Mediterranean cuisine at **FISHTALES** (1621 SE Bybee Blvd; 503/239-5796). **STICKERS ASIAN CAFE** (6808 SE Milwaukie Ave; 503/239-8739) offers tasty good value. For a special treat, eat at **CAPRIAL'S BISTRO** (7015 SE Milwaukie Ave; 503/236-6457), where one of Portland's favorite chefs, Caprial Pence, cooks up eclectic Northwest fare with her own special touches.

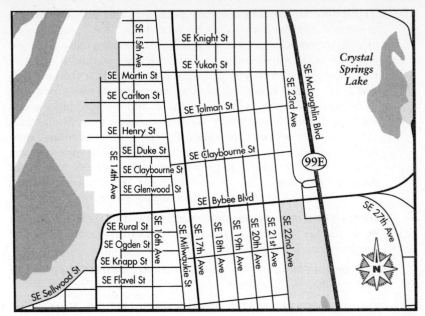

SE Knight St
SE Yukon St
SE 15th Ave
SE Martin St
SE Carlton St
SE Tolman St
SE Henry St
SE Duke St
SE Claybourne St
SE Claybourne St
SE Glenwood St
SE Bybee Blvd
SE 14th Ave
SE McLoughlin Blvd
SE 23rd Ave
Crystal Springs Lake
99E
SE 27th Ave
SE Rural St
SE Ogden St
SE Knapp St
SE Flavel St
SE 16th Ave
SE Milwaukie St
SE 17th Ave
SE 18th Ave
SE 19th Ave
SE 20th Ave
SE 21st Ave
SE 22nd Ave
SE Sellwood St
N

WESTMORELAND

Museums

AMERICAN ADVERTISING MUSEUM / 211 NW 5th Ave; 503/226-0000
Who could forget Burma Shave signs, Will Vinton's California Raisins, and Texaco's sign of the flying horse? All-American artifacts are preserved at AAM—the first museum of its kind in the world. Time-line displays chart the development of advertising from the 15th century to the present. Memorable moments from radio days replay continuously—not just commercials but broadcasts that marked the course of history, such as FDR's final oath of office and CBS's Bob Trout announcing the end of World War II. Video recordings of the all-time best TV commercials can keep you glued in place all day. Periodic rotating exhibits bring Portland some of the best print and broadcast advertising around. Admission varies, depending on the current exhibit. *Mon–Fri by appointment only, Sat noon–5pm; www.admuseum.org; map:K5* &

CHILDREN'S MUSEUM / 4105 SW Canyon Rd (across from the Oregon Zoo); 503/823-2227 Although for years Portland's Children's Museum has been housed in a quaint but cramped old building just south of downtown Portland, by the time this book is published it will have occupied roomier digs in the old OMSI building in Washington Park, near the zoo.

This is the museum that's not really a museum; it's a play and learning center for children from babies up to preteens. The "please touch" exhibits include a fantasy forest where babies can crawl into a giant nest and reach for birds overhead or grab at falling leaves; a child-size grocery store, complete with shopping baskets, canned goods, a checkout line, and a cash register where kids can ring up groceries; a water room that features everyday objects like kitchen tools and car windshield wipers used in unexpected and wacky ways; and a giant tone tower, which makes music as kids climb from place to place. Older children can experiment with video technology in Story Studios, and everyone loves the drop-in art center. When you get hungry, you can get real food at the museum's restaurant. Call for updated hours and admission charges. *Tues–Sun 9am–5pm; www.pdxchildrensmuseum.org; map:HH7*

END OF THE OREGON TRAIL INTERPRETIVE CENTER / 1726 Washington St, and other locations in Oregon City; 503/657-9336 See Top 20 Attractions in this chapter.

OREGON HISTORY CENTER / 1200 SW Park Ave; 503/222-1741 See Top 20 Attractions in this chapter.

OREGON MARITIME CENTER AND MUSEUM / 113 SW Naito Pkwy; 503/224-7724 When Portland was founded in the early 1840s on the banks of the Willamette River, the town thrived because of its deep harbor—any ship that could come into the mouth of the Columbia could go all the way to Portland, and shipping was by far the cheapest way to move cargo. The Maritime Museum celebrates this history; its largest exhibit is the tugboat *Portland*, the last steam-powered stern-wheel tugboat built in the country (it's moored on the Willamette just across Tom McCall Waterfront Park from the museum's building). Here you can see the crew's quarters and the engine room, then climb up to the Pilot House, 32 feet above the water, for a great view. Exhibits in the museum building include model sailing ships, Liberty ships, and stern-wheelers; photographs from Portland's ship-building heritage; and navigational instruments. The museum's library has an extensive collection of maritime books and photographs; and the museum store sells maritime publications and gifts. Admission is $4 for adults, $3 for seniors, $2 for students 8–17, $10 for families. Children under 8 are free. *Wed–Sun 11am–4pm (May–Aug), Fri–Sun 11am–4pm (Sept–Apr); www.tele port.com/~omcm/index.phtml; map:I7*

OREGON MUSEUM OF SCIENCE AND INDUSTRY (OMSI) / 1945 SE Water Ave; 503/797-4000 See Top 20 Attractions in this chapter.

OREGON NIKKEI LEGACY CENTER / 117 NW 2nd Ave; 503/224-1458 This small museum in the heart of what was once Portland's Japantown serves as a focal point for preserving and understanding the history of the

PORTLAND'S BRIDGES

Engineer and writer Henry Petroski describes Portland as an open-air bridge museum: in total 12 bridges (plus two railroad bridges) span the Willamette River, from the cathedral-like **St. Johns Bridge** on the north to the **Oregon City Bridge** on the south. The city features all three bridge types, all three movable span types, bridges that are close to one another (most within ³⁄₁₀ of a mile), and midtown bridges with short and safe approaches for pedestrians.

While all are interesting, some are unique. The **Steel Bridge** is the only vertical-lift bridge in the world with twin decks capable of independent movement. The lower rail-road deck, normally kept in the raised position, moves independently of the upper deck, which carries cars, pedestrians, bicycles, and the city's light rail trains. The **Hawthorne Bridge** is the world's oldest vertical-lift bridge still in full operation, and the **Fremont Bridge** is America's longest tied-arch bridge, with no in-water pier supports. Its 902-foot tied-arch midspan was built off-site and assembled on Swan Island, a mile down-stream from the bridge site. Engineers from around the world came to watch as its 6,000 tons were raised 175 feet above the river at a rate of 7 feet per hour.

For an insider's look at Portland's bridges, go on one of Sharon Wood-Wortman's bridge tours. Call her office at 503/222-5535 or see Waterfront Bridge Walks in the Walking Tours section of this chapter. —*Sarah Thomas*

Japanese and Japanese-Americans in Oregon, from the arrival of the first Issei in Oregon in the 1880s, to the thriving communities in the 1930s, to their displacement in the internment camps of World War II and postwar resettlement. With such rotating exhibits as "In This Great Land of Freedom: Issei Pioneers of Oregon," "Nikkei Artists," and "A League of Their Own: Oregon Nissei Baseball," plus a resource library of books and videotapes, educational programs and speakers, and performances of groups such as Portland Taiko, the center educates the public about the cultural and historical legacy of the Japanese. Call ahead for exhibit infor-mation and hours. Admission is free. *Mon–Fri 10am–3pm; map:K6* &

PORTLAND ART MUSEUM / 1219 SW Park Ave; 503/226-2811 See Top 20 Attractions in this chapter.

WORLD FORESTRY CENTER / 4033 SW Canyon Rd (in Washington Park); 503/228-1367 The talking tree inside the World Forestry Center in Washington Park is strictly for children: the 20-foot-high fir tells them (literally) about its natural functions. Permanent exhibits focus on old-growth stands in the Pacific Northwest and tropical rain forests (in coop-eration with the Smithsonian Institution). Periodic shows feature such things as Oregon woodworkers and carvers, specimens of 200-million-year-old logs preserved as petrified wood, James Audubon's original engravings, and a hands-on exhibit about paper making. Admission is $4.50 for adults, $3.50 for children and seniors, free for 5 and under. *Every day 9am–5pm (Memorial Day through Labor Day), 10am–5pm (after Labor Day to Memorial Day), closed Thanksgiving and Christmas; www.worldforestry.org; map:HH7* &

Art in Public Places

Public art is everywhere in this city—thanks to the patronage of its citizens and a program that requires all new large-scale commercial and public building construction to include public art in the budget. Every City of Portland office building, lobby, and park boasts its signature mural, sculpture, painting, relief, or fountain. With artwork spread out across the city, it's best not to cram a tour into an afternoon. Choose a few arty blocks, stop for a soda along the way, and enjoy.

No matter where you plan to wander, the first place to hit is the **PORTLAND OREGON VISITORS ASSOCIATION** (corner of SW Salmon St and Naito Pkwy; 503/222-2223; map:F5; in summer 2001, POVA will move to Pioneer Courthouse Square), open Monday through Saturday during business hours; there you can pick up a free map of the city's public art offerings. Following are some public art highlights around the city.

The famous **PORTLAND BUILDING** (1120 SW 5th Ave; map:F3) is a provocative landmark. The first major work by architect Michael Graves, it has been described with adjectives ranging from "brilliant" to "hideous." Kneeling above its entrance on SW Fifth Avenue is Raymond Kaskey's monumental *Portlandia*. In 1985, locals cheered as the nation's second-largest hammered-copper sculpture (only the Statue of Liberty is larger) was barged down the Willamette River, trucked through downtown, and hoisted to a ledge three stories up. Most Portlanders have forgotten that *Portlandia* is fashioned after Lady Commerce, the figure on the city seal.

Directly across the street from *Portlandia* is Don Wilson's abstract limestone sculpture *Interlocking Forms*. Nearby is **CITY HALL** (1220 SW 5th Ave; map:F3), whose east courtyard contains the oldest of Portland's artworks: petroglyphs that were carved into basalt rock near Wallula, Washington—estimated to be some 15,000 years old. Inside the nicely renovated City Hall are numerous interesting pieces of art, including Jim Blashfield and Carol Sherman's *Evolution of a City*—a photographic tour through time. One of the city's most familiar landmarks is the bronze *Elk* by Roland Perry, set in the fountain on SW Main Street between Third and Fourth Avenues (map:F3), which once served as a watering trough for both horses and humans and remains the primary watering hole for the Portland Police's mounted patrol. The **JUSTICE**

CENTER (between SW 2nd and 3rd Aves and SW Madison and Main Sts; map:F4) houses a fine 19th-century Kwaguilth carving of an eagle and an array of contemporary pieces. At the entrance are Walter Dusenbery's untitled travertine sculptures representing the various paths to justice. Near them is a wall of stained glass windows by Ed Carpenter.

On SW Yamhill Street between Third and Fourth Avenues (map:G4), the **SIDEWALK** speaks, thanks to author/artists Katherine Dunn and Bill Will. Engraved in the right-of-way are thought-provoking phrases and quotes, ranging from a Pablo Picasso quip to "Step on a crack, break your mother's back." Across the parking lot to the north is Gary Hirsch's *Upstream Downtown*, 18 colorful aluminum fish that decorate the south side of the parking structure at SW Third Avenue and Alder Street. Finally, backtrack a bit to catch John Young's *Soaring Stones* on SW Fifth Avenue between Yamhill and Taylor Streets.

The centerpiece of downtown is **PIONEER COURTHOUSE SQUARE** (map:H3), where Portlanders gather any (and every) hour of the day. The amphitheater-style design of the square is well suited to people-watching. Just before noon the *Weather Machine*, a shiny sphere atop a 25-foot pole, plays a musical fanfare and sends forth one of three creatures, depending on the day's weather. When it's clear, you'll see the sun figure Helia; on stormy days, a dragon; and on gray, drizzly days, a great blue heron. Equally popular is the bronze sculpture by J. Seward Johnson, *Allow Me*, a life-size replica of a businessman with an umbrella.

At SW Yamhill and Morrison Streets, on either side of the historic **PIONEER COURTHOUSE** building, look for Georgia Gerber's delightful bronze bears, beavers, ducks, and deer wandering down the sidewalk and playing in small pools of water (map:G3).

The **TRANSIT MALL** on SW Fifth and Sixth Avenues (map:F3) is lined with sculptures, including Kathleen McCullough's *Cat in Repose* (a children's favorite) and Norman Taylor's notorious *Kvinneakt*, the nude that Portlanders know as former mayor Bud Clark's accomplice in the "Expose Yourself to Art" poster. At the southern end of the transit mall, Portland State University has created a **CITY-BLOCK SIZED PLAZA** in the center of its **COLLEGE OF URBAN AND PUBLIC AFFAIRS** (between SW 5th and 6th Aves and SW Montgomery and Mill Sts; map:D2), with a variety of attractive stone sculptures and stair-stepping fountains.

Some of Portland's best privately financed artwork is set inside the **PACIFIC FIRST FEDERAL CENTER** (SW Broadway between Taylor and Yamhill Sts; map:G2): Larry Kirkland's suspended woven panels cascade into the lobby, catching the changing light throughout the day. More of Kirkland's work, including an intricately carved staircase and an enormous golden light fixture on the second floor, can be found a few blocks up at the **CENTRAL LIBRARY** (801 SW 10th Ave; map:H2).

In the inviting, newly renovated **SCULPTURE GARDEN** on the north side of the **PORTLAND ART MUSEUM** (1219 SW Park Ave; map:F1), you can see rotating exhibits of historic and contemporary sculpture from the museum's collection.

A modern application of trompe l'oeil effects can be seen from the South Park Blocks between SW Madison and Jefferson Streets. The Richard Haas murals on the south and west walls of the **OREGON HISTORY CENTER** (1200 SW Park Ave; map:F2) depict figures from Oregon history: Lewis and Clark, Sacajawea, fur traders, and pioneers who journeyed westward on the Oregon Trail. For another artistic rendering of the Lewis and Clark expedition, visit the lobby of the **GOVERNOR HOTEL** (SW 10th Ave at Alder St; map:I2), where artist Melinda Morey's sepia-toned murals cover the south wall.

FOUNTAINS abound in Southwest Portland—here are some to consider. The smallest are the ornamental bronze drinking fountains found all around the downtown core, which are called **BENSON BUBBLERS** after lumberman and civic leader Simon Benson, who gave them to the city in 1917, hoping the people would drink water instead of whiskey. The city's most popular fountain may be the ever-changing **SALMON STREET SPRINGS**, in Waterfront Park where SW Naito Parkway and Salmon Street meet (map:F5). To the southwest, in front of the Keller (formerly Civic) Auditorium (on SW 3rd Ave between SW Market and Clay Sts; map:D3), is the **IRA KELLER FOUNTAIN**, better known as the Forecourt Fountain. It is a cool resting place in the middle of downtown—a full city block of waterfalls and pools built specifically with summer splashing in mind. Less well known but equally fun to play in is the **LOVEJOY FOUNTAIN** (between SW 3rd and 4th Aves on SW Hall St; map:C2), which was built to resemble a small, cascading mountain stream. In Old Town stands Portland's first piece of public art, the 1888 bronze and granite **SKIDMORE FOUNTAIN** (SW 1st Ave and Ankeny St; map:J6); two bronze caryatids hold an overflowing bowl above their heads.

For a different perspective on Portland's public art, take a MAX ride across the river. The **OREGON CONVENTION CENTER** (NE Martin Luther King Jr Blvd and Holladay St; map:M9) is home to one of the state's most impressive public art collections. From the sound garden, created with bronze bells and chimes donated by Portland's Pacific Rim sister cities, to local artist Lucinda Parker's painting *River Song*, the works at the Oregon Convention Center define the spirit of the state's people. The vision is universal, as seen in Kristin Jones and Andrew Ginzel's *Principia*, a pendulum hanging in the center's north tower above a 30-foot halo of suspended rays and a circular blue terrazzo floor inlaid with brass and stones; provincial, as in a series of 30 etched and color-filled plaques noting key events and figures in Oregon history, by Terrence O'Donnell,

Dennis Cunningham, and John Laursen; and witty, as in Elizabeth Mappelli's enameled-glass panels of Oregon waterfalls, installed above men's-room urinals. Particularly telling and provocative is Seattle artist Buster Simpson's outdoor installation facing NE Martin Luther King Jr Boulevard. The work in progress is a nurse log pulled from Bull Run Reservoir; seedlings sprout from the irrigated, decaying wood, generating a bit of forest in the middle of the city.

While in Northeast Portland, don't miss the works scattered around the **LLOYD CENTER** mall, including Larry Kirkland's fountain *Capitalism*. Outside the **ROSE GARDEN** stadium, children love *Essential Forces*, which may or may not qualify as art: a computerized fountain emits some 500 jets of water—a gift to the city from Trail Blazer owner and high-tech tycoon Paul Allen. Further east, at **GRANT PARK** (NE 33rd Ave between Knott St and Broadway; map:FF5), Beverly Cleary's children's books come alive in the **BEVERLY CLEARY SCULPTURE GARDEN FOR CHILDREN**, where cast bronze statues of Ramona Quimby, Henry Huggins, and Henry's dog Ribsy cavort through a fountain, inviting real kids to join them.

Galleries

Portland's gallery scene continues to flourish with a healthy mixture of young, emerging artists and older, established artists. Much of the energy is due to the contagious success of **FIRST THURSDAY**, when many galleries stay open late on the first Thursday of each month to welcome roaming visitors to their shows; and artists who aren't exhibiting take to the streets in search of patrons, setting up their own wares along the sidewalks. On this night, great people-watching opportunities go hand in hand with grazing, strolling, and browsing.

Galleries can be found in every corner of the city and suburbs, but many cluster in two areas: downtown and the Pearl District. **DOWNTOWN**, numerous galleries line the streets of the Yamhill and Skidmore historic districts, between SW Naito Parkway and SW Third Avenue. The **PEARL DISTRICT**, once an aging industrial center north of Burnside, roughly between NW 10th and 14th Avenues, has become ground zero for the gallery scene. Warehouses and industrial storefronts have become galleries, artists' lofts, restaurants, and art-oriented businesses.

ALYSIA DUCKLER GALLERY / 1236 NW Hoyt St; 503/223-7595 This intimate and stylish gallery, tucked into the heart of the Pearl District, features small shows of consistently fine quality. Located as it is among furniture boutiques and restaurants, Alysia Duckler makes a fine stop on a leisurely stroll. *Tues–Sat; map:K3*

THE ART GYM / Marylhurst College, 10 miles south of Portland on Hwy 43; 503/699-6243 Once a gymnasium, this 3,000-square-foot space at Marylhurst College is a well-respected showcase (and testing ground) for the work of the Northwest's rising stars and established artists. Christine Bourdette, Lee Kelly, Lucinda Parker, Tad Savinar, and Mel Katz have all shown here. The Art Gym (in the B.P. John Administration Building) occasionally mounts major retrospectives, but there is always a place here for the experimental. Group and alumni shows and student thesis presentations round out the year of exhibits. *Tues–Sun; map:NN5*

AUGEN GALLERY / 817 SW 2nd Ave; 503/224-8182 As one of the largest and most comprehensive galleries in Portland, Augen caters to the tastes and budgets of a diverse clientele with a variety of art—from prints by Robert Motherwell and Jim Dine to paintings by regional artists. Monthly exhibits occupy the central space on the main floor. *Mon–Sat; map:H5*

BLACKFISH GALLERY / 420 NW 9th Ave; 503/224-2634 Over the last two decades, Blackfish has gained a loyal following among Portlanders, and it is a fixture on the First Thursday circuit. Housed at the edge of the Pearl District, at the sign of the wooden fish, Blackfish is the country's oldest artists' cooperative, primarily displaying the latest works of its 24 members in monthly shows. Media, as varied as the members' styles, run from figurative sculpture and weaving to abstract painting. *Tues–Sat; map:K3*

BLUE SKY GALLERY AND NINE GALLERY / 1231 NW Hoyt St; 503/225-0210 These two galleries share a space in the Pearl District. Blue Sky, which opened in 1975, displays outstanding contemporary and historical photography. The contemporary selections often show considerable wit, in distinct contrast to the seriousness of more traditional photography shows. The Nine Gallery, in an adjoining room, is a cooperative run by 10 local artists who take turns dreaming up installations. *Tues–Sat; www.blueskygallery.org; map:L2*

BULLSEYE CONNECTION GALLERY / 300 NW 13th Ave; 503/227-0222 Portland is fast becoming well known for its artists who work in glass. Many of the pieces in this stunning loft space are created by artists working in residence at the Bullseye Glass Factory in Southeast Portland. *Tues–Sat; map:K1*

BUTTERS GALLERY LTD. / 520 NW Davis St; 503/248-9378 This classy Old Town gallery features monthly exhibits by nationally known—as well as local—artists, including painters David Geiser and Frank Hyder from, respectively, New York and Philadelphia; sculptor Ming Fay; and Portland painter Ted Katz. Highlights might include exhibits by West Coast artists in glass. *Tues–Sat; www.buttersgallery.com; map:K5*

CONTEMPORARY CRAFTS GALLERY / 3934 SW Corbett Ave; 503/223-2654 The oldest nonprofit gallery in the nation (established in 1937) has undergone a renovation that, for the first time, allows its permanent collection to be on view. Perched on a hillside in a building that affords spectacular city views from its decks and windows, the gallery presents shows reminding us that the line between craft and art is a hard one to distinguish. Here are displayed textiles, furniture, and ceramics that go far beyond functional. *Tues–Sun; map:HH6*

ELIZABETH LEACH GALLERY / 207 SW Pine St; 503/224-0521 This airy space in the historic Hazeltine Building is well suited to large-scale sculpture, of which all too little is seen in Portland galleries. But the excellent exhibits here are equally strong in two-dimensional works. Northwest contemporary painting and photography get top billing—you'll find such figures as Christopher Rauschenberg, Norie Sato, and Terry Toedtemeier. *Tues–Sat; map:I5*

FROELICK ADELHART GALLERY / 817 SW 2nd Ave; 503/222-1142 Once part of the Augen Gallery, and still connected to it, this attractive, long space boasts an unusually strong roster of artists in both sculpture and two-dimensional media. The room lends itself well to solid, generous one-person shows featuring a number of excellent artists once associated with the celebrated Jamison-Thomas Gallery, which no longer exists. Not to be missed. *Tues–Sat; map:H5*

INTERSTATE FIREHOUSE CULTURAL CENTER / 5340 N Interstate Ave; 503/823-4322 A performance space, gallery, and workshop space make up the body of this multifaceted arts showcase, located in a refurbished 1910 firehouse. The emphasis is on the work of the city's artists from all heritages, and often the IFCC scores with shows not likely to be seen at other venues. The Kwanzaa celebration in December is a major event. *Tues–Sat; map:EE6*

LAURA RUSSO GALLERY / 805 NW 21st Ave; 503/226-2754 Laura Russo maintains a strong commitment to contemporary artists from the Northwest, and she represents many of the most respected ones. Russo does not shy away from the controversial and experimental. This handsome, bright, must-visit gallery is one of a handful with space enough for large-scale works. *Tues–Sat; map:FF7*

LITTMAN GALLERY AND WHITE GALLERY / Smith Memorial Center, Portland State University; 503/725-5656 The Littman Gallery has earned an excellent regional reputation for its engaging photographic exhibits and has long been a regular stop for gallerygoers. Down the corridor from the Littman is the space known as the White Gallery, where primarily two-dimensional works are displayed. *Mon–Fri; map:D1*

MARK WOOLEY GALLERY / 120 NW 9th Ave; 503/224-5475 This young and spirited upstairs gallery puts on great shows and knows how to throw a preview party (on the Wednesday before the First Thursday art walk). The work found here is almost always kinetic and dynamic. There is quite a range, but often the work is mixed-media and three-dimensional. *Tues–Sat; www.amzcom/mwooley; map:K3*

OREGON COLLEGE OF ART AND CRAFT / 8245 SW Barnes Rd; 503/297-5544 In every corner of the Oregon College of Art and Craft—on the grounds, in the modern but rustic structures, in each classroom—there is eye-pleasing design and detail. The Hoffman Gallery is entered through a gate of elaborate, swirling wrought iron. Featured artists work in various combinations of fiber arts, ceramics, glass, metal, and wood; occasionally, students' work is featured. The adjacent sales gallery displays and sells beautifully crafted gifts. Before leaving OCAC, stop at the Hands On Cafe (see review in the Restaurants chapter). Your visit's incomplete without a look at the rest room. *Every day; www.ocac.edu; map:GG9*

PACIFIC NORTHWEST COLLEGE OF ART / 1241 NW Johnson St; 503/226-4391 When PNCA moved into spacious new digs on the northern edge of the Pearl District in 1999, the gallery space was expanded considerably. The cavernous space is split into two galleries—the Manuel Izquierdo gallery and the Philip Feldman gallery space. There is always something interesting going on, whether it be a retrospective of Oregon printmaker Gordon Gilkey, a new media exhibit, or an open-studio show of student work. *Every day; www.pnca.edu; map:M1*

PDX GALLERY / 604 NW 12th Ave; 503/222-0063 This tiny independent gem is fast becoming one of the most well-respected galleries in the Pearl. Here you might encounter a show of fiery interiors by painter James Lavadour or the very fine work of such up-and-coming Portland artists as Erik Stotik and Molly Vidor. *Tues–Sat; map:L2*

PHOTOGRAPHIC IMAGE GALLERY / 240 SW 1st Ave; 503/224-3543 This is the place to go for fine prints by such well-known photographers as Phil Borges and Galen Rowell. Exhibits rotate monthly, featuring contemporary photographers from all around the country, including Portland's own Christopher Burkett, Edward Thomas, and Karry Thalmann. There is a small but excellent selection of books and cards as well. *Mon–Sat; www.photographicimage.com; map:I5*

PULLIAM DEFFENBAUGH GALLERY / 522 NW 12th Ave; 503/228-6665 The diversity and quality of the contemporary art selections featured in this Pearl District gallery are often stimulating and rewarding. The gallery prefers figurative, expressionistic works from Northwest artists such as painters Curtis Phillips, Max Grover, Kay French, and Ken Kelly, and printmaker Yuji Hiratsuka. There's also a downtown location (507 SW Broadway; 503/228-8208). *Tues–Sun; map:L2*

QUINTANA GALLERY / 501 SW Broadway; 503/223-1729 The only Portland gallery dedicated to Inuit and Northwest Coast Native American arts, this downtown establishment features contemporary and antique works—sculptures, carved masks, and totems from such Northwest Coast and Canadian tribes as the Haida, Kwaguilth, and Tlingits. Also Native Alaskan arts. *Tue–Sat; www.quintanagalleries.com; map:K4*

SK JOSEFSBERG GALLERY / 403 NW 11th Ave; 503/241-9112 This consistently fine gallery is dedicated to the photographic arts. It may present a show of surf photography one month and rarely seen Soviet photography the next. A recent show presented the gorgeous work of Martine Frank, an obscure member of the Magnum Photo Group. *Tues–Sat; www.skjstudio.com; map:L2*

Gardens

Portland has been called the gardening capital of the United States. That may or may not be true, but there's no disputing the fact that it is a fantastic place to get your hands dirty. The Willamette Valley's mild climate makes for a long growing season that supports a variety of plant life about which most American gardeners only fantasize, and the diversity, expertise, and wild enthusiasm of the local green thumbs make it fertile ground in more ways than one.

Accomplished Portland gardeners are not a recent phenomenon. In 1889 the nation's first rose society was established here, soon followed by the first primrose and rhododendron societies. By the 1920s, Portland boasted more garden clubs than any other city in the nation; they now total more than 20.

This predilection for plant life means that visitors will encounter gardens in unexpected places. A small bamboo garden, for example, is tucked between exhibits at the **OREGON ZOO** (see Top 20 Attractions in this chapter). There are more than 101 named varieties of camellias on the **UNIVERSITY OF PORTLAND** campus. A third-floor courtyard in **GOOD SAMARITAN HOSPITAL** includes a rose garden; the **KAISER PERMANENTE CLINIC** in Rockwood (503/669-3900) maintains a sinister garden of common poisonous plants, designed to alert parents to backyard dangers.

The **COMMUNITY GARDENS PROGRAM** (503/823-1612) took root in Portland in the 1970s; it has spread to 21 neighborhood locations. Both year-round and summer 20-by-20-foot plots are available; some gardens have waiting lists. For those who would rather look than dig, the

FRIENDS OF PORTLAND COMMUNITY GARDENS has established a demonstration site at Fulton Garden (SW 3rd Ave and Barbur Blvd) featuring raised beds, irrigation and composting methods, heirloom seeds, and new plant varieties. A backyard wildlife habitat cozies up to the **CLINTON GARDEN** (SE 18th Ave and Clinton St), and a demonstration orchard spreads its limbs next to the Gabriel Garden (SW 41st Ave and Canby St).

The following gardens are among the city's horticultural highlights—all free and open daily, unless otherwise noted.

BERRY BOTANIC GARDEN / 11505 SW Summerville Ave; 503/636-4112 Berry's quarter-acre rock garden is more than an extraordinary accumulation of alpine plants, it is also part of this Dunthorpe garden's nationally recognized effort to preserve endangered plant species of the Pacific Northwest in their native habitats. Three other plant groups (primulas, rhododendrons, and Northwest natives) are featured on the 6-1/4-acre estate of Mrs. Rae Selling Berry. Groups may schedule tours with volunteer guides—please call at least two weeks in advance. Admission is $5 for adult nonmembers; members and children under 12 are free. Call ahead to tell them you're coming and to get directions. The garden is partially wheelchair accessible. *Every day during daylight hours; visitors center open Mon–Fri 9am–4:30pm; www.berrybot.org; map:JJ6* &

CRYSTAL SPRINGS RHODODENDRON GARDEN / SE 28th Ave, 1 block north of SE Woodstock Blvd; 503/771-8386 Kodachrome was invented for places like this. Normally, this nationally acclaimed garden near Reed College is a peaceful green retreat for bird-watchers and neighborhood strollers. In April, May, and June, however, Crystal Springs becomes an irresistible magnet for color-happy camera and video buffs, as some 2,500 rhododendrons, azaleas, and companion plants blaze on the 7-acre grounds. Japanese maples, sourwood trees, and fothergillas paint the garden in fall, and the spring-fed lake, home to a sizable colony of waterfowl, is a year-round attraction. Although the garden is free to view on Tuesdays and Wednesdays and every day after 6pm, a $3 admission fee is charged Thursday through Monday, March through Labor Day; children under 12 are free. The annual plant sale and show is held on Mother's Day, when loads of Portlanders traditionally promenade through at peak bloom, and Crystal Springs is *the* spot for a spring wedding. *Every day dawn to dusk; www.portlandparks.org/parks/crysspringsrhodgar.htm; map:II5*

THE ELK ROCK GARDEN OF THE GARDEN OF THE BISHOP'S CLOSE / 11800 SW Military Ln; 503/636-5613 This 13-acre estate at the edge of the exclusive Dunthorpe neighborhood serves as the headquarters of the Episcopal Diocese of Oregon, which explains the name: "close" is a British

GARDEN OF THE AWAKENING ORCHID

As of September 2000, Portland became home to the largest urban classical Chinese garden in the country, the **Garden of the Awakening Orchid** (between NW 2nd and 3rd Aves and NW Everett and Flanders Sts; 503/221-8131; www.chinese garden.org). Designers and artisans from Portland's sister city, Suzhou (an ancient city 50 miles west of Shanghai know for its compact, intricate urban gardens), planned and built the garden, which was funded by a combination of private, foundation, and government monies.

Although tall buildings ring the garden, inside the walls lie an oasis of beauty and calm that covers an entire city block. Serpentine walkways lead you over the bridges and lake, through open colonnades and into serene courtyards and pavilions, such as "Flowers Bathing in Spring Rain" and "Celestial House of Permeating Fragrance." Meticulous rock groupings and Chinese and Northwest native trees and shrubs create a landscape that stays fixed though the visitors' view—framed through windows, doors, and lattice screens—continually shifts. A rockery with waterfalls embodies the Chinese gardening philosophy that a garden must encompass water and mountains.

From the garden's teahouse, an elegant two-story Chinese gable-roofed building, you can have a bird's-eye view of the garden. (Every visible component therein, from the granite blocks to the elaborate carvings to the 300 tons of cloud-shaped rock, was made or mined in China, with on exception: the cobbles in the pond.) All of the garden's elements are linked by the Central Lake, whose Moon-Locking Pavilion is reached by crossing a zigzagging bridge. If you're lucky enough to stand here on a clear night under a full moon: the shadow of the tile-roofed pavilion will frame the reflection of the moon in a breathtaking show that gives "city lights" a new meaning. *Every day 9am–6pm; www.portlandchinesegarden.org; map:K5* —Sarah Thomas

term for an enclosed place or garden around a church or other sacred place for quiet and meditation, where monks used to march in peace. This garden's genesis, however, dates back 75 years to the collaboration between its owner, Scottish grain merchant Peter Kerr, and New York landscape architect John Olmsted, son of Central Park designer Frederick Law Olmsted. Together they created an exquisite terraced garden facing Mount Hood and overlooking pristine Elk Rock in the Willamette River. Both native and rare plants are featured, including a multitude of madrones and 70 varieties of magnolia. Other highlights are lily ponds, a landscaped watercourse fed by a natural spring, a large rock garden, a formal boxwood-hedged terrace, and some of the finest specimens of wisteria you're likely ever to see. Tread respectfully. *Every day 8am–6pm in summer, 8am–5pm in winter; www.diocese-oregon.org/theclose/; map:JJ6*

GARDEN OF THE AWAKENING ORCHID / Between NW 2nd and 3rd Aves and NW Everett and NW Glisan Sts; 503/228-8131 See "Garden of the Awakening Orchid" sidebar in this chapter. *Every day 9am–6pm; map:K5*

THE GROTTO / NE 85th Ave and Sandy Blvd; 503/254-7371 Out-of-towners sometimes introduce longtime Portlanders to the Sanctuary of Our Sorrowful Mother, commonly known as the Grotto. Tended by Friars of the Order of the Servants of Mary (the Servites), the Grotto is both a religious shrine and a lovely woodland garden. Mass is held daily year-round in the chapel; from May to September, Sunday Mass faces the Grotto itself, a fern-lined niche in the 110-foot-tall cliff, which houses a marble replica of Michelangelo's *Pieta*. Throughout the 62-acre grounds, rhododendrons, camellias, azaleas, and ferns shelter religious statuary, providing both the prayerful and the plant lover with ample material for contemplation, while giant sequoias tower above. Upper-level gardens and a panoramic view of the Cascades and the Columbia River (seen from floor-to-ceiling windows in the Meditation Chapel as well as from the gardens) are reached via a 10-story elevator ride ($2). In December, the Grotto radiates with its spectacular Festival of Lights. *Every day except Thanksgiving and Christmas; www.thegrotto.org; map:FF3*

HOME ORCHARD SOCIETY ARBORETUM / 19600 S Molalla Ave, Oregon City Adjacent to the John Inskeep Environmental Learning Center (at Clackamas Community College) is a dazzling assortment of fruit-bearing plants. The Home Orchard Society cultivates dwarf fruit trees, with terrific samplings of apple and pear varieties. If you've been wanting to add a blueberry bush to your yard—or a kiwi vine, persimmon, papaw, or plum-apricot cross—this is the place to decide on the variety. *Tues and Sat approximately 8:30am–12:30pm (Mar through Oct); www.wvi.com/~dough/hos/hos8.html; map:QQ2*

HOYT ARBORETUM / 4000 SW Fairview Blvd; 503/228-8733 See Top 20 Attractions in this chapter.

INTERNATIONAL ROSE TEST GARDEN / Washington Park, SW Park Pl, a block west (uphill) of Vista Ave; 503/823-2223 See Washington Park in the Top 20 Attractions section in this chapter.

JAPANESE GARDEN / 611 SW Kingston Ave; 503/223-1321 See Washington Park in the Top 20 Attractions section in this chapter.

JOHN INSKEEP ENVIRONMENTAL LEARNING CENTER / 19600 S Molalla Ave, Oregon City; 503/657-6958 What was once an 8-acre plot of ravaged land—the wastewater lagoons and parking lots of a berry-processing plant—is now home to shady paths, ponds, and wildlife habitat in an urban setting. The learning center at Clackamas Community College demonstrates environmentally sound solutions to landscape problems, incorporating recycled plastic "logs" in footbridges and utilizing solar- and compost-heated greenhouses in the nursery. Kids flock to the ponds, home to three kinds of turtles (red-eared sliders, western pond, and painted) as well as ducks; parents appreciated the more delicate butterfly garden. The observatory's 24-inch refractor telescope is open during cloudless Friday and Saturday evenings. *Every day dawn to dusk; www.clackamas.cc.or.us; map:QQ2*

LEACH BOTANICAL GARDEN / 6704 SE 122nd Ave; 503/761-9503 The emphasis on native Northwest plants in this garden is fitting: one of the garden's creators discovered two genera and 11 species in Northwest wildernesses. Well-known amateur botanist Lilla Leach and her husband, John, began their 5-acre garden along Johnson Creek in the early 1930s; today it is home to 2,000 species and cultivars of both native and nonnative plants, as well as a variety of different habitats, including a sunny rock garden; a cool, shady riparian area; and a xeric plant display. The Leaches' 1930s manor house can be rented for weddings, receptions, and meetings. *Tues–Sat 9am–4pm, Sun 1pm–4pm, with tours at 2pm Wednesdays and 10am Saturdays; www.portlandparks.org/parks/ leachbotanicalgar.htm; map:HH1*

Parks and Beaches

Portland Parks and Recreation offers a wide variety of naturalist-led excursions in many of the regions parks, greenspaces, and waterways, including hikes, walks, bicycle rides, bird-watching trips, and kayaking and canoe trips. Pick up their brochure, *Outdoor Recreation,* at libraries and stores around town or at 1120 SW Fifth Avenue, room 1302, or call 503/823-5132.

BLUE LAKE PARK / Blue Lake Rd at N Marine Dr and 223rd Ave, Trout-dale; 503/797-1850 or 503/665-4995 Although there is a 5-acre natural wetlands area here, most of Blue Lake Park's 185 acres is unabashedly developed, with plenty of parking, swimming, boat rentals, volleyball courts, paved paths, playfields, and other facilities. Every Wednesday in summer, from 2pm to 2:45pm, kids can drop by for activities such as Asian drumming and folktales, Northwest birds of prey, a globe-trotting comedy cowboy show, or Tears of Joy puppet theater. Park admission is $3 for cars and free for walkers and cyclists (no pets). *Every day 8am–sunset* &

COUNCIL CREST PARK / Top of Marquam Hill, a 10-minute drive south-west of downtown—follow SW Vista Ave from W Burnside St, then continue on SW Talbot Rd Set atop one of the tallest peaks in the Tualatin Mountains, Council Crest Park is valued for its nearly panoramic views of the Coast Range and the Cascades. Park at the top, although sometimes, frustratingly, it's closed at sunset due to vandalism. The Marquam Hill Trail crosses through the Douglas firs and maple forest on the northwest side of the hill. *Map:HH7*

ELK ROCK ISLAND / SE 19th Ave and Bluebird St, Milwaukie Each spring, high waters on the Willamette impede access to this pristine island, but at other times you can step from Milwaukie's Spring Park across the gravel-scrubbed bedrock to the island. Great blue herons feed in the little bay between the island and Spring Park. Migrating Canada geese graze on the shelf of grass on the island's west side. A sublime natural rock formation cascades out of the oak forest on the northwest end, while the deepest waters of the Willamette (home to many sturgeon) slice by. Local lore attributes the name to Native Americans driving elk over the bluff and floating them to the island for processing. Watch for poison oak if you've a notion to wander into the woods. *Map:KK4*

FOREST PARK / Boundaries: north of W Burnside St to NW Newberry Rd, west of NW St. Helens Rd (Hwy 30) to SW Skyline Rd; 503/223-5449 In 1948, after more than 40 years of citizen effort, 4,200 acres of forestland were formally designated Forest Park. The land had survived logging, wildfire burns, subdivision into private lots, and an aborted scenic-road project. Now expanded to more than 5,000 acres, Forest Park is the largest city park in the nation. The forest wilderness includes 50 miles of trails and 30 miles of gated roadways for mountain biking along northwest Portland's Tualatin Mountains, and is an easy 10-minute drive from downtown. Leif Erikson Drive, an 11-mile gravel road that stretches from NW Thurman Street to Germantown Road, is all that remains of an ambitious real estate agent's 1914 plans for a subdivision. Now closed to cars, the popular hiking, running, and mountain-biking lane is bumpy in spots but affords good views north; it parallels the Wildwood Trail. An indispensable reference to the park is Marcy Cottrell Houle's *One City's Wilderness: Portland's Forest Park*, which includes maps, park history, and flora and fauna checklists. *www.parks.ci.port land.or.us/Parks/ForestPark.htm; map:DD9–FF7*

HOYT ARBORETUM / 4000 SW Fairview Blvd; 503/228-8733 See Top 20 Attractions in this chapter.

KELLEY POINT PARK / N Kelly Point Park Rd and N Marine Dr This is an isolated park across the channel from Sauvie Island at the convergence of the Willamette and Columbia Rivers. Biking, hiking, and wildlife viewing are best in the spring and fall. In the summer, Kelley Point is inundated with picnickers and sunbathers. Despite abundant wildlife, the slow-moving waters are polluted, and water experts advise against swimming and fishing. As in all urban-area parks, leave your valuables at home and lock your car. *Map:AA9–BB6*

MARY S. YOUNG STATE PARK / Hwy 43, just south of Marylhurst College, West Linn Along the Willamette River, this suburban refuge is stalwartly defending itself from surrounding development. A favorite of urban birders, the 160-acre park has baseball diamonds, soccer fields, picnic spots, 2 miles of dense forest trails, a half-mile bike path, and restrooms. The state maintains it in as close to its original natural condition as possible. *Map:MM5*

OXBOW REGIONAL PARK / 8 miles east of Gresham via SE Division St and Oxbow Pkwy, Gresham; 503/663-4708 or 503/797-1850 In the oxbow bends of the Sandy River Gorge, old-growth forests and wildlife thrive (in part because no dogs are allowed—not even on a leash). Formally the park covers more than 1,000 acres, but the ecosystem appears to extend upstream to the Sandy River Preserve (owned by the Nature Conservancy) and downstream to the YMCA camp. The Sandy River is part of the National Wild and Scenic River system; evidence exists that Native Americans lived here 9,000 year ago. The second weekend in October every year, the park hosts its annual Salmon Festival, focusing on the spawning salmon. One of the state's finer winter steelhead fisheries is in the Sandy River, with 4 miles of access in the park's boundaries. About 15 miles of hiking trails follow the river and climb the ridges, and some of them are open to horses. The park includes 45 camping sites, probably the closest public campground to Portland proper. Call the park for information on special Sandy River fishing rules. Year-round interpretive hikes, programs, films, and lectures are available to groups and the public; call for reservations.

POWELL BUTTE / SE Powell Blvd and 162nd Ave Plenty of horses, mountain bikes, and hikers share the trails in this park, and on sunny days the trails can be downright crowded. From the meadows at the 630-foot summit, you can see north to Mount St. Helens and south to Mount Jefferson. A 2-mile loop circles the volcanic mound on the way to the top. Watch out for poison oak. *Map:JJ1*

ROOSTER ROCK STATE PARK / Take I-84 east to exit 25; 503/969-8254 On a warm weekend, all 1,800 parking spaces for this mile-long sandy beach are full. The familiar Crown Point viewpoint rises on the other side of I-84. There's a logged-off swimming hole in the Columbia River, a boat launch, and docks for boats and anglers. On the far east end, a separate beach has been designated "clothing optional." When the east wind is blowing, windsurfers crowd the beaches. Park admission is $3 per car. *www.prd.state.or.us/parks.html*

SAUVIE ISLAND WILDLIFE MANAGEMENT AREA / At the confluence of the Willamette and Columbia Rivers (10 miles northwest of Portland via Hwy 30), on north end of Sauvie Island; 503/621-3488 The hinterlands of Sauvie Island offer great birding opportunities, but in the past two decades, both human and car traffic in this area have tripled. To finance toilets, parking, a viewing platform, and maintenance, the Oregon Fish and Wildlife Commission charges $3.50 daily and $11 annually for car-park permits for this 12,000-acre state wildlife preserve. Walton Beach, one of the few sandy beaches on the Columbia, is located at the end of the paved portion of NW Reeder Road. Warrior Rock Lighthouse is a 3-mile hike from the north unit parking facility. Non-wildlife-related activity is discouraged; open fires are prohibited, and there are no picnic facilities. *Open year-round are the road to Warrior Rock Lighthouse, bird-watching areas at Coon Point and NW Reeder Rd, the Columbia River beaches, and the eastside viewing platform; the rest of the park is closed from Oct 1–Apr 15; map:AA9*

SILVER FALLS STATE PARK / 20024 Silver Falls Hwy SE, east of Salem; 503/873-8681 It's a 1½-hour drive southeast of Portland and can't really be considered a Portland park. But it's certainly a park Portlanders love visiting to see the (at least) 10 waterfalls that drape Silver Creek Canyon, 4 of which you can walk behind without getting soaked. South Falls, the most spectacular, is a short walk from the lodge and main parking area. Farther up Highway 214, parking is available within a few hundred yards of Winter Falls, North Falls, and Upper North Falls. The essence of Silver Falls State Park, however, is best taken in from the 7-mile Silver Creek Canyon Trail, constructed in the 1930s by the Civilian Conservation Corps. A conference center makes this a favorite meeting and retreat spot. The park has more than 25 miles of trails for hiking and 14 miles of horse trails. More than 100 campsites of varying degrees of sophistication offer overnight accommodations. *www.prd.state.or.us/parks.html*

SMITH AND BYBEE LAKES WILDLIFE AREA / North Portland Peninsula between Delta and Kelley Point Parks In industrial North Portland, this designated natural area encompassing nearly 2,100 acres of lakes and wetlands is yet another haven where urbanites can hike, watch wildlife, and listen to birds call—the bird blinds offer a good place to spy on wildlife, especially blue herons in the slough. *Map:CC7–CC8*

SPRINGWATER CORRIDOR / 16.8 miles, from Sellwood east to Boring A true gem among Portland parks, the abandoned Springwater rail line—also known as the Bellrose Line—is a favorite pedestrian and mountain-biking path and an important link in the Forty-Mile Loop Trail. Its paved surface also accommodates strollers and wheelchairs. *www.parks.ci.portland.or.us/parks/springwatercorridor/swaterwelcome.htm* &

TOM MCCALL WATERFRONT PARK / On the west side of the Willamette River from the Marquam Bridge north to the Steel Bridge; 503/823-2223 See Top 20 Attractions in this chapter.

TRYON CREEK STATE PARK / 11321 SW Terwilliger Blvd; 503/636-9886 or 503/636-4398 Like Forest Park, the Tryon Creek canyon was threatened with a housing project. Thanks to the Friends of Tryon Creek State Park, a citizens' group organized to raise money to buy the land, it is now a park consisting of 645 protected acres between Lewis and Clark College and Lake Oswego. There are 14 miles of intersecting trails, including the paved half-mile Trillium Trail—the first all-abilities trail in an Oregon state park—and a 3-mile bike trail along the park's border with Terwilliger Boulevard. The Nature Center features a bookstore, exhibits, and a meeting room. The Trillium Festival is hosted in early spring, when these delicate flowers blossom. *The park is open every day from dawn till dusk; the Nature Center is open Mon–Fri 9am–5pm, Sat–Sun 9am–4pm; www.teleport.com/~tryonfrn; map:KK6* &

Organized Tours

MOTOR TOURS

ART: THE CULTURAL BUS, AKA TRI-MET BUS 63 / 503/238-7433 ART hits all the city's cultural hot spots: the Portland Art Museum, Oregon History Center, OMSI, and the Oregon Zoo, to name a few. Wildly designed by beloved Portland artist Henk Pander and his sons, Arnold and Jacob, ART is itself a masterpiece. Prices are the same as for all Tri-Met buses.

E & E SPECIALTY TOURS / 503/655-4351 This tour company offers minivan tours around Portland ($20) as well as a variety of favorite day trips outside the city: full- and half-day Columbia Gorge tours ($45 and $25, respectively), Mt. Hood Loop ($45), Mount St. Helens ($53), and the Northern Oregon Coast ($45). Or, you can design your own tour. If you have fewer than three people in your group, prices go up slightly.

ECOTOURS OF OREGON / 1906 SW Iowa St; 503/245-1428 You don't have to be politically correct to book a tour with these folks, but if you pride yourself on being politically progressive, you'll definitely want to check out their tours. As its name implies, this tour company specializes in environmentally and culturally conscious tours, including a full-day Old Growth Forests and Mountain Walks tour; a Native American Cultural tour to the Warm Springs Indian Reservation, where participants are guests of a tribal member; Rafting in White or Calm Water; and a Mount St. Helens Volcano Tour. Not all tours are active—they'll also take you on an evening Microbrewery Tour or a full-day Winery Tour. Or custom-design your own tour. *www.ecotours-of-oregon.com*

EVERGREEN–GRAY LINE OF PORTLAND / 503/285-9845 This touring agency offers several bus-tour choices, including a northern Oregon coast tour, three Portland city tours, a 4½-hour tour to Multnomah Falls and the Columbia River Gorge, and a 9-hour tour that includes the gorge, Timberline Lodge, and Mount Hood. Pickup can be arranged from any major hotel. Children under 12 are half price. Call for tour times and days. Reservations are required. *www.grayline.com*

PORTLAND PARKS AND RECREATION HISTORICAL TOURS / 503/823-5132 These educational day trips sponsored by the Outdoor Recreation Department of Portland Parks and Recreation cover a gold mine of historic places: the Oregon Trail, Lewis and Clark's route to Astoria, the Columbia Gorge, Portland cemeteries, and four- and five-day trips to eastern Oregon to see Native American petroglyphs, rock carvings, and the Lost Blue Bucket Gold Mine. Portland historian and writer Dick Pintarich leads the popular van tours. Most span the entire day (8am to 7pm), give or take a few good stories. April through October only. Reservations required. For more information, pick up the Parks and Recreation brochure *Outdoor Recreation* at libraries and stores around town or at 1120 SW Fifth Ave, room 1302.

VANGO TOURS / 503/292-2085 Like other minvan tour companies, VanGo will take you just about anywhere you want to go around Portland and northern Oregon: half-day city trips, half-day Columbia Gorge tours, full-day Mount Hood Loop trips, full-day Oregon Coast tours, and more. Call for details.

WALKING TOURS

PETER'S WALKING TOURS / 503/665-2558 Former elementary school teacher Peter Chausse offers walking tours of the downtown area, any day of the week. A knowledgeable and enthusiastic guide, Chausse focuses on the city's art, architecture, parks, fountains, and history and emphasizes his points with hands-on activities such as sidewalk rubbings and using magnets to see whether a building is made of cast iron or not. A 2½-hour, 1½-mile tour costs $10 for adults, $5 for teens, and nothing for children. Call to reserve a time.

PORTLAND PARKS AND RECREATION ART AND ARCHITECTURE WALKING TOURS / 503/823-5132 Portland Parks and Rec sponsors a variety of tours around Portland that focus on architectural history, public art and what's new in the various downtown neighborhoods. For more information, pick up the Parks and Recreation brochure *Outdoor Recreation* at libraries and stores around town or at 1120 SW Fifth Ave, room 1302.

PORTLAND PUBLIC ART WALKING TOUR / 503/823-5111 Request the map at the Regional Arts and Culture Council (620 SW Main St, Ste 420), the Oregon Convention Center (NE Martin Luther King Jr Blvd and Holladay St), the main lobby of the Portland Building (1120 SW 5th Ave), or the Portland Oregon Visitors Association (SW Naito Pkwy and SW Salmon St). See Art in Public Places in this chapter for more information on public art and architecture.

URBAN TOUR GROUP / 503/227-5780 For more than 25 years, schoolchildren and adults alike have learned Portland history from UTG volunteers. Teachers, round up the kids—school groups are free. Private tours cost $5 per person ($25 minimum); reservations are a must. Tourists can choose one of three stock tours or have one custom made.

WATERFRONT BRIDGE WALKS / 503/823-5132 There are few cities that offer such diverse bridgework as Portland, and fewer yet that feature tours by such a lively and devoted guide as Sharon Wood-Wortman, whose *Portland Bridge Book* was first published in 1989 (and sadly is now out of print). In addition to the tours offered through the Portland Parks and Recreation Department, Wood-Wortman also offers private tours; call her office (503/222-5535) for information.

BOAT TOURS

See River Cruises in the Top 20 Attractions section of this chapter.

TRAIN AND TROLLEY TOURS

MOLALLA MINIATURE TRAIN–PACIFIC NORTHWEST LIVE STEAMERS / 31803 S Shady Dell Dr, Molalla (southeast of downtown Portland); 503/829-6866 All-volunteer hobbyists drive these miniature trains along a 0.7-mile route. Passengers can bring their own lunches and relax in the shaded picnic area, admiring the fine, detailed antique trains. *Sun and major Mon holidays noon–5pm (May–Oct); www.pnls.org*

MOUNT HOOD SCENIC RAILROAD / 110 Railroad Ave, Hood River; 541/386-3556 or 800/872-4661 The restored Pullman cars of the Mount Hood Railroad chug from Hood River to Parkdale, March through December, linking the Columbia Gorge to the foothills of Mount Hood. Tickets are $22.95 for adults, less for seniors 60 and over and children 2–12. The Saturday dinner train is $69, and the Sunday brunch $56. The spring run gives rail riders spectacular views of blossoming orchards; there's also a Native American Celebration that features dancers from the Warm Springs Reservation, a Western Train Robbery and Country Barbecue (don't worry—the sheriff comes to the rescue); and in December the Christmas-tree train gives riders the chance to join Santa and Christmas carolers on the train and buy a tree, which is loaded onto the train. Call to get a full list of seasonal and special events. *www.mthoodrr.com*

OREGON ZOO RAILWAY / Oregon Zoo, 4001 SW Canyon Rd; 503/226-1561 The zoo railway boasts the only surviving railroad post office in the country, so mailing a postcard while you're on board is a must. A round-trip ticket to ride the train from the zoo to the Rose Garden costs $2.75, $2 for seniors and children 3–11 (in addition to zoo admission). You'll get a dose of history and some nice scenery along the 35-minute loop, which runs in warm-weather months; in spring the route is shorter. *Map:HH7*

SAMTRAK / 503/653-2380 A bright red-and-white open-air train allows you to take in the riverine scenery of the Oaks Bottom wetlands between OMSI and the legendary Oaks Amusement Park near the Sellwood Bridge. The round trip takes about an hour; you can get off to enjoy the sights and return on a later trip. Board the train at OMSI (1945 SW Water Ave), at the Oaks Park Station (SE Oaks Parks Dr at the foot of SE Spokane St), or at the Sellwood Station (8825 SE 11th Ave). Round-trip fare is $5 for ages 13 and up, less for youngsters. *ed–Sun 11am–5pm (mid-June–Labor Day), Sat–Sun 11am–5pm (after Labor Day–mid Sept); wheelchairs can board at the OMSI station*

VINTAGE TROLLEY / 503/323-7363 Four oak-paneled and brass-belled trolleys—replicas of the city's old Council Crest trolley—follow the MAX route (catch the trolley at any light rail station), from Lloyd Center to the downtown turnaround at SW 11th Avenue and back. Top speed is 35 miles an hour, and the round trip takes about 40 minutes. The trolley is free. Vintage Trolley is owned by PGE and operated by Tri-Met. *Sun 12noon–6pm*

WILLAMETTE SHORE TROLLEY / 503/222-2226 The Willamette Shore Trolley has been running along the river from downtown Portland to Lake Oswego since 1990, keeping the track warm for eventual mass transportation development. Two trolleys, one built in 1902 in Blackpool, England, and another 1932 model from Portland, run for 7 miles from RiverPlace to the State Street terminal in Lake Oswego. Round-trip tickets are $7 for adults, $6 for seniors, $4 for children 3 to 12. Charter runs are available for large groups. Reservations are required for the December Christmas boat-watching tour and the Fourth of July trip to watch fireworks. Call for current schedule.

SHOPPING

SHOPPING

Neighborhoods, Districts, and Malls

DOWNTOWN PORTLAND

Portland has a "Big Town, Little City" complex—and thank goodness! After kicking the mall mentality that has plagued most American cities in the last two decades—driving business out of the city and into the suburbs—Portland has gone out of its way to maintain a lively downtown. Through careful urban planning, the growth of the city's downtown has prospered into a pedestrian-friendly retail oasis for both the local community and travelers from near and far. Buses, light rail, and trolley cars crisscross the city's core, making it incredibly easy to maneuver to the big shops that we expect from a big city, as well as to the little shops that give the city its character we know and love.

A few big department stores (Nordstrom, Meier & Frank, Saks Fifth Avenue) and the Pioneer Place mall (as well as its new expansion) attract the lion's share of attention, but there's also a large number of boutiques, specialty shops, and chains to entice shoppers. (For shopping highlights in the downtown area, see the Exploring chapter.)

MEIER & FRANK / 621 SW 5th Ave, Downtown (and branches); 503/223-0512 The family-friendly Meier & Frank department store has been a marketplace mainstay since 1857. That's when two enterprising families opened a multifloored department store in the middle of downtown Portland on SW Fifth Avenue and Morrison Street. Now, nearly 150 years later, the eight resourceful outlets that make up the Meier & Frank chain are owned by the St. Louis–based May department store company (and the St. Louis operator is who you will get if you call the switchboard). The original flagship store still offers many signature services you expect from a downtown department store: a beauty salon, a bridal registry, picture framing, jewelry repair, a travel agency, and a photography studio—as well as the unexpectedly delightful ladies-who-lunch Georgian Room Restaurant. *Every day; www.maycompany.com; map:H3*

NORDSTROM / 710 SW Broadway, Downtown; 503/224-6666 Nordstrom shoppers, beware. This isn't the Nordy's you grew up with. Slowly shifting the emphasis away from service, Nordstrom no longer offers the exemplary "At Your Service" concierge desk at the downtown store—it comes out only at Christmastime and during the big sales. But speaking of sales, thank goodness this retail giant can still hook you up with ball gowns and beauty brands at prices that are almost too good to be true. Other pluses: the helpful sales staff follows current fashions and knows the merchandise they're selling (and they dress to emphasize that point).

Keep an eye out for the famous sales—the anniversary sale in July and the half-yearly sales for women and men—notorious for great deals and outrageous crowds. The downtown location was Oregon's first, but the Washington Square branch may be its largest—and most elegant. The Nordstrom Rack (401 SW Morrison St, downtown; 503/299-1815; map:H4 and 8930 SE Sunnyside Rd, Clackamas; 503/654-5415; map:KK3) carries clearance merchandise from nearby Nordstrom stores at up to 70 percent off. *Every day; www.nordstrom.com; map:H2*

SAKS FIFTH AVENUE / 850 SW 5th Ave, Downtown; 503/226-3200 The Northwest got its very first look at this distinguished New York–based department store when the 47th branch opened in 1990 in the (then) brand-new Pioneer Place. Now, a decade later, Saks has expanded its retail reach with a three-story shop in the newly expanded Pioneer Place. From elegant special-occasion dresses to cutting-edge sportswear, Saks offers top quality, style, and taste. Sales help is attentive, and if they don't have your size, they'll gladly order it for you. The 5th Avenue Club offers customers personal shopping services, including wardrobe consultation and gift selection, at no extra charge. Sales are frequent, and Saks's own label offers some of the best values anywhere on both shoes and apparel. For high-end women's fashions in sizes 14 to 21, make sure to check out Salon Z, tucked neatly above the new men's store. *Every day; www.saks fifthavenue.com; map:G4*

NEIGHBORHOODS

Shoppers flock in droves to **NW 23RD AVENUE** (from W Burnside north to NW Thurman St; map:GG7) for chic apparel, arty gifts, myriad housewares, and a coffee stop on practically every block. The **PEARL DISTRICT** is the place to take a peek at unique items for the house and garden as well as to watch what's developing in the old Blitz-Weinhard Brewery, the new home to shops and loft dwellers who will take possession sometime in early 2002. Down toward the river is the restored **SKIDMORE/OLD TOWN** (between Naito Pkwy and 4th Ave from SW Oak to NW Glisan Sts; map:H5–L5), which has a few good shops, a couple of dependable Greek restaurants, and some fine galleries. On weekends, Skidmore livens with the Saturday Market.

Southwest of town is the charming **MULTNOMAH VILLAGE** (just off SW Multnomah Blvd on SW Capitol Hwy; map:II7), with a quaint, small-town personality revolving around several eateries, an excellent bookstore, a few arty shops, and about a dozen antique stores. Alongside the Willamette is the **WATER TOWER AT JOHNS LANDING** (between the Ross Island and Sellwood Bridges on SW Macadam Ave; open every day and weekday evenings; map:II6), with three stories of interesting shops. Cross the Sellwood Bridge into the city's southeast corner to find **SELLWOOD** (SE Tacoma St and 13th Ave; map:II5), which is inundated with stores selling country antiques. **WESTMORELAND** (northeast of Sellwood), which has as its hub the intersection of SE 17th Avenue and Bybee Boulevard, continues to grow in restaurants and specialty shops.

The **HAWTHORNE** area (SE Hawthorne Blvd between about SE 30th and 45th Aves; map:GG5) has that thrown-together look—great for browsing. Scavengers can spend hours pawing through secondhand record shops and vintage clothiers, just down the street from an Italian foods specialty shop, a top-drawer cookbook store, and natural-fiber boutiques. To the north, **NE BROADWAY** (east from NE 7th Ave; map:FF5) has experienced a renaissance of its own, with clothing, kitchenware, and book shops; a good wine store; a brewpub; and more than a half-dozen better-than-average restaurants.

SUBURBAN MALLS

Long a fixture of Portland life, the **LLOYD CENTER** (east across the Broadway Bridge, bordered by NE Broadway and Multnomah St, and NE 9th and 16th Aves; open daily; map:FF5) remains the state's largest mall. A multimillion-dollar renovation in the last decade put a glass roof over the entire structure (including the ice rink); these days there are three levels with nearly 200 shops. Nordstrom is the foremost anchor store; Meier & Frank and Sears are also there. Lloyd Center's proximity to downtown (connected by MAX light rail), as well as to the Oregon Convention Center and the Rose Quarter, have all helped give this formerly faltering mall a new life.

The west side is crawling with malls. Between Beaverton and Tigard is the largest, **WASHINGTON SQUARE AND SQUARE TOO** (just off Hwy 217; open daily; map:II9). A food court, lots of specialty shops, and the essential Nordstrom (the newest in town) are the big draws.

BEAVERTON TOWN SQUARE (off SW Canyon Rd and SW Beaverton-Hillsdale Hwy off Hwy 217; open daily; map:HH9), marked by its clock tower, and the **BEAVERTON MALL** (take SW Walker Rd exit off Hwy 217; open daily; map:HH9) are smaller westside shopping stops.

Back across the river lie **MALL 205** (take the SE Stark St exit off I-205; open daily; map:GG3), with a much-needed remodel in progress, and the booming **CLACKAMAS TOWN CENTER** (take the Sunnyside Rd exit from I-205; open daily; map:KK3), best known as the place where Tonya Harding learned to skate. Up north is **JANTZEN BEACH CENTER** (just off I-5 at Jantzen Beach; open daily; map:BB6), which stands out from the crowd with a 72-horse merry-go-round in the center of the mall ($1 a spin).

Ringing the city are a number of wonderful factory outlets. The Columbia River hamlet of Troutdale beckons eastbound traffic to the **COLUMBIA GORGE PREMIUM OUTLETS** (450 NW 257th Wy; 503/669-8060; www.premiumoutlets.com), which features an amazing array of stores, including Levi's, Gap, American Tourister, and Adidas. Lace up your walking shoes because once you start, it's hard to stop at **WOODBURN COMPANY STORES** (1001 Arney Rd, Woodburn; 1-888-664-SHOP; www. woodburncompanystores.com). This Willamette Valley mall houses one of the best selections of high-end retailers, featuring top designers such as Banana Republic, Ralph Lauren, Tommy Hilfiger, and Timberland.

Shops from A to Z

ANTIQUES

CIRCA, A.D. / 1204 NW Glisan St, Pearl District; 503/221-1269 Forget using your frequent flyer miles to search the dusty back roads of Europe. Circa has done it for you by bringing 19th-century furniture from France, Sweden, and assorted points unknown to the Pearl District's ground zero: NW 12th Avenue and Glisan Street. Friendly staff, too. *Tues–Sat; map:L2*

THE GENERAL STORE / 7987 SE 13th Ave, Sellwood; 503/233-1321 Make tracks to this antique shop, which features a signature display room: a vintage red train caboose. The General Store has been in business for a long time, and the selection (and refinishing techniques) shows it: Victorian and Early American walnut, mahogany, pine, and oak furniture. Dressers, trunks, and especially large furniture—a dining room table that seats 12 or a high-backed bed frame—are relegated to a larger upstairs room. *Thurs–Sun and by appointment; map:II5*

GEORGE V / 4741 SE Hawthorne Blvd, Hawthorne; 503/234-3932 Lovers of merry old England need not pack their bags to relish British-flavored delights. George V Antiques specializes in enough original European antique home furnishings to fill an entire home in high turn-of-the-19th-century style. Furniture, candlesticks, odd-looking items that seem to have no particular purpose at all—they are all here. But if you can't find what you are looking for, inquire with the shopkeepers—they might be willing to look for it on their next trip overseas. *Wed–Sun; www.georgevantiques.citysearch.com; map:GG3*

GERALDINE'S / 2772 NW Thurman St, Northwest; 503/295-5911 You could drive up and down Thurman Street a million times and still never notice this little antique shop tucked between a pottery gallery and a tapas restaurant. Once you discover it, however, you'll frequent Geraldine's to peruse the ever-changing display of attractive furnishings: English pine dressers, freestanding full-length mirrors, iron bed frames, antique braids and trim, and outdoor garden gates worthy of indoor display. Tucked in here and there are bed linens, wire baskets, and other curiosities. A weekend must-stop for Portland society mavens. *Mon–Sat; map:GG7*

HOLLYWOOD ANTIQUE SHOWCASE, ANTIQUE ALLEY / 1969 NE 42nd Ave, Hollywood; 503/288-1051; 2000 NE 42nd Ave, Hollywood; 503/287-9848 The Hollywood District, the only neighborhood in Portland to be named after a Byzantine rococo movie palace, is home to two movie-star-quality antique malls. Hollywood Antique Showcase houses more than 70 dealers and fills over 10,000 square feet. On the main level are collectibles, from Depression-era glass to jewelry, while the basement showcases good-quality furniture and home accessories. Across the street you will find Antique Alley; located in the basement of the hub-bubby 42nd Street Station, this is a fun place to find funky junk and cool pieces from the baby boomer era. *Every day; map:FF4*

JERRY LAMB INTERIORS AND ANTIQUES / 2304 NW Savier St, Northwest; 503/227-6077 A former Pearl District landmark, this nifty showroom has gone uptown and moved its entire operations to the always-busy avenue of NW "Trendy-Third." Here interior designer/local legend Jerry Lamb displays his outstanding collection of Oriental antiques—especially porcelains—and fine, mostly English and American, furniture housed in what once was a photography studio. The perfect setting to show off picture-perfect embroidery and woodblock prints from China or Japan, and hundreds and hundreds of porcelain pieces—Imari, blue and white Canton, celadon, and Rose Medallion. *Tues–Fri; map:GG7*

PARTNERS IN TIME / 1313 W Burnside St, Pearl District; 503/228-6299 Cut a path to this cultural crossroads (both literally and figuratively) located in the middle of brewpubs, gay bars, and music venues. Most everything here is pine—European pine from England, Austria, Holland, and Germany—though there are a small number of newer pieces done in period style. In addition to the furniture (armoires, tables, chairs, benches, dressers, nightstands), you'll also find Oriental rugs of all ages plus decorative objects (Turkish pots, painted wooden boxes, and papier-mâché trays) and gift items (books, soaps, candlesticks). *Every day; www.partnersintimeantiques.com; map:J1*

SELLWOOD PEDDLER ATTIC GOODIES / 8065 SE 13th Ave, Sellwood; 503/235-0946 A super-sized version of grandma's attic, this 5,000-square-foot space has a little bit of everything craftily crammed into it. The emphasis here is on vintage clothing and jewelry, glassware, china, sterling silverware, lamps, and quilts. There's also a fair amount of furniture. The back room is full of dusty tools and salvageable house parts. *Every day; www.sellwoodpeddler.com; map:II5*

APPAREL

AUBERGINE / 1100 NW Glisan St, Pearl District; 503/228-7313 This gallerylike store features elegantly casual clothing in innovative fabrics.

Owners Margaret Block and Tanya Doubleday regularly travel to New York in search of unique designs, including Dosa silk pieces based on traditional Indian and Korean layering, simple styles in unusual fabric hybrids by Su-zen, and Lilith pieces designed for layering woven fabrics over stretch garments. *Mon–Sat; map:L1*

BARBARA JOHNSON CLOTHING OUTLET / 18005 SW Lower Boones Ferry Rd, Tigard; 503/620-1777 If you're a sample size (from 6 to 12), you're in luck, because Barbara Johnson is the place where sales reps unload their merchandise. Women's dresses, suits, blouses, and lingerie are priced 20 percent above wholesale, and well-known brands (Sigrid Olsen, Carol Anderson, Marisa Christina) hit the racks here one to two seasons ahead of the stores. *Mon–Sat; www.barbarajohnsons.com; map:MM9*

CERISE / 2417 SE Hawthorne Blvd, Southeast; 503/238-1540 Local designer Patricia Harrington recently opened her workroom and retail space in this beautiful Victorian house. Harrington's Arabian Knight label features natural-fiber pieces, including exquisite kimonos and other luxurious loungewear, hand-knit hats, pillows, and refurbished furniture. Jewelry and gift items designed by local craftspeople augment the stunning wares (and the dressing room's divine). *Weds–Sat, Mon, Tues by appointment; cerise@inetarena.com; map:HH5*

CHANGES—DESIGNS TO WEAR / 927 SW Yamhill St, Downtown; 503/223-3737 An extension of the Real Mother Goose, this shop carries clothing designed by regional and national artists. Goose management is always on the prowl for the new and the wonderful, so there are often great surprises: blocked silk shirts, tooled leather purses, burned velvet scarves, hand-woven suits cut to flatter real women's bodies. Earthy and unusual jewelry complements all of the above. This is a great destination for window shoppers as well as collectors. *Mon–Sat; map:H2*

EASY STREET / 16337 SW Bryant Rd, Lake Oswego; 503/636-6547 Here's where you'll find glitzy evening dresses and spunky accessories to wear with them. Mothers of the bride and groom favor this shop, which has been dressing women for special occasions for 22 years. There's a decent selection of sportswear, too. *Mon–Sat; map:MM7*

ELIZABETH STREET / 635 NW 23rd Ave, Northwest; 503/243-2456 If you—like the buyers here—find inspiration in the pages of *InStyle Magazine*, this is your kind of place. This Portland boutique strives to stay current by snatching up the latest by contemporary designers: Rozae Nichols separates in luxe fabrics, Trina Turk pieces featuring innovative textures and patterns, and Tono Sutono designs. From leather pants and killer jeans to sassy dresses, unique watches, and sunglasses aplenty, Elizabeth Street stays ahead of the curve. *Every day; map:GG7*

GIRLFRIENDS / 904 NW 23rd Ave, Northwest; 503/294-0488 Tailored to the young and slender, this shop carries a solid collection of cotton T-shirts, chic dresses, sweaters, and trousers, as well as pajamas and stockings (not to mention soaps, scents, dishes, and candles). Think of it as slumber-party wear—and then some. Shoppers' companions can rest on a sofa, sampling coffee, candy, and newspapers provided by the savvy management. *Every day; www.girlfriendsboutique.com; map:GG7*

IRVING'S / 2322 NW Irving St, Northwest; 503/243-5300 The owners of Elizabeth Street and Zelda's Shoe Bar teamed to open this ultrahip men's shop in the back space of the former. You'll find great denim, outerwear, and a branch of Zelda's for men that carries just the right lug-sole shoe—or Harley boot—for the occasion. *Every day; map:GG7*

JANE'S OBSESSION, JANE'S VANITY / 728 NW 23rd Ave, Northwest; 503/221-1490; 521 SW Broadway, Downtown; 503/241-3860; Two elegant lingerie outlets owned by Jane Adams feature the best in European bras, panties, garter belts, nightwear, and accessories. Acquired every January in Paris, elegant bits of silk and lace are displayed on racks, in glass cases, and across the walls. The central downtown store (Jane's Vanity) is pricier than Jane's Obsession, which features younger, trendier attire. *Mon–Sat; map:GG7; map:I3*

LA PALOMA / 6316 SW Capitol Hwy, Hillsdale Shopping Center; 503/246-3417 Kim Osgood and Mike Roach oversee one of the city's best finds for women's natural-fiber clothing and imaginative accessories. The emphasis is on easy-care pieces that pack well, a must for well-dressed adventurers. Brands such as Flax, Jam's World, and Mishi mean breezy linens and 100 percent cotton separates and sweaters. There's also Indonesian batik and ikat clothing and silver jewelry from Southeast Asia. *Every day; www.palomaclothing.com; map:II7*

LENA MEDOYEFF STUDIO / 3200-B SE Hawthorne Blvd, Hawthorne; 503/230-7259 Portland designer Lynn Solomson learned her craft from a woman in a small town in Guatemala during a stint in the Peace Corps—not exactly your average fashion schooling. Her luxurious creations are equally extraordinary. She employs exquisite fabrics (lots of silk and hand-stitched, ornate textiles) from Calcutta, Kashmir, and Hong Kong in straightforward dresses, skirts, blouses, jackets, and pants. Spoil yourself rotten in the rich beauty of Solomson's recently opened studio/retail space amid her infectious enthusiasm. *Wed–Sat, Sun–Tues by appointment; www.lenadress.com; map:HH5*

MARIO'S / 921 SW Morrison St, Downtown; 503/227-3477 For more than 60 years, men demanding the best in designer fashion have shopped Mario's. Armani, Vestimenta, Hugo Boss, Canali, and Zegna suits keep elegant company here with fine sweaters, top-notch cotton shirts, and tasteful Friday casual wear. *Every day; www.marios.com; map:H2*

MATISSE / 1411 NE Broadway, NE Broadway; 503/287-5414 Anyone who revels in femininity will adore this enchanting store; it's the bedroom/walk-in closet of girly-girl dreams. Stunning dresses (from formal to casual), adorable separates (not to mention vibrant tees and tanks), and silk and rayon dresses fill the racks; romantic necklaces and other accessories displayed in antique cases accent the gorgeous garments. *Every day; map:FF5*

THE MERCANTILE / 735 SW Park Ave, Downtown; 503/223-6649 Owner Victoria Taylor loves fashion, and her store seems at once a gallery of her favorite up-to-the-minute styles and an elegant, comfortable shopping destination. Clothing here suits mature women looking for tailored, upscale style as well as young professionals looking for sophisticated, contemporary fashion. The sprawling space houses everything from evening and sportswear to eclectic accessories and household objects. *Every day; map:H2*

MIMI AND LENA / 823 NW 23rd Ave, Northwest; 503/224-7736 Named for the grandmothers of the two shop owners, Mimi and Lena specializes in contemporary dresses that range from simply casual to bridesmaid dressy (think Nicole Miller). Local designs available here include rustic printed dresses by Kara-Line and adorable `e•ko logic hats made from recycled knits. Mimi and Lena also offers a large collection of feminine footwear (including white dress shoes that are beautiful, not chintzy) and unique jewelry. *Every day; www.mimiandlena.com; map:GG7*

M. SELLIN LTD. / 3556 SE Hawthorne Blvd, Hawthorne; 503/239-4605 M. Sellin carries natural-fiber clothing cut to wear easy and still look sophisticated—classic Northwest style. Eileen Fisher, Flax, and Tommy Bahama are the names on the labels; sizes range from petite to plus. Thirty different styles of shoes decorate store shelves near an eye-catching selection of linen handbags, ethnic jewelry, stockings, scarves, and scrunchable hats. *Every day; www.msellinltd.com; map:GG4*

NORM THOMPSON / 1805 NW Thurman St, Northwest; 503/221-0764 We'd be remiss in not telling you about Norm Thompson's two stores—in Northwest Portland and at the airport (503/249-0170). The clothes range from conservative to rigid and are of standard quality, but devotees appreciate the predictability of the designs. From comfy big polo dresses to slacks and pastel shirts, from sturdy luggage to shoes, slippers, and gift foods, everything here is beautifully displayed. *Every day; www.normtom.com; map:GG7*

ODESSA / 611 NW 13th Ave, Pearl District; 503/223-1998 It's easy to forget that you're in Portland while shopping at Odessa; the fashion lies ahead of the game, relative to most local offerings, and the space feels like a SoHo gallery. Shop here for coveted fashions spied in the latest magazines—not the high-end couture lines, but the more affordable, hip styles from young designers. Browse the racks in the minimalist, airy store for sumptuous evening wear, the sweater or blouse you won't find anywhere else for six months (if ever), or a new pair of slim-fitting Earl jeans. The latest footwear and unique jewelry add to the appeal. This style destination, located in the arty Pearl district, has even been featured in national fashion magazines. *Mon–Sat; map:GG6*

PHILLIP STEWART / 1202 SW 19th Ave, Goose Hollow; 503/226-3589 After running the show for more than 23 years, Phillip Stewart sold his eponymous store to a former employee, Jim Maer. Expect to find the same fine wool jackets and gabardine trousers, as well as more custom lines and updated sportswear, displayed like treasured objects through the main floor of this historic-house-turned-shop. Hidden away in Goose Hollow, this is one beautifully tailored secret, with more than 300 choices of fabric for custom shirts and other garments. *Mon–Sat; pstewart@ xann.com; map:GG6*

POKERFACE / 128 SW 3rd Ave, Old Town; 503/294-0445 Formerly a vintage shop in Northeast Portland, Poker Face's current downtown digs suit the hip, urban stock to a T. Look for young designers with an edge— Final Home, Levi's Red, and Diesel—as well as swanky duds for a night of clubbing or a rock 'n' roll show. Shoes, bags, and other street-smart accessories fit in just fine. *Every day; map:J5*

THE PORTLAND PENDLETON SHOP / 900 SW 5th Ave, Downtown; 503/242-0037 Believe it or not, Pendleton has dusted off its look at the end of the 20th century. The shop, in the Standard Insurance Building, offers the most complete collection of Pendleton clothing anywhere in Oregon, including petite sizes, skirt-and-shirt matchables, and summer silk and rayon combinations. Of course, it wouldn't be Pendleton without the wool chemises and blankets, endearingly familiar to virtually every Northwesterner. *Mon–Sat; www.pendleton-usa.com; map:F2*

SHEBA HOUSE OF ELEGANCE / 2808 NE Martin Luther King Jr Blvd, Ste K, Northeast; 503/287-8925 Assefash Melles's shop recently moved to the beautifully renovated Standard Dairy Building, but the dramatic ethnic pieces from Africa, Indonesia, and Portland remain. There's some alternative office and career wear here, plenty of caftans, and unique evening looks, as well as great jewelry by local artisans. *Every day; map:FF6*

SPARTACUS LEATHERS / 300 SW 12th Ave, Downtown; 503/224-2604 Spartacus is sort of the anti–Victoria's Secret; lingerie in this sex shop is more S&M leather than dainty satin. The selection is vast and, to the store's credit, not all geared toward the whips-and-chains crowd. There are racks of sexy, elegant nighties and robes, nice bras and panties, and a wide range of men's underwear in addition to the wilder stripper-inspired and novel garb. *Every day; www.spartacusleathers.com; map:J1*

3 MONKEYS / 803 NW 23rd Ave, Northwest; 503/222-9894 Jam-packed with contemporary garb and accessories for the teen and twentysomething set, shoppers peruse both floors for flirty dresses, slinky black evening wear, wild lingerie, cute purses, inexpensive jewelry, and bright wigs and separates. Don't miss the bin of thrifty vintage scarves upstairs. *Every day; map:GG7*

TUMBLEWEED / 1804 NE Alberta St, Alberta St; 503/335-3100 Local designer Kara Larson opened this delightful store in the flourishing and eclectic Alberta Street neighborhood to showcase her rustic, prairie-inspired Kara-Line dresses adored by the alt-country crowd. The timeless, sizeless dresses are romantic and feminine, yet comfortable and cowboy boot–worthy. (Kara even has a few vintage black pairs for sale.) Wild Carrots gingham jumpers for the toddler set, beautiful beaded jewelry, novel wallets and journals, and dresses and separates by other local designers are also charmingly displayed here (and, yes, there's real tumbleweed). Down-home tunes fill the air in this sunny space. *Tues–Sun; www.kara-line.com; map:EE5*

VERGOTIS CLOTHIER / 1433 NE Broadway, NE Broadway; 503/284-4065 Local designer Kelli Vergotis showcases her sleek creations and those of like-minded designers in this inviting store. Audrey (and Katharine) Hepburn–inspired style resonates in the classy yet contemporary garments, which are cut impeccably to flatter real women's bodies (as opposed to merely those of teenagers and supermodels). An intriguing array of designer jewelry complements stunning dresses and swanky separates. Besides the great wardrobe options, the giant mirrors and antiques make the place feel like a dressing room for glamour queens—that includes you. *Tues–Sun; map:FF5*

BAKERIES

BEAVERTON BAKERY / 12375 SW Broadway, Beaverton (and branch); 503/646-7136 Beautiful (and delicious) wedding and birthday cakes are what BB is best known for, but the crusty monastery whole wheat loaf, onion-cheese fougasse bread, and apple-cinnamon loaf are addictive staples. Lines are often longer at the larger Broadway store than at the Lake Oswego location (16857 SW 65th Ave, Southlake Center; 646-7136); take a number, or pick up a cake at any number of local markets. *Every day; map:HH9*

GABRIEL'S BAKERY / 123 SW Broadway, Downtown; 503/225-1655 The two former Gabriel's shops have consolidated into one central location at the corner of SW Broadway and W Burnside. The new venue still offers what fans remember from the old: a rotation of 15 different bread varieties and a panoply of muffins, plus scones and bagels for the morning crowd. Gabriel's also serves soups, salads, and sandwiches for lunch, so it's a good place to consider when you take a break from browsing at Powell's Books, just up the street. *Mon–Sat; map: J4*

THE GERMAN BAKERY / 10528 NE Sandy Blvd, Parkrose; 503/252-1881 This is the only place in town to find traditional German breads, butter cookies, and pastries. Sit at one of several tables and sample some desserts: creamhorns, Black Forest and Bienenstich cakes, and German tea cookies. *Tues–Sat; map:FF2*

GRAND CENTRAL BAKING COMPANY / 2230 SE Hawthorne Blvd, Hawthorne (and branches); 503/232-0575 The spacious, airy spot is a great place to start the morning with a jammer, apricot scone, or slice of pumpkin bread. Grand Central also serves sandwiches in its Hawthorne and Multnomah locations and an extended menu at the branch near Lloyd Center. But it is best known for its bread, some of the first—and best—representatives of the revival of artisan baking in Portland. Specialty breads, such as fresh herb or walnut-thyme, are sold only at the bakery, but the rustic Italian baguettes and hearty sour white, among others, are also sold at better grocery stores throughout the city. Other branches are located in the Lloyd District and Multnomah Village. *Every day; map:GG5*

GREAT HARVEST BREAD COMPANY / 810 SW 2nd Ave, Downtown (and branch); 503/224-8583 Looking to buy the freshest loaf of bread in town? Go where the wheat is ground, and the flour milled, daily. Breads of substance, character, and a healthy amount of fiber are harvested at this Montana-based franchise. Free samples of the whole crop are always available, as well as warm bread by the slice slathered with butter. In the morning, long lines form for no-cholesterol bran muffins, and you'll want to try the sweet, gooey cinnamon rolls—at least once. Good cookies, too! There's also a branch in Clackamas (8926 SE Sunnyside Rd; 503/659-5392; map:KK3). *Mon–Sat; map:F4*

JACIVA'S CHOCOLATES AND PASTRIES / 4733 SE Hawthorne Blvd, Hawthorne; 503/234-8115 Behind the retail area, Jack Elmer, Swiss-trained chocolatier and pastry chef, and his wife, Iva Sue, craft fine Swiss chocolates sold across the country. With their own recipes they create chocolates that Grandma would envy. They also stock the shop with billowy éclairs and exquisitely decorated cakes (the lemon is legendary, but there's also a chocolate mousse dome to prompt indecision), as well as less dramatic coffee cakes, Danishes, and muffins. There's even a room where brides and grooms can sample wedding cakes (pictures and "dummy cakes" help you decide). *Mon–Sat; map:GG4*

MARSEE BAKING / 1323 NW 23rd Ave (and branches); 503/295-5900 Marsee's look and feel has changed only slightly since the first one settled in Portland at the north end of NW 23rd Avenue, despite several recent changes in ownership. Now in addition to bagels, baguettes, hearty breads, tarts, cakes, cookies, and pastries, there's also a deli case filled with prepared sandwiches and a whole new line of—dare we say—supermarket-looking (but better tasting) cakes. Neighborhood branches are peppered throughout the city: downtown, NE Broadway, Sellwood, Lake Oswego, Tanasbourne, and even the Portland airport. With espresso, juices, and ample seating, they're places that are conducive to lingering. *Every day; map:FF7*

PEARL BAKERY / 102 NW 9th Ave, Pearl District; 503/827-0910 Standards for bread have not only proofed but risen to an incredible height in Portland since the Pearl set up shop in 1997. Now, it's hard to believe that there was ever a time when the light-filled bakery wasn't here. The irresistible pastries and the incredible artisan breads are leavened by traditional methods, hand-formed, and baked in the huge ovens in the back. For lunch there's a delicious selection of sandwiches in the case: eggplant on ciabatta, pears and gorgonzola on walnut levain, and smoked turkey on a Kaiser roll. Consider yourself forewarned: a visit to the bakery in the afternoon means limited choices; if there's something you absolutely have to have, go early. *Mon–Sat; www.pearlbakery.com; map:K3*

ROSIE'S BOULANGERIE / 1406 SE Stark St, Southeast; 503/232-4675 You might happen upon Rosie's late of an afternoon and find a single item sitting alone in the display case. This is not a sign that Rosie Lindsey is lazy—far from it. Rather, it's an indication of the popularity of this new bakery that things tend to sell out fast. Rosie's Boulangerie takes its cues from France, as the name suggests, and the French influence is everywhere apparent, from the buttery baguettes to the pastry-and-coffee breakfasts customers enjoy while standing at the counter. From simple breads to fine pastries, everything here speaks of Lindsey's integrity and artistry—so if you come across a lone item in the display case when you walk in, hurry up and buy it before another customer comes along. *Tues–Sat; map:GG5*

RUBY MOUNTAIN BAKERY / 3240-B SE Hawthorne Blvd, Hawthorne; 503/231-0062 This diminutive shop with its low-profile storefront is easily overlooked, but you'd do well to seek it out. Owner Becky Kole, who spent 13 years as the head baker at Papa Haydn's, has a deft touch with European tortes and fine pastries, from Sacher torte and chocolate praline dacquoise to lemon roulade and chocolate-dipped macaroons. She takes carrot cake to new heights, and her tarte Tatin and German chocolate cake are stellar. Cole's artfully assembled creations look as good as they taste, and you can enjoy her cakes and tortes by the slice at the bakery or take home a whole one. Give her two days' minimum notice for a custom order, and you'll be delighted by the results. *Wed–Sun; rubymtn@emailcom; www.rubymountain.homepage.com; map:GG5*

BODY CARE

AVEDA LIFESTYLE STORE AND SPA / 500 SW Washington, Downtown; 503/248-0615 If you're familiar with Aveda products, you know what to expect: cutting-edge, richly scented products packed with essential oils and other plant-derived ingredients for your skin and hair. The entire Aveda line—makeup, cleansers, and hair care products—is sold at the front of this attractive space in the Fifth Avenue Suites Hotel; full spa service is available in back. *Every day; www.aveda.com; map:I5*

COREEN SALOME / 808 NW 23rd Ave, Northwest; 503/827-8693 This cool "post-minimal apothecary" ups the ante for skin and hair care shopping. Coreen Salome carries a wide variety of domestic and imported products, including some lines you'd be hard-pressed to find anywhere else in town. Everything from Dead Sea salts and organic detanglers to Japanese jelly bath mixes; light-sensitive products are even tucked in slick brown UV-protection bags approved by the U.S. Pharmacopeia and lauded by fashionistas. *Every day; www.coreensalome.com; map:K3*

ESCENTIAL LOTIONS & OILS / 710 NW 23rd Ave, Northwest (and branch); 503/248-9748 or 800/750-6457 This is the perfect place to put together a gift basket for someone (including yourself) who loves luxurious baths and essential-oil-scented skin treats. Bonus: customers choose their own scents to be added to unscented potions by the friendly and knowledgeable staff. A vast array of soaps, classic shaving supplies, cosmetics, and incense round out the heady mix. A second branch (3638 SE Hawthorne Boulevard; 503/236-7976; map:GG4) is located in the Hawthorne District. *Every day; map:GG7*

THE PERFUME HOUSE / 3328 SE Hawthorne Blvd, Hawthorne; 503/234-5375 The ultimate in olfactory stimulation: Chris Tsefelas's Perfume House has been praised by the likes of Yves St. Laurent and Jean Patou as the finest in the world. You can sniff exquisite scents, from rare Russian perfumes to Corina from the Patrician House, introduced at the 1962 Seattle World's Fair and considered one of the greatest perfumes ever created. Prices range from $2 for a sample-size vial to $8,500 worth of L'Air d'Or. *Mon–Sat (closed Mon June–Aug, open Sun in Dec); www.theperfumehouse.com; map:GG5*

ZIVA SALON-STORE / 610 NW 23rd Ave, Northwest; 503/221-6990 Don't be surprised to feel like a New York City pro hair stylist or esthetician while shopping in this vast body-care emporium; Ziva stocks an unbelievable selection of products for your locks and skin, as well as pro tweezers, styling tools, and heavy-duty metal cases to tote your goods in. Lines like Bumble & Bumble, Rene Furterer, Phytologie, L'Occitaine, Dermalogica, Sebastian, and KMS are just the tip of the iceberg. Salon and spa services are available in back. *Every day; www.zivanet.com; map:GG7*

BOOKS AND MAGAZINES

ANNIE BLOOM'S BOOKS / 7834 SW Capitol Hwy, Multnomah; 503/246-0053 A paragon of independent bookstores, this cozy shop attracts readers from all over the west side (and even some book lovers who cross the river). Staff recommendations pepper the extensive selection of fiction, parenting,

and children's literature, which surrounds a colorful play area at the back of the store. The Judaica section is quite strong, and special orders are no problem. Comfy armchairs, a house cat, and a complimentary cup of tea make you feel at home. Magazines, cards, and puppets, too. *Every day; ablooms@teleport.com; www.annieblooms.com; map:II7*

BARNES & NOBLE / 1231 NE Broadway, NE Broadway (and branches); 503/335-0201 With six locations in the Portland-Vancouver area, these megabookstores place a savvy emphasis on comfort. Most stores have book groups, author readings, story hours for children; call for details. *Every day; www.bn.com; map:FF5*

BORDERS BOOKS AND MUSIC / 708 SW 3rd Ave, Downtown (and branches); 503/220-5911 A sunny operation that combines books, music, and coffee, this national chain—presents itself as a community-oriented, user-friendly shop in the downtown core. Branches in Beaverton and Tigard. *Every day; www.borders.com; map:G4*

BROADWAY BOOKS / 1714 NE Broadway, NE Broadway; 503/284-1726 Despite its proximity to Barnes & Noble, Broadway Books is thriving in this Northeast neighborhood. Together, Gloria Borg Olds and Roberta Dyer have been in the book biz in Portland for more than three decades, and they provide personal, educated service. There's a sizable selection of biographies and memoirs, the shop's specialty, but also fiction, Judaica, and contemporary fiction. They're pros at the special order, if the book you want isn't in stock. *Every day; map:FF5*

A CHILDREN'S PLACE / 4807 NE Fremont St, Beaumont; 503/284-8294 A change in ownership and a move to new quarters have shifted this store's emphasis, with toys, puzzles, and craft supplies complementing an extensive selection of books for your pint-size bookworm. The selection varies from classics to gimmicks, and it's an excellent resource for educators, who receive a 20 percent discount. If you're buying a gift, the helpful clerks take the time to find the perfect book among the hundreds of volumes that pack the place—whether the recipient wants a book to chew on (lots of cardboard titles) or to thumb through. *Every day; kids-books@jps.net; www.snapdragonbooks.com; map:FF4*

FUTURE DREAMS / 1800 E Burnside St, Southeast; 503/231-8311 The stuff of Future Dreams is one part sci-fi and one part comic art. New and used magazines, books, and comics range from classic favorites to esoteric, hard-to-find titles. Cover all your bases with a good selection of back issues combined with a reservation service for new volumes. *Every day; fdb@hevanet.com; map:FF5*

THE GREAT NW BOOK STORE / 1234 SW Stark St, Downtown; 503/223-8098 Good karma, good books, good people. This rambling store offers hidden treasure troves around every corner. GNW boasts the largest exclusively used-book inventory in the city, and so it makes sense that they also offer appraisals among their services (one of the few bookstores in town to do so). The strengths are Western Americana, first-edition modern and older literature, and sports—specifically baseball, mountain climbing, and golf. There's a rare-book room full of treasures, too. Book buying by appointment. *Every day; gnw@greatnorthwestbooks.com; www.greatnorthwestbooks.com; map:J2*

HAWTHORNE BOULEVARD BOOKS / 3129 SE Hawthorne Blvd, Hawthorne; 503/236-3211 Roger and Ilse Roberts invite the public into their Hawthorne home to browse their used and antiquarian books. They're particularly fond of classic literature and American history. A fireplace (when lit) makes it tough to leave. *Tues–Sun; hbb@teleport.com; map:GG5*

IN OTHER WORDS / 3734 SE Hawthorne Blvd, Hawthorne; 503/232-6003 Another bookstore on the book lover's miracle mile-and-a-half that is Hawthorne Boulevard, IOW distinguishes itself with a community-oriented, feminist approach. All the books are written by women. The nonprofit store provides its patrons with feminist, gay/lesbian, and holistic literature not available at mainstream retail venues, as well as "women-positive" videos to rent. An extensive selection of children's books gets your young friends off to a good start. The atmosphere is cheerful and calming, with a wonderfully dreamy painting in the public rest room. *Every day; othrwrds@teleport.com; www.inotherwords.com; map:GG5*

LAUGHING HORSE BOOKS / 3652 SE Division St, Southeast; 503/236-2893 Activists, heretics, and visionaries run this politically progressive and environmentally oriented nonprofit bookstore/coffeehouse collective. Stop in or call for a schedule of events—discussion groups, speakers, and community potlucks that focus on social change (health care in Guatemala, war-tax resistance, rain-forest protection struggles). Find their book tables at progressive events, such as Earth Day celebrations and Tibetan freedom rallies, throughout the metropolitan area. *Mon–Sat; map:HH5*

LONGFELLOW'S BOOKS / 1401 SE Division St, Southeast; 503/239-5222 Tucked between a school and a residential neighborhood, this gem of a used-book store will delight the dedicated book browser. Jon Hagen has run Longfellow's for the past 20 years and is quick to help both regular and new customers find their area of interest. A nice selection of the books we remember from childhood (juvenile boys' and girls' series), as well as National Geographic maps, Western Americana, collectible sheet music, and "ephemera." *Mon–Sat; longfellowsbookspdx@hotmail.com; map:HH5*

LOOKING GLASS BOOKSTORE / 318 SW Taylor St, Downtown; 503/227-4760 This much-loved shop—now over a quarter century old—with a skylit and polished tri-level interior is probably one of the nicest-looking bookstores around. But it's more than a pretty place, with a selection of titles other stores might skip over: offbeat comic books and contemporary graphic arts, as well as science fiction (plus notable psychology, health, and modern literature sections). Ask to be put on the mailing list for the newsletter and holiday catalog. *Mon–Sat; lookglas@teleport. com; map:G3*

MORRISON BOOKS / 530 NW 12th Ave, Pearl District; 503/295-6882 David Morrison has made a name for himself in two ways: by selling high-quality, used books on art, architecture, and design, and also by speaking out against bigger, monopolizing bookstores. His shop in the Pearl District houses a wide selection of general antiquarian books, boasts the largest collection of used photography books in the city, and also has a fine cache of rare and out-of-print titles. *Tue–Sat; morrison@ teleport.com; www.teleport.com/~morrison; map:K2*

MURDER BY THE BOOK / 3210 SE Hawthorne Blvd, Hawthorne; 503/232-9995 *The* place to go for lovers of mystery, thriller, and spy fiction. Books are divided by genus, so you'll find Kate Fanslar in the Cherchez la Femme section and more than 50 Northwest mystery writers in On the Homefront (many signings, too). Knowledgeable staff members take the time to listen to your preferences and turn you on to new authors. New and used volumes to buy, sell, barter, and kill for—so to speak. *Every day; info@mbtb.com; www.mbtb.com; map:GG5*

NEW RENAISSANCE BOOKSHOP / 1338 NW 23rd Ave, Northwest; 503/224-4929 Two adjacent Victorians house approximately 15,000 titles and a varied selection of paraphernalia to help people take that next spiritual step, whether it be recovery, growth, business prosperity, or self-transformation. Browsers must pay homage to the multiple shelves of tarot books. The top floor houses a meditation room and a small selection of used books. Lectures, tarot readings, or discussions led by "intuitive counselors" are also part of the scene. In the interest of the younger set, the play area has been expanded and there are holographs, science toys, fairy costumes, and books on children's spirituality. Other things that add material conflict to nonmaterial enlightenment: chimes, rainbow crystals, jewelry, tapes, and videos. *Every day; map:FF7*

OREGON HISTORY CENTER MUSEUM STORE / 1200 SW Park Ave, Downtown; 503/306-5230 Books remain the emphasis at this store operated on the street level of the Oregon History Center, despite the broad nonbook inventory (T-shirts, jewelry, calendars, and other tourist take-home items). The bookstore sells a fine selection of regional history books, perhaps the best in the state, including a good selection of children's history books and the society's own quarterly journal. If a book won't do, there's a substantial collection of maps and postcards depicting early Oregon. Upstairs, an extensive photo library offers reproductions of historical photographs. *Every day; www.ohs.org; map:F2*

OREGON MUSEUM OF SCIENCE AND INDUSTRY (OMSI) STORE / 1945 SE Water Ave, Southeast; 503/234-4358 In addition to a great selection of thought-provoking, fun, science-oriented toys, games, puzzles, and project kits, the OMSI store boasts an awesome selection of science books. Virtually every major category is here, from astronomy to zoology, with books targeted at every age and knowledge level. *Tue–Sun; www.omsi.org; map:D8*

PERIODICALS AND BOOK PARADISE / 3315 SE Hawthorne Blvd, Hawthorne; 503/234-6003 Two stores combined under one roof—Periodicals Paradise (formerly on Powell) and Book City—means more to look at and less room to do it in. As far as magazines go, with close to a million issues in stock, it's very likely one of the largest collections of its kind in the West. Issues published within the past year sell for 75 percent off the cover price. And when it comes to books, you'll find anything from mysteries to religion, health to children's books—no special area of depth, but a wide range of books within many topics. *Every day; mookeymags@aol.com; map:HH4*

PORTLAND STATE UNIVERSITY BOOKSTORE / 1880 SW 6th Ave, Downtown; 503/226-2631 Not just for students, the cooperatively run PSU Bookstore has been the city's major supplier of textbooks for more than 40 years; however, the stock of children's, computer, business, fiction, and reference books attracts even Ivy League alumni. Test and study guides, too. *Mon–Sat; psubook@bkst.pdx.edu; www.psubookstore.com; map:C1*

POWELL'S BOOKS FOR COOKS AND GARDENERS / 3747 SE Hawthorne Blvd, Hawthorne; 503/235-3802 Optimally located next door to Pastaworks, this shop is a delight. Cookbooks are the thing here: new, used, coffee-table, rare, and remaindered. There are lots of savvy things for the kitchen, too—colorful dishes and table linens, mixing bowls, retro refrigerator magnets, whisks, and lots of whatnot you simply can't live without. Noted cookbook authors pass through for signings and demonstrations; local chefs also give demonstrations here. Finally, there's a large gardening section, replete with accessories such as chimes and pots—and, of course, books galore. *Every day; www.powells.com; map:GG5*

POWELL'S CITY OF BOOKS / 1005 W Burnside St, Downtown (and branches); 503/228-4651 Powell's will always be top dog in Portland, despite the many omnipresent national-chain superstores that vie for attention. Even those who prefer smaller, more intimate bookstores find themselves lured to Powell's. See Top 20 Attractions in the Exploring chapter for branch listings. *Every day; www.powells.com; map:J2*

RICH'S CIGAR STORE / 820 SW Alder St, Downtown; 503/228-1700; 706 NW 23rd Ave, Northwest; 503/227-6907 Perhaps the best place in town to find a huge and thorough selection of national and foreign newspapers and magazines and, of course, tobacco. The charm of the tobacco stands of bygone days is missing, but it is replaced by a comprehensive selection of periodicals and a helpful staff. *Every day; info@richs cigar.com; www.richscigar.com; map:I3, map:FF7*

THINGS FROM ANOTHER WORLD / 4133 NE Sandy Blvd, Hollywood (and branches); 503/284-4693 With five stores in the greater metro area stocking trading cards (sports and otherwise), comic books, lead miniatures, Japanese toys, and sci-fi and fantasy literature, you're never far from meeting any alien's needs. Formerly Pegasus Books. Branches are located both in town (Northwest and Southeast) and in the suburbs (Beaverton and Milwaukie). *Every day; www.tfaw.com; map:FF5*

TITLE WAVE BOOKSTORE / 216 NE Knott St, Northeast; 503/248-5021 Ever wonder where old library books end up? More than 20,000 volumes from the Multnomah County Library sell for bargain prices here at the old Albina Library. The volunteer staff organizes the books (including encyclopedia sets) by—what else?—the Dewey decimal system. Lots of choices for young and old alike. There are also magazines, CDs, books on tape, and videos. *Mon–Sat; map:FF5*

TWENTY-THIRD AVENUE BOOKS / 1015 NW 23rd Ave, Northwest; 503/224-5097 Bob Maull's friendly demeanor is part of what makes this Northwest Portland store so appealing. It's just what a bookstore should be: low-key and well organized, with a strong sense of its authors. Contemporary fiction predominates in the original store area, while the adjoining room makes lots of space for lovely gardening and design books. Author readings occur frequently, so call for details. *Every day; books23@teleport.com; map:FF7*

CANDY AND CHOCOLATE

GODIVA CHOCOLATIER / Pioneer Place, Downtown; 503/226-4722 New digs in the new Pioneer Place mean more space to display the full line of Godiva products, and it's not just chocolate anymore at this nationwide chain with links in many major cities. In addition to the beautifully wrapped and displayed boxed sets of candy, the gold-tinted shelves are lined with Godiva coffee, cocoa, biscuits, biscotti, and novelties like chocolate cigars. Expansion, however, hasn't reduced the quality; you can still linger over the case of exquisitely sculpted chocolate starfish, seashells, and flowers, as well as an irresistible assortment of truffles, glacéed fruit, and, when in season, chocolate-dipped strawberries. Expensive, but worth it. *Every day; www.godiva.com; map:H4*

MOONSTRUCK CHOCOLATIER / 608 SW Alder St, Downtown (and branch); 503/241-0955 One thing about selling chocolates is that you don't need a lot of space, just enough room to ogle and queue. This small retail shop showcases probably the prettiest chocolates in town—and the tastiest. Some Moonstruck truffles—many hand-dipped—are spiked with such heavenly fillings as raspberry Chambord, Clear Creek pear brandy, and Grand Marnier; others, such as the cinnamon-latte and bittersweet chocolate truffles, are equally intoxicating and worthy of addiction. Another shop is located just inside the Red Lion at the Portland airport (503/335-8385). *Mon–Sat; www.chocaholic.com; map:H4*

SWEETS, ETC. / 7828 SW Capitol Hwy, Multnomah Village; 503/293-0088 Multnomah Village just wouldn't be the same without a candy store on its main street. Expect to find a good mix of old and new: hard candies, saltwater taffy, malt balls, chocolate turtles, penguin gummies, truffles. If you prefer to sit for a spell with your ice cream cone or Italian soda, there are a couple of seats. Of special interest: sugar-free and kosher candy. *Every day; map:II7*

CARDS AND STATIONERY

OBLATION PAPERS AND PRESS / 516 NW 12th Ave, Pearl District; 503/223-1093 There's no other place in town like this one when it comes to buying paper—or is that *fresh* paper? A peek from the retail space into the working studio reveals a day in the life of the papermaker and letterpress printer. Beautiful handmade floral paper, hand-tooled photo albums, cards, fountain pens, and French wax seals make up the bulk of the merchandise, but there's also custom-designed invitations and announcements to behold. Papermaking and book arts workshops, too. *Tues–Sat; info@oblationpapers.com; www.oblationpapers.com; map:L1*

PRESENT PERFECT / Pioneer Place, Downtown; 503/228-9727 This downtown destination for gift wrapping offers cheery papers sold by the sheet, laminated gift bags, bows, and ribbons—even a roll of tape and scissors for last-minute wrapping jobs at the guest wrap table. Stationery here also hits a higher plane; the knowledgeable staff can help you wade through a mammoth selection of cards—some exquisite handmade works of art—for every mood and occasion. Creative party invitations and matching favors will get any celebration rolling. *Every day; map:G4*

PRESENTS OF MIND / 3633 SE Hawthorne Blvd, Hawthorne (and branch); 503/230-7740 One-stop shopping for birthdays and other occasions: in addition to a well-rounded and frequently rotated selection of cards, you'll find everything you need to wrap a gift and a range of gifts to wrap (picture frames, candles, photo albums, blank books, jewelry, and scarves). There are also balloons and lots of things to stuff in a piñata—glow-in-the-dark insects, plastic fish, hair clips, candy necklaces, stickers, rubber stamps, and so on. A second store on Belmont (the Stamp Pad; 3423 SE Belmont; 503/231-7362; map:GG4) carries everything you need for stamping—paper, ink, and a huge selection of rubber stamps. *Every day; map:GG5*

WHAM! / 617 NW 23rd Ave, Northwest; 503/222-4992 Lots of pop culture cards, but toys too. Remember sea monkeys, stink bombs, and potato guns? And what about Gumby, the original yogi? There's also racks and racks of postcards, T-shirts, and refrigerator magnets galore. *Every day; map:GG7*

CHILDREN'S CLOTHING AND ACCESSORIES

BAMBINI'S CHILDREN'S BOUTIQUE / 16353 SW Bryant Rd, Lake Oswego; 503/635-7661 And what a boutique it is! If you're looking for the perfect thing for the kids to wear to a wedding or another special occasion, look no further. Extraordinary garments in silk, taffeta, and linen, with matching accessories, make you wish for more dress-up events (as well as a longer line of credit on your Visa). It's the only store in the Northwest stocking the Pampolina line from Germany; other popular European and domestic lines include Miniman, Catimini, Clayeaux, Baby LuLu, and Hartstrings. *Mon–Sat; map:KK6*

GENERATIONS / 4029 SE Hawthorne Blvd, Hawthorne; 503/233-8130 As befits its SE Hawthorne Boulevard location, this store carries a mix of colorful cotton garments, new and secondhand. Its bread and butter, however, lies in mainstream brands like Cotton Caboodle, Flapdoodles, and MulberriBush. Items range from organic-cotton gowns for newborns to adorable jumpers, fleece jackets, and cute pants and top ensembles for boys and girls (up to size 4). There's a small selection of used items in the back of the store, plus good-as-it-gets maternity wear. *Mon–Sat; www.citysearch.com/pdx/generations; map:GG5*

HAGGIS MCBAGGIS / 6802 SE Milwaukie Ave, Westmoreland; 503/234-0849 Never has shopping for the 4-foot and under crowd been so much fun. While you discuss "room to grow," the knowledgeable shoe people follow your children around—through the play house, down the slide, along the purple path—buckling and tying. In addition to one of the best selections (think variety, think European brands) of kids' shoes, there are also whimsical hats, colorful tights, and a multitude of must-have, don't-need accessories. If splurging for infants is a pastime, you won't be disappointed with the hand-knit cashmere booties and velvet bibs. And if an award for Best Changing Room in the Universe existed, this shop would win—hands down, bottoms up. *Tues–Sun; mcbaggis@aol.com; map:JJ5*

HANNA ANDERSSON / 327 NW 10th Ave, Pearl District (and branch); 503/321-5275 Hanna Andersson—best known around the country for its catalog of Swedish-style cotton clothing for kids, moms, and now dads, too—is one of Portland's brighter retail success stories; with colors this vivid and fabric this sturdy, how could it be anything but? The quality of Hannas (as the goods are known) is usually very high, and the styles are irresistible. And for the family who likes to dress alike, there are pj's, T-shirts, and sweatshirts in every size. Buy reduced-priced irregulars and last season's stock at the spacious outlet store in Lake Oswego's Mountain Park neighborhood (7 Monroe Pkwy, Oswego Town Square; 503/697-1953; every day; map:LL7). *Every day; www.hannaandersson.com; map:L2*

LADS AND LASSIES FROCKS AND BRITCHES / Beaverton Town Square, Beaverton; 503/626-6578 A move to the other side of the mall hasn't altered what this shop has to offer—beautiful clothes for infants, toddlers, boys up to size 7, and girls up to size 14. The sales staff will treat your kids like heirs to the throne, and the toy and book departments rival those of fine toy stores, as does the doll collection. *Every day; map:HH9*

MAKO / 732 NW 23rd Ave, Northwest; 503/274-9081 Colorful cotton sweaters, vests, and hats hand-knit by Mako and her sister are one of the biggest draws to this shop under the stairs, but there's also practical rain gear, colorful bathrobes, flashy underwear, a fanciful sock collection, and shelves of toys, puzzles, and bath accessories for kids. Everywhere you look, it's lots of cotton—a great selection of rainbow-hued leggings and T-shirts—at everyday prices. *Every day; mtmako@home.com; map:GG7*

SECOND TO NONE / 6308 SW Capitol Hwy (Hillsdale Shopping Center), Hillsdale; 503/244-0071 Tucked into the Hillsdale Shopping Center, this children's shop features a good selection of used clothing (often name brands like Guess, Gap, and Hanna Andersson) and colorful new cottonwear and polar fleece jackets. Costumes for dress-up, too. Unfinished and hand-painted wooden toy chests and child-size chairs, American Girl clothes and accessories (some custom made), and used goods such as car seats and toys in good condition set this store apart from other consignment shops. *Mon–Sat; map:II8*

WATER BABIES / 3272 SE Hawthorne Blvd, Hawthorne; 503/232-6039 After a long tenure in Sellwood, Susan Hays moved her shop to its new location on Hawthorne. Though a departure from the old store—

smaller, less merchandise, and no rice box—there's still the same good stuff: clothes and accessories for preemies to size 7 (including all-cotton undies, swimwear year-round, and bright pile jackets), as well as a thoughtful selection of books and cloth and wooden toys. Both you and your child will appreciate the sale rack. *Tues–Sun; map:HH5*

COFFEE AND TEA

BRITISH TEA GARDEN / 725 SW 10th Ave, Downtown; 503/221-7817 Shop here for a tea party—there's plenty of plum cake, English tea biscuits, gooseberry preserves, Terry's York Chocolate Oranges, and, yes, tea. Scones with Devonshire cream and a hot pot of Earl Grey are perfect in the middle of a hectic day (there are plenty of tables), and on bright afternoons, you can explore the secret garden behind the Tea Garden. Ask to be put on the mailing list to receive the monthly newsletter of special events, such as tea leaf readings or children's and literary teas. *Every day; anglofare@aol.com; map:H2*

PEET'S COFFEE & TEA / 1441 NE Broadway, NE Broadway (and branch); 503/493-0192 To the delight of many of Portland's Northern California transplants, Berkeley-born Peet's Coffee & Tea has brought its signature dark-roasted style north. The opening day of its NE Broadway store lived up to its anticipatory buzz, with droves of curious coffee hounds snatching up pounds of beans, and since then, Portlanders haven't been able to get enough. With such a positive response, Peet's wasted no time in opening a second location, this time downtown (508 SW Broadway; 503/973-5540; map:I3). Whichever side of the river you find yourself on, you'll find consistent coffee, knowledgeable employees, and a respectable selection of coffee and tea accessories. And if you're lucky, you might stop in while the staff is holding a free tasting of Central American coffees or Chinese green teas. *Every day; www.peets.com; map:FF5*

TAO OF TEA / 3430 SE Belmont St, Belmont; 503/736-0198 In the yin-yang cycle of life, sipping tea out of a ceramic vessel to the sound of trickling water is the natural antidote to sucking coffee out of a paper cup to the backdrop of an accelerating motor. The Tao of Tea, a pretty little tea room bedecked with colorful cushions and tea-lined walls, offers sweet respite from the chaos of modern life. Here, what cup you drink out of has everything to do with the kind of tea you order: green, black, white, scented, oolong, or herbal. A range of Eastern flavors comprise the menu, and everything goes well with a cup of tea. Be sure to check out the adjacent Leaf Room, where you can get a closer look at the Tao's impressive tea offerings and sample some of the more exotic varieties. You can also choose from a wide selection of teaware, from Yixing pots to yerba mate gourds. *Every day; tea@taooftea.com; www.taooftea.com; map:GG4*

THE TEAZONE / 510 NW 11th Ave, Pearl District; 503/221-2130 Nestled discreetly in the heart of the Pearl District, the TeaZone is the perfect place to kick back with a book and a wonderfully flavorful tea from the far reaches of the world. The refreshingly enthusiastic and knowledgeable owners of this tasteful tea shop have carefully fashioned a menu of more than 50 loose-leaf teas, and they are more than happy to tell you about each variety (or you can read from the incredibly descriptive menu). The selection is pretty eclectic, with everything from Dragonwell green tea to South American yerba mate. Whatever your infusion, you're sure to be enlightened and impressed, and you might just decide that oolong is indeed your cup of tea. *Every day; www.teazone.com; map:L2*

WORLD CUP COFFEE & TEA / 1740 NW Glisan St, Northwest; 503/228-4152 In a town where coffee roasters are as ubiquitous as breweries, World Cup Coffee & Tea has made quite a name for itself. The key to its coffee? Freshness. World Cup's beans are roasted on-site daily, and the menu is teeming with delectable concoctions, like the World Cup Espresso, a velvety blend of arabica beans with a bittersweet aftertaste, and the Cubano, a smooth espresso made from combining raw sugar with ground coffee before pulling a shot. On the tea side, World Cup offers about 12 loose-leaf varieties, including oolongs, green teas, black teas, and herbal infusions. Several are organic, and there are some interesting blends, such as a light, fruity green Earl Grey tea. And in case you've got the munchies, World Cup offers wonderful pastries and desserts, as well as impressive sandwiches grilled to order. *Every day; map:GG6*

ETHNIC AND SPECIALTY FOODS

ANZEN ORIENTAL GROCERS / 736 NE Martin Luther King Jr Blvd, Northeast; 503/233-5111 For all things Japanese—fish and nori for sushi, pickled ginger, live geoduck, fresh yellowfin tuna, and octopus— Anzen is the place. The stock goes well beyond just food: if you're looking for lacquered dishes, rice cookers, or Japanese books and magazines, Anzen is still the place. In fact, there's upward of 10,000 items, including prepared deli foods (sushi and bentos among them), plenty of packaged and canned goods (including shelves of various soy sauces), and a large selection of sake and Asian beers. *Every day; map:FF6*

BECERRA'S SPANISH AND IMPORTED GROCERIES / 3022 NE Glisan St, Northeast (and branches); 503/234-7785 The groceries come from Mexico, Southern California, South America, and Spain, and Becerra's customers come from as far away as Spokane. Mexican white cheeses are a specialty, as is the store's own beef and pork chorizo. Look here for things you might have a hard time finding elsewhere: quince paste, chipotle peppers, and bottled cactus. Becerra's also has some of the specialty kitchenware you'll need to take full advantage of the foodstuffs—tortilla presses, for example—and lots of music and videotapes (in Spanish, of course). Other branches are on E Burnside and N Lombard. *Every day; map:FF5*

ELEPHANTS DELICATESSEN / 13 NW 23rd Pl (Uptown Shopping Center), Northwest; 503/224-3955 One of the city's favorite spots for gourmet sandwiches, salads, and other fare, Elephants is often bustling to the point of pandemonium at lunchtime. If you have an order totaling $40 or more—for office or family, say—you can phone it in, Elephax it (503/238-8143), or even order on-line. Order by 10am and you'll get it delivered by noon. The kitchen also bakes 20 different kinds of breads, voluptuous desserts, and an impressive selection of sumptuous take-home dinner entrees. *Every day; feedback@elephantsdeli.com; www. elephantsdeli.com; map:FF7*

FONG CHONG & CO. / 301 NW 4th Ave, Chinatown; 503/223-1777 This is one of Portland's busiest Chinese markets, perhaps because of the succulent roasted and barbecued pork and ribs and the Peking duck available for takeout, cooked at the adjoining Cantonese restaurant of the same name. Narrow aisles bulge with sacks of rice, teas, noodles, seasonings, and sauces from China, Hong Kong, and Taiwan. *Every day; map:K5*

KRUGER'S SPECIALTY PRODUCE / 735 NW 21st Ave (City Market NW), Northwest (and branch); 503/221-3004 A few exotics—edible flowers, baby bok choy, purple potatoes—are mixed among more familiar (and some organic) produce. Kruger's also sells bulk and packaged natural foods and gourmet items, from breakfast cereals to dried pasta in the shape of artichokes or bicycles. Unforgiving prices, but high-quality produce. A second outlet is in the Irvington Market (1409 NE Weidler St; 503/288-4236; map:FF5). *Every day; map:GG6*

MARTINOTTI'S CAFE & DELICATESSEN / 404 SW 10th Ave, Downtown; 503/224-9028 There was a time not that long ago when Martinotti's was Portland's only Italian foods shop, with one of the first espresso machines in town. Even though the city is now saturated with many Italian venues (restaurants, shops, cooking classes, pottery, etc.), there's still a place for what the Martinotti family has to offer: a decidedly Italian grocery of good tastes, good smells, and good products. See Armand for wine, Dixie for catering, and Frank for lunch and the latest in microbrews. The wine selection is rich in Burgundies, Bordeaux, and port, as well as fine examples of Italian varieties. For everyday shopping, there are oodles of dried pastas and sundry other imports: Italian tomatoes, olive oil, chocolate, and cookies. *Mon–Sat; map:J2*

THE PORTLAND GROWING SEASON

Visiting farmers markets has become a highlight of the year in food for thousands of Oregonians. The outdoor gatherings of growers have become immensely popular of late—their number has increased fourfold in the last decade—and with good reason. The quality of the produce, much of it rare and unusual, is unparalleled, and it tastes all the better when you know that you're directly supporting family farms. Prices are generally (and fittingly) higher than for the tasteless stuff you find with year-round monotony at the supermarket, but growers often uphold the tradition of throwing in a few extra ounces, known as "giving good weight."

The highest-profile farmers market in the city is the **Portland Farmers Market**, which is held on Saturday mornings (8am to 1pm), April through October, on the southern end of the South Park Blocks (SW Park Ave and Montgomery St, by Portland State University; 503/705-2460; www.portlandfarmersmarket.com), and midday Wednesday (10am–2pm) at the northern end (SW Park Ave and Salmon St, by the Arlene Schnitzer Concert Hall). It's nowhere near the biggest, but it's one of the oldest (it was established at the foot of the Albers Mill grain elevators alongside the Willamette in 1992), and its central location and two-day-a-week-schedule make it a more prominent part of city life than most of the other markets. In addition to awe-inspiring produce, including organic and heirloom vegetables and loads of fruit and nuts from all over the region, the PFM boasts baked and dairy goods, organically raised meat and seafood, fresh wild mushrooms, herbs, and flowers. On any given day (call for a schedule), there are cooking demonstrations, advice on soil management, and a variety of special events.

The most popular farmers market is the **Beaverton Farmers Market** (SW Hall

PASTAWORKS / 3735 SE Hawthorne Blvd, Hawthorne (and branch); 503/232-1010 Pastaworks is all things Italian: fresh pastas, pesto and mushroom sauces, dozens of olive oils, herbed and aged vinegars, whole-bean coffees, take-home entrees, delectable desserts, exotic cheeses, aged prosciutto—and the best (and most expensive) Italian wine section in town. Some bottlings are so esoteric they escape mention even in Italian wine books—so don't hesitate to ask for help from the staff. The original Pastaworks on Hawthorne has expanded its inventory of kitchenware; Reidel glassware, Spanish pottery, wooden salad bowls and cutting boards, and top-notch cooking utensils are just some of the things that can turn a quick stop for a loaf of bread into an hour of browsing. There's also a branch at City Market NW (735 NW 21st Ave; 503/221-3002; map:GG7). *Every day; info@pastaworks.com; www.pastaworks.com; map:GG5*

Blvd between 3rd and 5th Aves; 503/643-5345), the state's largest agriculture-only market (as opposed to those that sell crafts as well): on any given Saturday (8am to 1:30pm, May through October) in the peak season, nearly 10,000 people will descend upon a hundred vendors and lunch booths, to the sound of country music and the buzz of their own excited conversation. (From July to September there's also a Wednesday market.)

Other bustling farmers markets in the immediate area include those in Gresham (NE Roberts Ave between 4th and 5th Aves; 503/695-2698); Hillsboro (Courthouse Square, NE 2nd Ave and Main St; 503/844-6685), Hollywood (NE Hancock St between 44th and 45th Aves; 503/233-3313); Lents (SE 91st Ave and Foster Rd; 503/227-5368); and Tigard (SW Hall Blvd and Oleson Rd; 503/244-2479). That's by no means an exhaustive list; there are others, including an all-organic market that sprouts up on Wednesday afternoons (2pm–7pm) outside the People's Food Co-op (3029 SE 21st Ave; 503/232-9051). The state's Department of Agriculture publishes an up-to-date directory on the Web at www.orda.state.or.us; it's a good idea to check before you head out, since some markets change location and others have irregular (i.e., non-Saturday) schedules. One caution: It's not just the vendors that have to get up early in the morning to make it to market—you'd better, too, if you want to get there in time for anything but the leanest pickings. That means arriving around opening time, which is generally 8 or 9 o'clock. These markets have become so popular so fast that even though there are more than ever before they're nowhere close to meeting demand. For all those who love fresh food—and who don't mind not sleeping in on a Saturday morning—that's a very good sign. —James McQuillen

SHERIDAN FRUIT CO. / 408 SE Martin Luther King Jr Blvd, Southeast; 503/235-9353 Founded in 1916, this is one of the last remnants of the city's old Produce Row. Neighborhood locals know it for more than well-priced produce, however: there's also a wide and eclectic selection of bulk foods and a full-service meat market. The director of the cooking-class program has left to open a business of her own, leaving the kitchen to be used for preparing more in-house deli foods (it's crazy here during the weekday lunch hour, when the neighborhood stops in for a bite), but there's still plenty here to attract both novice and die-hard foodies. With improvements in the cheese, meat, and wine departments, prices have crept up, but there are still good deals to be had, and lots of items you won't find elsewhere. *Every day; map:GG5*

TRADER JOE'S / 4715 SE 39th Ave, Southeast (and branches); 503/777-1601 California-based Trader Joe's continues to expand its presence in Portland; the latest addition is a store in the Hollywood District. It's the best place in town to look for inexpensive, high-quality olive oils, vinegars, sauces, beer, and wine. You'll find good prices on some perishables, like milk and cheese, and even bouquets of fresh-cut flowers, but otherwise the fresh stuff is limited. The two other branches reside in Beaverton and Lake Oswego. *Every day; www.traderjoes.com; map:FF4*

UWAJIMAYA / 10500 SW Beaverton-Hillsdale Hwy, Beaverton; 503/643-4512 For the lover of Asian food, the name means "heaven." This is no hole-in-the-wall ethnic specialty shop, but a full-size supermarket chock-full of imported rarities, superb fresh seafood, and hard-to-find produce for Asian recipes. Looking for long Chinese green beans? Piles of fresh lemongrass? Curry leaves? This is the place. The offerings are mostly Japanese, from food to housewares to books (a branch of the Japanese Kinokuniya bookstore chain is on the premises), but there's an ample supply of Southeast Asian and Chinese ingredients as well. There's even a Japanese restaurant—Bush Soba—on-site. *Every day; www.uwajimaya.com; map:II8*

ZUPAN'S MARKET / 2340 W Burnside St, Portland Heights (and branches); 503/497-1088 Here's a cross between Fred Meyer and City Market NW, where you can buy toilet paper and fresh lychees in the same stop. The produce section is stupendous—14 different varieties of apples in peak season, fresh water chestnuts, champagne grapes, and seasonal exotic mushrooms. The market is open 24 hours a day, every day but Christmas, and contains a deli, bakery, meat counter, and wine section. Nothing is bargain-priced. *Every day; www.zupans.com; map:GG7*

FLORISTS AND NURSERIES

ALAMEDA ORCHIDS / 404 NW 12th Ave, Pearl District; 503/295-6899 Satiate your craving for exotic bloomers at Gary Brown's exquisite floral shop. Besides rare and hard-to-find plants that can cost up to $500, there are also more reasonably priced potted orchids that start at $25. At any one time there are around 150 orchids in bloom in the store—some fragrant, some not. Other varieties of cut flowers are for sale outside on the sidewalk. *Every day; map:L2*

THE BOVEES NURSERY / 1737 SW Coronado St, Lake Oswego; 503/244-9341 Customers can wander under towering firs and among hundreds of types of rhododendrons in the display garden, examining neatly labeled mature samples of prospective purchases. The star rhodies and deciduous azaleas bloom nearly six months of the year, but trees, hardy perennials, and Northwest natives are no less visible. Catalog on request. *Wed–Sun*

(closed Jan and mid-Aug–mid-Sept, except by appointment); bovees@ teleport.com; www.bovees.com; map:KK5

CORNELL FARM / 8212 SW Barnes Rd, West Slope; 503/292-9895 The Dutch Colonial house, built in 1926, with its towering monkey puzzle tree and lovely flower gardens, is the centerpiece of this 5-acre nursery. The gardens support 300 varieties of roses. Owner Ed Blatter's folks still live in the house, but the former goat and strawberry farm now grows 700 varieties of perennials and 150 varieties of annuals—garden flowers tended by a sales staff of 12-plus gardeners. Growing beds are open to the public, and neighbors walk here daily, but give Ed's parents a break— please don't ring the doorbell. Across the road from the Oregon College of Art and Craft. *Every day; map:HH9*

FLOWERS TOMMY LUKE / 1225 NW Everett St, Pearl District; 503/228-3140 This high-volume florist's shop is a Portland tradition, with designs from standard FTD to airier English garden arrangements. Recently it has combined its various locales into one glorious Pearl District location. In addition to a larger showroom, there are select gifts (including pottery and Vance Kitara vases) and a second floor full of beautiful home furnishings. *Mon–Sat; map:K2*

GERANIUM LAKE FLOWERS / 555 SW Oak St (US Bancorp Tower), Downtown; 503/228-1920 Painter and floral artist Kim Foren has built an oasis of blooms right in the middle of a bank tower. A brightly colored space, Geranium Lake gems come directly from the garden and match perfectly with great gewgaws for those looking for a hip edge in floral display. You won't find any baby's breath here. Worldwide delivery is available. *Mon–Sat; geraniumlake@bigplanet.com; www.geranium lake.com; map:J4*

GIFFORD-DOVING FLORISTS / 704 SW Jefferson St, Downtown (and branch); 503/222-9193 Gifford-Doving (family-owned since 1938) stocks one of the better selections of cut flowers in town, and in the late afternoon, it is one of Portland's busiest florists. At the two downtown shops (the second is on SW Market St), there are usually several kinds of greens on hand as well, making this a favorite source for do-it-yourself arrangers. *Mon–Sat; www.giffordflorist.com; map:F2*

POPPYBOX / 3433 NE Fremont St, Irvington; 503/280-1228 Take a look at the colors and the airy design of Portland's newest neighborhood garden store, and you'll swear that Martha Stewart herself was the contractor. The plants stocked here in customer-friendly fashion—with many of each kind together, so it's easy to find what you're looking for or be struck by something new—are no less easy on the eyes. There are many striking and uncommon varieties, making Poppybox a good place to get inspired as you design your garden. There's also plenty of good advice, from the store's own brochures or from its friendly staff, and fine tools, pots, and other horticultural accessories. One caveat: prepare for a radical cashectomy on your wallet. *Every day; map:FF5*

PORTLAND NURSERY / 5050 SE Stark St, Southeast (and branch); 503/231-5050 You can't buy the arabica bush here, but you can drink its brew while shopping on the weekend at the city's most abundant nursery. Scads of good-quality plants and supplies fill the 5-acre grounds; on sunny days it seems like half of Portland is here. The perennials are especially bountiful, but many unusual trees and shrubs—witch hazels and franklinia trees—are stocked as well. The store's reputation owes much to its knowledgeable and helpful staff, ready to track down the answers to any questions they can't immediately resolve themselves. Powell's Books supplies the gardening lit at the SE Stark Street store; a second branch (9000 SE Division Street; 503/788-9000; map:HH3) specializes in ponds and houseplants. *Every day; www.portlandnursery.com; map:GG4*

SAMMY'S FLOWERS / 218 NW 13th Ave, Pearl District; 503/222-9759 After a long stint at Durst's Thriftway, this floral institution has moved to the Pearl District. A choice of more than 50 varieties of cut flowers, plus a larger selection of tropicals, spills out onto the former loading dock that marks the entrance to Wieden & Kennedy. Sammy and her crew of hip workers will happily wrap up a mixed bouquet for less than you might expect—under $15. No longer open 24 hours a day, the shop still keeps later hours than most (7am to 10pm), and it also offers delivery. *Every day; map:K1*

TUALATIN RIVER NURSERY / 65 S Dollar St, West Linn; 503/650-8511 Owners John and Lori Blair have created a shopping destination known for its relaxed atmosphere: there's a lovely pathway, a coffee shop that serves espresso and light meals featuring homegrown vegetables, and some years there's been a children's garden and summer concert series. On Saturdays, November through Christmas, the nursery features tamales, so you can keep your strength up while you browse through perennials as good as you'll find anyplace in Portland, and annuals with new and interesting foliage. Call during the winter to be sure someone's around. *Every day; map:OO5*

WILDFLOWERS ON HAWTHORNE / 3202 SE Hawthorne Blvd, Hawthorne; 503/230-9485 More aptly called a flower shop than a florist (although they do deliver), this enchanting store sells flowers in many forms. The small but lovely selection of fresh-cut flowers tends toward the wild and seasonal varieties—snapdragons and veronica in the summer, branches of vine maples and rose hips in the fall. There are also bouquets of dried larkspur, lavender, and roses, and handmade wreaths. In the back are shelves lined with jars of herbs, spices, and delicious herbal tea blends. Don't hesitate to ask for guidance; the staff is both knowledgeable and helpful. *Mon–Sat; map:GG5*

FURNITURE

BADER & FOX SOFA FACTORY / 3400 SE 122nd Ave, Southeast; 503/761-6135 At this little-known furniture outlet, home furnishings (chairs, sofas, etc.) are manufactured from scratch, and old pieces can be refurbished with a freshly updated look and upgrades like down-filled cushions. Bader & Fox can even re-create the designs you see in upscale, glossy magazines—for a fraction of the price. Detailing is superb, and prices are competitive. But take the time to double-check your dimensions—once you buy it, it's yours. *Mon–Sat; map:HH1*

FULL UPRIGHT POSITION / 1200 NW Everett St, Pearl District; 503/228-6190 F.U.P. is less a furniture store and more a lofty layout for the ultimate young urbanite. The specialty here is classic mid-century modern furniture. Located in the Pearl District, within the comfortably cushy environs of Portland's most buzz-worthy advertising agency, Wieden & Kennedy, this store offers a beautifully stark display of contemporary chairs, sofas, tables, and home accessories from the world's top furnishing designers/architects: Eames, Jacobsen, Breuer, Le Corbusier, Aalto, Starck. If they don't have it, the fully functional F.U.P. can also do special orders. But a word of warning for those who are ready to move up from the world of Ikea and Pottery Barn: start saving your pennies; this stuff isn't cheap. *Every day; www.fup.com; map:K2*

GOODNIGHT ROOM / 1517 NE Broadway, NE Broadway; 503/281-5516 This is the place to shop for a child's "home." A newcomer to a growing market—children's home accessories—this colorful store houses almost everything to outfit, or at least decorate, a child's nursery or bedroom: furniture, linens, bumpers, hand-painted mirrors, lamps, and pint-sized rocking chairs. If, however, you don't have a grand to spend on a Maine Cottage dresser, at least stop by for one of the less expensive items: step stools, bath toys and towels, whimsical bibs, Groovy Girl dolls, hand puppets, books, and games. Also a great resource for hooking up with artists who paint kids' furniture and murals—just ask one of the friendly shopkeepers. *Every day; map:FF5*

THE HANDWERK SHOP / 8317 SE 13th Ave, Sellwood; 503/236-7870 Customers become fast friends at this welcoming store located at the southwest tip of Sellwood's antique row. Mission oak furniture, textiles, and pottery from the Arts and Crafts period vie for space with distinguished artwork and antiques in-the-making. Here co-owner and master craftsman Brent Willis makes Morris chairs, settles, accent tables, and picture frames in the spirit of design legend Gustav Stickley. His life and business partner, Linda, runs the shop and gives expert design advice to inquiring local bungalow owners and fans. *Thurs–Sun and by appointment; map:JJ5*

J. D. MADISON RUG & HOME CO. / 1307 NW Glisan St, Pearl District; 503/827-6037 In the race for space, J. D. Madison Rug & Home Co. is clearly a front runner. On the cutting edge of cohabitation, this home furnishing outlet is the culmination of the pared-down aesthetic of its owner, Todd Dewey. An inviting, living room–sized showroom—where everything is up for grabs—it's the retail equivalent of an upscale eatery and a store with a "look" that could be described as maximum minimalism. Each item is infused with the highest impact, no matter how small. Furniture and rugs—from the hottest designers of Tibetan rugs in the country to a virtual couture line of handcrafted floor coverings—provide the bulk of Dewey's inventory. *Every day; map:L2*

THE JOINERY / 4804 SE Woodstock Blvd, Woodstock; 503/788-8547 The Joinery, for many years, has been a fine place to find custom-made Mission and Shaker style furniture. In addition to tables and chairs, this spacious showroom also retails well-hewn wooden accessories (mirrors, boxes, and spinning tops) from all over the world. You might wait four to five months for your new treasure—but it will be well worth it. *Mon–Sat; www.thejoinery.com; map:HH5*

KINION FURNITURE COMPANY / 1230 SE Grand Ave, Southeast; 503/221-1574 Choose among 50 mostly cherry samples crafted in Kinion's McMinnville workshop and shipped straight to Kinion's Southeast store. You'll find beautifully made contemporary renditions of Shaker furniture with a little Mission and Arts and Crafts thrown in for good measure. Kinion's traditional joinery techniques guarantee furniture that is built to last—if not forever, for a very long time. *Mon–Sat; www.kinionfurniture.com; map:D6*

P. H. REED FURNITURE / 1100 NW Glisan St, Pearl District; 503/274-7080 Upscale upholstered furniture and sophisticated Italian lighting dazzle the eye at this furnishing boutique that feels like a neighborhood art gallery. Owner Pieter Reed represents local artists/furniture makers, so expect up-close looks at one-of-a-kind, cast-glass side tables, hand-loomed carpets, and incredible lamps. Directly across Glisan Street, Reed has given the same attention to detail to the most intimate of surroundings. P. H. Reed Bedroom (1101 NW Glisan St; 503/227-1742) makes sweet dreams come true with a truly adorable/seductive selection of bed and bedding accessories. *Tues–Sun; map:K2*

REJUVENATION HOUSE PARTS / 1100 SE Grand Ave, Southeast; 503/238-1900 A Portland institution, this store has built a national reputation (and a booming catalog business) around superior reproductions of turn-of-the-century and Craftsman-style light fixtures and Mission-style furniture. You'll also find salvaged doors, windows, tubs, and, of course, kitchen sinks. And if you are having trouble getting started, the well-versed staff can offer a wealth of advice. There's a variety of workshops for the basic do-it-yourself weekend warrior or the most accomplished pro. Another Portland legend, Powell's Books, supplies interior design and building books to this space saver that has firmly established itself as the home refinishers' hangout. Most recent additions include an upstairs seconds room and the Daily Cafe, a delicious place to break for coffee or lunch while you're shopping (located in the southwest corner of the building; see review in the Restaurants chapter). *Every day; store@rejuvenation.com; www.rejuvenation.com; map:EE5*

SIMON TONEY AND FISCHER / 105 SE Taylor St, Southeast; 503/721-0392 David Simon and Bill Toney designed and built custom cabinetry and fine furniture in Portland for 21 years before they opened their Pearl District showroom in 1994 with designer (and partner) Susan Fischer. Making the decision to place their entire operation under one roof, this talented trio recently moved to a larger (albeit harder-to-find) space in Southeast Portland, between First and Second Avenues on SE Taylor Street. For anyone who wants to see a luminous collection of tables, beds, and cabinetry made from rarely used woods—walnut, pear, yew, and chinquapin—many of which are indigenous to Oregon, it's worth visiting the new showroom. Each board at STF is handpicked with care and crafted into one-of-a-kind pieces that feature painterly finishes fused with just a hint of artistically placed color. The result is astonishingly beautiful furniture. *Tues–Sat; map:L2*

GIFTS

CALLIN NOVELTY SHOP / 1013 SW Washington St, Downtown; 503/223-4821 This little shop of ha-ha's employs a staff of expert magicians who can show you how to pull off pranks (or at least your finger) in style. Not so much a gift shop, Callin's is a prop shop for adolescent schemes and dreams and for anyone who spent their childhood buried in the back pages of a comic book. Among the boomer-era gag gifts this novel novelty shop offers up: sea monkeys, magic rocks, and X-ray specs sure to make your friends blush. *Mon–Sat; map:I5*

DAZZLE / 704 NW 23rd Ave, Northwest; 503/224-1294 From the horse-of-a-different-color mascot to an interior that suggests a Southwest store decorated by Salvador Dali, Dazzle's chaotic collection of kitschy collectibles certainly lives up to its name. And it's the perfect pick-me-up for those who need to perk up their life/home/dearest loved one with something they won't find anywhere else. Besides tasteful tchotchkes, look for colorful objets d'art from both local and international artists. *Every day; map:GG7*

DISH N DAT / 827 NW 23rd Ave, Northwest; 503/279-8946 A fun place to shop for a special wedding gift, if you're big enough to give it away once you've brought it home. In addition to whimsical tableware, Finnish and Swedish glasses, and truly lustrous Swid Powell lustreware, there's everything you might need to make or serve a cocktail—from shakers to olive picks—except the booze. When baby makes three, mark the occasion with the ultimate plate and cup set. *Every day; www.dishndat.net; map:GG7*

FRIENDS LIBRARY STORE / 801 SW 10th Ave, Downtown; 503/306-5911 Multnomah County's Central Library not only makes room for its own Starbucks but also houses its own gift shop. Operated by the Friends of the Multnomah County Library, this is a niche-filled nook full of everything for the book lover—colorful bookends, tiny book lights, and writing implements (both costly and not), as well as children's gifts and jewelry. But, hey, you aren't going to find any books—you have to check those out. Open during library hours. *Every day; www.folstore@ europa.com; www.friends-library.org/store; map:H2*

GREG'S / 3707 SE Hawthorne, Hawthorne; 503/235-1257 At first glance—or whiff—this seems to a shop that takes bathing out of the hygiene realm and into the movies, with its abundant selection of perfumed soaps and candles. A closer look, however, reveals its additional treasures: vintage French and Vogue postcards, Asian papers, colorful lanterns, beaded lamps, silk baby booties with embroidered dragonflies, enamelware buckets, and lots of funny little things to make you laugh— from the broad and eclectic range of cards to the dish filled with tiny gilded feet. If you see something you like that is not soap, by all means buy it; owner Greg Klaus and his shopkeep always seem to be unpacking boxes and moving stuff around, which means that when you come back, it may not be around. *Every day; map:GG5*

MADE IN OREGON / 921 SW Morrison St (the Galleria), Downtown (and branches); 503/241-3630 If it's made, caught, or grown in this state, it's sold at Made in Oregon. Visitor essentials include smoked salmon, berry jams, chocolate, and hazelnuts that can be packed for traveling along with souvenir wooden slugs, myrtlewood, and warm and cozy Pendleton Woolen Mill blankets. Nine stores branch out through the metropolitan area (usually in malls), including one at the Portland airport. For a catalog, call 503/273-8498 or 800/828-9673. *Every day; www.madeinoregon.com; map:H2*

THE NATURE STORE AT PORTLAND AUDUBON SOCIETY / 5151 NW Cornell Rd, Northwest; 503/292-9453 Going bird-watching in Belize? Before you take flight, be sure to swoop down to this resource center and gift shop on the edge of Forest Park, within the Audubon sanctuary. Inside, there's the cool odor of birdseed and a treasure trove for naturalists: worldwide field guides, natural history books, binoculars, bird feeders, and more. About one-third of the book inventory is children's books; there are also stuffed animals, model insects, and jigsaw puzzles. *Every day; general@audubonportland.org; www.audubonportland.com; map:FF8*

TOPANIEN / 7832 SW Capitol Hwy, Multnomah Village; 503/244-9683 Nadine Lefkowitz's world-friendly shop brings global treasures to the comfy confines of the Multnomah Village. Alongside a colorful stock of beeswax sheets for candle making, educational gifts from the world over include wall hangings, noise-making toys, and necklaces. And for the home there's a collection of conversation starters: tablecloths, vases, and frames. *Every day; map:JJ7*

TWIST / 30 NW 23rd Pl, Northwest (and branch); 503/224-0334 Lauren Gulau and Paul Schneider started their business as a cooperative clay outlet in Eugene, Oregon, and over the years have turned it into a spectacular gallery displaying some of world's top jewelry designers alongside truly unique American Arts and Crafts artifacts. The gallery space in Northwest Portland focuses on exclusive designers, delicate glassware, hand-painted ceramics, crafts, and a smattering of furniture twisters. While the Pioneer Place shop (700 SW 5th Ave; 503/222-3137; map:G4) is geared for the traveler, it maintains the same level of quality merchandise and mystique. *Every day; map:GG7*

URBINO / 521 NW 23rd Ave, Northwest; 503/220-0053 It's hard not to feel great pangs of retail lust while wandering through this sunny, good-smelling shop. Owners Rob Friedman and Stacey Mattraw have assembled a collection of all things beautiful for home, body, and spirit—artful dinnerware, jewelry, furniture, candlesticks, lemon verbena soap, and more, mostly handcrafted on this side of the Atlantic. There are also antique toys and other special gifts for children—such as the perfect oatmeal-brown bear. Don't miss Urbino Home (638 NW 23rd Ave, NW; 503/220-4194; map:GG7) down the street; this sumptuous outpost for furniture and interior accessories is filled with fine fabrics, one-of-a-kind lamps, custom-upholstered furniture, and more. *Every day; map:GG7*

HARDWARE

A-BALL PLUMBING SUPPLY / 1703 W Burnside St, Northwest; 503/228-0026 A-Ball's surprise-filled windows have amused passing motorists while attracting customers for nearly 30 years. A locally founded, nationally recognized emporium of posh porcelain goods, this on-the-ball spot sells high-end kitchen fixtures as well as bathroom fittings. If the fine claw-footed tubs are out of your price range, consider a towel bar or a toothbrush holder. *Mon–Sat; www.a-ball.com; map:GG6*

1874 HOUSE / 8070 SE 13th Ave, Sellwood; 503/233-1874 Local architectural remnants that homeowners ripped out and discarded decades ago have found a new home at the 1874 House. A jumble of mint-condition light shades and fixtures, antique as well as reproduction hardware, windows, shutters, and mantels all wait to be reinstalled in the bungalow of your dreams. A tad bit younger than most of its contents, this place has been around for more than three decades. *Tues–Sat; map:II5*

ENVIRONMENTAL BUILDING SUPPLIES / 1331 NW Kearney St, Pearl District; 503/222-3881 Not just another paint store, EBS is the source for hard-to-find floor coverings and finishes, plant-based finishes from Germany, and linoleum from Holland, all safe for the home and easy on the environment. Also in store: New Zealand wool carpets and sustainable hardwoods. Markus Stoffel and Abigail Mages opened this Pearl District store in 1993 with a mission to provide environmentally safe building resources—both products and helpful information. *Mon–Sat; ebs@ecohaus.com; map:N1*

HIPPO HARDWARE AND TRADING COMPANY / 1040 E Burnside St, Southeast; 503/231-1444 Hip, hippo, hooray! This place can hook you with a kitchen sink—and just about every other house part you can think of. Built on the foundation of buying, selling, and trading, Hippo is always on the prowl for architectural elements—doors, windows, molding, and trim—as well as hardware from the 1800s through the 1940s. Pre-1970s lighting fixtures and plumbing materials in good shape are also accepted into the collection. Packed with architectural gems, Hippo is also home to a wonderfully quirky staff that keeps you smiling as you sort through organized bins of clutter. If you can't find something, ask for help. If they don't have it, they just might be able to splice, cut, or file something to fit. The first hardware store on the Internet. *Mon–Sat; www.hipponet.com; map:GG5*

WINKS HARDWARE / 903 NW Davis St, Pearl District; 503/227-5536 We're not too sure that Jayne Kilkenny's father intended to stock 50,000 items when he opened this hardware store in 1909. But everything, from 1,000 sizes of springs to 70 different types of hammers, gives Winks a full house for your house. With its impressive assortment of outdated, odd, and useful things, Winks caters to the trade (hence the weekday-only hours), but experienced sales clerks happily share advice with do-it-yourselfers. About as old-fashioned as it gets today; if you're lucky, you'll get taken behind the counter. *Mon–Fri; map:K3*

WOODCRAFTER'S / 212 NE 6th Ave, Northeast; 503/231-0226 This is where Portland's builders and woodworkers spend their fun money—a friendly warehouse filled with tools, wood stains, and high-quality lumber, mill ends, and hardwood carving blocks. An enormous book section (with back issues of *Fine Homebuilding*) serves as an unofficial library for do-it-yourselfers and craftspeople—and makes this the logical destination after an episode of *This Old House*. Free demonstrations of wood turning and other specialized techniques on most Saturdays. *Mon–Sat; map:GG6*

HEALTH FOOD STORES

FOOD FRONT / **2375 NW Thurman St, Northwest; 503/222-5658** Pony up $150 for a lifetime membership at this cooperative grocery, and you'll receive a rebate at the end of each year based on your total purchases; if you work here eight hours a month, you'll receive a 15 percent discount. Bulk foods for the health-conscious, and trendier fare (Sichuan noodle salad, Vietnamese steamed buns, European chocolates) for the gourmand. The wines are selected thoughtfully and priced conservatively, there's plenty of excellent organic produce, and the deli section turns out great sandwiches. *Every day; map:FF7*

NATURE'S NORTHWEST / **3535 NE 15th Ave, Northeast (and branches); 503/288-3414** You know the gentry have landed when Nature's opens a branch in your neighborhood. This store used to be the place for crunchy-sprouty bulk food and garden supplies, but today the line between health food and gourmet fare (or beauty products and housewares, for that matter) has blurred. The latest addition to the Nature's chain—itself a part of Wild Oats Markets, Inc.—is a superstore in Northeast Portland, complete with a deli, gifts, fresh flowers, espresso, a bakery, meat and cheese counters, beer and wine, cooking classes, a wellness center (movement classes and lectures, with a traditional pharmacist and naturopath on staff), and a day spa. The superstores in Vancouver and Lake Oswego host cooking classes, and the Lake Oswego store also has a day spa and pharmacy (Vancouverites have to settle for a salon). All stores offer plenty of organic produce, free-range meat and poultry, and high prices. *Every day; www.wildoats.com; map:FF5*

NEW SEASONS / **7300 SW Beaverton-Hillsdale Hwy, Raleigh Hills (and branch); 503/292-6838** Customers familiar with the Nature's stores may feel a sense of déjà vu at New Seasons, and with good reason. The store was established by former Nature's employees who defected when Wild Oats took over and who wanted to keep the principles of local ownership and good relations with local suppliers alive. There's an abundance of fresh local produce and meats here, as well as a good deli section and bakery. In keeping with the store's neighborhood mission, there's also plenty of the prepackaged stuff that you expect in a grocery store, so you don't have to go to three different shops for your organic produce, gourmet cheese, and Oreos. A second branch in Sellwood (1214 SE

Tacoma St; 503/230-4949; map:JJ6) opened within a year of the first store—a sign of things to come—and a third is scheduled to open next in Northeast. *Every day; map:II8*

PEOPLE'S FOOD CO-OP / 3029 SE 21st Ave, Southeast; 503/232-9051
A $180 share in this co-op gets you 4 percent off your purchases at the register, and you can also volunteer at the store for up to 19 percent off, plus steep case discounts. Even if you don't buy into the place, you can come anytime for excellent all-organic produce. This small temple of health and sustainability makes a point of getting food made from organic ingredients whenever possible—just don't come for your fish and meat shopping, because this is a vegetarian establishment. From April until Thanksgiving, People's expands its offerings with an organic farmers market on Wednesdays afternoons. And as of this writing, it's heading toward expanding its offerings on a permanent basis, with an addition that will double the size of the store come 2001. *Every day; map:HH5*

HOME ACCESSORIES

THE ARRANGEMENT / 4210 NE Fremont St, Beaumont; 503/287-4440
This friendly shop in the Alameda/Beaumont neighborhood beckons with an ever-changing flow of decorative items for the home. The helpful staff is more than happy to work with your colors, fabrics, photos, or whatever else might be your source of inspiration to create just the right dried-flower wreath or silk-flower table arrangement to fit your personal home decor. There are plenty of other things to find too: jewelry, casual wear, cards, and holiday decorations. *Every day; map:FF4*

BLUE PEAR / 1313 NW Glisan St, Pearl District; 503/227-0057 In the beloved former Jamison/Thomas Gallery sits an upscale home decor store full of oh-so-delectable treasures: fabric-covered, museum-quality furniture, display-worthy platters and dishes, fine tableware, and commissioned tiles. The Pear is just one of the many must-stops on a lazy afternoon tour of the Pearl District. *Mon–Sat; www.Blue-Pear.com; map:L1*

THE COMPLEAT BED & BREAKFAST / 615 NW 23rd Ave, Northwest; 503/221-0193 This is a store where you can indulge in some civilized pampering; you'll find enough luxurious linens and billowy comforters to supply sweet dreams for a lifetime. If it's not on the shelf, pick out fabric—Waverly or other top-drawer lines—and they'll make it to order. A large selection of Crabtree & Evelyn toiletries as well. *Every day; www.compleatbed.com; map:GG7*

DIECI SOLI / 304 NW 11th Ave, Pearl District; 503/222-4221 Featuring artful treasures for the table smack-dab in the middle of the Pearl's gallery and furniture store district, Dieci Soli carries an enormous selection of gorgeous hand-painted Italian pottery—from espresso cups to jardiniere. Local artist Suzy Root's whimsical painted tiles are displayed here as well, and a recent remodel brought a larger selection of fine linens, as well as April Cornell clothing, to the second floor. *Every day; www.dieci-soli.com; map:K2*

FRENCH QUARTER / 1444 NE Broadway, NE Broadway (and branch); 503/284-1379 "Crème de la crème" best describes this duo of boutiques catering to Francophiles who don't want to use up their frequent flier miles in search of a gift, but still want to wrap themselves in Parisian panache. Every square inch of the French Quarter is filled with something to lust after: plush bath mats, unbelievably soft flannel (100 percent cotton, unbleached, undyed) sheets, aromatic candles, fancy French soaps and bath salts, colorful towels, downy bathrobes, and dreamy pajamas. The original flagship-style boutique is located at the corner of NE 15th Avenue and Broadway; the second shop resides between cafes and artists lofts—so French—in the Pearl District (536 NW 14th Ave; 503/223-3879; map:L1). *Every day; www.eurolinens.com; map:FF5*

HUNT & GATHER / 1302 NW Hoyt St, Pearl District (and branch); 503/227-3400 Treasures from around the globe make for an interesting mix of home accessories at this Pearl District favorite. Beyond global goodies for the table, Hunt & Gather features custom-made, deliciously decadent down sofas as well as chairs sure to be the focus of any elegant home. Check out their nifty candle selection, too. More furniture, fewer accessories can be found at the eastside shop, Sofa Table Chair (2337 E Burnside; 503/231-2782; map:GG5). *Every day; www.huntgather.com; map:L2*

PENDLETON WOOLEN MILLS STORE / 8550 SE McLoughlin Blvd, Milwaukie (and branch); 503/535-5786 This is the drop-off spot for products from the research and development department of the Pendleton Woolen Mills. Prototypes for new products—from Pendleton wool–upholstered furniture to theme blankets—land here at discount prices. A shop annex offers fabric, buttons, elastic, and other sewing goods such as 1-cent buttons and 25-cent zippers. If you have the time, be sure to check out the outlet store in Washougal, Washington (off Hwy 14 on 217th St; 800/568-2480). *Mon–Sat; www. pendleton-usa.com; map:JJ5*

PRATT & LARSON TILE CO. / 1201 SE 3rd Ave, Southeast; 503/231-9464 With what seems to be miles of tile lining every surface, this is one of the country's largest custom tile manufacturers. And this inviting space is more like a large working studio rather than a factory, with local artists in the loftlike space above the showroom creating one-of-a-kind tile art. Michael Pratt, a potter, and Reta Larson, a fabric artist, combine their considerable talents to produce a distinctive line of tiles in hard-to-find colors such as cherry, celadon, and ocher. Accent with imported tile—16th-century-style Portuguese tiles, bird- and floral-motif tiles from France, or iridescent slate from India—for stunning results. For bargain tiling, check out their seconds room, where mistakes are practically given away. *Mon–Sat; www.prattandlarson.com; map:E9*

IMPORTS

ARTHUR W. ERIKSON FINE ARTS / 1030 SW Taylor St, Downtown; 503/227-4710 This astonishingly eclectic mélange of ethnographic objects (with a Native American focus) will appeal to the novice and experienced collector alike. A boar's-tusk necklace from New Guinea, 2,000-year-old bronze bracelets from the Mediterranean, and Kashmiri shawls are just a few of the out-of-the-ordinary offerings. *Wed and by appointment; map:H1*

CARGO / 1301 NW Glisan St, Pearl District (and branch); 503/827-7377 Welcome to another world. Welcome to Cargo. Where else will you find all the world's treasures under one roof? Some of the big-ticket home furnishing items: Chang dynasty beds or a Ming dynasty puppet theater (with puppets) for just under $10,000, or entire walls from a faraway island in Indonesia. Also for the home: folding iron chairs, seed baskets from Borneo, Indonesian hutches, Mexican pottery and glassware, and funky doodads from everywhere else fill this eclectic store right up to its rafters. A shopping oasis for those in search of creating a homespun Shangri-la. The store on NW 23rd Avenue stocks smaller stuff, mostly clothing and accessories. *Every day; www.cargoinc.com; map:L1*

EYE OF RA / 5331 SW Macadam Ave, Johns Landing; 503/224-4292 For many women shoppers, a trip to Portland without a stop at this boutique isn't really a trip at all. Robin Busch's Johns Landing hot spot features vividly hued clothing imported from Southeast Asia, Africa, and India—as well as Mishi cotton basics and unique kimonos. There's also a wide array of jewelry, one-of-a-kind tribal furnishings, textiles, and folk art. Trunk shows and sales are scheduled throughout the year. *Every day; map:HH6*

SCANDIA IMPORTS / 10020 SW Beaverton-Hillsdale Hwy, Beaverton; 503/643-2424 Finnish glassware, gleaming brown stoneware by Arabia, and heavy pewter candelabras from Denmark dazzle at surprisingly low prices. Homesick Scandinavians can buy birthday cards in their native languages, good Swedish mint pastilles, linens, and enough candles for a hundred Santa Lucia nights. *Mon–Sat; www.scandiaimports.com; map:HH9*

SIGNATURE IMPORTS / 638 SW Alder St, Downtown (and branch); 503/222-5340 With several stores in Oregon—including one in Northwest (920 NW 23rd; 503/274-0217; map:GG7)—Signature Imports is doing a bang-up business in the import trade. About 75 percent of the merchandise is from Latin America: colorful sweaters, jewelry, and clothing. It also carries rough-hewn furniture and gorgeous handblown glass from Mexico, masks from Ghana, and whimsical, handcrafted figures from the district of Oaxaca. Although you have seen much of their stuff in other shops, you can shop at this import store with a clear conscience—Signature supports cottage industries and has its own knitting co-op in Bolivia, so craftspeople benefit directly from their labors. *Every day; signatureimports@aol.com; map:H3*

TEN THOUSAND VILLAGES / 3508 SE Hawthorne Blvd, Hawthorne; 503/231-8832 The creed of this nonprofit organization—"fair-trade handicrafts from around the world"—manifests itself as a store full of eye-catching crafts and home accessories. Mexican pottery, colorful Haitian metal sculpture, handmade paper from Bangladesh, Vietnamese ceramics, and nesting dolls from India are only some of the Third World countries and crafts represented. A great place to buy a small gift for a child or a huge, hand-woven rug for your home. *Mon–Sat; www.tent housandvillages.com; map:GG5*

TRADE ROOTS / 1831 NE Broadway, NE Broadway; 503/281-5335 Folk art at this friendly shop includes brightly painted coconut-shell masks from Mexico, Peruvian amulets, and hand-woven place mats from Nepal. Gauzy skirts, embroidered vests, batik dresses, and other colorful apparel (including pieces from Putumayo), plus lots of silver jewelry—all at good prices. A small collection of Native American pottery makes this a great place to find a gift for someone who has everything. And for a child's room, consider suspending one of the colorful mobiles, larger-than-life butterfly kites, or star lanterns. *Every day; www.traderoots.com; map:FF5*

JEWELRY AND ACCESSORIES

CARL GREVE / 731 SW Morrison St, Downtown; 503/223-7121 Exclusive representation of the world's top jewelry designers is the specialty of the house at the fourth-generation, family-owned Carl Greve. And above all the glittering jewels (and up a starry stairway) is another one of Carl Greve's crowning achievements. The second-floor gift boutique is a fantasyland of shimmering china, stemware, and home accessories—musts for everyone from brides and grooms to grandes dames. Like the jewels and gems, much of it is also exclusive to this chic boutique. Many of CG's trunk shows and events are the talk of the social season. *Mon–Sat; www.carlgreve.com; map:H3*

DAN MARX / 511 SW Broadway, Downtown; 503/228-5090 For more than a century, Portlanders and visitors have been buying from Dan Marx, Oregon's oldest jewelry store. Clean-lined jewelry, gorgeous colored stones and diamonds, and the staff's quiet politeness set the tone. Eighteen-karat gold and platinum is used throughout this immaculate little family-owned shop full of small and delicate treasures. *Tues–Sat; map:H3*

GARY SWANK JEWELERS / 840 SW Broadway, Downtown; 503/223-8940 Custom designer Gary Swank does on-the-spot creations—bold earrings or necklaces like something from an Egyptian tomb—and he'll set anything from a diamond to a scarab. A great selection of newly minted wristwatches, as well as his coveted collection of antique timepieces (restored to perfect ticking order), are an extra lure for ladies and gentlemen. *Tues–Sat; www.garyswank.com; map:G3*

GOLDMARK / 1000 SW Taylor St, Downtown; 503/224-3743 A swell fellow, Cal Brockman, owner and operator of Goldmark, loves working with customers to create one-of-a-kind jewelry designs. Endlessly fascinated with the variety of colored gemstones, he has been designing, updating, and restyling jewelry for 25 years. *Tues–Sat and by appointment; map:H1*

MARGULIS JEWELERS / 800 SW Broadway, Downtown; 503/227-1153 David Margulis designs fetching pieces in 18- and 22-karat gold as well as platinum, many of which are inspired by classical themes: Heracles-knot bracelets, Celtic-style rings adorned with granulation, and elegant pearl earrings that resemble those in a Rubens painting. This family-owned business was the first to sell estate jewelry in Portland, and it offers pieces culled from around the world. Although it was established in 1932, this is hardly a traditional shop. Sleek, glossy, and very spacious, it features a spectacular view of Pioneer Courthouse Square. *Mon–Sat; david.margulis@margulis.com; www.margulis.com; map:G2*

THE REAL MOTHER GOOSE / 901 SW Yamhill St, Downtown (and branch); 503/223-9510 An American Crafts Gallery of the Year award winner, this fairy-tale shop is stocked full of singularly delightful artworks with a Northwest edge and attitude. A jewelry designer and gold-smith are on staff here to design wedding rings as well as other custom pieces; this is also a popular stop for holiday shoppers and travelers seeking choice gifts that reflect the region's spirit. The furniture gallery at the spacious downtown store carries contemporary pieces, in creative blends of fine (and sometimes exotic) woods, and there's a branch at the Portland airport for buying distinctive Northwest gifts on your way out of town. *Mon–Sat; map:H2*

VISAGE EYEWARE / 810 NW 12th Ave, Pearl District; 503/944-5475 Tucked into a corner of the Pearl District, Craig Valline's new shop has garnered a reputation as *the* place in town to buy glasses. You'll find unique and eclectic specs, ranging from minimalist to avant-garde, with brands such as Wood, Gold of Paris, Kesselstein-Cord, and Selima Optique. With an optometrist on site, you can update your prescription and your image at the same time. The focus here is on quality, and the prices reflect that. *Tues–Sat or by appointment; www.visageeyeware.com; map:W1*

ZELL BROS. / **800 SW Morrison St, Downtown; 503/227-8471** In 1912, brothers Julius and Harry Zell opened a small jewelry store near Portland's Union Station. Today, a marble building downtown houses the Zell empire: three floors of jewelry, Swiss watches, sterling silver, china, and crystal. *Mon–Sat; map:H3*

KITCHENWARE

IN GOOD TASTE / **231 NW 11th Ave, Pearl District; 503/248-2015** Gayle Jolley did more than just move her cooking school to the Pearl District from its original location at Sheridan Fruit, she broadened the concept of good taste by adding a catering and takeout kitchen and retail space for premier kitchen utensils and specialty food. This is the place to splurge on the good stuff—like professional cookware or Scharffen Berger chocolate—for the foodie in your life (especially if it's you). And do check out Jolley's cooking classes, taught by well-known local chefs and cooking professionals, which combine learning with dining. Also worth noting: lunch 11:30am to 3pm, Monday through Saturday in the Bistro, with an inviting menu along the lines of Cobb Salad, panini sandwiches, a bistro burger, and goat cheese tart—for dining in or carryout. *Mon–Sat; map:K2*

KITCHEN KABOODLE / **8788 SW Hall Blvd, Beaverton (and branches); 503/643-5491** Top-of-the-line cookware, tons of gadgets, and beautiful, reasonably priced tabletop ware make Kitchen Kaboodle a favorite haunt of food enthusiasts. Out-of-the-ordinary accessories, like salt and pepper shakers in the shape of tomatoes, are complemented by purely practical tools and appliances. Most of the stores have furniture, too: cherry dressers, ash side tables, and custom-made couches. Kitchen Kaboodle's biannual sale has been known to turn even the best-mannered into shopping sharks. Also branches downtown, on NE Broadway, and in Northwest. *Every day; www.kitchenkaboodle.com; map:II9*

MEATS AND SEAFOOD

EDELWEISS SAUSAGE COMPANY AND DELI / **3119 SE 12th Ave, Southeast; 503/238-4411** This crowded, nose-pleasing store is famous for its German foods and sundries (as well as those from other European countries) and for its wonderful meat and cheese case—where else can you find butterkase? Stacked chockablock are dozens of varieties of sausages (try the spicy beer version), Black Forest hams, and some of Portland's best bacons. Ask for a taste, or take out a sausage sandwich for lunch. Anyone nostalgic for Germany or Austria will delight in the European chocolates, preserves from Austria, and—be still, my rapidly congealing heart—German butter in the freezer. *Mon–Sat; map:GG5*

GARTNER'S COUNTRY MEAT MARKET / 7450 NE Killingsworth St, Northeast; 503/252-7801 This is the no-flourishes, serious-about-meat store. Busy but truly pleasant counter people staff a large, open preparation and display-case area. Roasts, steaks, chops, and house-smoked hams and bacons fill the L-shaped meat case. Aromatic smells spice the air, and meat saws whir in the background. Enthusiasm and pride imbue the store with a feeling of quality and value. *Tues–Sat; map:EE3*

NEWMAN'S FISH CO. / 1409 NE Weidler St (Irvington Market), Lloyd Center (and branch); 503/284-4537 Hands down, fins up, Newman's is the best place in town to buy fresh fish. The staff is knowledgeable, energetic, and pleasant; helping customers learn to buy and prepare fish is a priority of the owners. The variety is noteworthy, and freshness is a given. Admire the fresh whole salmon, the Oregon lox, the beautiful green-lipped mussels, Manila clams, and scampi (when available). Call ahead for fresh Dungeness crab and Maine lobster, which isn't thrown into the boiling water until you order it. At the Irvington Market location, peruse the small selection of poultry and red meat. The westside location is housed inside City Market NW (735 NW 21st Ave; 503/221-3002; map:GG7). *Every day; map:FF5*

OTTO'S SAUSAGE KITCHEN & MEAT MARKET / 4138 SE Woodstock Blvd, Woodstock; 503/771-6714 The deli in the front of this Germanic shop draws in lots of folk from the neighborhood for lunch, but what this solid, good-natured store is famous for is its smoked meats and homemade sausages. The smoked meats are delicious, the stuffed chicken breasts—Florentine, Cordon Bleu, or stuffed with wild rice—are from Otto's own recipe, and the sausages (ground and stuffed in the back room) are out of this world. Don't pass up the hams: smoked or dry-cured. There's an evenly balanced wine selection with excellent French choices and good sparkling wines. Beers, too. *Mon–Sat; map:II4*

PHIL'S UPTOWN MEAT MARKET / 17 NW 23rd Pl (Uptown Shopping Center), Northwest; 503/224-9541 If there was such a thing as a "meat boutique," this would be it. This small black-and-white-tiled shop, with white porcelain display cases, butcher blocks, and fan-type butcher scales, sells meats and poultry of the highest quality, and there's a small seafood selection, too. Here you can find beautiful cuts of meat, from domestic lamb (leg, rack, chops, kebabs), to pork and beef, including a choice of ground beef—round or chuck, shaped into patties or not. Check out the wines on your way in; on your way out, buy a skewer of moist, grilled chicken (Monday through Saturday) to munch on the way home. *Tues–Sat; map:FF7*

VIANDE MEATS AND SAUSAGE CO. / 735 NW 21st Ave (City Market NW), Northwest; 503/221-3012 Formerly known as Salumeria di Carlo, the renamed Viande Meats and Sausage Co. carries on with unchanged high standards for quality. Prosciutto-style ham, marinated chicken, fresh sausages (such as the classic Italian pork with fennel, Moroccan-style lamb, Spanish chorizo, and Thai chicken), and a fantastic porchetta—stuffed pig—fill the small case in the front of City Market NW. There's also fresh Oregon poussin, or young chicken, something not commonly sold in retail meat markets. The delicious sausage sandwiches, messy with grilled peppers and onions, are available for takeout Monday through Thursday—and usually sell out by 2pm. *Every day; map:GG7*

WHITE'S COUNTRY MEATS / 1206 SE Orient Dr, Gresham; 503/666-0967 Gresham residents highly recommend this establishment: it's a straightforward, good-quality meat store with its own smokehouse and processing facilities. Expect fresh, honestly trimmed, reasonably priced meats. A variety of roasts, steaks, and ground meats are available; the poultry and pork look better than at most other meat counters. *Tues–Sat.*

MUSIC (CDS, RECORDS, AND TAPES)

CROSSROADS / 3130-B SE Hawthorne Blvd, Hawthorne; 503/232-1767 This cooperative of 35 vendors in a storefront is modeled much like an antique mall. That makes sense, considering that they specialize in collectibles and hard-to-find records—they even offer a computerized record-search service. If you need *Meet the Beatles* on the black label, green label, red label, or Apple label to complete your collection, pay this place a visit. It will definitely be worth the trip. *Every day; www.xro.com; map:GG5*

DJANGO'S / 1111 SW Stark St, Downtown; 503/227-4381 The first used-record store in Portland, this place has the look and feel of the record stores of the '70s: lots of posters for sale, Grateful Dead on the sound system, and loads of vinyl LPs. But Django's is a lot more than a trip down memory lane; it's a Portland landmark that stocks lots of used CDs and records in all styles of music. Take heed: the racks get picked over quickly, making some titles difficult to find. *Every day; www. django.com; map:I2*

EVERYDAY MUSIC / 1313 W Burnside St, Pearl District (and branches); 503/274-0961 This large space on downtown's Burnside Street—a short walk up from Powell's Books—is well stocked with CDs, cassettes, and LPs from the worlds of rock, jazz, and dance music (this spot sports a next-door store that carries a great classical selection). Most everything is used and priced quite fairly. There is a smattering of listening stations, and all genres are well represented. Other branches are in Beaverton and on NE Sandy Boulevard. *Every day (including Christmas); www.every daymusic.com; map:J1*

LOCALS ONLINE.COM / 916 W Burnside St, Downtown; 503/227-5000
All types of music from the Pacific Northwest can be found at Locals Online.com (formerly known as Locals Only). CDs from platinum-earning acts such as Nirvana and Alice in Chains sit on racks opposite hand-labeled tapes of shows at local hangouts. Jazz, folk, and other sounds, too. They'll gladly let you listen before you buy. *Tues–Sat; www.localsonline.com; map:I6*

MUSIC MILLENNIUM / 3158 E Burnside St, Laurelhurst (and branch); 503/231-8926 Since 1969, the independently owned Music Millennium has stayed competitive with larger record chains. Its stock is truly impressive: an amazing variety of rock CDs, from ABBA to Zuzu's Petals, plus separate areas for collections, oldies, rap, jazz, blues, reggae, country, and New Age. The Burnside store has a separate classical music annex. Big-name musicians coming through town occasionally stop in to meet their fans and play a mini-set. Special appearances at the Northwest shop, too (801 NW 23rd Ave; 503/248-0163; map:FF7), as well as a sound kiosk. *Every day; www.musicmillennium.com; map:GG5*

OZONE RECORDS / 1036 W Burnside St, Downtown; 503/227-1975
Ozone may be just down the street from Django's, but in certain music circles it's in a whole different stratosphere. Loads of local music is always blaring in the background, and the catchword is "cutting edge"—everything experimental, industrial, and alternative. Locals, out-of-town bands, and scene makers hang out at the Ozone every weekend. Great selection of concert T-shirts too. *Every day; www.ozonerecords.com; map:J2*

PLATINUM RECORDS / 104 SW 2nd Ave, Old Town; 503/222-9166 This DJ-centric shop is the place to go for dance music and hard-to-find musical genres. The stock is mostly LPs—not surprising, since DJs don't mix with cassettes. There is also a good selection of DJ equipment, including mixers, PA systems, and a few glittering disco balls. *Every day; www.platinum-records.com; map:J6*

REVERB / 3623 SE Hawthorne Blvd, Hawthorne; 503/736-9110 New and used LPs are mixed together with a smaller number of CDs and cassettes. Most prices are reasonable, and there are unquestionably a few finds to be found. In addition to rock, there are sections for country, jazz, gospel, and, lo and behold, "zither." *Every day; rmusic@uswest.net; map:GG5*

2ND AVENUE RECORDS / 400 SW 2nd Ave, Downtown; 503/222-3783
Stacks and stacks of boxes containing tapes and CDs of rap, metal, alternative, punk, and rock crowd every square inch of this store. For years, 2nd Avenue Records has been a browser's paradise. If you don't have the time to wade through it all, ask Cathy Hagen or John McNally: they'll know where to find what you want. *Every day; map:H5*

OUTDOOR GEAR

ALDER CREEK KAYAK SUPPLY / 250 NE Tomahawk Island Dr, Jantzen Beach; 503/285-0464 If it floats and you paddle it, Alder Creek probably sells it—whether it's a canoe, sea kayak, or river kayak. Demos in the nearby Columbia River are free (note to self: this is a great way to find out how much you're willing to lug around on the dock). The store carries an extensive line of gear, books, and videos and emphasizes group and private instruction and guided tours. *Every day; acks@teleport.com; www.aldercreek.com; map:CC6*

ANDY & BAX SPORTING GOODS / 324 SE Grand Ave, Southeast; 503/234-7538 This is it—ground zero for the sports lover/camper or for the person who just likes to wear campy sport clothes. Huge helpings of personality are split three ways between rafting and whitewater equipment, piles of Army/Navy surplus, and family camping and cold-weather gear. From commercial inflatables to information on guides and beginner classes, Andy & Bax is one of Portland's better rafting and whitewater resources. Reasonable prices and some awesome bargains (read: European army surplus blankets for cheapie cheap). *Mon–Sat; www. andyandbax.com; map:GG5*

ATHLETIC DEPARTMENT / 3275 SW Cedar Hills Blvd, Beaverton; 503/646-0691 This was the original Nike store at the beginning of the running boom, when both runners and Nike were considered (slightly) demented. When Nike turned its massive marketing attention to a full line of specialty stores, ex-Nike employee Danny Adams bought this shop. He hasn't changed it much. As far as he knows, it is—along with the Bend branch of the Athletic Department—the only non-Nike-owned Nike-only store in the country. *Every day; map:HH9*

BICYCLE REPAIR COLLECTIVE / 4438 SE Belmont St, Belmont; 503/233-0564 The Bicycle Repair Collective has only a handful of peers nationwide. It sells parts and accessories, rents work space, repairs bikes, and gives classes on bike repair and maintenance. For $50 a year or $5 an hour, cyclists can tune their bikes and adjust their chains. *Mon–Sat; map:GG4*

THE BIKE GALLERY / 3645 SW Hall Blvd, Beaverton (and branches); 503/641-2580 The Bike Gallery is to cycles what Saks is to clothes. With humble origins as a small, family-run shop, it's now one of the country's finest bike dealers. Whether you're in the market for a bike (road, mountain, crossover, tandem, child's, or adult), Burly, or jogging stroller, all sales are guaranteed. Branches throughout the city (NE Sandy, Downtown, Lake Oswego, and Gresham); the Beaverton store also carries Nordic ski gear when in season. *Every day; bikeclub@bikegallery.com; www.bikegallery.com; map:HH9*

BOB'S BICYCLE CENTER / 10950 SE Division St, Southeast; 503/254-2663 Bob's started as a small BMX store and is now one of the largest cycling shops in the Northwest. The stock has grown to 2,000-plus bikes (everything from BMX to touring), and the store even sponsors a mountain-biking race team. Eighteen staff members in one store cater to customer needs, from free bicycle fits to full-service bike repairs. *Every day; www.bobsbicyclecenter.com; map:GG2*

COLUMBIA SPORTSWEAR / 911 SW Broadway, Downtown (and branches); 503/226-6800 While Gert Boyle, mother figure and CEO of Columbia Sportswear, has become a national icon through savvy advertising and an insistence that everyone dress warmly, her business has exploded internationally. This is Boyle's flagship store: 16,000 square feet of outdoor apparel and footwear reflecting the latest in high-tech fabrics and technologies. Got a sport? She's got the shoes, the socks, and the practical advice. Outlet stores in Sellwood (1323 SE Tacoma St; 503/238-0118; map:JJ6) and Lake Oswego (3 Monroe Pkwy; 503/636-6593; map:LL7) carry irregulars, closeouts, and overstocks of active outdoor apparel and footwear fresh from the factory, at 30 to 50 percent below retail prices. *Every day; www.columbia.com; map:H2*

COUNTRYSPORT / 126 SW 1st Ave, Downtown; 503/221-4545 For the fly-fishing aficionado, Countrysport is a simple yet gorgeous store, with antique reels, bamboo fly rods, wicker creels, and canoe chairs all displayed on hardwood floors. Clothing includes waxed-cotton rainwear, lamb's-wool sweaters, canvas shirts, and fleece. There's a huge selection of flies, feathers, and thread, and practical gear (float tubes, pontoon boats) as well. Fly-fishing classes and guided tours are available. A weekend-minded retreat in the middle of the downtown work force. *Every day; www.csport.com; map:I7*

EBB & FLOW PADDLESPORTS / 0604 SW Nebraska St, off Macadam near Willamette Park; 503/245-1756 Donna Holman is Portland's sea-kayaking expert. The co-founder of OOPS (Oregon Ocean Paddling Society), she's refined her line of sea kayaks and canoes based on 16 years of renting them; if they don't hold up, out they go. The shop is intimate—boats and gear squeezed into a small space—with a warehouse full of boats behind the shop. You can put a kayak on a portage cart, wheel it across the street to Willamette Park's boat ramp, and try out different kinds of paddles to ensure a perfect fit. Whitewater instruction for all levels of experience. *Tues–Sun; www.ebbnflow.citysearch.com; map:JJ6*

FAT TIRE FARM / 2714 NW Thurman St, Northwest; 503/222-FARM This shop, located at NW 27th and Thurman, has the advantage of having immediate access to Portland's (and the nation's) largest municipal playground: Forest Park. Mountain biker wannabes can rent a bike and helmet here, load up on equipment, grab a water bottle and a fistful of Power Bars, and, on Thursdays at 6pm, take a guided tour through the park. Free park maps available. Mountain bikes, bike accessories, clothes, literature, and miscellany for sale. Friendly, informed staff. Easy parking. *Every day; www.fattirefarm.com; map:GG7*

KAUFMANN'S STREAMBORN FLY SHOP / 8861 SW Commercial St, Tigard; 503/639-6400 Kaufmann's has been Portland's consummate fly shop for more than two decades. The knowledgeable staff can outfit you for fishing on the Clackamas, or they can equip you for specialty fishing trips, local or abroad. Along with one of the finer selections of flies in the country, Kaufmann's offers fishing classes and fly-tying materials. Its free catalog has made the store world renowned. *Mon–Sat; www.kman.com; map:KK9*

THE MOUNTAIN SHOP / 628 NE Broadway, NE Broadway; 503/288-6768 This store may well be the area's best one-stop shopping center for downhill gear. It's certainly the most unabashed, with three floors of ski stuff to help you perfect your style. They also outfit backcountry ski lovers, as well as those who would rather go up (or down) the mountain without skis. *Every day; www.mountainshop.net; map:FF5*

NIKE TOWN / 930 SW 6th Ave, Downtown (and branches); 503/221-6453 This state-of-the-art store/showcase displays all the latest from the entire Nike line. Fans come not only to buy but to gawk at this runner and sport lovers' freak fest. The sideshow stops, however, when it comes to outfitting athletes. The young and fit clerks—athletes one and all—know what they're talking about and will gladly help you find what you need. And though you'll rarely find stuff on sale, there's plenty to purchase no matter your budget. For less show and better prices, shop at the Nike Factory Store (2650 NE Martin Luther King Jr Blvd; 503/281-5901; map:FF5). The Nike store on the mini-retail row at Portland's International Airport (503/284-3558) packs as much as it can into a small space. *Every day; www.nike.com; map:G3*

OREGON MOUNTAIN COMMUNITY / 60 NW Davis St, Old Town; 503/227-1038 OMC is a four-season outfitter: in the winter this popular Old Town outdoor store stocks up with skis; in summer, look for packs, tents, sleeping bags, and rock-climbing equipment. Other outdoor clothing and equipment are available year-round. The sales staff has a tremendous amount of outdoor experience. *Every day; map:K6*

PACESETTER ATHLETICS / 4306 SE Woodstock Blvd, Woodstock; 503/777-3214 If you wear your old running shoes to this store, the staff will check them out and, based on how you wore them down, recommend a new pair. Some of the area's better athletes work in this store, so the merchandise reflects a slightly more technical bias than that of the typical running store. In addition to offering more than 115 models of running shoes,

Pacesetter sponsors a 30-person racing team. Customers who are not as fast or knowledgeable as the staff will like the casual, helpful atmosphere. Student discounts. *Mon–Sat; www.pacesetterathletics.com; map:HH4*

PLAY IT AGAIN SPORTS / 9248 SW Beaverton-Hillsdale Hwy, Beaverton (and branches); 503/292-4552 For moms and dads, Play It Again is a great (and inexpensive) godsend. This store targets kids who are growing too fast to wear sports stuff out and beginners who don't want to pay a fortune to try out a new sport. You'll find new and used sports equipment (skis to backyard games). The location, next door to Valley Ice Arena, assures a fine stock of hockey and ice-skating equipment—in-line skates, too. The branches are in Clackamas and on NE Halsey Street and SE 82nd Avenue. *Every day; www.playitagainsports.com; map:II8*

REI / 1798 Jantzen Beach Center, Jantzen Beach; 503/283-1300 REI (Recreational Equipment Inc.) is one of the nation's largest sports-minded cooperatives. It specializes in clothes and equipment for mountaineering, backpacking, skiing, cycling, water sports, and walking. The staff is knowledgeable and helpful; A onetime $15 fee earns roughly 10 percent cash back on non-sale purchases. *Every day; www.rei.com; map:BB7*

RIVER CITY BICYCLES / 706 SE Martin Luther King Jr Blvd, Southeast; 503/233-5973 Open since 1994, this bike shop may well be the finest wheel winder in town. With an 11,000-square-foot showroom, including an indoor test track, it's certainly the largest. The friendly experts who run River City stock the store with all kinds of riding gear: tricycles, tandems, mountain and road bikes, helmets, shoes, a huge clothing section—you name it. A great place to outfit the family. *Every day; www.rivercitybicycles.com; map:G9*

RUNNING OUTFITTERS / 2337 SW 6th Ave, Lair Hill; 503/248-9820 At the foot of the popular Terwilliger Boulevard running route, two blocks from Duniway Park's track, is the city's oldest running-only store (formerly Terwilliger Athletic Gear)—smaller than your garage, but well stocked. Owner Jim Davis is, of course, an avid runner, and his store has an almost cultlike following. *Mon–Sat; map:HH6*

SHOES

AL'S BOOTS & SHOES FOR MEN / 5811 SE 82nd Ave, Southeast; 503/771-2130 This family-run business has been outfitting men (and women who eschew heels) for 53 years. Durable cowboy boots and steel-toes are plentiful, and there's also a range of hiking boots and other styles. This is where hard laborers shop for footwear that can take a beating, but the friendly and knowledgeable staff treats hipsters seeking the perfect black boot with equal respect. *Mon–Sat; www.alsshoes.citysearch.com; map:J3*

BIRKENSTOCK FOOTPRINTS OF OREGON / 730 SW 11th Ave, Downtown; 503/227-4202 Descend the stairs and you're met by the chatter of canaries, Birkie the house cat, and a collection of the world's most comfortable walking shoes. In the last few years, the hipness quotient of Birkenstocks has skyrocketed (there's even jewelry), but if your tastes run to sleeker designs, there are other options here as well: Finn Comfort and Haflingers. *Every day; www.birkenstock.com; map:H2*

HALO / 1425 NE Broadway, NE Broadway; 503/331-0366 This intimate, newish shoetique is a pleasant addition to the style-conscious, thriving NE Broadway area. Incredibly rich leather styles range from updated Mary Janes to ultra-feminine heeled sandals and other classy styles for women of impeccable taste (and a couple hundred dollars to spend). Hunker down on the comfy couch and find the glass slipper that fits. Men's shoes, unique leather wallets and other accessories are worth a look, too. *Every day; map:FF5*

IMELDA'S DESIGNER SHOES / 1431 SE 37th Ave, Hawthorne; 503/233-7476 Heads up, shoehorses. Here's a store that prides itself on carrying lines you won't find at department stores (in addition to others that you will), but at prices that allow more than an occasional indulgence. Owner Pam Coven strives for a mix of fashion-forward lines for men and women, with an emphasis on designer labels. The helpful staff will even call you when the new BCBG line comes in. Leather handbags, jewelry, and hosiery too, all a half block from colorful Hawthorne Boulevard. *Every day; map:GG5*

JOHNNY SOLE / 815 SW Alder St, Downtown; 503/225-1241 John Plummer's got sole. Even better, the Portland entrepreneur keeps a close watch on the fashion trend-o-meter and stocks his once-tiny shoe boutique—now a two-story, sprawling shoe mall—accordingly. Here you'll find Italian and Spanish imports, steel-toed work boots, sexy women's flats and heels, those beloved Fluevogs, and classy Kenneth Cole styles. (The funkiest stuff is upstairs.) There's also a decent selection of street-smart accessories. *Every day; map:I3*

MODA / 615 SW Park Ave, Downtown; 503/227-6522 Michael Jolley's Moda features cutting-edge footwear for women. With lines such as Calvin Klein, Via Spiga, and Robert Clergerie, the look is European but the prices are affordable. There's also a notable selection of clothing by Nicole Farhi, Shoshanna, Iceberg, Chaiken, and others. *Every day; map:H2*

ODDBALL SHOE COMPANY / 1639 NW Marshall St, Northwest; 503/827-7800 A recent move to Northwest has yielded more room to stretch out for the big guys, with shoes sizes 12 and up. From sporty Adidas sneakers to Donald Pliner dress and casual footwear—as well as brands like Kenneth Cole, Hush Puppies, and Doc Marten—there's lots to choose from. And tall-size clothing, too. *Mon–Sat; map:GG6*

ZELDA'S SHOE BAR / 633 NW 23rd Ave, Northwest; 503/226-0363 This bar serves only the most contemporary shoes—straight up—to a well-heeled clientele thirsty for style. Sleek copper counters display a carefully chosen selection emphasizing designer looks in European leathers. Vans and a few sportier styles occasionally appear as blue-plate specials. *Every day; map:GG7*

TOYS

BRIDGES: A TOY AND BOOK STORE / 402 N State St, Lake Oswego; 503/699-1322 This spacious Lake Oswego store should serve as a model for other toy stores: it's well organized, it has lots of toy set-ups for kids to engage in while grown-ups shop, and there's enough room to move without knocking the baby into a display. In addition to all the name-brand toys (Playmobil, Brio, Ambi), the store also carries dress-up clothes, jazzy Hula Hoops, and a long aisle of things to make and do (beads, tie-dye, clay), as well as big-ticket items like a wooden rocking rowboat or a life-sized-for-a-kid baseball mitt lounge chair. In the adjoining Baby Bridges Boutique and Bookstore, you'll find a wide selection of developmental toys for babies on the fast track, as well as a thoughtful selection of books (from board to bored/young adult) and clothes for a special occasion. The new Raleigh Hills store (6559 SW Beaverton-Hillsdale Highway; 503/292-1311; map:II8) is not as large but is just as well thought out. *Every day (Lake Oswego), Mon–Sat (Raleigh Hills); susan sullivan@uswest.com; www.bridgestoys.com; map:LL6*

CHILD'S PLAY / 907 NW 23rd Ave, Northwest; 503/224-5586 You haven't lived until you've witnessed this shop's own band of stuffed primates singing "I'm a Bongo-Playing Monkey." Choose from a great selection of uncommon American and European toys for every stage of a child's development, from rattle shaking to puzzle building. While there is a nice selection of dolls (Ginny, Madame Alexander, and the hard-to-find American Girls Collection) and doll accessories, we gravitate toward the strong art and science sections. Go often (and well before Christmas) to see Child's Play at its finest. *Every day; www.toysinportland.com; map:GG7*

FINNEGAN'S TOYS AND GIFTS / 922 SW Yamhill St, Downtown; 503/221-0306 The biggest and best toy store in town, Finnegan's can keep you and your child enthralled for the better part of an afternoon. A part of this spacious, always stimulating store is set aside for test drives of the windup cars, flip-over monkeys, and whatnot. Look for Ambi rattles, Playmobil gear, Brio trains, dollhouses, craft supplies, wooden and floor puzzles, board games, dress-up clothes (including a number of amusing animal snouts), and a great selection of puppets and stuffed animals. *Every day; www.FinnegansToys.com; map:H2*

KIDS AT HEART / 3445 SE Hawthorne Blvd, Hawthorne; 503/231-2954
A move up the street has made a world of difference to a toy shop that before seemed pretty perfect. Not only is there more room to shop without bumping into the displays, but there's also added shelf space to display more of the same great stuff: lots of Brio and Playmobil, dollhouses, puppet theaters, dress-up helmets and fairy garlands, glow-in-the-dark soccer balls, MagiCloth paper dolls, dolls, and stuffed animals. A quick stop on the way to a birthday party yields the perfect less-than-$10 gift: Gerti balls, craft kits, finger puppets, harmonicas, maracas, and cards, too. *Every day; map:GG5*

PAINT THE SKY KITES / 828 NW 23rd Ave, Northwest; 503/222-5096

Enter this colorful store through the curtain of wind socks hanging on the front porch, and find yourself amid a friendly collection of kites and other stuff to fly in the great blue yonder: boomerangs, flying disks (aka Frisbees), banners, and flags. Kite-making supplies for do-it-yourself types, as well as juggling equipment, razor scooters, and Beamo Frisbees round out the inventory. *Every day; www.paintthesky.com; map:GG7*

TAMMIE'S HOBBIES / 12024 SW Canyon Rd, Beaverton; 503/644-4535
Tammie's is always abuzz with enthusiastic hobbyists. It's one of the only Portland stores to carry German LGB electric train sets (and spare parts). Few outgrow the yearning for radio-controlled race cars, airplanes, and boats. You'll also find models of all sorts, a paint center, and a full range of paintball supplies. *Every day; www.Tammies.com; map:HH9*

THINKER TOYS / 7784 SW Capitol Hwy, Multnomah; 503/245-3936 Tye and Joan Steinbach have been putting smiles on the faces of children and their parents for years. A recent move and expansion (one block from the original space) means a store that's 2.7 times larger, with lots of things to entertain the kids while the adults shop: a built-in Snow White's play hut, a magic mirror on the wall with a basket of dress-up clothes, and plenty of play tables. The type of merchandise hasn't changed—Brio, dress-up clothing, puzzles, baby toys—there's just more of it. The shop in Westmoreland (1626 SE Bybee Blvd; 503/235-2970; map:JJ5) features a lot of the same toys and games in a smaller space. *Every day; map:JJ7*

VINTAGE AND CONSIGNMENT

ACT II EXCLUSIVE RESALE BOUTIQUE / 1139 SW Morrison St, Downtown; 503/227-7969 There are labels in this highbrow, low-key store that

scream "no one can afford me." You can. Armani, Donna Karan, Valentino, and St. John take a sharp markdown here. You will also find some pretty nifty knockoffs, too. *Tues–Sat; map:I1*

AVALON ANTIQUES / 203 SW 9th Ave, Downtown; 503/224-7156
Avalon is one-stop shopping, especially for men. It's easy to walk out of this well-stocked vintage emporium with a dashing suit, dress shirt, shoes, fedora, watch, and tie. From Victorian to '50s-era wear, the selection for both men's and women's clothing is outstanding. Those who adore '20s styles will be especially pleased. Antique lockets, scarves, and other accents are quite impressive, and the staff is knowledgeable and friendly. Come here for the perfect, personal gift for someone special. *Every day; map:J3*

BUFFALO EXCHANGE / 1420 SE 37th Ave, Hawthorne; 503/234-1302
This funky resale shop primarily carries used, contemporary garb and shoes for guys and gals, but there's also a slew of new bags, belts, and cheap jewelry for the young and trendy. The vintage racks holds the occasional treasure, but customers are more likely to walk out with a J. Crew sweater or a Gap shift than anything truly retro. *Every day; www.buffalo exchange.com; map:HH5*

CHEAP DATE / 1027 SW Morrison St, Downtown; 503/226-2616 Cheap Date is the recently added extension to Ray's Ragtime next door. The difference between the two is the '60s and '70s focus of the former. Cheap Date has one of the best boa collections in town and lots of crinoline skirts, not to mention plenty of wild getups from the pre-disco and disco days. This is vintage shopping at its most fun. *Every day; ragtime@ pacifier.com; www.raysragtime.com; map:I2*

DECADES VINTAGE COMPANY / 328 SW Stark St, Downtown; 503/223-1177 Impeccable men's and women's vintage fashions from the '30s to the '70s are nicely displayed here. Gorgeous dresses and well-tailored trousers, vintage eyeglass frames, costume jewelry, and deco bar collectibles await shoppers who value quality and cut. *Every day; www. decadesvintage.com; map:I5*

LADY LUCK VINTAGE / 1 SE 28th Ave, Southeast; 503/233-4041 There's nothing demure here—Lady Luck specializes in the sexier side of vintage. Wild nighties, gold heels, and dreamy evening wear are plentiful in this large store. There's a pink glamour corner in the back with dressing rooms where countless racks of gauzy gowns and slinky black numbers hang for your perusal. (Think Sophia Loren.) The store offers a little something for the men, too. *Every day; map:GG5*

RAY'S RAGTIME / 1021 SW Morrison St, Downtown; 503/226-2616 Hundreds of gowns and glittery party dresses are arranged chronologically in this downtown shop. There's also an excellent collection of costume jewelry and tons of fine men's suits and ties. Hawaiian and bowling shirts are a favorite with bargain-hunting Californians and Japanese.

ODDS AT THE END OF THE TRAIL

Portland is packed full of interesting shops, but some of them are, well, just plain odd. For a souvenir off the beaten track, or to simply explore Portland's more eclectic or goofier side, you'll want to check out the following. Though some could be squeezed into a category, most of these shops stand alone when it comes to filling a niche.

Wacky Willy's Surplus Store (2374 NW Vaughn St; 503/525-9211; every day; www.wackywillys.com) This no-man's retail land is unlike any store in Portland. Every time you try to label it (surplus store, museum, novelty shop) another strange and oddly wonderful item will catch your eye and make you wonder (or laugh out loud) about what exactly you should do with it. The business card boasts that they buy and sell "any type of merchandise," which explains a shifting inventory that might include 27,000 pieces of itty bitty Plexiglas, 100 old-fashioned dial telephones, Desert Storm postcards, and tiny purple and pink army guys (40 for a buck). Popular with artists, teachers, mechanics, electricians, hobbyists, and clutter bugs. A second store in Hillsboro can be found at 2900 SW Cornelius Pass Road (503/642-5111).

The **Button Emporium** (914 SW 11th Ave; 503/228-6372; Tues–Sat; www.buttonemporium.com) One of the area's most unusual shops, the Button Emporium is a fabric lover's must-stop. Literally hundreds of thousands of buttons, from the everyday to the exotic, are up for grabs, along with a wide assortment of antique ribbons and trims. Sign up for one the various hand-crafting specialty classes.

Desperado (1321 NW Hoyt St; 503/294-2952; every day) Although the Pearl District may seem like an unlikely place for a Western-themed boutique, "boutique" is the operative word. It carries cowboy boots, dress-up Western apparel, jewelry, wool blankets, and lots of nostalgic stuff for kids to fill up your saddle bag: cowboy pj's, leather chaps, and deerskin moccasins.

Beauty for the Beast (3832 NE Sandy Blvd; 503/288-5280; every day) This Northeast salon du chien is the perfect place to pamper your pooch. Choose between do-it-yourself pet washing or indulging in the full-service grooming salon. When you're done doing doggy's do, you can shop at the bowwow-tique for treats, sweets, and other gifts.

Bazaar of the Bizarre (5667 NE Glisan St; 503/235-3552; Mon–Sat) A treasure trove of truly tantalizing tidbits, some with a high gross-out factor. The proximity to Providence Medical Center may or may not explain the amazing array of anatomically correct reproductions of hearts, brains, and eyeballs. There's also a fair share of hard-to-find toys and an impressive collection of things that glow in the dark.

—*Byron Beck*

Every day (closed Sun from Halloween to Christmas); ragtime@ pacifier.com; www.raysragtime.com; map:I2

RED LIGHT CLOTHING EXCHANGE / 3590 SE Hawthorne Blvd, Hawthorne; 503/963-8888 Red Light is a fine addition to the bustling Hawthorne strip. The palatial store is filled with all manner of his and hers vintage and retro wear at fair prices: '70s rock tees and polyester shirts to '60s gowns and skirts, black wingtips to go-go boots, and everything in between. Pick up a fancy hat, a bowling bag, or a new pair of shades to accent your new-old look. You won't leave this store empty-handed. *Every day; www.vintageclothes.com; map:HH5*

RETREAD THREADS QUALITY CLOTHING / 931 SW Oak St, Downtown; 503/916-0000 Fun, retro casual wear from the '60s to early '80s is the emphasis at Retread Threads. There are plenty of campy T-shirts, wild jeans, and old-man cardigans. The jewelry, shades, and other accessories here are equally playful, and even the new inventory (about half of the store's stock) stays true to the old school in style and feel. *Every day; www.retreadthreads.com; map:J3*

TORSO BOUTIQUE / 64 SW 2nd Ave, Old Town; 503/294-1493 In many vintage stores, you have to hunt for the great buys. At Torso, the Prince of Vintage, John Hadeed, displays his vintage collection so well that you must first just stand and gawk. From Victorian black to '70s brights, all the pieces are in great shape; prices do reflect this. *Wed–Sun, and by appointment; www.torsovintages.com; map:I6*

WINE, BEER, AND SPIRITS

BEAUMONT WINES / 5015 NE Fremont St, Beaumont; 503/331-3991 Kimberly Bernosky, Lee Medoff (a winemaker himself), and their faithful dog, Che, preside over one of Portland's newest, most attractive, and most interesting wine shops. Education is a focus here: there are wine classes every other Wednesday featuring intriguing flights of eight or more wines, drop-in tastings for a small fee on Fridays, and free tastings on Saturdays. Bernosky and Medoff have a nose for uncommon finds—obscure labels and little-known or emerging winelands—and an awareness that many wine lovers operate on a beer budget, so you'll find plenty of unusual and inexpensive bottles. *Tues–Sat; www.beaumontwines. com; map:FF4*

BURLINGAME GROCERY / 8502 SW Terwilliger Blvd, Burlingame; 503/246-0711 If this market doesn't carry the bottled beer you're after, you're probably out of luck. Owner Tom Calkin and his staff strive to stock every beer available in the state, including some obscure European labels at bargain prices (and look for closeout specials: great beers that sold poorly in the Portland market are frequently available for a song). The wine section is also very strong, from West Coast wines to Bordeaux to Italian reds, and there are usually free tastings on Saturday. You can also pick up milk, eggs, and a loaf of bread here; it is a grocery, after all. *Every day; www.burlingamegrocery.com; map:HH6*

CLEAR CREEK DISTILLERY / 1430 NW 23rd Ave, Northwest; 503/248-9470 With a gorgeous copper still, fruit from his family's Hood River orchards, and other local ingredients, Stephen McCarthy creates impeccably crafted versions of a variety of classic European liquors. He is best known for his pear brandy, a colorless ambrosia that's available with and without a pear in the bottle, but his range extends from a Calvados-style apple brandy to grappa to Oregon's first single-malt whiskey. He also makes framboise (raspberry eau-de-vie), kirschwasser (cherry brandy), and slivovitz (plum brandy). Clear Creek is open daily during the week, but it's best to let them know you're coming. *Mon–Fri; www.clearcreek distillery.com; map:FF7*

E&R WINE SHOP / 6141 SW Macadam Ave, Johns Landing; 503/246-6101 Ed Paladino ("E") and Richard Elden ("R") arrived on the Portland wine scene in 1999 with a splash, and their shop has instantly become a necessary stop on every Portland wine lover's pilgrimage. Their selection is large—but well laid out, so as not to be overwhelming—and they bring a level of personal attention that makes the place feel like home. They have a lengthy newsletter that offers appraisals of wines from an illustrious panel of food and wine personalities—not to mention their own thoughts on wine and a variety of other subjects. There are tastings, both paid and free, as well as books, accessories, and foodstuffs, including excellent dried pasta. *Tues–Sat (every day in Dec); erwines@earthlink.net; www.erwines.citysearch.com; map:II6*

GREAT WINE BUYS / 1515 NE Broadway, NE Broadway; 503/287-2897 Longtime owner Rachel Starr recently sold her shop to John Kennedy and Dawn Bolgioni, who have dressed it up in the warm Mediterranean colors that have become de rigueur for local wine shops. More important, they've substantially beefed up the offerings, which include a thoughtfully chosen sampling from the world's major wine regions, with particularly good Northwest, Spanish, and Italian sections. There are some bargains to be had and still plenty of friendly advice. If you'd like to open your purchase right then and there, you can avail yourself of a small seating area in the front of the shop to sip and watch the world go by. *Every day; www.greatwinebuys.citysearch.com; map:FF5*

LINER & ELSEN WINE MERCHANTS / 202 NW 21st Ave, Northwest; 503/241-9463 For wine lovers all over Portland, the day Bob Liner and Matt Elsen sold their shop in order to go over to the dark side of the wholesale wine business was a sad day indeed. The duo, part savvy wine lovers and part vaudeville team, did a great job of raising the level of Portland's wine consciousness in the most entertaining way. Current owner Bob Scherb knew he had big shoes to fill—four of them, in fact—but he's done his best to keep Liner & Elsen among the city's top wine shops. He's wisely kept the services customers came to rely on, such as regular tastings, a witty and informative monthly newsletter that previews special bottle and case prices, premium wine glasses, and temperature-controlled storage lockers. *Mon–Sat; info@linerandelsen.com; map:GG7*

MOUNT TABOR FINE WINES / 4316 SE Hawthorne Blvd, Hawthorne; 503/235-4444 The genial Sandy Thompson runs this low-key, tastefully appointed shop that caters to impecunious oenophiles and wealthy wine lovers alike. His monthly broadsheet advertises a healthy selection of reasonably priced wines, and Friday tastings take your palate around the world for a nominal fee. Mount Tabor Fine Wines also has premium bottles in a temperature-controlled walk-in cellar; you may appreciate that the lighting inside is subdued, so other customers are less likely to see you drooling over the Silver Oaks and Leonettis. *Tues–Sat; mttabor1@aol. com; www.mttaborfinewines.com; map:HH4*

WIZER'S LAKE OSWEGO FOODS / 330 1st St, Lake Oswego; 503/636-1414 What looks like an average, low-profile supermarket actually has one of the best selections of wine and biggest retail cellars in Portland. Although not as robust as in past years, this wine department has a wide array of domestic and imported wines with a vast repertoire of sale items. Talk to Tom Reider, the wine guy for the past 12 years, and do explore the cellar—an inventory book should be available for perusal (it's a treat to imagine owning one of the rare sweethearts from the collection, with vintages back to 1934). Groceries, too, of course. *Every day; www. wizers.com; map:KK5*

WOODSTOCK WINE AND DELI / 4030 SE Woodstock Blvd, Woodstock; 503/777-2208 Proprietor Gregg Fujino is one of Portland's friendliest and most astute wine sellers. Together with Jim Clark, he takes seriously the tasks of tasting, cataloging, and researching wine. And there's plenty to taste, catalog, and research in this capacious shop; fortunately, it's highly organized, and the stock is so well selected that you could close your eyes, grab the closest bottle, and be pleasantly surprised. Woodstock Wine and Deli also has a restaurant kitchen and informal bistro fare, which may inspire you to linger over your shopping and certainly makes the many wine tastings last further into the evening. Located near Reed College, this shop is a great place to dine, browse, and learn. *Mon–Sat; map:HH4*

PERFORMING ARTS

PERFORMING ARTS

Theater

The theater scene in Portland, as topsy-turvy as one could imagine as the decade closed, has begun to show signs of righting itself. With the closing of longtime player Portland Repertory Theater, many wondered how the rest of the city's companies would fare, but not to worry; the show has gone on—with new performance spaces and artistic directors enhancing the story. At any given time, the offerings usually include a long-running local hit, an imported Broadway blockbuster, the debut of an original play, a finely wrought version of a classic, and a foray into experimental theater. Plus, there are a couple of notable theaters (Imago is one) that appeal to children and adults alike. Check local newspapers for current schedules.

ARTISTS REPERTORY THEATRE / 1516 SW Alder St; 503/241-1278 One of the better small theaters in town features some of Portland's more acclaimed actors and directors under the salubrious influence of artistic director Allen Nause. The focus is on American plays, especially brand-new and relatively new ones. A sparkling black-box theater built in 1998 has given ART a dream space to work in; the stage and seating can be reconfigured for each play, further stretching the creative experience. *www.artistsrep.org; map:G1*

IMAGO THEATRE / 17 SE 8th Ave; 503/231-9581 This whimsical movement-based theater company will delight young and old (as it has in New York as well as Portland) with its blend of mask, mime, and vaudeville. Whether it's comical penguins in a game of musical chairs, a paper bag adrift in a breeze, or two-faced crocodiles, Imago theater captures the spirit of engaging, imaginative theater. *Map:GG5*

NORTHWEST CHILDREN'S THEATER / Northwest Neighborhood Cultural Center, 1819 NW Everett St; 503/222-4480 Sometimes a dose of Winnie the Pooh for the holidays is just the ticket—and here's the place to get that ticket. NCT presents several plays each year and runs a theater school for the city's youngest thespians. *www.nwcts.org; map:GG7* &

OREGON CHILDREN'S THEATER COMPANY / Various locations; 503/228-9571 Everyone from Stuart Little to Willy Wonka to the Velveteen Rabbit comes to life in the hands of this talented group. A handful of plays each year are produced at Portland Community College's Sylvania campus and at Keller Auditorium. *www.octc.org*

PORTLAND BROADWAY THEATER SEASON / Various locations; 503/241-1802 PBTS is a big shot on the local theater scene, importing some of the touring blockbuster shows from Broadway. Extravaganzas

PICA

During its roaming, formative years in the mid-1990s, the Portland Institute of Contemporary Art (PICA) gained a reputation for bringing truly edgy artists and performers to town, ones that local audiences never expected to see this side of New York City. Now, under the tireless leadership of executive director and curator Kristy Edmunds, the cutting edge arts group has found itself a permanent address (219 NW 12th Ave; 503/242-1419; map:K2) and a base of operation. PICA's spacious new galleries, housed in the same building as local ad giants Wieden & Kennedy, are located at the very pulse of Portland's creative center, the Pearl District. Thus situated, PICA can continue doing what it does best: commissioning artists to develop work and designing exceptional performance seasons for its audiences.

A typical season might include anything from New York theatrical group Elevator Repair Service to a screening of early 20th-century avant-garde films with live accompaniment by Tom Verlaine. PICA's first exhibition in their new space was a gutsy show titled *Fictional Cities* by two young contemporary French artists, each fascinated in their own way with themes of cities and migration. This show was followed by a salon-style art show open to all local artists who cared to participate.

Every autumn, PICA hosts an annual fund-raising event called the Dada Ball. The ball is a social high-point—a celebration of the weird and the wonderful not to be missed for its creative and conceptual costuming. Performances still take place all over town; for upcoming performances and current shows, check the *Oregonian* and *Willamette Week*, or visit www.pica.org.   —*Michaela Lowthian*

like *Rent, Cabaret,* and *The Sound of Music* sell out, no matter which local stage they hit (performances are often at the Keller Auditorium). Tickets are sold through the Portland Opera.

PORTLAND CENTER STAGE / Newmark Theatre, Portland Center for the Performing Arts, 1111 SW Broadway; 503/274-6588 Portland's largest, poshest theater company—formerly affiliated with the Shakespeare Festival in Ashland—has an exciting new director in Chris Coleman, who came from Atlanta to take over in 2000. Always professional and occasionally distinguished, Portland Center Stage is on a par with the country's best regional theaters. The excellent production values alone (sets, lights, costumes) guarantee a satisfactory experience, and seasoned actors from across the United States light up the stage. Coleman promises to bring first-rate drama to Portland audiences. *www.pcs.org; map:G2*

STARK RAVING THEATRE / 3430 SE Belmont St; 503/232-7072 Portland's scrappiest little theater—and one of its riskier and most innovative—has found a bright new home for its gritty, in-your-face productions, just around the corner from the Tao of Tea. Everything from Shakespeare to dramas and monologues by young local playwrights can be found under one roof in the Theater! Theatre! building. Check the reviews: chances are, if a show sounds good, it might just be the best theater ticket in town. The Starkers pull in the drama awards formerly reserved for more conservative and richer companies, and the quality has gone up without any sacrifice to the integrity of the uncompromising productions. To learn more about the annual New Rave Festival, a summertime fest of new work by local playwrights, check the web site. *www.starravingtheatre.org; map:GG5*

TEARS OF JOY / Dolores Winningstad Theatre, Portland Center for the Performing Arts, 1111 SW Broadway; 503/248-0557 This Vancouver, Washington–based company (with offices also in Portland) has been around for a long time, thrilling audiences with its over-the-top puppet-enhanced tellings of classic tales and original works alike. Winner of numerous awards, Tears of Joy is a local treasure; everything they do is a class act. *Map:G2*

TYGRES HEART SHAKESPEARE COMPANY / Dolores Winningstad Theatre, Portland Center for the Performing Arts; 1111 SW Broadway; 503/288-8400 Things are looking up for this eight-year-old troupe under new artistic director Nancy Doherty. The company, known for coming up with risky concepts—a *Taming of the Shrew* with an all-female cast, a *Comedy of Errors* set in Maine—recently proved with their excellent staging of *Macbeth* that they have crossed over troubled waters and landed on much safer shores. *www.tygresheart.org; map:G2*

Classical Music and Opera

During the symphony season, Portland audiences have many opportunities to hear classical music, both by the powerhouse Oregon Symphony Orchestra and by smaller orchestras, ensembles, and choral groups in town. But it's during the summer when the audience may have the best opportunity of all: Chamber Music Northwest is a month-long celebration of classical music that is among the finest festivals of its type in the nation (see listing). If you're lucky enough to be in town during July, investigate ticket availability. The rest of the year, rely on listings in local newspapers to direct you to the best performances.

CHAMBER MUSIC NORTHWEST / Catlin Gabel School, 8825 SW Barnes Rd and Reed College, 3203 SE Woodstock Blvd; 503/294-6400 A talented group of musicians recruited from New York's Chamber Music Society of Lincoln Center and other Big Apple ensembles puts this month-long summer festival in a class with the best in the nation. More than two dozen concerts, held at Reed College or the Catlin Gabel School, range from solo recitals to evenings for small orchestra, from Bach to Bartók, and from chamber music staples (Brahms, Schubert, Beethoven) to surprises of the repertoire. The variety of the programs is extensive, and the range of music broad. Especially with difficult and unusual pieces, the players go far beyond the routine festival standard and show their joy in working together. At various times throughout the year, artistic director David Shifrin brings in other touring chamber groups as well; watch for these in the *Oregonian* or call for information.

CHORAL CROSS-TIES / Various locations; 503/736-3374 Conductor Bruce Browne, who also leads the Portland Symphonic Choir (see Oregon Symphony Orchestra), has put together a superb 24-voice professional chorus. In repertoire ranging across four centuries, his polished singers—soloists in their own right—move with ease from the Renaissance to the 21st century, from motets to love lyrics. Call for performance schedule.

OREGON REPERTORY SINGERS / Various locations; 503/230-0652 Twenty-seven years of innovative concerts have given Gilbert Seeley's 50-voice ensemble a reputation for creative programming. Seeley specializes in new commissions and neglected classics (such as Frank Martin's *Mass)* and in intriguing combinations of pieces, but he is also a gifted orchestral conductor. The group's collaborations with various local ensembles (on works by Haydn, Bach, Mozart, and Handel) are high-quality programming staples. Call for performance locations.

OREGON SYMPHONY ORCHESTRA / Arlene Schnitzer Concert Hall, 1037 SW Broadway; 503/228-1353 In recordings and concerts, conductor (until he retires in 2005) James DePreist has made a name for himself with his colorful renditions of the large orchestral masterpieces of the late 19th and early 20th centuries: works by Rachmaninoff, Richard Strauss, Tchaikovsky, and Respighi. An all-star roster of visiting soloists and recitalists—from Kathleen Battle, Yo-Yo Ma, and James Galway to Ray Charles, Bobby McFerrin, and Pink Martini—supplements the symphony's offerings; the Portland Symphonic Choir chimes in a couple of times each year, and a pops series fills out the 39-week season. *www.orsymphony.org; map:G2*

PORTLAND BAROQUE ORCHESTRA / Various locations; 503/222-6000 One of America's premier baroque orchestras has gained enormous

PINK MARTINI

Pink Martini is perhaps Portland's hottest musical exponent of international chic. And as the name implies, a Pink Martini concert never fails to deliver a vibrant, stylish good time to its audience. The 10-piece band, which tours both nationally and abroad, still manages to play many sold-out concerts in Portland each year and is enjoying the continued success of its first full-length album, *Sympathetique*.

Much of this groups' success and appeal is due to the inimitable talents of its artistic director and pianist, Thomas Lauderdale. Vocalist China Forbes lends her strong and lovely voice to the music, often singing in French or Spanish. The result is a frothy mix of percussion, brass, and strings. One moment the band might play a big band bossa nova number, and the next a catchy reworked version of Barry Manilow's "Copacabana." Pink Martini is one of the few bands we know that blends classical chamber music, Cuban jazz, and an occasional French dance hall song—appealing to young and old alike.

Pink Martini performed alongside Elton John and Ringo Starr at the 1998 Cannes Film Festival, and it's not unusual to hear strains from *Sympathetique* playing in the background of such television shows as *Felicity* or *The West Wing*. From the rumba to the waltz, from Taiwan to Spain, from the Hollywood Bowl to Broadway, Pink Martini jetsets across the musical globe, thankfully always arriving back in Portland. What they bring back is never kitschy and always first class. Check www.pinkmartini.com for upcoming concerts. —*Michaela Lowthian*

stature in recent years under the baton of English superstar violinist Monica Huggett. The Portland early-instrument experts tackle music written between 1600 and 1825 in performances designed to re-create the sound of period ensembles. Visiting soloists on trumpet, cello, violin, harpsichord, and recorder, plus a crack 24-voice chorus, conspire in brisk versions of Monteverdi, Bach, Handel, Telemann, Vivaldi, Mozart, Haydn, and Beethoven. Call early for tickets; many concerts sell out in advance. The season runs from October through April. Friday-night concerts are held at the First Baptist Church on the corner of SW 11th Avenue and Taylor Street downtown; most Saturday and Sunday concerts are held at Reed College.

PORTLAND OPERA / Keller Auditorium, 222 SW Clay St; 503/241-1802
Over the years, Portland's homegrown opera company has lived up to its self-description: "anything but stuffy." Staples of the repertoire—Verdi, Mozart, Puccini—are juxtaposed with a season-ending Broadway offering, such as *Porgy and Bess* or *Show Boat,* and occasional premieres and less-heard 18th- and 19th-century works. Operatically speaking, it's

the only game in town, and tickets go quickly, so call ahead. *www.portlandopera.org; map:D3*

THIRD ANGLE NEW MUSIC ENSEMBLE / Various locations; 503/228-1353 (Oregon Symphony box office) Although it's been around for more than 15 years, Third Angle is finally in the limelight. Under the leadership of artistic director Jeff Peyton, Third Angle specializes in contemporary chamber music, with an emphasis on work by American composers—and, refreshingly, not just those of European decent. So you might hear a commissioned work by Guyanian master drummer Obo Addy (who makes Portland his home) or a concert devoted entirely to the work of New Romantic composers. Whatever you hear, it's sure to be polished and provocative. Inquire about performance locales. *www.third angle.org*

Dance

With the creation of **WHITE BIRD** (503/245-1600; www.whitebird.org) in 1997, the Portland dance scene got a much-needed lifeline. This nonprofit organization brings dancers of national note—Bill T. Jones, Paul Taylor, Mikhail Baryshnikov—to the city, and sponsors the work of local dancers as well. Besides the much-celebrated Oregon Ballet Theatre and the White Bird season, there are a handful of other notable dance performances to watch for, both local and national; check local newspaper listings.

ARTE FLAMENCO DANCE COMPANY / Various locations; 503/647-5202 This small company is the closest you will find to *puro flamenco* in Portland. They can most often be found dancing, singing, and playing in the informal settings of taverns, nightclubs, and festivals, but they also offer several full-length concerts throughout the year, in which their colorful costumes, wild music, and soulful dancing can reach an audience of all ages with the timeless drama of Spain's premier folk art. Call to inquire about the next fiesta, and take the kids.

DO JUMP! EXTREMELY PHYSICAL THEATER / 1515 SE 37th Ave; 503/231-1232 These tremendously energetic dancers explore acrobatic movement on everything from hand trucks to ladders, breaking down the boundary between audience and performers. The resident company of the Echo Theater, Do Jump also performs at other locations; call for current info, or check the web site. *www.dojump.org; map:HH4*

NORTHWEST AFRIKAN AMERICAN BALLET / Various locations; 503/287-8852 This company, under the inspired direction of Bruce Smith, appears in local college tours and as a regular feature of the Rose Festival. Typically, a dozen athletic dancers, clad in the gorgeous fabrics of West Africa and bangles of the Caribbean, re-create village dance festivals celebrating marriage, coming of age, harvest time, and the passing of the seasons. To the irresistible beat of a virtuoso drum contingent, the dancers jump, slide, shimmy, and shake in unison, then square off in bouts of solo fireworks. Not to be missed.

OREGON BALLET THEATRE / Various locations; 503/222-5538 This energetic company of talented dancers wowed critics in New York with its strong blend of classical and modern ballet when it toured there in 2000. The company is a wellspring of youth and daring that never fails to satisfy both the cravings of Portland's classical ballet fans for traditional fare and the appetites of the MTV generation. Director James Canfield concentrates on his own choreography and that of visiting artists, and he supplements new pieces with reworkings of American classics by the likes of Agnes DeMille, Jerome Robbins, and George Balanchine. Canfield and company takes plenty of chances; in 1999 OBT choreographed a dance to the music of techno star Talvin Singh. Of course, each year there's the obligatory annual run of *The Nutcracker,* but it was entirely remade in 1993 (from costumes to choreography to characters)—and met with resounding critical praise. *www.obt.org.*

OSLUND AND COMPANY / Various locations Artistic director and choreographer Mary Oslund puts a concert together when the spirit moves her, which is several times a year. Recently she developed a strong work commissioned by PICA, the Portland Institute of Contemporary Art. Oslund enlists some of Portland's best modern dancers, excellent scenery and lighting, and quirky, original dancing to live, newly composed music. The spirit of these evenings is both postmodern and avant-garde; the collaboration of musicians, poets, visual artists, and filmmakers puts Oslund in the best tradition of innovative collaborative art. Check the dance listings in the *Oregonian* or *Willamette Week,* or reach Mary through the Conduit Contemporary Dance Studio, 503/221-5857.

Film

For a city of its size, Portland has quite a few movie screens. While still small, the number of art and novelty film venues is ever-growing, making it possible to see a variety of films that the studio-bound theaters fail to book. For complete movie listings, check the entertainment section of the *Oregonian* (503/221-8327; www.oregonlive.com) or *Willamette Week* (503/243-2122; www.willametteweek.com).

BROADWAY METROPLEX / 1000 SW Broadway; 503/225-5555, ext 4607 True, it's a multiplex, but there are some nice touches here: old Portland theater marquees hang in the lower lobby, continuous classic film footage entertains the queue, and there's a coffee bar. Plus, its downtown location is central to its popularity. By the way, don't hang up when you call this theater (or any of the other Regal Cinema houses) and reach the *Oregonian*'s automated information service; punch in the extension, and eventually you'll get what you called for. *Map:G3*

CINEMAGIC / 2021 SE Hawthorne Blvd; 503/231-7919 This rep house serves up the classics, but it's not so much retro as eclectic: you might see *The Sound of Music, The Cell, Lawrence of Arabia,* or *But I'm Only a Cheerleader.* A jukebox in the lobby features movie soundtracks. And that's real butter on the popcorn. *Map:GG5*

CINEMA 21 / 616 NW 21st Ave; 503/223-4515 Portland's best movie house is one of a dying breed—the single-screen neighborhood theater. This spacious repertory-style house is equipped with a balcony, a crying room (for the kids, not the three-hanky movies), and rocking-chair seats, plus air conditioning that really works. Films range from outrageously bad B movies to longer runs of recent art-house releases to lefty documentaries and the occasional premiere. Pick up one of the theater's three-month calendars—and watch for the annual festival of animation. *Map:FF6*

FOX TOWER 10 / SW Park Ave and Taylor St; 503/225-5555, ext. 4604 Opened late in 2000, this Regal theater is big (with 10 auditoriums), is centrally located smack in the middle of the downtown core, and is outfitted with the kinds of amenities modern movie-goers appreciate: tiered seating, a retractable armrest for snuggling with your popcorn partner, and digital everything. Although it's billed as primarily an alternative film theater, check the listings; you might find a major Hollywood release here too. *Map:H3*

KOIN CENTER CINEMAS / SW 3rd Ave and Clay St; 503/225-5555, ext 4608 Hollywood releases, foreign films, and art-house movies appear on KOIN's six screens (two of which are minuscule). Get there early or take a bus—parking on the neighborhood streets can be a problem, although the garage across the street is usually open. Parental bonus: crying rooms are available in two of the theaters. *Map:E3*

LAURELHURST THEATER AND PUB / 2735 E Burnside St; 503/232-5511 It doesn't get much better than this: $3 admission plus a slice of Pizzicato pizza (see review in the Restaurants chapter) and a draft microbrew. Prescott Allen and Woody Wheeler have transformed what was once a very sticky theater showing a selection of movies most likely already out on video into a happening place. They removed rows and rows of seats to make room for tables in the four separate theaters, where newly released and held-over movies are shown. Compared to the popular McMenamin theaters, which for the most part feel like pubs with a large screen, Laurelhurst feels like a real theater where it just so happens you get to drink beer. The $4 special gets you a pint—with six choices on tap—and a bag of popcorn. No one under 21 admitted after 4pm (don't let it go to your head if you get carded; it's policy here). *MC, V; no checks; every day; beer and wine; map:GG5*

LLOYD CENTER AND LLOYD CINEMAS / Lloyd Center, upper level; 503/225-5555, ext. 4601; 1510 NE Multnomah Blvd; 503/225-5555, ext 4600 With 10 screens in the mall and 10 across the street, the Lloyd Center is the biggest movie site in the city. Both theaters are owned by the Regal Cinemas theater chain. The films are traditional Hollywood fare, but the Lloyd Cinemas building is remarkable for such features as its long, neon-lit interior boulevard and luxe espresso bar. *Map:FF5*

MCMENAMINS THEATRE PUBS / Various locations; 503/225-5555, ext. 8830 What may well be Portland's favorite movie theater chain isn't actually a movie theater chain at all: it's a group of McMenamins brewpubs that show movies—and if the film is especially good, the places remain more or less quiet. Besides, you gotta love the concept: a pint of suds and a big screen. Drink a Ruby Tuesday and maybe have a Communication Breakdown burger to go with it while you watch a recent release. Admission is at most $3, and children are allowed during matinees. Here are the four options: the **MISSION** (1624 NW Glisan St; map:L1) was the original brewpub/movie venue; the **BAGDAD** (3710 SE Hawthorne Blvd; map:HH5) is in the heart of the Hawthorne neighborhood; the **KENNEDY SCHOOL** (5736 NE 33rd Ave; map:EE5) is—like it sounds—in a one-time elementary school; and scenic **EDGEFIELD** (2126 SW Halsey, Troutdale) is a great place to spend the whole day. *www.mcmenamins.com*

THE MOVIE HOUSE / 1220 SW Taylor St; 503/225-5555, ext 4609 Here's a first-run art house owned by the big guys, Regal Cinemas. It's a charming, uncomfortable old theater with inscrutable Egyptian decorations on the walls. In the upstairs lobby, board games and card tables are thrown together, and there's an outdoor balcony for summer. The staff is exceptionally congenial. *Map:I1*

NORTHWEST FILM CENTER / 1219 SW Park Ave; 503/221-1156 A steady menu of art films, independent features, and documentaries is offered at the center, along with guest filmmakers showing their recent work. This nonprofit corporation, a branch of the Portland Art Museum, also presents the annual Portland International Film Festival, which shows dozens of new films from every corner of the world, and the Northwest Film and Video Festival, highlighting local work, in November. *www.nwfilm.org; map:F1*

ROSEWAY THEATER / NE 72nd Ave and Sandy Blvd; 503/287-8119 The city's best-preserved throwback to the days of spacious neighborhood cinemas is this family-operated, Northeast Portland gem. High-ceilinged and elegant, with generous leg room, comfy seats, wide aisles, and a classy, gleaming lobby, the Roseway shows second-run imports and American films of quality. Go for the sheer pleasure of the place—especially if you haven't seen the movie they're offering. *Map:FF4*

Literature

Long before Amazon.com, or Barnes and Noble superstores, or Oprah, even—for almost as long as anyone in Portland can remember, there has been **POWELL'S**: open 365 days a year and rumored to have broken up the marriages of people who spent too much time in its endless aisles. But although it is the nation's largest brick-and-mortar literary institution, Powell's—in the Portland book community—is only part of the story. The City of Roses boasts dozens of independent new-book shops and probably just as many, if not more, dealers in used and rare books (not to mention the bookstore chains, which have arrived in full force). And the Friends of the Multnomah County Library each fall conducts an enormous used-book sale that raises as much as $150,000 for the library.

Why does Portland have such a voracious hunger for the written word? Perhaps it's the weather, the sort that doesn't exactly make you want to head for the tennis courts. Among local booksellers, Powell's (1005 W Burnside St; 503/228-4651; www.powells.com; map:J2) is especially influential: it underwrites dozens of literary projects and events. More evenings than not, readers flock to its Pearl Room upstairs for appearances or readings by local and national authors.

But many other bookstores besides Powell's, including Annie Bloom's, Twenty-Third Avenue Books, and Borders, host **WRITERS ON TOUR**. Open-mike readings are regularly scheduled at coffeehouse venues on both sides of the river. Check the calendar listings in local newspapers.

It's no surprise, then, that bookish events are big news here. Portland is one of the few cities in the country to have its own nonprofit literary organization. **LITERARY ARTS** (503/227-2583; www.literary-arts.org) enriches readers and writers in three ways: through fellowships, book awards, and the hugely popular **PORTLAND ARTS AND LECTURES SERIES**. Created in 1984, the series, which runs during the school year, surprises even the nation's best-known authors with the enthusiasm of its audience. Fiction writers such as David Sedaris, Michael Ondaatje, and Annie Lamott—as well as essayists, scientists, playwrights, and poets (even radio personalities; in 2001 Terry Gross appears)—take the stage, not only to read from their work but also to talk about the writing life. This series, and its spin-off in Seattle, may be the finest of its kind in the United States.

Check the newspapers, too, for the location of the next **POETRY SLAM**. Poetry as competition, as spectator sport, as interactive art form is alive and well in this entertaining, amusing, and sometimes moving event in which poets recite their stuff to a noisy crowd of aficionados, who then choose a winner. Local competitors head to regional and even national slams. Often there's a monthly slam at **BERBATI'S PAN** (231 SW Ankeny St; 503/248-4579); call to find out when the next one is scheduled.

After 28 years, the **MOUNTAIN WRITERS SERIES** (www.aracnet.com/~pdxmws) has become one of the largest poetry reading series in the country, offering readings, workshops, and lectures by distinguished writers. The series maintains the **MOUNTAIN WRITERS CENTER** (3624 SE Milwaukie Ave; 503/236-4854), where you can hear readings, read a literary journal, attend a talk by an accomplished writer or poet, or just hang out.

Finally, you need not be a full-time student to take advantage of Lewis and Clark College's **NORTHWEST WRITING INSTITUTE** (503/768-7745), headed by writer and local literary stalwart Kim Stafford, with its ever-evolving list of courses and workshops.

NIGHTLIFE

Nightlife by Feature

ALL AGES
All Coffee Houses
Bridgeport Brew Pub
Quest
The Pine Street Theatre
Roseland Theater
Up Front FX

BAR GAMES/BILLIARDS
Bar of the Gods
Berbati's Pan
Laurelthirst Public House
The Matador
Medicine Hat Gallery
McMenamins
The Pine Street Theatre
Ponderosa Lounge at Jubitz
    Truck Stop
Produce Row Café
Pub at the End of the Universe
Rialto Poolroom Bar and Cafe
Sam's Hollywood Billiards
Quest
Ringler's
Uptown Billiards Club

BLUES/FOLK
Aladdin Theater
Laurelthirst Public House

CABARET
Cobalt Lounge
Dante's

CIGARS
The Brazen Bean
Greater Trumps

COCKTAILS/MARTINIS
The Bar at Atwater's
The Benson Hotel Lobby Court
The Brazen Bean
The Heathman Hotel
Embers Avenue
Saucebox
Wilf's

COMEDY
Harvey's Comedy Club

COUNTRY
Ponderosa Lounge at Jubitz
    Truck Stop

DANCE FLOORS
Biddy McGraw's
Cobalt Lounge
The Crystal Ballroom
Downtown Deli and Greek
    Cusina
Embers Avenue
Medicine Hat Gallery
The Ohm
Polly Esther's
Up Front FX
The Viscount Ballroom

DIVE BARS
Hung Far Low
The Matador
Space Room

GAY/LESBIAN
The Egyptian Club
Panorama

HAPPY HOUR/
LATE-NIGHT GRUB
The Bar at Atwater's
Cassidy's
Cobalt Lounge
Fellini
Harborside Pilsner Room
Jake's Grill/Jake's Famous
    Crawfish
The Lotus Cardroom
McCormick & Schmick's
Molly Maguire's
Paddy's
Suki's Steak House
Virginia Cafe

JAZZ
The Bar at Atwater's
The Benson Hotel
Brasserie Montmarte
The Heathman Hotel
Jazz de Opus
Produce Row Cafe

KARAOKE
The Alibi
Bush Garden
Chopsticks Express
The Grand Cafe/Andrea's Cha
    Cha Club

LATIN/SALSA
The Crystal Ballroom

The Grand Cafe/Andrea's Cha
    Cha Club
The Viscount Ballroom

PIANO BAR
Henry Ford's
McCormick & Schmick's
Wilf's

POETRY, LIVE
Berbati's Pan
Cafe Lena
Coffee Time

PUBS/ALEHOUSES
Biddy McGraw's
Bridgeport Brew Pub
Captain Ankeny's Well
Goose Hollow Inn
Horse Brass Pub
Laurelthirst Public House
The Lucky Labrador
McMenamins
Old World Pub and Brewery
Portland Brewing Co.'s Brew-
    house Taproom and Grill
Produce Row
Pub at the End of the Universe
The Rock Bottom Brew Pub
The Tug Boat Brewery

PUNK
Medicine Hat Gallery
Satyricon

REGGAE/
WORLD BEAT
Aladdin Theater
The Crystal Ballroom
Edgefield
Kennedy School
The Red Sea

RETRO
The Alibi
Bar of the Gods
Beuhlahland
The Crystal Ballroom
The Gypsy
Henry Ford's
The Pied Cow
Polly Esther's
Space Room
Wilf's

ROCK
Aladdin Theater
Berbati's Pan
Cobalt Lounge
The Crystal Ballroom
Laurelthirst Public House

The Pine Street Theatre
Roseland Theater

SMOKE-FREE
Aladdin Theater
Harvey's Comedy Club
Uptown Billiard Club

VIEW
The Bar at Atwater's
Harborside Pilsner Room

WINE BARS
The Empire Room
M Bar

Nightlife by Neighborhood

ALBERTA
Medicine Hat Gallery

BELMONT
The Pied Cow
Tao of Tea

DOWNTOWN
Anne Hughes Coffee Room
The Bar at Atwater's
The Benson Hotel Lobby Court
Brasserie Montmartre
Bush Garden
Cassidy's
The Crystal Ballroom
Downtown Deli and Greek
    Cusina
The Heathman Hotel
Higgins Bar
Huber's
Jake's Grill/Jake's Famous
    Crawfish
The Lotus Cardroom
The Market Street Pub
McCormick and Schmick's
Panorama
Polly Esther's
The Red Sea
Rialto Poolroom Bar and Cafe
Ringler's Annex
The Rock Bottom Brew Pub
Saucebox
The Tug Boat Brewery
Up Front FX
Veritable Quandary
Virginia Cafe

GOOSE HOLLOW
Goose Hollow Inn

HAWTHORNE
Bagdad Theater and Pub
The Barley Mill Pub
Bar of the Gods
Cafe Lena
Common Grounds
    Coffeehouse

Diedrich Coffee People
The Empire Room
Greater Trumps
Space Room

HOLLYWOOD
Old World Pub and Brewery
Sam's Hollywood Billiards

LADD'S ADDITION
Palio Dessert and Espresso
    House

NORTHEAST
Beuhlahland
Biddy McGraw's
Chopsticks Express
Kennedy School
Laurelthirst Public House
Ponderosa Lounge

NORTH PORTLAND
The Alibi
Ponderosa Lounge at Jubitz
    Truck Stop

NORTHWEST
The Blue Moon Tavern
The Brazen Bean
Diedrich Coffee People
Coffee Time
The Gypsy
L'Auberge Bar
The Matador
M Bar
Mission Theater and Pub
Paley's Place
Papa Haydn
Portland Brewing Co.'s
    Brewhouse Taproom
    and Grill
The Ram's Head
Ringler's
Torrefazione Italia
Uptown Billiards Club
Wildwood Bar

**OLD TOWN/
CHINATOWN**
Berbati's Pan
Captain Ankeny's Well
Cobalt Lounge
Dante's
Embers Avenue
Fellini
Harvey's Comedy Club
Hung Far Low
Jazz de Opus
The Ohm
La Patisserie
Quest
Roseland Theater
Satyricon
Shanghai Tunnel
Wilf's

PEARL DISTRICT
Bridgeport Brew Pub

RIVERPLACE
Harborside Pilsner Room

SOUTHEAST
Aladdin Theater
The Egyptian Club
The Grand Cafe/Andrea's Cha
    Cha Club
Horse Brass Pub
The Lucky Labrador
Papa Haydn
The Pine Street Theatre
Produce Row Café
Pub at the End of the Universe
Rimsky-Korsakoffee House
The Viscount Ballroom

SOUTHWEST
Fulton Pub and Brewery
Henry Ford's

TROUTDALE
Edgefield

NIGHTLIFE

Music, Clubs, and Lounges

ALADDIN THEATER / 116 SE 11th Ave, Southeast; 503/234-9698 An astute promoter pulled off magic worthy of a genie at this spot. The Aladdin, formerly a notorious porn parlor, became a concert hall featuring nationally known acoustic, ethnic, and genre-blurring acts. The touring artists who appear here today appeal to the crowd that once loved rock 'n' roll and now flocks to mellower, more highbrow popular music. Here they can enjoy it in a comfortable midsize space with seats and no smoking. *No credit cards; checks OK; open during events only; beer and wine; map:HH5*

THE BENSON HOTEL LOBBY COURT / 309 SW Broadway, Downtown; 503/228-2000 It's always fun to have a drink in one of your town's nicest hotels—you can pretend you're from some foreign port, just in for the weekend. This is where Bill Clinton usually stayed when he was in town; perhaps he too had a drink in the opulent Benson lobby court while pretending to be a visiting dignitary from Pakistan. The lobby is dark, lined with imported Russian walnut, and furnished with sinkingly comfortable black leather chairs. The Benson offers 28 different kinds of martinis and jazz Tuesday through Saturday. *AE, DC, DIS, MC, V; no checks; every day; full bar; www.showman.com; map:J3*

BERBATI'S PAN / 231 SW Ankeny St, Old Town; 503/248-4579 This popular club was originally just a second thought on the part of the owners of the adjoining Greek restaurant, but it has grown considerably both in physical size and prominence over the last few years. Featuring a long bar, large dance floor, and separate cafe and pool and game rooms, the Pan has become one of Portland's favorite live music venues. Showcasing acts ranging from burlesque cabarets to local band and smaller national touring acts, like Jonathan Richman or Mike Watt, the schedule's always full of interesting offerings. Check out the ping-pong enlivened happy hour, 5 to 7pm Monday through Friday. (See also review in the Restaurants chapter.) *AE, MC, V; checks OK; every day; full bar; map:J6*

BRASSERIE MONTMARTRE / 626 SW Park Ave, Downtown; 503/224-5552 At this dressed-up downtown spot you might catch a few Blazers hanging out late at night in their extra-long finest, or see a few head-over-high-heels couples doing their best crayon scribblings on the paper tablecloths (prize-winning drawings decorate the walls). The columnous, high-ceilinged decor is splendid, and the jazz is free. The Brasserie is packed with the professional crowd after work and into the evening; late-night partiers straggle in for early-morning eggs or something else that suits their fancy from the full bistro menu served until 3am on weekends, 1am Sunday through Thursday. (See also review in the Restaurants chapter.) *AE, DIS, MC, V; no checks; every day; full bar; map:H3*

BUSH GARDEN / 900 SW Morrison St, Downtown; 503/226-7181 You might not expect to find such a scene in the middle of a serene Japanese restaurant (complete with low tables), but this is one of the most jamming karaoke spots around, Monday through Saturday nights. Bold college students, good-time Asian businessmen, and lovely Nordstrom clerks take turns fulfilling their secret rock-star dreams on the stage. There's no charge to wail along with the video. It's fun if you're up there belting it out, and its equally (if not more) amusing just to sip a sake and watch. (See also review in the Restaurants chapter.) *AE, DC, DIS, MC, V; no checks; every day; full bar; map:H3*

CHOPSTICKS EXPRESS / 2651 E Burnside St, Northeast; 503/234-6171 This divey lounge in the back of a fast-food Chinese restaurant has become the karaoke bar of choice for Portland's rock 'n' roll haute monde. Catch local quasi-celebrities—perhaps members and associates of the critics' darling, Quasi, or the girls from Sleater-Kinney—belting 'em out on the checkered dance floor, starting at 9pm Monday through Saturday. *MC, V; no checks; every day; full bar; map:GG5*

COBALT LOUNGE / 32 NW 3rd Ave, Old Town; 503/225-1003 The former home of one of Portland's dirtiest dives has been cleaned up considerably and now showcases a wide variety of entertainment, from the longstanding Thursday-night Exotica-Go-Go (featuring artful semi-stripping by go-go girls and boys dancing to the grooves of local turntablists) to local and touring rock bands. The cavernous, retro-flavored space has excellent acoustics and a large enough dance floor, making it one of the better clubs for live music. *MC, V; no checks; every day; full bar; map:J6*

THE CRYSTAL BALLROOM / 1332 W Burnside St, Downtown; 503/778-5625 The icing on the McMenamin brothers' cake, this refurbished dance-parlor-cum-rock-club-cum-whatever is a sensory experience to sink your feet into. Notice first the floating dance floor that can make you feel slightly seasick during a particularly raucous rock show but light on your feet during a ballroom dance soiree. Then notice the attention to detail; artistic motifs abound on the walls, re-creating the room's past incarnations as a dance parlor, soul shack, and hippie hangout. The offerings are eclectic: alternative rock shows, neo-hippie bands, ballroom dancing complete with lessons. Every so often during a break in the activities, the McMenamins' marching band comes tromping through the audience, buzzing a trombone by your ear. On the second floor, visit the recently opened Lola's Room for a respite during big shows upstairs, or

THE PORTLAND SOUND: FULL OF SAD HOPE

Pinning down Portland's musical sound is like swinging at a star—you're not going to be able to hit it. The diverse musical landscape resists pigeonholing and is reflected in the city's varied nightlife. At Jimmy Mak's (300 NW 10th Ave; 503/295-6542; map:K2), the jazz drumming of **Mel Brown** attracts throngs; at the Paris Theater (6 SW 3rd Ave; 503/224-8313; map:J6) a few blocks over, young rebellious punks gather to hear **Five Cent Refund**; and at Cobalt Lounge (see review in Music, Clubs, and Lounges in this chapter), young rave kids tune in to the drum 'n' bass night. But from a commercial perspective, at least, the Portland sound is definable. It is a sound full of sad hope, as Academy Award nominee **Elliott Smith** penned in his song "Miss Misery" for the movie *Good Will Hunting*. This beautifully melodic tunesmith captures the essential wilting heart of the city. Although Smith no longer lives here, the days he spent alone writing songs in dank Portland bars are now a part of local music lore.

Smith's female counterpart might be **Rebecca Gates**, formerly of the Spinanes, who has since left Portland for New York. Within the spectrum of this sound—what some might call "indie" or "alternative" rock—there is a whole canon of Portland bands, among them the all-girl group **Sleater-Kinney**, the divorced duo **Quasi**, college favorite the **Pinehurst Kids**, and oldies **Pond, Hazel,** and **Heatmiser**. But the city's biggest act plays a more accessible, mainstream sound. Pop-rock smash **Everclear**, a chart-topping Portland favorite, uses its guitar rock ditties to address political, racial, and class issues. Front man Art Alexakis has been an outspoken advocate for social responsibility, making peace with himself and his critics. On the other end of the commercial stick—but perhaps as potentially popular—is British favorite the **Dandy Warhols**, whose greedy brand of psychedelic rock is as decadent as it is disaffected. And speaking of disaffected, who could forget **Courtney Love**, the indefatigable social climber who spent many a night at the rock club Satyricon? Hers is a wild legacy not soon forgotten.

For a quick musical history lesson, visit **Dan Sause** at Locals Online.com (916 W Burnside St; 503/227-5000; map:I6). An Oregon native and former guitarist, Sause has witnessed the changing face of local music, pinpointing the days when the outrageous Sweaty Nipples ruled, when record label Tim Kerr ascended, and when the grunge scene first made inroads. His store is chock-full of local music, including a few talented bands from Eugene—the Cherry Poppin' Daddies (of "Zoot Suit Riot" fame) and hippie-rockers Calobo. **Dan Reed**, formerly of glamour rock band the Dan Reed Network that toured with the Rolling Stones, can also provide perspective. As part owner of new nightclub the Ohm (see review in Music, Clubs, and Lounges in this chapter), Reed has helped spearhead an electronic musical movement within the city's youth culture. Reed's love for rock has not faded but mutated into a postmodern affair with challenging electronic rhythms and soothing ambient soundscapes, making room for groups such as Imogene, Systemwide, Dahlia, and Imix Records to flourish.

Another sound altogether, hip hop has also dropped anchor in P-town. Portland native **Marlon Irving** of the group Lifesavas recently joined Blackalicious, and has toured internationally with the crew. **Cool Nutz** and **Bosko** have also carved out a place in the music industry as producers and rappers on the Jus Family Records label. Their dedicated entrepreneurial spirit has paved the way for young upstarts such as Proz and Conz and Bleek. Hip-hop DJs are also popular at local nightclubs, with Five Fingers of Funk spin master **DJ Chill** and **DJ Mello-Cee** heading up the list. Pick up a current copy of *Willamette Week* or the A&E guide (published in Friday's *Oregonian*) to get the lowdown for your next musical throwdown. —*Ethan Machado*

to check out local bands on off nights. *AE, DIS, MC, V; no checks; open during events only; full bar; map:J1*

DANTE'S / 1 SW 3rd Ave, Old Town; 503/226-6630 This steamy, sexy hangout is dark and red enough to make you assume that everyone in there is positively drop-dead gorgeous. An open oil-drum fire blazes near the windows; in the back, a naughty little stage flirts through its rich, red velvet curtains; and in between a glowing red bar smolders with anticipation of your imminent intoxication. Resistance is futile! Cabaret-style performances, live bands, and special events (theme parties, go-go girls, etc.) make this an excellent addition to the Portland nightlife programme. *MC, V; no checks; every day; full bar; map:J6*

THE EGYPTIAN CLUB / 3701 SE Division St, Southeast; 503/236-8689 Hey, ladies! Get funky at this Sapphic social club that comes complete with DJ dancing Thursday through Sunday, a wet T-shirt contest every Memorial Day, free pool on Tuesday nights, an ever-changing roster of special events (open mic, karaoke, dancers), and lots of Ellen DeGeneres talk. *MC, V; no checks; every day; full bar; map:HH5*

EMBERS AVENUE / 110 NW Broadway, between the Pearl District and Chinatown; 503/222-3082 Nothing can extinguish the Embers, though the brightness of this awesome disco has been somewhat diminished by the new dance clubs around town. The music mix is more '80s retro than house and industrial; gay and straight mix under the high-tech, pulsing lights and within the throbbing beat. Don't miss the fabulous drag shows, happy hour piano bar and goldfish-encased bar top in the quieter front-room. *Cash only; every day; full bar; map:J4*

THE GRAND CAFE/ANDREA'S CHA CHA CLUB / 832 SE Grand Ave, Southeast; 503/230-1166 The Grand Cafe is a strange place indeed. The sprawling interior is lined with mirrors and the color red. Occasionally the menu stretches into the stratosphere to include such delicacies as ostrich meat or bull's balls, which you can nibble while checking out the karaoke action. Downstairs in a smallish, wood-paneled basement party room, Andrea's Cha Cha Club is home to some of the happeningest Latin dance throwdowns around. You can get lessons, if you so choose, or jump right in with the big kids and pump your pelvis to recorded salsa music. *AE, DIS, MC, V; no checks; every day; full bar; map:GG6*

HARVEY'S COMEDY CLUB / 436 NW 6th Ave, Chinatown; 503/241-0338 The only continuous comedy-only club in town, Harvey's has all the intimacy of an auditorium, but the comedy is often first-rate, including some big national names—David Brenner, Will Durst, John Bizarre. And the joke's on you, pawns of nicotine—Harv's is a non-smoking establishment. *DC, DIS, MC, V; no checks; open during events only; full bar; map:L4*

HENRY FORD'S / 9589 SW Barbur Blvd, between Multnomah and Burlingame; 503/245-2434 A perfectly preserved remnant of the Rat Pack heyday, replete with chic, armless Herculon-covered couches in electric blue and orange, cozy club chairs, a picture window showcasing a postcard-perfect view of Mount Hood in the afternoons, and the odd but fascinating soap-bubble and flame jet fountain by night. Swoon to the golden voice of Lyle Chaffee, behind the keyboard of the unique piano-organ bar, on Thursday, Friday, or Saturday nights. (See also review in the Restaurants chapter.) *AE, DC, MC, V; checks OK; every day; full bar; map:II8*

JAZZ DE OPUS / 33 NW 2nd Ave, Old Town; 503/222-6077 The lighting is low and the mood is mellow in this sedate bar where tempting smells waft through from the mesquite grill next door at Opus Too. Check out the live jazz—maybe Tom Grant, maybe Patrick Lamb—every night of the week. *AE, DIS, MC, V; no checks; every day; full bar; map:J6*

THE LOTUS CARDROOM / 932 SW 3rd Ave, Downtown; 503/227-6185 Once a key player in Portland's nightlife scene, the Lotus has fallen out of favor with the hippest of hipsters. Still, some of the city's most beautiful women and sleaziest men knock back drinks in the barroom; in the middle restaurant section they nibble on the remarkably good appetizers such as black bean quesadillas and chicken pizza, including the $1.95 happy-hour food specials; and in the back they mob in a sweaty frenzy to a rotation of retro, '90s, new wave, disco, and '80s music. On weekends expect a cover. *AE, DIS, MC, V; no checks; every day; full bar; map:G4*

MEDICINE HAT GALLERY / 1834 NE Alberta St, Alberta; 503/460-3514 Another fine use of an old Portland meeting hall, this club hosts live music most every night, usually in the surf to punk vein. The stage—along with two bars, plenty of tables, and comfortable chairs—lives on the main floor; at the top of the grand staircase the balcony offers a full view of the stage and dance floor below, several couches and lounge chairs, and Yahtzee and other board games for those not terribly moved by the music below. A game room with several pool tables, pinball, and the like draws budget-minded hipsters down to the basement. *MC, V; no checks; full bar; map:EE5*

THE OHM / 31 NW 1st Ave, Old Town; 503/223-9919 This slick, Miami-style club features an outstanding sound system, surprisingly elegant and tasty food, after-hours dancing, and a bevy of beauties serving what is usually an unusually good-looking crowd. Entertainments vary from turntablist and DJ nights to live bands of all genres. The well-designed and artfully lit interior is complemented by outdoor seating in the alleyway out back. *AE, DIS, MC, V; no checks; every day; full bar; map:J6*

PANORAMA / 341 SW 10th Ave, Downtown; 503/221-7262 No Portland dance club will ever capture the essence of a Manhattan disco, but Panorama sure tries. It is one of *the* places to see and be seen in the city. Sophisticated grown-ups, young rebels, and lots of suburban slummers check each other out in the murky light, multiple bars, and fantasy decor of this once gay and now almost-completely-straight-on-weekends club. Next door (accessible for the same cover price) is the Brig, which used to be the place for gay men to meet and dance. Now the flocks from Panorama nest at the Brig as well, to take in the DJ mix of disco and new wave from the '70s and '80s, techno, trance, house, and progressive tunes. Adjoining the Brig is Boxxes, a dark boy-bar with big-screen porn and NTN Trivia, as well as several oddball events each week, like Drag Queen Dating Games. The newest addition to what has become a sprawling entertainment extravaganza is the Red Cap Garage, a partially open-air bar that makes an ideal spot to catch all the cruising on the Pink Strip. *AE, DIS, MC, V; no checks; Tues–Sun (Boxxes, Red Cap), Fri–Sat (Brig, Panorama); full bar; map:I3*

THE PINE STREET THEATRE / 215 SE 9th Ave, Southeast; 503/241-5862 This club was formerly known as Paradigm, which was formerly known as La Luna; let's hope that the Pine Street Theatre (which was the original name) is here to stay. Midsize touring bands play here before they make the leap to the coliseum circuit. With nary a bad seat (rather, standing spot) in the joint, this is a great place to enjoy your favorite band. More intimate rave-style DJ nights are usually held in the upstairs balcony space. Separate all-ages and 21-and-over areas, a game room, and a full restaurant in operation during events add to the attraction. *AE, DIS, MC, V; no checks; open during events only; full bar; www.thrasherpresents.com; map:GG5*

POLLY ESTHER'S / 424 SW 4th Ave, Downtown; 503/223-4241 This recently established Portland outpost of a popular national chain of retro dance clubs caters to the young and buff set. The ground floor is a shrine to the icons and sounds of the '70s, complete with a Saturday Night Fever–style dance floor. Upstairs, in the Culture Club room, the '80s are still in full swing. Expect a small ($5 or less) cover. *AE, DIS, MC, V; no checks; Wed–Sun; full bar; map:H4*

PONDEROSA LOUNGE AT JUBITZ TRUCK STOP / 10310 N Vancouver Wy, North Portland; 503/283-1111 There's more testosterone pumping through this truck stop than there would be on a battlefield, but the dance floor at the Ponderosa Lounge—lined with lit-up tailgates—offers burly drivers, cowboys, and others an outlet for their hormones and relief from highway stress. Live country/western bands play seven nights a week. If that's not entertainment enough, you'll find pool tables and video games off to the side. Handily, there's a motel and weigh station next door. *AE, DIS, MC, V; no checks; every day; full bar; map:CC6*

QUEST / 126 SW 2nd Ave, Downtown; 503/497-9113 All-ages dance clubs (meaning ages 16 to 21 only) seem to come and go in Portland, but Quest is solid as a rock. The kids who stand patiently in weekend lines to disco down '90s-style range from suburban cherubic to urban slick. Some of Portland's most wizardly DJs spin industrial, house, hip-hop, and retro Thursday through Sunday. This place is smokier than most, but heck, if you can't drink, you gotta indulge somehow; for those who don't dance, there's pool. *Cash only; open during events only; no alcohol; map:I5*

THE RED SEA / 318 SW 3rd Ave, Downtown; 503/241-5450 One of the more internationally and racially diverse crowds in town throbs in sweaty, cathartic unison on the expanded dance floor in this oddly shaped, right-angle hideaway behind an Ethiopian restaurant. By now regulars must be sick of play list staples by Peter Tosh and the same old soca tunes, but the newer, esoteric world-beat numbers that flow out of the speakers are nirvana for booty shakers. Amazing international acts play here to small audiences. The drinks are stiff, and the vibes and tunes continue even after the bartender stops pouring. *MC, V; no checks; every day; full bar; map:I5*

ROSELAND THEATER / 10 NW 6th Ave, Chinatown/Downtown; 503/224-2038 Once a two-story Apostolic Faith church, the Roseland is now a comfortable midsize concert hall for out-of-town acts. It's smoky, boozy, and noisy with heavy metal, rock, and folk music (some shows are for all ages). Whether you dance or not, be prepared to sweat, especially in the balcony, which commands an excellent view of the stage. The Roseland also has a full restaurant and bar, with separate stage, downstairs. *Cash only; open during events only; full bar; map:J4*

SATYRICON / 125 NW 6th Ave, Chinatown; 503/243-2380 This little punk club is one of the nation's longest-lived underground music venues, although with the increased club competition in town, it is no longer the only place to catch the subterranean buzz bands of yesterday, today, and tomorrow. Still, it feels like home, and the lore more than lingers. The adjoining consciously hip Fellini bar and restaurant extends the scene in another direction. *Cash only; every day; full bar; www.clubsatyricon. com; map:K4*

UP FRONT FX / 833 SW Naito Pkwy, Downtown; 503/220-0833 Cover the waterfront and cover all the bases by stepping into this 18-and-over club that sports a huge dance floor. House music is in da house, and on the weekend you'd better dress to impress. There's a full bar at the Up Front restaurant next door. *AE, DIS, MC, V; no checks; Wed–Sat; no alcohol; map:F5*

THE VISCOUNT BALLROOM / 722 E Burnside St, Southeast; 503/233-7855 Portland has an abundance of abandoned Masonic Temples, many of which have been converted to one use or another. By far, this rehab project is the most ambitious. The vision, still a work in progress, is to create a temple of dance: a dance studio on the ground floor, a grand ballroom on the second, and a supper club with dance performances on the third level. The art deco ballroom is lovely, ringed by a balcony and adjoining salons that are perfect for viewing the action from afar or enjoying a quiet tête-à-tête with a new partner. Live bands and DJs run the gamut from big band to salsa. Lessons free with cover ($6–$10) about half hour before the music starts. *MC, V; checks OK; every day; full bar; map:J9*

WILF'S / 800 NW 6th Av (inside Union Station); 503/223-0070 The gold-flecked red velvet wallpaper fell victim to Wilf's 1995 remodel, but this piano bar in the train station has retained its old-fashioned nightclub feel. They make an excellent Cosmopolitan here—served in its own beaker, nested in a bowl of ice. Solo pianists play Sinatra-like standards on Tuesdays, and Thursday through Saturday. *AE, MC, V; no checks; Mon–Sat; full bar; map:M4*

Bars, Pubs, and Taverns

THE ALIBI / 4024 N Interstate Ave, North Portland; 503/287-5335 You are lured here, hypnotized by the gallant pageantry of neon that throws a glow over Interstate Avenue. One doesn't need an alibi to go to the Alibi—it is simply one of Portland's best untouched landmarks, where the service is sharp and all the waitstaff wear palm trees on their shirts. Friendly karaoke hosts lead a wholesome lung-powered jamboree starting at 9pm on Wednesday through Saturday nights (with a complimentary midnight buffet on Saturday). Tip: Saturday nights are really busy, so if you're itching to bust a move, try the Thursday-night fest. *AE, DIS, MC, V; no checks; every day; full bar; map:EE6*

BAR OF THE GODS / 4801 SE Hawthorne Blvd, Hawthorne; 503/232-2037 From its name, you might expect an exalted temple of insobriety, but instead you'll find a small, dark, very personable hole-in-the-wall. Nods to its sobriquet are given in various depictions of the Bacchae, in the grapevine-wrapped beams, and in the regular mixing of an eclectic crowd that spans the breadth of Portland's social strata. Expect an unusual selection of beer and wine, from the ubiquitous PBR to rare imports (a full bar is planned for the future); a tasty if limited menu; a well-used pool table; and a climate-controlled back-porch area (with propane "palm tree" heaters for chilly nights) that's perfect for giving your honey a nibble on the ear. *MC, V; no checks; every day; beer and wine; map:HH4*

BEULAHLAND / 118 NE 28th Ave, Northeast; 503/235-2794 A museum-quality assortment of quirky old restaurant and bar fixtures have been hauled out of retirement and once again placed into service at Beulahland, creating an atmosphere rich with Mayberryesque character. A plethora of oddball signage and vintage advertising paraphernalia completes the mise-en-scène that draws the neighborhood's vintage-sporting

---

IN PRAISE OF HAPPY HOUR

Ah, the beauty of twilight! The golden glow at the end of the long day, bidding adieu to the sun and beckoning the night's respite from its harsh rays. Wait a minute! This is Oregon, land of rain and clouds, where the sun is as welcome as a long-lost best friend—or a half-priced martini! Even our darkest days are brightened by the arrival of happy hour, that mystical time, somewhere between 4 and 7pm, when drinks are doubled, food is free, and life is good. Despite the fact that Oregon's puritanical Liquor Control Commission has seen fit to ban the advertisement of such pleasantries, be it known by such synonyms as "social adjustment hour," "no rush hour," "twilight time," or even "pirate time," happy hour thrives in Portland.

The best happy hours combine more than just food and drink specials, bringing together many walks of life, from the dot-commer celebrating her IPO to the bike messenger nursing his tendinitis. **Paddy's** (65 SW Yamhill St; 503/224-5626; full bar; map:G5; $2.75 bar menu and microbrew pints; 3–6pm Mon–Fri and 10 pm to close every day) is a fine example. Pockets of Portland that would rarely, if ever, cross paths—except when lured by the promise of cut-rate sustenance—lean on the long bar, or gather in booths or at sidewalk tables, to sup on Caesar salad and quesadillas. At the

denizens. In keeping with the southern-fried atmosphere, it tends to get rather steamy rather quickly in here. But respite from the heat can be taken on the charming back patio. *MC, V; no checks; every day; beer and wine; map:GG5*

BIDDY MCGRAW'S / 6000 NE Glisan St, Northeast; 503/233-1178 If a sweaty, smoky, jigging joint fits the bill, Biddy's is your place. You'll swoon to hear half the patrons using a genuine shipped-over-from-the-land-o'-the-green brogue. And these folks haven't brought just the good times over from the Old Country, they've also brought their political beliefs: the whitewashed walls are decked with posters urging sentiments such as all-party peace talks. You can get your Guinness as well as a full spectrum of drafts and hard cider. Catch musicians going crazy—Celtic on some nights—and watch the crowd explode into a toe-to-the-sky frenzy. It has the same feel as the old location on Hawthorne, just more room to move on the dance floor, a full bar with lots of whiskeys, and a three-course Sunday-night dinner worth sitting down for. *MC, V; no checks; every day; full bar; map:GG5*

CAPTAIN ANKENY'S WELL / 50 SW 3rd Ave, Old Town; 503/223-1375 Named after the Portland sailor who left his stamp in Old Town, this pizza-and-potables pit stop has become a home for a different kind of traveler: on any given day you can catch a gaggle of bike messengers

---

Cobalt Lounge suits dig into $2 plates alongside purple-haired, beer-swilling punks (see review in the Music, Clubs, and Lounges section of this chapter; $3 menu of standard bar food, $2 well drinks and microbrews; 4–7pm Mon–Fri), where few toss down their gold cards, except when someone's picking up a round of four drinks for $8!

No matter what your budget allows, free food is always a welcome sight (even if you're not really sure what it is, at first glance). For the price of a beverage, a few bars serve mini-buffets or appetizers on the house during happy hour. **Suki's Steak House** (2401 SW 4th Ave; 503/226-1181; full bar; map:A2; $2 well drinks and $2.50 brews, 4–7pm Mon–Fri) supplements your lifestyle with gratis hors d'oeuvres—like chicken wings and mini tacos— and free pool to boot. **Molly Maguire's** (2400 NW 21st Ave; 503/222-3385; full bar; map:FF6; $1 pints of Pabst Blue Ribbon and $1.75 well drinks, 4–7pm Mon–Fri) also provides a small spread—mostly deep-fried, mostly yummy— for its patrons.

So instead of squeezing yourself into the maddening crowd on the MAX after a long day boxed in the office, take a break, relax over a cocktail or two, and you'll find the ride home far more pleasant than you ever dreamed possible. —*Jen Lane*

hanging around the outdoor tables or staring out of the glass-walled bar. (Bonus: Bike messengers have a unique fashion sense; you may pick up some trendy tips.) Captain Ankeny's offers a full bar, but is best known for its wide variety of beers (20 on tap, 20 in bottles), the $2 pints on Wednesdays, and the $1.50 slice-of-pizza deals and the fact that you can order up a pitcher as you watch downtown Portland passing by. *AE, MC, V; no checks; every day; full bar; map:J5*

CASSIDY'S / 1331 SW Washington St, Downtown; 503/223-0054 The dim, turn-of-the-century environs are conducive to heavy thoughts and heavier conversation. But it's a night-owl place, too; you can knock 'em back here until 2:30am and enjoy the company of the personable staff as well as off-duty barkeeps from the surrounding establishments. Keep an eye on the windows, as the entertaining antics of its colorful neighbors often transpire within full view of the bar. And for a late-night meal—maybe a grilled chicken club or a veggie burger—it doesn't get much better than this. *AE, DIS, MC, V; no checks; every day; full bar; map:J1*

DOWNTOWN DELI AND GREEK CUSINA / 404 SW Washington St, Downtown; 503/224-2288 By day it's a Greek deli, but every Friday and Saturday night the upstairs bar gets crazy. Arrive before 9:30pm to watch the transformation: at first the musical trio seems to be dozing off, but before long the host peps things up by giving Greek dancing lessons. By midnight the floor is packed with as many as 100 people caught up in frenzied dancing, ouzo drinking, and plate smashing ($2 a plate). *AE, DIS, MC, V; no checks; every day; full bar; map:H4*

FELLINI / 121 NW 6th Ave, Chinatown; 503/243-2120 How did Portland get so lucky? This place combines some of the best cheap bar food around (coming in for dinner isn't such a bad idea either, with choices like Bangkok Ho, a mound of crunchy vegetables in peanut sauce over brown rice, or Zapatistas, fire-roasted enchiladas) with a full bar and plenty o' beer on tap. Fellini is situated next to the punk club Satyricon (see review in this chapter), so expect the thumpy fuzz of booming bass to mix with your sloe gin fizz. Warning: The place is small, so be willing to order some food before you plunk yourself down at one of the tables, or you may annoy one of the already annoyed, but adorable, waitstaff. *MC, V; no checks; every day; full bar; map:K4*

GOOSE HOLLOW INN / 1927 SW Jefferson St, Goose Hollow; 503/228-7010 For decades, the Goose was a hotbed of political debate and discussion. It's not surprising that it remains a social institution, given who its owner is—former mayor J. E. Bud Clark. Join the hundreds who came before you and surreptitiously carve your initials into the dark wooden booths, or sink your teeth into one of the thick Reuben sandwiches that have made this place as much a classic as the proudly displayed "Expose

Yourself to Art" poster, featuring Mayor Clark flashing one of Portland's street sculptures. *MC, V; checks OK; every day; beer and wine; map:GG6*

THE GYPSY / 625 NW 21st Ave, Northwest; 503/796-1859 If you're looking for a little romance en route to the dance clubs downtown, dust off your best pick-up lines and head to this neo-retro hot spot. On Wednesday nights, $2 microbrews pull in a slew of proto-yuppies on the make, so if you're up for it, pull on your best Abercrombie and Fitch ensemble and prepare to shamelessly make eyes over your gin and tonic. Excellent collection of pinball art and Sputnik-style space-age fixtures, plus extra-comfy booths. *AE, DIS, MC, V; no checks; every day; full bar; map:GG7*

HARBORSIDE PILSNER ROOM / 0309 SW Montgomery St, RiverPlace; 503/220-1865 This is perhaps the best waterfront drinking-with-a-view spot in Portland. The crowd tends toward quick-draw cellular packers and those who adore them, but the beer selection is large—Full Sail itself is brewed right next door—and you can get a decent mixed drink as well. Park yourself either inside near one of the floor-to-ceiling windows, to look out onto the RiverPlace esplanade, or outside, to behold the scene on our own green Willamette. From 4pm to 6pm and 9:30pm to closing, there are killer happy-hour specials: chicken skewers, pizza, tacos—all less than $3 a plate with a $3 minimum drink. *AE, DIS, MC, V; no checks; every day; full bar; map:C5*

THE HEATHMAN HOTEL / 1001 SW Broadway, Downtown; 503/241-4100 The three bars in the Heathman are among Portland's most chic: there's the cool ambience of the Marble Bar, where symphony crowds rendezvous after the performance and executives convene for lunch; the high-ceilinged Lobby Lounge, as formal as a Tudor drawing room, with a fire blazing in the hearth and live music (jazz, piano) seven nights a week; and, upstairs, the Mezzanine Bar, where art shows from the Elizabeth Leach Gallery decorate the walls. For a delicious light meal, the bar menu—with choices like Cobb or Caesar salad, a bistro burger, Pacific oysters on the half shell, and crab cakes—is served in both of the ground-floor bars. *AE, DIS, MC, V; checks OK; every day; full bar; map:G2*

HORSE BRASS PUB / 4534 SE Belmont St, Belmont; 503/232-2202 Truly a slice of merry old England, the Horse Brass is a magnet for British expats and Portland's Anglophiles alike. It's also a favorite of the beer-geek crowd, as it features dozens of esoteric microbrews, imports, and always a couple of cask-conditioned ales. The knowledgeable, convivial bar staff will guide you to the perfect pint (although they'll flatly refuse any cocktail order more complex than gin and tonic!), which may be enjoyed over a hot game of darts on one of the four highly competitive boards. The Brass also serves an extensive selection of whiskeys, especially Scotch.

English pub fare, served until fairly late in the evening, couldn't be more traditional—especially in the sense that it's more filling than it is delicious. *AE, MC, V; checks OK; every day; full bar; map: HH5*

HUBER'S / 411 SW 3rd Ave, Downtown; 503/228-5686 This is supposedly Portland's oldest bar (it originally opened in 1879), and it's certainly one of the more interesting, but even something that worked so well for so long has found a way to improve. A fabulous rendezvous spot for famous, flaming Spanish coffees and turkey sandwiches (two great tastes that actu-ally go well together) finally overcame its only flaw—the small number of tables, which inevitably led to a long wait. Voilà! With the 1997 expansion (considered recent, given how long this place has been around), there's enough room to hold twice the number of patrons amid an open kitchen and window tables. Although the turkey is almost as famous as the table-side coffees—and the menu has more bird recipes than a post-Thanksgiving weekend—it's the show that lures regulars and tourists alike. *AE, DC, DIS, MC, V; no checks; Mon–Sat; full bar; map:H4*

HUNG FAR LOW / 112 NW 4th Ave, Chinatown; 503/223-8686 This small, dark bar in the back corner of a brightly lit restaurant (which, by virtue of its name, has made the pages of *National Lampoon*) is the place to meet friends pre-concert and post-dancing downtown. Economically disadvantaged subculture types come for the strong, cheap drinks and the sassy but stern waitresses. *MC, V; no checks; every day; full bar; map:L5*

JAKE'S GRILL, JAKE'S FAMOUS CRAWFISH / 611 SW 10th Ave, Downtown; 503/241-2100; 401 SW 12th Ave, Downtown; 503/226-1419 The Grill, located in the exquisitely refurbished Governor Hotel, does its father establishment, Jake's Famous Crawfish, proud. Career dressing dominates, but all walks of Portland life gravitate here after work to see the original 1909 mosaic tiled floor, slow-turning fans, gold-framed mirrors, and big-game heads staring down at the plates of onion rings on the bar. Jake's Famous Crawfish is much the same, but with a little less elbow room. Check out either spot for a happy-hour bar menu featuring great cheap eats—seafood cocktails, teriyaki chicken wings, cheeseburgers—each ringing in at $1.95 with the purchase of a $2 (or more, of course) drink. (See also reviews in the Restaurants chapter.) *AE, DIS, MC, V; no checks; every day; full bar; map:I2; map: I1*

L'AUBERGE BAR / 2601 NW Vaughn St, Northwest; 503/223-3302 Stepping into L'Auberge is like traveling back in time 25 years—when revamped houses set the stage for fine dining and chrome chairs were all the rage. Add to this a warm fireplace in the winter, a cool patio in the summer, the best sidecars in town, and well-executed bistro food, and you begin to understand why even '70s-phobes make the bar one of their haunts. Try the famous hamburger, which has caused more than a few vegetarians to rethink their platform. This is a sweet place for dessert, too. (See also review in the Restaurants chapter.) *AE, DC, DIS, MC, V; local checks only; every day; full bar; map:FF7*

LAURELTHIRST PUBLIC HOUSE / 2958 NE Glisan St, Northeast; 503/232-1504 If it were located near a college campus, this is the kind of place some would simply call home. Tavern by night, cafe by day, at the Laurelthirst there's always someone hanging out, either noshing on a late breakfast, playing pool with a pitcher, or listening to music into the wee hours. A beautiful antique bar and comfortable leather booths add to the zero-pretension atmosphere. On the billiards side, you can cram around a small table and catch up on gossip. In the main section, live bands—blues, rock, acoustic—keep the karma flowing and get people dancing. *MC, V; no checks; every day; full bar; map:GG5*

M BAR / 417 NW 21st Ave, Northwest; 503/228-6614 If you're in the mood for good conversation and a reasonably priced glass of beer or wine, squeeze yourself into what is by far the tiniest bar in town. The bar itself seats only five people (uncomfortably), but with all walls practically within reach, and certainly all tables within earshot, everyone weighs in on the topic at hand. Sidewalk seating is available for the claustrophobic. *Cash only; every day; beer and wine; map:GG7*

THE MATADOR / 1967 W Burnside St, Northwest; 503/222-5822 Every town worth its salt has at least one perfect dive bar, and Portland is no exception. The Matador has all the dive essentials: an old jukebox loaded with esoteric classics, cheap drinks that'll put hair on your chest, a couple of well-used pool tables, lots of booths, and plenty of seedy patrons to keep the adrenaline flowing. *MC, V; no checks; every day; full bar; map:GG7*

MCCORMICK & SCHMICK'S / 235 SW 1st Ave, Downtown; 503/224-7522 The piano bar here continues to pack in the corporate and advertising execs, who come after work for the astoundingly low-priced bar menu. The half-pound Tillamook cheddar burger happily feeds the hungry for a mere $1.95 with the purchase of a drink (1:30pm to 6:30pm weekdays, 9:30pm to closing every night; see review in the Restaurants chapter). You may need a pencil and paper to converse; this brass-and-oak bar is often packed and noisy. *AE, DIS, MC, V; no checks; every day; full bar; www.mccormickandschmicks.com; map:H5*

PRODUCE ROW CAFE / 204 SE Oak St, Southeast; 503/232-8355 You certainly don't have to change out of hiking clothes to hunker down at a rough-hewn table on the Produce Row patio and contemplate the selection of 200 bottled beers, 29 drafts (mostly micros), and fresh cider. The Row, much loved since its beginnings in the early '70s, is a friendly spot to mix with a melange of Portlanders, from skatepunks to stevedores, dot-commers to dentists. Monday-night jazz and Tuesday-night bluegrass jam sessions draw supportive friends and music lovers, while the open mic on Wednesday nights attracts hopeful musicians. Summertime finds the back deck filled with those enjoying a pitcher under an open sky framed by the neighborhood's industrial walls as trains rattle past. *No credit cards; checks OK; every day; beer and wine; map:GG5*

PUB AT THE END OF THE UNIVERSE / 4107 SE 28th Ave, Southeast; 503/238-9355 It's a hard place to find if you don't live in the neighborhood or if you didn't go to Reed College, but this pub is worth a little crosstown navigation. Students and locals yuk it up, play some pool, avoid being bulls'-eyed by the continuous dart games going down, and get downright comfy in this lounge-away-from-home atmosphere. *MC, V; checks OK; every day; beer and wine; map:GG5*

RIALTO POOLROOM BAR AND CAFE / 529 SW 4th Ave, Downtown; 503/228-7605 From the hustler to the novice, all levels of pool player gather at this favorite downtown billiards hall. With 16 regulation-size tables, generously pouring bartenders, and a moody atmosphere that recalls *The Color of Money,* it's easy feel like Paul Newman or Tom Cruise as you saddle up to crack that next rack. The hall also features off-track betting in a separate area, somewhat appropriate considering that in the 19th century poolrooms were specifically set up as betting parlors for horse races. *AE, MC, V; no checks; every day; full bar; map:I4*

SAM'S HOLLYWOOD BILLIARDS / 1845 NE 41st Ave, Hollywood; 503/282-8266 A mural outside of men enraptured in a billiards game quickly tips off visitors that inside lurk pool sharks. But not just Minnesota Fats types find joy here. Indeed, all sorts congregate at Sam's on the weekends to test their hand-eye coordination on 10 regulation-size (plus a couple snooker) tables. Weekly nighttime tournaments heat up the action, and for those early-to-rise pool addicts the hall now serves breakfast in the recently added dining area. *MC; no checks; every day; full bar; map:FF4*

SAUCEBOX / 214 SW Broadway, Downtown; 503/241-3393 The artfully appointed interior is awash with well-coiffed up-and-comers, enjoying the expensive but perfect cocktails that can be had alongside tasty appetizers such as sweet potato spring rolls (see review in the Restaurants chapter). When the kitchen closes, the DJ turns up the hot house wax. Exceptionally attractive staff accept the moony stares of their devoted public as their due, without being the slightest bit pretentious or conceited about it. *AE, DIS, MC, V; local checks only; Tues–Sat; full bar; map:J4*

SHANGHAI TUNNEL / 211 SW Ankeny St, Old Town; 503/220- 4001
Word is that Portland is riddled with a maze of tunnels just below its blacktop, leftovers from the days when Puddletown was a rip-roaring port of call for sailors and smugglers. Most of the tunnels were bricked up long ago, but at this subterranean hipster oasis, you can enjoy a PBR or Spanish coffee, a game of pool, or a bowl of noodles while you're waiting for your ship to come in. *MC, V; no checks; Tues–Sun; full bar; map:J6*

SPACE ROOM (AT THE BRITE SPOT) / 4800 SE Hawthorne Blvd, Hawthorne; 503/235-8303 In Portland, it's become common for subculture types to discover a tacky neighborhood bar of old-time drinkers and turn it into their own. The Space Room at the Brite Spot is a textbook case: during the Ronald Reagan years, the clientele was decidedly middle-aged—except for a single table in the corner, where an isolated group of punks looked up from their cheap and effective Long Island iced teas only long enough to plug another Patsy Cline tune at the jukebox. For years now, this dark and smoky dive—lit by the red Saturn lamps above the bar—has been made up of almost 100 percent twentysomethings, still coming for the economical, strong drinks. *MC, V; no checks; every day; full bar; map:GG5*

UPTOWN BILLIARDS CLUB / 120 NW 23rd Ave, Northwest; 503/226-6909 Uptown Billiards is a find for pool aficionados who detest cigarette smoke clouding their vision: it's a smoke-free cueing zone in Northwest Portland's tony zone. With 10 immaculate replicas of French-style billiards tables, exposed brick walls, and a liberal supply of pool stools, this hall is the ideal place to shoot some serious stick. On occasion the club hosts a cigar night, but afterward they air it out, erasing any malodorous memories. *AE, MC, V; no checks; every day in winter, Tues–Sat in summer; full bar; map:GG7*

VERITABLE QUANDARY / 1220 SW 1st Ave, Downtown; 503/227-7342
The narrow, galley shape of this exposed-brick-and-dark-wood bar encourages body contact. By day, you rub up against corporate types and politicos who come for the efficient business lunches; by night, a dressed-up crowd moves in and transforms the VQ into a sultry late-night spot—despite efforts to turn this into more of a dining destination (see review in the Restaurants chapter). Steel yourself for some brazen once-overs when you enter. Outside seating means you can wear your sunglasses while you're scamming. *AE, DC, DIS, MC, V; no checks; every day; full bar; map:E4*

VIRGINIA CAFE / 725 SW Park Ave, Downtown; 503/227-0033 The VC is almost a guarantee for a good time, and the happy-hour specials grow addictive. Comfy in a worn-shoe way, the place is popular, and at times it's nearly impossible to find a seat. Among the diverse clientele are present college students and post-college types, slumming local business folk, and moms who've been shopping the sales at Meier & Frank. *MC, V; no checks; every day; full bar; map:H2*

Brewpubs

BRIDGEPORT BREW PUB / 1313 NW Marshall St, Pearl District; 503/241-3612 The Ponzi family's vision of producing beer as good and as complex as their wine was realized in 1984 upon the opening of this self-contained brewery and pizza pub. After several expansions, and a change in ownership, this former cordage factory (replete with gargantuan wooden rafters) remains a favorite nighttime spot for hanging out with a 20-ounce pint of thick, creamy Black Strap Stout or a floral India Pale Ale. Creative, ungainly pizza slices plus oversize Caesar salads add to the appeal. The Pearl District locale near cobblestone streets and busy loading docks is the essence of Northwest living—especially on a drizzly, hazy spring night. No smoking allowed except on the dock outside. The private room upstairs accommodates up to 200 people. *MC, V; checks OK; every day; beer and wine; www.bridgeportbrew.com; map:N1*

THE LUCKY LABRADOR / 915 SE Hawthorne Blvd, Southeast; 503/236-3555 Opened by a band of Bridgeport Brewing Company defectors, this eastside hangout follows a path similar to its crosstown model, with an easygoing atmosphere and flavorful, British-inspired brews. Instead of pizza, big burly sandwiches and curried bento dishes take center stage. A spacious covered outside area is perfect for chilling with your favorite canine. Speaking of lovable mutts, several brews are named after dogs: Black Lab Stout, Dog Day India Pale Ale, and the Top Dog Extra Special Ale. For private parties, customers can reserve a night in "The Kennel," which hosts small (up to 60) private banquets. *DIS, MC, V; checks OK; every day; beer and wine; map:GG5*

MCMENAMINS (HEADQUARTERS) / 2126 SW Halsey St, Troutdale; 503/669-8610 Like the old Roman Empire, the McMenamins' pub chain (spawned in 1983 when Mike and Brian McMenamin opened the Barley Mill Pub) continues to expand into all corners of the Northwest. Its heart, however—or its Vatican City, if you will—is the **CRYSTAL BALLROOM** (see Music, Clubs, and Lounges in this chapter), a renovated entertainment venue glowing with so much history that the founders commissioned an entire book to be written about it (which is available to peruse at Ringler's). Underneath the ballroom lies **RINGLER'S** (1332 W Burnside St; 503/225-0543; full bar; map:J1), a youthful hot spot to shoot pool and practice your pick-up lines.

From this dance-happy epicenter, all roads lead out to at least one other McMenamins. While each pub has its own quirky traits, they all maintain a few sacred characteristics; namely, great beer and wine (produced at the McMenamins' local brewery and winery, of course), crispy fries and burgers, and a relaxed hippie-meets-yuppie vibe. At the **MISSION THEATER AND PUB** (1624 NW Glisan St; 503/223-4031; beer and wine; map:L1), sink into a comfy couch and sip on one of those trademark intoxicants while enjoying a second-run film. Similarly, the **BAGDAD THEATER AND PUB** (3710 SE Hawthorne Blvd; 503/230-0895; beer and wine; map: HH5) offers cheap dollar films in a cavernous big-screen environment reminiscent of cinema's halcyon days. At the pub adjacent to the theater, neighborhood residents gather at the outdoor tables, just right for gawking at the passing tourists. Around the corner from the Bagdad lies **GREATER TRUMPS** (1520 SE 37th Ave; 503/235-4530; beer and wine; map:HH4), a smoky yet alluring port and cigar room. The McMenamins' signature mosaic design and recurrent court jester theme mark both theaters.

Less cinematic and more pragmatic is the **FULTON PUB AND BREWERY** (0618 SW Nebraska St; 503/246-9530; beer and wine; map:II7), a compact eatery with a functional and friendly flower-trimmed beer garden out back. **THE BLUE MOON TAVERN** (432 NW 21st Ave; 503/223-3184; beer and wine; map:GG7) and **THE BARLEY MILL PUB** (1629 SE Hawthorne Blvd; 503/231-1492; beer and wine; map:HH5) are casual lunch and dinner neighborhood joints with sidewalk seating. **THE MARKET STREET PUB** (1525 SW Park St, Ste 100A; 503/497-0160; full bar; map:E1) caters to urbanites and Portland State students alike. Equally upscale—if upscale could be applied to a pub chain—is **THE RAM'S HEAD** (2282 NW Hoyt St; 503/221-0098; full bar; map:GG7), fronting bustling NW 23rd Avenue.

Perhaps the hippest of the pubs is **RINGLER'S ANNEX** (1223 SW Stark St; 503/525-0520; full bar; map:J1), an old radio station wedged into a pie-cut corner, redesigned into a three-level den of revelry. The dank basement bar is moody and intriguing, lit predominantly by dripping candles, while the top seating area offers a nice view out. Two other historic properties are operated in Portland—the Kennedy School and Edgefield. The **KENNEDY SCHOOL** (5736 NE 33rd Ave; 503/249-3983; full bar; map:EE5) is a pub, performance space, movie theater, and bed-and-breakfast housed in a charming old elementary school the brothers rescued from the bulldozers. **EDGEFIELD** (2126 SW Halsey St, Troutdale; 503/669-8610; full bar) is a rambling former poor farm located in the wilds of Troutdale. It too combines multiple pubs and restaurants, along with a working vineyard, distillery, live stage, movie theater, and B&B. *AE, DIS, MC, V; checks OK; every day*

OLD WORLD PUB AND BREWERY / 1728 NE 40th Ave, Hollywood; 503/249-5779 The city's newest microbrewery and pub features clean, well-varnished wooden lines and an airy, open feel. Its unlikely location—hidden away across the street from a Bank of America just off Sandy Boulevard—belies the tasty treats found inside. A pint of Hollywood Honey Ale or a Welsh Oatmeal Stout goes a long way to complement the wildly varied menu, which ranges from healthy-sized enchiladas and British bangers to delicious grilled turkey sandwiches. Plop down in one of two leather sofas while playing a game of pool or enjoy a more formal meal in the dining area. *AE, MC, V; checks OK; beer and wine; map:GG5*

PORTLAND BREWING COMPANY'S BREWHOUSE TAPROOM AND GRILL / 2730 NW 31st Ave, Northwest; 503/228-5269 Founded in 1986, Portland Brewing Company has survived financial turmoil and a glutted, cutthroat microbrew market. After selling its Pearl District pub (the Flanders Street Brewery and Pub), it tightened its belt and refocused on what it does best: making quaffable specialty beers and running a convivial restaurant adjacent to its brewing facilities. The company's flagship MacTarnahan's Ale continues to be its Scottish beacon of light. Its seasonal brews, such as the German-style Oktoberfest, are equally robust and drinkable. The Taproom itself is highlighted by two large copper kettles and a menu that features honey beer steamer clams and baby back ribs prepared with the brewery's Haystack Black Porter. *AE, MC, V; checks OK; every day; beer and wine; www.portlandbrew.com; map:GG7*

THE ROCK BOTTOM BREW PUB / 206 SW Morrison St, Downtown; 503/796-2739 They boldly came north from Boulder, Colorado, in 1995 with a gutsy idea: to bring a chain of Rocky Mountain brewpubs to the very city known for starting the microbrew trend. Corporate interlopers always are met with suspicion around these parts. But such wariness has done little to deter the masses from making this one of the city's favorite yuppie bars, where young professionals gather to talk shop over a Blonde Ale or a Nut Brown Ale and down gargantuan plates of food better than one might expect. *AE, MC, V; no checks; every day; full bar; map:H5*

THE TUG BOAT BREWERY / 711 SW Ankeny St, Downtown; 503/226-2508 Producing only a few barrels of various malted elixirs each week, this most microscopic of microbreweries serves up its delicious homebrew in a cozy room lined with books and staffed by the owner's gregarious relatives. The $2.50 pints attract a wide swath of Portland, from visiting CEOs shacking up at the nearby Benson to graying hippies en route to Saturday Market. Tuesday through Saturday there's music—solos or duos—small acts for a small bar. *No checks; Mon–Sat; beer and wine; map:I3*

Coffee, Tea, and Dessert

ANNE HUGHES COFFEE ROOM (IN POWELL'S BOOKS) / 1005 W Burnside St, Downtown/Pearl District; 503/228-0540, ext 234 It doesn't seem to matter what's going on—gorgeous weather, a major holiday, or a renovation—the Anne Hughes Coffee Room is never empty. Here patrons gather to read, write, or stare pensively out the window. The coffee is good (Kobos), as are the cookies and pastries, brought in mostly from Delphina's and Brenda's Baked Goods. The coffee room keeps the same hours as the bookstore—and it's a good thing; Powell's just wouldn't be the same without it. *Cash only; every day; no alcohol; map:J2*

THE BRAZEN BEAN / 2075 NW Glisan St, Northwest; 503/294-0636 The setting is pure nouveau Gothic—tables tucked into various nooks and crannies surrounded by deep, saturated colors; velvet; and lots of candles. Movie-set types of all ages commingle with Gen Xers to smoke cigars (there's a humidor on premise; ask your server if you care to see it), linger over a wide range of beverages—champagne, beer, cocktails, single-malt Scotch, ports, coffee drinks, and tea—and nibble on the kinds of foods that go perfectly with drinks. Most of the menu consists of antipasto-type fare: crostini, plates of smoked meats and cheeses, an artichoke quesadilla. For dessert there's chocolate silk pie, apple pie, and messy but delectable chocolate fondue for two. *AE, MC, V; no checks; Mon–Sat; full bar; map:GG7*

CAFE LENA / 2239 SE Hawthorne Blvd, Hawthorne; 503/238-7087 This art-cluttered poetry den pays homage to poets both dead and alive. Tuesday-night poetry readings draw an eclectic crowd with bohemian tendencies, while what looks like the entire surrounding neighborhood files through the door for breakfast on weekends. The general consensus is that once you get a seat, it's yours for the rest of the day—or if you pen something worthwhile, maybe a lifetime. You can hear the strumming of an acoustic guitar during weekday dinners and eavesdrop on conversations revolving around anarchy, feminism, and Bukowski any day of the week. The espresso drinks are fine and the house coffee divine; sweets run the gamut from layered cakes to oversize cinnamon rolls. *No credit cards; checks OK; Tues–Sat; beer and wine; map:GG5*

COFFEE TIME / 710 NW 21st Ave, Northwest; 503/497-1090 Just in case you simply can't wait until morning for your daily caffeine fix, there's Coffee Time, open 24 hours a day, seven days a week. And if you think there's absolutely no reason to be drinking coffee in the wee hours of the morning, think again. Visit this coffee shop at any hour of the day or night, and you'll find buzzing yuppies and mellow hippies coexisting in a strangely natural way. And in addition to the colorful clientele are the interesting activities, from free-association poetry readings to local musicians playing impromptu blues. And the coffee? Well, it's just fine, but you'll quickly realize that Coffee Time is much more than a place to get a double latte to go—it's a certified hangout. *No credit cards; checks OK; every day; no alcohol; map:GG7*

COMMON GROUNDS COFFEEHOUSE / 4321 SE Hawthorne Blvd, Hawthorne; 503/236-4835 While it's easy to lament what Common Grounds used to be—namely, undiscovered—progress has not been wholly bad. Yes, they've packed too many tables in for the average paranoid writer, and sometimes there's a wait for a table (what next, reservations only?), but it is still one of the best coffeehouses in town. An excellent magazine rack, worn couches for lounging, windows for daydreaming, and delicious coffee—Torrefazione, served in a real mug—define the standards, while a panini grill and an expanded menu add to the welcome changes. And, as with any coffeehouse worth its weight in arabica, there's nothing shy about the dessert case: ginger-banana cake with cream cheese frosting, chocolate mousse, lemon squares, and an assortment of cookies name only a handful of the offerings. *Cash only; every day; no alcohol; map:GG4*

DIEDRICH COFFEE PEOPLE / 533 NW 23rd Ave, Northwest (and branches); 503/221-0235 Jim and Patty Roberts' Coffee People has come a long way since its humble beginnings on NW 23rd. Now owned by corporate mammoth Diedrich Coffee, the greater Portland enterprise totals some 24 outlets, including 9 drive-through Motor Mokas and a gig at PDX called Aeromoka (perfect for catching a high-flying buzz before boarding). CP's lengthy menu includes almost every kind of coffee concoction you could dream up, as well as Prince Puckler's ice cream from Eugene and a selection of pastries from various Portland bakeries. The cookies are old-fashioned favorites—chocolate chip, snickerdoodle, peanut butter—and are made in-house. The coffeehouses in Northwest Portland and in the Hawthorne District (3500 SE Hawthorne Blvd; 503/235-1383; map:GG5) provide modish backdrops for a late-night rendezvous. *AE, MC, V; checks OK; every day; no alcohol; www.coffee people.com; map:GG7*

THE EMPIRE ROOM / 4260 SE Hawthorne Blvd, Hawthorne; 503/231-9225 The Empire Room is a stylish place to stall, linger, or stop by after you've been someplace else but you're not quite ready to go home. Soft lights, small tables, a very chic waitstaff clad in black, and jazzy music provide the ambience of a French salon. This is not a place to dine but to nibble; the menu features more drinks than dishes. And although much of the food lacks finesse, it serves its purpose as a conduit for softening the blow of wine on an empty stomach. The best things on the menu are those that accompany either wine or coffee: the cheese and fruit plate, a sun-dried tomato and smoked mozzarella spread served with bread, a bowl of olives or pistachios, and rich chocolate desserts. *AE, DIS, MC, V; local checks only; Mon–Sat; beer and wine; map:GG4*

LA PATISSERIE / 208 NW Couch St, Old Town; 503/248-9898 In the era of hip and swank coffeehouses, La Patisserie appears dated (as in "totally '80s"), but it's still a fun place to hang out. This second-floor, dark-paneled eatery and espresso bar above Jazz de Opus was one of the first of its kind. The desserts are good, as is the espresso, but given the wide choice of Allann Brothers coffees brewed to order—by the cup or pot—it is worth trying something new. The Celebes, for example, is wonderfully rich and tasty, especially paired with a slice of French silk pie. *MC, V; no checks; every day; beer and wine; map:J6*

PALIO DESSERT & ESPRESSO HOUSE / 1996 SE Ladd Ave, Ladd's Addition; 503/232-9412 This may be the closest you get to great coffee and desserts without feeling like you've left the comforts of home. Palio is cozy and ambient, and it's situated in the comfortably quaint Ladd's Addition neighborhood. Candles and dim vintage lights warmly illuminate this neighborhood den, and lest you get bored, there are toys, games, and books galore—from Michael Crichton to Jonathan Swift. The desserts change regularly, but they're always decadently sweet, and you're sure to find a luscious chocolate cake of some sort. *AE, MC, V; checks OK; every day; no alcohol; map:GG5*

THE PIED COW / 3244 SE Belmont St, Belmont; 503/230-4866 This is where Jeannie—as in *I Dream of Jeannie*—would hang out now if she were into 70s self-parody. The front room of this colorful Victorian bears a strong resemblance to her bottle, with its bay window dressed in beads, lace curtains, and low couches with pillows covered in leopard-print fabric. Neo-hippies, retro-bohemians, and bookish types come here to read *The New York Times,* play cards, and ponder over a cup of coffee—is it half full or half empty? This is the ultimate coffeehouse: the food is cheap, the cappuccinos are delicious, and there's always a chocolate dessert that's satisfyingly rich. Add to that a license for serving dessert wine and imported beer, and a delightful courtyard lit by candles and lanterns, and there's no better place to while away a summer evening. *Cash only; Tues–Sun; beer and wine; map:GG5*

RIMSKY-KORSAKOFFEE HOUSE / 707 SE 12th Ave, Southeast; 503/232-2640 Laughter and music from the resident piano greet the ear at the threshold of this grand old mansion. The place is nearly always filled with young lovers sharing ice cream sundaes (Rasputin's Delight is a favorite) or a decadent mocha fudge cake. The Cafe Borgias are exceptional: coffee, chocolate, and orange harmoniously mingle in one cup. You might drive right by this place—there's no sign marking its presence— but once inside, with a string trio playing in the background and a proper cup of coffee to sip, you may not want to leave. *No credit cards; checks OK; every day; no alcohol; map:FF6*

TAO OF TEA / 3430 SE Belmont St, Belmont; 503/736-0198 Enter the Tao of Tea and you'll soon forget where you are. Trickling water, meditative music, exotic teapots, and Asian-influenced decor instantly draw you into another world. The tea selection seems endless (more than 120 types), with the finest varieties of oolong, green, white, red, and black teas, as well as fruit and herbal infusions. The eclectic (all vegetarian) food menu is designed to complement the tea selection, and the green tea, bean curd, and mango ice cream assortment finishes your palate nicely. The adjacent Leaf Room offers a more in-depth look into tea and tea accessories. *DIS, MC, V; checks OK; every day; no alcohol; tea@ taooftea.com; www.taooftea.com; map:GG4*

TORREFAZIONE ITALIA / 838 NW 23rd Ave, Northwest (and branches); 503/228-1255 This is Portland's own Little Italy. The terracotta tile floors, warm yellow walls, and hand-painted earthenware, not to mention the frequently overheard dialect and rich smell of dark-roasted coffee—well, put another notch in the belt for Mediterranean vogue. This is a popular hangout for neighborhood locals, Eurobabes, and Italian wannabes. Classic crunchy, sweet biscotti go perfectly with a foamy cappuccino or cup of coffee. On balmy days the breeze blows through the plate-glass windows, which are open to the street. The east-side shop (1403 NE Weidler St; 503/288-1608; map:FF5) offers the same delicious coffee and large leather chairs for lounging; the newest branch, in the Pearl District (1140 NW Everett St; 503/224-9896; map:K2), caters to day trippers, closing at 7pm every night. *MC, V; checks OK; every day; no alcohol; www.titalia.com; map:GG7*

ITINERARIES

ITINERARIES

Portland is Oregon's largest metropolitan area, but it's a compact, walkable city, and even on a short stopover, visitors can get a sense of what makes it such a livable, well-loved place. This chapter outlines a three-day tour of the City of Roses plus an alternative family day and another for a day in Vancouver, Washington, just north of Portland. The itineraries include suggestions for meals and for evening entertainment. Information about most of the places shown in boldface can be found in other chapters of the book (Restaurants, Shopping, Exploring, and Nightlife).

DAY ONE

Spend this first day exploring the sights and shops of downtown Portland, arguably one of the busiest and healthiest downtown cores in the country. The best way to get around is on foot, but driving from area to area is not difficult either, although parking can be hit or miss. Tri-Met buses in the downtown core's **FARELESS SQUARE** are free, as is the MAX train; just board at any stop and ride within the parameters of the Willamette River on the east side, I-405 on the west and south, and NW Irving Street on the north. For further information, call Tri-Met (503/238-7433).

MORNING: Start with breakfast on Broadway, a one-way street that runs north to south, past such quintessential Portland sights as **PIONEER COURTHOUSE SQUARE** (between SW Morrison and Yamhill Streets), **NORDSTROM** (710 SW Broadway; 503/224-6666), and the **HEATHMAN HOTEL** (corner of SW Broadway and Salmon St; 503/241-4100). In fact, king salmon hash at the **HEATHMAN RESTAURANT AND BAR** (reserve through the hotel) is a tasteful—and tasty—way to begin the day, although if coffee and a pastry are all you need, **PAZZORIA,** about five blocks north, just off SW Broadway (next to Pazzo, 625 SW Washington St; 503/228-1695) is a fine, fast choice. After breakfast, stretch your legs in **TOM MCCALL WATERFRONT PARK,** one of Portland's showpiece greenspaces, sandwiched between the Willamette River and a busy north-south thoroughfare, the Naito Parkway. Start just south of the **RIVERPLACE HOTEL** (1510 SW Harbor Wy; 503/228-3233) and walk north on the promenade, browsing the row of retail shops. A picturesque marina is set alongside the river here, too; procure a frozen yogurt or a cup of coffee, find a bench, and enjoy the passing boat show.

Continue your walk north along the sidewalk; you'll pass close to the **SALMON STREET SPRINGS,** with its waterworks show that's a playground for squealing children throughout the summer months. Continue on beneath the Burnside Bridge and, if it's a weekend day between early March and the end of December, you'll want to pause here at the **SATURDAY MARKET,** for great people-watching, better-than-average booth food, and loads of handmade Oregon craft items to take home to Kansas or Kyoto—from beaded earrings to fireplace pokers.

AFTERNOON: Lunch at the Saturday Market is satisfying and fun, but if it's a weekday and there's no sign of a food booth in sight, make your way to **DOGS DIG VEGETARIAN DELI** (212 NW Davis St; 503/223-3362), where the vegetarian takeout fare is healthy and delicious (not necessarily in that order); for more of a sit-down option, head to the longtime favorite **BIJOU CAFE** (132 SW 3rd Ave; 503/222-3187) for a memorable burger or salad. After lunch, take in the new **GARDEN OF THE AWAKENING ORCHID**—a classical Chinese Garden—between NW Second and Third Avenues, and NW Everett and Flanders Streets (enter at NW 3rd Ave and Everett St). The garden, which opened in late 2000, is a meditative place, and you might be compelled to spend all afternoon here, sipping tea in what may be the most authentic classical Chinese teahouse in the country, run by the able tea masters of the **TAO OF TEA** (admission to the garden is $6). If not, make tracks to the elm-lined **SOUTH PARK BLOCKS.**

PORTLAND STATE UNIVERSITY anchors this string of well-tended blocks at the south end; at the north end sits **SOUTHPARK** (901 SW Salmon St; 503/326-1300), where you can try a glass of Oregon wine or eat a blood-sugar-boosting midafternoon dessert. Art lovers should steer toward the **PORTLAND ART MUSEUM** (1219 SW Park Ave; 503/226-2811), and history buffs can go across the street to the **OREGON HISTORY CENTER** (1200 SW Park Ave; 503/222-1741).

Shoppers will be happy to know they can skip the museums altogether, but hit the **MUSEUM SHOPS**, both of which are excellent (the art museum shop is off the courtyard; the historical center's is right on SW Broadway). Almost any time is shopping time at **PIONEER PLACE** (on the blocks between SW 3rd and 5th Aves and SW Yamhill and Morrison Sts), but many downtown stores close at 6pm, so you'll want to plan to finish by then.

EVENING: Make a dinner reservation at **HIGGINS** (1239 SW Broadway; 503/222-9070), where local ingredients receive reverential treatment under the careful eye of local food master Greg Higgins; it's located just off the South Park Blocks in the same block as the Oregon History Center. Or go down SW Broadway to the Benson Hotel's **EL GAUCHO** (319 SW Broadway; 503/227-8794), a new restaurant where steak is the main attraction. End the evening with a nightcap high atop the city at **ATWATER'S** (111 SW 5th Ave, 30th floor; 503/275-3600) in the US Bancorp building (lovingly known as the Big Pink, for its pinkish glass exterior). Or arrange to see a music or theater performance in the **PORTLAND CENTER FOR THE PERFORMING ARTS' WINNINGSTAD THEATRE** (1111 SW Broadway; 503/796-9293) or across Main Street at the **ARLENE SCHNITZER CONCERT HALL** (phone number is the same). If neither of those options appeals, take a walk along SW Broadway; here you'll notice that even in the waning hours of the evening, pedestrians (residents, late workers, tourists, and gadflies) are still enjoying the city's very vital downtown.

DAY TWO

On the second day, discover the area **IN AND AROUND NORTHWEST PORTLAND**, especially NW 23rd and 21st Avenues, and the arty **PEARL DISTRICT**. Once more, we prefer walking to other modes of transportation, and although the I-405 freeway divides the two areas, there are several easy foot passages that cross from the neighborhood on the west side of the freeway to the Pearl on the east. However, other options abound: driving gives you the most flexibility, but Tri-Met bus 15 (to NW 23rd Ave) goes from downtown to NW Thurman Street in a quick 20 minutes—and you don't have to park the bus. The new **PORTLAND STREETCAR** should be up and running in 2001, and that also will be a quick trip from the downtown core.

MORNING: Begin this day with a four-square breakfast at **BESAW'S** (2301 NW Savier St; 503/228-2619). Or, for lighter fare, pick up a cranberry cornmeal scone and a coffee at **MARSEE BAKING** (1323 NW 23rd Ave; 503/295-5900). Thus fueled, head south along NW 23rd Avenue. **WINDOW SHOPPING** here is pure pleasure, especially in the area south of Good Samaritan Hospital. Many of the street's original Victorian-era houses have been developed into boutiques and shops, and there are plenty of cool cafes and coffee stops interspersed (one caveat: some shops don't open until 11am). One store that's pure Portland is longtime tenant **MUSIC MILLENNIUM** (801 NW 23rd Ave; 503/248-0163), where you can get Pink Martini's new CD. Another is **URBINO** (521 NW 23rd Ave; 503/220-0053), with its beautiful albeit pricey inventory of goods for your home. Zigzag along NW 23rd (there are shops for 10 blocks straight, and then some) as long as you can stand it, but before you leave the neighborhood be sure to poke into **TWIST** (30 NW 23rd Pl; 503/224-0334), where the selection of dishes, jewelry, furniture, and tabletop items made mostly by American craftspeople would be notable in any city. (To get here, turn west off of NW 23rd Avenue onto W Burnside St, and double back onto the half-block-long NW 23rd Pl.)

If you follow NW 23rd Avenue across W Burnside Street, it becomes SW Vista Avenue. One of Portland's more exclusive neighborhoods, Portland Heights, is just off this route. SW Vista is also the easiest way to get to the **WASHINGTON PARK ROSE GARDEN** or to the **JAPANESE GARDEN** from Northwest Portland. Walk a couple of blocks up—up as in climb—SW Vista Avenue to Park Place and turn right. Here you can catch bus 63 to take you up into Washington Park (or if you haven't climbed enough already, continue your hike). Disembark at the tennis courts to visit either the rose garden (just down the hill to your left) or the Japanese garden (uphill on your right). Or stay on the bus until it reaches the big parking lot near the **OREGON ZOO** and the **WORLD FORESTRY CENTER**. From here you can also check out **HOYT ARBORETUM**, where dozens of species of trees are labeled. One of Portland's longest, most woodsy hiking trails is the **WILDWOOD TRAIL**; it starts near the **VIETNAM VETERANS' LIVING MEMORIAL**, near the forestry center, and will take you through Washington Park and beyond.

AFTERNOON: Lunch at the Oregon Zoo's **CASCADE GRILL RESTAURANT** is possible—and not bad, really, for zoo food—even if you don't actually enter the zoo. Or head back down to Northwest Portland—to NW 23rd Avenue and Everett Street, exactly—for outstanding Thai food at **TYPHOON!** (2310 NW Everett St; 503/243-7557). Another can't-miss restaurant choice is **PAPA HAYDN**, at NW 23rd Avenue and Irving Street (701 NW 23rd Ave; 503/228-7317), where you can get a salad and a voluptuous dessert and have a good view of the people parade along the street. (Both of these restaurants have outdoor seating—a nice choice come summer.) You should know, too, that along NW 21st Avenue—two blocks east of 23rd Avenue—are many excellent restaurants that serve lunch and dinner, including **WILDWOOD** (1221 NW 21st Ave; 503/248-9663), for a distinguished meal made of local foods; **SERRATTO** (2112 NW Kearney St; 503/221-1195), a lovely place to linger over a leisurely Italian lunch; and **BASTA'S** (410 NW 21st Ave; 503/274-1572), in a reformed fast-food restaurant, for heavenly pasta and other Italian fare.

After lunch, walk east on NW Everett Street or Lovejoy Street to the Pearl District. A onetime warehouse and light industrial area, the Pearl is caught up in a renaissance. This neighborhood continues to be gentrified, with new structures going up among once-decrepit buildings that now house work/live lofts, advertising and high tech offices, and arty retail space (especially art galleries and furniture stores). Be sure to hit NW Everett, Glisan, or Hoyt Streets, but don't overlook the cross streets either. A few places to be sure to check out are **PICA** (Portland Institute for Contemporary Art; 219 NW 12th Ave, No. 100; 503/242-1419), in the elegant Wieden + Kennedy—of advertising fame—building; **IN GOOD TASTE** (231 NW 11th Ave; 503/248-2015), where foodies run amok; and—if there's a child in your life, **HANNA ANDERSSON** (327 NW 10th Ave; 503/321-5275), for Swedish cotton clothing via Oregon.

EVENING: These days the Pearl District has almost as many restaurants as art galleries. We suggest two places for dinner: either **CAFE AZUL** (112 NW 9th Ave; 503/525-4422), where the haute Mexican cuisine rarely fails, or **BLUEHOUR** (250 NW 13th Ave; 503/226-3394), for elaborate surroundings and Mediterranean-style food. There are plenty of options for lingering over a cocktail here too: ¡**OBA!** (555 NW 12th Ave;

NATIVE AMERICAN HISTORY

When explorers Meriwether Lewis and William Clark pushed through to the mouth of the Columbia River at present-day Astoria almost 200 years ago—in 1805, to be exact—the greater Willamette Valley and the Columbia Gorge area were home to dozens of Native American tribes. These days it's not always easy to locate a place to learn about any given tribe's cultural heritage, but there actually are a number of excellent museums and cultural sites focusing on Native American history not far from Portland.

About a two-hour drive from Portland over the scenic Mount Hood Highway (Highway 26), the award-winning **Museum at Warm Springs** (Hwy 26 at Warm Springs; 541/553-3331; www.tmaws.org), was built by three tribes (Wasco, Paiute, and Warm Springs) and is located on the Warm Springs Reservation. The well-designed museum introduces visitors to the tribes of the Columbia River Gorge through stunning beadwork, songs, stories, and historical and contemporary exhibits. Stay overnight at **Kah-Nee-Ta Resort** (541/553-1112; www.kah-nee-taresort.com), which is owned by the Confederated Tribes of Warm Springs and sits on Highway 3, off Highway 26 in the Warm Springs River canyon. Among Kah-Nee-Ta's charms are its hot-spring-fed swimming pools, fine restaurant, spa, gaming facility, and golf course.

On the next day, head north to the Columbia River on Highway 97. Cross the Columbia at Bigg's Junction and travel up the hill to the **Maryhill Museum of Art** (35 Maryhill Museum Dr, Goldendale, WA; 509/773-3733; www.maryhillmuseum.org) to see the fine collection of Klickitat and Wasco baskets. You might then continue on Highway 97 an hour north, past Mount Adams (the Yakama tribe's sacred mountain, Pahto, returned to them by President Nixon), to the **Yakama Nation Cultural Heritage Center** (280 Buster Rd, Toppenish, WA; 509/865-2800). Another option is to head two hours east to the spectacular **Tamustalik Cultural Institute** (on the Umatilla Indian Reservation, just east of Pendleton, off I-84 on Hwy 331; 541/966-9748). This museum tells the story of the Oregon Trail migrations from the perspective of the resident Cayuse, Nez Perce, and Walla Walla Indians. A popular "trail trash" exhibit shows belongings dumped off the wagons by weary pioneers.

On the return to Portland via I-84, you'll want to stop at the **Columbia Gorge Discovery Center** at Crate's Point (just west of The Dalles—watch for signs; 541/296-8600; www.gorgediscovery.org). For centuries, the area around The Dalles was a major Native American trade center. In the early 1800s, it was home to Hudson's Bay Company trappers, and later the area served as a pioneer staging ground for the last leg of the Oregon Trail. The best exhibit is a 33-foot working model of the Columbia River that removes the current dams to expose Celilo Falls, an immense basalt chasm of roaring waterfalls and the traditional fishing grounds of the Columbia River tribes.

Indian commerce and wealth were already well established when the Hudson's Bay Company built its Northwest trading headquarters on the Columbia River at Fort Vancouver. At the **Fort Vancouver National Historic Site** (10 minutes north of Portland off I-5; 1501 E Evergreen Blvd, Vancouver, WA; 800/832-3599; www.nps.gov/fova/), visitors can see the stockade and tour five major restored buildings: an Indian trade shop stocked with replicas of trade goods, the chief factor's residence and kitchen, a blacksmith shop, a bakery, and a shipping warehouse filled with furs. There's also a period vegetable and flower garden.

Multnomah County is named for the tribe that once occupied this area; explorers Lewis and Clark reported sighting Chinook villages all along the Columbia River from the Gorge to the Pacific Ocean. You won't find much information about the Chinooks in Portland, although **Powell's City of Books** (1005 W Burnside; 503/228-4651; www.powellsbooks.com) offers more than 5,000 new and used books by and about Native Americans, and the **Oregon History Center** (1200 SW Park Ave; 503/222-1741; www.ohs.org) has collections of basketry, beadwork, leatherwork, and stone representing Northwest tribes, as well as more than 1,000 photographic images of Indians in its library.

Farther afield, near the mouth of the Columbia River outside Astoria, is **Fort Clatsop National Memorial** (follow the well-marked signs from Hwy 101 at Warrenton; 503/861-2471; www.nps.gov/focl), where Lewis and Clark's bacon was saved one cold winter by the Clatsop band of Chinooks.

Most Northwest tribes lost their land and economic strength to the newcomers. Today they're gaining it back through casinos, whose revenues help fund interpretive centers, traditional and contemporary art, and other tribal enterprises. Two of the largest casinos are near the Oregon Coast—**Spirit Mountain** at Grand Ronde (800/760-7977; www.spirit-mountain.com), and **Chinook Winds** at Lincoln City (888/CHINOOK; www.chinookwindscasino.com)—and both offer big-name entertainment.

For information on current Native American tours, powwows, rodeos, and other events, or for maps and brochures, contact the Portland office of the Affiliated Tribes of Northwest Indians (1827 NE 44th Ave, Suite 130; 503/249-5770) or visit the group's web site at www.atni.org. —*Kim Carlson*

503/228-6161) is a popular dinner and night spot, as is **PARAGON** (1309 NW Hoyt St; 503/833-5060). If a fussy dinner isn't what you're needing, consider pizza and a pint at one of the city's longtime microbreweries, **BRIDGEPORT BREW PUB** (1313 NW Marshall St; 503/241-3612).

If you walk on NW 10th Avenue toward W Burnside, you'll come to **POWELL'S CITY OF BOOKS** (1005 W Burnside St; 503/228-4651); there's also an entrance at the corner of NW 11th Avenue and Couch Street. Depending on how you feel about books and shopping, you could spend a whole day here or be overwhelmed immediately, but start with an evening trip, when the store is hopping and there may be an author reading in the Pearl Room. Don't think twice about walking around with a map (even natives do it, since major remodeling seems to enlarge the store on a regular basis), available at the front door.

Still not ready to call it a day? Stop by the **CRYSTAL BALLROOM** (1332 W Burnside St; 503/778-5625) to see what's playing; it could be anything from bluegrass to bossa nova. The dance floor here is on springs, making an evening of dancing an energizing treat.

DAY THREE

To get the full flavor of Portland, you'll want to spend some time across—and on—the Willamette River. This day starts with a visit to three east-side neighborhoods and ends with a cruise on the river. You may want a car on this day, since the neighborhoods are not adjacent to one another.

MORNING: One of the best breakfasts in town is at **ZELL'S: AN AMER-ICAN CAFE** (1300 SE Morrison St; 503/239-0196), but perhaps more convenient—since you'll start the day in the residential neighborhood of **IRVINGTON**—is for you to grab a hearty cinnamon roll and a fresh orange juice at the **GRAND CENTRAL BAKING CO.** (1444 NE Weidler St; 503/288-1614), which is on the edge of Irvington (Zell's is about 20 blocks south). One of Portland's oldest neighborhoods, Irvington is chock-full of mansions and rambling old houses—most in good repair with appealing gardens. In **GRANT PARK** (on NE 33rd Ave, between Broadway and Knott St, adjacent to Grant High School), you'll find statues of Beverly Cleary's characters from her Ramona series. These beloved statues are not visible from the street; you'll have to walk into the park to find them. (Klickitat Street, where Ramona lives, is about four blocks to the north.) Many shops line NE Broadway between 14th and 28th Avenues, but the traffic along this four-lane conduit to I-5 and downtown is heavy, making for noisy walking. A few shops to duck into: rumpled maybe, but frumpy never **MATISSE** (1411 NE Broadway; 503/287-5414), for beautiful women's clothing; and **FRENCH QUARTER** (1444 NE Broadway; 503/284-1379), where the linens—and everything else—are imported from the Continent. There's a lot of coffee in this neighborhood—**PEET'S, TORREFAZIONE, STARBUCKS**; you should have no problem staying on your feet.

AFTERNOON: Lunch is in the **HAWTHORNE DISTRICT**, about 30 blocks south of Irvington. One of the joys of this street is its ambience, a cheerful hippieness that ages gracefully—and it's a real neighborhood, where Gen Xers hanging at one of the strip's many music stores mingle on the street with octogenarians on their way to the Fred Meyer pharmacy. **BREAD AND INK CAFE** (3610 SE Hawthorne Blvd; 503/239-4756) is a longtime neighborhood bistro, where the burgers and homemade ketchup are legendary (not to mention the cassata for dessert). It's a place where almost everyone feels at home. After lunch, take in the used book and music stores, funky furniture vendors, and **PASTAWORKS** (3735 SE Hawthorne Blvd; 503/232-1010), where you can buy the makings of a grand meal (or at least some accoutrements to take home on the plane). It may come as no surprise that there's a **BEN AND JERRY'S** (corner of SE 36th Ave and Hawthorne Blvd; 503/234-2223) in this neighborhood, with some of the richest and most politically progressive ice cream in town.

At some point in the afternoon, you'll want to head south again, to the **WESTMORELAND** neighborhood, where there's more shopping and **CAPRIAL'S BISTRO** (7015 SE Milwaukie Ave; 503/236-6457), a renowned, informal dinner spot owned by cooking show host and chef extraordinaire Caprial Pence and her husband, John. If you'd like to stay for dinner—and we recommend you do—but haven't reserved far in advance, you might still find a spot at the counter. Not hungry yet? The heart of Westmoreland is at the intersection of SE Bybee Boulevard and Milwaukie Avenue. If you take SE Bybee to the west here, and follow it as it curves around and becomes SE 13th Avenue, you've reached **SELL-WOOD**, with its multitude of antique stores.

EVENING: If you haven't already had dinner with Caprial, consider a dinner cruise on the Willamette River. The *Portland Spirit* (503/224-3900) docks at Tom McCall Waterfront Park, near the Salmon Street Springs fountain. A river cruise is a great way to get a sense of this city on the water and of the many bridges that connect Portland's west and east sides (you'll pass right under several of them, depending on your route). Most dinner cruises are two- to three-hour events starting at 7pm, but if you still have a little life in you after this busy day, check out the nightlife in the same place you started this three-day tour, the **HEATHMAN RESTAURANT AND BAR**.

DAY WITH CHILDREN

Kids and grown-ups alike should appreciate the following itinerary, which is best accomplished with a car.

MORNING: Load up everyone for breakfast at the **ORIGINAL PAN-CAKE HOUSE**, 10 minutes south of downtown (take the Barbur Blvd exit from I-5; the restaurant is immediately on your left). This Portland landmark is popular with tourists, businesspeople, students, grandparents and grandchildren, neighbors—well, you get the picture. Allow plenty of time to be seated, although service from that point is snappy. Afterward, take I-5 south to I-205 and head east, to historic Oregon City. Watch for the giant covered wagon off to the right (exit 10); this is the **END OF THE OREGON TRAIL INTERPRETIVE CENTER** (1726 Washington St, Oregon City; 503/657-9336). Call ahead to plan your arrival in time for a staging of the multimedia presentation; otherwise, there's not a lot to see besides the well-stocked gift store and some worthwhile hands-on displays.

AFTERNOON: They sat still for breakfast (maybe longer than you might have wished if there was a wait at the Original Pancake House), so the airy and spacious **OREGON MUSEUM OF SCIENCE AND INDUSTRY (OMSI)** (1945 SE Water Ave; 503/797-4000) might be a good place to head for lunch and the early afternoon hours. There are plenty of permanent and rotating exhibits here and a special room for the under-three crowd, plus a perfectly adequate restaurant at which to fortify the troops. If the sun is shining and no one wants to go inside, head to the **OREGON ZOO** (4001 SW Canyon Rd, in Washington Park; 503/226-1561). The zoo's new Pacific Northwest areas allow visitors to observe fauna that's native to this part of the country, and there are plenty of exotic creatures from farther afield (naked mole rats, anyone?). Finish the afternoon with a visit to the world's first **NIKE TOWN** (930 SW 6th Ave; 503/221-6543), a museum cum shopping experience, where everything is made by Portland's own mega shoe company. (OK, Nike headquarters are actually in Beaverton.)

EVENING: At dinnertime, head to NW 23rd Avenue, where there are a couple of pizza options. A quirky but fun place for excellent New York–style pies is **ESCAPE FROM NEW YORK PIZZA** (622 NW 23rd Ave; 503/227-5423), although be warned: its list of toppings is basic and its seating options are limited. A more practical choice might be **PIZZICATO** (505 NW 23rd Ave; 503/242-0023), where the toppings tend toward the pesto/sun-dried tomato/kalamata olive school (but of course, they have plain cheese also), and where there's lots of seating. Kids and grown-ups alike will enjoy walking along the street, with the little white lights twinkling in the trees overhead. **PAPA HAYDN** (701 NW 23rd Ave; 503/228-7317) is a good place to stop in for dessert. (Don't think your kids can deal with the line? Take them inside for a peek at the dessert case, and you might be surprised what they'll endure.) For a city view, and a final cap on a busy day, follow NW 23rd Avenue across W Burnside Street to where it becomes SW Vista Avenue, and follow the signs for Scenic Drive. This route takes you up to **COUNCIL CREST PARK**, at 1,073 feet the highest place in Portland, and a great spot for viewing the city lights spread out below.

DAY TRIPS

DAY TRIPS

Columbia River Gorge Scenic Area: Oregon Side

Take I-84 east from Portland; Hood River is 1 hour east, The Dalles another half hour beyond.

In 1792 Boston trader Robert Gray and his crew became the first white people to sail on a strip of then-wild water that flowed into the Pacific Ocean. They named it the Columbia, after their ship, and proclaimed it a "noble river." After a week or so, they sailed out to sea without much of a second thought; Gray barely acknowledged his find when he returned to Massachusetts. Historians note that Gray sailed on rather hastily because he didn't find any sea otter pelts to buy from the native people on the banks of the river. Would he have lingered a bit if he'd sailed the *Columbia Rediviva* as far east as the majestic Columbia River Gorge? This landscape, with its magnificent waterfalls, dramatic cliffs, and rock formations cut by the river, is enough to make nature lovers want to explore every crevice.

Driving in the gorge (just east of Portland) was at one time not for the queasy, because of the narrow, winding highway. These days, most of the traffic goes down I-84, leaving the beautiful old **COLUMBIA RIVER SCENIC HIGHWAY** (aka Highway 30)—an engineering marvel that originally went from Portland to Mosier—for the take-your-time wanderers. Portions of the old highway near Bonneville Dam and Hood River have recently been restored for **HIKERS AND CYCLISTS**; call the Oregon Department of Transportation (503/731-8200) for details and maps; see also the Hood River section in this chapter.

From Portland, taking a drive on the Columbia River Scenic Highway is an easy 20-mile trip from Troutdale east (from I-84, take exit 14). If it's after 2pm on Sunday (or dinnertime any other day of the week), you can stop off at **TAD'S CHICKEN 'N' DUMPLINGS** (a mile east of Troutdale on Hwy 30; 503/666-5337). Another option is the McMenamins' establishment **EDGEFIELD** (2126 SW Halsey St, Troutdale; 503/669-8610), a unique hostelry and eatery that occupy a site formerly used as a poor farm.

Once you're on the scenic highway, popular viewpoints and attractions are numerous: **CROWN POINT**, 725 feet above the river, features a stone visitors center with gorgeous views and, sometimes, tremendous winds. **LARCH MOUNTAIN**, 14 miles upriver from Crown Point, is one of the best sunset-watching spots in western Oregon, excluding the summit of Mount Hood. A short trail leads to Sherrard's Point—the summit—a rocky promontory jutting out from the mountaintop. From here there are spectacular 360-degree views of Mount Hood, Mount Adams, Mount St. Helens, Mount Jefferson, the Columbia River Gorge, and all of Portland.

Back down on I-84, you'll pass **MULTNOMAH FALLS**, the second-highest waterfall in the country at 620 feet (in two steps). The wood and stone Multnomah Falls Lodge, at the foot of the falls, was designed in 1925 by the notable architect Albert E. Doyle (of Portland's Benson Hotel fame). Now a National Historic Landmark, the lodge houses a naturalists and visitors center. The large restaurant (503/695-2376) serves good breakfasts (brunch on Sundays), lunch, and dinner but does not have overnight facilities. **ONEONTA GORGE** is a narrow, dramatic cleft through which a slippery half-mile trail winds to secluded Oneonta Falls; this rugged trail, mostly through the actual streambed, is suitable only for the adventurous.

BONNEVILLE DAM, the first federal dam on the Columbia, offers tours of the dam itself, the fish ladders (seen through underwater viewing windows), and the locks (541/374-8820). You can tour the **BONNEVILLE FISH HATCHERY** (next to the dam; 541/374-8393) all year-round, but the best time is September through November, when the chinook are spawning. Be sure also to visit the outdoor pond where the huge, 10-foot sturgeon reside. The **BRIDGE OF THE GODS**, in the old river town of Cascade Locks, is now steel, but at the site is a fine little museum that recounts the Indian myth about the original, legendary arching-rock bridge that collapsed into the Columbia River long ago. The locks themselves are a sight worth seeing; the stonework is beautiful and the scale awesome, accentuated by the small figures of the people who fish off the walls. The **STERN-WHEELER COLUMBIA GORGE** (503/223-3928) departs three times daily in the summer from the locks marina, stopping at Bonneville Dam and Stevenson Landing if there are passengers waiting; the cost is $12.95 per person for the narrated tour.

HOOD RIVER

Near the bustling town of **HOOD RIVER**, fruit orchards are everywhere. Sunny weather combines with substantial moisture (about 31 inches of rain annually)—perfect for cultivating pears, apples, and plums. It's pastoral indeed, but there's drama, too: 30 miles to the south, 11,235-foot Mount Hood looms, but from the town itself the stunning views are of Washington's 12,326-foot Mount Adams.

And then there's the **WINDSURFING**, which, in the past 20 years has transformed this once-sleepy town into a kaleidoscope of color. In summer you can't miss the board sailors dotting the river with their brilliant sails and lending the town a distinctly touristy feel. They've come since the 1980s because of the roaring winds that blow opposite the Columbia River current, making Hood River one of the world's top three windsurfing destinations (Hawaii and Australia are the other two). While Hood River reaps all the sailboard mythology, in fact the waters on the Oregon side of the Columbia are reportedly tame compared to those off the Washington banks, where boardheads claim the wind "really pulls." Hence, the hottest sailors circumvent rocky shores and industrial areas to surf off points on the river's north bank such as Swell City and Doug's Beach. To find them, follow the streams of vans and wagons piled high with boards and masts, tune in to radio station KMCQ-104 for the local wind report, or call 541/386-3300 for a recorded message.

Two fine spectator spots are located right in Hood River. The **HOOD RIVER WATERFRONT CENTRE EVENT SITE** is a grassy park with a small sandy beach and unrestricted access to the Columbia (from I-84 follow the signs). Sailing is somewhat easier at the **COLUMBIA GORGE SAILPARK** at Port Marina Park, which features a marina, rental shop, and cafe with enclosed porch. (After all, who wants to dine in the wind?) For lessons or for information on wind conditions, sailboard rentals, or launching spots, investigate the multitude of sailboard equipment shops, including **HOOD RIVER WINDSURFING** (in Doug's Sports, 101 Oak St; 541/386-5787) and **BIG WINDS** (207 Front St; 541/386-6086). **KERRITS** (316 Oak St; 541/386-4187) makes colorful and practical activewear for women (that is, the suit remains on your body when you fall off your board); Kerrits recently added a line of kids' clothing that includes knock-your-socks-off polar fleece and equestrian gear. Down the street, **WINDWEAR** (504 Oak St; 541/386-6209) sells probably the most stylish onshore clothing in town, at boutique prices.

As longtime residents strongly attest, there was life in Hood River before the windsurfers arrived. The **HOOD RIVER COUNTY MUSEUM**, located at Port Marina Park (541/386-6772), is open daily, April through late October, with a small suggested donation. The museum exhibits, among other things, Native American artifacts of the region. The **MUSEUM OF CAROUSEL ART** (304 Oak St; 541/387-4622) is a labor of love that restores and displays carousels from around the world. The museum recently relocated from Portland into an 18,000-square-foot bank building and may take some time to fill the space, but the operators' enthusiasm makes up for any in-transition feel. Admission is $5 for adults and $2 for kids. The local **VISITOR INFORMATION CENTER**, tucked inside the Hood River Expo Building (405 Portway Ave; 800/366-3530), is a friendly place to find information but is sometimes closed on winter weekends.

In town, you'll find a notable independent bookseller, **WAUCOMA BOOKSTORE** (212 Oak St; 541/386-5353); the **COLUMBIA ART GALLERY** (207 2nd St; 541/386-4512), which exhibits the work of contemporary local artists; and **WY'EAST NATURAL FOODS** (at 5th and Oak Sts;

541/386-6181), where locals and passers-through alike shop for organic produce and Nancy's Yogurt. **PUBLIC REST ROOMS** are located at Second and State Streets, on the ground floor of the city hall. The **LIBRARY PARK**, just up from where Oak intersects with Fifth, sports a great view of both the town and river. For the best picnic food around, cross the Columbia to Bingen and head east a mile to the deli at **MOTHER'S MARKETPLACE** (415 W Steuben, Bingen; 509/493-1700). The cheerful owners are on a health food mission and will give you samples of their homemade vegan cheeses, sandwiches, and fresh fruit shakes.

The region's bountiful orchards and beautiful landscape are celebrated during the wonderful small-town **BLOSSOM FESTIVAL**, held annually in mid-April. **THE MOUNT HOOD RAILROAD** (800/872-4661) makes two- or four-hour round trips—and dinner-train excursions—from the quaint Hood River Depot into the heart of orchard country; call for the schedule. You can buy the fruit of the orchards at **THE FRUIT TREE** (4140 Westcliff Dr; 541/386-6688), near the Columbia Gorge Hotel; at **RIVER BEND COUNTRY STORE** (2363 Tucker Rd; 541/386-8766); or at one of the many fruit stands that dot the valley. **RASMUSSEN FARMS** (3020 Thomsen Rd, 1 mile off Hwy 35; 541/386-4622), in addition to selling seasonal fruit, also has a pumpkin patch and U-pick flower fields. For wine tasting, visit **HOOD RIVER VINEYARDS** (4693 Westwood Dr; 541/386-3772), known for its pear and raspberry dessert wines. Beer aficionados head for the **FULL SAIL TASTING ROOM AND PUB** (506 Columbia St; 541/386-2247) for handcrafted Full Sail ales and light meals. The outdoor deck (with live music on weekends) is an apt place for tired board sailors to unwind while keeping the river in sight.

PANORAMA POINT, a half mile south of Hood River on Highway 35, has the best view of the valley leading to Mount Hood. For another breathtaker, go east on I-84, exit at Mosier, and climb to the **ROWENA CREST VIEWPOINT**, on old Highway 30; the grandstand Columbia River view is complemented by a wildflower show in the **TOM MCCALL PRESERVE**, maintained by The Nature Conservancy.

The area's newest **HIKING AND BIKING** option is the 6.5-mile restored section of the Columbia River Scenic Highway connecting Hood River to Mosier. The highway was decommissioned in 1953, and the **TWIN TUNNELS** were plugged with gravel to keep the curious out. A lengthy and expensive effort reopened—and reinforced—the Twin Tunnel trail in the summer of 2000. To reach this spectacular trail, follow the signs to the parking lots at I-84's Highway 35 exit in Hood River, or exit 69 in Mosier. You'll need $3 in correct change for the parking fee machine.

Hood River locals head to **THE MESQUITERY** (1219 12th St; 541/386-2002) for substantial barbecue. At **BIG CITY CHICKS** (1302 13th St; 541/387-3811), the menu incorporates satays from Thailand, curries from India, Mexican moles, and more—but only for three seasons; they're closed in the winter. Fans of Purple Rocks Art Bar will find it's been replaced by **BRIAN'S POURHOUSE** (606 Oak St; 541/387-4344). Besides a clever name, the Pourhouse has steaks, fish, pastas, desserts made in-house, and, of course, microbrews. **BETTE'S PLACE** (416 Oak St; 541/386-1880), a diner-type cafe that's been serving practically the same menu for more than 20 years—bear-claw pastries, patty melts, and banana splits—has been discovered by the out-of-town crowd. Outside the city limits, on the way up to Mount Hood, is **SANTACROCES' ITALIAN RESTAURANT** (4780 Hwy 35; 541/354-2511), where the Santacroces bake their own bread, make their own Italian sausage, and serve the best pizza in the valley—all with good humor. Mike Caldwell, a former employee of the landmark Stonehedge Inn, loved the place so much he bought it. Now, the new **STONEHEDGE GARDENS** (3405 Cascade Dr; 541/386-3940) has been slightly upgraded, and the menu reaches farther afield—to Asia even—than ever before.

The first opening of the old gorge highway was crowned in 1922 by lumber baron Simon Benson's luxury lodging, the **COLUMBIA GORGE HOTEL** (4000 Westcliff Dr; 541/386-5566 or 800/345-1921). It is Hood River's grandest structure, and its dining room is the town's fanciest restaurant. In 1990 the turn-of-the-century **HOOD RIVER HOTEL** (102 Oak St; 541/386-1900) was restored to its former role as a simple but comfortable country hotel. Eight kitchen suites are available, but for those who don't want to cook, the small dining room serves up reasonably priced meals that are strong on local fruit and fish. An inexpensive alternative is the modest **VAGABOND LODGE** (4070 Westcliff Dr; 541/386-2992), located next door to the Columbia River Gorge Hotel—ask for a cliffside room.

THE DALLES

Twenty minutes east of Hood River is **THE DALLES**, a particularly historical stop along this stretch. In the 1840s, the Oregon Trail ended here; goods from wagons were loaded onto barges for the final float to Portland. Later, Fort Dalles was here; an **1850 SURGEON'S HOUSE** at the fort is now a museum (15th and Garrison Sts), with exceptional relics from the pioneer trails. Architecturally, the town is much more interesting than others nearby, with nicely maintained examples of Colonial, Gothic Revival, Italianate, and American Renaissance styles.

At **THE DALLES DAM** (2 miles east of The Dalles, off I-84; 541/296-9778), a visitors center has informative displays on Lewis and Clark and the fishing industry. A free tour train departs from the center and makes stops at the dam, the powerhouse, fish ladders, and a picnic area.

The **BALDWIN SALOON** (1st and Court Sts; 541/296-5666), built in 1876, has been a steamboat navigational office, warehouse, coffin storage site, and saddle shop; today it's been restored to its original use as a restaurant and bar. It's gorgeous, and the food is great too. If **BAILEY'S PLACE** (515 Liberty St; 541/296-6708) seems familiar, it's because the owner simply moved the staff, wines, and menu of the popular Oly's Supper Club into the 1865 Victorian that is now Bailey's. Though known for its prime rib, the restaurant serves up fresh seafood as well; try the razor clams in summer. For a bit of pampering and home cooking, reserve one of the two rooms at the **LIBERTY HOUSE** (514 Liberty St; 541/298-5252). At ease in an 1892 Victorian, the Liberty House has a pleasant garden and tea room.

The excellent **COLUMBIA GORGE DISCOVERY CENTER/WASCO COUNTY HISTORICAL SOCIETY** sits on Crates Point (5000 Discovery Dr; 541/296-8600). Exhibits focus on the life and use, past and present, of this stretch of the Columbia, from how the Native Americans used the river to its current popularity as a windsurfing spot (there's even a board you can ride that simulates surfing the river). The location is stunning and the architecture noteworthy; even the cafe is above average.

Columbia River Gorge Scenic Area: Washington Side

Drive east from Portland on I-84; cross to the Washington side at Bridge of the Gods (toll 75 cents for autos), about 45 minutes east of Portland.

One gorge attraction on the Washington side of the Columbia River worth visiting is the impressive **SKAMANIA LODGE** (1131 Skamania Lodge Wy, Stevenson; 509/427-7700). Skamania was constructed in the early 1990s with the help of a $5 million grant to spur economic development on the Washington side of the river. Built in the style of the old Cascade lodges, with big timbers and river rock, it's not meant to be a four-star resort (there's no valet parking, turndown service, or private decks, and only one pressed log in the fireplace). But the common rooms are grand, the conference center works well, and the setting in the woods overlooking the river is pleasant indeed.

Skamania is a huge hostelry—195 rooms—and the amenities are numerous: bar, restaurant, lap pool, saunas, outdoor hot tub, 18-hole public golf course. The Forest Service's small room in the massive lobby offers **MAPS** and info on area recreation, wildflower and geology books, and so on. A day pass ($10 for adults, $5 for kids) buys you entrance to the pool, hot tub, and workout center without being a hotel guest; anyone can hike the trails. **SUNDAY BRUNCH** in the restaurant draws folks from a one-hour radius for a spread that includes fresh crab, smoked salmon, omelets made to order while you watch, and miles of pastries and desserts.

The **COLUMBIA GORGE INTERPRETIVE CENTER** (509/427-8211), located just below the lodge on Highway 14, displays the history of the gorge via a nine-projector slide show that re-creates the gorge's cataclysmic formation. It also features Native American fishing platforms and a 37-foot-high replica of a 19th-century fishing wheel. Admission is $6 for adults and $4 for kids.

At **CARSON HOT SPRINGS** (509/427-8292), about 15 minutes east of Stevenson, people come to take the waters—mineral baths and massages. The women's side is much more crowded than the men's, so if your entourage is mixed, the men will finish sooner. To avoid this problem, reserve a massage in advance ($67 for the bath, wrap, and one-hour massage). For bath and wrap only, the price is $12. There are also rooms at the lodge and cabins to rent—nothing fancy—for reasonable rates ($35–$60).

About 100 miles east of Portland, the eclectic **MARYHILL MUSEUM OF ART** (on Hwy 14, 13 miles southwest of Goldendale, Washington; 509/773-3733) is a massive neoclassical edifice, perched rather obtrusively upon the river's barren benchlands. Built to be the palatial residence of the eccentric Sam Hill, it is now a museum with an unlikely assortment of exhibits, including a stunning collection of Rodin sculptures.

In 1907, Hill bought 6,000 acres here near Goldendale, with the intention of founding a Quaker agricultural community. When that failed to materialize, Hill lost interest in living in the "ranch house" named after his wife and daughter. The museum came about through a little help from his friends: famed dancer Loie Fuller (also a close friend of Rodin) encouraged Hill to turn his mansion into an art museum, art collector Alma Spreckels became Maryhill's principal benefactor, and Queen Marie of Romania (whom Hill met during their shared philanthropic work in Europe after World War I) offered Maryhill much of her royal and personal memorabilia and graced the dedication of the Maryhill Museum in 1926.

With one of the largest collections of Rodin works in the world (78 bronze and plaster sculptures and 28 watercolors), three floors of classic French and American paintings and glasswork, unique exhibitions such as chess sets and 19th-century royal Romanian furnishings, and splendid Native American art, the museum makes for quite an interesting visit. Along with its permanent collection, the museum hosts a number of traveling collections, often featuring Northwest artists. **CAFE MARYHILL** on the lower level serves espresso, pastries, and sandwiches; peacocks roam the lovely landscaped grounds. Take time, also, to explore the intriguing sculptural overlook on the east side of the museum grounds. Maryhill is open daily from March 15 to November 15.

Four miles east of the museum on Highway 14 is another of Sam Hill's eye-catching creations, a full-scale replica of the inner third of **STONEHENGE**, built to honor the World War I veterans of Klickitat County. About 3 degrees off center, Hill's Stonehenge (not stones but poured concrete) actually functions as an observatory. It embodies Hill's personal vision: a pacifist, he considered his monument a statement on the human sacrifices made to the god of war.

Just 20 minutes north of Goldendale on Highway 97 is the **GOLDENDALE OBSERVATORY**(509/773-3141), a popular spot when comets drop by. High-powered telescopes offer incredible celestial views through unpolluted skies. Open Wednesday through Sunday.

Mount Hood

About 50 miles east of Portland; take I-84 east to the Wood Village/Gresham exit; follow that exit south to Burnside Street; turn left at the intersection and continue through the mountain towns of Sandy, Welches, and Rhododendron to Government Camp. Timberline Lodge is another 6 miles up the mountain. Allow 90 minutes' driving time from Portland to Government Camp.

At 11,235 feet, Mount Hood is not the highest in the chain of volcanoes in the Cascade Range, but it is one of the most developed—in part because it's a short drive east from Portland. According to geologists, Mount Hood still conceals hot magma and is bound to spew at some point. For now, though, all's peaceful in the towns scattered on its flanks. On the way up, between Gresham and Government Camp, **SANDY** (named for the nearby river), with its white-steepled church, weekend country market, and fruit stands, makes a nice stop. Here you'll find **ORAL HULL PARK**, designed for the blind but a pleasure for the sighted as well, with splashing water and plants to smell and feel. You'll need permission to walk through the garden unless you are a guest at the conference lodge here (503/668-6195). The knowledgeable staff at busy **OTTO'S CROSS COUNTRY SKI SHOP** (38716 Pioneer Blvd; 503/668-5947) will outfit you with whatever ski gear or snowshoes you need to get up the hill. Farther east you'll pass through the aptly named town of **RHODODENDRON** (look for blooms in June).

From Highway 26 at Government Camp, a 6-mile road twists its way to stunning **TIMBERLINE LODGE** (elevation 6,000 feet), with its impressive frontal views of Mount Hood's glaciers. The massive timber-and-stone lodge was constructed by government workers in the 1930s, who completed the monument in just 15 months. Throughout the building are structural and decorative pieces made by hand from native materials: the 100-foot-high chimney and enormous central fireplace were fashioned out of volcanic rocks from the mountain, the hand-wrought andirons were made from old railroad tracks, and the hardwood chairs and tables were hand-hewn from Oregon timber. The lodge's rooms with fireplaces get booked early, so call well in advance (800/547-1406). The **CASCADE DINING ROOM** (503/622-0700) serves an array of notable Northwest fare and is popular; reservations are suggested. (Other more modest dining options are also available.) For lodgers dying to shop, the **GALLERY** on the ground floor has locally made handicrafts and more images of Mount Hood than you can imagine. The Forest Service offers historical tours of the lodge at midday on weekends, and a self-starting movie shows the lodge's history daily.

One of the best hiking trails in the area, the **TIMBERLINE TRAIL**, leads 4.5 miles west from Timberline Lodge to flower-studded **PARADISE PARK**. The Timberline Trail is a 40-mile circuit of the entire peak that traverses snowfields as well as ancient forests. The lower parts can blaze with rhododendrons (peaking in June) and wildflowers (peaking in July); all are easily reachable from trails that branch out from the lodge.

Mid-May to mid-July is the prime time for **CLIMBING** Mount Hood, a peak that looks deceptively easy, although its last 1,500 feet involve very steep snow climbing. **TIMBERLINE MOUNTAIN GUIDES** (541/312-9242) in the Wy'east Day Lodge equips and conducts groups of climbers to the summit for a whopping $350 per person. The climb starts early in the morning; allow four to six hours to go up and two or three to come down.

FAM For those looking for an easier route up the mountain, the **MAGIC MILE SKY RIDE** chair lift hoists the brave and the curious to the 7,000-foot line year-round, weather permitting. All they ask is that you pay $6 ($3 for kids), wear sturdy shoes, and—no matter how warm you feel in the parking lot—bring a jacket. At the top of the lift you can buy a barbecue lunch, look though the powerful **TELESCOPE,** or find your favorite vantage point for a magnificent view. Call 503/222-2211 for weather conditions, and see Timberline's web site (www.timberline lodge.com) for ever-changing year-round activities.

The nearby **SILCOX HUT** (503/219-3192) has been gutted and restored to its original stone-and-timber glory. Six cubicles off the large central room provide sleeping quarters for 22. Organize a dozen or more of your best friends: in winter you can ride up on a Sno-Cat, have dinner, stay overnight, wake up to breakfast, and then ski down to the lodge—all for $100 per person, or $90 if you bring your own sleeping bag.

Just east of the town of Government Camp on Highway 26, the meadows of **TRILLIUM LAKE** beckon picnickers. A scenic and accessible walking trail circles the entire lake, passing through patches of trillium in the spring and columbine in the summer. In early August **HUCKLE-BERRY** pickers wander the trails from the Clark Creek Sno-Park in search of their beloved berries. In winter you can take the kids sledding at the **SNOW BUNNY LODGE** on the north side of the highway. Mount Hood has options for skiers of every ability: **MOUNT HOOD MEADOWS, SKI BOWL, TIMBERLINE,** and **COOPER SPUR.** The biggest, Mount Hood Meadows (off Highway 35; watch for signs), is also Portland's favorite for beginners and schussers alike. **COOPER SPUR SKI AREA** (on Cooper Spur Rd, off Hwy 35; 541/352-7803) has gentle slopes perfect for children, and the year-round **INN AT COOPER SPUR** (541/352-6692) has rooms, cabins with fireplaces and hot tubs, and a restaurant renowned for its huge steaks and rough-hewn service. Another dozen or so miles down Cooper Spur Road is the 1889 **CLOUD CAP INN**, a log landmark at the timberline on the north flank of Mount Hood. No longer a hotel, it's anchored to the mountain by cables, and the view alone is worth the detour. If the inn happens to be occupied by a search and rescue team (which is common in the summertime), you can ask if they have time to give you a tour. The lodge is also an access point for the Timberline Trail. Call the Ranger Station in Hood River (541/352-6002).

For information on any of the ski areas or on other Mount Hood activities, call the **MOUNT HOOD INFORMATION CENTER** (503/622-3360).

Sauvie Island

Take Highway 30 west from I-405; allow 20 minutes to drive to the Sauvie Island bridge, on your right.

Pastoral Sauvie Island, with its farms, orchards, produce stands, waterways, and wildlife—just 20 minutes from downtown Portland on Highway 30W—is a quick escape for bicyclists, bird-watchers, anglers, and boaters.

The island enticed the Multnomah Indians to make it their summer and fall home with its edible *wappato* root. You too can graze at in-season U-pick farms, or buy **FRESH PRODUCE** from one of the local markets, such as the **SAUVIE ISLAND FARMS MARKET** (503/621-3988) or the **PUMPKIN PATCH** (503/621-3874). Be warned, though: On rainy days the broad, golden fields of the island turn into mud farms, so take your rubber boots if you're going to pick. To **BIKE** around the island, park your car at the east end of the bridge (you can't miss the lot), and from there take the 12-mile biking loop. At the halfway point, if you're feeling energetic, take the 5-mile side trip down to the Columbia. There are several bird-watching turnouts along the loop.

The northern half of the island is a **GAME REFUGE** of sorts. From October through January duck hunters show up, making it no place to hang around—for you or the ducks. At other times, the marshes and open fields make a fine playground for you to enjoy the bountiful wildlife. Look for red foxes, black-tailed deer, great blue herons, geese, ducks, bald eagles, and migrating sandhill cranes. **REEDER ROAD** extends to the northern shore's sanctioned Collins Beach Clothing Optional Area and other short sandy beaches that freighters and small pleasure craft pass by. The western branch of the road follows the dike of the Multnomah Channel, passing the historic Bybee-Howell House, humble houseboats, rickety marinas, and the old site of the Hudson's Bay Company's Fort William (abandoned in 1836; nothing remains), and then eventually dead-ends. You'll want to purchase a **PARKING PERMIT** (daily or yearly) if you plan to venture to the refuge or beaches; permits are available at the grocery on your left immediately as you cross over the bridge onto the island.

The **BYBEE-HOWELL HOUSE**, in Bybee-Howell Territorial Park, was built in 1858 by James F. Bybee on a donation land claim and was sold to neighbor Benjamin Howell in 1860. The Classic Revival–style, two-story house has nine rooms and six fireplaces. The hands-on **AGRICULTURAL MUSEUM** displays agricultural equipment used in cultivating and harvesting crops, a complete harness shop, dairy equipment, and hand tools for working wood, leather, and metal. In the adjacent **PIONEER ORCHARD**, there are more than 115 varieties of apple trees—many of them unknown to modern-day orchardists—brought here by pioneers. (House and museum open noon to 5pm weekends only, from the first Saturday in June through Labor Day.) Admission is a suggested $2 donation. The park makes a lovely place for a summer picnic and can be rented for special events. An especially nice fall tradition is the **WINTERING-IN FESTIVAL** at Bybee-Howell House—complete with gallons of fresh apple cider. Call the Oregon History Center (503/222-1741) for information.

Oregon Coast

ASTORIA

Take Highway 30 west from I-405. Astoria is about 75 minutes from Portland.

Situated on the tip of a peninsula where the Columbia River reaches the sea, **ASTORIA** has a unique, edge-of-the-world flavor. With its Victorian architecture, natural beauty, and rich Native American and immigration history, Astoria offers much to the visitor.

SIXTH STREET RIVER PARK, with its always-open, covered observation tower, provides the best vantage point for viewing river commerce, observing river pilots as they board tankers and freighters, and watching seals and sea lions search for a free lunch. Downtown, **ART GALLERIES** are tucked in next to the fishermen's bars and mom-and-pop cafes, and there are a few notable restaurants as well. Bed and breakfasts have pro-liferated, particularly in the lovely Victorian homes on the steep hillsides overlooking the river. Note that unpretentious Astoria claims about 10,000 residents, and its downtown all but shuts down on Sundays.

The history of U.S. exploration and settlement here begins with Cap-tain Robert Gray, who sailed up the river in 1792, naming it after his ship, the *Columbia Rediviva*, which saw only 10 miles of the river before turning back to sea. In 1805–06, Lewis and Clark spent a miserably rainy winter at Fort Clatsop, now restored as the **FORT CLATSOP NATIONAL MEMORIAL** (6 miles southwest of Astoria; 503/861-2471). Besides audio-visuals and exhibits in the visitors center, there are living history demon-strations (musket firing, candle making) during the summer.

Five years later, in 1910, New York fur trader John Jacob Astor, one of America's wealthiest individuals, sent to the Northwest the fur-trading company that founded **FORT ASTORIA**. The fort had all but disappeared by the mid-19th century but now has been partially reconstructed (at 15th and Exchange Sts).

The city of Astoria really dates back to the late 1840s, when it began to thrive as a customhouse town and shipping center. The well-main-tained Victorians lining the harbor hillside at Franklin and Grand Avenues provide glimpses of that era. Now Astoria is a museum without walls, an unstirred mix of the old and new that finds common ground along the busy waterfront—once the site of canneries and river steamers, now an active port for oceangoing vessels and Russian fish-processing ships. Salmon and bottom-fishing trips leave from here.

The first stop for most visitors is the **ASTORIA COLUMN**, atop Cox-comb Hill, Astoria's highest point. The climb to the top is 164 steps but is well worth it: from there you have an endless panoramic view of the harbor, the Columbia estuary, and the distant headlands of the Pacific. Spiral murals of the region's history wrap around the column. To get there, drive up to the top of 16th Street and follow the signs.

The **COLUMBIA RIVER MARITIME MUSEUM** (on the waterfront at the foot of 17th St; 503/325-2323) is the finest museum of its type in the Northwest. The 1951 Coast Guard *Lightship Columbia* is moored out-side, and inside are restored small craft and thematic galleries depicting the Northwest's maritime heritage: fishing and whaling, fur trading, nav-igation, and shipwrecks. Admission is $5 for adults, with discounts for seniors and children.

Three other museums devoted to Astoria's history are operated by the Clatsop County Historical Society (503/325-2203). One is the **CLATSOP COUNTY HERITAGE MUSEUM** (16th and Exchange Sts) in the 1904 city hall building. The **FLAVEL HOUSE** (8th and Duane Sts) is the city's best example of ornate Queen Anne architecture, built by the

Columbia River's first steamship pilot, Captain George Flavel. Tea and scones are served periodically at the Flavels' grand dining room table; call the historical society in advance for information. The **UPPERTOWN FIRE-FIGHTERS MUSEUM** (2986 Marine Dr) houses an extensive collection of fire-fighting equipment dating back to 1879. One admission ($5 and less) gets you into all three of these museums.

Astoria's intelligentsia frequent the **PACIFIC ROOM GALLERY** (108 10th St; 503/325-5450), which offers pleasing regional art and espresso, and the owners have recently added a deli and fine wine. **LUCY'S BOOKS** (240 10th St; 503/325-4210) is a good browse, and **PERSONA VINTAGE CLOTHING AND ANTIQUES** (100 10th St; 503/325-3837), with its high-quality merchandise, is a special treat. **JOSEPHSON'S SMOKEHOUSE** (106 Marine Dr; 503/325-2190) prepares superb hot-smoked and cold-smoked seafood, including salmon, tuna, and sturgeon. Buy fresh seafood at **FERGUS-MCBARENDSE** (at the foot of 11th St; 503/325-0688).

The best meals in town—fresh and vegetarian-oriented, but with plenty of seafood—can be found at the **COLUMBIAN CAFE** (11th St and Marine Dr; 503/325-2233), where chef Uriah Hulsey presides like a prince in his palace; for adventure, try his Chef's Mercy, a surprise pot-pourri of the day's best fixings. The place to go for Sunday brunch and the catch of the day is the **CANNERY CAFE** (at the foot of 6th St; 503/325-8642), which sits on pilings right over the water. The **RIO CAFE** offers inspired south-of-the-border cuisine (125 9th St; 503/325-2409). The Cajun chef at **HOME SPIRIT BAKERY AND CAFE** (in the old Victorian at 1585 Exchange St; 503/325-6846) makes his pastas and ice cream from scratch, and a local forager delivers wild mushrooms and watercress daily. Locals love the new **T. PAUL'S URBAN CAFE** (1119 Commercial St; 503/338-5133) for its big salads and fresh clam chowder.

Bed-and-breakfast inns are plentiful in Astoria. The **BENJAMIN YOUNG INN** (3652 Duane St; 503/325-6172 or 800/201-1286) has five lavishly decorated guest rooms, and stellar views of the Columbia River. The Finnish innkeepers at the **ROSE RIVER INN BED & BREAKFAST** (1510 Franklin Ave; 503/325-7175 or 888/876-0028) lend a European flair to their lodging; ask about the sauna paneled in Alaska yellow cedar. The reasonably priced and rambling **ROSEBRIAR INN** (636 14th St; 503/325-7427) has 11 rooms, each with a private bath.

Astoria is a natural starting point for excursions to the Oregon and Washington coast. You can see panoramic views of both from the **SOUTH JETTY LOOKOUT TOWER**, Oregon's northwesternmost point. **FORT STEVENS STATE PARK**, 20 minutes southwest of Astoria on Highway 101, is a 3,500-acre park offering 604 campsites, 7 miles of bike paths, uncrowded beaches, and **YURTS** (rigid-walled, domed tents) for rent. (The yurts in Oregon state parks have light, heat, and sleep space for eight people. For reservations and information, call Reservations Northwest; 800/452-5687). Walk the beach to see the rusted hulk of the British schooner *Peter Iredale,* wrecked in 1906. Fort Stevens, built at the mouth of the Columbia during the Civil War as part of Oregon's coastal defense, was fired upon in June 1942 by a Japanese submarine. It was the only military fort in the continental United States to see action during that war.

CANNON BEACH TO GARIBALDI

Take Highway 26 west from Portland; Cannon Beach is just south of the intersection with Highway 101. Allow 90 minutes' driving time from Portland.

CANNON BEACH relishes its reputation as the Carmel of the Northwest. This artsy community with a hip ambience has strict building codes that prohibit neon and ensure that only aesthetically pleasing structures of weathered cedar and other woods are built. During the summer the town explodes with visitors who come to browse local galleries and crafts shops or rub shoulders with the coastal intelligentsia on crowded Hemlock Street. Its main draw is the spectacular beach—wide, inviting, and among the prettiest anywhere. Dominating the long, sandy stretch is **HAYSTACK ROCK,** one of the world's largest coastal monoliths. It's impressive enough just to gaze at, but check it out at low tide to observe the rich marine life in the tidal pools.

ECOLA STATE PARK (on the town's north side) has fine overlooks, picnic tables, and good hiking trails. If you climb to Tillamook Head, you can see the Tillamook Rock Light Station, a lighthouse built offshore under difficult conditions more than 100 years ago and abandoned in 1957. Today it is a columbarium (a facility for storing cremated remains) called "Eternity at Sea." No camping is allowed along the trail, except for summer campsites atop the Head.

Shopping is a favorite pastime in Cannon Beach, and there are enough stores along Hemlock Street, the main drag, to keep you busy until the tide goes out. **GALLERIES** are also numerous on N Hemlock. Especially good ones are **WHITE BIRD,** featuring a variety of arts and crafts (503/436-2681); **HAYSTACK GALLERY,** with prints and photographs (503/436-2547); and **JEFFREY HULL WATERCOLORS,** in Sandpiper Square (503/436-2600). **GREAVER GALLERY** (on S Hemlock St; 503/436-1185) has beachy paintings and prints.

The **COASTER THEATER** (108 N Hemlock St; 503/436-1242) presents good summer plays, as well as local and out-of-town shows in the winter. Also, the **HAYSTACK PROGRAM IN THE ARTS** (in Portland; 503/725-8500), offered through Portland State University, conducts workshops for adult students at the Cannon Beach grade school.

There are several good restaurants in town. Reserve for dinner at **THE BISTRO** (263 N Hemlock St; 503/436-2661), which specializes in unpretentious, delicious seafood, or at **KALYPSO** (140 N Hemlock St; 503/436-1585), where meals are inspired by the Mediterranean. For a special treat, drive 15 minutes north to Gearhart, to the excellent **NORTH STAR RESTAURANT AND LOUNGE** (1200 N Marion Ave, Gearhart; 503/738-3370). Everyone visiting Cannon Beach should make time for at least one breakfast at the **MIDTOWN CAFE** (1235 S Hemlock St; 503/436-1016).

There is a confusing array of lodging options in Cannon Beach, but two can't-miss choices are the clean and comfortable **ARGONAUTA INN** (188 W 2nd St; 503/436-2601), which is right on the beach, and the nicely refurbished **CANNON BEACH HOTEL** (116 S Hemlock St; 503/436-1392), which is on the main road through town and three blocks from the beach.

TOLOVANA PARK, nestled on Cannon Beach's south side, is more laid-back and less crowded than its neighbor. Leave your vehicle at the Tolovana Park Wayside (with parking and rest rooms) and stroll the uncluttered beach. At low tide you can walk all the way to Arch Cape, some 5 miles south, but take care: the incoming tide might block your return. The tidy and cute oceanfront **SEA SPRITE GUEST LODGING** (280 Nebesna St; 503/436-2266) has five units. More extravagant is the **STEPHANIE INN** (2740 S Pacific St; 503/436-2221), an elegant 46-room hotel.

Just south of here is **OSWALD WEST STATE PARK**, with one of the finest campgrounds on any coast in the world. You walk a half mile from the parking lot (where wheelbarrows are available to carry your gear) to **TENT SITES** among old-growth trees; the ocean, with a massive cove and tide pools, is just beyond. No reservations, but the walk deters some of the crowds who might otherwise come.

Low-key **MANZANITA** is gaining popularity as a second home for in-the-know Portlanders. The attractions are obvious: the adjacent Nehalem Bay area is a windsurfing mecca, and **NEHALEM BAY STATE PARK**, just south of town, offers hiking and bike trails as well as miles of little-used beaches. Overlooking it all is nearby **NEAHKAHNIE MOUNTAIN**, with a steep, switchbacked trail leading to the 1,600-foot summit, boasting the best viewpoints on Oregon's north coast. Hundreds of miles of Coast Range logging roads offer unlimited mountain-biking thrills. Yurts are available for rent in the park.

Besides a great beach, Manzanita has great food. The sweet **BLUE SKY CAFE** (154 Laneda Ave; 503/368-5712) has a menu that is far-flung and ambitious—and lacks any pretension. Guests usually fill up the eight tables at the **JARBOE'S** (137 Laneda Ave; 503/368-5113), where the offerings are limited but excellent. The best pizza on the north coast can be had at **CASSANDRA'S** (60 Laneda Ave; 503/368-5593). For a pampered, adults-only retreat, try the **INN AT MANZANITA** (67 Laneda Ave; 503/368-6754).

ROCKAWAY BEACH offers little in the way of quaintness, but the beach is splendid, especially at the TWIN ROCKS area south of town.

Several establishments in GARIBALDI sell the area's freshest seafood. MILLER SEAFOOD, on Highway 101 (503/322-0355), is the easiest to find; salmon, lingcod, and bottom fish are featured. SMITH'S PACIFIC SHRIMP CO. (608 Commercial Dr; 503/322-3316) sells fine shrimp and has viewing rooms. And in nearby BAY CITY, ARTSPACE (Hwy 101 and 5th St; 503/377-2782) is a gallery and bistro where oysters are always artistically rendered; or you can make a quick stop at DOWNIE'S CAFE (9320 5th St; 503/377-2220) for a rich, chunks-o'-clam chowder.

TILLAMOOK TO NESKOWIN

From Portland, take Highway 26 west to Highway 6 at Banks. Exit to Highway 6 and follow it to Tillamook. Allow 90 minutes' driving time from Portland.

TILLAMOOK is dairy country par excellence. On the north end of town along Highway 101 sits the home of Tillamook cheese, the TILLAMOOK COUNTY CREAMERY ASSOCIATION (503/842-4481). Loads of tourists come for the self-guided tour and for scoops of rich ice cream in waffle cones. For less kitsch—but no ice cream—you might go about 1 mile south on Highway 101 to the BLUE HERON FRENCH CHEESE COMPANY (2001 Blue Heron Dr; 503/842-8281), where you can sample a variety of cheeses and other Oregon-made specialty foods, and taste wine.

The PIONEER MUSEUM (2nd St and Pacific Ave; 503/842-4553) occupies three floors of the 1905 county courthouse in Tillamook. Shipwreck buffs will be particularly interested in the artifacts (including huge chunks of beeswax with Spanish markings) from an unnamed 18th-century Spanish galleon that wrecked near the base of Neahkahnie Mountain. Adult admission is $2.

MUNSON FALLS NATURAL SITE, Oregon's newest state park, is 7 miles south of Tillamook (turn off Hwy 101 to Munson Creek Rd) and features a 319-foot waterfall (Oregon's second tallest). Traveling south from Tillamook, you have a choice. One option is to stick close to the water, following the 22-mile THREE CAPES SCENIC DRIVE, arguably Oregon's most beautiful stretch of coastline. The narrow, winding road skirts Tillamook Bay, climbs over CAPE MEARES, traverses the shores of Netarts Bay, and runs over CAPE LOOKOUT, the westernmost headland on the north Oregon coast. The trail from the parking lot at the cape's summit meanders through primeval forests of stately cedar and Sitka spruce. The lower side of the drive provides spectacular ocean vistas. Down at sea level, the desertlike dune landscape presents a stark contrast to Cape Lookout's densely forested slopes. The road to PACIFIC CITY and the route's third cape, CAPE KIWANDA, runs through lush, green dairy country. All have excellent camping facilities, and Cape Lookout has yurts as well.

You'll pass through two towns on this route: the first is **OCEANSIDE**. In the evening, slip into **ROSEANNA'S OCEANSIDE CAFE** (1490 Pacific St; 503/842-7351) for a wedge of Toll House pie topped with Tillamook ice cream, then roll into one of the 17 rooms at the **HOUSE ON THE HILL** (1816 Maxwell Mountain Rd, on Maxwell Point; 503/842-6030).

About 20 miles south of Oceanside, the dory fleet comes home to **PACIFIC CITY**, where salmon-fishing boats are launched from trailers in the south lee of Cape Kiwanda. This town is also known for another kind of fleet: hang gliders that swoop off the slopes of the cape and land on the sandy expanses below. The region's second Haystack Rock (Cannon Beach has the other) sits a half mile offshore. Even if you've never visited before, this area may look familiar: the late Ray Atkeson, a nationally acclaimed Oregon photographer, made Cape Kiwanda the most photographed spot on the Oregon Coast. **ROBERT STRAUB STATE PARK** sits at the south end of town and occupies most of the Nestucca Beach sand spit. The Nestucca River flows idly to the sea right outside the **RIVERHOUSE RESTAURANT** (34450 Brooten Rd; 503/965-6722), a calming, apple-pie sort of place. Gargantuan cinnamon rolls and loaves of crusty bread can be had nearby at the **GRATEFUL BREAD BAKERY** (34805 Brooten Rd; 503/965-7337). At the secluded **EAGLE'S VIEW BED AND BREAKFAST** (37975 Brooten Rd; 503/965-7600), all five guest rooms have private baths. As you might guess, the panoramas are grand.

If you decide to forgo the Three Capes Scenic Drive, Highway 101 will steer you from Tillamook through Nestucca dairy land, some of the most fertile in the state. Nestled in the heart of the Nestucca River valley is **CLOVERDALE**, the town that became famous for a 1986–87 battle with state officials over two roadside signs (featuring Clover the Cow) that violated a state signage law. Outside Cloverdale, in the middle of nowhere, is the historic 1906 **HUDSON HOUSE BED & BREAKFAST** (37700 Hwy 101 S; 503/392-3533). Just south, in the diminutive town of **NESKOWIN** (the final port of refuge before the touristy 20-mile stretch from Lincoln City to Newport), stands **THE CHELAN** (48750 Breakers Blvd; 503/392-3270), attractive, substantial, cream-colored adobe condominiums right on the beach.

OTIS is barely more than a junction, but the busy **OTIS CAFE** (you can't miss it; 541/994-2813) and its down-home breakfasts, shakes, and homemade pies—good enough to have been touted in *The New York Times*—have put this tiny town on the map.

LINCOLN CITY TO CAPE FOULWEATHER

Take Highway 99W (Barbur Blvd) from Southwest Portland, and follow it through the Portland suburbs to Yamhill County. Pass through Newberg and Dundee. For the most expedient trip, take the Highway 18 bypass around McMinnville, then continue to Lincoln City. Allow 2 hours from Portland.

If local business owners have their way, **LINCOLN CITY** may someday have a more "beachlike"—thus more tourist-friendly—name. Most locals seem happy with the name as is, though, and it hasn't stopped hordes of Willamette Valley residents from converging on Lincoln City year-round. Whale-watchers appreciate the nearby viewpoints, shoppers hunt for bargains at the huge **OUTLET MALL** on the east side of Highway 101, and others simply pass through before dispersing to quieter points north and south. This is a good place to pop in your favorite tape—the congestion all the way south to Newport may slow you down a bit.

Lincoln City offers little in the way of outstanding lodgings, although the scene is slightly improved over years past. The upscale, oceanfront **O'DYSIUS HOTEL** (120 NW Inlet Ct; 541/994-4121 or 800/869-8069) contains 30 sizable units outfitted with such amenities as fireplaces, whirlpool baths, and down comforters. Consistently the finest place to dine is **BAY HOUSE** (5911 SW Hwy 101; 541/996-3222), where the food, like the view, is worth savoring. The **BLACKFISH CAFE'S** (2733 NW Hwy 101; 541/996-1007) bustling open kitchen turns out exemplary clam chowder—and much more. At the hip **CHAMELEON CAFE** (in new digs at 2185 NW Hwy 101; 541/994-8422), you can go Mexican or Mediterranean—depending on your mood. Part deli, part bistro, the **SALMON RIVER CAFE** (4079B NW Logan Rd; 541/996-3663) features three inspired meals a day. At the **LIGHTHOUSE BREW PUB** (4157 N Hwy 101; 541/994-7238), expect the same pub grub as at any McMenamins establishment—and beer made on the premises. Two good stops are **BARNACLE BILL'S SEAFOOD MARKET** (2174 NE Hwy 101; 541/994-3022), famous for smoked fish—salmon, sturgeon, albacore, and black cod—and fresh seafood, and **CATCH THE WIND KITE SHOP** (266 SE Hwy 101; 541/994-9500), the headquarters for a coastal chain of excellent kite stores.

GLENEDEN BEACH is home to the innovative restaurant **CHEZ JEANNETTE** (7150 Old Hwy 101; 541/764-3434), where flower boxes decorate the windows and whitewashed brick walls lend a French country inn ambience. The buildings at **SALISHAN LODGE** (7760 N Hwy 101; 800/452-2300)—perhaps the coast's best-known resort—blend well with natural landscaping that lessens the visual impact on the hillside. The beach, a half mile away, is a splendid strand of driftwood and gulls. A standard of excellence is adhered to throughout the resort.

Once a charming coastal community, **DEPOE BAY** today is mostly an extension of Lincoln City's strip development. Driving south down Highway 101, it's hard to tell where one community ends and the other begins. Fortunately, some of the original Depoe Bay, including its tiny harbor, remains intact. During the **GRAY WHALE MIGRATORY SEASON** (December through April), the leviathans cruise within hailing distance of the headlands. In the week between Christmas and New Year's, and then again during Oregon schools' spring break, knowledgeable volunteers from the Hatfield Marine Science Center in Newport staff 23 **VIEWING SITES** along the coast, answering whale-related questions and sharing binoculars. To get closer to the action, consider a **WHALE-WATCHING CRUISE**; Zodiac Adventures, Inc. (800/571-6463) is one of several operations offering trips. Zodiac charges $30 for the 90-minute tour. Another place to watch whales is from your nicely appointed room at the **CHANNEL HOUSE** (35 Ellingson St; 800/447-2140), a small, neat inn perched right on the rocks. Breakfast is included with your room, but for lunch or dinner, you'll want to check out **TIDAL RAVES** (279 NW Hwy 101; 541/765-2995), a cliffside restaurant that serves imaginatively prepared seafood.

CAPE FOULWEATHER (at Milepost 131.5), christened by famed British explorer Captain James Cook when he sailed by in 1778, is aptly named: fog often enshrouds it, even though sunny skies may appear just to the north and south. Reach the cape by the Otter Crest Loop, 2 miles south of Depoe Bay. The 500-foot cliff is an inspiring viewpoint for watching birds, sea lions, and surf. Adjoining it is the **LOOKOUT GIFT SHOP AND OBSERVATORY** (541/765-2270), a rarity: its gifts are carefully selected items from craftspeople around the world. On the Otter Crest Loop, in a 100-acre parklike setting, is the **INN AT OTTER CREST** (541/765-2111), with exquisite, lush landscaping (including marine tidal gardens) and adequate condominium resort facilities.

NEWPORT

Allow 1 hour to drive south from Lincoln City to Newport on Highway 101.

The 1998 departure of Keiko, the rescued whale star of the *Free Willy* movies, was a triumph for the activists who worked to reintroduce him to his native Iceland waters. For the folks on the central Oregon coast, the orca's departure marked the end of a titanic tourist boom. **NEWPORT** has taken the transition in stride by investing heavily in projects to help it remain worthy of the worldwide attention it received during Keiko's tenure.

The **OREGON COAST AQUARIUM** (2820 SE Ferry Slip Rd; 541/867-3474) has transformed Keiko's pool to a $6.9 million exhibit called "Passages of the Deep." Visitors walk through a 200-foot underwater tunnel suspended in a simulated ocean, and are armed with a printed species

SAVING OPAL CREEK, OREGON STYLE

What do environmentalists, a Republican senator, a mining company, loggers, a high-tech billionaire, and the Forest Service have in common? Apparently, these unlikely allies are pleased with the outcome of the long struggle over the fate of Opal Creek, an old-growth forest east of Salem.

The fight to save one of the nation's last pristine watersheds goes back to the mid-1970s and at times reached custody-battle levels of drama rivaling the spotted owl controversy. Along the way, Mark Hatfield pushed conservation legislation through the U.S. Senate at the end of his illustrious career, activists gave thousands of hours, computer mogul Paul Allen kicked in a cool $1.5 million, and logging communities accepted a promise of $10 million to replace lost timber revenues. The 1998 prize: a 34,132-acre Wilderness and Scenic Recreation Area designation for Opal Creek's centuries-old woodlands. Friends of Opal Creek now use the land to educate students on the value of old-growth forests and practice "sustained activism" to make sure the designation sticks.

A mountain bike is a great way to cover the 3 miles from the gate up to the quaint mining town of Jawbone Flat, where the trail begins (the way back is all downhill). Anyone there can point out the spot where a white water pipe marks the trailhead, across the Battle Ax Creek bridge and up a lane to the right. From there, it's about 3 miles on an unauthorized but well-traveled trail to the cedar grove, which has trees up to 250 feet high and 1,000 years old. Here the trail fades, requiring cross-country travel on steep terrain. The hiking is predictably rigorous in spots; practically the only old growth left is in places that are difficult to log. It's 13-plus miles for the round-trip hike; start early, bring a lunch, and dawdle in the forests. Help the Friends of Opal Creek, who are working to keep the area from being "loved to death"—tread lightly.

A two-hour drive from Portland, Opal Creek is 36 miles east of Salem via progressively more primitive roads. To get to Opal Creek, drive south from Portland on I-5, take the North Santiam Highway exit (Oregon Hwy 22), and drive east for about 25 miles. At a flashing yellow light between the state forestry department and the Swiss Village Restaurant (look for the Elkhorn Recreation Area sign), turn left and drive 21 miles due north up the Little North Fork Santiam River. When you cross the national forest boundary, the Little North Fork Road becomes Forest Service Road 2207. At the only major fork in the road, bear left on Forest Service Road 2209. Watch for deer as the road surface deteriorates into rutted dirt. Park at the gate; chances are good that you'll have lots of company.   —*Jennifer Jane Sargent*

guide to help them identify the live sharks, bat rays, and hundreds of fish they meet eye-to-eye. The exhibit includes nice touches such as swaying kelp and a glass floor (so it seems you're walking on water), and is more lively—if less famous—than its predecessor. The aquarium's 39-acre site is world class, with a walk-through aviary, a sea otter pool, and a wetlands area. Admission is $9.25 for adults and $4.75 for children 4 to 13.

Nearby, the newly refurbished **HATFIELD MARINE SCIENCE CENTER** (2030 SE Marine Science Dr; 541/867-0100) features a replica of a tide pool, educational programs, and a full range of free nature walks, field trips, and films, especially during the summer Seatauqua program; admission is by donation. **MARINE DISCOVERY TOURS** (541/265-6200) has a privately owned 48-passenger vessel that operates as a floating classroom. You can sign up for eco-tours that vary from scouting oyster beds to marine bird-watching and ocean exploration.

Several boat operators will take you closer to the maritime action. Most **FISHING CHARTERS** provide bait and tackle, clean and fillet your catch, and even smoke or can it for you. Many operators have initiated whale-watching excursions as well as half- and full-day fishing trips. **SEA GULL CHARTERS** (343 SW Bay Blvd; 541/265-7441) and **NEWPORT SPORT FISHING** (1000 SE Bay Blvd; 541/265-7558 or 800/828-8777) are two popular operators; expect to pay $16 to $20 for a two-hour whale-watching tour, and $50 to $100 for a day of fishing.

Newport's thriving arts community is perhaps the biggest on the coast. The **NEWPORT PERFORMING ARTS CENTER** (777 W Olive; 541/265-2787) is an attractive wooden structure that hosts music, theater, and other events, some of national caliber. The **VISUAL ARTS CENTER** (839 NW Beach; 541/265-6540) offers an oceanfront setting for exhibits and classes. **YAQUINA ARTS CENTER** next door (541/265-5133) showcases arts and crafts. Worthwhile **GALLERIES** on SW Bay Boulevard along the waterfront include the **OCEANIC ARTS CENTER** (444 SW Bay Blvd; 541/265-5963) and the **WOOD GALLERY** (818 SW Bay Blvd; 541/265-6843). The former offers mostly jewelry, paintings, pottery, and sculpture; the latter, functional sculpture, woodwork, pottery, and weaving.

For cheap thrills, veer off Highway 101's commercial strip and seek out the **BAY FRONT**, where fishing boats of all types—trollers, trawlers, shrimpers, and crabbers—berth year-round. Nearby, take a drive out on the **SOUTH JETTY ROAD** for sea-level views of harbor traffic. A walk through the congenial Nye Beach area offers glimpses of the old and new in Newport, a potpourri of Newport's professionals, tourists, writers, and fishermen. For a bird's-eye perspective of boats, bay, and ocean, take a drive through **YAQUINA BAY STATE PARK**, which wraps around the south end of town.

On a sunny day, request an outdoor table overlooking the bay at the **CANYON WAY BOOKSTORE AND RESTAURANT** (1216 SW Canyon Wy; 541/265-8319). Another longtime favorite is the **WHALE'S TALE** (452 SW Bay Blvd; 541/265-8660), where you can try a fresh jalapeño omelet or a plate of Yaquina oysters.

Even though there are a number of places to stay in Newport, you won't want to drop into town without a reservation. For maximum quaintness, check out the **SYLVIA BEACH HOTEL** (267 NW Cliff St; 541/265-5428), a nearly century-old hotel that for the last 15 years or so has enjoyed what must be its happiest and most imaginative incarnation: each room is decorated to commemorate a different author. Book lovers also appreciate the Sylvia Beach's dramatic bluff-top location and delicious family-style breakfasts. Next door, the newer **NYE BEACH HOTEL & CAFE** (219 NW Cliff St; 541/265-3334) has 18 tidy guest rooms that each feature private bath, fireplace, willow loveseat, balcony, and ocean view.

Champoeg–Aurora

About 30 miles south of Portland, off Interstate 5, near the Willamette River; watch for signs. Aurora is nearby but on the east side of Interstate 5.

The road to **CHAMPOEG** (pronounced "shampooey"), off Interstate 5 south of Portland, winds through amber farm fields with green patches of fir and oak forests, past browsing cattle and horses, and leads to some of the state's most significant historic sites. Champoeg was the home of the Calapooya Indians before fur traders and settlers arrived in the early 1800s. In 1843, settlers here voted to form the first provisional government of the Oregon Country. Now the **CHAMPOEG STATE HERITAGE** **AREA** is a 568-acre park on the Willamette River. For a $3 per vehicle fee, picnickers, kids on bikes, Frisbee throwers, and volleyball players enjoy the park on summer weekends. The excellent **VISITORS CENTER** (8239 Champoeg Rd NE, St. Paul; 503/678-1251) tells of Champoeg's role in Oregon's history. The **MOTHER'S PIONEER CABIN** (open Monday, Friday, and Saturday) is run by the Daughters of the American Revolution. There, visitors can admire an authentic log cabin and kids can knead bread dough, card wool, and make fires using flint and steel just as pioneer children did. Admission is $2 for adults, $1 for children.

Just west of the park entrance is the **NEWELL HOUSE** (503/678-5537), a replica of the 1852 original, which serves as a museum of Native American and pioneer artifacts. On the grounds are the Butteville Jail (1850) and a pioneer schoolhouse. Call for hours (closed November through February). Admission is $2 for adults, $1 for children 11 and under.

The town of **AURORA**, midway between Portland and Salem on the east bank of the Willamette, is a well-preserved turn-of-the-century village that's been put on the National Register of Historic Places. It's also a well-known antique center. Two dozen or so clapboard and Victorian houses line a mile-long stretch of Highway 99E, and more than half of them have been made into antique shops (most are closed Mondays). The town is fortunate to have as its only restaurant the popular **CHEZ MOUSTACHE** (21527 Hwy 99E; 503/678-1866), which has for many years served French Continental cuisine.

In 1856 a Prussian immigrant, Dr. William Keil, led a group of Pennsylvania Germans here to establish a **COMMUNAL SETTLEMENT** of Harmonites (Aurora is named for his daughter). Property, labor, and profits were shared, and the society prospered under his autocratic rule. Farming sustained the economy, but outsiders knew the colony for the excellence of its handicrafts: furniture, clothing, tools, embroidered goods, baskets, and clarinet reeds. After a smallpox epidemic in 1862 and the coming of the railroad in 1870, the colony gradually weakened.

The **OLD AURORA COLONY MUSEUM** (503/678-5754), at the corner of Second Avenue and Liberty Street, recounts the history of the town with five buildings: the ox barn, the Karus home, the Steinbach log cabin, the communal washhouse, and the farm equipment shed. Among the museum's annual events, Colony Days in August and a quilt show in October are standouts. (Open different days depending on the season; call ahead.) Admission is $3.50 for adults, $1.50 for children ages 6 to 18. Group tours are available by prior arrangement.

McMinnville and Vicinity

Take Hwy 99W from Southwest Portland; follow it through the Portland suburbs of Tigard and King City to Yamhill County. Allow 1 hour driving time to McMinnville.

To explore **MCMINNVILLE** and surrounding **YAMHILL COUNTY** is to partake in a banquet for all the senses. Hillsides are painted with the seasonal brights of deciduous trees, the local wineries are redolent with fermenting grapes, and fruit stands along Highway 99W beckon with perfectly ripened produce. For food lovers especially, this region is bliss.

There are cultural riches here as well. The town of McMinnville—like the Oregon Trail that brought the early white settlers to this region—celebrated its 150-year anniversary in 1993. Best known as a farm center and the home of **LINFIELD COLLEGE**, a liberal arts college that's been there almost as long as the town that surrounds it, McMinnville also has a historic hub, known as the **DOWNTOWN HISTORIC DISTRICT**. Pick up a walking-tour map at the Chamber of Commerce (417 NW Adams; 503/472-6196); it points out many late-19th-century and early 20th-century buildings of interest up and down Third Street.

If the folks at the soon-to-open **EVERGREEN AVIATION EDUCATIONAL INSTITUTE** (on the Hwy 18 bypass at McMinnville airport; 503/472-9361) have their way, you will equate **HOWARD HUGHES' SPRUCE GOOSE** with the Portland/McMinnville area. The *Spruce Goose* is the largest aircraft in the world and was built to carry 750 men into World War II battle. The plane has a 335-foot wingspan and took so long to build that the war ended before the plane was completed. The institute will have a '40s-style cafe, a movie theater, and 40 other planes on display. (And no, you won't be able to step into the *Spruce Goose*; it's for viewing only.)

Reserve in advance a table at the popular, quarter-century-old **NICK'S ITALIAN CAFE** (521 E 3rd St; 503/434-4471), where both à la carte meals and marvelous five-course dinners are served in a convivial atmosphere. Nick's minestrone soup is the only menu item served every night—ask about the scrumptious salt-grilled salmon. Another possibility is **KAME** (228 N Evans St; 503/434-4326), a local favorite for simple, savory Japanese food.

The **GOLDEN VALLEY BREWERY AND PUB** (980 E 4th St; 503/472-1921) prides itself on its recent major remodel, including a crowd-pleasing 100-item menu of burgers, gourmet pizza, ribs, Northwest fish, salads, and homemade sausages. The full bar includes British-style brews and homemade Oregon wines. The **HOTEL OREGON** (310 NE Evans St; 888/472-8427), in recent years refurbished and run by the McMenamin brothers of brewpub fame, is a great place to stay, whether you're going on the cheap or splurging.

Beyond McMinnville, about 10 minutes by car along Highway 18, is Bellevue, home of a couple of art galleries, including the thriving **LAWRENCE GALLERY** (503/843-3633; www.lawrencegallery.net), with an outdoor garden where you are welcome to picnic among the sculptures (and buy one if you'd like). Inside, paintings, jewelry, prints, and pottery are among the fine works by some 200 artists. The **OREGON WINE TASTING ROOM** (503/843-3787) is also here. This facility may be the only place in the state where you can sample under one roof wines from more than 50 different Oregon wineries—with an impressive and long roster of Oregon pinot noirs. Put your new wine knowledge to good use as you order lunch at **FRESH PALATE** (503/843-4400), above the gallery. Eating on the deck feels like dining in the treetops; Northwest cuisine, crab cakes, and sandwiches are all made from scratch. Another gallery of note nearby is **FIRE'S EYE** (19915 SW Muddy Valley Rd; 503/843-9797), where the art is well chosen and adventurous.

For those who yearn to see the Yamhill Valley from the air, Vista Balloon Adventures (503/625-7385) offers daily, dawn-departure **HOT-AIR BALLOON RIDES**. The tickets ($179 per person, $160 per person with a group of four) include one hour of flying over wine country, from just above the trees to 3,000 feet, and a fussy postflight fête that includes lunch and glasses of the local favorite, Argyle sparkling wine.

Wine Country

Yamhill County is home to several wineries and small towns. Allow a day to see it properly; you can drive on Highway 99W from Southwest Portland.

Oregon's rolling hills—with their with good sunlight exposure, soil composition, and drainage—are choice locations for vineyards. Winemakers are at work in Oregon as far south as Ashland and as far east as Milton-Freewater, but the majority are clustered west and southwest of Portland in the northern Willamette Valley. Once best known for its hazelnut and prune crops, the state nowadays boasts some of the finest vineyards on the West Coast and has a growing international reputation for **PINOT NOIR** and **PINOT GRIS**.

The wineries themselves are delightful to visit for those with even a passing interest in wine. In all seasons, there is much to take in, from misty hills reminiscent of a Japanese woodcut to flaming fall colors to the harvesting of the small, intensely flavored grapes. Almost all have tasting rooms staffed by either winery owners or workers with intimate knowledge of the wines and production methods. Facility tours are often available—to be sure, you may want to call ahead. And, of course, there are the wines to sample, which may include vintages not available elsewhere or small lots from grapes in scarce supply. Do take along bread, cheese, and other wine-friendly foods to enjoy. Calling in advance is always recommended; some wineries close for the month of January.

Start your wine tour by making a dinner reservation at tiny **TINA'S** (503/538-8880), along 99W in Dundee, or at **RED HILLS PROVINCIAL DINING** (503/538-8224)—both are excellent, creative restaurants. The newer and much celebrated **JOEL PALMER HOUSE** (600 Ferry St, Dayton; 503/864-2995)—also a superb choice—is making a name for itself with one key ingredient: mushrooms. (See reviews in the Restaurants chapter.)

Once dinner is arranged, just enjoy the ride along Highway 99W— the state's official wine road. Local produce stands still dot the roadside in summer, and the wineries, antique shops, and galleries (see McMinnville and Vicinity in this chapter) will give you many options to follow your whims as you pass through these lush green hills. In Lafayette, drop into the former **LAFAYETTE SCHOOLHOUSE** (503/864-2720), now a 100-dealer antique mall.

Here are some notable wineries along 99W: just out of Portland, **REX HILL VINEYARDS** (30835 N Hwy 99W, Newberg; 503/538-0666) has produced a number of vineyard-designated pinot noirs that received critical attention. Its location is splendid, with perennials in bloom even when the grapevines are not, making this one of the state's best visitor

EXPLORING LOCAL WINERIES
OUTSIDE YAMHILL COUNTY

WEST OF PORTLAND: There are several wineries due west of Portland worth visiting, so pack a picnic and head to the Tualatin Valley for a good day trip. **Ponzi Vineyards** (14665 SW Winery Lane, Beaverton; 503/628-1227) was designed by Richard Ponzi with striking results. His bottlings (especially pinot noir, pinot gris, and dry riesling) are first-rate. Open every day; call ahead. **Oak Knoll Winery** (29700 SW Burkhalter Rd, Hillsboro; 503/648-8198) is one of Oregon's oldest and largest producers, famous for fruit and berry wines, plus award-winning pinot noir and riesling. Great picnic grounds; open daily. The beautifully reconstructed facilities at **Laurel Ridge Winery** (46350 NW David Hill Rd, Forest Grove; 503/359-5436) are open daily (closed in January). Taste their excellent sparkling wine and good gewürztraminer and riesling on the site first chosen by a German winemaking family in the 1800s.

SALEM AREA: Salem, the state capital, lies just shy of an hour south of Portland. North and west of Salem are several of the newer vineyards and wineries. While a few are still developing their drop-in tasting trade, there are a couple that welcome visitors: **Bethel Heights Vineyards** (6060 Bethel Heights Rd NW, Salem; 503/581-2262) has a lovely location and a tasting room that commands an incredible view. Its wines have won several awards; try the pinot noir, chenin blanc, and riesling. Hours vary throughout the year; call ahead to confirm tasting hours. **Cristom** (6905 Spring Valley Rd NW, Salem; 503/375-3068), around the corner from Bethel Heights, also makes a noteworthy pinot noir; call for hours. **Schwarzenberg Vineyards** (11975 Smithfield Rd, Dallas; 503/623-6420) is noted not only for its pinot noir and chardonnay but also for its setting near a wildlife preserve. Open weekends only.

facilities. The tasting room is open daily from February through December. In **DUNDEE**, you can't miss the tasting room of **ARGYLE** (691 Hwy 99W, Dundee; 503/538-8520), which is producing some of the best sparkling wines in the region as well as fine dry riesling. **ERATH VINEYARDS WINERY** (9409 NE Worden Hill Rd, Dundee; 503/538-3318) is one of the pioneer Oregon wineries, noted for wonderful pinot noirs. Dick Erath doesn't look or act anything like a stereotypical winemaker, and his successful (and good-value) wines seem to prove that doesn't matter. His winery is in a beautiful setting, just up the hill from Crabtree Park (good for picnics). **SOKOL BLOSSER** (5000 Sokol Blosser Ln, Dundee; 503/864-2282) is one of Oregon's more commercially successful wineries. High on a hill overlooking the Yamhill Valley, **CHATEAU BENOIT WINERY** (6580 NE Mineral Springs Rd, Carlton; 503/864-2991) is best known for its sparkling wines and sauvignon blanc. Open year-round, this facility has an astonishing view.

A number of wineries are open to the public only on Thanksgiving and Memorial Day weekends. **THE EYRIE VINEYARDS** (503/472-6315), **ADELSHEIM VINEYARD** (503/538-3652), **ST. INNOCENT** (503/378-1526), **KEN WRIGHT CELLARS** (503/852-7070), and **PANTHER CREEK CELLARS** (503/472-8080) all make killer pinot noir, and most offer case discounts over the holiday weekends. (Call for hours and directions.)

Mount St. Helens National Volcanic Monument

Allow 1 hour for the drive north from Portland on I-5. Driving directions for each part of the monument are given below.

The flat-topped **MOUNT ST. HELENS**, about an hour's drive north of Portland and east of I-5, enthralls visitors. On a clear day it is well worth the trip to see the 8,365-foot remains of the volcano, as well as the vegetation that's sprouted since St. Helens' incredible eruption of May 18, 1980 (it's 1,300 feet shorter than before the blast). There are two areas to explore, and each is reached by a different highway. One area is the south and east sides of the volcano, where climbers ascend and where there are caves to brave; and the other is the west side, where a string of visitors centers educate about the blast and the area's regrowth. All visitors must display a **MONUMENT PASS** at developed recreation sites; these passes are $8 per person for three days ($4 for seniors, free for children under 15) and can be purchased at visitors centers and information stations throughout the area.

SOUTH AND EAST SIDES

Follow I-5 north about 25 minutes from Portland and take the Woodland exit. Travel east on Highway 503, but before leaving Woodland, check out the map at the visitors center; the St. Helens area has a confusing range of attractions, and it may help to orient yourself at the beginning of your trip.

There are two possibilities for spelunking at the **APE CAVES** on Forest Service Road 8303, an hour from Woodland: the moderately difficult lower cave, which is three-quarters of a mile long, and the more challenging 1½-mile-long upper cave. This lava tube, the longest in the continental United States, was formed 1,900 years ago in a St. Helens blast. Rent lanterns and gather more information at the **APES HEADQUARTERS**, open daily from mid-May until the end of September. For a dramatic view of a vast pumice plain, travel east another hour and 45 minutes to the **WINDY RIDGE VIEW-POINT**, situated within 4 miles of the volcano.

For information on **CLIMBING** St. Helens, call the **CLIMBING INFOR-MATION LINE** (360/247-3961). You'll need to buy a $15 climbing permit—a few are available on a daily basis, but it's best to reserve in advance. Most climbers take one of two trails (Butte Camp or Monitor Ridge) up the south face—more of a rugged hike than real alpine climbing, but an ice ax is still recommended. The all-day climb (8 miles round trip) is ideal for novice alpinists; the only big dangers are some loose-rock cliffs and the unstable edge around the crater. In winter you can ski down.

WEST SIDE

Follow I-5 north about 40 minutes from Portland, take the Castle Rock exit, and go east on the Spirit Lake Memorial Highway (Highway 504).

Just off the freeway, before you begin the ascent to the ridge, you can see the 25-minute Academy Award–nominated *The Eruption of Mount Saint Helens* projected on the **CINEDOME'S** (360/274-8000) three-story-high, 55-foot-wide screen. The rumble alone, which rattles your theater seat, is worth the $6 admission (less for children). About 5 miles east of I-5, on your way up to the volcano, sits the oldest of the visitors centers in the Mount St. Helens area, the wood-and-glass center at **SILVER LAKE** (360/274-2100). Built shortly after the eruption, this center commemorates the blast with excellent exhibits, a walk-through volcano, hundreds of historical and modern photos, geological and anthropological surveys, and a film documenting the area's destruction and rebirth.

The second visitors center, complete with cafe, gift shop, and bookstore, sits atop the windswept **COLDWATER RIDGE**, some 38 miles west (360/274-2131). It's a multimillion-dollar facility with a million-dollar view—of the crater just to the west, the debris-filled valley of the Toutle River's North Fork, and new lakes formed by massive mudslides. The speed and heat of the blast, estimated at 600 miles per hour and up to 500 degrees in temperature, scalped at least 150,000 acres surrounding the mountain. The Coldwater Ridge center focuses on the astounding biological recovery of the landscape. From the visitors center, you can descend the short distance to Coldwater Lake—where there is a picnic area and boat launch—or take a guided interpretive walk.

The **JOHNSTON RIDGE OBSERVATORY** (360/274-2140) is located at the end of Spirit Lake Memorial Highway, about 8 miles beyond Coldwater Ridge. (Call to be sure the facility is open; it closes in winter.) This futuristic-looking structure, within 5 miles of the crater, offers the best views of the steaming lava dome inside the crater—unless, of course, you climb the volcano.

Two visitors centers can be visited without the Monument Pass: Cowlitz County's **HOFFSTADT BLUFF** center (milepost 27 on Spirit Lake Memorial Highway; 360/274-7750), which explores the lives and deaths of those most directly affected by the blast, and Weyerhaeuser's **FOREST LEARNING CENTER** (at milepost 33.5; 360/414-3439), which focuses on the land's recovery in the wake of the eruption.

Every gift store along the way offers something of interest besides tourist trinkets: the family that owns **19 MILE HOUSE** in Kid Valley (360/274-8779) serves some of the best fresh fruit cobblers you'll ever eat—the owners claim rhubarb converts worldwide. Around the corner you'll get a look at Blair Barner's **MUD-FILLED A-FRAME**; he calls his business—helicopter rides and a souvenir shop featuring on-site glass blowers—North Fork Survivors (360/274-6789). No fancy hotels yet, but Mark Smith's **"TENT AND BREAKFAST"** in the blowdown area is a real kick, and we give it four stars—as will families looking for fun lodgings. You sleep in roomy Beckel wall tents, with a chuck-wagon dinner and breakfast beside the lake ($150 per person, $285 per couple; Mount St. Helens Adventure Tours, 360/274-6542). Smith provides fishing gear, cedar-strip canoes, fishing permits, van tours, cross-country ski trips, and guided hunting trips. The friendly proprietors at **VOLCANO VIEW MOUNTAIN BIKE TOURS** (360/274-4341) will outfit you with a bike and take you on a tour of some of the lesser-traveled areas around St. Helens—lunch included.

RECREATION

RECREATION

Outdoor Activities

Portland is one city whose citizens really can have it all. Large enough to have outstanding restaurants and a lively arts scene, the city still manages to maintain a connection to its beautiful natural setting. Proud and protective of their parks and greenspaces, Portlanders are never more than a few minutes away from a quick getaway to go bird-watching, kayaking, or cycling. A little farther afield, they have the magnificent scenery of the Pacific coast and the snowy slopes of Mount Hood. As the city continues to grow and freeways clog with newcomers and old-timers alike, harried drivers at least know that where the traffic jams end, the fun begins.

OUTDOOR RECREATION, published three times a year by Portland Parks and Recreation (1120 SW 5th Ave, Rm 1302; 503/823-5132; www.parks.ci.portland.or.us; map:F3), is a comprehensive guide to seasonal recreation programs. There is something in it for everyone: from cross-country ski trips, fly-fishing, and whale watching in winter to hiking, paddling, biking, tot walks, and historic bridge tours in summer. Pick it up free at libraries and outdoor stores. **METRO GREENSCENE,** another triannual guide to the great outdoors, focuses on wildlife habitats (call Metro to receive a copy; 503/797-1850).

BICYCLING

In recent years, *Bicycling* magazine has twice rated the City of Roses the most bike-friendly city in the country. Why? The diverse topography—flat and breezy stretches on the east side, steep and breathless hills on the west—has something for every cyclist, and many streets have bike lanes. In Portland, a lot of people bike to work, and urban messengers work on bikes, as do some of the neighborhood police patrols. Want to know the quickest and safest bike route to your destination? Grab a copy of the map "Bike There," published by Metro and available at area cycle shops ($6) and at Powell's Travel Store (in the southeast corner of Pioneer Courthouse Square, SW 6th Ave and Yamhill St; 503/228-1108; map:H4). You can take your bike on any Tri-Met bus or MAX train if you purchase a permanent $5 pass, available at the Tri-Met office in Pioneer Courthouse Square (503/238-7433). Buses and trains are outfitted with racks to make the going easy.

Cyclists looking for organized 30- to 100-mile rides at a touring pace should call the **PORTLAND WHEELMEN TOURING CLUB** hotline (503/257-7982). As many as 120 people show up for group and nongroup rides—several each week and at least one nearly every day of the year—and you don't have to be a member to pedal along. The **BEAVERTON**

BICYCLE CLUB (503/649-4632), which sponsors road, track, and criterium events, has a strong group of junior riders but no age limit. The **OREGON BICYCLE RACING ASSOCIATION** (OBRA) acts as a clearinghouse for race information for the 23 competitive clubs in Oregon. Call the OBRA hotline for event information (503/661-0686; www.obra.org). From May to mid-September, races are held at **PORTLAND INTERNATIONAL RACEWAY** (West Delta Park; 503/823-RACE; map:DD7) on Tuesday nights—women and masters on alternate Mondays—and at the **ALPENROSE DAIRY VELODROME** on Thursday nights (6149 SW Shattuck Rd, 503/244-1133; map:II8). The velodrome is the second shortest in the country (hence heroically steep) and is situated next to a working dairy farm. Admission is free for spectators. Classes are offered on Wednesdays, and fixed-gear bikes are available to rent.

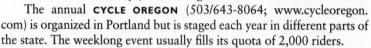

The annual **CYCLE OREGON** (503/643-8064; www.cycleoregon.com) is organized in Portland but is staged each year in different parts of the state. The weeklong event usually fills its quota of 2,000 riders.

In the interest of protecting environmentally sensitive areas, **MOUNTAIN BIKING** is restricted to a handful of marked trails in the metropolitan region, but the available choices are well managed and rewarding. Mountain bike trail maps are available from **PORTLAND PARKS AND RECREATION** (1120 SW 5th Ave, Rm 1302; 503/823-5132) for Forest Park, Powell Butte, and the Springwater Corridor. Fat-tire cyclists looking for like minds can call PUMP (**PORTLAND UNITED MOUNTAIN PEDALERS**, 503/357-7558), whose motto is "Mountain biking is not a crime," for information on organized year-round weekend rides or to be put on a mailing list for their newsletter (see also the Leif Erikson Drive listing). The **BIKE GALLERY** (1001 SW Salmon St; 503/222-3821; map:G2; and 5329 NE Sandy Blvd; 503/281-9800; map:FF4) organizes free Wednesday-night rides during the warm months and weekend rides throughout the year. Usually beginner or intermediate mountain bike rides fill the program, but some road rides are also organized. WAM (**WOMEN'S ASSOCIATION OF MOUNTAIN BIKERS**, 503/829-8487) stages Tuesday night rides in Forest Park during the summer and weekend rides throughout the year. Men are welcome on some of the rides.

Although one avid **CYCLOCROSS** racer has described that sport as "ballet on wheels," a less biased observer might see it as a mud festival for people who just can't get off their bikes—even for a few months each year. (Cylocross first gained popularity in Europe, as a means of breaking up the winter doldrums between racing seasons.) There are six or so races in the annual **FAT TIRE FARM CROSS CRUSADE,** which runs early October through December. A typical cyclocross course includes paved roads, gravel, and single-track trails and takes riders through mud bogs, over barriers, down sharp slopes, and up steep, short hills. Racers spend about 30 percent of the race running with their bikes slung by their sides or over their shoulders. Interest in the sport has grown remarkably over the past five years; more than 200 racers, and an equal number of spectators, show up, rain or shine. For race information, contact Fat Tire Farm Mountain Bike Company (2714 NW Thurman St; 503/222-3276; map:GG7).

The following are a few favorite mountain and road bike routes in the area. For more rides and details, ask the resident experts at a local bike shop or pick up a copy of *Bicycling the Back Roads of Northwest Oregon* by Philip N. Jones or *Rubber to the Road* by Peter Marsh.

BANKS/VERNONIA STATE PARK / 25 miles west of Portland on US 26 to the Manning trailhead; 503/324-0606 An old railroad has been converted to a 21-mile-long trail in the eastern foothills of the Coast Range in Washington and Columbia Counties. The northern part of the trail near Vernonia is paved, but the rest of the trail has some missing links where cyclists are diverted to gravel roads, so it's best to ride the trail with a fat-tire mountain bike.

HAGG LAKE / 7 miles southwest of Forest Grove; 503/359-5732 From early spring to October, cyclists swarm the well-marked bike lane around man-made Henry Hagg Lake in Scoggins Valley Park. The loop follows gentle hills and fields for some 10 miles, passing numerous picnic and swimming spots. Ambitious cyclists can start in Forest Grove and take the Old TV Highway to Scoggins Valley Road. Open sunrise to sunset.

LEIF ERIKSON DRIVE / End of NW Thurman St to NW Germantown Rd Fat-tire affinity? Forest Park's Leif Erikson Drive is your kind of place. This 11-mile gravel road twists along the park's north side. For the first 6 miles, the road threads in and out of gullies, offering occasional spectacular views of the Willamette River and Northeast Portland; the last 5 miles are the most isolated and peaceful. Leif Erikson is rough going, but possible, on touring bikes. Although the fragile Wildwood Trail is off-limits, four other areas are open for mountain biking. Take the cutoff to NW Skyline Boulevard via Fire Lane 3 (just past the 3-mile marker), NW Saltzman Road (6 miles), Springville Road (9 miles), or NW Germantown Road (11 miles). Then loop back on the precariously busy Highway 30, or continue to Bonneville Road and Fire Lanes 12 and 15. If you yearn to tread the terrain but don't own gear, Fat Tire Farm Mountain Bike Company (2714 NW Thurman St; 503/222-3276; map:GG7), located about a mile from the Leif Erikson gate into Forest Park, will rent you everything you need. PUMP (503/357-7558) organizes year-round, after-work rides. Meet at the gate to Leif Erikson Drive at 6pm Wednesday evenings. *Map:DD9–GG7*

A NEW PATH ON THE EAST SIDE OF THE WILLAMETTE

Only time will tell whether Portland's newest recreation corridor will be the envy of cities everywhere—or another shining example of an expensive government boondoggle. But it's a good bet anyone who likes to walk, run, or ride a bicycle will consider the $30 million it will cost to be a wise investment in the future livability of the city.

A portion of the East Bank Esplanade, a massive trail-building project on the east side of the Willamette River, opened in late 2000. When the north connection to the Steel Bridge is completed in 2001, it will give the downtown lunch crowd the option of walking or riding a 3-mile loop along the river's edge by crossing the Steel and Hawthorne Bridges. Additional trail work, from the Hawthorne Bridge past the Oregon Museum of Science and Industry and on to Oaks Park, is also scheduled to be completed in 2001. That will complete the connection from the downtown riverfront to the Springwater Corridor.

The **Springwater Corridor** is a former rail line that was converted to a recreation trail in the 1990s. It runs 16 miles from the Eastmoreland area of Portland all the way to Boring in Clackamas County. When the connections are complete, Portland will have a dedicated bicycle/walking trail that runs 21.75 miles from downtown to the southeast edge of the city's urban growth boundary. Eventually, the trail will extend into the Mount Hood National Forest, but that will take several more years.

The showcase of the East Bank Esplanade is a 1,000-foot-long floating walkway, the longest of its kind in the country. Because Interstate 5 and the Southern Pacific Railroad run so close to the east bank of the Willamette River, the only way to build a trail was to make it run over water. By the way, the river is 90 feet deep beneath the walkway. Vegetative screening and sound barrier walls will help buffer trail users from the highway and rail noise. The floating walkway is 18 feet wide and sturdy enough to support the city's police horses, which will be used to patrol the area.

Besides offering a dynamite view of the downtown skyline and the many fireworks shows that are staged over the river, the esplanade will help rejuvenate Portland's long-neglected inner Southeast neighborhoods. The trail and some adjacent public spaces will help alleviate the city's shortage of outdoor event space. Arts groups were trying to rent facilities before construction was even completed.

Portland city managers hope the trail will help raise the consciousness of its citizens regarding water quality issues. Even though the Willamette has a nasty reputation for pollution, the worst areas are lower down in the main harbor. The city's worst sewage overflow outlet is near the Steel Bridge, but those problems are gradually coming to an end as the city's sewer system is rebuilt. Workers reported seeing river otters while building the walkway, and they were challenged to keep beavers from eating the new trees they planted.

—*Terry Richard*

MARINE DRIVE / Kelley Point Park at confluence of Willamette and Columbia Rivers to east end of N Marine Dr Just across the Willamette from Sauvie Island, Kelley Point Park anchors a favorite ride that follows the Columbia east along the airplane-swept flats of N Marine Drive. Most riders take the river road, but you can also cross the Columbia River on I-205 (there is a bike lane) into Washington and back to the bike path alongside roaring I-5 via Evergreen Highway and Columbia Way. The bike lane across the Columbia is part of the I-205 bike path, which extends 15 miles south to the Clackamas River in Gladstone. *Map:AA9–BB6*

SAUVIE ISLAND / Sauvie Island, 10 miles northwest of Portland via Hwy 30 On this ride, the ends justify the means. Endure 10 miles of pedaling alongside 18-wheelers through the mostly industrial section of Highway 30 from Northwest Portland to Sauvie Island (or shuttle your bike on Tri-Met bus 17 or on your car), and you'll be rewarded. The island offers a bicycle-friendly—as long as you ride single-file—12-mile loop with many scenic offshoots. Forgo the head-down hammer for a chin-up view of farm animals, U-cut flower and vegetable farms, blue herons, and more. Be sure to visit Howell Territorial Park, a 100-acre park rich in cultural and natural history. Metro Regional Parks has added a new rest room building and interpretive displays that explain how some of Oregon's earliest pioneers lived. During summer weekends, tours are available of the historic Bybee House, an authentically restored and furnished farmhouse of the 1850s. *Map:CC9.*

SKYLINE BOULEVARD / Skyline Blvd between NW Cornell and Rocky Point Rds This 17-mile loop requires pedaling an elevation gain of 1,400 feet, but Skyline Boulevard is truly the most scenic ridge-top road around, offering broad views of the Willamette Valley. Begin in Portland or in Beaverton (the climb is about the same either way). Turn off NW Cornell onto 53rd Drive or Thompson Road for a peaceful (albeit steep and winding) climb to Skyline. Pack a few dollars and plan to stop for microbrews and a view at the Skyline Tavern (8031 NW Skyline Blvd; 503/286-4788; map:FF9) or for burgers, fries, and malts at the Skyline Restaurant (1313 NW Skyline Blvd; 503/292-6727; map:GG8). *Map:DD9–GG7*

SPRINGWATER CORRIDOR / Portland Parks and Recreation; 503/823-2223 Since 1990 when the City of Portland acquired the land, nearly 17 miles of abandoned rail line between Milwaukie and Boring have been open to mountain bikers, hikers, and horseback riders. The wild and weathered rail bed was replaced by a tamer, smooth surface called "sandseal." While mountain bikes are still the best two-wheel bet in the corridor, narrow road-bike tires can also negotiate the trail. The paved surface runs from Westmoreland east to Gresham. Signals, crosswalks, and warning signs add a modicum of safety. Trailheads and toilets are located at SE Johnson Creek Boulevard, SE Hogan Road, and at the Main City Park in Gresham. *Map:JJ1–JJ5*

BIRD-WATCHING/WILDLIFE VIEWING

Water makes Portland a wildlife haven. The infamous rainfall results in lush vegetation, and the confluence of the Columbia and Willamette Rivers lures myriad waterfowl. Streams, lakes, and wetlands form an emerald necklace around the metropolitan area, and there's a regional effort to protect these wildlife habitats and promote responsible use of natural areas. Three times a year, Metro's Regional Parks and Greenspaces Department publishes *Metro GreenScene,* a guide to hikes, benefit concerts, history tours, biking, river trips, and other organized activities that increase awareness of local wildlife habitats. To receive a copy, call Metro (503/797-1850).

From blue herons to beavers, minks to muskrats, an impressive array of wildlife calls Portland home. Every glove compartment should include a copy of the *Oregon Wildlife Viewing Guide* ($10; available at bookstores and from Defenders of Wildlife in Lake Oswego 503/697-3222, or Falcon Press, 800/582-2665). Many **VIEWING SITES** are marked with state highway signs depicting binoculars. For nature unleashed, venture to Powell Butte, Sauvie Island Wildlife Management Area, or Kelley Point Park. Here are a few other notable natural areas.

BEGGARS-TICK WILDLIFE REFUGE / SE 111th Ave and Foster Rd Named after a native sunflower, the Beggars-Tick Wildlife Refuge serves as a wintering habitat for a diversity of waterfowl: wood duck, green-winged teal, and hooded merganser, to name a few. The refuge provides a permanent residence for muskrats, raccoons, and other species. *Map:II5*

HERON LAKES GOLF COURSE / 3500 N Victory Blvd; 503/289-1818 Built around wetlands, the course is home to blue herons as well as other waterfowl. Ask for permission and directions at the pro shop and, once on the course, be sure to keep your eyes open for birdies of the round, white, dimpled sort. *Map:CC7*

OAKS BOTTOM WILDLIFE REFUGE / Trailheads: SE 7th Ave and Sellwood Blvd (Sellwood Park); SE Milwaukie Blvd and Mitchell St These 160 acres of woods and wetlands form the first officially designated wildlife refuge in Portland. The walk, just short of 3 miles, begins in Sellwood Park. More than 140 species of birds have been spotted here, among them the great blue heron, which feeds on carp in the Bottom. Others include pileated woodpeckers and warblers (spring) and greenbacked herons (spring and summer). *Map:HH5*

PORTLAND AUDUBON SOCIETY SANCTUARY / 5151 NW Cornell Rd; 503/292-6855 Every birder in the state ends up here eventually—in part for the winged species that flock to the woods surrounding the facility and in part for the selection of excellent naturalists' books in the store (503/292-9453). This 160-acre sanctuary is surrounded by the vast wildness of Forest Park and connects to the Wildwood and Macleay Park trails. The trails wrap around a pond and follow the creek. The Audubon House features a nature-oriented store, an interpretive area, and a viewing window overlooking the feeding platforms for local songbirds. Year-round, the Audubon Society sponsors free field trips as a way of fulfilling its mission to teach people about how special nature is. During winter, spring, and summer vacations, the sanctuary offers educational nature classes for kids. To listen to the weekly updated Rare Bird Alert message, call and ask for extension 2. *Map:FF7*

ROSS ISLAND / Willamette River, just south of Ross Island Bridge The Willamette River island just south of downtown actually includes the complex of Ross, Hardtack, East, and Toe Islands. All but one are owned by Ross Island Sand and Gravel. The company's dredging permit expires in 2005, and gravel mining is slowly being phased out. On the northwest side of privately owned Toe Island is a 50-nest great blue heron rookery in a black cottonwood grove. The rookery can be viewed only by boat or with binoculars from the mainland. The best shoreside views (try for winter, when the trees are leafless) are from the Willamette Greenway, just north of Willamette Park. Look for belted kingfishers nesting on the island's steep banks, as well as beavers and red foxes. Bald eagles have also nested on the island in the past. The nearest boat ramp is in Willamette Park, but please don't land on the island. To join an organized kayak tour, contact the **PORTLAND RIVER CO.** (0315 SW Montgomery St; 503/229-0551). *Map:HH5*

WALLACE PARK / NW 26th Ave between Pettygrove and Raleigh Sts If you loved Alfred Hitchcock's classic *The Birds,* you won't want to miss Wallace Park in late September and early October. For about a two-week period during their migratory route south, Vaux's swifts roost in the several-story-tall chimney of Chapman School on the west side of the park. Each evening thousands of birds circle the chimney and then drop down inside, one by one, for the night; at sunrise they fly out just as dramatically. Spectator conversation usually revolves around the swifts that flew in first: can they actually sleep at the bottom of the pile, and what happens if one bird becomes claustrophobic? *Map:GG7*

CAMPING

Portland residents who want to get away for a quiet weekend camping trip need not drive far. Visitors from outside the city also have the opportunity to explore the city sights, its restaurants, and other attractions while staying inexpensively in a nearby campground. Metro, the Portland area's regional government, has recently upgraded the closest campground to the city at Oxbow Regional Park. Other campgrounds less than an hour's drive from downtown are managed by the Oregon and Washington state park systems and by Clackamas County. Campsite fees range from $12 to $20, depending on the season and the amenities.

OXBOW REGIONAL PARK (6 miles E of Gresham via SE Division St; 503/797-1850) has long been a favored spot for fishing on the Sandy River, hiking through old-growth forests, studying nature (especially the fall chinook salmon run), and simply getting away from the surrounding hubbub. Recent improvements to the campground make the park much more attractive to campers. Installation of a new water pumping and treatment system allowed Metro to construct two new rest room buildings, complete with hot running water, showers, and flush toilets. The campground was expanded to include 45 campsites. It is open year-round but does not take reservations. Pets are not allowed in the 1,200-acre park.

The Oregon Parks and Recreation Department manages three state parks close to Portland that have campsites. **MILO MCIVER STATE PARK,** 4 miles west of Estacada, has 44 electric sites and 9 primitive tent sites. The main attraction is the park's Clackamas River frontage and its trail system for hikers and equestrians. **CHAMPOEG STATE PARK,** 30 miles south of Portland and 7 miles east of Newberg, has 46 full-service sites, 12 tent sites, and 6 yurts. The park preserves a historic settlement on the banks of the Willamette River. **AINSWORTH STATE PARK,** 37 miles east of Portland in the Columbia River Gorge, has 45 sites. Reservations are available at McIver and Champoeg. Only Champoeg is open all year. For reservations, call 800/452-5687. For state park information, call 800/551-6949.

The Washington Parks and Recreation Department has three parks with campgrounds within an easy drive of Portland. **PARADISE POINT STATE PARK,** located on the East Fork of the Lewis River 16 miles north of Vancouver, has 70 standard sites and another 9 primitive sites. **BEACON ROCK STATE PARK** has 34 sites 35 miles east of Vancouver in the Columbia River Gorge. **BATTLE GROUND LAKE STATE PARK,** 19 miles northeast of Vancouver, has 35 electrical sites and another 15 walk-in tent sites. Battle Ground Lake is open for camping all year, but the other parks are seasonal. Reservations are taken May through September for Battle Ground Lake and Paradise Point, but not for Beacon Rock. Washington state parks use the same reservation service as Oregon (800/452-5687). For information on Washington state parks, call 800/233-0321.

Clackamas County offers camping at **BARTON PARK,** 9 miles west of Estacada on the Clackamas River, **METZLER PARK,** 5 miles south of

Estacada on Clear Creek, and at **FEYRER PARK**, 3 miles southeast of Molalla on the Molalla River. Barton is the largest with 96 sites. Camping season runs May through September. For reservations at all three, call 503/650-3484, or for information call 503/353-4415.

CANOEING/KAYAKING

Four rivers converge in the Portland area. Boaters paddle kayaks and canoes at a leisurely pace along the shores of the **WILLAMETTE** and **COLUMBIA RIVERS**, watching for blue herons, which nest along the banks. Whitewater kayakers surf the rapids of the **SANDY** and **CLACKAMAS RIVERS**. Pick up a copy of *Oregon's Quiet Waters: A Guide to Lakes for Canoeists and Other Paddlers*, by Cheryl McLean and Clint Brown; it includes more than a dozen lakes within two hours of Portland. Another must-read for Portland paddlers is the second edition of *Canoe and Kayak Routes of Northwest Oregon*, by Philip N. Jones. The **OREGON OCEAN PADDLING SOCIETY** (OOPS) fills a niche, too; the club has 300 active members (no phone, but check out their web site, www.teleport.com/~orops/; or inquire at PO Box 69641, Portland, OR 97201).

South of the city, canoe and kayak rentals are available from either of two shops on opposite sides of the Willamette. On the west side, across SW Macadam Avenue from Willamette Park, **EBB & FLOW PADDLE-SPORTS** (0604 SW Nebraska St; 503/245-1756; map:JJ6) rents canoes, kayaks, and accessories for $20 to $45 a day. The store offers sea kayaking classes and family and private lessons. On the east side, there's the floating **SPORTCRAFT MARINA** (1701 Clackamette Dr, Oregon City; 503/656-6484; map:OO4), which rents flatwater kayaks, canoes, and motorboats. The marina's history dates to the 1920s, when it was just a floating moorage; enterprising high school students augmented their allowances by offering rowboat rides. And though it started as a specialty store for whitewater enthusiasts, **ALDER CREEK KAYAK AND CANOE** (250 NE Tomahawk Island Dr; 503/285-0464; map:CC6) now rents and sells a variety of inflatable kayaks, touring canoes, and whitewater and flatwater kayaks and offers trips, tours, and classes.

CLIMBING

On July 19, 1894, aided by the complex carbohydrates of an old-fashioned bean bake, 193 persons climbed Mount Hood and initiated themselves as members in the **MAZAMAS** (909 NW 19th Ave; 503/227-2345; map:FF6). Now 3,000 members strong, the Mazamas is Oregon's biggest climbing group and the standard local means of acquiring mountain- and rock-climbing skills. This safety-conscious organization is a superb resource, offering seasonal group climbs, weekly lectures at its clubhouse, midweek rock climbs, day hikes, and other adventurous activities both in and outside of the Northwest.

Throughout the year, avid rock climbers—as well as those just starting out—hone their skills at local indoor climbing facilities: the **PORT-LAND ROCK GYM** (2034 SE 6th Ave; 503/232-8310; map:GG5) and **STONEWORKS CLIMBING GYM** (6775 SW 111th Ave, Beaverton; 503/644-3517). The Portland Rock Gym accommodates a 40-foot lead wall; it has 8,000 square feet of climbing, 25 top ropes, and 12 lead routes. The newer Stoneworks features 13 roped sections of wall and a large bouldering area. **CLUBSPORT OREGON** (18120 SW Lower Boones Ferry Rd, Tualatin; 503/968-4500; map:NN9), a sports megastore that includes basketball and volleyball courts and a soccer/hockey field, also boasts the highest indoor rock-climbing wall (45 feet) in the Portland area.

OREGON MOUNTAIN COMMUNITY (OMC; 60 NW Davis St; 503/227-1038; map:K6) rents and sells ice and alpine climbing gear as well as rock shoes. Check out the piles of adventure literature lining the entrance for info on classes and trips, and see the For Sale bulletin board for gear. **RECREATIONAL EQUIPMENT INC.**—better known as REI— (1798 Jantzen Beach Center; 503/283-1300; map:CC7) rents shoes, sells climbing equipment, and occasionally holds classes. The **PORTLAND PARKS AND RECREATION** spring/summer schedule of events (1120 SW 5th Ave, Rm 1302; 503/823-5132; www.parks.ci.portland.or.us; map:F3) includes rock-climbing classes in Portland and at Smith Rock State Park, and mountaineering ascents of Mount Hood and Mount St. Helens. Free mountaineering slide shows and lectures are a regular feature of the Mazamas, REI, and the **MOUNTAIN SHOP** (628 NE Broadway; 503/288-6768; map:FF6).

The following are a few of the major climbs (alpine and rock) within three hours of Portland. For a more complete list, talk to the experts at one of the local rock gyms or outdoor stores. Both of the definitive sources for climbing around Portland—*Portland Rock Climbs: A Climber's Guide to Northwest Oregon,* by Tim Olson, and *Oregon High: A Climbing Guide,* by Jeff Thomas—are out of print; consider yourself lucky if you find a used copy. A guide to the volcanoes is *Climbing the Cascade Volcanoes,* by Jeff Smoot.

BROUGHTON'S BLUFF / Lewis and Clark State Park, above the east bank of the Sandy River While it pales in comparison to the beauty and quality of Smith Rock, Broughton's Bluff is just 30 minutes from Portland and offers about 200 midrange to difficult climbs. A new trail was cut in 1990, and the rock is relatively clean. The southwestern exposure protects climbers from the cold winds of the Columbia River Gorge.

HORSETHIEF BUTTE / 2 miles east of The Dalles bridge, on Hwy 14 in Washington Here's a good practice spot, a basaltic rock mesa offering corridors of short climbs and top-rope challenges.

MOUNT HOOD / 50 miles east of Portland; information center in Welches; 503/622-4822 When British navigator Captain George Vancouver first spied Mount Hood from the mouth of the Columbia River in 1792, he thought it must have been the highest mountain in the world. At just over 11,235 feet, Mount Hood is not even the highest in the Cascades, but its beautiful asymmetry and relative ease of ascent make it one of the busiest peaks in the country. Still, unpredictable weather and very steep snow climbing (the last 1,500 feet) require either a skilled guide or solid mountaineering skills. In summer, smart climbers start early, finishing before the heat of the day turns the snow to mush. **TIMBERLINE MOUNTAIN GUIDES** (541/312-9242) are based, in summer, at the Wy'east Day Lodge at Timberline. The primary guide service on Mount Hood, this group teaches mountaineering, mountain-climbing, and ice-climbing courses; rock climbing is taught at Smith Rock State Park and in the Columbia Gorge.

MOUNT ST. HELENS NATIONAL VOLCANIC MONUMENT / 55 miles northeast of Portland; 360/247-3900 (Mount St. Helens Headquarters) or 360/247-3961 (climbing hotline) See the Day Trips chapter.

SMITH ROCK STATE PARK / 9 miles northeast of Redmond on Hwy 97, 3 hours southeast of Portland; 541/548-7501 Its extreme difficulty (the welded tuff volcanic rock is sometimes soft enough to tear off in your hand), stunning scenery, and arid climate have helped make Smith Rock a mecca for world-class climbers. The park is open year-round, but rock climbers are busiest February through November, before and after the rainy season. There are more than 1,000 routes in the park (as well as a few great hiking trails and scenic vistas), something for all abilities. The nationwide climbing consensus is that "Just Do It" is one of the hardest in the country, although several other less famous, but just as difficult, routes have been put up in the park in recent years. Bivouac camping only (hike-in sites; showers available; no reservations) along the Crooked River.

FISHING

To maintain a minimum number of spawning chinook salmon, the Oregon Department of Fish and Wildlife has issued quotas on Portland-area waters. It used to be that from February through June, fanatical anglers would line their boats from bank to bank across the Willamette, wait for the river's monsters to bite, and be rewarded with 10- to 30-pound salmon. In recent years, quotas of 3,000 or 6,000 fish caught after April 1 have brought the season to a close by mid-May. Indeed, the fishing week has been limited to two days in some instances. Even so, there is a lot of fun to be had—industrious fishermen will take to other, legal waters or spend the off days roaming through the gear at **GI JOE'S** (1140 N Hayden Meadows Dr; 503/283-0318; map:DD6; many additional locations throughout the Portland area).

Fishing in Portland is a year-round sport. The Clackamas and Sandy Rivers lure a steady stream of fishermen to their banks and wading pools for spring chinook salmon and summer and winter steelhead. The Willamette River is a good place to catch warm-water species such as bass, bluegill, and crappies; Blue Lake Park in the east Portland suburb of Fairview and Smith and Bybee Lakes in North Portland are also good bets. For more info on the best bets for local fishing, pick up a copy of the ninth edition of *Fishing in Oregon,* by Madelynne Sheehan and Dan Casali, at a local outdoor store. Hogliners and other anglers can find salmon and steelhead tag information at the **OREGON DEPARTMENT OF FISH AND WILDLIFE** (www.dfw.state.or.us/; 503/872-5268, a 24-hour automated number that provides answers to often-asked questions); also, pick up the annual regulations at fishing goods stores. **OUT-OF-STATE FISHERMEN** can call 800/ASK-FISH for information. The state sponsors a **FREE DAY OF FISHING** on an early Saturday in June. The Oregon State **MARINE BOARD** (435 Commercial St NE, Salem, OR 97310; 503/378-8587) publishes a guide to the lower Columbia and Willamette Rivers, as well as a statewide facilities guide that includes information on boat ramps, parking, and types of fishing available.

GUIDE SERVICES are numerous and easy to find under Fishing Trips in the Yellow Pages. For home river specialists, try Jack's Snacks and Tackle (1208 E Historical Columbia River Hwy, Troutdale; 503/665-2257) on the Sandy River, the Clackamas River Fly Shop in Milwaukie (12632 SE McLoughlin Blvd; 503/794-7122; map:KK5), and Countrysport Limited (126 SW 1st Ave; 503/221-0543; map:I7) near the Willamette River in downtown Portland.

Two local sport-fishing groups have been especially active in watching over area fish populations. The **ASSOCIATION OF NORTHWEST STEELHEADERS** (PO Box 22065, Milwaukie, OR 97269; 503/653-4176) promotes fishery enhancement and protection programs, river access, and improved sport-fishing. Since 1958, the **OREGON BASS AND PANFISH CLUB** (503/282-2852) has promoted preservation of, improvement of, and education about warm-water fishery in Oregon. Thanks to the club's efforts, access to warm-water fishing—which has been diminishing due to the amount of shoreline that is privately owned—may be stabilizing.

GOLFING

Portland has more golfers than greens—but more courses are being built all the time. Currently, about 55 golf courses are less than an hour's drive of the city center, though half are private, including the most spectacular courses: the Columbia Edgewater Country Club (2138 NE Marine Dr; 503/285-8354; map:DD5), Portland Golf Club (5900 SW Scholls Ferry Rd; 503/292-2778; map:II8), Riverside Golf & Country Club (8105 NE

33rd Dr; 503/282-7265; map:DD5), and Waverley Country Club (1100 SE Waverly Dr; 503/654-9509; map:KK5).

The following are the best of the public courses in the Portland area.

CEDARS GOLF CLUB / 15001 NE 181st St, Brush Prairie, WA; 360/687-4233 or 503/285-7548 Just north of Vancouver, the Cedars offers a long, rolling challenge with a lot of water hazards. Nice clubhouse facilities.

EASTMORELAND GOLF COURSE AND DRIVING RANGE / 2425 SE Bybee Blvd; 503/775-2900 Bordered by the Crystal Springs Rhododendron Garden and blessed with venerable trees and lovely landscaping, the second-oldest golf course in the state is a technically challenging championship course. In 1991 Eastmoreland was named one of the top 25 public golf courses in the nation by *Golf Digest*. (For tee times call 503/292-8570 and ask about the free online reservation service at www.thegolfnetwork.com.) *Map:II5*

HERON LAKES GOLF COURSE / 3500 N Victory Blvd; 503/289-1818 Designed by renowned golf course architect Robert Trent Jones Jr., Heron Lakes is a championship-quality public golf facility with two 18-hole courses. Great Blue has been described as one of the hardest courses in the Northwest—thanks to water and sand on every hole. The Green Back is a bit less challenging and retains the old, economical rates. Located just 15 minutes from downtown, Heron Lakes is one of the busiest courses in the city. *Map:CC7*

PUMPKIN RIDGE: GHOST CREEK COURSE / 12930 NW Old Pumpkin Ridge Rd, North Plains; 503/647-9977 Pumpkin Ridge's recent claims to fame have been hosting the 2000 U.S. Junior Amateur, the 1997 U.S. Women's Open, and the1996 U.S. Men's Amateur Championship, which Tiger Woods won so easily that he had to turn professional in order to find a challenge. The Women's Open will be back in 2004. *The Business Journal* ranked it as the toughest course in the Portland area in 2000. And in 1996, *Golf* magazine rated it the fifth-best golf course in America. Designed by Robert E. Cupp, Pumpkin Ridge (20 miles west of Portland off Highway 26) features natural areas and views of both the Cascades and the Coast Range. A second course at Pumpkin Ridge—Witch Hollow—is private.

THE RESERVE VINEYARDS AND GOLF CLUB / 4805 SW 229th Ave, Aloha; 503/649-8191 Opened in 1997, the Reserve is a 36-hole, semi-private golf facility with two courses, one designed by John Fought and the other by Robert Cupp. Fought's is a championship, traditional, 7,300-yard course with 114 bunkers; Cupp's is a slightly less difficult, open-design course with lots of water and trees. *www.reservegolf.com*

HIKING

Oregon offers superlative hiking. The cascading waterfalls of the Columbia River Gorge, the alpine lakes of the Cascades, the desolate peaks of the Wallowas, majestic Mount Hood, and the rugged Oregon Coast—all (except the Wallowas) are within easy access of Portland. To really get away, however, you barely need to leave the city limits. A 24-mile hike, the Wildwood Trail, begins in Northwest Portland in Forest Park; it's part of a 140-mile hiking/biking/ running loop around the city. Looking for company? Metro's Regional Parks and Greenspaces Department publishes a seasonal guide to organized outdoor activities, including hikes. To request a copy of *Metro GreenScene,* call 503/797-1850.

For tramping farther afield, good maps of hikes in the gorge and around Mount Hood can be found at the U.S. Forest Service office (800 NE Oregon St; 503/872-2750; map:GG6) and at local outdoor stores. Parking lots at some trailheads are notorious for car break-ins—don't leave anything valuable behind.

The following are a few of the better close-in hikes.

KELLEY POINT PARK / N Kelly Point Park Rd and N Marine Dr See Parks and Beaches in the Exploring chapter. *Map:AA9–BB6*

LOWER MACLEAY PARK / NW 29th Ave and Upshur St Balch Creek is one of the few creeks that still flows unfettered down the heavily developed West Hills. Lower Macleay Trail connects NW Upshur Street to Forest Park's long Wildwood Trail, but hikers can make a 2-mile loop up Balch Canyon by taking a right at the first trail intersection, at the stone hut, then right again at the second intersection, near an open meadow, ending up on NW Raleigh Street. A short northeasterly walk through the Willamette Heights neighborhood takes you to the Thurman Bridge above the park; take the stairs on the east side of the bridge back down to the starting point. At the park, the creek disappears unceremoniously into a drainpipe. *Map:FF7*

MARQUAM NATURE PARK / Trailheads: Council Crest Park, SW Sam Jackson Park Rd (just west of the Carnival Restaurant); SW Terwilliger Blvd, near the OHSU School of Dentistry A series of trails makes this one of the best hilly hiking areas in the city. From the parking lot and shelter off SW Sam Jackson Park Road (just west of the Carnival Restaurant), the trail to the right climbs 900 feet to Council Crest. To walk to the Oregon Zoo, continue over the top to the intersection of SW Talbot and Patton Roads. A short downhill trail leads to a Highway 26 overpass. The trail to the left of the shelter follows an old roadbed up and around Oregon Health Sciences University, crosses Marquam Hill Road, and comes out on Terwilliger Boulevard. At Terwilliger and SW Nebraska, the trail departs from the bike path and goes under Barbur Boulevard and I-5, coming out in John's Landing, four blocks from

Willamette Park. A third trail, a 1½-mile nature loop, also begins at the shelter; follow the signs. The trails are all remarkably quiet and peaceful; however, be forewarned: it's becoming more common to round a corner on a trail and stumble upon folks making their homes in the woods. *Map:GG7*

OAKS BOTTOM WILDLIFE REFUGE / **Trailheads: SE 7th Ave and Sellwood Blvd (Sellwood Park); SE Milwaukie Blvd and Mitchell St** The trail can be damp at times—you're in a wetland—but what an inner city escape. See Bird-Watching/Wildlife Viewing in this chapter. *Map:HH5*

SPRINGWATER CORRIDOR / **Portland Parks and Recreation; 503/823-2223** One of the region's best rails-to-trails hikes. See Bicycling in this chapter. *Map:JJ1–JJ5*

WILDWOOD TRAIL, FOREST PARK / **Main trailheads: W Burnside gravel parking area, Washington Park, NW Cornell Rd, NW Thurman St; 503/823-2223** One of the country's longer natural woodland trails winding through a city park, the Wildwood Trail is Portland's cherished refuge for hikers and runners. The shady route through groves of fir and aspen officially begins at the World Forestry Center (near the Oregon Zoo) and travels north, linking such attractions as the Hoyt Arboretum, Pittock Mansion, and the Portland Audubon Society Sanctuary before it plunges into the less-trodden territories of Forest Park. It ends some 30 miles later, at NW Newberry. Many spurs cross the trail, joining it to various neighborhoods and parks. The first 10 miles are well used; the last are good for solitude. Large, glass-encased maps of the entire trail are situated at convenient locations along the way. The Hoyt Arboretum Tree House has brochures and maps. Many of the trail-marked trees—bearing a green diamond—have a mileage marker posted higher up on the trunk. The best place to pick up the southern end of the Wildwood Trail is at its origin, at the World Forestry Center near the Vietnam Veterans' Living Memorial and the light rail stop at the Oregon Zoo. The trail travels north and crosses W Burnside, then climbs up to the Pittock Mansion or farther north to NW Cornell Road (and the Audubon sanctuary). Another option is to explore the branching trails of the Hoyt Arboretum in Washington Park. You should know that these are the most used parts of the trails, and they are also very hilly. Another trail begins across the Highway 26 overpass and continues south, connecting the Wildwood Trail to panoramic Council Crest. A walk on this uncrowded mile-long trail is best when timed with the setting sun.

The central 10 miles of the trail (from NW Cornell to NW Germantown Rd) is a departure from the comforting rest stops of zoo, arboretum, mansion, and gardens. This part—a favorite for runners and walkers training for marathons—is composed of long, solitary stretches of rolling hills with just a few brutally steep sections. Bring plenty of water, as there are no drinking fountains. Get to the central section via NW Cornell, 53rd Avenue, or the Leif Erikson gate at the end of NW Thurman Street (hike Leif Erikson Road up to the Wild Cherry Trail, which climbs to Wildwood). To reach the northern 10 miles, hike north from Germantown Road and access it from the BPA road along Skyline Boulevard. While the weather in recent winters has damaged many sections of Wildwood (especially its access trails), thanks to an amazing trail crew, repairs are fast and thorough. The ultimate guide to the park's trails is *One City's Wilderness: Portland's Forest Park,* by Marcy Cottrell Houle.

HORSEBACK RIDING

Although Oregon is about as west as you can get, it's not the romantic wild west of the Rocky Mountains. Still, look hard enough and you can find a horse to ride, a sunset to ride into, and bliss along the trail.

HILL TOP RIDING STABLES / SW 204th Ave and Farmington Rd, Beaverton; 503/649-5497 The last public riding stable in the Portland metro area, Hill Top has 50 wooded acres, plus an indoor arena. Cost is $20/hour; make your reservation on the day you want to ride. Once clients are known, they can rent horses and ride on their own.

FLYING M RANCH / 10 miles west of Yamhill on Highway 99W, watch for signs; 503/662-3222 Known for its Old West down-hominess, the Flying M is a great place to take the kids (over age 8) riding. The fee is $17 per hour on weekends or $12 midweek, including a guide. Pony rides for the younger set are available. For more adventuresome travel, a handful of two-day overnight rides up Trask Mountain are scheduled each summer, including all meals, lodging, and the singing cowboy's campfire songs at the top of the mountain. Flying M also takes private groups on overnight trail rides and has special steak dinner, breakfast, day-long and starlight rides. Call for information.

MOUNTAIN SHADOWS RANCH / 5 miles east of Cascade Locks (exit 51 from I-84, then ½ mile west); 541/374-8592 Located in the Columbia River Gorge a 45-minute drive east of Portland, this ranch offers trail rides year round, weather permitting. One-hour rides cost $25 for one or $45 for two. The ranch also keeps an interesting array of emus, Nubian goats, mules, llamas, and peacocks.

ICE SKATING

Even in the deep of winter, you'd be hard pressed to find naturally occurring ice in the Portland area. Skaters settle for indoor mall rinks, of which there are several.

 **CLACKAMAS ICE CHALET / Clackamas Town Center, Clackamas; 503/786-6000** Yes, Tonya Harding practiced here. That was back in the

1980s and early 1990s, when her triple axel was more famous than her dubious domestic dealings. Set in the center of one of Portland's major shopping malls, the rink offers 6- and 12-week figure skating and hockey lessons. Public skate admission (including rentals) is $7.50 for kids 17 and younger, and $8.50 for adults. The rink sits on the lower level of the mall's food court, thrilling the lunchtime crowd. *Map:KK3*

LLOYD CENTER ICE CHALET / Lloyd Center Mall, NE Portland; 503/288-6073 For more than 30 years, only the Portland sky covered the ice rink at Lloyd Center, but in 1990, the rink and the mall went undercover. The facility includes a pro skate shop, where group and private lessons are available. Public skate admission (including skate rentals) is $7.50 for kids 17 and younger and $8.50 for adults. *Map:FF5*

MOUNTAIN VIEW ICE ARENA / 14313 SE Mill Plain Blvd, Vancouver, WA; 360/896-8700 The new star among Portland metro-area ice rinks, Vancouver's twin ice sheets opened in 1998 and quickly became the in place to skate. Portland's junior hockey team, the Winter Hawks, uses it for practice. Frequent public skate sessions cost $6, or $3 for children under age 5, plus $2.25 for skate rental.

VALLEY ICE ARENA / Valley Plaza Shopping Center, 9250 SW Beaverton-Hillsdale Hwy, Beaverton; 503/297-2521 This rink is the largest recreational skating rink on the Portland side of the Columbia River and has been a fixture at the Valley Plaza Shopping Center for more than 30 years. Lessons are available, and skate rentals are free with a $7 admission (children under 4 skate free). Public skating most weekday mornings, afternoons, and weekends. *Map:HH9*

RIVER RAFTING

The local rafting season generally runs from May to October. Outfitters rent the necessary equipment to run the four closest whitewater rivers—Clackamas, Sandy, White Salmon, and Klickitat—as well as the Deschutes, the busiest of all. Since river conditions can change rapidly, inexperienced rafters should stick to guided trips.

CLACKAMAS RIVER / The upper Clackamas River is one of the most challenging runs so close to a major American city. The 13 miles from Three Links to North Fork Reservoir, just above Estacada, has Class IV water. Bob's Hole is a favorite play spot for kayakers. For a guided trip, arrange an excursion with **BLUE SKY WHITEWATER RAFTING** (800/898-6398). The 21½ miles of the lower Clackamas, from McIver State Park near Estacada to Clackamette Park at the confluence with the Willamette, in Oregon City, provides a good introduction for beginners; it's so placid that inner tubers float it during summer, although cold water during spring runoff makes it potentially dangerous because of the risk of hypothermia. Shorten the trip by using Clackamas County boat facilities at the communities of Barton or Carver.

DESCHUTES RIVER / Located two hours southeast of Portland, the Deschutes is an extremely popular day trip, especially for the 12-mile "splash and giggle" section on either side of Maupin. The river's lower section can be run as a pair of three-day trips—53 miles from Warm Springs to Sherars Falls and another 44 miles to the Columbia River. With more than 100,000 boater days each summer, the Deschutes has plenty of outfitters. Maupin's big four rental companies are **ALL STAR RAFTING AND KAYAKING** (800/909-7238), **DESCHUTES RIVER ADVENTURES** (800/723-8464), **DESCHUTES U-BOAT** (541/395-2503), and **DESCHUTES WHITE WATER SERVICE** (541/395-2232).

SANDY RIVER / One of the most reputable rental outfitters is **RIVER TRAILS CANOE AND RAFT RENTALS** (336 E Columbia River Hwy, Troutdale; 503/667-1964), through which, for $55 per raft, up to four people can float the relatively calm section of the Sandy from Oxbow Park 7½ miles to Lewis and Clark State Park, or the more challenging 8 miles from Dodge Park to Oxbow Park. In May and June, more confident rafters can run the longer section that starts 11½ miles from Dodge Park at Marmot Dam, which is designated an Oregon Scenic Waterway and includes Class III rapids.

WHITE SALMON RIVER / Less than a two-hour drive from Portland, **PHIL'S WHITE WATER ADVENTURE** (38 Northwestern Lake Rd, White Salmon; 800/366-2004) offers guided day trips on the White Salmon, which enters the Columbia River across from Hood River. White Water runs three trips a day down the White Salmon, recently designated a Wild and Scenic River. From April to October, spend three hours floating through inspiring scenery. Fed by springs, White Salmon has rapids in Class II, III, and IV. Prices start at $55 per person; call for reservations. The Klickitat, the next river to the east, is primarily run by rafters with their own gear, or with a fishing guide during the steelhead season.

For those on their own, a good place to start gathering equipment and information is **ANDY & BAX SPORTING GOODS** (324 SE Grand Ave; 503/234-7538; map:GG5), Portland's premier rafting store.

ROLLER AND IN-LINE SKATING/ROLLER HOCKEY/SKATEBOARDING

Remember when skates buckled over your shoes and off you went down the road? Talk about 20th century—things have changed. Roller skating has been joined by roller hockey, in-line skating, and "aggressive skating"—the name for what those amazing kids who skateboard down railings, catching some serious air, and (miraculously) landing back on their boards are doing. In Portland, most action of this sort takes place beneath the east side of the **BURNSIDE BRIDGE**, which is pretty much maintained and monitored by those who skate there. Two park districts have also created places to ride. The Tualatin Hills skateboard park (off NW Blueridge Dr at NW 158th Ave and Walker Rd, Beaverton) is part of the Tualatin Hills Park and Recreation District (503/645-6433). The City of Tualatin's skateboard park is part of the Tualatin Community Park (SW Tualatin Rd and Boones Ferry Rd; 503/692-2000, ext. 932).

For roller hockey players, the best bets can be found at **CLUBSPORT OREGON** and **SKATE WORLD**. For up-to-date information on the best half-pipes, skate parks, and roller hockey leagues, try **CAL SKATE** (210 NW 6th Ave; 503/248-0495; map:K6). In-line skaters who long for open skies have a few options to choose from in Portland: Tom McCall Water-front Park (see Top 20 Attractions in the Exploring chapter), Springwater Corridor (the paved section in Gresham; see the Bicycling section in this chapter), and the bike pathway along I-205.

CLUBSPORT OREGON / 18120 SW Lower Boones Ferry Rd, Tualatin; 503/968-4500 This sports megastore has a year-round, weekend roller hockey league. To play in a league game—open to members of ClubSport and "free agents" (nonmembers)—players must have all hockey equipment as well as in-line skates. For indoor in-line skating practice, check out the "No Stick Time" free skate on Friday, Saturday, and Sunday mornings for members only. Skating is available Thursday through Sunday, as a soccer turf is rolled out for use Monday though Wednesday. *Map:MM9*

OAKS AMUSEMENT PARK / Foot of SE Spokane St, north of Sellwood Bridge on the east riverbank; 503/236-5722 Although the Northwest's largest roller-skating rink normally stays open year-round (even though the park closes in winter), floods during the winter of 1996 necessitated a temporary closure. Damage was kept to a minimum, however, thanks to the rink's floating floor, which is designed so that it can be cut away from the wall to float atop rainwater. A live DJ rocks the rollers Friday through Sunday nights, and a giant Wurlitzer pipe organ entertains the rest of the time (it's closed on most Mondays). A full session costs $5. The rink's available for private parties; call ahead. *Map:II5*

SKATE WORLD / 1220 NE Kelly Ave, Gresham; 503/667-6543; 4395 SE Witch Hazel Rd, Hillsboro; 503/640-1333 Skate World describes itself as a "clean, family-oriented, modern skate center," and the rinks welcome all sorts of patrons and parties—recently a local dentist threw a skating party for all his patients. There's a roller hockey league for both kids and adults at the Hillsboro branch. Prices range from $3.95 to $6.75, including rentals.

ROWING

The Willamette is to Portland what the Charles is to Boston. When the weather is good, it's best to get on the water at sunrise—later, barges and motorboats turn smooth water to chop. Most rowing takes place between the Sellwood and Fremont Bridges, and boathouses on this stretch of water are at a premium. **OREGON ROWING UNLIMITED** (503/233-9426) offers youth programs, coaching, and rack space at Oaks Park. For lessons, check with **LAKE OSWEGO COMMUNITY ROWING** (503/699-7458) or, for sculling lessons, the **RIVERPLACE ROWING CENTER** (503/221-1212, ext. 309).

RUNNING/WALKING

Regardless of the weather, Portlanders like to run—a lot. And those who don't run walk. The **OREGON ROADRUNNERS CLUB** (4840 SW Western Ave, No. 200, Beaverton; 503/646-7867) is the premier running/walking club in the Northwest with 1,300 active members at $30 per year for individuals, or $40 per family. The club coordinates spring and summer running programs for youths, sponsors running clinics, and publishes a magazine and newsletter. ORRC puts on 14 local races—including the Thanksgiving Turkey Trot at the Oregon Zoo. For race information (updated monthly), call the ORRC Hotline (503/223-7867). The annual **PORTLAND MARATHON** is held each year in late September or early October. Training clinics (free and fee-based) are held year-round, although the pace picks up in the spring and summer (503/244-0902; www.portlandmarathon.org and www.teamoregon.com).

COUNCIL CREST PARK / Top of Marquam Hill SW Hewett, Humphrey, and Fairmount Boulevards form a figure eight, creating one of the more popular recreation paths in the city. People walk, run, cycle, even roller-ski here. The most heavily used portion is 3½-mile SW Fairmount Boulevard, which circles Council Crest Park, a moderately hilly course that on a clear day overlooks virtually everything from the Willamette Valley to Mount St. Helens. Take SW Hewett Boulevard to avoid the busier Humphrey Boulevard during rush hour—making, in fact, a figure nine. *Map:HH7*

DUNIWAY PARK AND TERWILLIGER BOULEVARD / North end of SW Terwilliger Blvd to Barbur Blvd and I-5 Runners have worn grooves into the lanes of the Duniway track, which now holds water like a drainage ditch. Up one terrace, however, is the quarter-mile sawdust track. The track has certain conveniences—the adjacent YMCA, an exercise and stretching area, public toilets—but parking is not one of them. At 5pm you won't find a space, legal or illegal, for your car in the tiny lot. Terwilliger continues all the way to Lake Oswego, although few trot that far, due to the hills and hard asphalt surface. *Map:GG6–II6*

GLENDOVEER GOLF COURSE / 14015 NE Glisan St; 503/253-7507 The sawdust trail around the circumference of the 36-hole golf course measures 2 miles 95 feet, according to one coach who measured it for his team's workouts. The north and south sides border sometimes busy streets, but the east-end trail curves through a miniature wildlife refuge in woods overrun with well-fed (and fearless) rabbits. Open daylight hours. *Map:FF1*

GREENWAY PARK / SW Hall Blvd and Greenway St, Beaverton A suburban common, Greenway is surrounded by fairly new commercial and residential developments. The 2½-mile trail follows Fanno Creek to SW Scholls Ferry Road, where the asphalt ribbon doubles back. *Map:HH9*

LAURELHURST PARK / SE 39th Ave between Ankeny and Oak Sts Once a gully and swamp, Laurelhurst is now a lovely 25-acre parkland where paved and gravel trails crisscross under elegant shade trees, and a pond set amid manicured lawns holds ducks. The mile path rings the park, but pay attention to the kids on bikes and roller skates. *Map:FF4*

LEIF ERIKSON DRIVE/FOREST PARK / NW Thurman St to Germantown Rd Runners share this road with hikers, dog walkers, and cyclists—but no motorized vehicles. See Bicycling or Hiking (Wildwood Trail) in this chapter. *Map:DD9–FF7*

MOUNT TABOR PARK / SE 60th Ave and Salmon St The only volcano within city limits in the Lower 48 has one of the better eastside views of Portland's West Hills and Mount Hood. Tabor was named in honor of a faraway twin peak in the Biblical Palestine. Asphalt roads loop up the hill (the upper roads are for bikes and walkers only). Dirt trails stretch for 1 to 5 miles. *Map:GG3*

POWELL BUTTE / SE Powell Blvd and 162nd Ave (unmarked street) A hilly run on an open butte. See Parks and Beaches in the Exploring chapter. *Map:JJ1*

TOM MCCALL WATERFRONT PARK AND WILLAMETTE PARK / West bank of the Willamette River, stretching 3-1/4 miles south from downtown Portland Noontime runners flock to the promenade in what's considered by many to be the city's front yard. It runs only 1-3/4 miles north to the Broadway Bridge from RiverPlace; however, south of RiverPlace (after a brief interruption) the path reappears along the river to Willamette Park, making a round trip of 6½ miles. *Map:A6–K6*

TRYON CREEK STATE PARK / 11321 SW Terwilliger Blvd, 1 mile off Hwy 43 in Lake Oswego; 506/636-4398 Lots of trail to get lost on here. See Parks and Beaches in the Exploring chapter. *Map:KK6*

TUALATIN HILLS NATURE PARK / 15655 SW Millikan Blvd, Beaverton; 503/644-5595 Fortunately, the Tualatin Hills Park and Recreation District has left St. Mary's Woods virtually untouched since it purchased the 200 acres from the Catholic archdiocese of Portland in the mid-1980s. Deer trails work their way through the woods, but the path (clearly marked) makes a 1-mile loop on the west bank of Beaverton Creek. If it's wet out, the dirt trail is likely to be quite muddy. The new Nature Park Interpretive Center is the focal point of the 1½-mile paved and 3-mile dirt trail system. Westside light rail stops at the park's north entrance.

SAILING

Scores of speedboats chop up the water on the Willamette River, making a simple Sunday sail a fight for survival, especially against the wakeboarders and jet skis in the stretch of river just upstream from downtown. And while sailing on the Columbia is certainly pleasant, windsurfing gets more attention on that river these days, upstream from Portland in the Columbia River Gorge. Nevertheless, sailing is a business for the following organizations, which specialize in rentals and instructions.

ISLAND SAILING CLUB / 515 NE Tomahawk Island Dr; 503/285-7765 This members-only Columbia River club, located east of Jantzen Beach, offers instruction for American Sailing Association certification and rentals (20- to 30-foot crafts). Members are welcome at the club's two Washington locations. Charters are available; open year-round. *www.islandsailingclub.com; map:CC6*

PORTLAND SAILING CENTER / 3315 NE Marine Dr; 503/281-6529 Primarily an American Sailing Association certified school, the center allows students at all skill levels to practice the particulars of tacking and jibbing on a range of boats. The center also rents to certified parties, when its boats are available, and offers brokered charters far beyond the banks of the Columbia—to Baja or the San Juans, for example. The staff is terrific. Hours are 10am to dusk, seven days a week, all year round. *Map:CC4*

WILLAMETTE SAILING CLUB AND SCHOOL / 6336 SW Beaver Ave; 503/246-5345 The club is a family affair, costing $250 to join and $180 per year. The club-owned school offers adult and youth classes. Most popular are the weekend and Thursday evening classes from May into September and the weeklong, $125 youth session during the summer. *Map:JJ6*

SKIING: CROSS-COUNTRY/SNOWSHOEING

The popularity of cross-country, or Nordic, skiing has outpaced the availability of new groomed trails, Sno-Parks (designated parking areas), and trail information. Many maps list the popular or marked trail systems, but Klindt Vielbig's guide, *Cross-Country Ski Routes of Oregon's Cascades,* offers a more comprehensive listing. Snowshoeing, which often uses the same locations as cross-country skiing, is booming at

Mount Hood, as it is everywhere else. Snowshoers should walk along-side ski tracks so they don't obliterate them. Portland has more than a dozen ski clubs, which have banded together to form the Northwest Ski Club Council (503/243-1332).

BEND RANGER DISTRICT / 180 miles southeast of Portland; 541/388-5664 Fifteen miles west of Bend on the road to Mount Bachelor, the U.S. Forest Service's Swampy Lakes trail system has warming huts and exquisitely beautiful (if hilly) terrain. Six more miles up Century Drive is the Sno-Park for Dutchman Flat, a trail system that connects to Swampy Lakes. Together, the systems are the best-planned web of trails in Oregon.

MOUNT HOOD / It takes more than looking out the window to assess weather conditions at Mount Hood. Miserable weather in Portland sometimes shrouds excellent Nordic conditions on the mountain. Snow reports can be dialed at the mountain's ski areas (the snow is rarely the same at all three): Timberline (503/222-2211), Mount Hood Meadows (503/227-SNOW), and Skibowl (503/222-BOWL). In Portland, call 800/977-6368 for road conditions. Of the three downhill ski areas, only **MOUNT HOOD MEADOWS** (off Highway 35, watch for signs; 503/337-2222) has a Nordic center, featuring 15 kilometers of cross-country and snowshoe trails; when the Nordic trails are groomed, the fee is $9.

The Portland chapter of the **OREGON NORDIC CLUB** (PO Box 3906, Portland, OR 97208; 503/222-9757; www.onc.org) operates the popular weekend Nordic center at **TEACUP LAKE**, on the east side of Highway 35, across from the Mount Hood Meadows parking lot. The 20 kilometers of groomed trails are open to the public for a small donation. The Nordic Club schedules year-round weekend activities, including hiking, backpacking, and cycling. The Barlow Pass Sno-Park nearby has the highest elevation (4,800 feet) of any Nordic ski trail system at Mount Hood.

South of Highway 26, just past the Timberline Lodge turnoff (watch for signs), the **TRILLIUM LAKE BASIN** is especially popular. Local resident David Butt voluntarily grooms the two main areas, Trillium Lake Road and Still Creek Campground Loop, as well as six other trails. For trail information and other Sno-Park areas, check with the **MOUNT HOOD INFORMATION CENTER** in Welches, about 60 miles east of Portland, 503/622-4822.

SANTIAM PASS / 86 miles southeast of Salem at Santiam Pass; 541/822-3381 (McKenzie Ranger District) or 541/549-2111 (Sisters Ranger District) The U.S. Forest Service trail system at Ray Benson Sno-Park near the Hoodoo ski area is one of the most extensive in the state, with warming huts (and wood stoves) at the trailhead and beyond.

SOUTHWEST WASHINGTON / 76 miles east of Portland, 26 miles north of Carson, WA; 509/427-3200 (Wind River Ranger District) or 360/247-3900 (St. Helens Ranger District) Oregon winter parking permits are valid for Sno-Parks in Washington. Along the Upper Wind River the terrain is generally rolling, through heavy clear-cuts and forested areas (20 miles of groomed, well-marked trails; be sure to check whether the road has been plowed). Two areas south of Mount St. Helens are both accessible from Forest Service Road 83. Recommended are the Marble Mountain–Muddy River area and the Ape Cave–McBride Lake–Goat Marsh area. Unmarked roads through gentle. wide-open areas offer extensive views of the mountain itself.

SKIING: DOWNHILL

MOUNT HOOD MEADOWS / Off Highway 35 (watch for signs); 503/227-7669 (from Portland) or 503/337-2222 Sixty-eight miles east of Portland, Meadows offers the most varied terrain of all Mount Hood ski areas—from wide-open slopes for beginners and novices to plenty of moguls and steep, narrow chutes for the experts. This ski area is big; there are 82 runs, including one that goes on for 3 miles. Lift lines can be long on weekends, but four high-speed express lifts get skiers up the mountain in a hurry. The rope tow is free. There are two day lodges, and night skiing is offered Wednesday through Sunday.

MOUNT HOOD SKIBOWL / Just off Highway 26 at Government Camp; 503/222-2695 With 210 acres under lights, Skibowl is one of America's largest night ski areas. It's also the state's lowest-elevation ski area, which means it suffers during seasons with light or late snowfall, but recent winters have been epic. The lower bowl suits beginners and intermediates, while the upper bowl is challenging enough to host ski races and draws the region's very best skiers for extreme-steep challenges. Also, a snowboard park includes an in-ground half-pipe for the aboveground hardcore. Five rope tows, four double chairs. Ski Bowl is closer to Portland than the other areas: 53 miles east on Hwy 26.

TIMBERLINE / Follow the signs from Government Camp; 503/231-7979 (from Portland) or 503/272-3311 North America's only year-round ski area. See Mount Hood in the Day Trips chapter.

SWIMMING

Water, water everywhere—but the Portland Parks and Recreation Department discourages swimmers from plunging into the Willamette River. Although cleaner than it was in the early half of this century, the Willamette contends with sewer system overflows after rainstorms and barge traffic. The Columbia River, however, has two popular wading areas, at Rooster Rock State Park and Sauvie Island (see Parks and Beaches in the Exploring chapter).

EXTREME FUN ON MOUNT HOOD

When the snow melts and skis get stashed in the closet, the fun is only beginning at Government Camp. Located on busy US 26, Skibowl has taken advantage of its location—50 miles east of Portland—and the privately owned land that surrounds its base lodges by operating Action Park (503/222-2695), an extreme-sport theme park that brings it nearly as much business as winter's snow. Most other Oregon ski areas are on land managed by the U.S. Forest Service, which frowns on the city-type attractions that Skibowl offers.

Actually, the Mount Hood National Forest is a willing partner with the Action Park, giving its blessing to such attractions as scenic horseback rides, a mountain biking park, a dual alpine slide, and hay rides on the federally owned ski slopes. Down in the parking lots, which are privately owned, the Action Park has enough activities to keep a junior high school class buzzing for the summer.

If you dare, begin with a tumble off the 100-foot free-fall bungee tower. If that's not enough, go for an 80-foot fling on the reverse rapid-riser bungee jump. Indy karts, kiddy jeeps, trampolines, miniature and Frisbee golf, Velcro fly trap, body Nerfing, batting cages, and a 40- by 60-foot play zone offer fun for all ages. The mountain bike park has 40 miles of trail and is served by the only two chairlifts in Oregon that transport bicycles. Scenic helicopter rides take off from the parking lot for a bird's-eye view of Mount Hood.

The Action Park also stages music concerts and rents out to company picnics. The Multorpor Lodge offers fine dining with a European flair on weekend evenings, and a mountainside barbecue dishes out plates of burgers, sausages, and carnival-type food.

Located in the Cascades, the Action Park's weather isn't always perfect. Any good weather that falls on a weekend, between the park's opening on Memorial Day to the Fourth of July, is considered a blessing. But once Oregon's summer weather takes hold, usually right after July 4, long stretches of brilliant sunshine are more common than the cloudy skies that usually return to stay in October. The park is open daily through Labor Day and on weekends in September.

Six miles up Mount Hood from the Action Park, Timberline Lodge attracts young skiers and snowboarders by the thousands from around the United States, Europe, and Japan to the only year-round ski area in North America. When the morning's training is completed, more than a few youngsters head down to the Action Park for some real fun off the snow.

—*Terry Richard*

The few indoor public pools in the city are busy during the winter. Every year, thousands of children take swimming lessons through **PORT-LAND PARKS AND RECREATION** (503/823-SWIM); Wilson High School's pool in Southwest Portland and the Sellwood Pool in Southeast—both outdoor pools—are two of the more popular. Admission is $2.50 for admission; 2 years and under, free with parent.

The largest indoor swim spot is **NORTH CLACKAMAS AQUATIC PARK** (7300 SE Harmony Rd, Milwaukie; 503/650-3483 (hotline) or 503/557-7873; map:LL4), where there are attractions for all ages. Four-foot waves roll into one pool, and older kids can dare the twister and drop slides. There's a heart-shaped whirlpool for adults, and an outdoor sand volleyball court. Admission isn't cheap: $24 for a family; $9.99 for adults; $6.99 for ages 9 to 17; $4.99 for ages 3 to 8; under age 3 free (less for the lap pool only; all prices discounted two hours before closing). Lessons and aquatic exercise programs are available.

Most high schools have pools, but public access is usually limited to the summer months. Both the Mount Hood Community College and Tualatin Hills Aquatics Centers can handle many swimmers (see listings). The following are the better public pools in the area.

COLUMBIA POOL / 7701 N Chautauqua Blvd; 503/823-3669 One of Portland's largest indoor pools is actually two 25-yard pools side by side. The shallow one ranges from 1½ to 4 feet deep; the deep pool slopes to 7 feet. *Map:DD7*

DISHMAN POOL / 77 NE Knott; 503/823-3673 This indoor public pool's best feature is its 10-person whirlpool. *Map:FF6*

HARMAN SWIM CENTER / 7300 SW Scholls Ferry Rd, Beaverton; 503/643-6681 A hot spot in the Tualatin Hills Parks and Recreation Department's award-winning swim program—literally. At 88 degrees, the water's extra 4 degrees make it noticeably warmer than the other pools in the district. Swimming instruction for all ages. The pool runs the area's largest water therapy program for disabled or physically limited individuals. *Map:HH9*

METRO FAMILY YMCA / 2831 SW Barbur Blvd; 503/294-3366 Its location next to the Duniway Park track and running trail makes the Barbur YMCA extremely popular (avoid parking headaches and take one of the many buses that stop here). The pool is available for lap swimming whenever the YMCA is open (except for a brief period on Tuesdays and Saturdays). A $10 day pass entitles visitors to the use of the entire facility. Members of the Southeast and Northeast YMCAs are welcome free anytime; members of other YMCAs are entitled to 21 free visits, and after that it's $10 a day. Water step-aerobics and swim lessons are available to members. *Map:A1*

MOUNT HOOD COMMUNITY COLLEGE / 26000 SE Stark St, Gresham; 503/491-7243 The Aquatics Center runs four pools: an outdoor 50-meter pool (June to early October) with morning, noon, and evening lap swims; an indoor 25-yard six-lane pool; a very warm (90 to 92 degrees) 4-foot-deep pool for the physically impaired; and an oft-used hydrotherapy pool. Fee is $3 per visit; annual memberships are available for families ($240) and individuals ($180). Summer passes are also available.

MOUNT SCOTT COMMUNITY CENTER / 5530 SE 72nd; 503/823-3183 A spanking new Portland Parks facility—open in 2000—the community center has a 25-yard pool with six lanes. Another play pool has a slide, a lazy river, and a water vortex. Walk-in rates are $3 for adults, $2.25 for teens, and $1.75 for children. *Map:KK4*

OREGON CITY MUNICIPAL SWIMMING POOL / 1211 Jackson St, Oregon City; 503/657-8273 Lap swimming, swimming lessons, and water exercise classes are all available in this 25-meter, six-lane indoor pool. Open year-round. *Map:OO4*

SOUTHWEST COMMUNITY CENTER / 6820 SW 45th Ave; 503/823-2840 This attractive new Portland Parks facility in Gabriel Park has a 25-yard pool with six lanes. Children have their own pool with a slide and fountain structure. *Map:II8*

TUALATIN HILLS PARKS AND RECREATION SWIM CENTER / 15707 SW Walker Rd, Beaverton; 503/645-7454 At 50 meters long, this is Portland's largest enclosed public swimming pool. It's part of a large recreation complex in the Sunset Corridor, where the facilities include covered tennis courts, playing fields, and a running trail. $4 per swim for adults; $3 for children. Memberships and lessons are available.

TENNIS

Portland is well supplied with public tennis courts. Portland Parks and Recreation has 110 outdoor courts at 40 sites. Washington Park, which has six lit courts above the Rose Garden—and a waiting line on warm weekends—is a favorite. For a nominal fee, one-hour court reservations can be made May through September for individual outdoor courts at Grant, Portland Tennis Center, and Washington Park. Otherwise it's first come, first served—and free.

In addition, the city owns two indoor tennis centers. The excellent **PORTLAND TENNIS CENTER** (324 NE 12th Ave; 503/823-3189; map:GG5) was the first municipal indoor court in the Western states financed by revenue bonds. It has eight outdoor and four indoor courts ($7.25 each for singles on weekends and after 4pm; early weekday play is $6.50). At **ST. JOHNS RACQUET CENTER** (7519 N Burlington St; 503/823-3629; map:DD8), everything is under cover: three indoor tennis courts ($15 per court for adults, $10 for juniors) and Portland's only public racquetball courts (there are three; $10 per court).

Other area **INDOOR COURTS** that are open to the public, though some require more than a full day's advance notice, include Glendoveer Tennis Center (NE 140th Ave and Glisan St; 503/253-7507; map:FF7); Lake Oswego Indoor Tennis Center (2900 SW Diane Dr, Lake Oswego; 503/635-5550; map:KK6); Tualatin Hills Parks and Recreation District Tennis Center (15707 SW Walker Rd, Beaverton; 503/645-7457); and Vancouver Tennis and Racquetball Center (5300 E 18th St, Vancouver, WA; 360/696-8123; map:BB5). Weekdays are a better deal.

Here are a few of the better courts in the area (call Portland Parks and Recreation for others; 503/823-2223).

West Side
GABRIEL PARK: SW 45th Ave and Vermont St; map:II8
HILLSIDE: 653 NW Culpepper Terr; map:GG7

Southeast
COLONEL SUMMERS: SE 20th Ave and Belmont St; map:HH5
KENILWORTH: SE 34th Ave and Holgate Blvd; map:HH4

Northeast
ARGAY: NE 141st Ave and Failing St; map:FF1
U. S. GRANT: NE 33rd Ave and Thompson St; map:FF5

WINDSURFING
See Columbia River Gorge Scenic Area in the Day Trips chapter.

Spectator Sports

MULTNOMAH GREYHOUND PARK / NE 223rd Ave and Glisan St, Fairview; 503/667-7700 You've seen the Kentucky Derby, right? Well, here dogs run instead of horses, the track is smaller (no race is longer than 770 yards), and instead of a jockey urging the animals on, the greyhounds chase a mechanical rabbit. The season runs from May to October. Admission is free. Children under 12 are allowed during Sunday matinee.

PORTLAND MEADOWS / 1001 N Schmeer Rd; 503/285-9144 It's possible to catch live horse racing at the Meadows (call for a schedule), but if the timing isn't right, you can always watch simulcasts of greyhound and horse racing. *Map:DD6*

PORTLAND FIRE / Rose Garden Arena; 503/797-9601 The Women's National Basketball Association landed in Portland during the summer of 2000 when the Fire made its debut in the Rose Garden, and their 10–22 record shows this young team has room for improvement. Ticket prices range from $5 to $30, with all seats in the lower bowl of the arena. The season runs late May until August. *Map:O7*

PORTLAND BEAVERS / PGE Park, SW 20th Ave and Morrison St; 503/553-5555 Portland rejoined the Triple A Pacific Coast League for the 2001 season when Portland Family Entertainment bought the Albuquerque Dukes as the cornerstone of its refurbishment plans for Civic Stadium, now known as PGE Park. The Dukes are now the Beavers, and the Beavs have a polished place to play ball. The PCL schedule runs April through September. This league remains the last stop before many players move up to the major leagues. *Map:GG7*

PORTLAND TRAIL BLAZERS / Rose Garden Arena; 503/231-8000 (season tickets only), 503/224-4400 (single tickets), or 503/321-3211 (events hotline) Owned by Paul Allen, one of the country's richest men and a self-avowed basketball nut, the Trail Blazers have become one of the most powerful organizations in the National Basketball Association. Allen's having the money and being willing to spend it guarantees the Blazers a solid nucleus of talent that should keep them in contention for the NBA championship for as long as he is writing the checks. *Map:O7*

PORTLAND WINTER HAWKS / Memorial Coliseum; 503/238-6366 See tomorrow's NHL players today in the WHL (Western Hockey League). This developmental league grooms young hockey players for the big time, but the Winter Hawks already think their team is the best. The 72-match season runs from October through March, with admission prices ranging starting at $11.50. Tickets are available at all Ticketmaster locations and at the box office. Some matches are held at the Rose Garden Arena. *Map:O7*

CONFERENCES, MEETINGS, AND RECEPTIONS

CONFERENCES, MEETINGS, AND RECEPTIONS

Most hotels and many restaurants have private meeting rooms for rent. The following is a list of other rental facilities appropriate for business meetings, private parties, and receptions. Private functions can also be held at the Multnomah County Library (call the branch nearest you to reserve a room), most museums, Portland State University (which has numerous halls, auditoriums, and meeting rooms), and other educational facilities. A good resource, too, is the Portland Oregon Visitors Association (503/275-9750; www.pova.com).

EDGEFIELD / 2126 SW Halsey St, Troutdale; 503/669-8610 The former Multnomah County Poor Farm at Edgefield was acquired by the McMenamin brothers in the early 1990s, and they've turned it into a multiuse theme park offering everything from art to beer to wine to fine dining to cheap movies to blues concerts. There are also overnight accommodations. Twelve rooms are available for private functions, the largest of which seats 176 people (225 standing). Ask for the conference packet when you inquire. *www.mcmenamins.com* &

JENKINS ESTATE / 8005 SW Grabhorn Rd, Aloha; 503/642-3855 An Arts and Crafts–style house, stable, and gatehouse sit on 68 idyllic acres, 33 of which are landscaped and crisscrossed with trails. The general public is just as welcome as guests are to stroll the grounds, and trail maps are available. The gatehouse is perfect for small business meetings, and the main house can accommodate varying numbers of people, depending on room arrangements. The stable can handle even more guests on its two floors. The old stalls make for great breakout sessions during a meeting or can serve as intimate dining alcoves. Catering by the Jenkins Estate staff can provide breakfast, lunch, and snacks for corporate groups in any of these facilities during the week. Business dinners and appetizer events are also available weekday evenings. Weekends are usually reserved for weddings and social events. Make wedding reservations a year in advance. *www.thprd.org* &

MENUCHA RETREAT AND CONFERENCE CENTER / 38711 E Crown Point Hwy, Corbett; 503/695-2243 Nonprofit religious, cultural, educational, and governmental groups are welcome at this center, perched high on a bluff overlooking the Columbia River. Personal spiritual retreats and family reunions are also welcomed. Part of Portland's First Presbyterian Church, it has a kinder, gentler atmosphere than some of the other conference locales. Trails wind through Menucha's 100 wooded acres, and a swimming pool, volleyball court, and tennis court are available. The home-style cooking with fresh-baked bread is a draw. No alcohol is allowed in the dining room. *www.fpcpdx.org/menucha* &

MONTGOMERY PARK / 2701 NW Vaughn St; 503/224-6958 Montgomery Park is one of Portland's premier meeting places. There are numerous possibilities here: the Don Campbell Hall can accommodate as many as 300 people for a sit-down dinner, or if that's too grand, choose from three conference and meeting rooms. The (sometimes) sunny atrium is also available and can hold as many as 1,200 standing guests. *Map:FF6* &

OREGON CONVENTION CENTER / NE Martin Luther King Jr Blvd and Holladay St; 503/235-7575 Purposefully recognizable by its twin green towers (glowing when lit from within), this facility just across the river from downtown has 150,000 square feet of open exhibit space with numerous reception, banquet, and meeting rooms. The OCC is spacious—it has contained as many as 25,000 people at one time, although groups of 50 are welcome as well. Outdoor parking accommodates 900 cars; also, a MAX light rail stop at the front door makes a trip into downtown effortless—or it's a pleasant walk across the Steel Bridge. *www.oregoncc.org; map:M9*

OREGON MUSEUM OF SCIENCE AND INDUSTRY / 1945 SE Water Ave; 503/797-4671 After regular museum hours, this science center offers its facilities for private special events and can accommodate groups of 50 to 4,000. Located on the east bank of the Willamette River, it offers an extraordinary view of the downtown Portland skyline. The highlight of OMSI's event spaces are six large exhibit halls, filled with hands-on, interactive exhibits. There's also an outside courtyard, auditorium, and dining room. Catering is provided in-house. Groups can also rent the OMNIMAX Theater for private showings of motion pictures within a five-story domed screen with surround sight and sound. The Murdock Planetarium, with its astronomy and laser light shows, and the USS *Blue-back* submarine are also available. *www.omsi.org; map:HH6* & *(except submarine)*

PITTOCK MANSION / 3229 NW Pittock Dr; 503/823-3623 This Portland landmark leases space during the evening to recognized organizations, commercial and nonprofit alike. The mansion, in its lofty location high above the city, can accommodate 50 for a sit-down dinner or 250 for a standing reception; you'll need to hire the caterer. It's a popular locale—reserve a year in advance for the holiday season. The mansion is partially wheelchair accessible. *www.mediaforte.com/pittock; map:GG7*

PORTLAND CONFERENCE CENTER / 300 NE Multnomah St; 503/239-9921 Conferences, meetings, and receptions are a big business at this full-service, privately owned facility, whether the party's for 5 or 500. Twelve rooms include stage areas and teleconferencing equipment, and the location, adjacent to the Oregon Convention Center, is convenient. In-house catering is carried out by a large staff. The facility is partially wheelchair accessible. *www.portlandcc.com; map:N9*

PORTLAND'S WHITE HOUSE / 1914 NE 22nd Ave; 503/287-7131 or 800/272-7131 Weddings and private receptions are popular at this elegant bed-and-breakfast inn, the former mansion of local timber baron Robert F. Lytle. The White House features a 1,650-square-foot ballroom, with room for 100 dancers. If you'd like to stay over, the White House has nine lovely sleeping rooms with private baths. *www.portlandswhitehouse.com; map:FF5*

TRYON CREEK STATE PARK / 11321 SW Terwilliger Blvd; 503/636-9886, ext 21 A meeting room for 60 in the Nature Center at picturesque Tryon Creek is available (for a small charge) for retreats and meetings only. No parties, weddings, or receptions. Lovely setting, limited facilities. *Map:JJ6*

WORLD FORESTRY CENTER / 4033 SW Canyon Rd (Washington Park); 503/228-1367 Three facilities and a large outdoor plaza are available at the Forestry Center, which welcomes all kinds of parties, from class reunions to academic conferences (no proms, however). There are kitchen facilities and tables and chairs; you arrange for the catering. The largest building can accommodate up to 300 guests. The smallest seats up to 60, classroom-style. This is an exceptionally nice and very popular place. Planning a wedding? Make your reservations at least a year in advance. *www.worldforest.org; map:GG7* &

WORLD TRADE CENTER / 121 SW Salmon St; 503/464-8688 This recently renovated facility includes 20,000 square feet of flexible meeting space with a state-of-the-art auditorium, unique to downtown Portland, and a 10,000-square-foot covered outdoor plaza for summer evening events. These spaces are available for business meetings, wedding receptions, and other events. Full catering. *www.wtcpd.com; map:F5*

Index

We Stand By Our Reviews

Sasquatch Books is proud of *Best Places Portland*. Our editors and contributors go to great lengths and expense to see that all of the restaurant and lodging reviews are as accurate, up-to-date, and honest as possible. If we have disappointed you, please accept our apologies; however, if a recommendation in this 5th edition of *Best Places Portland* has seriously misled you, Sasquatch Books would like to refund your purchase price. To receive your refund:

1. Tell us where and when you purchased your book and return the book and the book-purchase receipt to the address below.
2. Enclose the original restaurant or lodging receipt from the establishment in question, including date of visit.
3. Write a full explanation of your stay or meal and how *Best Places Portland* misled you.
4. Include your name, address, and phone number.

Refund is valid only while this 5th edition of *Best Places Portland* is in print. If the ownership, management, or chef has changed since publication, Sasquatch Books cannot be held responsible. Tax and postage on the returned book is your responsibility. Please allow six to eight weeks for processing.

Please address to Satisfaction Guaranteed, *Best Places Portland*, and send to:
Sasquatch Books
615 Second Avenue, Suite 260
Seattle, WA 98104

Best Places Portland Report Form

Based on my personal experience, I wish to nominate the following restaurant, place of lodging, shop, nightclub, sight, or other as a "Best Place"; or confirm/correct/disagree with the current review.

_____

_____

_____

(Please include address and telephone number of establishment, if convenient.)

REPORT

Please describe food, service, style, comfort, value, date of visit, and other aspects of your experience; continue on another piece of paper if necessary.

_____

_____

_____

_____

_____

_____

_____

I am not concerned, directly or indirectly, with the management or ownership of this establishment.

SIGNED _____

ADDRESS _____

_____

_____

PHONE _____ **DATE** _____

Please address to Best Places Portland and send to:
SASQUATCH BOOKS
615 SECOND AVENUE, SUITE 260
SEATTLE, WA 98104
Feel free to email feedback as well: **BOOKS@SASQUATCHBOOKS.COM**

Best Places Portland Report Form

Based on my personal experience, I wish to nominate the following restaurant, place of lodging, shop, nightclub, sight, or other as a "Best Place"; or confirm/correct/disagree with the current review.

_____

_____

_____

(Please include address and telephone number of establishment, if convenient.)

REPORT

Please describe food, service, style, comfort, value, date of visit, and other aspects of your experience; continue on another piece of paper if necessary.

_____

_____

_____

_____

_____

_____

_____

I am not concerned, directly or indirectly, with the management or ownership of this establishment.

SIGNED
_____

ADDRESS
_____

_____

PHONE   **DATE**

Please address to Best Places Portland and send to:
SASQUATCH BOOKS
615 SECOND AVENUE, SUITE 260
SEATTLE, WA 98104
Feel free to email feedback as well: **BOOKS@SASQUATCHBOOKS.COM**